84676

D0990886

# Contact Points

*Published for the*
*Omohundro Institute of*
*Early American History and Culture,*
*Williamsburg, Virginia,*
*The Newberry Library, Chicago, and*
*The Historic New Orleans Collection*
*by the*
*University of North Carolina Press,*
*Chapel Hill and London*

# Contact Points

AMERICAN FRONTIERS *from*

*the* MOHAWK VALLEY *to the*

MISSISSIPPI, 1750–1830

*Edited by* Andrew R. L. Cayton *and* Fredrika J. Teute

The Omohundro Institute of
Early American History and Culture
is sponsored jointly by the
College of William and Mary
and the Colonial Williamsburg Foundation.
On October 25, 1996, the
Institute adopted the present name
in honor of a bequest from
Malvern H. Omohundro, Jr.

Library of Congress Cataloging-in-Publication Data
Contact points : American frontiers from the Mohawk Valley to the Mississippi,
1750–1830 / edited by Andrew R. L. Cayton and Fredrika J. Teute.
p.   cm.
"Published for the Omohundro Institute of Early American History and Culture,
Williamsburg, Virginia."
Includes bibliographical references and index.
ISBN 0-8078-2427-5 (alk. paper). — ISBN 0-8078-4734-8 (pbk. : alk. paper)
1. Frontier and pioneer life—United States.   2. United States—Territorial expansion.
3. Acculturation—United States—History—17th century.   4. Acculturation—United
States—History—18th century.   5. Indians of North America—Government
relations—To 1789.   6. Indians of North America—Government relations—1789–1869.
7. Indians, Treatment of—United States—History—18th century.   8. Indians,
Treatment of—United States—History—19th century.   I. Cayton, Andrew R. L.
(Andrew Robert Lee), 1954– .   II. Teute, Fredrika J.   III. Omohundro Institute of Early
American History & Culture.
E179.5.C597   1998       97-49510
973—dc21          CIP
AC
02 01 00 99 98   5 4 3 2 1

# PREFACE

The last decades of the twentieth century have witnessed a proliferation of work on native American experiences in the colonial and early national periods. During the same time, a new wave of interest in the backcountry produced studies on the edges of European-American settlement. As the centennial approached of Frederick Jackson Turner's seminal address, "The Significance of the Frontier in American History," delivered in 1893, Alan Taylor and I came up with an idea to hold a conference exploring new understandings of early American frontiers. James H. Merrell had pointed out in 1989 in a critique on colonial history and native American studies in the *William and Mary Quarterly* that, in spite of all the work accomplished, the various schools of scholarship had yet to integrate the results of each other's research. Alan and I proposed challenging scholars in relevant fields to transcend their own boundaries by applying other disciplines' perspectives to their work. The result was the conference "Crucibles of Cultures: North American Frontiers, 1750–1820," held in New Orleans in November 1994 and cosponsored by the Institute of Early American History and Culture, The Historic New Orleans Collection, and the Newberry Library. This volume of essays comes from the scholarly proceedings of that meeting.

In a preliminary exchange, James H. Merrell, Daniel K. Richter, Alan Taylor, and I considered an agenda and topics for a frontiers conference that would cross borders. That discussion was essential to laying out a format for the conference. Although the proposal languished for a while, fortune and many people smiled on the frontiers conference, encouraged it, and made it happen. Alan was steadfast in his support, and other scholars of early America responded with excitement and enthusiasm at the prospect of a conference that would look at frontiers as zones of cultural interactions. Conversations with Andrew R. L. Cayton, John Mack Faragher, Stephen Aron, Peter H. Wood, Theda Perdue, Colin Calloway, and David Edmunds, among others, kept the idea alive.

Essential to holding any conference is financial and institutional support. When Ronald Hoffman took over as director of the Institute of Early American History and Culture in mid-1992, he endorsed the proposal for the frontiers conference by promising to fund it. With his inimitable flair for shaping and facilitating conferences, Ron guided this one from the drawing board to reality. Frederick E. Hoxie, then director of the D'Arcy McNickle Center for American Indian History of the Newberry Library, now vice president for research and education, and Charles T. Cullen, the Newberry's president, agreed to join forces with the Institute to underwrite the costs. Fred Hoxie's insightful understanding and knowledge of native American studies had an important impact on the contents of the conference program. When the call for papers went out, a telephone call came in from Jon Kukla, director of The Historic New Orleans Collection. He proposed that New Orleans, as a major crossroads of early American cultures, would be an appropriate venue for the meeting and that The Historic New Orleans Collection should serve as host. These individuals and the sponsorship of their institutions made "Crucibles of Cultures" possible and determined its success.

The call for papers asked scholars to reflect on how contacts with others influenced groups' perceptions and practices or on how contact between two or more cultures created something new, in cultural patterns, gender behavior and order, spatial arrangements and land use, and power relations. The many fine proposals confirmed the vitality of frontier studies in early American history. At "Crucibles of Cultures," fourteen scholars presented work examining multicultural interactions in eastern North America from the late colonial to the end of the early national period. In recognition of all the participants, whose contributions made this an exciting and stimulating meeting, we have included the complete conference program at the back of this volume.

The final act was to shape a volume of essays from the conference papers. Andrew Cayton joined me in this undertaking, and I could not have asked for a collaborator more supportive, better humored, or more perceptive. A fine historian and good editor, he diplomatically prompted contributors to do the necessary revisions and gently prodded the other editor to get the volume done. Daniel K. Richter and James P. Ronda, as outside readers, gave insightful readings and valuable advice to authors and editors on the contents and shape of the book. Virginia Montijo Chew, the Institute's manuscript editor, has given the final polish to these essays, carefully copyediting them, collating texts, maps, and illustrations, all of which is a far more complicated affair for a multiauthored collection than for a monograph. She has managed the project with professionalism and the editors with patience, tying all the loose ends together and bringing it to completion.

Departing from the topical format of the conference, we have organized the essays in roughly their chronological and geographical order of development. We found that cumulatively the pieces created a powerful narrative from the mid-eighteenth-century imperial wars to the Era of Removal. Although the essays follow a sequence of frontiers, they envision no overarching continental design of either progress or conquest. European and American regimes colonized territory in many different parts of North America between the sixteenth and nineteenth centuries. Originally, we envisioned a conference that would encompass all North American frontiers from the beginning of the eighteenth century to the second quarter of the nineteenth. Ultimately, we decided this would be unwieldy and would diffuse the focus. For historical and thematic coherence, we formed the conference, and subsequently the collection, primarily around frontiers in the eastern half of North America. By limiting the regional framework from the Mississippi Basin eastward and the time frame between 1750 and 1830, we intended to establish overlapping cultural motifs and to allow deep exploration of contacts on contiguous frontiers. Still, there are unintentional omissions, such as Canada, Louisiana, and Florida. At the back of the volume, a bibliography of printed primary sources and of secondary works offers a select list of readings on frontiers mainly within the geographical regions and time period of the volume. We offer *Contact Points* as a convincing argument that frontiers are crucial arenas for studying America's past.

FREDRIKA J. TEUTE
*Editor of Publications*
*Omohundro Institute of Early*
*American History and Culture*

# CONTENTS

# MAPS

# Contact Points

ANDREW R. L. CAYTON & FREDRIKA J. TEUTE

# Introduction

## On the Connection of Frontiers

American frontiers have long been contested terrains. Indeed, the very concept of "frontier" is controversial. Like all labels, the term has meant many things to many peoples, its definition contingent upon the cultural perceptions of those using it and the spatial context in which they apply it. Frontier can mean a political boundary between two states or a physical, psychological, or intellectual barrier between the known and unknown. As a regional division between different racial and ethnic groups, frontier is often a fluid and permeable line. Constituted as a geographical border, frontier may invoke distinctions between occupied and unoccupied territory. Taken as a divide, frontier often sets up an invidious comparison between two sides, establishing one side as normative and casting the other in the dark as unknown, unoccupied, savage, dangerous.

In the history of North America, the most prevalent use of the word "frontier" has been to designate an area on the edge of Anglo-American settlement, defining the land beyond as unsettled and uncivilized. Not coincidentally, "frontier" acquired this meaning in the decades that followed the American Revolution. In the middle of the eighteenth century, British colonists referred to regions west of their settlements as the "backcountry," quite literally, the land behind them as they faced east toward Europe. It was only in the late 1700s and early 1800s, as American citizens began to contemplate the settlement or conquest of the North American continent, that they began to call areas beyond the pale of their civilization "frontiers."[1]

Explicit in Americans' formulation of frontier was the Enlightenment idea that societies develop in predetermined stages: scattered peoples give way to

---

1. Mitford M. Mathews, ed., *A Dictionary of Americanisms on Historical Principles* (1951; reprint, Chicago, 1956), s.v. "frontier"; John T. Juricek, "American Usage of the Word 'Frontier,' from Colonial Times to Frederick Jackson Turner," American Philosophical Society, *Proceedings*, CX (Philadelphia, 1966), 10–34.

farmers, who are eventually superseded by merchants, artisans, and city dwellers. The citizens of the United States would not simply populate North America; they would transform it into an extension of their vision of their new nation.[2] Indians, British, French, and Spaniards resisted these plans, and Anglo-Americans divided over their specific formulation. Still, the histories of the American Republic and the meaning of frontier have been intertwined ever since. Historians may dismiss eighteenth-century assumptions about development as ethnocentric—even racist—but they cannot deny that the European conquest of North America, and the frontiers it created, must be at the center of any analysis of the history of this continent.

*Contact Points* emphasizes the connection of frontiers to America's story, but not in traditional ways. The essays' authors share a revisionist notion of what constitutes a frontier. Influenced by a renewed appreciation of American pluralism and social difference, the contributors approach frontiers as zones rather than binary dividing lines. They see them as contested spaces, not as a stage in the progress of the world according to Europeans. In this book, the essence of a frontier is the kinetic interactions among many peoples, which created new cultural matrices distinctively American in their eclecticism, fluidity, individual determination, and differentiation. Attention centers, not on the ultimate domination by white Americans of the frontier, but on the multisided negotiations of power involved in forming that most distinctive of American landscapes, frontiers.

A century after Americans turned away from Europe to face the peoples and lands of North America, substituting frontier for backcountry, a historian wrote the quintessential statement about the importance of the frontier in the history of the United States. In July 1893, Frederick Jackson Turner, at the time a professor at the University of Wisconsin in Madison, delivered a paper titled "The Significance of the Frontier in American History" to an audience gathered in the new Art Institute in Chicago. The occasion was the American Historical Association's annual meeting, one of the "Congresses" held as part of the World's Columbian Exposition (or the Chicago World's Fair). In explaining what became known as his "frontier thesis," Turner succeeded in shifting study away from Western Europe as the primary source of American institutions to the West as the formative zone of American society. Turner argued that successive movement westward into expanses of "free" land removed pioneers

2. Peter S. Onuf, "Liberty, Development, and Union: Visions of the West in the 1780s," *William and Mary Quarterly*, 3d Ser., XLIII (1986), 179–213.

from European and eastern influences, that this regenerative frontier environment induced uniquely American traits of individualism and democracy, and that, with the populating of the entire continent, the American frontier had come to an end. Turner focused attention on the western edge of European American settlement as the determining factor in shaping democratic institutions, economic behavior, and social habits.[3]

Few, if any, scholarly papers have had the enormous impact of Turner's address. More than a hundred years after the meeting in Chicago, scholars still debate the validity of what he said there. Criticism has come from many directions. Most historians, including the contributors to this volume, find Turner's thesis fundamentally flawed in its ethnocentrism, triumphalism, gender bias, and linearity. Our intention, however, is not to add *Contact Points* to the very long list of books and articles attacking Frederick Jackson Turner. Indeed, he is rarely mentioned in the pages that follow, and none of the authors discusses whether her or his essay confirms or refutes Turner's thesis. Rather, this collection demonstrates the abiding significance of frontiers as a critical organizing principle in the history of North America.[4]

Over the last quarter of the twentieth century, historians have reconceptualized what frontier landscapes looked like and what happened there, even as their work, ironically, reinforced Turner's focus on the margins of settlement as central to comprehending America's past. Scholars have reenvisioned American borderlands as worlds of social diversity, innovative cultural adaptations, and political mutability. They have concentrated on less-celebratory

3. Frederick Jackson Turner, *The Frontier in American History* (1920), foreword by Wilbur R. Jacobs (Tucson, Ariz., 1986), ix–xix, 1–38. Using its definition of settled area as containing two or more people per square mile, the 1890 U.S. Census claimed a contiguous frontier line no longer existed. From these data, Turner posed these questions in his essay: With the frontier's closing, would its influence in Americanizing the country's inhabitants and institutions be dissipated and lost? What would replace the frontier as the driving force in American history? (See 1–3, 37–38.) This dark side of the frontier thesis was part of a turn-of-the-century, Progressive anxiety over America's future as a democratic society.

4. For a short anthology of the historiographical debates over the Turner thesis in the first half of the twentieth century, see George Rogers Taylor, ed., *The Turner Thesis concerning the Role of the Frontier in American History,* rev. ed. (Boston, 1956). For a current historiographical overview, see Gerald D. Nash, *Creating the West: Historical Interpretations, 1890–1990* (Albuquerque, N.M., 1991). For a reassessment of Turner and the debate between Turnerians and the New Western historians, see John Mack Faragher, ed., *Rereading Frederick Jackson Turner: "The Significance of the Frontier in American History," and Other Essays* (New York, 1994), 1–10, 225–241; and also see Wilbur R. Jacobs, *On Turner's Trail: One Hundred Years of Writing Western History* (Lawrence, Kans., 1994).

aspects of the expansionist process, especially on the ways in which peoples previously dismissed as uncivilized or ignored altogether resisted and survived the European conquest of North America. Ethnohistorians populated the continent with complex native American cultures, underscoring the obvious fact that North America was hardly empty in 1492 and after.[5]

Instead of positing a white, Anglo-Saxon civilization overcoming savagery or European-style settlement turning a wilderness into a garden, scholars have recognized that European penetration of the Western Hemisphere entailed the collision and convergence of several worlds. Emphasizing this point, public television programs, exhibits, and museum catalogs as well as numerous books commemorated the quincentenary of Columbus's voyages to the west, not as an act of discovery, but as invasion, contact, and exchange between different civilizations. Historians have attacked Turner for glorifying the westward expansion of European American males, who exploited natural resources, Indians, enslaved Africans, and women and children to aggrandize power and profit for themselves. This revisionist scholarship has exposed the human, environmental, and moral costs of colonial conquest.[6]

5. Because Turner's own historical research and writing focused on the late eighteenth and early nineteenth century in the East, primarily in the Ohio and Mississippi Valleys, his findings, putting aside his cultural biases, have congruence with early American scholars' historical observations. The lands and climates of the eastern woodlands were conducive to the hunting, trading, stock raising, and farming depicted in Turner's work. Fertile soils and extensive riverine systems supported human habitation and led to contact between indigenous and immigrant peoples. The counterweights of Indian, Spanish, French, and British systems maintained extensive interactions over a long period of time, which were conducive to the development of new types of behaviors and cultural adaptations in frontier areas. Later, Turner and other scholars extrapolated his hypothesis about the significance of the frontier in American history, applying it across the country to the arid and sparsely inhabited lands of the West, to the outback of Australia, and to Argentina's pampas. The extension of the thesis's scope beyond its original evidentiary base drained it of historical meaning. See Andrew R. L. Cayton and Peter S. Onuf, *The Midwest and the Nation: Rethinking the History of an American Region* (Bloomington, Ind., 1990).

6. See Patricia Nelson Limerick, *The Legacy of Conquest: The Unbroken Past of the American West* (New York, 1987), for a trailblazing and forceful articulation of the new views; see also the novelist Larry McMurtry's rejoinder, "How the West Was Won or Lost," *New Republic*, Oct. 22, 1990, 32–38, in which he dubbed the New Western history "Failure Studies." For a summary of some of the scholarly and educational activity generated by the Columbian quincentenary and its reoriented perspective, see James Axtell, "Columbian Encounters: Beyond 1992," *WMQ*, 3d Ser., XLIX (1992), 335–360.

New approaches to frontier history, however, amount to more than turning Turner's assertions on their head by transforming settlers into conquerors. Central to the whole revisionist enterprise is an insistence on variant perspectives on frontier experiences, envisioned as *frontiers* rather than *the frontier*. Historians have rejected the concept of a frontier line for its teleological determinism and ethnocentrism. Instead, they have located multiple sites of exchange among different groups, cultures, and nations.

The essays in *Contact Points* analyze the ways in which the interaction of diverse peoples on frontiers created new cultural forms. They challenge or complicate ideas of acculturation and conquest, considering a composite of frontiers with many meanings and patterns of existence. Abandoning the idea of distinct demarcations, the contributors have followed the lead of Leonard Thompson and Howard Lamar in *The Frontier in History* in coming to

> regard a frontier not as a boundary or a line, but as a territory or zone of interpenetration between two previously distinct societies. Usually, one of the societies is indigenous to the region, or at least has occupied it for many generations; the other is intrusive. The frontier "opens" in a given zone when the first representatives of the intrusive society arrive; it "closes" when a single political authority has established hegemony over the zone.

Thompson and Lamar concluded that the existence of a frontier depends on "three essential elements"; they include "territory; two or more initially distinct peoples; and the process by which the relations among the peoples in the territory begin, develop, and eventually crystallize."[7] This approach to the study of frontiers has influenced much of the scholarship on borderlands in North America since Thompson and Lamar's publication. It has allowed historians to consider human choices in frontier settings without foreclosing them by predetermining outcomes.

In searching out different actors' perspectives, frontier historians confront a particular challenge in the sources from which they construct their interpretations. They must rely on written documents generated mostly by Europeans. No matter the intentions of the original authors, their accounts distort the past from the vantage point of the ultimate winners. Because scholars are depen-

7. Leonard Thompson and Howard Lamar, "Comparative Frontier History," in Lamar and Thompson, eds., *The Frontier in History: North America and Southern Africa Compared* (New Haven, Conn., 1981), 7, 8. For a succinct restatement of this definition, see Gregory H. Nobles, *American Frontiers: Cultural Encounters and Continental Conquest* (New York, 1997), xii.

dent primarily on what Europeans recorded about these contact points, they have learned to employ indirect readings to interpret their observations of others. In filtering Europeans' cultural assumptions and political purposes, reading texts and objects for messages both projected and received, historians in several of the following essays reflect the successful appropriation of methods used by ethnographers, linguists, and students of material culture.

As historian Stuart B. Schwartz has explained, understanding and representing what happened on any frontier, or point of cultural encounter, involve complex layers of observation. There is the initial encounter in which the participants observe and represent each other. And then there is the encounter between the scholar and the sources the original participants left behind. Some historians and anthropologists contend that, although the travelers' accounts, letters, diaries, official correspondence, and treaty negotiations may tell us a great deal about the people who recorded them, they tell us next to nothing about the people they were observing. The representation of others is so dependent on the cultural discourse of the original observers that it cannot be seen as a reliable record of the past.

Other scholars vehemently disagree with this position. Some hold adamantly to the position that primary sources are valuable in and of themselves. A more sophisticated perspective—and the one that underlies most of the work included in this volume—accepts the biases and limitations of the historical record but argues that the sources, read carefully and cautiously, open windows on the past, revealing things that the participants might not have fully comprehended. Encounters with others forced people to recalibrate their previous understandings of themselves and their worlds. According to Schwartz:

> A dynamic tension between previous understanding and expectations and new observations and experiences was set in motion with each encounter, and modified as the encounters changed over time. Both sides might be convinced that their interpretations of the situation were correct, and sometimes cultural similarities caused more confusion than did differences. But it was the process itself that was crucial.[8]

Schwartz's final sentence captures the central point of much of the scholarship on North American frontiers written since the 1970s: historians find the

8. Stuart B. Schwartz, ed., *Implicit Understandings: Observing, Reporting, and Reflecting on the Encounters between Europeans and Other Peoples in the Early Modern Era* (Cambridge, 1994), 3.

significance of frontiers more in the process than in the outcome. In cis-Mississippi North America, New Indian historians such as James Axtell, James H. Merrell, Daniel K. Richter, Daniel H. Usner, and Richard White have stressed exchanges between Europeans and Indians in commerce, diplomacy, and society. For the most part, with the exception of Richter, they have de-emphasized warfare and violence. In their writings, frontiers emerge as complex places. Instead of traditional frontier accounts of white settlers combating and overcoming Indians, they have redirected attention to examples of inter-dependence, cultural convergence, and efforts, if only intermittently successful, at mutual understanding.[9]

Paralleling these concerns, the New Western history emerged in the 1980s with a clarion call to take the history of the trans-Mississippi West seriously. Scholars such as William Cronon, Patricia Nelson Limerick, Richard White, and Donald Worster claim national relevance for the set of problems they have defined for the West. More than students of Indians in colonial British and French America, they have explicitly rejected the questions and interpretations of earlier generations' Western scholarship. The new approach has strongly emphasized conquest as opposed to settlement, race and class instead of frontier equality and democracy, environmental degradation rather than progress, and government intervention in directing development in place of frontier self-reliance and autonomy. Because of these issues' persistence, New Western historians have rejected notions of the frontier as static. Instead, they have insisted on placing the West at the center of continuing debates over America's past and present direction.[10]

Influenced by New Indian and New Western scholarship, historians of British North America have begun to reframe their conceptual boundaries. Think-

9. James Axtell, *The European and the Indian: Essays in the Ethnohistory of Colonial North America* (New York, 1981); James H. Merrell, *The Indians' New World: Catawbas and Their Neighbors from European Contact through the Era of Removal* (Chapel Hill, N.C., 1989); Richard White, *The Middle Ground: Indians, Empires, and Republics in the Great Lakes Region, 1650–1815* (New York, 1991); Daniel K. Richter, *The Ordeal of the Longhouse: The Peoples of the Iroquois League in the Era of European Colonization* (Chapel Hill, N.C., 1992); and Daniel H. Usner, Jr., *Indians, Settlers, and Slaves in a Frontier Exchange Economy: The Lower Mississippi Valley before 1783* (Chapel Hill, N.C., 1992).

10. Limerick, *Legacy of Conquest;* Richard White, *"It's Your Misfortune and None of My Own": A History of the American West* (Norman, Okla., 1991); William Cronon, George Miles, and Jay Gitlin, eds., *Under an Open Sky: Rethinking America's Western Past* (New York, 1992); and Donald Worster, *Rivers of Empire: Water, Aridity, and the Growth of the American West* (New York, 1985).

ing in continental rather than national terms, early American historians are replacing the traditional historiographical focus on the evolution of the British colonies into the United States and its expansion westward with a broader view of North America as a mosaic of diverse Indian groups interacting with different European empires. If the emergence of the United States is the most decisive event in the modern history of North America, its development was neither as straightforward nor as inevitable as earlier generations of historians had assumed.[11]

No book more successfully encapsulates the revisionism of the New Indian and the New Western history than Richard White's *Middle Ground: Indians, Empires, and Republics in the Great Lakes Region, 1650–1815*. A sophisticated analysis of Indian-European contact between 1650 and 1815 in the Great Lakes region, referred to as *pays d'en haut* ("upper country") by the French, *The Middle Ground* portrays a world in between. There Algonquians and Europeans found common ground as they sought to accommodate each other's interests in order to further their own. Through a process of what White calls "creative misunderstandings," diverse peoples interpreted (or misinterpreted) others' cultures in attempts to overcome differences and to coexist. Arising from this mutual accommodation was a new set of cultural meanings and practices that facilitated extensive social and economic exchange and cultural mixing between Indians and Europeans. This world collapsed over the half-century between the Seven Years' War and the War of 1812. The elimination first of the French imperial presence and then of the British left Indians in the region without any counterweight to American expansion and domination. More committed to settled agriculture than the fur trade that had defined the structures of life in the pays d'en haut for more than a century, Anglo-Americans had little interest in accommodating the presence of either In-

---

11. Two significant works on the Spanish empire's influence on the continent are Ramón A. Gutiérrez, *When Jesus Came, the Corn Mothers Went Away: Marriage, Sexuality, and Power in New Mexico, 1500–1846* (Stanford, Calif., 1991); and David J. Weber, *The Spanish Frontier in North America* (New Haven, Conn., 1992). Edward Countryman has tried to analyze Indians' and Europeans' agency on their own terms rather than as counters in Anglo-American imperial expansion ("Indians, the Colonial Order, and the Social Significance of the American Revolution," *WMQ*, 3d Ser., LIII [1996], 342–362). Neal Salisbury has described a precontact North America as socially fluid, with numerous intercultural and trade transactions among various Indian groups over long distance, rather than as a static, culturally isolated set of distinct Indian societies ("The Indians' Old World: Native Americans and the Coming of Europeans," *WMQ*, 3d Ser., LIII [1996], 435–458).

dians or French. They were all too eager to render Indians as alien others, to be subordinated, eliminated, or, at best, assimilated to European civilized norms.

Published in 1991, *The Middle Ground*'s conceptual framework quickly became one of the most widely imitated in early American history. The trope of the middle ground offered a coherent and intelligible interpretive tool to replace the traditional linear model of frontier history. As a compelling counternarrative to the standard story of the inevitable progression of European American conquest, *The Middle Ground* provided a formula for comprehending a complex process of cultural exchange, agency, balance of power, and creation of new social forms among intersecting societies on the North American continent. This reconceptualization of the colonial past appealed to many American historians at the end of the twentieth century. Its portrayal of a multicultural society offered an alternative vision of peaceful coexistence and creative accommodation against the acculturationist presumptions of an expansive Anglo-American empire.

As an innovative application of ideas and theories lying behind the New Indian and New Western histories, *The Middle Ground* stands both as summation and exemplar of the conceptual impact these schools have had on historical approaches to and understanding of eastern North America. Yet, the effort to recover the past from perspectives other than that of British Americans has tended to homogenize the colonists/conquerors and reduce them to a single cultural stereotype. Frontier stories of the eastern woodlands necessarily must be grounded at least partially in the historiography of colonial British America, and an expanded comprehension of the transatlantic world has helped transform that field in the last quarter of the twentieth century.

Recognition of the diversity within the first British empire no longer permits writing of an American colonist, because there were many different kinds, distinguishable in their outlook by status, race, ethnicity, gender, and religion. Within the borders of British North America, Africans, English, Scots, Welsh, Irish, Dutch, Germans, Swedes, French, and Spaniards participated in their own series of cultural encounters. Diversity went well beyond ethnic types. Regional origins, religious beliefs, and environments encountered in North America divided English among themselves. Even when a coherent British identity was asserted in the mid-eighteenth century, many people, including some Scots and most Irish, dissented strongly, seeing themselves as having been conquered and colonized by the English. The variegated inhabitants of British

America had divergent views about the colonial empire in which they all lived.[12]

Anglo-American frontier studies have revealed bitter contests and occasionally violent confrontations over controlling the terms of backcountry settlement—propertyholding, religious beliefs, political participation, governmental intervention, and social status. As scholars such as Thomas P. Slaughter, Andrew R. L. Cayton, Alan Taylor, Rachel N. Klein, Michael A. Bellesiles, and Stephen Aron have shown, from Maine to Georgia and across the Appalachian Mountains, even as subjects of the British empire transformed themselves into citizens of the American Republic, they struggled with each other for the power to define the structures and ideas of their worlds.[13]

What went on within frontier arenas was in part an extension of the construction of power relations in larger political entities, be they empires, Indian leagues, states, or republics. Essential to probing internal power dynamics has been analyzing gender, race, and status hierarchies. Scholars have focused on gender as an important component of the social complexity of frontiers. In seventeenth-century Virginia, Kathleen M. Brown has identified a "gender frontier," where competing ideas about the proper roles of women shaped the patriarchal society that emerged by the eighteenth century. Central to the ordering of social relations on frontiers everywhere were the gendered constructions of Indian women. As Nancy Shoemaker has suggested, nearly all cultural differences were refracted through a gender lens, informing the contact experience and framing interpretations of words and actions. Understanding, mis-

12. Standard works that make this point include Bernard Bailyn and Philip D. Morgan, eds., *Strangers within the Realm: Cultural Margins of the First British Empire* (Chapel Hill, N.C., 1991); David Hackett Fischer, *Albion's Seed: Four British Folkways in America* (New York, 1989); Jack P. Greene, *Pursuits of Happiness: The Social Development of Early Modern British Colonies and the Formation of American Culture* (Chapel Hill, N.C., 1988).

13. Thomas P. Slaughter, *The Whiskey Rebellion: Frontier Epilogue to the American Revolution* (New York, 1986); Andrew R. L. Cayton, *The Frontier Republic: Ideology and Politics in the Ohio Country, 1780–1825* (Kent, Ohio, 1986); Cayton, *Frontier Indiana* (Bloomington, Ind., 1996); Alan Taylor, *Liberty Men and Great Proprietors: The Revolutionary Settlement on the Maine Frontier, 1760–1820* (Chapel Hill, N.C., 1990); Taylor, *William Cooper's Town: Power and Persuasion on the Frontier of the Early American Republic* (New York, 1995); Rachel N. Klein, *Unification of a Slave State: The Rise of the Planter Class in the South Carolina Backcountry, 1760–1808* (Chapel Hill, N.C., 1990); Michael A. Bellesiles, *Revolutionary Outlaws: Ethan Allen and the Struggle for Independence on the Early American Frontier* (Charlottesville, Va., 1993); Stephen Aron, *How the West Was Lost: The Transformation of Kentucky from Daniel Boone to Henry Clay* (Baltimore, 1996).

understanding, and labeling women's and men's functions were pivotal in structuring power relations between and within societies.[14]

Racial distinctions in eighteenth-century frontier encounters were entwined with status hierarchies. Evolving equations of race and status made by European Americans for Africans and Indians over the colonial and early national periods complicated relations between the latter two groups. Because of their enslavement, Africans' presence in American frontiers introduced yet another basis for forging alliances among subordinated groups or creating differences among them. Both Peter H. Wood and Daniel H. Usner have brought to light the crossovers between status and race played out among Indians, Europeans, and Africans on southern frontiers.[15]

Elites extended their control into border areas by relying on the labor of lower-status whites to occupy, defend, and clear the land. Often underlying power struggles between metropolitan authority and local autonomy was frontier settlers' sense of exploitation by wealthy nonresidents and political elites. Middle-class values of purchasing and owning private property eclipsed Indians', squatters', and tenants' alternative visions of holding property rights in common or by possession. As white settlement quickly expanded into the trans-Appalachian region, the new Republic colonized its internal frontiers by pitting the interests of Indians, African Americans, and lower-status whites against each other. Constructions of gender, racial, and status barriers, as much as physical borders, could serve as parts of imperial designs to divide peoples. That helps explain why, after decades of interaction, European Americans and Indians failed by the end of the eighteenth century to find common ground.[16]

The era encompassed in *Contact Points* closely fits the span of wars contesting control over much of North America and its inhabitants, from the Seven

14. Kathleen M. Brown, *Good Wives, Nasty Wenches, and Anxious Patriarchs: Gender, Race, and Power in Colonial Virginia* (Chapel Hill, N.C., 1996); Nancy Shoemaker, ed., *Negotiators of Change: Historical Perspectives on Native American Women* (New York, 1995).

15. Peter H. Wood, *Black Majority: Negroes in Colonial South Carolina from 1670 through the Stono Rebellion* (New York, 1974); Usner, *Indians, Settlers, and Slaves.* See also Nancy Shoemaker, "How Indians Got to Be Red," *American Historical Review,* CII (1987), 625–644.

16. Slaughter, *Whiskey Rebellion;* Taylor, *Liberty Men and Great Proprietors;* Aron, *How the West Was Lost;* Fredrika Johanna Teute, "Land, Liberty, and Labor in the Post-Revolutionary Era: Kentucky as the Promised Land" (Ph.D. diss., Johns Hopkins University, 1988). See also Alan Taylor, "Land and Liberty on the Post-Revolutionary Frontier," in David Thomas Konig, ed., *Devising Liberty: Preserving and Creating Freedom in the New American Republic* (Stanford, Calif., 1995), 81–108.

Years' War in 1754–1763 to the Mexican-American War in 1846–1848. In connecting the pace and type of settlement to long-term economic cycles, Carville Earle and Changyong Cao have connected the violent or gradual extension of frontiers with a cyclical model of economic expansion and contraction. Even more important, they conclude that the rate of white penetration into new areas was so negligible after the 1840s that the frontier was over by 1850. Their study places the most active conquest and settlement of continental territory between the 1720s and 1840s. These years witnessed the spatial expansion of Anglo-America with rapid economic and population growth and dramatic, often traumatic, movements of people. Although in the end Anglo-American conquest imposed national boundaries around the bulk of the continent, during much of the hundred years between the 1750s and 1850s the terms of relationships among various Indian and European peoples were under negotiation. The outcome at any given time or place was not predetermined; encounters were fluid and often occurred out of mutual needs and interests. The frontiers examined in *Contact Points* were at the center of a period in North America's history in which cultural and political definitions were neither self-evident nor foreclosed.[17]

The essays cover a range of territory from the Mohawk Valley in New York to the Mississippi Basin, the Susquehanna River to the Tallapoosa River. They deal with events from the era of the Seven Years' War and Pontiac's War in the 1750s and 1760s, across the Revolution and frontier warfare in the Ohio Valley at the end of the century, to the Redstick War of the 1810s and the Black Hawk War in the early 1830s. In this pressurized space of time and place, native Americans, European Americans, and African Americans shifted from multiple frameworks of imperial power relations to a single order of internal colonial structures. The new circumstances of an emerging American empire altered dramatically the balance of power and configuration of relations among the peoples meeting in America's eastern frontiers. Covering almost a century of coexistence, settlement, displacement, exchange, conflict, and war, the essays progress chronologically and spatially through these crucibles of change.

Beginning with the mid-eighteenth century in the mid-Atlantic colonies of Pennsylvania and New York, the first three essays look at cultural interchange on an expansive frontier. James H. Merrell focuses on the transformation of

17. Carville Earle and Changyong Cao, "Frontier Closure and the Involution of American Society, 1840–1890," *Journal of the Early Republic*, XIII (1993), 167. Earle and Cao argue that after 1850 the overwhelmingly predominant settlement pattern was migration into urban centers.

Shamokin, the Indian trading town on the Susquehanna River, into Fort Augusta and the attendant reordering of Indian-European American relations in the vicinity. On this same Pennsylvania frontier, Jane T. Merritt carefully dissects metaphors used in formal negotiations and ritual encounters for the extent and limits of their power to bridge barriers between native Americans and colonists. The shifting identities and barely visible traces of African Americans in the midst of Senecas and Mohawks suggest the fluidity of frontier New York society in William B. Hart's essay. Gregory Evans Dowd takes the reader to the South Carolina frontier during the Seven Years' War, where conflict galvanized ceremonies of gift giving and revealed profound antipathies lying beneath the surface gestures of good will. Over the next fifty years, Claudio Saunt argues, the effects of European American contact and capitalist development redefined gender relations within Creek society, intensifying internal tensions that resulted in the Redstick War in 1813.

In the Revolutionary Ohio Valley, fragmented Indian groups and diverse white migrants converged, competing over the same terrain. Stephen Aron portrays Kentucky as a common hunting ground for Indians and white men, giving way to divergent purposes as waves of settlers transformed the landscape. Looking at the polyglot nature of border society in Kentucky, Elizabeth A. Perkins seeks the ways in which residents identified themselves and negotiated differences, first blurring and ultimately sharpening distinctions between European and native Americans. Andrew R. L. Cayton scrutinizes the treaty negotiations leading up to the peace of Greenville in 1795 for the ways in which sentiment and civility structured power hierarchies in the early Republic.

The upper Mississippi Valley in the early nineteenth century contained remnants of various European and native American cultures. By examining labor patterns of Winnebagos, métis, and Anglo-Americans, Lucy Eldersveld Murphy correlates the degree of accommodation in creole communities with gender relations and kinship networks. John Mack Faragher tracks the transformation of multiethnic coexistence in Missouri to a dichotomized society of white masters and African American slaves cleansed of native American inhabitants. Finally, through her analysis of the popular play *Metamora* in the 1830s during Indian removal, Jill Lepore concludes that mythologizing Indian-white relations on historical frontiers provided the rationale for behavior on new American frontiers.

Collectively the essays in *Contact Points* narrate a history of cultural convergence and conflict while uncovering the complex strata of various frontiers. All landscapes reflect the arrangement of topographical and human elements through the eyes of the beholder. The frontiers explored in the following essays are terrains struggled over, not just militarily, economically, and socially, but conceptually as well. Diverse peoples ordered the land and the people on it in divergent ways, they called them different things, they used different names. Often, the meanings one group gave to a place made no sense to another group, even though they might have appropriated the same words for their own purposes.

In eastern North America, as *Contact Points* cumulatively reveals, Europeans, primarily British Americans, eventually controlled the discourse, giving names and meanings to terrain and peoples and imposing their landscapes on the land. One of the primary contentions of this volume is that this process was neither inevitable nor static. Indians might have given way to Europeans, women might have accompanied men as reluctant pioneers, African Americans might have come to frontiers as enslaved peoples, French and Spanish peoples might have lost territory. Nonetheless, they dramatically affected the outcome of these cultural encounters because they were active participants in what occurred in them.

The ways in which European American men thought about land, about other peoples, and about themselves were not what they would have been had they never encountered Indians or brought women and African Americans along. The encounters among European and Indian peoples in eastern North America created landscapes of their own. Each author, applying his or her own viewpoint, gives meaning to places and interactions. They, too, evoke landscapes, sometimes unsettled and chaotic, where appearances were not what they seemed and identities were fluid. At other moments, settings were clearly delineated, with possibilities limited and roles carefully scripted. The contributors provide participants' readings of each other and their own readings of the past.

In Hart's Mohawk Valley, at Merrell's trading post of Shamokin, around Perkins's stations in Kentucky, there were many opportunities for masquerade. Where borders were permeable, there was space to maneuver, and people took on and mistook identities. With the transformation of Shamokin into Fort Augusta, Aron's transition from woods to fenced fields in Kentucky, Cayton's treaty negotiations at Greenville, control over spatial arrangements realigned human relationships within them. As Saunt, Aron, Murphy, and Faragher all demonstrate, the Anglo-American ethos of private property rights separated the mixed economies and social relations of earlier creole frontiers from the emerging capitalist culture of the nineteenth century, under which binary gender and racial systems hardened. That the control over languages gave the power to shape meaning was recognized by all parties from Merritt's Pennsylvania frontier to Dowd's South Carolina to Cayton's Ohio. All involved understood that negotiations over peace and war were a life-and-death struggle over whose version of the terms of coexistence would prevail. In all these frontiers, inscribing places, food, clothes, people with defining names was important. As Perkins shows in Kentucky, this was the means by which people of varying backgrounds sorted themselves out, created common bonds, and increasingly differentiated themselves from others. Underlying the transformation of Aron's Kentucky hunters into farmers was a colonizing process that assimilated lower-class white males to Anglo-American normative elite values and polarized Indian-white relations. Lepore's concluding essay suggests that the dominant society deflected its own internal contradictions onto frontiers and then relegated those conflicts to the realm of memory.

As Indians have always known, as Turner hypothesized, and as New Indian and New Western historians have demonstrated, the dynamics and problems of American frontiers endure in spite of attempts to consign them to history. This volume provides examples of a New Frontiers studies that offers a pathway into the heart of North American history. Over the centuries, diverse peoples have constructed the contours of American landscapes through their interactions with each other in numerous contact points. None was more complex or ultimately more decisive than the frontiers that flourished in eastern North America from the middle of the eighteenth to the middle of the nineteenth century.

JAMES H. MERRELL

# Shamokin, "the very seat of the Prince of darkness": Unsettling the Early American Frontier

## Darkness Discovered

### "All was dark about Shamokin"

On September 16, 1745, the German colonists Martin and Anna Mack arrived at the Susquehanna River Indian town of Shamokin to set up a Moravian mission (see Figure 1). A difficult fall awaited them. Although some natives seemed friendly, sharing food and lending the newcomers a bed or an ear, these promising signs were all but buried beneath an avalanche of scorn, resentment, and rum. Even Indians who "rec[eiv]ed us very friendly" also "ask'd at the same Time when we intended to go away again?" Others, less polite, "were very Lightminded and Ridiculed us." And these opponents were sober; when Indians drank—and they were, Martin Mack observed, "for the most part drunk"—Shamokin went from unpleasant to frightening. Scarcely twenty-four hours after their arrival, the Macks heard "a great Noise in our Neighbourhood, the Indians . . . being all Drunk, Some of them came into our Hut, look'd very dismal and roar'd like the very Beasts." [1]

That was only a taste of things to come; during the next several weeks, the two often met "very Fierce and Bloody" natives who had mischief and may-

For comments and suggestions I am grateful to William Cronon, Clyde Griffen, Michael McConnell, and Richard White, to Stephen Aron and the participants in a colloquium in the Department of History at Princeton University, to the Colonial History Workshop at the University of Minnesota, and to Charles Cohen and the Early American History Colloquium at the University of Wisconsin, Madison.

1. Shamokin Diary, Sept. 17, Oct. 8, 12, 24, 1745, *Records of the Moravian Mission among the Indians of North America* (New Haven, Conn., [1978]), from original materials at the Archives of the Moravian Church, Bethlehem, Pa., microfilm, 40 reels, reel 28, box 217, folder 12B, item 1 (hereafter cited as *Moravian Records*, reel/box/folder/item). Two of these journals are in English; translations of the others are my own. I am deeply grateful to Beverly Smaby for checking my work.

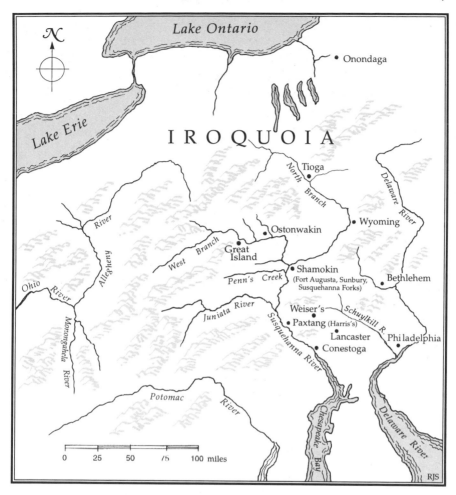

FIGURE 1

Shamokin and the Susquehanna Country. *Drawn by Richard Stinely*

hem, if not murder, in mind. The worst of these storms hit on a night in early November, near the end of the Macks' stay. A passing war party paused at Shamokin and, making a drum from an empty rum barrel, proceeded to dance—while emptying, apparently, another barrel of liquor. They were, Mack wrote, "so drunk, that they roar'd like Beasts, and had like to have pulled the Hutt over our Ears." Failing that, one warrior, "full of Fury," stormed in, "Snatch'd a great Fire Brand out of the Fire, and said he wo[ul]d burn the white People." The next morning, another yanked a backpack off the Macks' newly arrived Moravian replacement and heaved it into the woods, then snatched the newcomer's "Hat from his Head, . . . put it on . . . , and run away." On November 4, the Macks headed home to the Moravian town, Bethlehem, leaving to their shaken successor "this as yet wild People." Shamokin was, Martin Mack recalled with a shudder years later, "the very seat of the Prince of darkness."[2]

Mack was not alone in his assessment of the place. Soon after the Macks reached Shamokin, the Presbyterian missionary David Brainerd, who was staying in another part of town, dropped by to compare notes on the settlement— and, probably, to size up his competition. "He complain'd very much of [the Indians] that they were such wicked People, being always drunk," Mack wrote. "He did not know what he sho[ul]d do with them." "The Indians of this place," Brainerd later reported, "are accounted the most drunken, mischievous and ruffian-like fellows of any in these parts; and Satan seems to have his seat in this town in an eminent degree."[3]

Nowadays, it is hard to read such words without an indulgent smile or a contemptuous sneer for the misguided sensibilities of an earlier era. Which is worse: the missionaries' arrogance or their ignorance? These folk brought to Shamokin a Manichaean view of the world that pitted the forces of order (the people of Christ and of clearings) against the lords of misrule (the heathen denizens of the woods). Foot soldiers in that cosmic struggle, determined "to turn them [Indians] from darkness to light," they failed really to see the people who joined them for lunch and staggered toward them in the dark. In an age that paints the American frontier in shades of gray, it is tempting to dismiss

2. Ibid., Sept. 18, Oct. 16, 19, Nov. 2–3, 1745, 28/217/12B/1; John H. Carter, "The Moravians at Shamokin," Northumberland County Historical Society, *Proceedings and Addresses,* IX (Sunbury, Pa., 1937), 64. The firebrand episode might have been a ritual. The Indian, disarmed easily by the Macks' host, the métis Andrew Montour, then picked up (in succession) a gun and a stick, making the same threats and being disarmed each time. He finally sat quietly by the fire for a while before leaving the house. Fifteen years later, another Moravian encountered similar treatment at an Indian town farther up the Susquehanna River. See "Journal of Mr Christn. Fred Post, in Company with Teedyuscung, Mr John Hays, Isaac Still, and Moses Tattamy, to the Great Council of the Different Indian Nations, 1760," Historical Society of Pennsylvania, Philadelphia (hereafter cited as HSP).

3. Shamokin Diary, Sept. 25, 1745, *Moravian Records,* 28/217/12B/1. For the competition, see ibid., Oct. 25, 1745, 28/217/12B/1; Jonathan Edwards, *The Life of David Brainerd,* ed. Norman Pettit, The Works of Jonathan Edwards, VII (New Haven, Conn., 1985), 324. For David Brainerd's assessment, see Carter, "Moravians at Shamokin," Northumberland Co. Hist. Soc., *Procs.,* IX (1937), 62. See also Edwards, *Life of Brainerd,* ed. Pettit, 324–326, 420–425. For other Moravians' similar assessments, see Shamokin Diary, Jan. 5, 1748, *Moravian Records,* 6/121/4/1; and Travel Diary, Apr. 19, 1747, ibid., 6/121/9/2; J. T. Hamilton, trans., "Autobiography of Bernhard Adam Grube," Moravian Historical Society, *Transactions,* XI (Bethlehem, Pa., 1936), 203–204.

those who saw things in black and white as fools and cranks, if not imperialists and racists.⁴

We should resist the temptation if we hope to make sense of Shamokin and the Susquehanna frontier. For one thing, the Macks and David Brainerd were familiar with native Americans and therefore unlikely to suffer culture shock upon arriving at just any Indian town. Martin Mack came to Shamokin from more than two years at other missions, his wife grew up close enough to Indians to pick up Mohawk (and later added Delaware), and Brainerd brought with him to the Susquehanna River lessons picked up during sojourns among several other Indian groups beside the Delaware and the Connecticut.⁵

For another, missionaries were not the only ones Shamokin threw off balance. The town at the Forks of the Susquehanna was an easy place to find; it was also an easy place to get lost. One colonial fur trader there became so disoriented that he forgot what day of the week it was. Another veteran of the Indian countries, the Pennsylvania Indian agent Conrad Weiser, once was struck dumb by what he saw in Shamokin. Sent there by provincial officials to greet an Iroquois delegation, Weiser anxiously scanned the visitors' faces as their canoes approached the shore. "There is but two among them I Remember I have sien befor," he fretted. "All the rest ar Strangers to me." The Iroquois expert was momentarily stupefied. "I was troubled in my mind," he recalled, "dit not know what to say or what to doe."⁶

Even as Shamokin's Indian inhabitants helped Weiser recover from his stupor, they knew the feeling. Although they would not have agreed that the Prince of Darkness was in their midst, they knew well enough how darkness felt. After all, not ten miles upstream lay Otzinachson, "Demon's Den," where, natives said, "the evil spirits . . . have their seats and hold their revels."⁷ And sometimes

4. David Brainerd to Ebenezer Pemberton, Nov. 5, 1744, in Edwards, *Life of Brainerd*, ed. Pettit, 572, 579.

5. For the Macks' background, see "J. Martin Mack's Recollections of a Journey from Otstonwakin to Wyoming . . . in October of 1742," in William C. Reichel, ed., *Memorials of the Moravian Church*, I (Philadelphia, 1870), 100–101n. The name of Mack's wife is variously given as Anna, Annel, or Jeannette. For Brainerd, see Edwards, *Life of Brainerd*, ed. Pettit, 24–32, 58–62, 570–576, and pts. V–VIII.

6. Shamokin Diary, Dec. 27, 1747, *Moravian Records*, 6/121/3/3; Conrad Weiser to James Logan, Sept. 16, 1736, James Logan Papers, box 10, folder 62, HSP.

7. "Zinzendorf's Narrative of a Journey from Bethlehem to Shamokin, in September of 1742," in Reichel, ed., *Memorials*, I, 94. For the Iroquois sense of these places, see George R. Hamell, "Mythical Realities and European Contact in the Northeast during the Sixteenth and Seventeenth Centuries," *Man in the Northeast*, no. 33 (Spring 1987), 68–70.

malignant spirits did approach the heart of the village. "All was dark about Shamokin," said Sassoonan, a Delaware headman from the town, during one crisis; "we could not see at the Least Distance from Us." In fact, the first appearance of "Shahomaking" in the colonial records came in 1728, a time when there was "som Misc[h]if hac[h]in by the Indians" in those parts, Sassoonan was trading "hard words" with another local leader, and the town itself was said to have been abandoned.[8]

This report of Shamokin's demise was premature, but in the years to come "great noise" and "great Confusion" were no strangers there. One spring, a Nanticoke hunter, passing through the town, "complained very much" that the native inhabitants "were the most disorderly and drunken Indians he knew, and he would not live here for all the world." But the worst noise and confusion erupted in the fall of 1755, when Indians from over the western mountains brought war to the Susquehanna country by striking colonists settled just below the Forks. Shamokin at once became a cauldron of rumor and intrigue, of maneuvers and veiled threats. Converging on the town were Indians from throughout the Susquehanna Valley, there to discuss the bloodshed, native diplomats from Ohio and "a great number of strange Indians, . . . all painted Black," looking to enlist the Susquehanna peoples in their cause, and a band of almost fifty Pennsylvanians from downriver, led by the prominent frontier trader, John Harris, come to investigate the recent attacks. By winter, the combined pressure of these contending forces did destroy Shamokin. Abandoned and burned, the site greeted new tenants the following summer when Pennsylvania troops built an outpost they called Fort Augusta atop the ashes of the native settlement.[9]

8. *Minutes of the Provincial Council of Pennsylvania, from the Organization to the Termination of the Proprietary Government,* 10 vols., Colonial Records of Pennsylvania (Philadelphia and Harrisburg, Pa., 1851–1853), IV, 651 (hereafter cited as *MPCP*). Similar sentiments are ibid., IV, 684, V, 475, VI, 685, VII, 8; *Pennsylvania Archives,* 138 vols. (Philadelphia and Harrisburg, Pa., 1852–1949), 1st Ser., I, 214, 227 (hereafter cited as *PA*); *MPCP,* III, 330.

9. For "great noise" and "great Confusion," see Weiser, Report of Indian Conference at Shamokin, May 2, 1744, Records of the Provincial Council in the Pennsylvania State Archives, Executive Correspondence (Harrisburg, Pa., 1966), reel B2, item 377 (hereafter cited as Recs. Prov. Ccl., Exec. Corr., reel/item). For the Nanticoke hunter, see Shamokin Diary, Mar. 20, 1749, *Moravian Records,* 6/121/5/1. For attacks in the fall of 1755, see *MPCP,* VI, 645–661. The best history of Fort Augusta is William A. Hunter, *Forts on the Pennsylvania Frontier, 1753–1758* (Harrisburg, Pa., 1960), chap. 10. See also Thomas Lynch Montgomery et al., eds., *Report of the Commission to Locate the Site of the Frontier Forts of Pennsylvania,* 2 vols. (Harrisburg, Pa., 1916), I, 354–363. The town's demise can be followed in *MPCP,* VI, 783, VII, 154.

According to the frontier saga embedded in American memory, Fort Augusta was the dawn of a new day, the triumph of light over darkness. In fact, though, the place at the Forks defied conventional story lines; Augusta, too, had its share of darkness and noise. Colonel James Burd, arriving at the stronghold in December 1756, was appalled, when he "inquired into the State of the Garrison, . . . that no work has been done for some time" and the fort "was full of heaps of nusances." More than three years later, he returned to find, again, "every thing much out of order." Burd managed to escape the mess, but there was no escaping reports from subordinates informing him—yet again—that "all [is] in Confusion." [10]

Shamokin could, then, be a bewildering place, whether Indians or European colonists—or both—occupied it. In that very bewilderment and confusion lie Shamokin's mystery, and its significance. Perhaps it is time, some 250 years after the Macks got there, to return to the Susquehanna Forks and have a look around, to peer into the darkness and listen to the noise. Another visit to the place reveals how far this corner of the frontier departs from the epic Europeans told themselves (and us) about their adventures in North America. Although perhaps not as dramatic as the cosmic clash of good and evil, Shamokin's story is more complicated, and more interesting, suggesting as it does both the enduring pull of disorder and the enticing prospect of an altogether new order, a fragile rearrangement of disparate peoples. [11] At the same time, however, a visit to the town and to its replacement, Fort Augusta, helps explain why the older plot endures: within its denigration of natives and celebration of newcomers, its bombast and myopia, the grand narrative harbors a deeper truth about the early American frontier, a truth about the divide between Indian and colonist, a barrier these peoples had built and one they could not, would not, tear down.

-----

Some archaeologists believe that the fort partially covered the Indian town; see Deborah L. Nichols, "Field Report on the 1979 Excavations at 36Nb 71, Fort Augusta, Sunbury, Pennsylvania," Northumberland Co. Hist. Soc., *Procs.*, XXVIII (1980), 105. Others believe that the fort was just south of the town; see Barry C. Kent, *Susquehanna's Indians* (Harrisburg, Pa., 1989), 101. One contemporary account (*PA*, 2d Ser., II, 678) put the fort just downriver. Both could be right: soldiers might have built at the site where Shickellamy and the Moravian missionaries had lived, which was a short way from town (see below).

10. *PA*, 2d Ser., II, 642, VII, 441; Lt. Caleb Graydon to Col. James Burd, July 12, 1762, Shippen Family Papers, V, HSP.

11. The best account of such an intercultural arrangement—one that, under different circumstances, endured—is Richard White, *The Middle Ground: Indians, Empires, and Republics in the Great Lakes Region, 1650–1815* (New York, 1991).

## Darkness Explored: Shamokin

## "We find it verry Diffical[t] to larn anything"

The roots of that widespread sense of being adrift on a turbulent, forbidding sea can be found in the geography and history of this corner of the world.[12] The Susquehanna River that ran past Shamokin's front door stretches like a great tree up from the Chesapeake Bay, its branches reaching deep into the interior to brush the headwaters of other streams that flowed toward the Great Lakes and the Ohio country.[13] The river had long been an avenue for Indian warriors, traders, diplomats, and emigrants. In 1700, however, a Susquehanna traveler would have found the valley remarkably empty of inhabitants, the Susquehannocks and other local peoples having recently migrated or merged with the Five Nations Iroquois, masters of the river's headwaters.[14] This emptiness and this highway, combined with the Five Nations' habit of encouraging other peoples to live on the borders of Iroquoia, made the Susquehanna country attractive to Indian settlers. For much of the eighteenth century, there was, as one Iroquois observed in 1754, an "abundance of Indians . . . moving up and down" the valley. Various bands from the Delaware River, Shawnees from remote lands to the south and west, Conoys and Nanticokes from Maryland, Tutelos and Tuscaroras from Carolina, Senecas, Cayugas, and Oneidas from Iroquoia—people from these and other groups founded an archipelago of

12. *Shamokin*'s meaning is unclear. It has been interpreted as "the place of eels," "the place where gun barrels are straightened" (for the smithy Moravians established there in 1747), "Crawfish Place," "where antlers are plenty," and "the place of chiefs, or rulers." See George P. Donehoo, *A History of the Indian Villages and Place Names in Pennsylvania, with Numerous Historical Notes and References* (Harrisburg, Pa., 1928), 141–143, 186–190; David M. Oestreicher, "Surviving Historic Traditions of the Unami Delaware" (I thank Dr. Oestreicher for sharing his work with me and allowing me to cite it). Confusion deepens because *Shamokin* was only one of the names for the town or region at the Susquehanna Forks and because *Shamokin* or *Otzinachson* sometimes referred to the Susquehanna's West Branch or colonial settlements below the Forks. Usually, *Shamokin* was the town, *Otzinachson* the region. I focus on the village, aware of the larger context, since references to "the Indians at Shamokin and thereabout" were common (*MPCP,* IV, 641).

13. I embellish here on the "treetop" metaphor of Francis Jennings; see *The Ambiguous Iroquois Empire: The Covenant Chain Confederation of Indian Tribes with English Colonies from Its Beginnings to the Lancaster Treaty of 1744* (New York, 1984), 31–32.

14. Susquehannocks were the people inhabiting the Susquehanna Valley in the seventeenth century; after 1700, "Susquehanna Indians" meant the peoples of different tribes living along the Susquehanna River.

towns stretching from Conestoga and Paxtang in the south to Wyoming and Tioga, Ostonwakin and Great Island in the upper reaches of the river's two great branches.[15]

The fertile plain at the junction of these two streams (which European colonists called the North and West Branches) helped make the village at that site among the largest of the Indian islands. When Brainerd and the Macks arrived in 1745, the town's fifty houses, spread across both banks at the mouth of the North Branch and on an island between, held some three hundred Indians.[16]

In the site's very appeal lay an important source of Shamokin's darkness. Although the Iroquois claimed—and their man on the Susquehanna from 1728 to 1748, the Oneida leader Shickellamy, sometimes asserted—control of the region, in fact there was never a charter group of sufficient size or influence to set the terms on which newcomers would be accepted.[17] Shamokin was, throughout its life, clearly an Indian town—"The whites have nothing to say here," Shickellamy once said, "and no white is allowed to live here"—but which Indians? Though the settlement was probably founded by Delawares around 1720, a colonial map drawn a few years later denoted it an Iroquois town. By 1745, the identity of the place was more confusing still, with half of its inhabitants Delawares, the rest Tutelos and Iroquois: "Three different tribes of Indians; speaking three languages, wholly unintelligible to each other," sighed Brainerd, who knew none of them. Another missionary, Joseph Powell, suffered the same assault on his ears shortly after his arrival in January 1748. We

15. These migrations have been too little studied. But see Paul A. W. Wallace, *Indians in Pennsylvania*, 2d ed., rev. William A. Hunter (Harrisburg, Pa., 1986), chap. 14; Peter C. Mancall, *Valley of Opportunity: Economic Culture along the Upper Susquehanna, 1700–1800* (Ithaca, N.Y., 1991), chap. 2; Kent, *Susquehanna's Indians*, 70–108. In 1722, the Iroquois formally adopted these Tuscarora migrants, thereby becoming the Six Nations; see *MPCP*, VI, 116 (quotation).

16. John Bartram, *Observations on the Inhabitants, Climate, Soil, Rivers, Productions, Animals, and Other Matters Worthy of Notice; Made by John Bartram, in His Travels from Pensilvania to Onondago, Oswego and the Lake Ontario, in Canada . . .* (London, 1751), 14, 16; "Extracts from Mr. Lewis Evans' Journal, 1743," in T[homas] Pownall, *A Topographical Description of the Dominions of the United States of America*, ed. Lois Mulkearn (Pittsburgh, 1949), 169; Hunter, *Forts*, 522; David Brainerd, Diary, July 14–Nov. 20, 1745, 30, American Philosophical Society, Philadelphia (hereafter cited as APS).

17. For the idea of a "charter" group, see T. H. Breen, "Creative Adaptations: Peoples and Cultures," in Jack P. Greene and J. R. Pole, eds., *Colonial British America: Essays in the New History of the Early Modern Era* (Baltimore, 1984), 204–205.

"have hear so many Languages that we find it verry Diffical[t] to larn any-thing," Powell wrote. Indeed, he went on in despair, "Its rare to hear two Indi-ans talking in one Language."[18]

Poor Powell probably heard more than three languages that winter, for Shamokin was also a headquarters for Indians throughout the Susquehanna country. The council fire that the Iroquois kindled at the Forks made it a cen-ter for discussion and diplomacy. Six Nations ambassadors heading south sent word ahead to collect at that town "all the Indians about Shohomoakin," then paused there "to Settle their affairs" with these native neighbors. Around 1730, Pennsylvania got into the same habit, and over the next generation, when trouble broke out on the frontier, it was to Shamokin that provincial agents and Susquehanna Indian leaders repaired in order to patch things up. Here, observed one visitor to the village in the early 1740s, "the Indians have their Rendevous, and it is in some measure like the Hague in Holland."[19]

Home to some, headquarters for all, Shamokin was also a way station for travelers, further filling its houses with foreigners and its air with outlandish tongues. The passing scene was a carnival of peoples and cultures: Jeremias, a Moravian Indian from Bethlehem, whose getup drew stares and puzzled looks from the town's natives, and two warriors, whose fluent English, bearskin clothes, and fiercely painted faces elicited a similar reaction from missionaries; an Indian from up the West Branch, a snake tattooed on his face, hunting a stray cow, and two Pennsylvanians looking for horses; Indian fur traders from hundreds of miles away stopping by en route to Philadelphia and colonial traders passing through, going in the opposite direction. A Delaware war party, bound for battle in Catawba country on the borders of Carolina, halted one summer's night to dance in Shickellamy's house, taking turns planting hatch-ets into a post "on which a human head is carved," and one winter's day two warriors, sole survivors of another foray against Catawbas, paused to tell of their companions' being captured and skinned alive. One fall, Conrad Weiser showed up with the Moravian leader Count Nikolaus Ludwig von Zinzendorf,

18. Shamokin Diary, Aug. 2, 1747, *Moravian Records*, 6/121/3/1, Jan. 7–8, 1748, 6/121/4/1; Charles A. Hanna, *The Wilderness Trail; or, The Ventures and Adventures of the Pennsylvania Traders on the Allegheny Path . . .* , 2 vols. (New York, 1911), I, facing 192 (1727 map); Brai-nerd, Diary, 30. Brainerd knew Mahican but needed an interpreter to speak to Delawares (see Edwards, *Life of Brainerd*, ed. Pettit, 254 n. 2).

19. *MPCP*, VI, 116, VIII, 748–749; Weiser to Logan, Sept. 2, 16, 1736, Logan Papers, box 10, folders 59, 62; Weiser to ?, Jan. 24, 1745/6, Pierre Eugene DuSimitiere Papers, Indian Treaties, 966.F.24, Library Company of Philadelphia; "Zinzendorf's Account of His Experience among the Indians . . . ," in Reichel, ed., *Memorials*, I, 133.

who demanded that Indian "merry-making" cease so that he could pray; the following summer, Weiser was back, this time with the naturalist John Bartram, who ambled out of town in search of a nap or a swim and canoed upriver "to look for curiosities." These and untold numbers of other people, parading through, made the place babel's resort.[20]

To compound the confusion, even Shamokin's inhabitants were a peripatetic lot. It was not that in the fall they left town for months on end to hunt; most Susquehanna Indians did that. Rather, it was that few made Shamokin their home for long. Sassoonan, the Delaware headman who was living there in 1728 and was buried there nineteen years later, may hold the record for longevity; staying so long, he saw many of his people emigrate west across the mountains. In 1756, Tachnechdorus (John Shickellamy), the eldest son of Shickellamy, called Shamokin "our old place," neglecting to add that his family had only moved there around 1740. With such swirling, eddying human currents, it was hard to get one's bearings in Shamokin; the complexion of the spot could change from one visit to the next. Those Tutelos the Macks met in the fall of 1745, for example, were not even in Shamokin two years earlier or three years later.[21]

Ethnic antagonism furthered the sense of dislocation. Shamokin Iroquois were said to "despise" the Delawares living there, and during the 1740s Shickellamy belittled his Delaware neighbors, even announcing that Sassoonan was gravely ill, perpetually drunk, or hopelessly insane. In apparent retaliation for these and other slights, a Delaware conjurer bewitched and killed one of the Oneida's grandchildren, only to be done in later by an Iroquois who, the next day, strutted about the town proclaiming himself a hero. Moravians, picking up on the contention in no time, reminded each other that, in order to stay on good terms with everyone, "no partiality must be shown to Iroquois, Dela-

20. For Shamokin as way station, see "Br. Rösler's Relation," *Moravian Records*, 6/121/7/1; Shamokin Diary, Sept. 19, 1745, ibid., 28/217/12B/1, June 7, 1747, 6/121/3/1, Jan. 28, Apr. 4–5, 1748, 6/121/4/1, Jan. 25, 1749, 6/121/4/3, June 5–6, 1749, 6/121/5/2, May 15, 1755, 6/121/7/1; Travel Diary, Oct. 16, 1748, ibid., 30/225/2/1; "Zinzendorf's Narrative," in Reichel, ed., *Memorials*, I, 83–93, 101n; Bartram, *Observations*, 14–17 (quotation on 11).

21. Delaware migrations can be followed in C. A. Weslager, *The Delaware Indians: A History* (New Brunswick, N.J., 1972), chap. 10; Michael N. McConnell, *A Country Between: The Upper Ohio Valley and Its Peoples, 1724–1774* (Lincoln, Nebr., 1992), chaps. 1–2; Jennings, *Ambiguous Iroquois Empire*, pt. III. For Tachnechdorus, see *PA*, 1st Ser., II, 776. For the Tutelos, see "An Account of the Famine among the Indians of the North and West Branch of the Susquehanna, in the Summer of 1748," *Pennsylvania Magazine of History and Biography*, XVI (1892), 431; Travel Diary, Oct. 11, 1748, *Moravian Records*, 30/225/2/1.

wares or Tudelars." These German newcomers had good reason to be cautious, for some of the anger was directed at them. The suspicion and ridicule that Anna and Martin Mack found in some quarters of the town during the fall of 1745 would greet others from Bethlehem, too. To make matters worse, colonial fur traders fanned the flames of native resentment, cursing at missionaries and pointedly inviting them to leave.[22]

Add rum or whiskey to this volatile mix and the result could be explosive. Shamokin was by no means awash in liquor all the time, but drunkenness was a prominent feature of the social landscape. And, although drinkers sometimes were "merry," even "polite," more often they were menacing. "A drunken Indian is a desperate Creature," wrote one colonist, "and 10 others will run out of the way from a single [Indian] who is drunk and begins to behave wildly." In fact, in Shamokin the ratio usually was reversed: a handful of people, bent on abstaining, took to the woods, hid in the fields, even locked themselves in a storehouse in order to escape the blandishments of their intoxicated neighbors, who "plagued" them to join the crowd.[23]

When rum ruled, that crowd turned ugly. People plunged into fires and tried to tear a door off its hinges. With fists or firebrands, husbands beat wives, and mothers maimed children, leaving the little ones to "Cry Bitterly . . . in the Night"; other Indians "wrestled each other in the filth like pigs, and bellowed all night like mad beasts." Shamokin on the morning after one of these sprees was not a pretty sight. They "looked," wrote one who saw the survivors, "like they got up out of their graves."[24]

Swarms of peoples coming and going in pursuit of their own versions of happiness, unpleasantness between tribes and between those whites seeking souls and those after furs, rivers of rum—these combined to make the Indian settlement at the Forks a bewildering, sometimes scary place. But it was more

22. John W. Jordan, ed., "Bishop J.C.F. Cammerhoff's Narrative of a Journey to Shamokin, Penna., in the Winter of 1748," *PMHB*, XXIX (1905), 173–174, 176, 178 (quotation); *PA*, 1st Ser., I, 762; *MPCP*, V, 88; Shamokin Diary, June 8, July 2, 1747, *Moravian Records*, 6/121/3/1, Nov. 20–21, 1747, 6/121/3/3, Apr. 26, May 31, June 1, 1749, 6/121/5/2; Carter, "Moravians at Shamokin," Northumberland Co. Hist. Soc., *Procs.*, IX (1937), 67.

23. Shamokin Diary, Apr. 20, May 10, 1748, *Moravian Records*, 6/121/4/2, Feb. 1, 23, Mar. 13, 1749, 6/121/5/1, Jan. 12, 1749, 6/121/4/3, May 9, 13–14, 27, 1749, 6/121/5/2; Travel Diary, Oct. 15, 1748, ibid., 30/225/2/1.

24. Shamokin Diary, Feb. 23, Mar. 20, 1748 (child crying; this quotation has been reversed for the sake of clarity), *Moravian Records*, 6/121/4/1, Feb. 24, Mar. 7, 12, 1749, 6/121/5/1, Mar. 5, 1750, 6/121/5/2; Travel Diary, Oct. 15, 1748, ibid., 30/225/2/1. See Peter C. Mancall, *Deadly Medicine: Indians and Alcohol in Early America* (Ithaca, N.Y., 1995).

than simply the numbers or the diversity, the tension or the occasional violence that knocked Shamokin akilter. It was the sheer unpredictability of encounters there. Missionaries, who most keenly felt cut loose from their cultural moorings, recorded it best. For no reason that Moravians could fathom, one visiting war party delighted in terrorizing them while another "behav'd with greatest Sevillity." One colonial trader entering their house was "as a fish outof [*sic*] water," another "was verry Exact in behaviour." One day Moravians pronounced a Delaware family "very beloved Indians" and "candidates for the realm of God"; the next, Tutelos crowding in on the German visitors "looked very satanic and barbaric."[25]

Perhaps Susquehanna Indians felt less disoriented. After all, they knew the place better than missionaries, knew it as home and rendezvous, way station and trading post. Nonetheless, they, too, found the Forks capricious. Tutelos versed in the ways of Virginia Christians were puzzled by the Moravian practice of holding services on Saturday; "They woonder'd," wrote one missionary, that "we kept two Sundays, never said they knew that the white people kep[t] more then one." Nor was that all of the confusion missionaries sowed. One moved into Shickellamy's house and immediately instructed Indian dancers there "to desist" with their "noise," then went out to round up some others for a sermon; the next adopted a low profile, convinced that "it [is] not . . . our Buisness to compell the People" and noting that in any case sermons were "a Suspicious Thing amongst them." Similarly, one colonial trader would store his goods with Indians; the next might steal their horses, guns, and pelts.[26]

Part of Shamokin's strange, unsettling aura was the way peoples there shed some of the assumptions structuring native and European societies. Consider the place of women. As a rule, in neither Indian nor colonial culture did women take a visible role in public affairs. In and around Shamokin, however, influential women were common. The French-Iroquois métis "Madam Montour," for one, was a commanding presence in the Susquehanna country for two decades after her arrival in the late 1720s. So was her niece, "French Margaret," occasionally a resident of Shamokin when not driving packhorses loaded with furs to colonial markets. Another local trader was John Harris's wife, Esther, who for at least one winter ran a trading post near the Forks. No less novel was a Mahican woman, a sometime interpreter at Shamokin. Work-

25. Shamokin Diary, Feb. 1, Mar. 16, Apr. 12–13, 1748, *Moravian Records,* 6/121/4/1; Travel Diary, Oct. 10–11, 1748, ibid., 30/225/2/1.

26. Shamokin Diary, Oct. 24, Nov. 3, 1745, *Moravian Records,* 28/217/12B/1, Jan. 9, 1748, 6/121/4/1; Brainerd, Diary, 29–30; *PA,* 1st Ser., I, 758; *MPCP,* V, 87–88.

ing with that anonymous Mahican as a translator was Anna Mack, who also visited sick Indians, establishing credentials as a healer, still another uncommon position for a woman in those parts.[27]

Natural calamity wreaked further havoc with efforts to bring Shamokin to some semblance of order. The town at the Forks was hardly alone in finding itself prey to occasional disasters of one sort or another. Diseases that struck in late summer (in 1747, a fever killed Sassoonan and the Moravian John Hagen as well as a dozen or so of Shickellamy's kin), droughts, late frosts, and high winds that blasted the corn crop, snows that stopped hunters, floods that stole canoes from the riverbank—these did not single out Shamokin.[28] Nor did hunger, a frequent visitor throughout the Susquehanna country in late spring and early summer. And yet these forces might have been particularly powerful at the Forks. For one thing, the site and its water supply were dangerous toward fall. For another, the town's popularity as a meeting ground and way station depleted local food supplies. In 1745, Martin and Anna Mack learned that other recent arrivals, the Montours, were "almost starved for Hunger," and Madam Montour's son Andrew exclaimed that "he had never liv[e]d so poorly in his Life." "It is uncomfortable for Indians there," observed a colonial visitor, "for if they plant they cannot enjoy it, so many strange Indians pass through the town whom they must feed."[29]

27. For assumptions among Susquehanna Indian women that public affairs were the preserve of men, see Brainerd to Pemberton, Nov. 5, 1744, in Edwards, *Life of Brainerd,* ed. Pettit, 579. For French Margaret, see John W. Jordan, ed., "Spangenberg's Notes of Travel to Onondaga in 1745," *PMHB,* II (1878), 429–430 (which identified her as Madam Montour's sister); [Bernhard A. Grube], "A Missionary's Tour to Shamokin and the West Branch of the Susquehanna, 1753," *PMHB,* XXXIX (1915), 442–444; Shamokin Diary, Sept. 19, 1745, *Moravian Records,* 28/217/12B/1; Esther Harris is mentioned in Jan. 6, Feb. 25, Mar. 1, 23, Apr. 2, 8, 11, 1748, 6/121/4/1. On Anna Mack, see Jordan, ed., "Cammerhoff's Narrative," *PMHB,* XXIX (1905), 172–174. For the Mahican woman working with Mack, see Travel Diary, Apr. 21, 1747, *Moravian Records,* 6/121/9/2. Anna Mack's work is noted in Carter, "Moravians at Shamokin," Northumberland Co. Hist. Soc., *Procs.,* IX (1937), 64; Shamokin Diary, Oct. 15, 17, 1745, *Moravian Records,* 28/217/12B/1.

28. Weiser to Logan, Sept. 16, 1736, Logan Papers, box 10, folder 62; *PA,* 1st Ser., I, 661–662; Edwards, *Life of Brainerd,* ed. Pettit, 425; *MPCP,* V, 136–138, VI, 443; "Account of the Famine," *PMHB,* XVI (1892), 430–431; Jordan, ed., "Cammerhoff's Narrative," *PMHB,* XXIX (1905), 169, 174; Grube, "Missionary's Tour," *PMHB,* XXXIX (1915), 441–442; Shamokin Diary, Nov. 18, Dec. 2, 4, 1747, *Moravian Records,* 6/121/3/3, May 31, Aug. 30, 1755, 6/121/7/1.

29. Edwards, *Life of Brainerd,* ed. Pettit, 425; Letter from Shamokin, Aug. 25, 1747, *Moravian Records,* 6/121/8/6; John W. Jordan, trans., Bishop Cammerhoff's Letters to Zinzendorf,

No wonder people from all walks of life and all corners of early America thought Shamokin anything but a nice place to visit, much less live. Madam Montour, though she had spent most of her long life in Indian country, was decidedly uneasy when she settled in Shamokin that fall of 1745. "The old Woman laments much, that the Indians here are still so cold and dead," Montour confided to a colonist one day, "and that they know of nothing but drinking and Dancing." That very night, as if on cue, some of those drunks rousted the old woman from her house and drove her into the dark.[30]

## Darkness Explored: Fort Augusta

### "I am plagued with these Devilish . . . Indians"

The same gravitational forces that made Shamokin the largest Indian town in the Susquehanna country—a deserted, fertile plain at the junction of two major waterways—in 1756 determined that Fort Augusta, built and manned by provincial soldiers, would be the keystone in the arch of frontier forts protecting Pennsylvania from Indian raids. According to frontier mythology, this abrupt shift from Indian country to white outpost signals the victory of order over chaos, civilization over savagery. Shamokin, archetypal of wilderness, also seems to follow the script here, with its metamorphosis into a provincial fort and then a white settlement, a script that has Indians—and those advance guards of the civilizers, fur traders and Christian missionaries –disappear before the superior numbers, superior virtue, "superior genius of the Europeans."[31]

The surviving evidence of the fort certainly makes it look that way. Indeed, the colonial impulse to impose its own version of order on the region's land and peoples was evident before the first Pennsylvania troops glimpsed Shamokin's ashes. Colonel William Clapham, commander of the regiment heading up the Susquehanna in the summer of 1756, designed a carefully calibrated,

---

1747–1749, Letter VIII, Sept. 27–30, 1747, 89–90, HSP; Edward Shippen to Joseph Shippen, Aug. 1, 1756, Weiser to Burd, Apr. 21, 1757, Shippen Family Papers, II; Shamokin Diary, Oct. 17, Nov. 3, 1745, *Moravian Records*, 28/217/12B/1, June 9, 1747, 6/121/3/1, Apr. 11, 20, 1749, 6/121/5/2; Grube, "Missionary's Tour," *PMHB*, XXXIX (1915), 444.

30. Shamokin Diary, Sept. 17, 1745, *Moravian Records*, 28/217/12B/1.

31. J. Hector St. John de Crèvecoeur, *Letters from an American Farmer; and, Sketches of Eighteenth-Century America*, ed. Albert Stone (New York, 1981), 122.

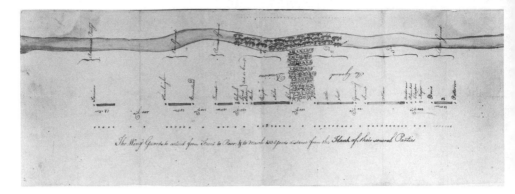

FIGURE 2

The Army's Line of March, 1756. *Captain Joseph Shippen described the army's orderly progress upriver:* *"We proceeded along with great regularity and caution, having a well concerted line of march, such as* *would prevent us from being surprized or surrounded. The whole body extended in length from front to* *rear a mile and a half and consisted of an advanced party, a van guard of 25 men, the provosts guard,* *the main body and a rear guard, each party from the other at the distance of 100, and 200 yds. and* *every man five yards from another marching always in one Indian file, each party having its own Wing* *Guards 150 yds. distance on the right or left flank as we marched on the East or West side of the River.* *The Fleet of Battoes always under the escort of the main body"* ("Military Letters of Captain Joseph Shippen of the Provincial Service, 1756–1758," Pennsylvania Magazine of History and Biography, XXXVI [1912], 388). Courtesy, The Historical Society of Pennsylvania, Philadelphia

"well concerted line of march" that, "with great regularity and caution," arranged troops on shore and supply bateaux on the river (see Figure 2). On reaching the Forks, the soldiers proceeded to build a square structure that, in its very size and shape, heralded the dawn of a new day (see Figure 3). As an added precaution, Clapham had the trees within half a mile of the stronghold cut down, then drew up modes of reconnoitering the perimeter "round the Edge of the Woods" (see Figure 4). Like his sketch, the piles of paper slips—noting each day's watch, password, and the weapons available—testifies to the newcomers' obsession with order.[32]

That obsession aspired to reach beyond the trees and troops to include everyone in the vicinity. Colonial women, too, were to be subdued. No more were they interpreters or traders, no more healers. Those at the garrison,

32. "Military Letters of Captain Joseph Shippen of the Provincial Service, 1756–1758," *PMHB,* XXXVI (1912), 388; Journal by Capt. Joseph Shippen at Fort Augusta, Shamokin, 1757–1758, Jan. 23, 1758, Small Books, no. 6, Shippen Family Papers, HSP (hereafter cited as Shippen Journal [1757–1758]); Morning and Evening Reports of the Garrison at Fort Augusta, Miscellaneous Items, Burd-Shippen Papers, APS.

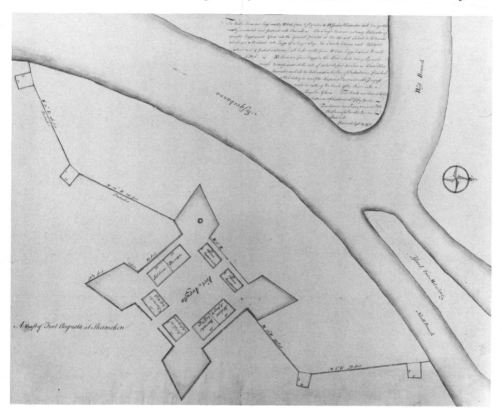

FIGURE 3

Plan of Fort Augusta. *The plan shows stockade lines running
to blockhouses near the river and other features announcing a new order at the Forks.
Courtesy, The Historical Society of Pennsylvania, Philadelphia*

mostly soldiers' wives, were to perform the traditional camp tasks of washing, mending, and cooking for the army. Last but by no means least, the extant documents reveal how the new masters of the Forks sought to control Indians. Instead of the haphazard, unpredictable contacts of an earlier day, encounters now would follow prescribed—and circumscribed—forms, preserved for posterity by massive account books that, line by line, recorded every transaction with natives.

In fact, however, all of these maps and diagrams, straight lines and ruled pages are misleading. Life at the fort was messier than the tidy paper trail suggests. The stronghold, although more imposing than Shamokin's buildings, proved no more immune to regnant forces of nature. Late summer remained a perilous time, carrying off soldiers as it once had done John Hagen, Sassoonan, and Shickellamy's kin. Torrential rains and blinding snowstorms still

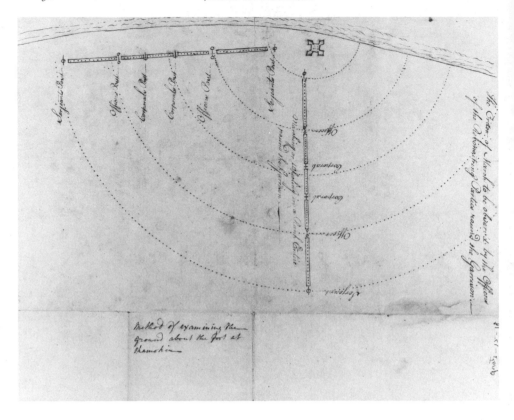

"The Order of March to be observ'd by the Officers of the Reconaitring Parties round the Garrison." *Describing the reconnaissance, Joseph Shippen wrote: "Every Morning before Sun-rise a Party of 50 Men goes out to reconnoitre the Ground for a mile and a half round the Fort, they take different Routs every time and march at the Distance of 6 or 7 Yards apart and all a Breast in one rank entire, so as to sweep a large space of Ground" ("Military Letters of Captain Joseph Shippen of the Provincial Service, 1756–1758,"* Pennsylvania Magazine of History and Biography, *XXXVI [1912], 397). Courtesy, The Historical Society of Pennsylvania, Philadelphia*

struck, slowing, stopping, even wrecking work on the edifice. "The Impetuosity" of a creek destroyed a bridge, and on the Susquehanna itself ice dams or floes in winter, like dry spells in summer, could ground bateaux bringing supplies—and the trappings of civilization—to what one homesick Pennsylvania officer called "this remote part of the World."[33]

The new tenants of the Forks also found that they could no more control

33. Hunter, *Forts,* 534; *PA,* 2d Ser., II, 648; "Military Letters of Shippen," *PMHB,* XXXVI (1912), 404–408 (see also 410).

the human traffic there than they could quiet the winter wind roaring down the West Branch. A sentry peering over Augusta's walls was likely to see all manner of Pennsylvania colonists go by, from a man searching for loved ones taken prisoner by Indians to parties hunting good "Land up the Susquehanna, . . . where some of them purposes to goe and settle." Shifting his gaze to the site just north of his post, that same sentry would spy thirty, or fifty, or more Indians from all over—Conestogas and Conoys, Delawares and "Delaware Negroes," Iroquois and Saponis—camping out there as they went about their usual round of activities. A war dance, a funeral "in the Indian Manner at the Indian Burying Ground," the "usual Chorus" of drunken song, traders crowding into the provincial trading post, ambassadors bearing wampum belts and tobacco pipes—all of these scenes and more still played on the local stage, as they had in Shamokin's day. As late as May 1765, a provincial officer remarked that Indians still were "continually coming and going."[34]

But it was less unforgiving nature or the sheer number of transients than the vagaries of humanity that defied order at the fort. Pennsylvania women, for example, undermined those bent on plotting and pursuing a strict regimen beside the Susquehanna. Like the dream of order, the nightmare of disorder appeared before the army made it to the Forks. En route upriver in July 1756, the regiment's chaplain, Charles Beatty, extracted a promise from Colonel Clapham "to leave the women behind ['especially those of bad character']." "Accordingly," Beatty wrote happily, "they were all ordered to be paraded" so that the unsavory could be weeded out. "But when this came to be done," the disappointed clergyman went on, "one of the officers pleaded for one, and another for another, saying that they could wash, etc., so that few were left of a bad character, and [even] these would not stay but followed that night, and kept with us."[35]

The independent streak continued at Augusta, where women did wash and mend clothes—then, much to the commander's dismay, hung them out to dry

34. Burd to T. Floyd, Military Letterbook of James Burd, 36, Shippen Family Papers; "An Account of the Captivity of Richard Bard . . . ," in Archibald Loudon, *A Selection of Some of the Most Interesting Narratives, of Outrages, Committed by the Indians, in Their Wars with the White People . . .*, 2 vols. (Carlisle, Pa., 1808–1811), II, 73; *PA*, 1st Ser., IV, 218. For Indians, see Shippen Journal (1757–1758), esp. Jan. 18, Feb. 18, Mar. 10, 1758; Hugh Mercer to Burd, Apr. 1, 1760, Graydon to Burd, July 20, 1761, July 12, 1762, Shippen Family Papers, V.

35. Charles Beatty, "Journal Kept in 1756," in William Henry Egle, *History of the Counties of Dauphin and Lebanon in the Commonwealth of Pennsylvania: Biographical and Genealogical* (Philadelphia, 1883), 55.

on the pickets and stockades. Nor were camp followers shy about advancing their own interests. In February 1758, several complained to the commander that sharing their husbands' rations invited starvation and soon started to get their own provisions.[36]

Indian women around Augusta also proved to have minds—and tongues—of their own. If the fort's architects intended to limit contacts solely to Indian men, they were to be disappointed. Native women were frequent customers in the provincial store, trading on their own account and probing for ways around rules against selling liquor. Another woman protested those illicit sales when her son got drunk, quarreled with the provincial storekeeper, and was hauled into the fort. Right behind came his mother, "very much enraged, asking what Right the White People had to tie her Son, Since they were the very people who Sold them the Rum, he was then Drunk with."[37]

Such open confrontations were rare, but every commander at Augusta found Indians—men and women—stubbornly resistant to military discipline. They drank. They complained about (and at least once tried to kill) the storekeeper. They insisted on toasts and formal farewells. "I expect we shall have our own Troubles with them," glumly predicted an officer contemplating the imminent arrival of one native delegation. "I am plagued with these Devilish . . . Indians that every now and then Interrup[t]s me," another moaned.[38]

Troublesome as Indians and Pennsylvania women were, it was Pennsylvania men who caused the most difficulty. The military chain of command created only the illusion of control. In fact, soldiers were hardly less fractious than Indian villagers had been. The officers feuded with the storekeeper (who spied on them through a peephole) and derided ragtag bands of "fickleminded disobedient Volunteer[s]" heading upriver to hunt Indians. Those same officers quarreled among themselves over pay, precedence, and promotion, throwing

36. Fort Augusta, Quartermaster's Ledger, APS; James Burd, Orderly Book, Fort Augusta, Mar. 12, May 10, 1757, APS; Shippen Journal (1757–1758), Feb. 6, 1758. See also PA, 2d Ser., VII, 479.

37. Graydon to Burd, July 12, 1762, Shippen Family Papers, V. For trading, see Shamokin, Ledger B, June 2–Dec. 15, 1759, Gratz Collection, case 17, no. 6, HSP; Fort Augusta, Ledgers A, B, 1762–1763, Gratz Collection, case 17, no. 20; Indian Commissioners Day Book, Shamokin, 1759–1760, ibid., case 17, compartment 5, no. 31; Indian Commissioners Day Book, Shamokin, 1760–1761, ibid., compartment 6; James Irvine to Burd, July 13, 1762, Letters, Burd-Shippen Papers.

38. PA, 2d Ser., VII, 444; Burd to Edward Shippen, July 25, 1757, Graydon to Burd, Apr. 23, 1762, Shippen Family Papers, III, V.

one another in the guardhouse and bombarding Philadelphia with charges and countercharges.³⁹

On one thing, however, all officers agreed: the troops they commanded were so different as to be almost another order of being. In 1758, Captain Peter Bard wrote that one recent batch of recruits beggared belief. "I think they exceed anything of men-kind I ever saw," the astonished and amused Bard remarked after reviewing the troops that July. "They look more like a detachment from the dead than the living. I would have given five pounds to have had Hogarth here when they were drawn up on parade," he scoffed to Colonel James Burd, "to have taken them off that I might have had the pleasure of giving you a view of them." Even those officers who were less contemptuous still considered common soldiers "working people" more inclined to "grumbel," curse, and rebel than build sturdy palisades or mount a proper patrol. At best, the troops were an endless source of trouble who drank rum they were assigned to guard and left their posts to bathe a toothache in the river or answer the call of nature in the bushes.⁴⁰

39. Graydon to Burd, Oct. 12, 1763, Shippen Family Papers, VI. For battles with the storekeeper, see Nathaniel Holland to Gov. Denny, Feb. 24, 1759, Recs. Prov. Ccl., Exec. Corr., B9/2094; Graydon to James Hamilton, Nov. 13, 1761, and Burd(?) to Hamilton(?), Feb. 5, 1762, Shippen Family Papers, V; James Irvine to "Gentlemen," July 13, 1762, Affidavit of Dennis McCormick, July 17, 1762, Burd-Shippen Papers. For the peephole, see *PA*, 1st Ser., IV, 88. Officers' squabbles are in Hunter, *Forts*, 514–516; *PA*, 2d Ser., II, 700–701, 704–708; Thomas Balch, ed., *Letters and Papers Relating Chiefly to the Provincial History of Pennsylvania; with Some Notices of the Writers* (Philadelphia, 1855), 64–65; Lt. Gov. Robert Hunter Morris to ?, [August 1756], Gratz Coll., case 15, box 18; Lt. Daniel Clark to Richard Peters, Nov. 3, 1756, Recs. Prov. Ccl., Exec. Corr., B7/1316; Edward Shippen to Burd, Mar. 26, 1757, Shippen Family Papers, II; "Military Letters of Shippen," *PMHB*, XXXVI (1912), 375–376, 391–394, 399–402, 407, 422.

40. Balch, ed., *Letters and Papers*, 125; Bard to Governor, Aug. 8, 1756, Gratz Coll., case 15, box 18. For desertions and mutinies, see Hunter, *Forts*, 502, 531, 535; Johnston to Hamilton, Oct. 16, 1760, Graydon to Burd, June 5, 1764, Shippen Family Papers, V, VII; *PA*, 2d Ser., II, 659–661, 666, 676–677, 692, 694, 696–697, 699, VII, 442; "Military Letters of Shippen," *PMHB*, XXXVI (1912), 377, 430, 432, 433, 435–437. Even as he complained of German recruits as "a parcel of Mutinous Dutch Rascals" (ibid., 432), Shippen sometimes acknowledged that the troops had reason—a lack of clothing, late pay—to protest (386, 448–449). See also Beatty, "Journal," in Egle, *Dauphin*, 54–55; Christian Busse to Weiser, Oct. 23, Nov. 13, 1756, Correspondence, Conrad Weiser Papers, I, 89–90, HSP. The number and quality of troops fluctuated considerably over the years, from as low as 30 to as high as 400, and from unseasoned and unwilling to "exceeding good Men" ("Military Letters of Shippen," *PMHB*, XXXVI [1912], 413; Hunter, *Forts*, 535). For misbehavior, see Court Martials,

The natural tendency in wartime to let the imagination run wild further wrecked colonial plans for a coherent new community at the Forks. The army's march upriver in the summer of 1756 brought a taste of what was in store. We had "many alarms, reports, and detentions," noted one anxious colonist en route, because there were "many traces of the enemy as near at hand." Scouts sent ahead to reconnoiter scampered back, having "imagined they were discovered and surrounded by the Indians." On the march itself, a little target practice by the "advance guard" put "the whole regiment . . . under arms, . . . expecting to engage every minute" with some unseen foe. On the river, meanwhile, jittery bateaux men poling provisions upstream took a flock of cranes standing on shore for an enemy war party.[41]

Arrival at the Forks did little to calm frayed nerves. Soon after the army reached its objective and began digging in, the night watch made a falling tree out to be gunshots and returned fire with cannon in the direction of the offending timber. Almost a year later, now with the fort fully in place to protect them, sentries were still so jumpy that they took "a large Rock tumbled off the Mountain into the River" for an enemy barrage.[42]

If these new denizens of the Susquehanna Forks could not distinguish Indians from birds or a falling tree from gunfire, they were not likely to be able to tell which natives were friendly and which were not. It is hard to blame colonial soldiers, however; some Indians did indeed disguise their hatred of Pennsylvanians behind a mask of friendship, winning flattery and gifts from the province, then turning on its people. One victim of the ruse met his end just downstream from Fort Augusta: scalped, his skull split open, "his Gun shattered in pieces," the man had "one of the provincial Tomhawks [presents given Indians at treaty councils] stick[in]g in his private parts" as a sort of calling card. Another colonist picked off in a firefight near the fort was, survivors of the ambush insisted, killed by "friendly" Indians who had just camped within sight of the outpost on their way home from a peace treaty in the frontier town of Lancaster.[43]

---

Nov. 24, 1763, Shippen Family Papers, VI; Joseph Shippen to the Officer of the Guard, Dec. 9, 1756, Misc. Items, Burd-Shippen Papers (and James Burd Commitment Order for Sgt. John McCew, n.d., ibid.); *PA*, 2d Ser., II, 626–628.

41. Beatty, "Journal," in Egle, *Dauphin*, 54–55; Journal of Joseph Shippen, Building of Fort Augusta, 1756, July 2, 1756, Small Books, no. 4, Shippen Family Papers (hereafter cited as Shippen Journal [1756]).

42. Shippen Journal (1756), July 20, 1756; *PA*, 2d Ser., II, 665.

43. Shippen Journal (1756), Aug. 23, 1756; *PA*, 2d Ser., II, 681–683.

Confusion reigned in the Susquehanna country not only because it was hard to distinguish Indian friends from foes; it was hard even to tell Indian from white. In July 1756, "one Baskins" learned this while canoeing on the Susquehanna. "He saw 5 Ind[ia]ns," the colonist insisted; "they spoke Delaware to him and he answ[ere]d them." It turned out that these were, not enemy warriors, but provincial scouts "dressed in Indian habit"; poor Baskins was neither the first nor the last to be fooled. European colonists on the Susquehanna frontier did more than wear Indian clothes and speak to each other in Delaware; they also painted or blacked their faces and went scouting with "orders to proceed regularly in an Ind[ia]n File etc. as usual." Indians, too, were adept at disguise, as when "a Hallooing in the Forks of the River[,] seemingly the call of an English Man," turned out to be the shout of a Delaware. No wonder Fort Augusta seemed as full of darkness and noise as Shamokin had been.[44]

## Darkness at Bay

### "A bless'd singing Hour in English, Dutch and Indian"

It is easy, from our perch, to see why the social currents on this part of the frontier ran hard toward confusion and chaos. Who can forget Anna and Martin Mack cowering in that hut as a storm of Indians broke over them or Joseph Powell assaulted by that cacophony of voices? A panicked Conrad Weiser searching the faces of those Iroquois approaching shore or Baskins peering no less anxiously at the figures he saw on that shore? These are powerful images, to be sure. But as the conversation in Delaware that Baskins had with some other Pennsylvanians suggests, Shamokin resists simplicity. Looked at from another angle, one can see that the peoples meeting there were also developing a shared language, a mutually comprehensible set of symbols and ways that rendered life at the Forks something more than the tumult the Macks and others made it out to be.

One way for us to fix that different angle of vision is to imagine a trip to Shamokin in, say, the summer or fall of 1748. Unless you came from Iroquoia and could float downriver, you would find just getting there to be something of an ordeal. Paddling upstream from John Harris's was no easy task: not only was the current against you, but, when the Susquehanna was low, the boulders in its bed lay exposed, making a canoe trip akin to wending through "a town

44. "Batteaux," n.d. [May–July 1756?], Shippen Family Papers, II; Shippen Journal (1756), July 4, 23, 1756; Shippen Journal (1757–1758), Mar. 24, 1758; Beatty, "Journal," in Egle, *Dauphin*, 55.

filled with houses." Going overland was no easier, for the hills were so steep that some riders formed a terrified human chain, each holding onto the coat of the one before, and some who started across on foot ended up crawling over on hands and knees.[45]

While picking your way through the river's rocks or up the mountain trails, you would begin to come upon Shamokin's people well before reaching the village itself. Here on the path are Indian women bound for some colonial settlement to buy liquor and Moravians heading the opposite way with beef from Bethlehem; there are other Moravians, and other Indians, en route from Weiser's farm or Harris's store with sacks of grain. Still other natives would be hauling, not grain, but the blacksmith's tools upriver to Shamokin. Farther along you might see a party of Tutelos and Cayugas heading out to trade or hunt and another band—Delawares and Iroquois, perhaps, or an Oneida war captain at the head of Shawnees and Tutelos—out to snatch scalps or prisoners from some remote Indian tribe.[46]

As you approached Shamokin itself from the south, you would first see the fences enclosing fields planted by Moravians and Shickellamy's family. One reason for the enclosures would also be obvious: horses were by now common in Shamokin. Indeed, two of Shickellamy's had helped haul rocks from the river and logs from the woods to build the Moravian house. That house, too, would now be in sight: eighteen feet by thirty feet, one and one-half stories high, the shingled structure stood a mere twelve paces from Shickellamy's, another log dwelling seventeen feet by forty-nine feet, built for him by colonists several years ago.[47]

45. Shamokin Diary, July 31, 1747, *Moravian Records*, 6/121/3/1, Nov. 4, 1745, 28/217/12B/1; "Zinzendorf's Narrative," in Reichel, ed., *Memorials*, I, 84–85.

46. Carter, "Moravians at Shamokin," Northumberland Co. Hist. Soc., *Procs.*, IX (1937), 67; Jordan, ed., "Spangenberg's Notes of Travel," *PMHB*, II (1878), 427–428; Jordan, ed., "Cammerhoff's Narrative," *PMHB*, XXIX (1905), 164, 168; "Account of the Famine," *PMHB*, XVI (1892), 430, 432; Shamokin Diary, Oct. 20, 27, 1747, *Moravian Records*, 6/121/3/3, Apr. 3, 1748, 6/121/4/1, Feb. 3, 1749, 6/121/5/1, May 7, Aug. 5, 1755, 6/121/7/1; *PA*, 1st Ser., I, 662, 758, II, 23; Jordan, trans., Cammerhoff's Letters, VI, Aug. 12, 1747, 60; Grube, "Missionary's Tour," *PMHB*, XXXIX (1915), 442.

47. Jordan, trans., Cammerhoff's Letters, V, June 29, 1747, 52, VI, Aug. 12, 1747, 60–61; Shamokin Diary, June 3, July 1, 1747, *Moravian Records*, 6/121/3/1, Mar. 9, 25, 1748, 6/121/4/1; Travel Diary, Oct. 13, 1748, ibid., 30/225/2/1; Jordan, ed., "Cammerhoff's Narrative," *PMHB*, XXIX (1905), 177; Carter, "Moravians at Shamokin," Northumberland Co. Hist. Soc., *Procs.*, IX (1937), 66–67. For Moravian house building, see Shamokin Diary, May–July 1747, *Mora-*

While you took in these sights, perhaps your ears would pick up the sound of Moravians at "a bless'd singing Hour in English, Dutch [German] and Indian" or Delawares at a feast who "Sing *Hee* 3 Times, w'ch they drill'd out very long."[48] Audible, too, would be the clang and clatter of the blacksmith at work along with the murmurs of Indian hunters and colonial traders waiting to have a horse shod, a hatchet made, or a gun fixed.

Which of these people stopped what they were doing to welcome you depended on who you were. Weiser or Count Zinzendorf or an Iroquois headman got elaborate greetings and handshakes; most visitors probably did not. Whether your arrival was formal or casual, there was the matter of where to stay. The town had designated "visitors' houses," but—again, depending upon who you were—Shickellamy, the Moravians, or a colonial trader and his Indian wife might offer you a bed.[49]

Once settled into your lodging, you can head out to see the sights. You eavesdrop as a Moravian answering to Anouhseráckeri or Ganachragéjat talks to an Indian named John Petty or John Watson in Delaware, Iroquois, English, or German. You drop by the Moravians' to watch the missionary men bleed an ailing Delaware or cut Shickellamy's hair while the women make shirts for the Indians. Out front, meanwhile, another German woman pounds corn at the stump mortar before the Oneida's house and, just beyond, an African American sent from Bethlehem splits rails to fence the headman's field.[50]

Like the Moravians, you then slip into the stream of visitors, stopping at houses where the woman is Mahican and her husband Shawnee, or Shawnee and Cayuga, or Tutelo and Oneida. Like Moravians, too, and like an Indian

---

*vian Records,* 6/121/3/1, Mar. 21–22, 1748, 6/121/4/1. The missionaries replaced this dwelling with one in another location during the spring of 1753 (6/121/6/1). For Shickellamy's house, see *PA,* 1st Ser., I, 661. The Oneida also had a summerhouse and a storehouse, which might have been the same building.

48. Shamokin Diary, Sept. 29, Oct. 24, 1745, *Moravian Records,* 28/217/12B/1, Apr. 13, 1748, 6/121/4/1.

49. Jordan, ed., "Cammerhoff's Narrative," *PMHB,* XXIX (1905), 177; Bartram, *Observations,* 15.

50. List of Indian Names, *Moravian Records,* 6/121/10/1; *PA,* 1st Ser., IV, 91; Shamokin Diary, July 11, 25, Aug. 1, 1747, *Moravian Records,* 6/121/3/1, Nov. 9, 1747, 6/121/3/3, Jan. 18, Mar. 27, 1748, 6/121/4/1, May 1, 1748, 6/121/4/2; Jordan, ed., "Spangenberg's Notes of Travel," *PMHB,* II (1878), 429–430; *MPCP,* V, 136–137; Jordan, trans., Cammerhoff's Letters, XIII, May 14–26, 1748, 92–93.

couple headed off with a bag of corn loaves, you cross to the island to drop in on people there. Back on the south bank there is a council to attend, where Delawares, Iroquois, and perhaps some Tutelos and Shawnees gather, settle themselves on bearskins, light a pipe, and "put every thing in order." Leaving that gathering, you visit the grave of John Hagen, near Sassoonan's along the shore. Late in the day there is another burial, this time for one of Shickellamy's grandchildren. Painted, dressed in a shirt Moravian women sewed and placed in a coffin Moravian men built, the little girl goes to the next world well stocked with necessities: a blanket to keep her warm, moccasins (along with leather, needle, and thread to make new ones), flint, steel, and tinder to build a fire, with a kettle to hang above it, and, to fill the pot, some bear meat and Indian corn.[51]

Our visit to Shamokin is, admittedly, idealized: the weather is good, the food is plentiful, the liquor is not. But it is no fabrication. Rather, it suggests some of the ways disparate peoples stitched together the fabric of a shared life. The marriages, hunts, councils, and war parties that crossed tribal lines, the linguistic and musical confluences, the Moravian women at Shickellamy's mortar, the Iroquois child in a shirt and a box made by German hands—all of these, amid the din made by so many different peoples, whisper possibilities of peace and harmony.

Returning to the same spot a decade later, you would find that a brutal frontier war had not altogether torn apart the fabric of understanding and common experience. On the river, you see Indians approaching Fort Augusta with a British flag in the bow of their canoe, firing two rounds in greeting and being answered by three huzzas from the garrison. Meanwhile, other natives, departing, are decked out in English clothes and, at their request, get not only those three cheers but also a farewell cannon salute. On shore, Pennsylvania soldiers patch the craft of other Indian visitors, just as the smithy repaired their tools and weapons.[52] Closer to the fort stands the provincial Indian store; busi-

51. *MPCP*, IV, 684; Shamokin Diary, Oct. 19, 1745, *Moravian Records*, 28/217/12B/1, Nov. 23, 1747, 6/121/3/3; Weiser to ?, Jan. 24, 1745/6, DuSimitiere Papers, 966.F.24. For Hagen's grave, see Travel Diary, Oct. 13, 1748, *Moravian Records*, 30/225/2/1; Jordan, ed., "Cammerhoff's Narrative," *PMHB*, XXIX (1905), 172–174; Jordan, trans., Cammerhoff's Letters, VIII, Sept. 27–30, 1747, 89, IX, Nov. 17, 1747, 105.

52. *PA*, 2d Ser., II, 661–662, 665, 678; Milita[r]y Letterbook of James Burd, 1756–1758, 41, Shippen Family Papers; "An Account of Sundrys . . . Delivered to (Andrew) a Dalaware Indian," Dec. 17, 1757, Recs. Prov. Ccl., Exec. Corr., B8/1703; Shippen Journal (1757–1758), Feb. 27–28, Mar. 16, 1758.

ness is brisk, with traders of many tribes drawn there to swap peltry or sell venison to the troops.[53]

These scenes suggest the kinds of everyday contacts that were part of Augusta life, especially when soldiers and their families (along with other families drawn there to serve the garrison) built houses outside the walls and when the gate itself apparently stayed open much of the time. Walking through that gate, you might come upon a council between Indians and colonists, talks where the smoke of a calumet pipe and the rattle of wampum belts—now, sometimes, with the Pennsylvania commander's initials woven into them—mixed with the rustle of paper passports or the scratch of a pen recording the speeches. Or you might see Toshetaquah (Will Sock) working with some curious colonist on a Conestoga-English vocabulary. Turn around and a Delaware is lending an officer his portmanteau while another arranges to stable his horse at the fort.[54]

Perhaps most striking of all the consonances there would be the garrison's penchant for going native. Following the lead of army scouts, those "Woodsmen" routinely clad and painted in Indian fashion already, colonists aimed more generally to "train up Officers and Men to fight the Indians in their own Way." This scheme, "to make Indians of part of our provincial soldiers," was popular among European colonial strategists on the Pennsylvania front. The troops "are very willing," wrote one officer. He might have added that, after a generation of contact in the Susquehanna country—contact that continued at Fort Augusta—those troops were also very able.[55]

53. *PA,* 8th Ser., VI, 4630; Fort Augusta, Ledgers A–B, Gratz Coll., case 17, no. 20; "Invoice of Four Bundles of Peltry and Furs," Apr. 7, 1763, ibid., case 14, box 10; Nathaniel Holland to Israel Pemberton, Dec. 18, 1758, Feb. 25, 1759, Jan. 1, Oct. 16, 1760, Philadelphia Yearly Meeting, Indian Committee Records, Friendly Association for Regaining and Preserving Peace with the Indians by Pacific Measures, I, 323, 469, III, 407, IV, 43, Quaker Collection, Haverford College Library (hereafter cited as Indian Committee Recs.); Hamilton to Graydon, Oct. 10, 1761, Graydon to Hamilton, Nov. 13, 1761, Burd(?) to Hamilton(?), Feb. 5, 1762, Shippen Family Papers, V.

54. *PA,* 1st Ser., IV, 627–628, 2d Ser., II, 662–663, 679–680, VII, 459; Hunter to Burd, June 7, 1763, Shippen Family Papers, VI; Shippen Journal (1756), July 28, 1756; Shippen Journal (1757–1758), Feb. 15, 1758; Holland to Pemberton, May 6, Aug. 7, 1760, Indian Committee Recs., III, 111, 503; "Fort Augusta, 25th January 1757, a Vocabulary in the Mingo Tongue Taken from the Mouth of William Sock a Canistogo Indian," APS; *MPCP,* VIII, 489–490.

55. Peters to Proprietaries, Apr. 30, 1756, Richard Peters, Letters to the Proprietaries, 1755–1757, 35, Gratz Coll. For the use of "Woodsmen" at the fort, see "Military Letters of Joseph Shippen," *PMHB,* XXXVI (1912), 421. See also S. K. Stevens et al., eds., *The Papers of Henry Bouquet* (Harrisburg, Pa., 1951–), II, 124 (see also 51, 61, 133; *PA,* 1st Ser., III, 213, 224).

## Darkness Revealed: The Antebellum Era

## "The Shadow may be often taken for the reality"

The British commander in Pennsylvania, General John Forbes, endorsed one plan to replace some troops' "coats and breeches" with "moccasins and blankets," then to "cut off their hair and daub them with paint and intermingle them with the real Indians." "As you justly observe," he wrote in a letter to a subordinate, this might trick the enemy into thinking that Britain's Indian auxiliaries were many, for "the Shadow may be often taken for the reality."[56]

Forbes might have been talking about Shamokin and the Susquehanna country, where shadows abounded. One shadow was the dissonance that the Macks and others found, which had its roots in the motley array of peoples collected there. Another was the harmony evident in our imaginary trips to the place, harmony grounded in cultural convergence and mutual interest. There is substance—"reality"—in both of these, of course: Shamokin and Fort Augusta *were* bewildering, there *was* common ground there. But it would be wrong to take either as the whole story. Behind the painted faces were colonists, not "real Indians," and neither colonist nor Indian ever forgot it. So it was at the Forks: beneath the general hubbub of folk from all over, beneath the surface of the social landscape of Indian town and then of provincial fort, lay a fault line with native Americans on one side, European colonists on the other.[57]

To be sure, the boundary between Indian immigrants and their European counterparts was blurred, and, in an effort to get along, leaders on both sides tried further to erase it. Time and again, Pennsylvania officials told Shamokin headmen that "we and you are as one People," and those Indians agreed that they and the colonists had "one heart, not divided into halves, but intirely the same without any Distinction." Powerful metaphors did not one people make, however, no matter how often invoked. Another visit to the Susquehanna Forks reveals the obdurate divisions that structured life in that place, the darkness lurking there, making all the talk of being one people just that: only talk.[58]

56. Stevens et al., eds., *Papers of Bouquet*, II, 124, 136.

57. For the limits to colonial borrowing of Indian ways, see James Axtell, "The Indian Impact on English Colonial Culture," in Axtell, *The European and the Indian: Essays in the Ethnohistory of Colonial North America* (New York, 1981), 274–275, 284–303. This is not to suggest that the fault line between Indians and colonists was identical to a geological fault line. Rather, it was as much a product of human action and thought as was the confusion and commonality.

58. *MPCP*, III, 336, IV, 308.

The cultural divide became most apparent once war came in 1755, but it was always present. Sometimes a frontier crisis sent tremors through the Susquehanna country that exposed it. In 1728, a rash of rumors about Indian attacks on the province prompted some Pennsylvania "borderers" to assume that "they might lawfully Kill any Indian whom they could find," as if all natives were the same. Some fifteen years later, a Susquehanna Shawnee, harboring a similar set of assumptions, again placed all Indians on one side of a line, Europeans on the other. When word reached a town on the West Branch in January 1743 that some Virginians had ambushed an Iroquois war party, a Pennsylvania trader there, fearing for his goods (and his life), tried to argue that "the Disorders that have happen'd are no ways owing to the People of Pennsylvania." "We . . . are not answerable for what the People of another Province may imprudently do." The colonist was unconvincing. In reply, "one of the Shawna's observed that the white People are all of one colour and as one Body, and in Case of Warr would Assist one another."[59]

Such assumptions about difference contained a deeper, more frightening belief about the savagery of those on the far side. When Shamokin Delawares killed a Pennsylvania trader named John Armstrong early in 1744, the trader's kinfolk and friends—experienced Indian hands, all—were convinced that they could find only the shoulder bone of the corpse because the murderers had devoured the rest. Soon thereafter, Delawares at Shamokin were persuaded to hand over the culprits when word came that the only other choice was to "separate [the suspects'] Heads from their Bodies . . . and carry them to Alexander [Armstrong, the victim's brother,] to roast and eat them, . . . as he wants to eat Indians." Delawares dining on John Armstrong's remains was about as unlikely a repast as the grieving brother cooking some native heads. But each, in a time of crisis, was ready to believe the worst about the other.[60]

Though killings laid bare the chasm between Indian and European, traces of that gulf can be found throughout the antebellum history of the Susquehanna Forks. They lie, for example, in widespread native suspicion of colonists. The missionary David Brainerd, who one day met up with a band of Susquehanna Indians while he was en route to the Forks, discovered that some "suspected that I had some ill design upon them, and [they] urged that the white people had abused them and taken their lands from them, and therefore they had no reason to think that they were now concerned for their happiness." Although Brainerd insisted that most Indians in this group were friendlier, his

59. *MPCP,* III, 304, IV, 631–633; *PA,* 1st Ser., I, 217.
60. *PA,* 1st Ser., I, 643; *MPCP,* IV, 685.

welcome at Shamokin suggests otherwise. "We are Indians, and don't wish to be transformed into white men," Shickellamy answered when pressed to let the missionary live there. "The English are our Brethren, but we never promised to become what they are. As little as we desire the preacher to become Indian, so little ought he to desire the Indians to become preachers. He should *not* build a house here; they don't want one." Nothing else in Brainerd's scouting trip made him any more optimistic about the prospect of sowing seeds of the true religion in Susquehanna soil. "These poor heathens," he reported on his return, "are extremely attached to the customs, traditions, and fabulous notions of their fathers." "'Twas not, [they say,] the same God made them who made the white people, but another who commanded them to live by hunting, etc., and not conform to the customs of the white people." [61]

That very fall, to the Moravians' delight, Shickellamy changed his mind about missionaries. Impressed by the Macks' willingness to help with the harvest, taken with their quiet, indirect campaign for Christ—no demands, no sermons—tempted by their talk of putting a smithy at his doorstep, the Oneida let the Moravians stay. Yet these pious folk, whose hopes for a meeting of minds and hearts were so high and whose gentle ways held such promise of closing the cultural distance, ended up falling farthest and striking hardest the stony ground of irreconcilable differences. For a decade, from the Macks' arrival to the missionaries' abandonment of the site one step ahead of enemy warriors in October 1755, a cadre of devoted men and women lived in Shamokin, learning languages, visiting and being visited in turn, stressing that their God was also the Indians' God. Yet, after ten years, the last missionary to leave echoed Martin Mack's first assessment of the place: it was still "wild." [62]

This is not to say that Moravians failed altogether. Shickellamy himself, shortly before his death in December 1748, traveled to Bethlehem for further instruction in the faith. As proof of his acceptance of Moravian ways, before heading home he discarded an amulet that he wore around his neck—the last vestige, Moravians rejoiced, of his pagan ways. Moreover, earlier that same year a woman had wept because, she said, she "could not understand and Speake with Sister Smith more." And toward the end of the Moravians' stay, a Conoy

61. Brainerd to Pemberton, Nov. 5, 1744, in Edwards, *Life of Brainerd*, ed. Pettit, 578, 580 (see also 576); Jordan, ed., "Spangenberg's Notes of Travel," *PMHB*, II (1878), 428.

62. Shamokin Diary, Sept. 29–30, Oct. 1, 6, 9–10, 14, 1745, *Moravian Records*, 28/217/12B/1; "Br. Rösler's Relation," Oct. 30, 1755, ibid., 6/121/7/1. For Moravian methods, see Shamokin Diary, Oct. 22, 1745, ibid., 28/217/12B/1; "Zinzendorf's Narrative," in Reichel, ed., *Memorials*, I, 65.

named Schafmann cast his lot with them, even going so far as to build a house next door to his new friends.[63]

Such hopeful signs only set in bolder relief the missionaries' failure, however. In his journey to Bethlehem and to the Moravian faith, Shickellamy had no Shamokin companions. Moreover, his death within days of returning from the Moravian capital (and less than a month after discarding the charm that, he believed, warded off sickness) was hardly an endorsement of the path toward Christ.[64] Similarly, the woman who wept was indeed trying to understand, but her tears of frustration suggest the imposing linguistic and cultural obstacles that faced even a willing listener. And, although Schafmann's enthusiasm certainly excited his Moravian sponsors, he was the exception that proved the rule: building his house by the missionaries', the Conoy also eschewed contact with other Indians.[65]

As Schafmann's isolation suggests, the seeds of the Moravian failure, and the larger significance of that failure, lay in their ultimate inability to shed their habits of thought and behavior in order to meet the Indian world on its own terms or at least to meet it halfway. For all the talk of plans "simply to sojourn in their towns, as friends," Moravians were out to redeem the Indians' world and illuminate its pagan darkness. Behind the strategy to just "Pray and Weep" while waiting for Indians to "open the Doors of their Hearts" to Christ was an aggressive campaign to remake the spiritual and natural world.[66]

That urge was clear even before the first Moravians reached Shamokin, for en route there in 1742 Count Zinzendorf and his companions indulged in

63. James H. Merrell, "Shickellamy, 'A Person of Consequence,' " in Robert S. Grumet, ed., *Northeastern Indian Lives, 1632–1816* (Amherst, Mass., 1996), 250–251; Shamokin Diary, Jan. 16, 1/48, *Moravian Records,* 6/121/4/1, Jan. 30, 1/49, 6/121/4/3, Apr. 22, 1/49, 6/121/5/2, Aug. 3, Oct. 30, 1755, 6/121/7/1.

64. Other inhabitants of Shamokin went to Bethlehem at one time or another, but I have found no evidence of other conversions. One might also ask how sincere Shickellamy's own conversion was (Merrell, "Shickellamy," in Grumet, ed., *Northeastern Indian Lives,* 250–251). That word spread of Shickellamy's visit just before his death, see Shamokin Diary, Feb. 19, 1749, *Moravian Records,* 6/121/5/1.

65. The Moravians' ability to get their message across might never have been very great. As late as June 1755, a Shamokin Indian complained that only one missionary could communicate effectively with the natives, and that one was rarely there (Shamokin Diary, June 8, 1755, *Moravian Records,* 6/121/7/1).

66. "Zinzendorf's Narrative," in Reichel, ed., *Memorials,* I, 65; Shamokin Diary, Sept. 15, Nov. 3, 1745, *Moravian Records,* 28/217/12B/1.

an orgy of renaming the landscape. Traveling through terrain still bearing an unmistakable Indian signature—not only names and paths but "a memorial stone" here, there drawings on trees, over there a warrior's grave—Moravians christened everything from campsites and springs to valleys and hills. Sleeping at *Pilger Ruh,* drinking from *Erdmuth's Spring,* fording *Benigna Creek,* scaling *Jacob's Heights,* those who followed found comfort in the familiar landmarks and took up where Zinzendorf's party had left off, carving initials into trees and adding to the stock of Susquehanna features with new names.[67]

Once Moravians settled in at Shamokin, the same impulses found various outlets. The house built in the summer of 1747, although it resembled Shickellamy's next door, nonetheless astonished local Indians—who often stood and watched it go up—with its cellar, chimney, wooden floor, coal house, and loft.[68] And that was just the beginning. Ignoring advice from their superiors to farm "in the Indian manner" so as to fit in, Moravians fenced and plowed fields, planted fruit trees, and built bridges.[69]

Furthering the missionaries' departure from the main currents of Shamokin life was their aloofness from that life. For all of the determination to make a home in Shamokin, Bethlehem was never far from Moravian minds. Not dwelling *in* Bethlehem, missionaries dwelt *upon* it, continually revisiting family and friends there in their prayers, their thoughts, even their dreams.[70] So intense was the longing to see friends from home that rumors of a visitor's

67. "Zinzendorf's Narrative," in Reichel, ed., *Memorials,* I, 82; Jordan, ed., "Spangenberg's Notes of Travel," *PMHB,* II (1878), 426–427, III (1879), 58; Travel Diary, October 1748, *Moravian Records,* 30/225/2/1; W[illia]m M. Beauchamp, ed., *Moravian Journals Relating to Central New York, 1745–1766* (Syracuse, N.Y., 1916); Grube, "Missionary's Tour," *PMHB,* XXXIX (1915), 442.

68. Shamokin Diary, June 10, 13, 22, 27, July 1, 2, 4, 8–11, 13, 16, 1747, *Moravian Records,* 6/121/3/1, Oct. 16, 23, 30, Nov. 10, 19, 1747, 6/121/3/3, Mar. 21–22, 1748, 6/121/4/1.

69. Jordan, ed., "Cammerhoff's Narrative," *PMHB,* XXIX (1905), 178 (quotation); Shamokin Diary, June 17, 25, July 13, 1747, *Moravian Records,* 6/121/3/1, January–April 1748, May 13, 18, 19, 1748, 6/121/4/2, Mar. 14–15, 1749, 6/121/5/1, May 9, 1749, 6/121/5/2, May 19, 1754, 6/121/6/2, Sept. 9, 1755, 6/121/7/1. A meadow is mentioned on June 20, 1755, 6/121/7/1. In addition, during the spring of 1754 Moravians spent a week cutting down the trees around their new house (May 12, 1754, 6/121/6/2). Whether the Indians' absence that week was coincidental is unclear.

70. This occurred especially, though by no means exclusively, on the Sabbath. See, for example, Shamokin Diary, Feb. 4, 11, Mar. 4, 11, 25, 1749, *Moravian Records,* 6/121/5/1. For Moravians' revisiting Bethlehem in their dreams, see June 19, 1747, 6/121/3/1. For doing so in their hearts, see Oct. 24, Nov. 22, Dec. 25, 1747, 6/121/3/3, May 14, 21, 22, June 1, 4, 18, 1748, 6/121/4/2.

approach were enough to keep eyes on the path to town or even to send someone down that path in hopes of meeting the longed-for traveler. When a visitor did reach Shamokin, anxiety gave way to ecstasy as the famished spirits devoured the fresh letters, greetings, and news, often keeping the newcomer up
talking late into the night. Sweet these reunions were; but their end was
marked by tears. Those left behind among the Indians were disheartened,
wrote one traveler recounting his own departure from Shamokin, "especially
brother Boehmer, who is not yet accustomed to the lonely way of life."[71]

At least one Moravian was lonesome when Indians left on the hunt and the
town stood empty. More often, however, missionaries watched natives leave
with relief, not regret, for, regardless of the Moravians' frequent professions of
affection for Indians, the German colonists loved Delawares, Iroquois, and
other native neighbors at arm's length. Building a house of their own made an
unambiguous statement of this desire for distance; placing it with Shickellamy's several hundred yards from town spoke still louder.[72] Loud, too, was
their steadily deepening isolation of their local shrine, John Hagen's grave. In
September 1747, Moravians laid the beloved Hagen to rest near Sassoonan. But
in the years to come, they set him farther and farther apart from Indians, first
putting a wooden fence around the plot, then covering it with a hut, and finally
surrounding it with a stone wall.[73]

71. Ibid., Dec. 28–29, 1747, 6/121/3/3, Dec. 19, 1748, Jan. 1, 1749, 6/121/4/3. For newcomers'
arrivals, see June 25, July 23, 1747, 6/121/3/1, Sept. 29, Oct. 12, 18, Nov. 2, 8, 1747, 6/121/3/3,
Apr. 18, May 1, 13, June 15, 1748, 6/121/4/2, Jan. 2–3, 1749, 6/121/4/3, Feb. 14–15, 1749 6/121/5/1,
May 1, 1749, 6/121/5/2, Jan. 21, Apr. 17, June 11, 1754, 6/121/6/2. See also Jan. 4, 1748, 6/121/4/1,
May 5, 1748, 6/121/4/2, June 28, 1754, 6/121/6/2.

72. Ibid., Sept. 24, 1755, 6/121/7/1. That Shickellamy did not live in town is suggested by
Shamokin Diary, Oct. 28, 1745, *Moravian Records*, 28/217/12B/1. The site of the Moravians'
house was said to be half a mile from the town (Timothy Horsfield to the Governor, Nov. 10,
1755, Timothy Horsfield Papers, 45, APS). Moravians visiting Indians after June 1747 commonly said they went "into the town" (Shamokin Diary, Aug. 31, Sept. 7, 28, 1755, *Moravian
Records*, 6/121/7/1). The Indians' dislike of visitors' living apart from the village was apparent at other Susquehanna towns. See "Mack's Recollections," in Reichel, ed., *Memorials*, I,
102–106; Jordan, ed., "Spangenberg's Notes of Travel," *PMHB*, III (1879), 58. The missionaries' location might have reflected not only their wishes but those of Indians. However eager natives were to have visitors staying in houses in town, they might have felt differently
about foreigners determined to settle in for a prolonged stay. See Daniel K. Richter, "'Some
of Them . . . Would Always Have a Minister with Them': Mohawk Protestantism, 1683–
1719," *American Indian Quarterly*, XVI (1992), 477–478.

73. Travel Diary, Oct. 13, 1748, *Moravian Records*, 30/225/2/1; Shamokin Diary, Mar. 26,
1749, ibid., 6/121/5/1, June 17, 1754, 6/121/6/2.

The missionaries' daily round further betrayed them. True, Moravians visited and welcomed Indians, fed them and sewed shirts for them, fixed their guns and shoed their horses. Yet, Moravians also refused a native's invitation to take a swig from a bottle, watched but did not join Indian dances, never considered marrying a local Indian, tended to shoo guests away as the day wore on—saying that "our house was not for the Indians to lodge in"—and sometimes surrendered to the urge to lecture Indians on their faults.[74]

However much they admired some Indians, however much they despised many colonists (especially fur traders), Moravian missionaries nonetheless divided the world into Indian and colonist. Their daily account of visits always distinguished *Weisse Leute* (white people) from *Indianer* (Indians). Few if any of those *Indianer* could peer over a German's shoulder as he wrote in his journal and read the dichotomous picture of Shamokin being set down there. But many could read a Moravian well enough nonetheless, and did not like what they learned. For every native happily pronouncing these Bethlehem missionaries different from other colonists, another was full of doubt.[75] The newcomers' plow, like their house, apparently generated uneasiness. So did the coveted blacksmith, who occasionally annoyed Indian traders by haggling over debts and insisting that he would accept only deerskins—not raccoon, not fox, not wildcat—in exchange for his work. Even Shamokin Indians borrowing a Moravian custom remarked (and thereby marked) the limits of their interest. Natives burying their dead in a coffin built by missionaries, for example, scolded the carpenters, saying that it was cruel to bury people, as Christians did, without the tools needed to survive in the next world.[76]

74. Shamokin Diary, Oct. 15, 24, 1745, ibid., 28/217/12B/1, June 7, 1747, 6/121/3/1, Mar. 28, 1749, 6/121/5/1; Travel Diary, Apr. 19, 1747, ibid., 6/121/9/2, Oct. 13–15, 1748, 30/225/2/1. On lodging, see Jordan, ed., "Cammerhoff's Narrative," *PMHB*, XXIX (1905), 177. For reluctance, see Shamokin Diary, Jan. 15, 22, 23, 30, Feb. 1, 5, May 20, 27, 28, 1749, *Moravian Records*, 6/121/5/2. Indians sometimes did stay (July 25, 1749, Feb. 8, 1750, 6/121/5/2, April–August 1755, 6/121/7/1). The occasional lectures are mentioned in Shamokin Diary, Sept. 20, 1745, ibid., 28/217/12B/1, Mar. 24, 1748, 6/121/4/1, May 16, 1748, 6/121/4/2.

75. For those saying Moravians were different, see Jordan, ed., "Cammerhoff's Narrative," *PMHB*, XXIX (1905), 172; Shamokin Diary, Nov. 3, 1745, *Moravian Records*, 28/217/12B/1, Dec. 8, 25, 1747, 6/121/3/3; Travel Diary, Oct. 14, 1748, ibid., 30/225/2/1.

76. Jordan, ed., "Cammerhoff's Narrative," *PMHB*, XXIX (1905), 172, 174–176. It may also be significant that no Indians helped the missionaries build their house, though Shickellamy did lend them two horses. For Indians watching the missionaries at work in the fields and exclaiming over the quality of the corn in those fields, see Shamokin Diary, May 12, June 8, 1748, *Moravian Records*, 6/121/4/2. The following spring, two Indian men asked

Other Indians thought missionaries not merely misguided but malevolent. One Susquehanna native "Spoke many Evill things of the Brethren." "Said the indians tould him in Knaden Hitt [Gnadenhütten, another Moravian mission in Pennsylvania] that the Brethren wanted to make them to Slaves, and that [when] thay . . . puld of[f] Sum Indian Corn Colbs of thare owne planting and a [Moravian] Brother met them and took it from them and Beate them." At the heart of these concerns about Moravians was the Indians' fear of losing their land to European intruders. In October 1745, the Macks confronted these Indian suspicions when a Shawnee named Neshanackcow turned on them to say: "You . . . are like the Pidgeons, when you come to a Place, 1 or 2 don't come alone, but imediat[e]ly a whole Company fly thither." [77]

Neshanackcow, like his fellow tribesman at that town on the Susquehanna's West Branch in January 1743, insisted that, whatever Moravians said about being different from other European colonists, white people were "all of one Colour and as one Body." Although missionaries protested these accusations, in fact some of them did have an eye out for likely places to start towns "if sometime the Proprietor should get the land" from Indians.[78] It would be surprising were Neshanackcow the only Susquehanna Indian to get wind of these musings, for natives were acutely sensitive to signs of invasion by colonial settlers. As early as 1733, Shamokin leaders warned off John Harris, who, calling it a trading post, had built a house and—betraying, the Indians argued, his real design—begun "clearing fields" at the mouth of the Juniata River, just forty miles downstream. For the next two decades, Indians, "very uneasy," watched as European colonists pressed up the Susquehanna toward Shamokin itself. In the spring of 1755, Tachnechdorus was outraged to find a family of German farmers putting up a house and planting crops on the very outskirts of town.[79]

---

Moravians to plow their field but refused a missionary's offer to teach them (May 20, 23, 1749, 6/121/5/2). Shickellamy, for one, pronounced himself pleased with the plowing in the summer of 1747, when he was eager to accommodate the newcomers in order to secure the services of their blacksmith (July 25, 1747, 6/121/3/1). See also Feb. 24, 26, 1750, 6/121/5/2.

77. Shamokin Diary, Oct. 31, 1745, *Moravian Records*, 28/217/12B/1, Mar. 6, Apr. 2, 1748, 6/121/4/1.

78. Travel Diary, Oct. 17, 1748, ibid., 30/225/2/1. See also Oct. 5, 1748; Reichel, ed., *Memorials*, I, 16n; Jordan, trans., Cammerhoff's Letters, IV, May 22–24, 1747, 30; "Extracts from Evans' Journal," in Pownall, *Topographical Description*, ed. Mulkearn, 168.

79. *MPCP*, III, 503, IV, 570, 572, 648; Jordan, ed., "Cammerhoff's Narrative," *PMHB*, XXIX (1905), 167, 169; *PA*, 1st Ser., II, 24; Shamokin Diary, May 2, 12, July 26, 1755, *Moravian Records*, 6/121/7/1 (see also July 2, Aug. 14).

Darkness Revealed: The War Years

"I thought to refuse any kind of Connection with them"

Even more than land encroachment, the outbreak of war in the autumn of 1755 laid bare the alienation that was always beneath Shamokin's surface. Like the occasional bloodshed earlier, the killing that began during that terrible fall unleashed hatreds, hatreds that, this time, would rule the Susquehanna for a generation, until the day Iroquois, Delawares, and the rest abandoned the valley forever. Indians, Pennsylvania borderers now asserted, had shown their true colors; all were enemies. It is time to get rid of those Iroquois families, our so-called friends, hanging around my house, John Harris urged Pennsylvania officials in late October, as "I don't like their Company." With old acquaintances like Harris in this humor, Shamokin Indians who followed the old paths "to the [colonial] Inhabitants" took their lives into their hands. Tachnechdorus, making his way down the Susquehanna to Pennsylvania in the spring of 1756, was "often insulted by the fearful ignorant people who have Sometimes told Sheckallimy to his face, that they had a good mind to Scalp him." "Your People are foolish," an enraged Pennsylvania loyalist, an Oneida leader named Scarouyady, told the provincial Council that same season. "At present your People cannot distinguish Foes from Friends; they think every Indian is against them; they blame us all without Distinction . . . ; the common People to a Man entertain this notion, and insult us wherever we go." [80]

Scarouyady predicted that a fort at the Forks would quiet the dreadful noise in the Susquehanna country. The stronghold, he said in Philadelphia that spring, would give Indians a "Place to go where they can promise themselves Protection." Fear, suspicion, murder: "All this," Scarouyady promised Pennsylvania, "will be set right when you have built the Fort." [81] It did not turn out that way, not least because the colonists who built and manned that fort agreed with John Harris, and their rage found brutal expression. On the army's march upriver in June 1756, "two Dutchmen, deserters . . . , sacreligiously mutilated an Indian in his grave." In January 1757, another party escorting two Indian messengers upriver to the fort had to seize one Manes, a sergeant who, claiming that he knew the two were actually Indian foes, grabbed his gun and swore

80. *MPCP*, VI, 655, VII, 6, 47, 51, 80, 244; *PA*, 1st Ser., II, 634, 777–778.

81. *MPCP*, VII, 80. Although Scarouyady and other Indians did request that Pennsylvania build a fort there, it should be noted that he and most of the others issuing the invitation were Ohio Indians; the Six Nations Iroquois never formally approved a fort at that site. See Hunter, *Forts*, 485–486, 519.

that "if he Should meet them in the woods he would as Soon kill them as the Greatest enemy he had."[82]

Manes and the two deserters were hauled in for their misdeeds, suggesting that at least some provincial officers still were somewhat immune to the epidemic of Indian hating sweeping the frontier. But commanders of the garrison at the Forks were hardly more enthusiastic about "our Dear Fr[ien]dly Indians at Augusta" than the troops were, and they were as eager to be rid of them as John Harris. Colonel Clapham's orders as he assembled his forces in June 1756 were clear: once you erect the fort, no Indian, "however friendly, should . . . be admitted but in a formal manner, and the guard turned out." Later instructions were even more strict: because they might get drunk or—worse—begin "making Observations on the Works and Strength of the Garrison, . . . the Indians should not be suffered to come unto the Fort." Officers were glad, in this case, to follow orders. "I thought to refuse any kind of Connection with them," wrote Lieutenant Caleb Graydon of some Delaware visitors.[83]

Complete segregation was impossible, as we have seen. Nonetheless, even as they followed the scripts of treaty councils and formal calls, officers did what they could to keep Indians at a distance and to maintain the barrier separating natives from colonists. Indian allies, traders, and scouts were almost always recorded, not as Job Chilloway, William Taylor, Telenemut, Kukywunham, or Lykins, but as "Job Chillaway, an Indian," "Telenemut, an Indian," "Indian William Taylor," "Kukywunham and Lykins 2 Indians." So deep ran the distrust that, when two Delaware men, three women, and five children—hardly a menacing bunch—showed up one day, the fort's commander canceled his review of the troops because "my Garrison [is] so small that I don't Choice to give them an opportunity of knowing my Numbers."[84]

The same urge for separation can be read in the plans for the fort itself. Just as the governor ordered Clapham to put up houses for visiting natives "at a convenient distance, under the command of the Guns," so the Indian store, too, went outside, in the shadow of the fort's walls (and its cannon) rather than within its confines.[85]

82. Beatty, "Journal," in Egle, *Dauphin*, 54; Court of Inquiry, Fort Augusta, Jan. 31, 1757, Shippen Family Papers, II.

83. Harris to Burd, Dec. 6, 1757, Shippen Family Papers, III; On Clapham's orders, see *PA*, 1st Ser., II, 667. See also Lt. Gov. Robert Hunter Morris to ?, September 1756, Gratz Coll., case 15, box 18; *PA*, 1st Ser., IV, 214, 2d Ser., VII, 462; Denny to Burd, Oct. 29, 1757, Shippen Family Papers, III.

84. *PA*, 2d Ser., II, 681, 685, VII, 459, 461, 464.

85. Ibid., 1st Ser., II, 667.

Placement of huts and store sent a clear signal of the colonists' vision of proper relations between Indians (however friendly) and whites. But the message sent by the construction of Fort Augusta—this is now English land—was clear in a host of other ways. Shamokin Indians had been worried about a solitary cornfield beside the Juniata in 1733; what must they have thought about the fort people's wholesale reformation of the landscape at the Forks? The straight lines, the right angles, the formidable walls of oak and pine, the seventy-foot flagpole—these were only the beginning. Year after year, work gangs ranging in size from several men to seventy and in skills from mere laborers to carpenters and colliers or masons and brickmakers set about taming what they considered wild terrain. They dug trenches and sawpits, a well and a magazine. They constructed a bakehouse and a "Necessary house." They ventured to the river to sow bluegrass on the banks, to haul stones and hunt lime, to build a wharf and a fish dam.[86]

At the same time, other construction crews set to work fashioning livestock pens. The forty-one cows brought with the army in the summer of 1756 were the first of a steady stream of domestic animals that included sheep and even chickens as well as cattle and hogs. One officer betrayed his priorities when he noted the arrival of a party from downriver consisting of forty-eight bullocks—and twenty-seven soldiers.[87]

A "Herdsman" was, then, a valuable member of the garrison. So was a plowman, for many of the colonists driving that first herd of livestock soon turned a hand to agriculture in order to make the garrison less dependent on food shipped up the Susquehanna. Only two weeks after arriving at the Forks, soldiers cleared "a large Garden" of several acres. The following spring, work details fenced this plot before fencing and plowing a ten-acre turnip patch nearby. Each year the agricultural regime expanded: turnips and watermelons in 1757, cabbage, potatoes, marigolds (for soup), and fruit trees in 1758, by 1760 oats and hay from a meadow. "We live in the hight of Luxury," boasted Lieutenant Graydon in June 1760, "especeliss abounding in strawberrys, Cream, Mutton, Lamb, Green Peas, salad[?], Butter of our own making etc. etc. etc. etc. etc. etc.

86. Military Letterbook of Burd, 8; *PA*, 1st Ser., III, 48, 66, 2d Ser., II, 654, 656, 659, 677, 687, 697–700, 703, VII, 479, 484; Shippen Journal (1757–1758), Dec. 22, 1757; Montgomery et al., eds., *Frontier Forts*, I, 360–361.

87. Beatty said that 20 cattle were with the regiment (Beatty, "Journal," in Egle, *Dauphin*, 55). For references to domestic animals, see *PA*, 1st Ser., III, 4, 14, 347, 515, 550, 568, IV, 122, 2d Ser., II, 672–704, VII, 462, 470, 471, 478–479. For chickens, see Hunter, *Forts*, 528; Balch, ed., *Letters and Papers*, 75.

etc." The following spring, Graydon again could scarcely contain his enthusiasm: "Every thing grows finely here and we have all more Occasion of Cooks than Phisycians."[88]

Men like Graydon spent more time detailing their achievements at the Forks than sounding the Susquehanna country to gauge the Indians' reaction to the course of events since the fall of 1755. But it is clear that Susquehanna natives followed a path of hatred, fear, suspicion, and estrangement akin to colonists'. When those fifty Pennsylvanians headed by John Harris arrived in Shamokin at the outbreak of war in October 1755, one Delaware who saw them asked another, "What are the English come here for?" "To kill us I suppose," was his companion's prompt reply.[89]

However much Scarouyady and some other Iroquois lobbied for it, Pennsylvania's plans to erect a stronghold at the Forks the following spring did little to reassure most Susquehanna Indians. "If built," they worried, "from thence the English would march up the Susquehanna, burn[?] all before them," and, meeting up with other colonial forces, "so drive off all the Indians." In the end, Scarouyady was wrong, the native doubters right: the fort heightened rather than relieved tension. So imposing was Augusta that native delegations bound for the garrison might send scouts to see if the troops there shot Indians on sight. A party bold enough to camp under the guns still might be reluctant to venture through the gate. "They would not come into the Fort to my House," wrote one officer in 1760, "least I should cut them all off."[90]

Just how alienated Indians remained, how keen they were to maintain their distance from colonists, became clear in May 1757. Earlier that spring, in an attempt to keep an eye on natives, Pennsylvania officials at the Lancaster treaty thought they had extracted from Indian ambassadors a promise to settle twelve native families near the fort. When, stopping at that stronghold on their way home, the Indians were told of this supposed deal, their speaker, a Susquehanna Oneida named Sagughsuniunt (Thomas King), was blunt. "We never made any such promise as you mention . . . ; we never intended to stay here. . . . We have all our friends and Relations at our Towns, and it would not be good

88. *PA*, 1st Ser., III, 15, 2d Ser., II, 669–670, 673, 684–685, 698; Bard to Governor, Aug. 8, 1756, Gratz Coll., case 15, box 18; Hunter, *Forts*, 528; Balch, ed., *Letters and Papers*, 125–126; Johnston to Burd, June 21, Aug. 1, 1760, Graydon to Burd, June 5, 1760, May 20, 1761, Mar. 5, Apr. 10, 1762, Shippen Family Papers, V.

89. *MPCP*, VI, 648.

90. Memorandum of Conversations with Indians, May 31, June 1, 1756, Recs. Prov. Ccl., Exec. Corr., B6/1171. See also *PA*, 1st Ser., II, 666, 2d Ser., II, 662, VII, 443.

for us to stay here and leave them there; . . . We are all going off to-day,"
Sagughsuniunt concluded, "and . . . none will stay here unless those that dye"
from the smallpox then raging through the delegation.[91]

Neither Sagughsuniunt nor his companions thought that by refusing Pennsylvania's offer this time they were abandoning the Forks to colonial control.
The spot was too precious, too sacred, to be relinquished. In 1754, an Iroquois
leader had told provincial officials: "We will never part with the Land at Shamokin and Wyomink; our Bones are scattered there, and on this Land there
has always been a great Council Fire." Once fire of another sort consumed the
town shortly after frontier war broke out the following year, Shamokin Indians scattered by the flames were in despair. His family made a mistake in "run-
ing away from Shamockin last fall into a Wildnessness," Tachnechdorus admitted in the spring of 1756; "we have lost ourselves."[92]

In order to find themselves again, Tachnechdorus and the others knew that
they had to get Shamokin back. It would not be easy. The sheer size of the fort
and the scope of colonial operations there proclaimed permanence. Indians
passing by saw the fruit trees and marigolds, the lime kilns and wharf, and got
the message. They watched as the fort's gravitational pull—its need for supplies
and skills as well as the protective power of its guns—drew other colonists to
the Forks. They noticed the "straight road round Shomocken Hill" that soldiers built and saw a survey party scouting the best route for a second highway
to run southeast, all the way to the Schuylkill River. They stumbled upon other
surveyors out to divide up the land and saw prospectors chipping ore samples
or chasing down rumors of a lead mine.[93]

91. *PA,* 2d Ser., II, 679.

92. *MPCP,* VI, 116 (and see Benjamin Lightfoot, Notes of a Survey, Pottstown to
Shamokin, 1759, 10, HSP); *PA,* 1st Ser., II, 776.

93. *PA,* 2d Ser., II, 648. For surveying, see Holland to Pemberton, May 6, Aug. 7, Oct. 16,
1760, Indian Committee Recs., III, 111, 503, IV, 43; John Armstrong to Hamilton, Nov. 19,
1760, Letters, Burd-Shippen Papers. For roads, see *PA,* 1st Ser., III, 560, 721, 728–730, IV, 362–
363; Lightfoot, Notes of a Survey, 3, 10; Peters to Mercer, Dec. 30, 1760, Shippen Family Papers, V. For the mine and crystal, see William Allen to Burd, July 10, 1762, Shippen Family
Papers, V. It is unclear who owned Shamokin. Conrad Weiser in 1754 apparently made a private purchase from the Shickellamys for the proprietors of the land on which the fort eventually would be built, but that was never done in formal treaty. See Hunter, *Forts,* 486–487,
508–509, 519–520; Letterbook of Richard Peters, 1737–1750, 381, 392, Richard Peters Papers,
HSP; Penn-Physick Manuscripts, XI, 58, 113, HSP; Penn Manuscripts, Indian Affairs, IV, 6,
HSP; Weiser to Peters, Mar. 11, 1755, Peters Papers, IV, 7; Peters to the Proprietors, Jan. 10,
1757, Penn MSS, Additional Miscellaneous Letters, I, 100, HSP.

Reading the fort and its ominous companions, Indians were "much alarm'd . . . and jealous," one Pennsylvania official noted as early as 1756, "that we intend by it to secure the possession of their unpurchased lands." Two years later, the Conestoga William Taylor, "furious," told Colonel James Burd at Augusta "that we [English colonists] had taken all the Indians' Lands from them, and that land on which Fort Augusta stands was theirs." That Schuylkill road crew only deepened suspicion; Indians camped at the Forks "are fearful," reported the surveyor, that "if the People get a Waggon Road there they [Pennsylvanians] will then come and settle their Land." By 1760, Indian skeptics had only to gaze westward across the mountains to the confluence of the Allegheny and Monongahela, where the shape of Shamokin's future lay. "You told me, when you was going to Pittsburgh, you would build a Fort against the French, and you told me you wanted none of our Lands," a Seneca reminded provincial officials during a treaty at Lancaster in 1762; "and that you promised to go away as soon as you drove the French away, and yet you stay there and build Houses, and make it stronger and stronger every day." [94]

At that same Lancaster council in August 1762, Indians tried to take Shamokin back before it, too, slipped forever into other hands. The council fire that the Iroquois had kindled there "is not yet out," insisted Sagughsuniunt, their speaker; "if any body stirs it, it will soon blaze." On behalf of "all the different Tribes of us present"—some six hundred people in all, including Tachnechdorus and others from old Shamokin—the Oneida made clear the Indians' refusal to share a common destiny with their European colonial neighbors. "You know I am not as you are," he said. "I am of a quite different Nature from you." To reflect that difference, Sagughsuniunt wanted the stronghold at the Forks evacuated and the land returned. He began by reminding Pennsylvania of its promise to "go away" from the fort when the war was over, or "at any time when I should tell you to go away." Now, he said; now is the time. Keep a "Trading House" there, by all means. Trade "is the way for us to live peaceably together." But "for you to keep Soldiers there, is not the way to live peaceable." Therefore, "call your Soldiers away from Shamokin." Sagughsuniunt was adamant: "I must tell you again these Soldiers must go away," he repeated; "We must press you to take away your Soldiers." [95]

94. *PA*, 1st Ser., II, 666, 2d Ser., II, 681 (see also Holland to Pemberton, Apr. 16, 1761, Indian Committee Recs., IV, 95); Lightfoot, Notes of a Survey, 10. See also *PA*, 8th Ser., VI, 4895–4896, 4990–4991, 5093; *MPCP*, VIII, 767.

95. *MPCP*, VIII, 742, 748–749, 752–753. The garrison's strength is in Hunter, *Forts*, 536–537.

Issuing these orders ten times more would not have helped. Pennsylvania stalled—the French conflict continues, we need the king's permission to withdraw—and the soldiers stayed. Indeed, a year after the Lancaster council, when another Indian war threatened, colonists made their priorities clear by doing precisely the opposite of what Sagughsuniunt had demanded: instead of razing the fort and leaving the store, they leveled the trading post and dragged its remains inside to strengthen the garrison. Inside, too, went the Pennsylvanians who lived near the Forks. But when friendly Indians in the vicinity tried to seek shelter among colonists, they were refused entrance "to the settlements." By the time the soldiers did at last leave, in June 1765, it was too late: European colonists were too many, and too entrenched, to remove.[96]

## Darkness Defeated

## "My Heart feels for the wandering Natives"

On June 27, 1775, precisely a decade after the last troops headed home, a young Presbyterian minister named Philip Fithian arrived at the Forks of the Susquehanna River. Fithian, a Princeton graduate recently employed as a tutor to Robert Carter's children at Nomini Hall in Virginia, was now searching the Shenandoah and Susquehanna Valleys for a pulpit to call his own. The Susquehanna Forks seemed a likely place. The town of Sunbury, laid out three years earlier, now boasted one hundred houses arranged on the Philadelphia model; its neighbor across the river's North Branch, the "infant Village" of Northumberland, "seems *busy* and *noisy* as a Philadelphia *Ferry-House*." Between the two stood Fort Augusta, still more or less intact.[97]

For an educated young gentleman from New Jersey and Princeton by way

96. *PA*, 2d Ser., VII, 464. For the closing down of trade, see also James Irvine to the Indian Commissioners, May–August 1763, Gratz Coll., case 14, box 10; Invoice of Goods Brought Down from Fort Augusta, Aug. 22, 1763, ibid.; *PA*, 2d Ser., VII, 459, 464. See also Bouquet to Hamilton, July 4, 1763, Hamilton to Bouquet, July 12, 1763, Robert Callender to Bouquet, [Aug. 2, 1763], in Stevens et al., eds., *Papers of Bouquet*, VI, 295, 306, 329. Discussions of the fort's future are in *PA*, 8th Ser., VII, 5740, 5743, 5772, 5853; Turbutt Francis to Samuel Hunter, June 28, 1765, Society Collections, Francis, HSP; Herbert C. Bell, *History of Northumberland County, Pennsylvania* (Chicago, 1891), 76.

97. Robert Greenhalgh Albion and Leonidas Dodson, eds., *Philip Vickers Fithian: Journal, 1775–1776; Written on the Virginia-Pennsylvania Frontier and in the Army around New York* (Princeton, N.J., 1934), 38 nn. 39 and 52–54, 63. See also "Journal of General James Whitelaw, Surveyor-General of Vermont," Vermont Historical Society, *Proceedings* (St. Albans, Vt., 1905–1906), 134; and Crèvecoeur, *Letters and Sketches,* ed. Stone, chap. VIII.

of Nomini Hall, the place had considerable appeal. There were enough men like himself to promise many happy hours drinking toddy or coffee "in the Company of Gentlemen where there is no Reserve" and where the talk could turn to "Books, and Litterary Improvements." Indeed, many of gentility's trappings could be found there, from Philadelphia newspapers and personal libraries to a garden and summerhouse, from paintings on the wall to ladies at the piano. To be sure, there were a few rough characters around: after all, the land on which the towns stood had been bought from the Indians only seven years ago, and some people had "'New Purchace' Manners." Still, Fithian, impressed by the "beautiful Prospect of *Sunbury*," was convinced that "in a few Years, [all] will be grand and busy." [98]

Fithian gave no hint of knowing that the site already had been, in its way, grand and busy. If the spot still bore traces of its Indian past, he did not mention them. What he did mention—indeed, what he dwelt upon—was the powerful effect of the Susquehanna landscape. Where once that landscape had evoked in colonists only terror, it now, for Fithian, was a delight. He marveled at its richness; he strolled or sat "on the cool dark Bank of the River," noting that "these shady Banks were made for Contemplation"; he ventured out in a canoe, sometimes entertaining those on shore with his *"Fife"*; he went for walks in the "Woods and Wilds," indeed could spend a whole day doing nothing "but ramble and stare about on the Wilds, and Luxeries of Nature's Bosom." There he admired the "musical" birds, the bells of cows, horses, and sheep "grazing through the Woods" that made "a transporting Vesper" and "a continued, and a charming Echo!" "The Woods are musical," the young man exclaimed, "they are harmonious." [99]

Climbing and walking, canoeing and riding around the Forks, Fithian found time, and occasion, to mourn the natives' loss. "My Wonder ceases that the Indians fought for these happy Valley's," he remarked after one stroll along the riverbank. Canoeing past Sunbury a few days later, Fithian "could not help thinking over with myself, how often the Savage Tribes, while they were in Possession of these inchanting Wilds, have floated over this very Spot. My Heart feels for the wandering Natives. I make no Doubt but Multitudes of them, when they were forced away, left these long-possess'd, and delightsome Banks, with swimming Eyes." [100]

98. Albion and Dodson, eds., *Fithian Journal, 1755–1776*, 40, 42, 45, 46, 47–49, 59, 63, 65.
99. Ibid., 40, 44, 50, 51, 52, 53, 55, 58. He also ventured out to gather huckleberries (61, 79) and wildflowers (71–72).
100. Ibid., 58, 63.

With Fithian we have come a long way from what the Macks had found a generation before, or even what his father-in-law, Charles Beatty, had glimpsed as the colonial army marched upriver in 1756. Where they saw darkness, he saw light; where they saw howling wilderness, he saw enchanting wilds; where they saw Indians, he saw none—and, seeing none, was free to indulge in a mourning ritual that soon would grow in popularity.[101]

But just as news of a copperhead striking a local farm woman took much of the pleasure out of Fithian's "rambling," so the powerful Indian presence near the Forks ultimately unsettled him. At Northumberland on July 17, he heard that some Indians were just then leaving town to head "up the Country" with "Eight Horse Loads of Powder." No doubt, the preacher fretted, this is part of "some infernal Stratagem!" "Poor I," he moaned, "unarmed and impotent, am going up" that way soon, too. Following a wagon road up the West Branch on July 22, he soon crossed onto "the 'Indian's Land'" and was now in the "Enemies Country."[102]

Signs of Indians were everywhere: two clearings along the river that once had been "Indian-Towns," "many 'Indian Camps'" and fireplaces, only recently vacated, trees "cut, by the Indians, in strange Figures." Bad as such signs were, actual Indians were infinitely worse. "Two Indians!" Fithian exclaimed on catching his first glimpse of some. "Young Fellows about eighteen," their "neat, clean Riffles" and deerskins were not enough to ease this wanderer's fear and contempt. "I cannot bring myself to a Pleasant Feeling," he shuddered, "when I look upon or even think of, these heathenish Savages."[103]

Unpleasant feelings all but overwhelmed Fithian one evening several days later. The minister was lodging with one Gillespie when "two Indian Boys bolted in" after dinner, toting fish. "Down they sat in the Ashes before the Fire"

101. See ibid., viii. Fithian married Beatty's daughter that fall. Almost a century after Fithian wrote, J. F. Meginness, a local historian, also had "no doubt" that Indians left Shamokin "with regret, and the dusky warrior as he turned into the forest, could not refrain from looking back at the spot he loved so well, that was to be abandoned forever." "The flames of the burning wigwams lighted up the gloom of the surrounding wilderness—the little pappooses clung closer to their mothers, and looked wistfully around"; see Meginness, *Otzinachson; or, A History of the West Branch Valley of the Susquehanna* . . . (Philadelphia, 1857), 74.

102. Albion and Dodson, eds., *Fithian Journal, 1775–1776*, 54, 61, 70.

103. Ibid., 70–71, 81, 82. That the tree marks consisted of "Diamond's—Deaths Heads—Crowned Heads—Initial Letters—Whole Names—Dates of Years—Blazes" suggests either that Fithian misread them as Indian marks or that the Indians again were demonstrating their considerable acquaintance with colonial forms.

to cook their catch, but scarce had the cooking begun when "they bit it off in great Mouthfuls, and devoured it with the greatest Rapacity." The two left, Gillespie turned in, and Fithian sat on a stool, writing of the "Shambles" and stench of his lodgings, when "Stop! O Stop—Sleep to night is gone—! Four Indians come driving in, each with a large Knife and Tom-Hawk—Bless me two other Strapping Fellows! . . . Six large Indians!" The young clergyman had seen enough: "For all this Settlement I would not live here," he cried; "for two such Settlements—not for five hundred a Year—nothing would persuade me—!"[104]

In his excitement and anxiety, Fithian scarcely noticed that Gillespie, finding his guests unremarkable, simply gave them food and chatted with them. But Gillespie and his Indian visitors belonged to the Susquehanna's past, not its future. In Fithian lay the future, in his elegiac rhapsody on the natives' absence and his open revulsion at their presence. Spiced with the accounts of atrocity then enjoying popularity—"all the People in these back Settlements . . . are very taleful of the Indian War," Fithian later noted—the Presbyterian traveler's pleasant musings and unpleasant feelings would be repeated again and again on other frontiers. As with the Macks and David Brainerd, Fithian's exclamations and excesses invite our indulgence or our contempt.[105]

But as with the missionaries, so with the minister: we should resist the temptation. True, in his assumption that Indians fought for the valley and were driven away Fithian missed the complexity of life at the Forks before his time. But in his belief that Indians belonged to a different world, a world not only alien but antithetical and hostile to his own, he shared the view that the Macks had brought to Shamokin in 1745, and the view that natives there had of them that fall. This conviction—shared by Neshanackcow and Shickellamy, Moravian missionary and provincial officer alike—was best expressed at the Lancaster treaty council in 1762 by Sagughsuniunt, the Susquehanna Oneida who once had refused to share Shamokin with colonists and now came to tell those colonists to get out: *I am not as you are, I am of a quite different nature from you.*

104. Ibid., 82–83.
105. Ibid., 154 (see also 164).

# Metaphor, Meaning, and Misunderstanding
## Language and Power on the Pennsylvania Frontier

In March 1753, a group of Nanticokes and Shawnees representing the Six Nations arrived from the Wyoming Valley on the Susquehanna River to present a proposal to the Moravian Brethren and baptized Mahicans and Delawares near Bethlehem, Pennsylvania. They met on a small hill above the town, where Partrik, the Shawnee speaker, holding a string of wampum three bands wide, stood up and solemnly addressed the Brethren and Indians in his own dialect: "Brothers! You must excuse me if I cannot express myself very well in the language." He proceeded to symbolically cleanse the eyes, ears, throats, and hearts of those present, so they might better comprehend the true sense of his message. To ensure that everyone understood the proceedings, there was a lengthy chain of interpretation. Robert White, a Nanticoke chief, translated each Shawnee speech into English, which Joseph Spangenberg, the Moravian leader, then translated into German, and the Indians Augustus and Nathaniel translated them from German into Delaware and Mahican.[1]

As strings of wampum were presented with each carefully crafted speech, meticulously recorded in German by the Moravians, Partrik's request unfolded: the Iroquois in New York wanted Delawares and Mahicans from the mission communities and Indian towns between Bethlehem and the Susquehanna River to move north to the Wyoming Valley, to live under the protection of their "Uncles," the Six Nations, and to act as a buffer between them and the increasing numbers of white settlers moving into the backcountry of Pennsylvania. For nearly ten years, the Six Nations had attempted to bring the scattered Indian communities of Pennsylvania into their sphere of influence. With

---

1. "Brüder, ihr müst mich entschuldigen, wenn ich mich etwa nicht so recht in der Sprache ausdrücken kan"; see *Records of the Moravian Mission among the Indians of North America* (New Haven, Conn., [1978]), from original materials at the Archives of the Moravian Church, Bethlehem, Pa., microfilm, 40 reels (hereafter cited as *Moravian Records*), Mar. 21, 1753, reel 35, box 323, folder 1, item 3, letter A; see also Mar. 23, 1753, reel 40, box 3500, folder 16. Unless otherwise noted, all translations from the German are mine.

their offer, they promised a permanent place of residence and protection, yet they also threatened retribution if their request was not heeded. At the end of the conference, a few Indian families from the Moravian mission agreed to move north, with the condition that they might live separately from non-Christian Indians and bring a missionary with them.[2]

However, after five long days of careful exchange, negotiation, and agreement, some meaning had been lost in translation. Shortly before the Nanticokes and Shawnees left Bethlehem, Partrik confronted Joseph Spangenberg about a metaphor he had employed three days earlier that "did not please them." The Moravian had told the Indians: "If we sit together and smoke our pipe, we always learn to understand each other better. Also if water drops fall repeatedly on a stone, they surely make a hole in the end; so it is with learning words." Spangenberg reassured the Shawnee that he simply meant that the constant repetition of words, like dripping water, would help them learn each other's language, and sharing common customs might help to convey the meaning of the words. Partrik, on the other hand, had assumed that he and his people were the stones, to be slowly worn down by a constant flow of white settlers with their strange languages and practices.[3]

This misunderstanding might have been a matter of poor translation that caused momentary confusion. But by the eighteenth century, many Indians and whites had garnered the language skills to translate words through participation in ethnic intermarriage, a thriving Indian trade, and missionary and political activities. The impressive panel of interpreters used at Bethlehem in 1753 is a case in point. Yet, even interpreters familiar with Indian and European languages and customs sometimes struggled with the ritualized language of treaty conferences. Even if they found equivalent words in the other language, the meanings of metaphors were not always transparent. Despite the explicit intention of the Moravian's metaphor—to build a bridge of communication—the implicit meaning, as Partrik had suspected, was also there.[4]

This essay explores the ways that Indians and whites in eighteenth-century Pennsylvania wrestled with translating and communicating their respective ideas and the ways these linguistic exchanges evolved. Until the mid-1750s,

2. Ibid., Mar. 22, 1753, reel 35, box 323, folder 1, item 3, letter E.

3. Ibid., Mar. 26, 1753, reel 40, box 3500, folder 16. "Wenn wir beysammen sizen, und unser Pfeiffe rauchen, lernen wir immer einander beßer verstehen. Wenn die Wasser-Tropffen auch auf einen Stein oft fallen, machen sie *doch* endlich ein Loch; so ists mit dem lernen der Worte"; see Mar. 23, 1753, reel 35, box 323, folder 1, item 3, letter H.

4. Nancy L. Hagedorn, "'A Friend to Go between Them': The Interpreter as Cultural Broker during Anglo-Iroquois Councils, 1740–70," *Ethnohistory*, XXXV (1988), 60–80.

native Americans and Euramericans relied upon language rather than physical force to negotiate with, persuade, convince, berate, cajole, or control each other. Throughout the eighteenth century, Indians, non-Indians, Christians, non-Christians, men, and women developed cross-cultural language skills in various venues—households, backcountry communities, and trading posts— where they attempted to understand each other and to control an increasingly contested common world. From the 1720s to the 1760s, a variety of ethnic groups moved into the region north and west of Philadelphia between the Delaware and Susquehanna Rivers. Delawares, Mahicans, Iroquois, Tutelos, Nanticokes, and Shawnees as well as English- and German-speaking peoples came together to form new communities, sometimes overlapping and sometimes defiantly separate, but invariably connected by interdependent social, economic, and political networks. Since it was not always clear who had greater physical or political power in the region, Euramerican colonists still needed the cooperation, even partnership, of Indians with whom they shared the land, resources, and sometimes a common adversary, the French. Language—both as lexicons and grammars to communicate ideas or as metaphors and representations to define social relations—became a powerful tool manipulated by all participants to control the parameters of this interdependency.[5]

In political arenas especially, metaphors and metaphoric language emerged as a potential point where divergent cultural meanings could intersect, as they did in 1753 at Bethlehem. According to theorist Paul Ricoeur, the meaning of a metaphor is relative. Since a metaphor signifies both what "is like" and what "is not," it is a space into which the speaker and the listener can read slightly different meanings, yet still recognize the resemblance. In the eighteenth century, metaphors were an important part of discourse between Indians and whites precisely because they allowed for these different meanings within a commonly used language. Thus the image of water dripping on stone was recognizable to both Spangenberg and Partrik, even as they interpreted it differently.[6]

Yet, metaphors and metaphoric language also emerged as a weapon to manipulate or exclude another politically. By the 1750s, both native Americans and Euramericans actively wielded gendered metaphors and derogatory or

5. See Michel Foucault, "Afterword, the Subject and Power," in Hubert L. Dreyfus and Paul Rabinow, *Michel Foucault: Beyond Structuralism and Hermeneutics* (Chicago, 1982), 208–226.

6. Paul Ricoeur, *The Rule of Metaphor: Multi-disciplinary Studies of the Creation of Meaning in Language*, trans. Robert Czerny, with Kathleen McLaughlin and John Costello (Toronto, 1977), 7, 80.

ideal representations to dominate diplomatic exchanges. Indeed, Spangenberg's graphic illustration of interaction between cultures yielded a drop of truth. Like water on rock, whites and Indians repeatedly flowed around, clung to, or slapped against each other. Even though this constant association provided the chance for better understanding, whites and Indians would conclude that their political and economic needs, unlike the meanings within a metaphor, did not always intersect. The Seven Years' War washed away the necessity of a British-Indian alliance, and, after 1763, language would forge new kinds of boundaries between peoples.

One of the first places that people learn languages and communication skills is in the family. On the colonial Pennsylvania frontier, households tended to be ethnically diverse. Not only did Mahicans and Delawares live with German missionaries, but often Indian families adopted white or other native captives and refugees to replenish populations decimated by war or disease. James Smith, a white captive adopted into an Indian family in western Pennsylvania between 1755 and 1757, recalled that in his household "three tongues were commonly spoke, viz. Caughnewaga, or what French call Iroque, also the Wiandot and Ottawa." Indeed, captivity and adoption not only changed the linguistic landscape for whites but sometimes redefined kinship ties and cultural practices as well. Especially if they had been taken as children, some white captives, returned home at the end of the Seven Years' War, could no longer speak the languages of their original homes. In August 1762, when five boys and two girls were returned to Lancaster, the clerk keeping records simply noted: "Children's names unknown, as they cannot speak English, or give any account from whence they were taken." Three years later, Indians from Ohio returned adopted whites from their communities. Adolescents who had been part of Indian families for five to ten years could not remember where they had been born but instead identified themselves as "Nosewelamh," "Wapatenequa," and "Neculissika." They had not just received new names; by learning new languages from their adoptive families, these young people had acquired new habits, emotions, mannerisms, and perceptions.[7]

7. James Smith, *An Account of the Remarkable Occurrences in the Life and Travels of Col. James Smith, during his Captivity with the Indians, in the Years 1755, '56, '57, '58, and '59,* ed. William M. Darlington (1799; reprint, Cincinnati, 1870), 142; *Minutes of the Provincial Council of Pennsylvania, from the Organization to the Termination of the Proprietary Government,* 10 vols., Colonial Records of Pennsylvania (Philadelphia and Harrisburg, Pa., 1851–1852), VIII, 750 (hereafter cited as *MPCP*); enclosure in George Croghan to General Thomas Gage, May 12, 1765, General Thomas Gage Papers, American Series, XXXVI, William L.

Like captivity, which could be a temporary condition with profound cultural results, sexual encounters between whites and Indians also embraced a brief moment of cultural exchange, fostering new language skills. For instance, a Delaware and Shawnee word list compiled at Fort McIntosh in 1785 contained a series of translations for phrases such as "I love you," "I must sleep with you," or "Will you sleep with me?" The list suggests that, over many years, soldiers and traders might have collected and passed on a vocabulary of desire to help them find female companionship on the frontier. Temporary companionship sometimes became more permanent. Cross-cultural liaisons and intermarriage provided political or economic alliances for native families and access to language skills that eased frontier relations among ethnic groups. Paxnous, a Shawnee chief present at the March 1753 conference in Bethlehem, could "talk good Delaware," most likely because he married a Delaware woman. Cayuga chief Gagohunt, living on the northern branch of the Susquehanna in the 1760s, understood Delaware, "since he had a Delaware wife," but could also speak Munsee (another Delaware dialect), "since he had lived among them." English trader Thomas McKee had a Shawnee wife who spoke "but little English" yet helped him maintain "a brisk trade with the Allegheny Country."[8]

As these examples of linguistic exchanges suggest, native women more often acted as agents for communication within the context of the home and community, where they held the balance of power as cultural brokers. Women taught adopted children as well as their own to speak the languages of the

---

Clements Library, University of Michigan, Ann Arbor. See also Floyd G. Lounsbury, "Iroquoian Languages," in William C. Sturtevant, gen. ed., *Handbook of North American Indians*, XV, Bruce G. Trigger, ed., *Northeast* (Washington, D.C., 1978), 336. Daniel K. Richter, *The Ordeal of the Longhouse: The Peoples of the Iroquois League in the Era of European Colonization* (Chapel Hill, N.C., 1992), 65–66, notes that by the 1660s two-thirds of the Iroquois population was thought to be adopted from outside the Five Nations.

8. *The Record of the Court at Upland, in Pennsylvania, 1676 to 1681 and a Military Journal Kept by Major E. Denny, 1781–1795* (Philadelphia, 1860), 479–485; *MPCP*, VII, 139–140; *Moravian Records*, reel 26, box 211, folder 16, item 1, "weil er eine Dellawar Frau hat," and "weil er war herunter ihnen gewohnt," Friedenshutten Diary, July 18, 1768, reel 8, box 131, folder 5; John W. Jordan, "Bishop J.C.F. Cammerhoff's Narrative of a Journey to Shamokin, Penna., in the Winter of 1748," *Pennsylvania Magazine of History and Biography*, XXIX (1905), 169. McKee's wife might have been a white woman raised by a Shawnee family, but she was always identified as Shawnee.

household. Because of their central roles in matrilineal kinship networks and communities, women were often the first to interact with outsiders who ventured into their villages. In 1748, for instance, Moravian Bishop John Christopher Frederick Cammerhoff met with Shickellamy, the representative of the Six Nations in Shamokin, to discuss how much the Moravian blacksmith could charge for his services and other matters about the Moravian presence in that trade town. But it was Shickellamy's daughter-in-law, a Mahican woman, who provided the essential link of communication between the various parties. "Bro. Mack translated my words [which were German] into Mohican to Logan's wife," wrote Bishop Cammerhoff of his negotiations; "she then into Shawanese to her husband, and he into Oneida for his father [Shickellamy]." White women also contributed to intercultural communication, since they often interacted with native women in their homes and communities, either as captives themselves or as missionaries and neighbors. When Jeanette Rau married Moravian missionary John Martin Mack in September 1742, the church was especially pleased because "her knowledge of the Mohawk and Delaware dialects rendered her an efficient assistant in the mission."[9]

Native women actively participated in social interactions with Euramericans, invited them into their homes and communities, and through their exchanges even witnessed and adopted a variety of white cultural practices. Yet, these social adaptations from a decidedly patriarchal society did not change or diminish the power that native women enjoyed. In their own homes and communities, these women already had an authoritative voice. The colonial encounter, as Natalie Zemon Davis has suggested, offered new means for native women to express their power. When Christianity brought changes to social practices in mission towns, native American women used "Christian forms and phrases" to enhance their status. Tawaneem, a Mahican woman baptized by Moravians in August 1743, took the name Bathseba and between 1747 and the 1770s became an active participant in several mission communities in the Pennsylvania backcountry. She learned German, enabling her to describe her spiritual beliefs to German missionary women. She also traveled away from her family and community in Gnadenhütten to visit unconverted Indian neighbors, speak with them on religious matters, bless newly baptized children, and translate other native women's professions of faith. Bathseba made herself an

9. Jordan, "Cammerhoff's Journey to Shamokin," *PMHB*, XXIX (1905), 174; John W. Jordan, "Rev. John Martin Mack's Narrative of a Visit to Onondaga in 1752," *PMHB*, XXIX (1905), 343.

undeniable presence in the community and the spiritual lives of Pennsylvania Indians.[10]

Whereas native women mastered new languages and communication skills to build bridges between interdependent communities, other people collected and preserved these same languages for their own purposes. Missionaries in New York, New Jersey, and Pennsylvania needed to use language skills to convert native Americans to Christianity; in doing so, they created written lexicons that document the efforts of Indians and whites to find some common understanding. A few Presbyterians, such as David Brainerd, took "considerable pains to learn the Delaware Language," though Brainerd always employed an interpreter when he preached. In comparison, the German Moravians, a Protestant pietistic sect who in 1740 migrated from Saxony to settle at Bethlehem, Pennsylvania, taught their missionaries the language skills needed to preach persuasively. Indeed, the Moravians instructed their missionaries: "Take all possible Pains to learn the Language of those Heathen, with whom they have to do. — They must be very careful what Interpreters they use at publick Sermons. — Until they shall be able to express themselves intelligibly to the Heathen, they must rather be contented with preaching by their walk and Conversation."[11]

Although they might communicate the word of a Christian God in a rudimentary way through "their walk and Conversation," the Moravians thought they would be most effective at conversion through native speech and the written word. Moravians sent male missionaries to Indian towns to study and record Iroquois, Mahican, and Delaware languages (Unami and Munsee were the two major Delaware dialects). John Heckewelder spent long days carefully paying "attention to [Delaware] discourses with each other on different subjects, and occasionally asking them questions, always watching for the proper opportunity, when they do not suspect your motives, and are disposed to be free and open with you." John Jacob Schmick, another Moravian who lived

10. Natalie Zemon Davis, "Iroquois Women, European Women," in Margo Hendricks and Patricia Parker, eds., *Women, "Race," and Writing in the Early Modern Period* (London, 1994), 255. Indeed, Davis describes the changes in lives of Iroquois and Huron women in the seventeenth century as a "Renaissance" "in regard to voice" (257). Carol Devens, *Countering Colonization: Native American Women and Great Lakes Missions, 1630–1900* (Berkeley, Calif., 1992), insists that native women, at least in the Great Lakes region, rejected missionary attempts to convert them and became, instead, "conservators of traditional ways" (113). I did not find that to be the case in Pennsylvania, where more Mahican and Delaware women than men were baptized by the Moravians.

11. David Brainerd's Journal, Nov. 20, 1745, 45, American Philosophical Society, Philadelphia, Pa. (hereafter cited as APS).

among the Mahicans, first in New York, then with a migrant group in Pennsylvania, carefully collected phrases in German and Mahican for his "Miscellanea Linguae Nationis Indicae Mahikan Dicta Cura Suscepta." He created a new vocabulary of salvation, which attempted to translate Christian theology into an understandable native lexicon. "G'máo maamschan'ma" ("I think about the Savior all the time") and "Schepòchqua˘ta-ha-sse~en" ("he was crucified") were among the more prominent concepts the Moravians wished to communicate.[12]

The native American dictionaries, word lists, and grammar books, so carefully committed to paper by missionaries, soldiers, and traders, perhaps do not tell us much about eighteenth-century Indian linguistics, but they do reveal something about the relationship between whites and natives and how Euramericans attempted to frame that encounter. For instance, intellectual works of the Enlightenment, such as Carolus Linnaeus's, *Systema Naturae* (1735), classified American Indians as less culturally evolved than Europeans. Native languages, like their cultures, were similarly thought of as deficient, able to communicate only very simple ideas. The Moravian leader Count Nikolaus Ludwig von Zinzendorf pitied "these poor people [the Indians], whose imperfect language is made inadequate for the expression of their new experiences, and of their views and wishes, as assistants in the Saviour's work." "Our language is divine in comparison with theirs." Yet, even while Zinzendorf advocated forcing Indians to speak and write German or English—because their own languages would never convey the intricacies of Christianity—his missionaries were actively learning native languages, writing poetry in Mahican, and translating Bible passages and prayers into Delaware. Indeed, they had to record and translate "imperfect" and "inadequate" native languages in order to bring about Indian conversions.[13]

Ironically, Indians held similar ideas about linguistic purity, and it made them critical of Euramerican efforts to commit their languages to paper. In

---

12. *Moravian Records*, n.d., reel 34, box 315, folder 3, item 7, in English; John Heckewelder, *History, Manners, and Customs of the Indian Nations, Who Once Inhabited Pennsylvania and the Neighbouring States*, rev. ed., ed. William C. Reichel (1876; facsimile reprint, Bowie, Md., 1990), xvii; "Ich dencke allezeit an den Heiland," and "er wurde gecreuzigt," in John Jacob Schmick (1714–1778), "Miscellanea Linguae Nationis Indicae Mahikan Dicta Cura Suscepta," 2 vols., [c. 1760], APS.

13. Robert F. Berkhofer, Jr., *The White Man's Indian: Images of the American Indian from Columbus to the Present* (New York, 1979), 38–49; Stephen J. Kunitz, "Benjamin Rush on Savagism and Progress," *Ethnohistory*, XVII (1970), 31–42; William C. Reichel, ed., *Memorials of the Moravian Church*, I (Philadelphia, 1870), 55.

July 1750, Gaschwehtio, a leader at Onondoga, told David Zeisberger that the Moravians should not try to learn Iroquois dialects in Shamokin, since the Indians there "sometimes drank very hard," and "they spoke miserably, but that here and in Anjot they spoke more beautifully, and had a much greater choice of words than Gajukas [Cayugas] and Sennekas [Senecas]." Indians were contemptuous, not to mention suspicious, of the methods whites used to learn and record native languages. Even though John Heckewelder was careful to keep his linguistic work a secret, one of his Indian informants finally told him to "throw the whole into the fire." "Never write one word down, before you have learnt to hear—The white people come among us, to write down words in our Language—and do write but no Indian can understand what they have written." He appeared to lament that Indians and whites would never understand each other until white men overcame their inability to listen.[14]

Yet, despite their impatience with writing-obsessed missionaries, Indians worked with whites to create a common linguistic ground. The Shawnee negotiator Partrik, although suspicious, had been willing enough to press Joseph Spangenberg for further explanation of a metaphor's meaning. Other native informants patiently repeated words and phrases to German missionaries or traders, so they might write them down. In March 1753, a young Shawnee, returning from the conference at Bethlehem, visited John Jacob Schmick at the Delaware town of Meniolagomekah. "He gave me to understand," Schmick noted, "that he wanted to speak words of his language to me, which I should write down, which I also did, the first that he said to me were these: Now we are like one man, together." This exchange of words and their meanings reminds us that the day-to-day contact between whites and Indians entailed constant negotiation. Just as Schmick's "Miscellanea Linguae" of Mahican words was a work-in-progress—the Mahican-German vocabulary list was literally unfinished, containing alphabetically arranged German words with no translations and many blank pages—language on the frontier continued to evolve as one group learned or appropriated the words and phrases of another. Native languages influenced German and English, and French, English, Dutch, and Swedish words crept into native usage. In the first half of the eighteenth century, at least, with the help of native women and religious men, whites and

14. William M. Beauchamp, ed., *Moravian Journals Relating to Central New York, 1745–66* (Syracuse, N.Y., 1916), 89–90; John Heckewelder to Peter S. DuPonceau, June 20, 1816, John Heckewelder Letters, 1816–1822, APS. On linguistic imperialism, see John Comaroff and Jean Comaroff, *Ethnography and the Historical Imagination* (Boulder, Colo., 1992), 250–255; and Eric Cheyfitz, *The Poetics of Imperialism: Translation and Colonization from* The Tempest *to* Tarzan (New York, 1991).

Indians were creating common languages and, perhaps, even becoming "like one man, together."[15]

Native women controlled the communication of meaning within the household, translating, interpreting, and passing on new ideas and practices to their families and neighbors. Missionaries also crossed cultural boundaries to exchange and record languages in religious contexts. But within frontier economies, men—Euramerican fur traders and Indian hunters—more often created and exchanged common languages. One could imagine, as John Mack Faragher has postulated, that a "pidgin tongue" might have developed, "based on Algonquian but employing many English, French, Dutch, and Scandinavian terms," whose primary purpose was to express "how much" or "how many." Practical words and phrases were probably passed among English traders or learned during apprenticeships, as Schmick's Mahican translations for "give me a tobacco pipe" and "as long as a finger" suggest. Then again, trade was not always conducted with rudimentary words or gestures. At the Pittsburgh trade store established by the Provincial Commissioners of Indian Affairs, James Kenny found that the "Delawars are mightly pleas'd that I have preferr'd thier Tongue in learning most of it so that I can converse a little with them." Indians also learned other languages and modes of communication to gain economic advantages. In January 1748, Moravian missionary Joseph Powell in Shamokin "Recd a letter from Snake an Indian up the [Susquehanna] River to whom we are somthing in Debt. said heed com down soon," presumably to collect what was owed him.[16]

15. "Er gab mir zu verstehen er wolte mir Worte von seiner Sprache sagen die solte ich auf schreiben welches ich auch that, das erste das er mir sagte war, dieses, Nun sind wir wie ein Mann, zu samen"; see Meniolagomekah Diary, Mar. 27, 1753, *Moravian Records,* reel 6, box 122, folder 3; Ives Goddard, "Eastern Algonquian Languages," in Sturtevant, gen. ed., *Handbook of North American Indians,* XV, Trigger, ed., *Northeast,* 77; Goddard, "Dutch Loanwords in Delaware," in Herbert C. Kraft, ed., *A Delaware Indian Symposium,* Anthropological Series No. 4 (Harrisburg, Pa., 1974), 153–160. See Philip Motley Palmer, *The Influence of English on the German Vocabulary to 1700,* and *The Influence of English on the German Vocabulary to 1800, a Supplement,* University of California Publications in Linguistics, VII, nos. 1, 2 (Berkeley, Calif., 1950, 1960), for examples of English-German exchanges.

16. John Mack Faragher, *Daniel Boone: The Life and Legend of an American Pioneer* (New York, 1992), 19; "Gib mir eine Pfeife Tobac," and "Wie ein finger lang," in Schmick, "Miscellanea Linguae"; John W. Jordan, ed., "Journal of James Kenny, 1761–1763," *PMHB,* XXXVII (1913), 169; Shamokin Diary, Jan. 17, 1748, *Moravian Records,* reel 6, box 121, folder 4, item 1, in English. John Heckewelder referred to a language he called "Swedish Delaware," but it is unclear whether this was actually a commonly used trade language; see Heckewelder to DuPonceau, Nov. 17, 1819, John Heckewelder Letters, 1816–1822.

Though trade towns might have been places where whites learned to speak a little Delaware and Indians, in turn, learned to write a little English, this linguistic exchange did not always imply complete understanding. Communication could easily turn to miscommunication, especially if the speaker were in a hurry and if the meanings of words were unclear. In a world where economic motives prevailed, as they did among Euramerican traders, concepts such as ownership might have been difficult to convey to Indian trade partners. John Jacob Schmick noted in his Mahican vocabulary list the phrases: "Mine—it is mine, the knife was mine, the horse was mine." These words of possession, useful to English traders, might have sent mixed messages to Indians, who had a different understanding of the use of available resources. To tell another man that "the knife was mine" or "the horse was mine" implied that the trader thought the Indian had borrowed or even stolen the items and should give them back. The difficulty in translating cultural ideas of ownership and the purpose of economic relations created suspicions between Indians and whites on the Pennsylvania frontier.[17]

Indeed, the very act of trying to communicate with each other paradoxically fueled new misunderstandings that could just as easily turn violent. In early 1757 at Fort Augusta, built on the Susquehanna River near the recently abandoned town of Shamokin, the commander compiled an innocuous list of Indian words. With the assistance of William Sack, a Mingo living in Conestoga, the commander recorded various translations for the time of day, weather conditions, the seasons, and numbers. One imagines that his patience must have worn thin, for William Sack was not known for his cooperative spirit among white Pennsylvanians, nor was he considered a likable fellow. The vocabulary list ends abruptly with an inadvertent comment on the commander's perception of his colonial encounter; he asked for the translation of "You lye."[18]

Just as native women, such as Bathseba, found new "forms and phrases" to express themselves within a Christian lexicon, native men also learned new ways to express their growing anger or distrust in their exchanges with whites. One white woman captive noted that her captors "cannot swear nor Curse in their own Language; all the Profanation of that sort, ever I heard among them,

17. Schmick, "Miscellanea Linguae." Besides German-Mahican translations, Schmick included a few English-Mahican translations and a few Delaware terms.

18. "A Vocabulary in the Mingo Tongue Taken from the Mouth of William Sack a Canestogo Indian," Jan. 25, 1757, APS. William *Sack* is also known as Bill *Sock* or sometimes as Conestoga Bill. He was killed in December 1763, along with the remaining Conestoga Indians, during the attack by the "Paxton Boys" from a nearby white community.

being in English, which (I suppose) they learned of our Traders, and the like." At Easton, Pennsylvania, in October 1758, the Delaware chief Teedyuscung came into the council room drunk and "called out in Indian and English that he was the head man and swore in English prodigiously." Cursing could be a powerful language to articulate strong emotions and feelings, such as injured honor or humiliation. With a sense of irony and anger, Ghesaont, speaking for the Iroquois in July 1721 to Governor William Keith of Pennsylvania, complained that traders carrying goods up the Susquehanna River treated their young warriors badly, "use them with ill Language, and call them Dogs, etc." "They take this unkindly, because Dogs have not Sense or understanding: whereas they are men, and think that their Brothers should not compare them to such Creatures." On one particular occasion, Ghesaont's young warriors decided to take the traders at their word and replied: "'If they were Dogs, then they might act as such:' whereupon they seiz'd a Cag of Liquor, and run away with it." Even as whites and Indians struggled to understand each other, even as they negotiated a common language to work and trade together, some could not help but curse and conclude "Shanowent": "You lie." [19]

In a world where Iroquois warriors and Pennsylvania traders insulted one another in one another's language, where attempts at mutual understanding could lead to violent misunderstanding, where Indians did not want to become stones worn down by white water, the diplomatic arena became an important and more formal place to negotiate their differences. In 1754, the struggle between England and France for control of the Ohio Valley and supremacy on the North American continent flared up once more. Delawares, distrusting both nations, attacked white settlements along disputed boundary lines between the Susquehanna River and the Forks of the Delaware, hoping to recover lost land. Between 1756 and 1763, the Pennsylvania governor and British agents held a series of treaty negotiations with Delawares and Iroquois, where the skills of cross-cultural communication, learned in the informal settings of homes and communities in the Pennsylvania backcountry, were tested.

For Iroquois and Eastern Algonquian cultures, the goal of treaty negotiations was to reach a consensus between parties. Everything that unfolded in the course of a conference became part of a mutual agreement, and it was assumed

19. Jean Lowry, *A Journal of Captivity of Jean Lowry and Her Children . . .* (Philadelphia, 1760), 13; "Extract from the Diary of Richard Peters," Oct. 12, 1758, in Julian P. Boyd, ed., *The Susquehannah Company Papers,* II (1930; reprint, Ithaca, N.Y., 1962), 20–21; "Particulars of an Indian Treaty between Sir William Keith and the Deputies of the Five Nations, July 5, 1721," 5–6, APS.

that certain problems such as land use, economic assistance, and political alliances, all important to community stability, would be renewed or renegotiated at regular intervals. Consequently, within the eighteenth-century colonial encounter, the power of language for Iroquois and Eastern Algonquian cultures rested on oral traditions, memory, and particular speech forms used for political persuasion. Ritual language was a means of harnessing personal power and obtaining spiritual assistance to influence other people and the particular situation.[20]

Indians customarily used strings and belts of wampum to preserve, remember, present, and perform these rituals and send messages between communities, as Partrik had done at Bethlehem. The strings both aided the memory, being a record of formal council proceedings, and added authority to the message. In many ways, wampum served as the written language of Northeastern American Indians; similar to a commission, it gave an individual power to speak, and its form—color, size, and design—indicated its function. Indeed, without wampum, the substance of a speech could be silenced. At a conference in Carlisle in 1753, where the Pennsylvania Commissioners of Indian Affairs met with Ohio Indians, the speaker apologized that the "Twightwees intended to say something to you; but they have mislaid some strings which has put their speeches in Disorder; these they will rectify, and speak to you in the afternoon."[21]

Like their Indian neighbors, whites also sought conflict resolution, friendship, and material assistance when negotiating with strangers. Instead of seeking consensus or the fluidity of an ongoing dialogue about mutual problems, however, the goal of a treaty conference generally was to negotiate for, and to claim, absolute legal control over land, resources, labor, or groups of people. In this world, where the emphasis lay on particular legal principles and the formal structures of government, neither resonance of voice, presentation of gifts, nor wampum was a key factor. The written word was. Deeds, commissions, receipts, petitions, ordinances, legislation, and court records embodied the power of language for Europeans. Within the political forum, written docu-

20. Gregory Evans Dowd, *A Spirited Resistance: The North American Indian Struggle for Unity, 1745–1815* (Baltimore, 1992), 3–4; Robert Steven Grumet, "Sunksquaws, Shamans, and Tradeswomen: Middle Atlantic Coastal Algonkian Women during the Seventeenth and Eighteenth Centuries," in Mona Etienne and Eleanor Leacock, eds., *Women and Colonization: Anthropological Perspectives* (New York, 1980), 47–48.

21. Michael K. Foster, "Another Look at the Function of Wampum in Iroquois-White Councils," in Francis Jennings et al. eds., *The History and Culture of Iroquois Diplomacy* (Syracuse, N.Y., 1985), 99–114; Penn Manuscripts, Indian Affairs, Oct. 2, 1753, I, 1687–1753, Historical Society of Pennsylvania, Philadelphia (hereafter cited as HSP).

ments were meant to capture the presumed permanence of an agreement. In August 1742, Governor George Thomas wondered why Cacowachico and Nochiconna, both Shawnee chiefs, did not remember what they had all discussed in council three or four years before, for the whites had "Records in Writing by which the memory of past Transactions are preserved for all Ages to come."[22]

That Indians invested ritual, oration, and memory with certain powers and whites invested codified legal systems and written words with other powers did not mean that each did not accommodate the other's political forms in the eighteenth century. When whites and Indians met in a common political arena to negotiate the legitimacy of land sales, the return of white captives, the creation of new community boundaries, and the prospects of peace, each learned effective ways to incorporate the other's language to communicate their needs. Both Indian and white men knew enough about the other's methods and technologies to manipulate the metaphors, ritual speech, and the written word in attempts to dominate the spaces of power in which they both operated. Euramericans accepted, used, and contributed to the forms and language of native rituals and ceremonies, such as the use of wampum. Indians also adapted new methods, such as the written word, to negotiate with whites.[23]

During the 1740s and 1750s, as Indians and whites struggled to understand each other, metaphors, especially, became an important point of entry to these negotiations. Native Americans often applied metaphoric kinship terms to their political relations. Whether they appealed to their "brothers," "cousins," "uncles," or "grandfathers" during a treaty conference, each of these symbolic kinship designations meant something specific about the role and responsibil-

---

22. Michel Foucault, "Truth and Power," in Foucault, *Power/Knowledge: Selected Interviews and Other Writings, 1972–1977*, ed. Colin Gordon (New York, 1980), 66; Governor George Thomas to Cacowachico and Nochiconna, Shawnees, Aug. 16, 1742, Richard Peters Papers, 1697–1845, I, pt. 2, HSP.

23. Foucault, "Truth and Power," in Foucault, *Power/Knowledge*, ed. Gordon, 66, asserts that modern technologies of power, such as writing, became important by the seventeenth and eighteenth centuries as part of new state policies and institutions (schools, police, armies, government administrations) that were created to control capital and the labor of men. Premodern technologies of power, on the other hand, included "signs of loyalty to the feudal lords, rituals, ceremonies, and so forth, and levies in the form of taxes, pillage, hunting, war, etc" (66). Native Americans, with their focus on kinship relations, rituals of condolence, and the need for retribution during war, seem to fit into Foucault's premodern category. The eighteenth century should be considered a period of crossover, however, where both modern and premodern technologies of power could be useful to both Indians and whites, depending on the circumstances.

ities of each party and set a hierarchy of authority within the meeting. But Eur-americans often misunderstood the meanings of these labels. "Father" was perhaps the most problematic metaphoric relationship that bound Indian and non-Indian communities. The Iroquois addressed the French governor in North America as Onontio, or father, because the Indians regarded the French "as their allies, protectors, suppliers, and as the mediators of their disputes." Whereas the French regarded their fatherly role as an extension of patriarchal authority, the Iroquois believed that fathers "had no power to command children." In a similar fashion, the Pennsylvania government sometimes misunderstood its relationship with Indians. In the early eighteenth century, the governor assumed that the Conestogas and Delawares looked upon themselves as "Children, Rather to be Directed by this Governmt," their father. The Conestogas had a very different view, perhaps based on a new understanding of Euramerican family relations, "for often Parents would be apt to whip their Children too severely, and Brothers sometimes would differ." Instead, the Conestogas wanted to be considered "as the same Flesh and Blood with the Christians," as William Penn supposedly had insisted, "and the same as if one Man's Body was to be divided in two Parts." There remained a gap between what the term "father" "was like" and what "father" "was not" in the minds of both parties, but they continued to use relational metaphors, perhaps because of these ambiguities, to describe and manipulate their political relationships.[24]

Whereas kinship terms determined or delineated the relative positions of authority for each party, other metaphors, such as the road, the Chain of Friendship, and the body, graphically depicted the current state of relations between Indians and whites. The road, especially, and the continual need to keep it open, conveyed the desire for clear communication, commerce, shared community, and friendship. The Chain of Friendship, which needed to "be kept bright and clean, without Rust or Spott," or council chambers, which had "grown dirty and wanted cleaning very much," also pointed to a common desire to meet often and reach an agreement.[25]

24. Richard White, *The Middle Ground: Indians, Empires, and Republics in the Great Lakes Region, 1650–1815* (New York, 1991), 36; Francis Jennings, *The Ambiguous Iroquois Empire: The Covenant Chain Confederation of Indian Tribes with English Colonies from Its Beginnings to the Lancaster Treaty of 1744* (New York, 1984), 44; *MPCP,* III, 46; [Charles Thomson], *An Enquiry into the Causes of Alienation of the Delaware and Shawanese Indians from the British Interest* (1759; reprint, Philadelphia, 1867), 9; Ricoeur, *The Rule of Metaphor,* 7, 80.

25. Carl Van Doren and Julian P. Boyd, eds., *Indian Treaties Printed by Benjamin Franklin, 1736–1762* (Philadelphia, 1938), 71, 140, 216; *MPCP,* III, 312, IV, 742–743; S. K. Stevens et al., eds., *The Papers of Henry Bouquet* (Harrisburg, Pa., 1951–), II, 188.

Other metaphors, such as those of the body, brought an intimacy to the political proceedings and drew on a desire for deeper understanding. A treaty or meeting often opened with a speech that symbolically cleansed the body, as at the meeting in Bethlehem. Ritual cleansing was necessary, for fear that "an Evil Spirit of great Power and Cunning" may have "blinded you and throwed Dust in your Eyes." At treaties, participants needed "the best Medicines" to cleanse "some Foulness [that] come into your heart through your Throat" or a "fine Feather . . . diped in that pure Oil which our Grandfathers formerly used on this Occasion" to wash out "the inside of your Ears, that you may hear what I am going to say to you." Even in more informal settings, metaphors of the body prevailed. A few weeks after the Six Nations invited the Moravian Indians to move to the Susquehanna River in March 1753, the baptized Mahicans and Delawares met to discuss the matter. Abraham, the leader of the Christian Mahicans, laid four strings and four belts of wampum on a table and formally addressed the Delawares: "Until now your eyes have been dark, I will wash them for you, so that you are able to see more clearly. I will clean your ears, so that you can hear well, I will make the inside of your heart pure and take all that is evil from it." [26]

Metaphoric language also extended to more complex ritual encounters between Indians and whites intended to mitigate violent confrontations or compensate for an unexpected death. For instance, Euramericans readily adopted the condolence ceremony, a native American ritual. When a family member or important leader died, somebody from outside the family or clan performed the ritual, which included wiping away the blood of the victim and the tears of the mourners and presenting gifts to cover the grave. The observance symbolically resurrected the deceased and restored the rational souls of the grieving survivors, after which they could return to their daily activities. The Pennsylvania government found that the condolence ceremony went a long way to maintain smooth relations with Indian allies, especially since they were often the direct or indirect cause of Indian grief. In 1744, the governor extended "a small present" to the local Iroquois chief Shickellamy "in order to weap of his dears, and Comfort his heart" after the death of his son "Unhappy Jake." When Shickellamy himself died four years later, Pennsylvania interpreter Conrad

---

26. "Capt. Newcastle's Report," June 1, 1756, Timothy Horsfield Papers, I, APS; Stevens et al., eds., *Bouquet Papers*, III, 509; "Bishers sind eure Augen dunkel. gewesen ich will sie euch auswaschen, dass ihr lauter gutes sehen könnt. Eure Ohren will ich reinigen, dass ihr lauter guts hören könt, Eure Inwendiges Herz will ich rein machen und alles böse heruns nehmen"; see Gnadenhütten Conference, Apr. 5, 1753, *Moravian Records*, reel 5, box 119, folder 1, no. 9.

Weiser gave his children and grandchildren "a small present in order to wipe off their Tears according to the Custom of the Indians." Indians did not just condole the death of other Indians; they performed these rites for white allies as well. In August 1736, Delawares came to Philadelphia and extended their condolences after the death of Governor Patrick Gordon. Upon the death of Conrad Weiser in 1761, Seneca George performed condolences and lamented: "Since his Death we cannot so well understand one another." [27]

By the 1750s, growing tensions between Indians and whites had created so many reasons to perform condolence ceremonies that they became standard practice for opening treaty conferences with Euramericans. The renewed hostilities between Indians allied with the French, Delawares, Iroquois, and white colonists in the Pennsylvania backcountry required condolences for "the Death of many . . . Counsellors and Warriors." In 1757, George Croghan met with 160 Iroquois, Nanticokes, Delawares, and Conestogas on the Susquehanna River to symbolically wipe the blood off the council seats and wipe the tears from their eyes before they would even consider further talk of peace. "With these Strouds," Croghan intoned, "wrap up the Bodies of your deceased Friends and bury them decently, covering their Graves with those Blanketts and half thicks." Scarouyady, an Oneida who acted as liaison for the increasingly powerful coalition of Ohio Indians, accepted the presents, thanking him and "our Brother Onas," who "wisely considered the Antient Custom of our Fore Fathers in condoling with us and mixing your Grief with ours." A month later, Croghan had to condole the Indians at Lancaster "on Account of some of their People who died of the Small Pox since they came here and gave them a Piece of Stroud to cover the Graves of the Deceased agreable to the Antient custom of the Six Nations." By May 1757, he reported that thirteen Indians had died of the illness since they came to Lancaster, though "none of the head Men." [28]

27. Matthew Dennis, *Cultivating a Landscape of Peace: Iroquois-European Encounters in Seventeenth-Century America* (Ithaca, N.Y., 1993), 81, 101. Dennis notes that the Jesuits first witnessed an Iroquois condolence ceremony in 1645, when the general purpose was to restore order and peace within the community and to prevent the beginning of a blood feud by the deceased's family (79). See *Pennsylvania Archives*, 138 vols. (Philadelphia and Harrisburg, Pa., 1852–1949), 1st Ser., I, 665–666 (hereafter cited as *PA*); Conrad Weiser to Richard Peters, Apr. 22, 1749, "Manuscript Papers on the Indian and Military Affairs of the Province of Pennsylvania, 1737–1775," microfilm, APS; *MPCP*, IV, 53, VIII, 631; James Sullivan et al., comps., *The Papers of Sir William Johnson*, 14 vols. (Albany, N.Y., 1921–1965), IX, 393.

28. Sullivan et al., comps., *Papers of William Johnson*, IX, 730, 732, 762, 771.

Metaphors brought Indian and white men together at treaty conferences and gave them a common language, a basis from which to mourn losses and build political alliances. English, Iroquois, Delawares, and white Pennsylvanians had learned each other's languages—perhaps even the subtler meanings of metaphors and methods; yet, by the late 1750s, they increasingly found they had dissimilar visions of the future. Metaphors instead began to mark the growing differences of people at war and sometimes took on a life of their own, becoming a means of excluding others politically. In the mid-eighteenth century, the Six Nations claimed that they had conquered the Delawares and Shawnees in battle and conferred on them the metaphoric status of "women." According to historian Francis Jennings, the term originally meant that Delawares were "assigned a political role of neutrality so as to be able to assume the peacemaker's role when warring tribes wanted to end their strife without losing face." But in the treaty negotiations of the 1750s, the Delawares' status as women marked them as subordinate, not permitted to sell land or negotiate directly with the British. British colonial governments, which had often been impatient with self-proclaimed or scattered native leaders in the Pennsylvania backcountry, welcomed this arrangement. By symbolically subordinating Delawares in the context of Indian-white relations, Pennsylvania could treat directly with an assumed political power, the Six Nations, who were much more cooperative when it came to selling land.[29]

The term "women" as applied to Delawares was nominally based on the restricted public role of Indian women. Historically, Indian women enjoyed a certain degree of economic autonomy and control within native households and communities. They owned longhouses, controlled material and agricultural resources, and passed on property to their children. Native women also attended treaty conferences, often seated prominently according to their individual status, and advised the men, but they had limited power to speak in political forums. Their restricted public role, however, did not diminish their authority at home. Yet, despite their persuasive voice in the community and their presence in public, during the 1750s Iroquois, white, and Delaware men turned the concept of native women's authority on its head as a means of shaming and excluding men from places of power within the diplomatic arena. Indians and

---

29. Jennings, *Ambiguous Iroquois Empire*, 301–302. For other discussions on the origin and development of the Delawares' status as women, see Heckewelder, *History, Manners, and Customs of the Indian Nations*, 57–58; and Jay Miller, "The Delaware as Women: A Symbolic Solution," *American Ethnologist*, I (1974), 507–514.

whites perhaps used their knowledge of the other's gender constructs to manipulate each other politically and, in turn, infused this metaphor with new
meaning. By repetition and exchange, these new gendered representations of
Indians, in the words of Paul Ricoeur, unleashed "the power that certain
fictions have to redescribe reality." [30]

It was not uncommon for Indians to invoke the term "female" and the char-
acteristics and roles associated with it in a derogatory manner to shame males.
James Smith, a white captive, recalled that, when he had helped some young
Wyandot women hoe a cornfield, the men in town laughed at him and said that
he "was adopted in the place of a great man, and must not hoe corn like a
squaw." At the treaty of Lancaster in 1744, representatives from Virginia and
Maryland attempted to negotiate a peace between the Six Nations and the
Catawbas to the south, who had been at war throughout the eighteenth century. The Catawbas refused the invitation, according to Gachadow, a Cayuga
chief, "and sent us word that we were but Women; that they were men and
double men for they had two Penises; that they could make Women of Us, and
would be always at War with us." Delawares in the Ohio Valley called the English "a parcel of old Women for that they could not travel without loaded
Horses and Waggons full of Provisions and a great deal of Baggage that they
did not know the Way to their Towns without Pilots and for these they must
be obliged to take Indians with them." So, it was perhaps not so unusual that
the Iroquois chief Canassatego admonished the Delawares in July 1742 for
being women. He used a recognizable gendered representation to shame and
embarrass Delawares publicly. "We conquer'd You," he insisted, "we made
Women of you, you know you are Women, and can no more sell Land than
Women. Nor is it fit you should have the Power of Selling Lands since you
would abuse it." [31]

Yet Canassatego's public declamation of Delawares' womanhood went beyond simply shaming a captive male for misunderstanding accepted native

30. Elisabeth Tooker, "Women in Iroquois Society," in Michael K. Foster, Jack Campisi,
and Marianne Mithun, eds., *Extending the Rafters: Interdisciplinary Approaches to Iroquoian
Studies* (Albany, N.Y., 1984), 114–123; J.N.B. Hewitt, "Status of Woman in Iroquois Polity be-
fore 1784," *Annual Report of the Board of Regents of the Smithsonian Institution Showing the
Operations, Expenditures, and Condition of the Institution for the Year Ending June 30, 1932*
(Washington, D.C., 1933); Grumet, "Sunksquaws, Shamans, and Tradeswomen," in Etienne
and Leacock, eds., *Women and Colonization: Anthropological Perspectives*, 43–62; Ricoeur,
*The Rule of Metaphor*, 7.

31. Smith, *An Account of his Captivity*, 45; MPCP, IV, 579, 580, 721; Deposition of John
Craig of Peters Township, Mar. 30, 1756, no. 78, Penn MSS, Indian Affairs, II, 1754–1756.

gender roles. The Iroquois leader was surely aware that the women of his family not only owned longhouses and personal property but were considered the "Truest Owners" of Iroquois land, since it was they who planted the crops and labored in the fields. Apparently, Indian diplomats felt the need to use specific European concepts of female gender, in which women could not own and sell land, to delineate Delawares' subordinate position in terms that Euramericans would clearly understand.[32]

Indeed, by using gendered representations politically, Iroquois, Delawares, and Euramericans—men and women alike—began to change the meaning of the political category of "women." After Delawares and Shawnees attacked the Pennsylvania and Virginia frontiers in 1755, the governors of both colonies begged the Six Nations to control the Delawares who were responsible. In January 1756, Robert Dinwiddie of Virginia told the Six Nations: "You looked upon [Delawares] as Women who wore petticoats; they never dar'd to do any thing of Importance without your leave, for they knew if they did you would Chastize them." If not punished, Delawares "will think themselves as good Men as you, and you will lose the name of being their Masters." In July, at Easton, Pennsylvania, the Six Nations again reminded Delawares: "You are our Women; our Fore-Fathers made you so, and put a Petticoat on you, and charged you to be true to us, and lie with no other Man; but of late you have suffered the String that tied your Petticoat to be cut loose by the French, and you lay with them, and so became a common Bawd, in which you acted very wrong, and deserve Chastisement." The Iroquois did not merely apply an alternative cultural category of femaleness in a political setting to convince whites to join them against Delawares. By the 1750s, Iroquois used these gendered representations to express the intimate and personal betrayal they felt as they wrestled to control Delawares.[33]

Despite the use of these gendered images within a political arena, the Six Nations were not very successful in controlling their "women." Delawares, instead, exploited the same images in order to manipulate Englishmen and Iroquois. They decided where and when they would be women. In September 1755, the Six Nations sent a black belt of wampum to entice Delawares to join them in war against the French. To secure the alliance, they "ordered their

32. Sullivan et al., comps., *Papers of William Johnson*, IV, 56, 58; Tooker, "Women in Iroquois Society," in Foster, Campisi, and Mithun, eds., *Extending the Rafters*, 114.

33. Robert Dinwiddie of Virginia to Gov. Morris, Jan. 2, 1756, no. 72, Penn MSS, Indian Affairs, II, 1754–1756; Gen. William Shirley to the Six Nations, January 1756, in Sullivan et al., comps., *Papers of William Johnson*, II, 414–415; Treaty of Easton, July 31, 1756, in Van Doren and Boyd, eds., *Indian Treaties Printed by Benjamin Franklin*, 148.

Cousins the Delawares to lay aside their petticoats and clap on nothing but a Breech Clout." Two months later, Delawares and Shawnees themselves insisted that they were "no longer Women, by which they mean no longer under [the Six Nations'] Subjection," and declared war against the English. Yet, by December, Delawares again wrapped themselves in their identity as women to exonerate themselves. They sent a message to Sir William Johnson: "'Tis true, brother, as you say, we are not at our own command, but under the direction of the six nations; we are women, our uncle must say what we must do; he has the hatchet, and we must do as he says." In the spring of 1757, however, Delawares and Shawnees in the Ohio Valley reversed their position and once more "looked upon themselves as Men" and were "determined to cut off all the *English*"; they warned that the Six Nations say no more about it, "lest we cut off your private Parts, and make Women of you, as you have done of us." Many whites thought that the Delawares' new alliance with French-allied Senecas in western Pennsylvania and New York originated from their anger at the Six Nations for making them women. It was clear, however, that Delawares could also manipulate their status as women for their own ends.[34]

Native American women, whose authority seemingly had been turned on its head to restrict the political powers of Delawares, also participated in producing and manipulating gendered images to control the actions of others. When they presented themselves in council, most often through male speakers, native women made it clear to their kinsmen what it meant to "act like a man." At two Indian conferences with Sir William Johnson near Albany in the early 1760s, a group of Tuscarora women assured him that they would give him "all the Assistance in the power of Women" toward his war effort against Indians in the West. To them, the "power of Women" included instilling "into the minds of their Children the Sentiments of Bravery, and Attachment to the En-

34. *MPCP,* VI, 615; Sullivan et al., comps., *Papers of William Johnson,* II, 681–682, IX, 310, 336; Treaty at Lancaster, in Van Doren and Boyd, eds., *Indian Treaties Printed by Benjamin Franklin,* 178; *PA,* 1st Ser., III, 193. The use of this cultural metaphor did not easily go away. It seemed that the Six Nations repeatedly took off the Delawares' petticoat and made them men. In January 1759, the Iroquois addressed the Delawares in Ohio, saying: "You know that I had made you women; I make you men. You must, therefore, listen to me and make peace as I do"; see Casteogain's Report, Jan. 4, 1759, in Sylvester K. Stevens and Donald H. Kent, eds., *Wilderness Chronicles of Northwestern Pennsylvania* (Harrisburg, Pa., 1941), 137. As late as 1796, there were reports that the Six Nations were *still* making men of the Delawares. John Heckewelder wrote that, during that year, "with great solemnity, [they] had again changed the latter, from the state of Women, to that of Men"; see Heckewelder to DuPonceau, Dec. 23, 1816, John Heckewelder Letters, 1816–1822.

glish" and sending their sons, husbands, and brothers to assist Johnson. They admonished their kinsmen to "be ever ready to follow, and observe his directions, and . . . when he sends you on Service, you will exert yourselves, and *act like Men,* and true Brothers." In other words, native women chose to exercise a very public role that reflected their private authority as mothers of men. They used representations that gave them a persuasive voice in common political arenas with native and white men and that might have also helped create pervasive new gendered images.[35]

Although the political metaphor of "woman" might have once simply symbolized Indian women's limited power to speak publicly, during the 1750s the meaning was changing. Through language Euramericans, Iroquois, and Delawares constructed and reconstructed what it was to "act like a woman." They had created a representation of woman that, when wielded politically, disenfranchised and dispossessed another of land. They had expanded the meaning of female gender to include a patriarchal view of the relative position of men and women as one of masters to slaves or servants. They also invoked an increasingly sexualized representation in which Delawares as women who acted on their own were no better than "common Bawds" and "Lewd Women" with no "modesty" who deserved chastisement. Through the use, repetition, exchange, and embellishment of gendered images in political places, the implicit meanings in these shifting metaphors perhaps eroded native women's power within their own communities. At the very least, this new category of "women" in politics belied the flexible public roles and practices that native women enjoyed and instead represented an identity that might be used to limit the options of individuals.[36]

Indians adapted and used images such as "women," which referred to European gender roles, in attempts to delineate the kinds of political relationships they wanted to establish with whites. Still, native Americans were becoming less certain whether Euramericans really understood the meaning of metaphors or the technologies by which they were conveyed. For instance, although

35. Sullivan et al., comps., *Papers of William Johnson,* Indian Council, Fort Johnson, July 1758, IX, 950, 958, X, 947, 959, XI, 41.

36. Karen Anderson, in *Chain Her by One Foot: The Subjugation of Women in Seventeenth-Century New France* (London, 1991), 5, postulates that, within thirty years of the French arrival, the status of women within Huron and Montagnais societies changed for the worse, because of the influence of European concepts of female gender. See Davis, "Iroquois Women, European Women," in Hendricks and Parker, eds., *Women, "Race," and Writing,* 243–258, for a different interpretation of the effects of cultural interaction on gender.

oral tradition and wampum belts had been a customary way to transmit messages between Indian communities, by the mid-1750s Indians began to employ
written documents as well as wampum to relay messages and address whites at
treaty conferences. This change was partly fueled by fear that non-Indians
might misinterpret the meaning of wampum. But it also marked the increasing need to control the outcome of these negotiations. Indeed, instead of a potential point where common meanings intersected and mutual understanding
emerged, by the late 1750s language had become a place of contention and political struggle.[37]

During the treaty negotiations of the 1750s, some Indians assumed that the
written word, which seemed to constitute political authority for Euramericans,
would be the most powerful way to approach and persuade white men. They
hoped that, through the written word, they might control the proceedings and
outcome of political negotiations. For example, when the Pennsylvania governor negotiated with Delawares to end their attacks on white settlements along
the frontier in the mid-1750s, the Delaware leader Teedyuscung emerged as the
most prominent speaker for several smaller Indian groups not directly affili-
ated with the Six Nations. In the fall of 1756, he stubbornly confronted the
colonial Council with the issue of title to Indian lands, rather than the conflict
at hand, and used the written word as a way to legitimize his own claims of
authority and ensure the fairness of the proceedings. After accusing the Province of taking Delaware lands illegally through the Walking Purchase of 1737,
Teedyuscung demanded copies of all deeds and documents "in order to prevent Misunderstandings." He wished to "have it in my Power to shew to others what has passed between this Government and me: What is committed to
Writing, [after all,] will not easily be lost, and will be of great Use to all, and
better regarded."[38]

To "have it in my Power," for Teedyuscung, did not simply mean obtaining

37. The Shawnees at Bethlehem in March 1753 had complained about an inappropriate
color that the Moravians had inadvertently used in a string of wampum they presented; see
*Moravian Records,* Mar. 26, 1753, box 323, folder 1, item 3. By 1779, the Delawares had
"thrown aside the use of wampum, . . . they had abandoned the communication of messages
through belts for communication through writing." "Despite past experiences with Americans who had purposefully misinterpreted written documents to them, the Delawares apparently preferred to take their chances with intentional deceptions rather than with unintentional blunders by Americans who did not know how to use wampum belts, calumets,
and war axes"; see White, *Middle Ground,* 383.

38. Van Doren and Boyd, eds., *Indian Treaties Printed by Benjamin Franklin,* 157, 163.

copies of the questionable deeds to interpret on his own. The Delaware leader also wanted to control the treaty's written record, or at least to monitor its accuracy and the way it was presented in public. After his initial complaint in the fall of 1756, Teedyuscung continued to accuse the Pennsylvania government "of having forged a Deed, and altered the Courses" of the Walking Purchase. In July 1757, Teedyuscung demanded that the governor let him have his own clerk to take notes during the treaty conferences, since his land claims were of "the utmost Importance and required to be exactly minuted." The governor, again trying to rein in Teedyuscung's power, denied the request because "no *Indian* Chief before him ever demanded to have a Clerk, and none had ever been appointed for *Indians* in former Treaties." Teedyuscung countered that having a clerk "was the most certain means to searching out the Truth, and of obtaining Justice to the Persons who should prove to be injured." Teedyuscung admitted that writing things down in council might be a new method for the Indians but that he aimed "by having a Clerk of my own, to exceed my Ancestors." [39]

Teedyuscung might have momentarily found justice in demanding copies of deeds and compiling a treaty record with his own clerk, but his power over the language and direction of the treaty negotiations was just as easily undermined or subverted by the provincial government. The Pennsylvania governor, even more successfully, manipulated public information about the conferences by controlling the translations of Indian speeches and curtailing any communication between Delawares and Euramericans. In April 1757, when Delawares met with the colonial Council in Lancaster, the governor ordered that neither Conrad Weiser, the interpreter for Pennsylvania, nor Teedyuscung's interpreter translate anything for the Indians without his explicit permission. The governor especially feared that Delawares would speak freely with Quakers, who supported and encouraged their demands for reparations for land taken at the Forks of the Delaware. Although the governor realized that he could hardly control the effects of conversation, since "almost all the Delawares speak English, and Teedyuscung We know does, . . . and might converse with whom they pleased," by regulating the public record of the treaties and

39. George Thomas and Richard Penn to Richard Peters, Dec. 8, 1757, Richard Peters Papers, 1697–1845, V, pt. 1; [Thomson], *Alienation of Delaware and Shawanese*, 110–111, 112 (Charles Thomson, the author of this treatise, was recruited as Teedyuscung's clerk); *MPCP*, VII, 656; Treaty of Easton, Aug. 1, 1757, in Van Doren and Boyd, eds., *Indian Treaties Printed by Benjamin Franklin*, 201.

the public image of Delawares that it conveyed he effectively obstructed their appeal to a higher British authority.[40]

Indians and whites adapted common linguistic forms and common strategies for power within the shared context of Indian and white political relations. As they exchanged and repeated metaphors and metaphoric language in this struggle to understand and control each other, they were able to untangle the meanings of exchanged words and phrases and uncover the underlying political and cultural motives. With comprehension, however, came disappointment. As each came to understand the actions or intentions of the other, hopes for finding a common ground faded. More and more, Iroquois, Delawares, Germans, and English invented ideal pasts for each other with their attendant histories and myths. They created representations of noble savages and peaceful William Penns—identities that seemed much more tangible and complaisant than the slippery, complicated, and demanding peoples who collided like water and rock. By appealing to these ideal images, each tried to compel the other to behave properly. Yet, as they increasingly used images of a mythical Golden Age, they simultaneously built the foundation for new boundaries of separation.

In the Euramerican version of the golden past, every Indian was the noble savage, the Lenni Lenape of the first meeting at Shackamaxon—eloquent, "full of words 'of more sweetness or greatness' than most European tongues." Indians were also supposed to adhere to the oral traditions of their forefathers. In October 1745, after a Mohawk interrupted the New York governor at Albany, Conrad Weiser took the wampum belts and reprimanded him: "I am Ashamed for our sakes and no doubt some of you are too, we ought to use one another well and not behave as Drunkards. I desire you will hear the Governor first and go to your Lodgings and agree upon an answer unanimously according to your old and good ways." The "old and good ways" did not include angry interruptions, nor did they include writing. Or so David Zeisberger thought when he refused to write a letter for some Onondagos in July 1753, saying: "If they had any message to send, they should do it by means of a belt, which was a much better and surer way than by letter." Indeed, to the governor of Pennsylvania, who admonished Teedyuscung in 1757 for requesting his own clerk in council,

40. Governor Denny to the Proprietaries, Apr. 9, 1757, *PA*, 1st Ser., III, 18, 107. See David Murray, *Forked Tongues: Speech, Writing, and Representation in North American Indian Texts* (Bloomington, Ind., 1991), 40.

writing for Indians was "quite a new Method, and was never practised before." He did not understand why Indians were not acting more like Indians.[41]

Indians in eighteenth-century Pennsylvania also constructed their own version of a golden past with every white man a William Penn. For the Conestogas, "old William Penn" might have loved all Indians, but "there was a singular love between him and the people who came with him, and the Conestogo Indians." On the other hand, Teedyuscung remembered that Penn had been "adopted and received into [the Delaware] Family as a Child." "Further that it had been formerly agreed to by all the Nations that the Delaware Country shod never be incommoded with War, but always enjoy an undisturb'd peace and Tranquillity." Even in the Ohio Valley, the myth of William Penn and the vision of a Golden Age held strong. In the fall of 1758, Ohio Delawares addressed the Pennsylvania governor: "Father, thy children remember the many good counsels we held with our grandfather William Penn when we first come in this country and with what great love You received us as your own children your own family and what peace and love we enjoyed with our grandfather." They had not only constructed the ideal white man, who compliantly maintained the peace, but also had given William Penn a revered status, adopting him as their "grandfather."[42]

During the eighteenth century, Indians and whites learned each other's languages in shared homes and communities and came together to negotiate their mutual needs and expectations. Together, Indians and whites in Pennsylvania

41. Stephen Greenblatt, "Learning to Curse: Aspects of Linguistic Colonialism in the Sixteenth Century," in Greenblatt, *Learning to Curse: Essays in Early Modern Culture* (New York, 1990), 19; Treaty of Albany, Oct. 8, 1745, Penn MSS, Indian Affairs, I, 1687–1753; Beauchamp, ed., *Moravian Journals Relating to Central New York*, 179; *MPCP*, VII, 689.

42. *MPCP*, VIII, 457; Christian Frederick Post, Journal, May 13, 1760, contemporary copy, HSP; C. F. Post's notes of his first journey to Ohio, July 15–Sept. 21, 1758, *Moravian Records*, reel 28, box 219, folder 3, item 1; Historical Society Collection, miscellaneous manuscripts, 1661–1931, Indians, HSP. William Penn was given the title "Onas" by the Iroquois and Delawares. Onas then became a personage, a role that was filled at various times during the eighteenth and early nineteenth century by different individuals connected with the Pennsylvania white political community, such as the Quakers. So, perhaps the ways that whites created the ideal Indian (the noble savage) were different from the ways Indians formally constructed and thought of an ideal personage (William Penn/Onas). But, this does not necessarily negate the existence of a perceived Golden Age of Pennsylvania Indian-white relations. Onas was an ideal white personage, which very few actual individuals were deemed worthy of assuming.

crossed cultural boundaries through language—Shawnees attempted to understand Delawares by way of Nanticokes who spoke English to Germans. Moravian missionaries on the Pennsylvania frontier used Indian languages to translate the Bible, sing songs of praise, and write poetry in hopes of converting natives, and Indians learned German and English to cope with the legal and diplomatic tangles of a changing world. All employed some of the same metaphors and technologies to promote cultural understanding but also to control the outcome of treaty negotiations. Military men sent speeches and belts of wampum to Indians along the Susquehanna, asking them to "be strong and dont Herken to the French to take up the Hatchet against the English," and Indian warriors shook hands with whites and "had no Wampum and on that accound did not know what to do, but[,] as is usual among the English," made "use of writings." In their struggle for power, Indians and whites borrowed or created common cultural languages that at times blurred the boundaries of difference between them. This was a world where white settlers on the frontier, asking the Pennsylvania governor for assistance against Indian attacks, could sound like Indians: "In these sad and lamentable Circumstances we betake ourselves to your Honour's compassion as to a kind and careful Father of whose tender concern for us we are well assured." And where Wappingers could sound like whites: "I am Chief of the Opies, and have a Commission for it, and if any other Indian pretends to be Chief, you must not regard it, for they have no Commission for it."[43]

But the exchange of metaphors, symbolic gestures, technologies, gendered images, and, finally, idealized representations, like drips of water, also wore away old cultural boundaries that ordered the eighteenth-century world. If Indians did not act like ideal Indians but instead used white political strategies within common political spaces or appropriated white actions and "behaved as Drunkards," if whites did not act like ideal whites but instead misinterpreted their responsibilities as "fathers" or "grandfathers" and incited war, then golden pasts, with their implied dark present, could become the basis for future racialized boundaries of differences. The ideal world of tolerant, caring white men and noble Indians also implied the existence of its opposite, a world inhabited by heartless white men and cruel ignoble savages.

By the 1760s, after a brief period of sharing metaphors and puzzling over their meanings, Indians and whites in Pennsylvania broke off their attempts at accommodation. With the end of the Seven Years' War, the Proclamation

43. Samuel Hunter to James Burd, June 14, 1763, Shippen Family Papers, VI, 21, HSP; Penn MSS, no. 104, June 14, 1756, Indian Affairs, II, 1754–1756; *MPCP,* VI, 533, VIII, 668–669.

of 1763 created a political line separating their communities. But it was not simply a physical boundary that marked a permanent rift between Indians and whites. The flexibility of the metaphor—a space where "brothers" and "cousins" once met on open roads with clear eyes—no longer held diverse cultural groups together. The political discourse that Delawares, English, and Iroquois had created and manipulated during the 1750s gave way to increasingly rigid linguistic exchanges. The passions of war had crystallized perceptions of an enemy other, and, more than any shared metaphor, racial rhetoric would shape the direction of Indian-white relations in the late eighteenth and early nineteenth centuries. After the Seven Years' War, Delawares and Shawnees moved north on the Susquehanna River or west to the Ohio Valley. The Iroquois retreated to New York to consolidate control over their remaining lands. Once they left the Pennsylvania frontier, a tide of white settlers rushed in. As Partrik had feared, the power of language had finally worn a hole in the stone.

# Black "Go-Betweens" and the Mutability of "Race," Status, and Identity on New York's Pre-Revolutionary Frontier

One November day in 1767, a delegation of Seneca warriors and their wives led by the war chief Onoghsoakta arrived at Johnson Hall (in present-day Johnstown, New York), the home of Sir William Johnson, the superintendent of Indian affairs in the Northern colonies, for a council meeting. Among the Senecas was "a free Negro [Mullatto]" named the "Sun Fish," who had lived at Kanaghiyiadirhe (present-day Belvidere, New York), a Seneca village, since the early 1750s.[1]

After conducting some general business with the warriors, Johnson drew the Sun Fish aside to a separate room, where the two men carried on a private conversation behind closed doors. There, the Sun Fish proceeded to tell Johnson news that had been passed to him by a Delaware headman while he was in Ohio country "on his Hunt" in 1765. The news, a litany of "jealous[ies]" and discontent among some of the western Indian nations and many of the nations "to the Southward," warned that a war belt was circulating among the Shawnees and the Delawares (Munsees and Unamis), the latter having become refugees in Ohio country following the Seven Years' War. The Delawares had the support of Creeks and Cherokees, who had strong desires to avenge the losses they had suffered during the war. The war belt called for an Indian uprising to remove the English once and for all from the colonies. The revolt

I wish to thank Fredrika J. Teute and Andrew Cayton for their keen editorial eyes and thoughtful comments and suggestions. I also wish to thank Jean M. O'Brien and Peter H. Wood for their insightful comments on an earlier draft of this essay, presented at the conference "Crucibles of Cultures: North American Frontiers, 1750–1820," November 18–19, 1994, sponsored by the Institute of Early American History and Culture, The Historic New Orleans Collections, and the Newberry Library. I also wish to thank Gloria Chun, Myra Armstead, Mario Bick, and other faculty and students at Bard College for their comments on an earlier draft of this essay.

1. James Sullivan et al., eds., *The Papers of Sir William Johnson,* 14 vols. (Albany, N.Y., 1921–1965), XII, 386 (hereafter cited as *Johnson Papers*).

would commence at Fort Pitt. Once the garrison was destroyed, the warriors would work their way eastward to Albany, pillaging all of the white settlements in their path and recruiting Indian allies along the way. Those Indians who chose not to join the revolt would be regarded as traitors and killed along with their English friends.[2]

The Sun Fish, a paid informant to Sir William Johnson, passed along information about an effort to rekindle Pontiac's War, which had virtually collapsed in 1765. Johnson, troubled by this news, gave the Sun Fish a copy of the *"Prince of Chote's"* speech. The recorded speech had earlier accompanied a Cherokee peace belt, which had circulated among the Six Nations of the Iroquois affirming a recently negotiated peace treaty between the Cherokees and the Iroquois. Because the conspirators would have to march through Iroquois country to reach Albany, Johnson wanted to block the possibility of Iroquois involvement in the revolt by reminding the Senecas of their commitment to keep the peace.[3]

Johnson instructed the Sun Fish to read the prince's speech to *"Addongot* and *Squissahawe,* the Two Chiefs of His Castle, least it might be delivered to them wrong." The Sun Fish promised to carry out Johnson's order and to bring him further news of "Stirring amongst the Indians." Before dismissing him, Johnson gave his informant "a handsome present . . . [of] four Strings of black Wampum to deliver to his Brother *Addongat"* as ransom for the release of a

2. *Johnson Papers,* XII, 387–388. For a brief discussion of Delaware refugees and Shawnees in Ohio country, see Gregory Evans Dowd, *A Spirited Resistance: The North American Indian Struggle for Unity, 1745–1815* (Baltimore, 1992), 21, 32, 51.

3. *Johnson Papers,* XII, 388–389. Dowd suggests that the Shawnees took their first "tentative steps" at rekindling Pontiac's War in 1767. The above conversation between Johnson and the Sun Fish, however, indicates that the Shawnees took steps a year after Pontiac's siege of Detroit in 1763–1764 and a year before the peace treaty negotiated between Pontiac and Johnson in July 1766. See Dowd, *Spirited Resistance,* 42. The identity of the Prince of Chota— Chota was commonly called the capital of the Cherokee nation—is a bit obscure. The prince might have been also known as the Little Carpenter, whom James Mooney labeled "the civil Chief of the Nation and well known as a friend of the English." See James Mooney, *Historical Sketch of the Cherokee* (Chicago, 1975), 32. It is possible, however, that William Johnson was referring to Oconostota, the nation's principal war chief. Oconostota, whom John Norton called "the Great Chief of Chote," was pro-French throughout much of the Seven Years' War but, like Attakullakulla, endorsed the 1764 peace treaty between the Iroquois and the Cherokee. See John Norton, *The Journal of Major John Norton, 1816,* ed. Carl F. Klinck and James J. Talman (Toronto, 1970), 136. Colin G. Calloway suggests that the Prince of Chota was another individual entirely; see Calloway, *The American Revolution in Indian Country: Crisis and Diversity in Native American Communities* (New York, 1995), 182–201, esp. 186–187.

captive, Peggy May Pole, who had been adopted by Addongat's sister. Johnson also wrote a "few lines to Captain MacLeod," the commissary of Indian trade at Fort Niagara, which he gave to the Sun Fish "by way of a Passport." The note read: "As the Bearer a Free Mullatto named the *Sun Fish* is employed by me to go of Errands and bring Intellegence. You will not Suffer him to be followed Should he go to Niagara upon business of his own, and behave Well."[4]

We know not much else of the Sun Fish. Presumably, he left with his Seneca wife and his fellow warriors and their wives and headed for Fort Niagara, where he resumed his activities as a cattle trader and freelance spy. In all probability, the Sun Fish accompanied his Seneca brethren the following month to their winter hunting and trapping grounds in Ohio country for a prolonged stay of several weeks or months. There he would be in a position to collect more intelligence. The historical record is silent on his exact movements, as it is about so much regarding the quotidian activities and behavior of persons of African and Indian descent on New York's frontier. We, therefore, must infer from the ethnographic record of Iroquois people the activities the Sun Fish most likely would have undertaken as a member of Seneca society.[5]

Herein lies the significance of the Sun Fish: he exercised dual identities on the frontier. At one moment Johnson identified him as Seneca and at the next mulatto. The frontier, where, according to Frederick Jackson Turner, American life underwent "perennial rebirth," was an open and fluid region in the decades preceding the Revolutionary War. Of necessity, convenience, and sheer pleasure, individuals appropriated cultural habits from others and in doing so altered their identity. Outsiders unfamiliar with frontier life found that the reshaped and reinvented identities violated their assumptions and preconceived notions about race, status, and identity contained in their racialized worldview, which was becoming more commonly held in the colonies.[6]

4. *Johnson Papers,* V, 795, XII, 389.

5. An early antiquarian, Orasmus Turner, identified the cattle trade at Fort Niagara and southern Ontario as the "personal business" of the Sun Fish. Turner also noted that the Sun Fish's wife was Seneca and that they had at least one biological child, a daughter. See Turner, *History of the Pioneer Settlement of Phelps and Gorham's Purchase* (Rochester, N.Y., 1852), 406. For evidence of Iroquois wives' accompanying their husbands to provincial council meetings, see *Johnson Papers,* II, 80, III, 707–708, 711–712, X, 241, XIII, 189, 251, 255–256. Readers interested in early ethnographic studies of Iroquois customs and practices, focused largely upon Seneca culture, should begin with Lewis Henry Morgan, *League of the Ho-de-no-sau-nee, or Iroquois* (1851; reprint, New Haven, Conn., 1954).

6. Frederick Jackson Turner, *The Frontier in American History* (1920; reprint, Huntington, N.Y., 1976), 2–3. For a brief study of "malleable identities" and "self-fashioning" on the

Cultural appropriation and identity alteration were practically uncontainable on the frontiers of the middle colonies. There the populations, Turner noted, reflected "the map of Europe in their variety." Contact between these European Americans and persons of Indian ancestry and of African descent led to almost limitless possibilities for social innovation and cultural transformation. The Sun Fish stands as an example of one who oscillated between identities—sometimes a Seneca warrior, husband, and father; at other times a free mulatto spy, informant, and cattle trader. His particular identity was dictated by his needs and the needs of others with whom he was in contact within a given situation.[7]

## The Frontier and the Mid-Eighteenth-Century Worldview

Frontiers were those regions that lay between two or more culturally distinct societies and beyond the immediate control of any one of them, where individuals or groups from these societies came into direct contact. The uncertain, changeable natural and social conditions of frontier life required that people rely upon and borrow from others who came from alien cultures. Borrowing was done of necessity as well as for convenience and ranged from securing necessary material goods to appropriating cultural habits. Anne Grant, who spent her youth on the frontier of the Mohawk Valley in the 1750s and 1760s, recalled years later that "there was an undefinable charm [to Indian life] . . . wrought in every one who dwelt for any time amongst them." The early European American settlers, she remembered hearing, had "found it convenient in several things regarding hunting, food, etc. to assimilate in some degree with the Indians." As a consequence of such assimilation and borrowing, some individuals transformed their sense of self.[8]

---

colonial frontier, see Richard White, "'Although I am dead, I am not entirely dead. I have left a second of myself': Constructing Self and Persons on the Middle Ground of Early America," in Ronald Hoffman, Mechal Sobel, and Fredrika J. Teute, eds., *Through a Glass Darkly: Reflections on Personal Identity in Early America* (Chapel Hill, N.C., 1997), 404–418.

7. Turner, *Frontier in American History*, 5, 28.

8. Anne Grant, *Memoirs of an American Lady: With Sketches of Manners and Scenery in America, as They Existed Previous to the Revolution*, 2 vols. (1808; reprint, New York, 1970), I, 242–243. For a study of "white Indians," that is, whites living on the frontier who lost sight of themselves and turned "savage," see James Axtell, *The European and the Indian: Essays in the Ethnohistory of Colonial North America* (New York, 1981), 168–206; and Axtell, *The Invasion Within: The Contest of Cultures in Colonial North America* (New York, 1985),

Those individuals who successfully borrowed from, negotiated with, and maneuvered within multiple cultures were truly multicultural. They engaged in acts of cultural innovation that included wearing the clothing of the "other," speaking the *lingua franca,* pidgin, or trade language of the local region, adopting the other's religion, and taking a spouse of the other's race or ethnicity. They transcended European American categories of racial labeling that were being used increasingly by whites in some of the towns and plantations on or near the eastern seaboard to fix Africans and Indians in a lower social status. To maximize one's life options on the northern frontier, one was required to hold a flexible worldview that did not pre-categorize individuals.

Cultural borrowers often practiced cultural habits that were specific to particular situations. Anthropologists have referred to this practice as constructing "situational ethnicity." Those who employ two or more identities typically live in biracial, bicultural, or bilingual households and at different times practice both a private and a public cultural identity. In order for their repertoire of identities to work, however, they must conform to the learned cultural habits of the ethnic groups with which they are identifying.[9]

Ethnicity, then, reflects culture—ways of knowing, ways of believing, and ways of communicating. The individual who practices situational ethnic identity, therefore, reflects the learned behavior, values, and beliefs of two or more ethnic groups. Sir William Johnson was a master of situational identities. During the summer, his "mode of living [was] that of an English gentleman at his country seat," Julia Grant, the mother of Anne Grant, recalled, whereas in the winter he wore "almost entirely [the Iroquois's] dress and ornaments." In donning Iroquois garb, Johnson did not suddenly lose sight of himself and turn savage. He was too firmly attached to the circles of English power to permit that to happen. On the contrary, he practiced being the other for his own comfort and from political necessity. As superintendent of Indian affairs, he found it politically expedient to identify himself as Iroquois. One man of French Iroquois ancestry—known as Jean Montour in European American circles and Hiokato in Iroquois society—declared that Johnson was so familiar with Iro-

---

302–327. Axtell focuses largely on white captives in Indian country who "crossed the cultural divide." Still, he acknowledges that many fur traders, trappers, and social "renegades" voluntarily exiled themselves to the frontier, where they adopted Indian ways. For a first-hand account of a white captive who adopted Indian customs, see James E. Seaver, comp., *A Narrative of the Life of Mrs. Mary Jemison . . .* (1824; reprint, Syracuse, N.Y., 1990).

9. For an analysis of "situational ethnicity," see Anya Peterson Royce, *Ethnic Identity: Strategies of Diversity* (Bloomington, Ind., 1982), 202–215.

quois laws, customs, and languages that "he was not like other white men, but an Indian like ourselves." Montour understood Johnson's situational ethnicity well. Montour, identifying himself as Indian, implied that ethnic identity was cultural and thus subject to appropriation and mutability.[10]

European American visitors to the frontier who held preconceived ideas about culture, race, identity, and status would have had difficulty reading men like Montour and the Sun Fish. Julia Grant relied upon predetermined categories of race and ethnicity for reading the social and cultural worlds she encountered there. Because she was unfamiliar with cultural borrowing on the frontier, her worldview was shaken during a visit to Johnson Hall in the early 1750s: "During my stay [Johnson] had Indian chiefs to dine with him several times. Their attire was the same as white people, and for the most part they conversed in English. This disappointed me, because I wished to sit at table with genuine Indians in blankets and leggings and talking nothing but their gibberish through an interpreter."[11]

Johnson's dinner guests undermined Grant's expectations of authentic Indian behavior that she brought with her to the frontier. These Iroquois diners did not wear the precontact garb of their ancestors that she expected, nor did they speak much in their native language. Their behavior inverted Grant's preconceived categories of true Indians and proper Indian behavior. Consequently, Grant believed that she was deprived of a genuine frontier encounter. On the contrary, she experienced the very thing that defined the frontier: fluidity of social interaction, creativity in cultural borrowing, and the possibility of self-transformation.[12]

10. For references to William Johnson's style of living, see Julia Grant, *Eight Years in America: Journal of an Officer's Wife,* cited in Augustus C. Buell, *Sir William Johnson* (New York, 1903), 44. For Montour's remarks, see ibid., 68, 68 n. 1, 79. For a study of cultural cross-dressing in this frontier region, see Timothy J. Shannon, "Dressing for Success on the Mohawk Frontier: Hendrick, William Johnson, and the Indian Fashion," *William and Mary Quarterly,* 3d Ser., LIII (1996), 13–42.

11. Grant, *Eight Years in America,* cited in Buell, *Sir William Johnson,* 44.

12. The headmen at Johnson's table were probably Mohawks, as they were the most acculturated of the Six Nations of the Iroquois. According to Johnson, the Mohawks, who had been located "next to our settlem[en]ts for sev[era]l years," had "lost [a] great part of [their Ancient usages], and have blended some with Customs amongst ourselves, so as to render it Extremely difficult, if not impossible to Trace their Customs to their origin." See Sir William Johnson to Arthur Lee, Feb. 28, 1771, in E. B. O'Callaghan, ed., *Documentary History of the State of New York,* 4 vols. (Albany, N.Y., 1849–1851), IV, 270 (hereafter cited as *DHNY*).

My thinking on the subversion of preconceived ideas about roles and cultural practices has been influenced by Barbara Babcock's work on "symbolic inversion." The symbols that

Grant's inability to find "genuine Indians" at Johnson Hall indicates that she perceived the world in racial terms. A racialized worldview constructed human differences as fixed, immutable, heritable, and nontranscendable. Uneven relationships of power were considered natural, even desirable. Grant's racialized Iroquois diners should have behaved like Indians from a precontact past. Their engaging in cultural change and innovation jarred with her expectations. Moreover, these Indians undermined her preconceived ideas about power relationships. Indians were not supposed to be on par with whites culturally. Because they appeared more white than Indian, Grant refused to see them as "genuine." In Grant's worldview, the speech and clothing of authentic Indians were supposed to remain primitive and, thus, inferior to those of whites.[13]

The European American racialized worldview was just beginning to emerge in the colonies in the middle decades of the eighteenth century. It would reach full maturity in the early nineteenth century, as many white Americans applied a range of heritable racial characteristics to a variety of perceived racial others, which included some Europeans. Some whites were beginning to articulate such racialized views in the mid-eighteenth century, believing that the behavior, moral qualities, and status of persons of African descent were universal, immutable, and heritable. Daniel Horsmanden, the judge presiding over the trial of the perceived 1741 slave uprising in New York City, offered evidence of a coalescing racialized worldview when he charged that all free and enslaved blacks were members of a "wicked race" and were a "brutish and bloody species of mankind." Horsmanden assigned sweepingly common characteristics to all persons of African descent.[14]

---

she focuses on, however, are a society's "commonly held cultural codes, values and norms" that might be "linguistic, literary or artistic, religious, social and political." The inversion that I see occurring on the frontier is about preconceived ideas on race, status, and identity that did not necessarily originate on the frontier but rather were brought there largely by European Americans. See Barbara Babcock, ed., *The Reversible World: Symbolic Inversion in Art and Society* (Ithaca, N.Y., 1978), 14. Also, Richard White's concept of the "middle ground" has been instructive. The middle ground, geographically the Great Lakes region in White's study, is that frontier region where "distinct people" came into contact and, in their efforts to communicate with and accommodate the other, entered mutually into "a realm of constant invention," where new meanings and new practices evolved. See White, *The Middle Ground: Indians, Empires, and Republics in the Great Lakes Region, 1650–1815* (New York, 1991), 50–53.

13. For an insightful theoretical treatment of race as a worldview, see Audrey Smedley, *Race in North America: Origin and Evolution of a Worldview* (Boulder, Colo., 1993), 13–35, 109.

14. Daniel Horsmanden, *The New York Conspiracy* (1744), ed. Thomas J. Davis (Boston, 1971), xvi, 11.

Conversion to Christianity could ameliorate the "wicked[ness]" and "brutish[ness]" of the inner souls of free and enslaved blacks, but it did not alter their outer condition. So argued Bishop Fleetwood of the Anglican Church, who contended as early as 1710–1711 that neither the "Laws of *God,* nor those of the *Land"* set slaves free. Rather, Christianity simply freed slaves from sin and from fear of death, not from "any State of Life, in which they had either voluntarily engaged themselves, or were fallen into through their Misfortune." Biblical law, colonial statutes, and the accident of birth—being the unfortunate descendants of Noah's cursed son, Ham—contributed to the immutability of blackness in the minds of those who held a racialized worldview.[15]

By the mid-eighteenth century, the dark brown skin of Africans stood as the mark of their inferior status in colonial American society. John Woolman, the eighteenth-century Quaker abolitionist, understood that slavery was based upon an unequal power relationship between Africans and European Americans. Africans were enslaved, he argued, "because we [whites] have Power to do it." He lamented the fact that "Slavery [had become] connected with the Black Colour, and Liberty with the White." The "Ideas of *Negroes* and Slaves are so interwoven in the Mind," Woolman wrote in the early 1760s, that it was commonly believed that "black Men . . . ought to serve white Men." Woolman's critique of slavery was actually a critique of the racialized worldview that was

15. William [Fleetwood], *A Sermon Preached before the Society for the Propagation of the Gospel . . . February 16, 1710/11* (London, 1711), cited in Frank J. Klingberg, *Anglican Humanitarianism in Colonial New York* (Philadelphia, 1940), 205–206. During the second half of the eighteenth century, with the rise of abolition sentiments, racial attitudes varied more sharply. In 1768, abolitionist Anthony Benezet wrote to Daniel Burton, the secretary for the Society for the Propagation of the Gospel in Foreign Parts, the Anglican Church's foreign missionary wing, asking that the slave trade end on the grounds that blacks were "free by nature, and as well as we the Objects of Grace." Burton acknowledged that slaves should be treated kindly but that the church could not endorse emancipation, for (1) the Bible endorses the validity of slavery through its "master-servant" references; (2) if slavery were deemed unlawful, masters would treat their slaves more harshly, and it would further constrain the SPG's teaching the principles of Christianity to slaves; and (3) slaves would not stand for that and would initiate bloody revolts. See Anthony Benezet to SPG, 1768, Miscellaneous Manuscripts, B, New-York Historical Society. For the rationales in favor of Christianizing free and slave blacks, see John C. Van Horne, ed., *Religious Philanthropy and Colonial Slavery: The Correspondence of the Associates of Dr. Bray, 1717–1777* (Urbana, Ill., 1985), 1–47. From the second half of the seventeenth century through much of the eighteenth, it was believed by many who supported missionary efforts that Indians, who were widely viewed as remnants of the lost tribes of Israel, could overcome their natural savagism if they simply adopted Christianity and English ways and manners.

taking hold in the American colonies. However, the frontier undermined pre-determined racialized categories. There, where social contact was open and fluid, fixed racial categories were not very useful in defining individuals who could assume more than one identity.[16]

## An African Presence on the Frontier

At the end of the 1920s—a decade that began with bloody racial violence and ended with racial theorists' defending their explanations for human nature, ability, and worth—historian James Hugo Johnston explained the long tradition of Indian-black relations and intermarriage by suggesting that common "conditions of life" and "kindred . . . sympathy" led to "consciousness of kind" that precipitated a "mystical bond." Henry Bibb might have concurred with Johnston. Bibb, who was enslaved for a brief time in the 1840s by a Cherokee master, claimed that he would "rather be a slave to an Indian, than to a white man," for Indian masters fed and clothed their slaves well, did not beat them, and, in general, treated them humanely. Nevertheless, few of us today would find Johnston's reductionist theory useful or satisfactory to explain the history of Indian-black relations. Safety, survival, and collective power offer more plausible explanations for the gravitation of blacks to America's frontiers and to Indian communities. Consider the hundreds of black maroons among the Seminoles during the early nineteenth century. They calculated that their chances of survival and autonomy were greater among native people than alone or among other creole Americans. Like the runaway slaves who joined them, the Seminoles were a people of color, but, more important, they were a people in opposition to the power and interests of white America. They welcomed the nearby presence of black maroons, who augmented their fighting ranks and, for a time, helped forestall their removal from Florida.[17]

16. John Woolman, *Some Considerations on the Keeping of Negroes* (1754, 1762; facsimile reprint, New York, 1976), 18, 36, 59, 60. Woolman was not completely free of racialized thinking. He referred to blacks as "inferior" and to Jews as "degenerate" (see 21, 37). On the other hand, Woolman did consider the baseness of slaves' lives, not as a natural, heritable quality of blacks (as would be the case in the nineteenth century), but rather as a product of the institution of slavery and its influence on white thinking. "Placing on Men the ignominious Title SLAVE, dressing them in uncomely Garments, keeping them to servile labour, in which they are often dirty, tends gradually to fix a Notion in the Mind, that they are a sort of People below us in Nature, and lead us to consider them as such in all our Conclusions about them" (52).

17. James Hugo Johnston, "Documentary Evidence of the Relations of Negroes and Indians," *Journal of Negro History,* XIV (1929), 26, 40; Kenneth W. Porter, "Relations between

We cannot equate the black presence on New York's frontier with the large black maroon communities in places like Florida, Jamaica, Haiti, or Surinam. Most black refugees to New York's frontier were men who traveled and arrived alone. They represented a small proportion of persons of African descent there, most of whom were slaves in European American frontier households and thus did not try to insinuate themselves into Iroquois society. The dominant black presence on the frontier consisted of servants and slaves in Dutch and English households. Many families owned at least one young black housekeeper, and the wealthier estates possessed a dozen or more slaves. A few free blacks set up households on the frontier as well. Warren Johnson, the brother of Sir William Johnson, noted in his journal in 1761 during a visit to the Mohawk Valley that "there are many free Negroes here who have good Estates." Among the first to arrive were the "Willigee Negroes," who, along with several Palatine families, were recruited in 1738 by Sir William Johnson to be one of several tenant families on his uncle Peter Warren's estate, which Sir William Johnson had been hired to manage and develop.[18]

---

Negroes and Indians within the Present Limits of the United States," *Journal of Negro History,* XVII (1932), 298. For a brief discussion of racial theories in the 1920s, see Thomas F. Gossett, *Race: The History of an Idea in America* (New York, 1965), chaps. 15, 16. Despite his encomium of his Cherokee master, Henry Bibb ran away at his earliest opportunity. See Bibb, "Narrative of the Life and Adventure of Henry Bibb, an American Slave, Written by Himself," in Gilbert Osofsky, ed., *Puttin' On Ole Massa: The Slave Narratives of Henry Bibb, William Wells Brown, and Solomon Northrup* (New York, 1969), 139–143 (quotation on 141). For a study of slavery among the Cherokees, see Theda Perdue, *Slavery and the Evolution of Cherokee Society, 1540–1866* (Knoxville, Tenn., 1979). On African Americans among Seminoles, see Kevin Mulroy, *Freedom on the Border: The Seminole Maroons in Florida, the Indian Territory, Coahuila, and Texas* (Lubbock, Tex., 1993), esp. 12–34, on forestalling removal. In his study of Catawba Indian–black relations, James Merrell explains the importance of examining the *context* of such relations, for example, power relations, the purpose of contact and the people involved, and the image that Indians had of themselves in relation to the other. Merrell's model is useful for understanding the attitudes Indians held toward blacks among them but leaves the roles, statuses, and identities of black maroons among Indians unexamined. See James H. Merrell, "The Racial Education of the Catawba Indians," *Journal of Southern History,* L (1984), 363–384.

18. For evidence of slaves on the frontier, especially at Johnson Hall, see *Johnson Papers,* I, 230, 337, III, 573, IX, 3, 121, X, 247, XII, 231–232, 1070, XIV (index), 405, 544–546. For Warren Johnson's "Journal," see ibid., XIII, 201. At one point, while the German families waited for their plots of land to be surveyed and divided, the Willigee Negroes went ahead and had their parcel surveyed but waited for Johnson to clear the land before moving onto it. Perhaps Johnson never cleared their land, or the Willigee Negroes had to clear it themselves as

Some slaves perceived that New York's frontier was a "free zone" and that crossing its boundary changed one's status from "unfree" to "free." Dutch and English slaveowners from the Connecticut River valley to the Mohawk Valley had to contend with the persistent problem of their slaves running away to their neighbors. Slave catching became a form of employment for young Mohawk men. In August 1773, Jelles Fonda, the owner of a store in the Mohawk Valley, paid Seth, a Mohawk warrior and frequent customer, "1 pound, 2 shillings of credit" toward his store account for "4 days going in search of my negro." [19]

Johnson Hall became a veritable clearinghouse for the exchange of information leading to the whereabouts of missing slaves, both black and *panis* (Indian), some of whom had been kidnapped in Indian raids, most of whom had run away. In 1767, Samuel Johnson of Stratford, Connecticut, wrote to Sir William Johnson, seeking his help in securing the runaway slave of his neighbor, Ephraim Nichols. The slave had nearly killed Nichols with a scythe a few years back, and now, for some odd reason, Nichols wanted him back. He had heard that his slave was last seen at Fort Augusta (Shamokin, present-day Sunbury, Pa.) "with a party of Indians, among whom he is supposed still to be pretending to be free." The slave, who was literate and skilled at forging passes, had also changed his name to "Sam," Nichols had heard. "If any of the Indians know of such a fellow," Samuel Johnson wrote, well aware of the role that Indians played as slave catchers, "and could secure him, his Master would fully reward them." [20]

---

best they could, for Peter Warren, in his instructions to his nephew, William, explained how to landscape to leave hedgerows. It was no more expensive to do a beautiful job, he intimated to Johnson, than "doing it in a slovenly Iregular Manner as to the land the Negroes possess" (ibid., I, 8, XIII, 3).

19. [Jelles Fonda?], *Indian Account Book, 1768–78,* New-York Historical Society, fol. 88. Seth was a highly acculturated customer. Among the items he purchased were women's stockings, white linen, gartering, buttons, ribbon, sugar, calico, powder, black strouds, broad calico, delftware, striped linen, and a small knife. In addition to his labor, Seth sold to Fonda cranberries and wheat, suggesting that he farmed. Fonda kept separate account books, one for white shoppers and another for Indians, blacks, and some Dutch, who might have been biracial or at least closely connected to Mohawk society. All shoppers bought similar items, including "Indian shoes" (see fols. 1, 3, 8, 22, 23, 43, 46, 51, 54, 60, 67, 69, 70, 86, pt. II, 87). Free and enslaved blacks known to Fonda also frequented his shop (see fols. 4, 17, 19, 20, 22, 31).

20. *Johnson Papers,* V, 587. See E. B. O'Callaghan, ed., *Documents Relative to the Colonial History of the State of New York,* 15 vols. (Albany, N.Y., 1853–1887), V, 635–639, 674–676, 796,

Advertisements for runaway slaves that appeared in colonial newspapers in New York reveal that fugitive slaves long sought safety and freedom among Indians on the frontiers of New York and Pennsylvania. As early as 1679, the "hue and cry" went out in New York for the runaway slave Jacob, who spoke "Good English, Dutch, good Mohawk and Mohegan." His master, Sven Theunisse, offered to pay a reward for his return, whether he was captured in "Indian or Christian territory." Judging by his linguistic skills, Jacob had previous contact with Indians living in the Upper Hudson and the eastern Mohawk Valleys and likely would have sought refuge with a Mohawk or Mahican family. In 1759, William Hunt placed an advertisement requesting the return of his slave, Bood, who had yet again run away, this time with another of Hunt's slaves and two other friends. The four were most likely headed "to some of the Indian Towns upon Sasquehannah, the Mollatto Bood, having been entertained by the Indians there several months, some years ago." Like Jacob, Bood could count on Indian friends to shelter him. In 1775, Isaac Ward of East Chester, New York, believed that his runaway slave, Robin, a man of mixed Indian and African ancestry, had set a course for "the North River [Hudson River], to get over among the Indians." Ward offered a reward of four pounds for his return if captured in East Chester, five pounds if taken in another county, and seven "if taken among the Indians." The highest fee for the return of Robin from Indian country reflected the high costs required for travel and for the purchase of trade goods as ransom to secure his release. The higher fee also represented an increased incentive for slave catchers to return runaways from In-

---

965 (hereafter cited as *DRCHNY*), for evidence of New York colonial officials' beseeching the Iroquois to return runaway slaves and the Indians' claiming ignorance of such runaways. For additional evidence of runaway slaves to Iroquoia, see *Johnson Papers,* I, 43, V, 32, XI, 156; and *DRCHNY,* V, 965, 968, VII, 732–733. *Panis* were far western Indians who had been captured in raids and sold to European Americans as slaves. Despite a law passed by the New York assembly in 1679 prohibiting the practice, whites in New York City owned Indian slaves well into the eighteenth century. Note two subsequent pieces of legislation that indicate the presence of Indian slaves. In 1715, the assembly prohibited "any Negro, Indian, or mulatto slave" from selling oysters in New York City. And, in 1717, the assembly revisited the issue of requiring the posting of manumission bonds for "Negroe, Indian, or Malatto Slaves." See Higginbotham, *In the Matter of Color,* 122–123, 129. On the frontier, the slave trade in panis flourished until the Revolutionary War. See *Johnson Papers,* II, 388, III, 321–322, 348, 355, 360–361, 382–383, IV, 485, VII, 650, VIII, 153–154, XIV (index), 450. Some of the Indian shoppers at Fonda's store appear to have been servants or slaves in Dutch American and Anglo-American households. See [Fonda?], *Indian Account Book,* fols. 22, 93.

dian country, from which slave masters often had great difficulty retrieving their slaves.[21]

It is tempting to explain Bood's and Robin's flights to Indian country by their mixed ancestry; they identified as either mulatto (black-white), as did the Sun Fish, or as mustee (black-Indian). Today we assume that William Johnson's reference to the Sun Fish as mulatto meant that he was of African and European ancestry. Jack Forbes, however, has pointed out that, throughout much of the Americas during the seventeenth and eighteenth centuries, mulatto meant an Indian-African mixture. Rather than speculate on the Sun Fish's genetic makeup, it is worth remembering that many dark-skinned persons of African descent as well as whites were easily integrated into Indian society and claimed Indian identity. It is reasonable to assume, however, that many mulattos who crossed over to Indian country were dissatisfied with their lots in Anglo-American society, as racial ideology in the British colonies exerted downward pressure on the status of people of color, even when free.[22]

Those slaves wishing to find free space had to pretend—that is, declare themselves—to be free. In the latter part of the eighteenth century, slaveowners from New York and New Jersey surmised that three-quarters of their slaves who had disappeared from home had run away in order to live as free, rather than to escape punishment or to visit family or friends. Their proof of status rested either with their word or with passes that were either forged or expired.[23]

21. See the slave advertisements in Graham Russell Hodges and Alan Edward Brown, eds., "Pretends to Be Free": Runaway Slave Advertisements from Colonial and Revolutionary New York and New Jersey (New York, 1994), xxv, 79, 179, Table 7 (in index).

22. On the evolution and various definitions of the term "mulatto," see Jack D. Forbes, Africans and Native Americans: The Language of Race and the Evolution of Red-Black Peoples (Urbana, Ill., 1993), esp. chaps. 5–7. On the evolution of terms designating color and race, see Winthrop D. Jordan, White over Black: American Attitudes toward the Negro, 1550–1812 (Chapel Hill, N.C., 1968), 91–98. For pictorial evidence of "black Indians," see Mulroy, Freedom on the Border; and William Loren Katz, Black Indians: A Hidden Heritage (New York, 1986). For an example of a white woman identified as Indian, see John Demos, The Unredeemed Captive: A Family Story from Early America (New York, 1994).

23. For runaways' "pretending to be free," see Shane White, "Somewhat More Independent": The End of Slavery in New York City, 1770–1810 (Athens, Ga., 1991), 127, Table 15. Slaveowners typically issued passes to their slaves when they sent them alone on business away from home. The pass identified the slave, his or her master, the slave's home or town, and the nature of the business that took the slave to another part of the province or to a neighboring colony. The pass was intended to distinguish slaves engaged in legitimate business from fugitives. Each colony passed laws by which to punish runaways. For a brief discussion

It was illegal for slaves to travel about alone without the permission of their masters and proof of their errands. On August 4, 1705, New York passed An Act to Prevent the Running Away of Negro Slaves Out of the City and County of Albany to the French at Canada. Slaves "found Travelling forty Miles above the Citty of Albany at or above a Certain place called Sarachtoge" unaccompanied by their masters could be put to death. The Sun Fish required a pass to travel across Iroquoia and around Niagara country so that other Englishmen unknown to him would not mistake him for a runaway slave, seize him, and enslave him. Admittedly, whites and Indians in the service of Johnson and other colonial officials required passes when on business in Iroquoia. Nevertheless, a Seneca warrior would not have required a pass to return home—unless there was a chance that he might be mistaken for a "Negro." [24]

## Inventing and Inverting Identities

Nowhere on New York's frontier were identities tried on and cast off with the ease of changing one's seasonal clothing more than at the various frontier homes of Sir William Johnson. White visitors to Fort Johnson, Johnson Hall, and his summer recreational home, the Fish House, anxiously found themselves deep "on this remote frontier, almost in the shade of primeval forest," far removed from civilization. Here, persons of Indian, African, and European heritage intermingled in a Rabelaisian world of myriad ethnicities, recast identities, and unexpected role playing. [25]

After 1747, the woman of the house was always a Mohawk: Caroline, the daughter of Old Abraham (brother to Hendrick), until 1754, and from 1754 to

---

of passes for black slaves in eighteenth-century New York, see Edgar J. McManus, *A History of Negro Slavery in New York* (Syracuse, N.Y., 1966), 111–112. In Virginia and South Carolina, slaves required "tickets" from their masters when out on business. See Lathan A. Windley, *A Profile of Runaway Slaves in Virginia and South Carolina from 1730 through 1787* (New York, 1995), 4–8. Slaves were not the only individuals who required passes. Free blacks, whites, and Indians in the employ of another in a region where the hired person might be taken for a stranger required passes.

24. [Charles Zebina Lincoln] et al., *The Colonial Laws of New York from the Year 1664 to the Revolution . . .* (Albany, N.Y., 1896), I, chap. 149, 582. See also A. Leon Higginbotham, Jr., *In the Matter of Color: Race and the American Legal Process, the Colonial Period* (New York, 1978), 121 (see also 100–150 for other "black codes" passed in New York during the colonial period).

25. Grant, *Eight Years,* cited in Buell, *Sir William Johnson,* 44.

Johnson's death in 1774, Molly Brant, also referred to as "the brown Lady John-son," who was the sister of Joseph Brant. Between these two common-law wives, Johnson had at least a dozen métis (Indian-white) children.[26]

Johnson's workers, who were engaged in the daily operations of his estates, formed a motley, multiethnic crew. To manage his plantation, Johnson hired an Irish *bouw-master,* or overseer, named Flood, who monitored the work of fifteen enslaved black farm hands. (Johnson also employed more than fifty white workers.) Johnson had his tailor outfit the slaves in modified Iroquois garb, fashioning their blankets into coats to make fieldwork easier. A dwarf named Billy, of uncertain ethnicity, entertained guests with his expert violin playing. The gardener, whose ethnicity is also unclear, answered to "Old Daddy Savage," which suggests that he might have been Iroquois or métis. A German butler named Frank was in charge of seeing to the needs of Johnson and his family. A pair of white dwarfs, perhaps twins, with the surname of Bartholo-mew, waited on guests. An Irish schoolmaster, Wall, taught "manners and rudiments of English" to Johnson's métis children and the white children of his tenants. And a mustee waiter, John Abiel, accompanied Johnson whenever and wherever he traveled. Rather than call his servant by his proper name, Johnson referred to Abiel as "Pontiac," intended either as a comment on his servant's rebellious behavior or to belittle the Ottawa warrior of the same name, who, in protest to the English victory in the Seven Years' War, led a multinational Indian uprising against English settlements along the Western frontier from Niagara to Virginia from 1763 to 1764.[27]

A variety of languages, dialects, and argots were spoken at Johnson Hall and understood by many. The Sun Fish would have had little trouble communi-cating with people there. He was fluent in at least three languages: Seneca (and probably other Iroquois dialects), either Unami or Munsee, a Delaware lan-guage spoken by the Delaware refugees in Ohio country, and English, in which he was literate, learned perhaps from a minister in the course of receiving cate-chetical lessons when a youngster. He also must have known the trade lan-guages spoken by French, Iroquois, Algonquian, and English traders in the polyglot region of Fort Niagara and southern Ontario. The Sun Fish's linguis-tic skills affirmed his Seneca identity and were critical to his success as a go-

26. W. Max Reid, *The Mohawk Valley: Its Legends and Its History* (New York, 1901), 118–122; Buell, *Sir William Johnson,* 52, 55.

27. Reid, *The Mohawk Valley,* 121–122; Jeptha R. Simms, *Trappers of New York; or, A Bi-ography of Nicholas Stoner and Nathaniel Foster* (Albany, N.Y., 1851), 23–24, 281–282; Buell, *Sir William Johnson,* 86 (Buell referred to Abiel as Johnson's "half-breed orderly"); William Elliot Griffis, *Sir William Johnson and the Six Nations* (New York, 1891) 199–202.

between. Cultural brokers and go-betweens were required to be multilingual, for they provided the valuable service of cross-cultural communication. Many acquired fluency in various languages as traders, trappers, *coureur de bois,* and even as victims of kidnapping.[28]

A successful go-between had to demonstrate that he not only could talk the talk of the cultures for which he was brokering but he also had to possess a solid command of the cultures' social, cultural, and diplomatic etiquette. A firm grasp of language skills and cultural knowledge would instill trust and confidence toward the broker in the two or more parties with whom he was dealing. The Sun Fish's Seneca brethren and Delaware informants trusted him with the news they fed him, which they probably expected him to deliver to Johnson. They could also be certain that the news the Sun Fish brought to them from abroad was bona fide, straight from Johnson's mouth to the Sun Fish's ear. Likewise, Johnson trusted the Sun Fish to deliver accurately the prince of Chote's speech to his brothers Addongat and Squissahawe, "least it might be delivered to them wrong." In short, the Sun Fish was successful as a broker because his language skills and his understanding of the various cultures' practices permitted him to interpret the other's language and intentions in a way that was meaningful to the hearers.[29]

Consider the counter example of a young warrior who, while traveling to Albany in 1771, visited Sir William Johnson at Johnson Hall. The young Indian "produced a Pass from the Lt. Governor of Pensilvania." Johnson must have been suspicious of the pass, for he asked the young man a series of questions and learned that the Indian had been in Ohio country visiting Shawnee family and friends. He was now on his way to Albany, "the place with which he was best acquainted," to seek employment as "a Battoe Man." From the answers

28. Persons of African descent operated as go-betweens and linguisters among the Muscogulges of the old Southwest and the Lumbees of North Carolina. For a study of black Muscogulges, especially as linguisters, see J. Leitch Wright, Jr., *Creeks and Seminoles: The Destruction and Regeneration of the Muscogulge People* (Lincoln, Nebr., 1986), 73–99. For a study of the Lumbees of the Carolinas, see Gerald M. Sider, *Lumbee Indian Histories: Race, Ethnicity, and Indian Identity in the Southern United States* (Cambridge, 1993). For a study of black go-betweens among Indians in the Lower Mississippi region, see Daniel H. Usner, Jr., *Indians, Settlers, and Slaves in a Frontier Exchange Economy: The Lower Mississippi Valley before 1783* (Chapel Hill, N.C., 1992).

29. Nancy L. Hagedorn, "'A Friend to Go between Them': The Interpreter as Cultural Broker during Anglo-Iroquois Councils, 1740–70," *Ethnohistory,* XXXV (1988), 60–80. Many historians have incorporated sections on "cultural brokers" in their ethnohistories. For a study in which brokering plays a central role, see White, *Middle Ground.*

that the young man gave, Johnson determined that he was not Shawnee, for "he could give little or no Acc[oun]t of that country, or the People," nor was he able to "prove his assertion from any knowledge of the Language, or other particulars concerning his Tribe in the Shawnese Nation." Furthermore, Johnson concluded that this young warrior was actually a panis, who had been sold by other Indians to whites in the East. A slaveowner or a slaver had already claimed this young man, Johnson learned, and planned to sell him to the West Indies— one of the more inhumane fates, in Johnson's opinion, to befall a slave.[30]

This young warrior attempted to alter his identity in order to remain free. Ironically, the frontier was not a safe place for him. Had he truly been familiar with Albany, as he claimed, he would have been aware of the kind of cultural maneuvering that distinguished the greater region, but at which he failed. The young panis most likely lived in a region dominated by an Indian society that experienced little direct contact with others from a culturally distinct society. Whether the pass he carried was actually written for him is unknown. What is known, however, is that, unlike the Sun Fish, he could not convince those knowledgeable of multiethnic frontier cultures and practices of his identity, for he lacked the necessary language skills and cultural knowledge of the Shawnee society in which he purported to stake his claim.

The young panis appeared to be utterly unattached by kinship to the Shawnees. He could give no account of Shawnee society, which meant perhaps that he could not name some of the important headmen whom Johnson knew. An important factor for the Sun Fish's citizenship in Seneca society rested with his kinship relations. Iroquois marriage and adoption customs ensured that non-Senecas by birth would enjoy the same rights and privileges as native-born Senecas. Through matrilocal laws and customs, the Sun Fish would have become a member of his wife's clan. Matrilineal laws would have dictated that their biological daughter be a member of her mother's clan, which would have further solidified the Sun Fish's kinship ties.[31]

30. William Johnson to Golds Borrow Banyar, June 28, 1771, *DHNY*, II, 570. Johnson was so horrified by the prospect of this young panis being shipped to the West Indies that he vowed to see if he could not arrange to have him work off his debt to his master as a boatman in Albany.

31. The Iroquois tradition of adopting non-native peoples into their communities in order to shore up sagging populations and replace dead kin—and of extending to those adoptees (excluding panis) full rights and privileges of citizenship—is well known. By the 1670s, for example, the majority population within the Mohawk and Oneida nations were not native born. Nevertheless, full rights and privileges were extended to these nonethnic Mohawks and Oneidas. For analyses of Iroquois marriage, adoption, and population pat-

Marriage into Indian society carried distinct political, economic, and social advantages resulting from newly forged kinship ties. William Johnson well knew this when he took his two Mohawk wives, Caroline and Molly. Johnson used his marriage to them to establish ties in Mohawk society—particularly at Canajoharie—which in turn lent him a credible presence and voice in the affairs of the Six Nations of the Iroquois, a critical asset to his office of superintendent of Indian affairs. Jean Montour (Hiokato) believed that Johnson secured his identity as "an Indian like ourselves" beyond knowing Iroquois customs and the language by having "in his house . . . an Indian woman [Caroline], and his little children [who] are half-breeds, as I also am." [32]

Kinship constituted the basic determinant of Iroquois identity. Family membership and clan affiliation (a collection of related extended families) established one's sense of self. The family, constituted matrilineally (through descent on the mother's side) and matrilocally (in the household of the wife's and her mother's family), meant that women held a great deal of influence in matters that were social, economic, and to some degree political. Women were the keepers of the family and, therefore, made all decisions affecting the family, including adopting captives. As keepers of the fields, women provided the bulk of the family's nutritional needs through the crops they raised and the plant foods they gathered—which they also had the power to withhold, such as when they disagreed with warriors over the need for war. Because mothers knew well the temperaments of the boys and men in their families, elder clan mothers selected the replacements for the Great Council of the League, a body of fifty leading headmen, which deliberated matters of peace affecting all six nations. Women, therefore, were key members of Iroquois society. They governed one's identity, provided for one's family, and determined the makeup and temperament of the Great Council, which weighed matters affecting the health and welfare of Iroquois people. [33]

---

terns, see Daniel K. Richter, *Ordeal of the Longhouse: The Peoples of the Iroquois League in the Era of European Colonization* (Chapel Hill, N.C., 1992), chaps. 1, 2; Anthony F. C. Wallace, *The Death and Rebirth of the Seneca* (New York, 1972), chaps. 2–4; Morgan, *League of the Iroquois,* chap. 4.

32. Buell, *Sir William Johnson,* 68, 68 n. 1, 79–80.

33. For the role and status of women in Iroquois society in the eighteenth century, see Joseph François Lafitau, *Customs of the American Indians Compared with the Customs of Primitive Times* (1724), ed. William N. Fenton and Elizabeth L. Moore, 2 vols. (Toronto, 1974, 1977), I, 335–336, 338–339, 341–344, 347–348, 355–361, II, 47–52, 54–72, 94–97; Wm. Guy Spittal, ed., *Iroquois Women: An Anthology* (Ohsweken, Ontario, 1990).

One woman who resided among the Mohawks in the mid-eighteenth century was, like a Mohawk matriarch, keeper of the family, family provider, and politically important to both Mohawk and European American men. But she was not identified—and probably did not identify—as Mohawk. "Mrs. Eghye (Eve) Pickerd . . . an old Mulatto Woman . . . of Canajoharie" lived with some of her children and grandchildren as tenants of the Mohawks on the Canajoharie Flatts. She supported her family with a tavern that she operated from her home. Though Eve was identified as mulatto, she had kinship ties to the Mohawks. In 1764, Jelles Fonda recorded in his Indian account book that he sold rum to "the Caughnawaga Indian who is married to Eves Daughter." We do not know definitively if Fonda's "Eve" is Eve Pickard, though it is quite likely. She was certainly known to Fonda. In January 1765, Eve's grandson, Cobus (Jacobus) Maybe, eager to get a deed to the land on which he lived with his grandmother, invited three Canajoharie Mohawks and a fourth from another nation to his grandmother's house, where he got them drunk. He then piled them into a sleigh and, in the dead of winter, without the warmth of blankets, "carried them to Jelles Funda's house in order to bring them to Albany to sign a Deed for the Land they live[d] on." [34]

Linguistic evidence further supports the supposition that Eve Pickard held kinship ties to Mohawk society. Several leading white men in the region certified that Eve Pickard "understood the Indian language well." This suggests that she was not a native speaker but rather had acquired fluency in Mohawk. Her frequent contacts with Mohawk relatives and customers from Canajoharie and Caughnawaga would have afforded her ample opportunity to develop a strong command of the Mohawk language. Eve was so fluent in Mohawk and so closely connected to Mohawk society that she was called into court on at least two occasions to testify on behalf of the Mohawks in land-fraud cases. At both hearings, Eve, who was also literate in English, was asked to explain what she

---

34. [Fonda?], *Indian Account Book,* fol. 66; *Johnson Papers,* XI, 555–556. The village of Caughnawaga that Fonda referred to is probably the village located near present-day Fonda, and, hence, near his store, and not the Caughnawaga (Kahnawake) village near Montreal, which émigrés to Canada in the late 1660s and early 1670s named after the former village. See Francis Jennings et al., eds., *The History and Culture of Iroquois Diplomacy: An Interdisciplinary Guide to the Treaties of the Six Nations and Their League* (Syracuse, N.Y., 1985), 222. Other members of the Pickard family included Joseph Maybe and John and William Pickard. See *Johnson Papers,* XI, 469 n. 1, 555–556, XII, 333. There is no mention of Mr. Pickard, Eve's husband.

was told were the true feelings of the Canajoharie headmen toward these land claims.[35]

Ironically, Eve Pickard and her family had earlier become the focus of a land-claim dispute that oddly called into question her identity. In the early 1760s, some of the Canajoharie headmen evidently tried to remove her and her tavern from their community, for in February 1761 Eve brought to William Johnson a deed for eleven hundred acres of wooded and cleared flat land, signed by three Indians from Canajoharie, as proof that the land belonged to her. The signatures, however, were obtained fraudulently. Three days before Johnson saw the deed, Eve Pickard and her grandson, Cobus, had brought the three Mohawks to her home, where, foreshadowing the same trick that Cobus would attempt four years later, they plied them with so much rum that the three men could not recall later signing the deed—a deed that Eve had predated September 1760. When Johnson informed the Canajoharie headmen of what had happened, they flew "into a violent passion" and railed "against the deceitfullness, and unbrotherlike behaviour of the *white people* towards them."[36]

Eve Pickard, like the Sun Fish, carried dual identities, except that hers were "mulatto" and "white." It is unreasonable to assume that the Iroquois constructed their world in a bifurcated way: as "Indian" and "white." Certainly the young warriors employed as slave catchers knew that they were looking for men whose skin was a shade of brown. Some of the Senecas, the most western of the Iroquois and, thus, those with the least direct contact with the institution of black slavery, understood the burgeoning racialized worldview of the white colonists. In 1765, a Seneca warrior equated blackness with servitude when he warned his brethren not to convert to Christianity, for to do so would lead to

---

35. For Eve's testimony in 1762 that the Canajoharie Mohawks accused Mr. Collins, a surveyor, of trespassing on their property to do a "moonlight survey," see *Johnson Papers,* XIII, 276. For evidence of Eve's testifying against George Klock in 1763, see ibid., X, 995–997. In the Klock case, Eve was asked to swear that "not one Principal Sachim of Conajohare Signed the first Deed" that Klock had in his possession. The signers, it seems, were "2 Men, their Wives, 2 of their small Children and two Lads under Age," all from the "lower Mohawks" (Tiononderoge, or Fort Hunter), not from Canajoharie where the land lay. None had the authority to sign off on land deeds. An Oneida named Jacob confessed to being "made Drunk by U [George] Klock and Signed it [the deed]."

36. *Johnson Papers,* III, 339, X, 220 (emphasis on "*white people*" is mine), XI, 555–556, 556 n. 1, 960, XII, 288 n. 4; Isobel Thompson Kelsay, *Joseph Brant, 1743–1807: Man of Two Worlds* (Syracuse, N.Y., 1984), 122. It is not clear whether the three Mohawk men whom Cobus plied with liquor in 1761 were the same three he made drunk in 1765.

their sinking "so low as to hoe the corn and squashes in the field, chop wood, stoop down and milk cows like *negroes* among the Dutch people." He was no less perceptive than John Woolman in recognizing white attitudes toward darker skin.[37]

What can account, then, for the Mohawk headmen's identifying Eve Pickard as white? The answer rests, not with her physical appearance, but rather with her behavior: Eve Pickard engaged in the white crime of land stealing. The immediate reaction of the Mohawks, therefore, was to identify her and her behavior as white.

Eve Pickard was a multicultural person, able to maneuver within European American and Mohawk societies. Because of her cultural sophistication, she was also able to circumvent and take advantage of the demands that each side placed on her. Her strong linguistic skills made her an indispensable go-between. The Mohawks needed her to be their mouthpiece at court, and the European Americans needed her as a window to the Canajoharie community. No wonder, then, that the Canajoharie headmen had such difficulty dislodging her and her family.

Over the next several years, the headmen brought to Johnson a series of complaints against Cobus and Eve. At one point, the Canajoharie Mohawks became so frustrated with Johnson's inability to remove the Pickards and so fed up with Cobus's abusive language and threats to burn down their village that they preemptively burned the Pickard house. Not until 1767, when the governor of New York threatened them with legal action, did Eve and Cobus agree to leave.[38]

37. Samuel Kirkland, *The Journals of Samuel Kirkland . . .* , ed. Walter Pilkington (Clinton, N.Y., 1980), 24, as cited in Axtell, *The Invasion Within,* 164–165. The ethnicity or race of Cobus Maybe, also identified as "Cobus Pickerd," is not known. He shared the last name, however, of the Mabees (also "Mebee") of Schenectady, who arrived in that town in 1684. The Mabees held slaves for generations, down through the eighteenth century. Perhaps Eve and her children and grandchildren were descendants of white and black Mabees. For Cobus identified as "Pickerd," see *Johnson Papers,* XII, 245. On the Mabees of the Mohawk Valley, see John J. Vrooman, *Forts and Firesides of the Mohawk Country* (Johnstown, N.Y., 1951), 119–121; and Reid, *The Mohawk Valley,* 73, 75. The Mohawks had the most frequent direct contact with free and enslaved blacks, whom they encountered at Fonda's store, at church, at Johnson Hall, in Albany and Schenectady, and at the various farmsteads scattered across the frontier. For Indian-black contact at church, see various letters of John Ogilvie, *Records of the Society for the Propagation of the Gospel in Foreign Parts: The Journals, 1701–1850,* 50 vols. (London, 1964), microfilm, XII, 307–309, XIII, 182–185, 202–204, XIV, 106–107; John Wolfe Lydekker, *The Faithful Mohawks* (New York, 1938), 74, 83–86, 90–91.

38. *Johnson Papers,* IV, 645, XI, 555–556, 926. Cobus did not disappear, however. Cadwallader Colden, the acting governor of New York in the mid-1760s, received a petition from him in 1767 asking for Indian land (ibid., XII, 756).

Not all persons of color who attempted to insinuate themselves as brokers into the lives of Indians on the frontier were successful at negotiating the delicate cultural and political balance that existed there. Sam Tony, for example, fled slavery in Maryland in the 1740s and took up residence among the Indians at Otsiningo (Chenango, present-day Binghamton) on a branch of the Susquehanna River. By 1764, Tony's influence there had become so widespread that Johnson admitted that Tony had "acquired much influence" over the Otsiningo Indians. Johnson had known of Tony's residence on the Susquehanna for some time, but now in the face of a possible pan-Indian uprising led by Pontiac, Johnson wanted him and all other "incendiaries" removed from the frontiers. They "spread dangerous and Treasonable reports amongst these Indians," Johnson fumed, and in doing so "alienate their Affections from the English by assuring them that we design shortly to fall upon and destroy all the Indians in alliance with us."[39]

The Indians at Otsiningo heeded Johnson's demand for Tony and turned him over. We do not know why the Otsiningos agreed to do so: a prearranged quid pro quo with Johnson? Or perhaps Tony did not possess the advantages of the Sun Fish. Surely, his usefulness to the Otsiningos would have been limited, as he was unable to venture into English country to gather intelligence in the manner of the Sun Fish. Sam Tony also did not have a patron, as the Sun Fish had in Johnson, who could protect him and vouch for him. Johnson blamed the Otsiningo Indians for being naive and foolish in imagining that "those who have lived amongst Whites are consequently acquainted with their intentions." Too many incendiaries, Johnson complained, "continually spread the most Villainous reports, forgetting the Country to which they owe their attachment." Sam Tony, an independent-minded runaway who was unable to sustain a reinvented identity on the frontier, probably would have found great irony in Johnson's assessment that slaves owed their allegiance to England.[40]

Mitigating factors that tied a person of African descent to two or more cultures in contact were essential for that person to have reinvented his or her identity and status. Marginality to even one of the societies, as in the case of Sam Tony, almost guaranteed no change in status and, therefore, no option for maneuverability, as with the Sun Fish and Eve Pickard. The graphic example of a slave involved in a capital crime on the frontier in Michigan is instructive.

In May 1766, a black slave, identified as "an English Negro belonging to Mr. Sterling Merchant" of Fort Saint Joseph near Detroit, was apprehended

39. Ibid., XI, 165–166, 174.
40. Ibid.

for killing two Potawatomi women. John Campbell, the commissary at Detroit, was unsure about how to handle this case. His problem was this: Should he send the "English Negro" back to Albany to stand trial, according to English law? The mutiny act stated that in murder cases that occurred *at a fort* beyond civil jurisdiction, the suspect must be taken to the nearest "Inhabited Country and delivered up to the first Civil Magistrate." Or should Campbell have the slave stand trial at Saint Joseph's, which would have violated the mutiny act, but would have satisfied the Potawatomis? If he sent the slave to Albany, Campbell reasoned, he risked having the Potawatomi relatives "believe he [the slave] is sent on purpose out of the Way," which would look like a cover up. If he had the slave "tried here [Fort Saint Joseph] and if condemned to suffer death, his being made an example of in the presence of the Indians," Campbell believed, then that "wou'd have a very good effect." But there was no getting around its extralegality.[41]

Campbell deferred to General Thomas Gage, who deferred to Sir William Johnson. Gage told Johnson that he believed it was in the best interest of all if the Saint Joseph's Indians simply put the English Negro to death; it would save a lot of trouble. Johnson understood the Indian concept of revenge killing: the death of a family member had to be avenged either with the death of the perpetrator, or of a member of his family, or with a payment of a scalp, goods, or wampum. Campbell and Johnson were also aware of seething tensions between the Potawatomis and the English at Fort Saint Joseph; two English traders had been slain by suspected Potawatomis several months before. To cool tensions all around and to satisfy Potawatomi mourning needs, Johnson told Gage that the mutiny act was flawed, for it provided "little Justice for the Indians, and therefore it is better never to Send down the Negroe, than to Send him to be acquitted here for want . . . of all the necessary Law proofs."[42]

Sterling's slave was dispensable because he had no kinship ties and no linguistic skills that would have made him valuable to either the English or to the Potawatomis. His status was fixed and his identity unambiguous: Sterling's Negro was a slave. Johnson deemed him easily replaceable. Order at the frontier fort was more important than justice for the slave. Therefore, he was exempt from the mutiny act but subject to, as most slaves were, the arbitrary law of whites. As with some identities, some laws designed to serve justice on the

41. Ibid., V, 160–161, 271–272.
42. Ibid., V, 160–161, 271–272, XII, 115.

frontier were interpreted flexibly, creatively, and situationally, and always with power relations in mind.[43]

## The Negro Headman and the Search for Identity

It would be irresponsible to claim that every person of African ancestry on the frontier reinvented him- or herself. We do not have enough solid evidence to make such a claim. But we can say that, for some, the frontier offered opportunities for self-transformation that were not available to them in the more established communities to the east. For others, we can only speculate, as with the Cayuga headman identified in the 1750s as "The Negro." We do not know what the Negro looked like or whether, in fact, he was of African descent. But we do know that he was fluent in Cayuga, that he was a sachem, or headman, and that, like the Sun Fish, he was a repository of news.

Like the Sun Fish, the Negro was an informant who came to Fort Johnson from time to time to deliver news about the French to "Brother Warraghy-jagey," the name (which means "he who does much business," or "he who undertakes great things") that the Iroquois gave to Sir William Johnson when they adopted him in 1746. In 1756, at the outbreak of the Seven Years' War, the Negro told Colonel Butler that the fort at Oswego was under attack by the French. Butler wrote to Johnson that "Several Gentlemen" who heard the Negro's story laughed at it. Butler, however, believed it to be true. Why the discrepancy? Were the "Gentlemen" not aware of the kinds of personal transformations that occurred on the frontier? Was the Negro too Negro to them? Conversely, Butler might have had confidence in the Negro's news, because the colonel was aware that the Negro had just returned from Onondaga, the League Council seat for the Six Nations. He would not have been invited there had he not been a Cayuga of some standing. We cannot answer definitively whether or not "the Negro" was a cognomen, used as a racial marker for the Cayuga headman. We can say that he identified—and was identifed—as Cayuga and that perhaps he carried another persona from the perspective of others.[44]

The Sun Fish and other individuals of African descent on the late-colonial

---

43. See Bibb, "Narrative," 129–130, for an example of arbitrary rule exercised by the master.

44. *Johnson Papers,* II, 544, 672, IX, 955–956; Reid, *The Mohawk Valley,* 114; Kelsay, *Joseph Brant,* 58. The Negro's possible counterpart in the Southeast was "The Black Factor," a Lower Creek chief who was of African ancestry. See Wright, *Creeks and Seminoles,* 75–77.

Iroquois–New York frontier carried more than one identity because the frontier was an open and fluid arena. It afforded them the opportunity to maneuver in and around the cultures of two or more distinct societies in contact, if they possessed the necessary connections, skills, and knowledge to prove themselves invaluable to the societies. Without the proper linguistic skills, knowledge of the other's diplomacy and culture, and kinship ties, one was as disposable as Sterling's Negro.

Frontier informants, tavernkeepers, and incendiaries, who were phenotypically of African descent but culturally multivalent, should prod us into examining how the openness and fluidity of contact on the frontier contributed to acts of creative self-transformation. These individuals should raise questions for us about the usefulness of "race" as a category of biological demarcation linked to social status on the colonial frontier. One simple and basic question is: What language, what words, should we use when talking about these people? Blacks? Mulattos? Persons of African ancestry or descent? Identities were reformulated situationally; the Sun Fish oscillated between Seneca and mulatto. Some forms of behavior were inversions for both outsiders and insiders, which undermined their preconceived ideas about the other's behavior. Mohawk headmen who spoke English and wore European-style clothes were not genuine Indians. The act of land stealing whitened Eve Pickard's mulatto identity. And with the burgeoning racialized worldview, growing racial assumptions that link appearance with status and identity on the frontier prove increasingly problematic: a young traveling warrior from the West is actually a slave, a mulatto tavernkeeper is white, and a Cayuga headman is called the Negro.[45]

We need to conceive of the frontier as a place where not just American society was reborn perennially but where many individuals cast their identities. We cannot know for certain why some of these individuals, particularly those of African ancestry, engaged in acts of self-transformation or why others transformed them, except to say that they were most likely done for survival, for convenience, for gain, and for sheer pleasure. If we fail to consider the frontier in these terms, we risk underestimating and underevaluating the potential of the frontier to make possible the social and cultural rebirth of individuals, especially of African descent.

There is a coda to the story of the Sun Fish. He evidently tried to leave Seneca society later in his life when the Senecas and other Iroquois nations

45. Two studies that acknowledge the complexity of the multiracial frontier are Usner, *Indians, Settlers, and Slaves;* and Timothy Silver, *A New Face on the Countryside: Indians, Colonists, and Slaves in South Atlantic Forests, 1500–1800* (Cambridge, 1990).

grew impoverished after the Revolutionary War. An early antiquarian, relying on oral testimony, placed the Sun Fish and his family on a farm near Tonawanda Creek sometime after the war. Ebenezer Allan, a fellow cattle trader in Canada and at Fort Niagara, and perhaps the Sun Fish's business partner, married one of the Sun Fish's mustee daughters. Through his bride's dowry, Allan seized most of the Sun Fish's land holdings. The son-in-law did permit his father-in-law to live in a small cottage on the farm that formerly belonged to the Sun Fish. Allan even gave the Sun Fish a small pension. In time, however, feeling perhaps socially or economically impoverished or alienated from his family, the Sun Fish removed himself from the farm and resettled with a familiar Seneca community at Tonawanda. Moving back might have felt like coming home.[46]

46. Turner, *History of the Pioneer Settlement of Phelps and Gorham's Purchase*, 406.

# "Insidious Friends"
## Gift Giving and the Cherokee-British Alliance in the Seven Years' War

*The gift, to be true, must be the flowing of*
*the giver unto me, correspondent to my flowing unto him.*
—*Ralph Waldo Emerson*

In June 1754, during the outbreak of the American phase of the Seven Years' War, Governor James Glen of South Carolina boasted with considerable exaggeration that, because of his efforts, the Cherokees and other neighboring Indians were "not only in perfect Peace and Friendship with one another, but were never more strongly attached to the British Interest." "If this were to be disputed, let Facts speak; they come when we send for them, they go when they are bid and they do whatever is desired of them." If Glen's facts speak to us as they did to him, then they invite examination. The Cherokee Indians, numerous, well armed, and in command of the southern end of the Appalachian Mountain Chain, did stand that June among the best and most powerful of Great Britain's Indian allies. No people as independent and numerous had been a better and more consistent friend of the British colonies. During the Yamasee War (1715–1717), Cherokees had rescued the colony from destruction. In 1730, Cherokee leaders had traveled to London to make a treaty with Great Britain. So certain did the British-Cherokee alliance seem in the early years of the Seven Years' War that settlers from the heavily raided interiors of Virginia and Pennsylvania migrated to the South Carolina piedmont in order to live

An early version of this essay was presented at the annual meeting of the American Society for Ethnohistory in 1989. The University of Connecticut's association of history graduate students heard a more recent version in 1997. Special thanks to Guthrie Sayen for his comments on that draft. My thanks to James Axtell for his helpful comments and to Fredrika Teute and Andrew Cayton for helping me to see what the essay was really about. Thanks are also due to the University of Notre Dame and the Smithsonian Institution, both of which funded the research. William L. Anderson and James Lewis, eds., *Guide to Cherokee Documents in Foreign Archives* (Metuchen, N.J., 1983) helped the author locate PRO materials.

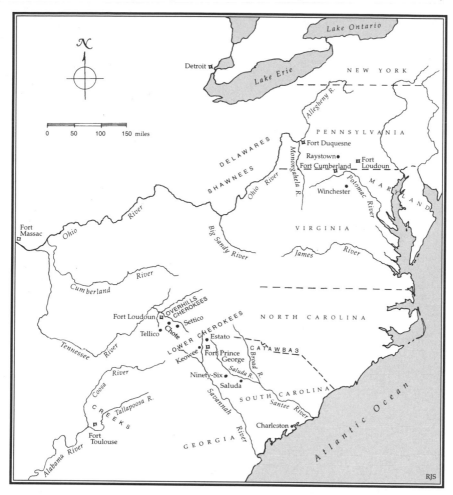

FIGURE 1
The Cherokee-British Alliance, 1756–1759.
*Drawn by Richard Stinely*

under the shelter of the Cherokees' mountains. Before 1759, no Indian people would contribute a larger body of warriors or a more important service to British efforts. Glen had reason to see great potential for cooperation, familiarity, and understanding in South Carolina's relations with the Cherokees, yet by 1759 the Cherokee War (1759–1761) would violently mark its end. None of the forces routinely examined as causes of colonial-Indian war—French intrigue, backcountry settlers' hostility, or Indian resistance to colonial expansion—satisfactorily explains the implosion of the alliance. All these forces imperiled the good relationship, but all were still negotiable in 1759. No longer negotiable was the structure of the partnership itself.[1]

Essential to the alliance, while it lasted, were gift exchanges. They formalized and sustained the relationship between these native American and European partners. Cherokees attributed great importance to gifts and favors; so, too, did Britons and British colonists. During the Seven Years' War, as the alliance faced its crucial test, disputes over "presents," and the way they were given or withheld, erupted in colonial council chambers, military staging grounds, and backcountry cabins. These arguments dramatized more fundamental confrontations. Gift exchanges between allies became focal points for controversy because they embodied, for both peoples, relations of friendship, leadership, power, and domination. The history of these exchanges between Cherokees and Britons (including British colonists) during the Seven Years' War reveals that their increasing familiarity bred less love than disaffection: that their very strong effort at cooperation put their coexistence in jeopardy. The relationship, though close, though contracted with promises, and though meant to endure, was a misalliance between partners who came to know each other too well.

Since the 1980s, there has been a tremendous rise of interest in the coexistence of Indians and colonists in North America. Powerful new images, employed in the titles of several works, have enlivened our interest in Indian adaptation, accommodation, and survival. The image most flattered with imitation, Richard White's "middle ground," is particularly elusive and powerful. In White's usage, the term stands in part as a metaphor for the French-Indian alliance centered in the "upper country" of the Great Lakes between 1680 and 1760, but he also suggests that "the middle ground was not simply a phenomenon of the *pays d'en haut*." The middle ground was, White tells us, a "search for accommodation and common meaning," one in which "peoples adjust their differences through what amounts to a process of creative, and often ex-

1. James Glen to Robert Dinwiddie, June 1, 1754, in William L. McDowell, Jr., ed., *Documents Relating to Indian Affairs*, [I], *May 21, 1750–August 7, 1754* (Columbia, S.C., 1958), [II], *1754–1765* (Columbia, S.C., 1970), Colonial Records of South Carolina (hereafter cited as *DRIA*, I, II), I, 526. By the southern "backcountry" in the 1750s I mean that region of the Carolina and Virginia interior settled by Europeans in the 1740s and 1750s above the coastal or tidewater "plantation zone." These Europeans and European-Americans represented the "southward influx of intermingled English, Scotch-Irish, and German pioneers from Virginia and Pennsylvania." They did not constitute a single subculture, and I do not treat them as such. The European influx into the South Carolina backcountry was vigorous in the 1740s and 1750s. See D. W. Meinig, *The Shaping of America: A Geographical Perspective on 500 Years of History*, I, *Atlantic America, 1492–1800* (New Haven, Conn., 1986), 225.

pedient, misunderstandings," but from which "misunderstandings arise new meanings and through them new practices—the shared meanings and practices of the middle ground."[2]

The interest in coexistence and mutuality has powerfully influenced historians of the British colonies as their understanding of frontiers has shifted from linear to spatial, human, and relational terms. Many early Americanists are gazing upon the exhilarating prospects, among them Edward Countryman. Indians in Eastern North America, writes Countryman, became in the eighteenth century "part of the composite extended British polity." As the British networks integrated them, Indians developed their own "patterns of authority, reciprocity, obligation, custom, and privilege that their members used within the imperial framework. These patterns were recognized as much by imperial authority as by themselves." Indians "who lived in and beyond the Appalachians had a place in the empire's social order and a claim on its rulers' protection." The American Revolution, which unleashed backcountry settlers and eastern speculators, overthrew the "empire's social order" and the "extended polity." Even White's middle ground, most vital when inhabited by French officials but still extant when British officials awkwardly took up the French role of the Indians' father during the Revolution, finally collapsed in

2. Richard White, *The Middle Ground: Indians, Empires, and Republics in the Great Lakes Region, 1650–1815* (New York, 1991), ix, x; Darcee McLaren, "Living the Middle Ground: Two Dakota Missionaries, 1877–1912," *Ethnohistory*, XLIII (1996), 277–305; Germaine Warkentin, "Discovering Radisson: A Renaissance Adventurer between Two Worlds," in Jennifer S. H. Brown and Elizabeth Vibert, eds., *Reading Beyond Words: Contexts for Native History* (Peterborough, Ont., 1996), 43–70; Joel W. Martin, "Indians, Contact, and Colonialism in the Deep South: Themes for a Postcolonial History of American Religion," in Thomas A. Tweed, ed., *Retelling U.S. Religious History* (Berkeley, Calif., 1997), 172–173. Martin, 152, also draws attention to new metaphors. One of these metaphors is included in the work of Francis Jennings, who by the 1980s elaborated on the relationship of the Iroquois League and the British colonists. He borrowed their own phrase, "the Covenant Chain," for the title of his trilogy: *The Invasion of America: Indians, Colonialism, and the Cant of Conquest* (Chapel Hill, N.C., 1975); *The Ambiguous Iroquois Empire: The Covenant Chain Confederation of Indian Tribes with English Colonies from Its Beginnings to the Lancaster Treaty of 1744* (New York, 1984); *Empire of Fortune: Crowns, Colonies, and Tribes in the Seven Years War in America* (New York, 1988), xxii. For other key metaphors titling works, see James H. Merrell, *The Indians' New World: Catawbas and Their Neighbors from European Contact through the Era of Removal* (Chapel Hill, N.C., 1989); and Frederick E. Hoxie, *Parading through History: The Making of the Crow Nation in America, 1805–1935* (New York, 1995). The seminal article in the current trend may well be James Axtell, "The Scholastic Philosophy of the Wilderness," *William and Mary Quarterly*, 3d Ser., XXIX (1972), 335–366.

the aftershocks of the American victory. The highlighting of imperial accommodations to Indian custom obscures persistent, even fundamental, divisions of the sort that disrupted the Cherokee-British alliance as early as the 1750s.[3]

Before and during the Seven Years' War, New France's achievements among Indians provoked British envy in the Southeastern colonies. Governor Glen, ambitious for South Carolina and well aware of French activities in the interior, sought to imitate French methods and to become the leader of an extensive network of Indian alliances. Among Glen's fondest memories of his term in office had been councils held with the Cherokees at the towns of Ninety-Six and Saluda in 1746 and 1755, towns that formed a kind of literal middle ground, according to historian Tom Hatley, between Charleston and the Cherokee Lower Towns. There Glen met the Cherokees "in the woods" to settle disputes. Like a French officer acting the part of the father in the pays d'en haut, Glen had mediated fragile peace agreements between the Indian nations within his reach.[4]

3. Edward Countryman, "Indians, the Colonial Order, and the Social Significance of the American Revolution," WMQ, 3d Ser., LIII (1996), 342–362, esp. 354; Countryman, Americans: A Collision of Histories (New York, 1996), 57–58; White, Middle Ground, 305–412. Tom Hatley points out that the backcountry of South Carolina often formed around the trading places that first welcomed Cherokees, Britons, and others. He sees in the expansion of settlement the primary cause for the collapse of the alliance; see Hatley, The Dividing Paths: Cherokees and South Carolinians through the Era of Revolution (New York, 1993), 80–81, 83–87.

The middle ground should not become a synonym for frontier, reasonably defined by Howard Lamar and Leonard Thompson as "a territory or zone of interpenetration" among "previously distinct societies." Almost anything could happen on a frontier—even the emergence of a middle ground. Nonetheless, the one is not the other. Frontiers appeared wherever new settlers did; middle grounds were unusual, isolated, and fleeting in eastern North America. See Lamar and Thompson, "Introduction," in Lamar and Thompson, eds., The Frontier in History: North America and Southern Africa Compared (New Haven, Conn., 1981), 7; Stephen Aron, "Lessons in Conquest: Towards a Greater Western History," Pacific Historical Review, LXIII (1994), 143. For the middle ground in the British North American colonies, see, for example, Timothy J. Shannon, "Dressing for Success on the Mohawk Frontier: Hendrick, William Johnson, and the Indian Fashion," WMQ, 3d Ser., LIII (1996), 26; "Dialogues on the Middle Ground" (session at the First Annual Conference of the Institute of Early American History and Culture, June 2–4, 1995, Ann Arbor, Mich.).

4. Hatley has called Glen's vision one of a "mingled destiny," and no historian has done more to examine the potential, unrealized for the most part, for mutuality and coexistence between Cherokees and South Carolinians. See Hatley, The Dividing Paths, 79. For a critical yet favorable view of Glen's Cherokee policy in South Carolina, see W. Stitt Robinson, James

The Cherokee-British alliance showed certain other features of the middle ground: close familiarity, frequent communication, and mutual need. Conocorte, the highly respected and aged civil leader of the powerful Overhills Cherokee town of Chote, embraced Glen in 1754 in deeply intimate terms: "I now think I am with you, and that I live with you, and my thoughts are very good about it. . . . I shall live much longer having my Brother to assist me, for I reckon we are both as one Flesh and Blood." But under the strains of the impending war, the cohabitation proved less a good marriage than a turbulent, unsatisfying affair. Far from the "creative, and often expedient, misunderstandings" that characterized White's *pays d'en haut*, clear understandings emerged between the Cherokees and Britons who launched joint ventures during the Seven Years' War. Each partner came to understand the other's material demands. Each came to understand British claims to dominance and Cherokee assertions of importance and autonomy. Britons learned that Cherokees sought not only good rewards but also respect for their risky contribution to the war effort; Cherokees learned that Britons thought good Indian allies would fight in due subjection and "on the cheap." As these terms became clear, negotiation became impossible, and each side began to behave in a manner that struck the other as unacceptable, probably hostile, and even malevolent. Britons resorted to martial power and economic coercion to establish their claims to superiority, authority, and mastery. Cherokees resorted to their own versions of martial power as well as to sacred power to establish their claims to autonomy, importance, and honor. By late 1759, the erstwhile allies recognized that they shared no middle ground, ended their misalliance, and resorted to war.[5]

Doubtless it might have been otherwise, for individual women and men among both peoples bucked the forceful trends. When a woman slipped away

---

*Glen: From Scottish Provost to Royal Governor of South Carolina* (Westport, Conn., 1996), 85–105. On the conferences, see *South-Carolina Gazette,* May 26, 1746, in William Sumner Jenkins, ed., *Records of the States of the United States* (hereafter *RSUS*), supplement, S.C., Na, reel 3; Glen to Cherokee Indians, Nov. 15, 1752, in "South Carolina, Journal of the Proceedings of His Majesty's Honourable Council" (hereafter cited as SCJHMC), 1752–1754, *RSUS*, S.C. E.1p, reel 6, 13–15; and South Carolina Council, Minutes, Dec. 27, 1755, in Colonial Office Papers, series 5, vol. 471, fols. 383–385b, in United Kingdom, Public Record Office, Kew, England (hereafter cited as CO5/volume). For perhaps the fullest examination of French practices by a southern colonist, see Wilbur R. Jacobs, ed., *The Appalachian Indian Frontier: The Edmond Atkin Report and Plan of 1755* (1954; reprint, Lincoln, Nebr., 1967), 4–13.

5. SCJHMC, 1754–1756, *RSUS*, Apr. 3, 1754, S.C. E.1p, reel 7, pt. 3, 181–186; White, *Middle Ground,* x; Jennings, *Empire of Fortune,* 218.

from her Cherokee village in 1759 and warned the Long Canes folk of South Carolina of an imminent Cherokee attack, or when a settler named "MTeer" and his "half-breed" friend John Downing tried to smuggle necessaries to Downing's Cherokee mother and sisters while war engulfed them, their affections challenged stark boundaries in ways that fascinate us today. But for each of these, thousands of others were ready by 1759 to kill or to endorse killings. It is fair, given the attractive alternative, to inquire more deeply into the road taken.[6]

Despite the rhetoric of alliance, neither South Carolinians nor Cherokees rushed to render each other support when the American phase of the Seven Years' War began in 1754. Backcountry South Carolinians and the Commons House of the colony, for their parts, heartily distrusted the Cherokees. As recently as 1751, the colony had been swept up by false alarms of Cherokee hostilities. That year, a frightening event that began with substantial trappings of the middle ground cast a shadow that still darkened Cherokee-British relations. On May 4, 1751, Isaac and Mary Gould welcomed two traveling Indians, who said they were Shawnees, into their farm cabin on the Saluda River in South Carolina's piedmont. Isaac, who actually spoke Shawnee, sat at the table with his guests until midnight, sharing tobacco and talk. At daybreak the two visitors murdered Isaac and his two children, also fatally wounding Mary, though she survived long enough to tell the story. Cherokees had no hand in the killings, but backcountry Carolinians were quick to implicate them in other so-called outrages of that year. In 1753, as tensions between the British and French colonies increased, the Gould ghosts returned to haunt Cherokee-British relations. That spring, another set of murders and a rape by unspecified "Northern Indians" rekindled backcountry fear and grief, firing the colony with new rumors of Cherokee hostilities. In June, South Carolina militia, patrolling the piedmont, captured six Ohioan Shawnees. These at first claimed to be Cherokees; the militia saw through the lie and brought the prisoners in chains to Charleston. Governor Glen assumed that the Shawnees had intended

6. Hatley, *The Dividing Paths*, 89–90. Hatley's account of the woman is based on a memoir. But see the similar incident of 1760 in the examination of Aron Price, SCJHMC, 1757–1760, *RSUS*, Feb. 2, 1760, S.C. E.1p, reel 8, 157–158. For MTeer and Downing, see S.C. Council, Minutes, Nov. 15, 1760, CO5/477, fols. 27–28. For traders who continued an illegal trade with the Cherokees during the Cherokee War, see S.C. Council, Minutes, Jan. 7, 1762, CO5/477, fol. 109.

to raid Carolina's other Indian allies, the Catawbas and the remaining Indians in the lowcountry, commonly called "Settlement Indians," though he could not prove they had come with hostile designs. Personally interrogating them, he accused them—without evidence—of the Goulds' murder, now two years past. Aware that he had "no positive proof" of the Shawnees' misdeeds, he jailed them.[7]

The detention infuriated the Ohio Valley Shawnees and contributed to their alienation from the British in the early years of the Seven Years' War. Its arbitrary nature also disturbed the Cherokees, who worried about colonial hostility to Indians. That became clear in the summer of 1753 during a Charleston conference to which Glen had invited leading Cherokees. Glen had prepared hard for the meeting. Sensing the lack of common conventions between Britons and Cherokees, and wishing literally to highlight the potential of British generosity, Glen had devised a ritual to brighten the proceedings: the lighting of a candle upon the exchange of presents. As if he recognized that the timelessness of ceremony brings order to relationships, he sought to portray himself as the giver of gifts, the leader on whom Cherokees depended and could depend.[8]

He was soon disappointed. Cherokees surprised him by insisting that he free the Shawnees into their hands, something he refused to do. He told them that the detention, a matter between South Carolina and the Shawnees, was

7. For the Gould killings, see SCJHMC, 1750–1752, *RSUS*, May 11, 1751, S.C. E.1p, reel 5, pt. 2, 76–79; Affidavit of Mary Gould, May 8, 1751, and John Fairchild to Glen, May 10, 1751, *DRIA*, I, 48, 126–127. For the Shawnees, see S.C. Council, Minutes, Apr. 7, 13, June 13, 18, Aug. 23, 1753, all in CO5/469, fols. 66b–68, 72–74, 118b–123b, 124–129, 172–173. After complaints from the Pennsylvania governor James Hamilton, Glen sent two of the six north. See Glen to Hamilton, Oct. 3, 1753, Glen to the Heads of the Creek Nation, Dec. 14, 1753, S.C. Council to Lieutenant Governor Dinwiddie, Nov. 12, 1753, Hamilton to Glen, Dec. 6, 1753, all in *DRIA*, I, 463, 464, 467–468, 471; Hamilton to Glen, Oct. 30, 1753, Hamilton to Six Nations at Ohio, n.d., *Minutes of the Provincial Council of Pennsylvania, from Its Organization to the Termination of the Revolution*, Colonial Records of Pennsylvania, V (Harrisburg, Pa., 1851), 696–698, 705–706.

8. Greg Dening, *Mr Bligh's Bad Language: Passion, Power, and Theatre on the Bounty* (New York, 1992), 27. On the Shawnees, see George Croghan, "Croghan's Journal, 1754," in Reuben Gold Thwaites, ed., *Early Western Travels, 1748–1846 . . .*, 32 vols. (Cleveland, Ohio, 1904–1907), I, 74; John C. Fitzpatrick, ed., *The Diaries of George Washington, 1748–1799*, 4 vols. (New York, 1925), I, 50; Marquis de Duquesne à Claude-Pierre Pécaudy de Contrecoeur, 18 Juillet, 1754, in Fernand Grenier, ed., *Papiers contrecoeur et autres documents concernant le conflit anglo-français sur l'Ohio de 1745 à 1756* (Quebec, 1952), 220. On Glen's ritual, see S.C. Council, Minutes, July 5, 1753, CO5/469, fols. 142–149.

"no business of theirs." The Cherokees pressed the matter further. They pointed out that Shawnees would retaliate, possibly by attacking Carolinian traders in the Cherokee nation. They thought there was no need to alienate the Shawnees, with whom both they and the British were currently at peace. Asserting their own independence and importance, they proposed to mediate between Shawnees and Carolinians. For good measure, they took the opportunity to complain about abusive traders. Glen admitted none of this, but the heated discussion upset the warm ritual he had planned. Glen learned that Cherokees considered themselves up to the diplomacy of mediation, up to leading as well as to being led.[9]

As Cherokees returned from the meeting to their nation, rumors spread through the South Carolina piedmont that the Indian diplomats had plundered a household on the Little Saluda River. The charge, though false, would recur in like form throughout the early years of the Seven Years' War. As Cherokees descended to visit Glen in Charleston, or as they moved through the valleys and piedmont to join the British armies in Virginia, Maryland, and Pennsylvania, they had to pass through an ambivalent colonial backcountry. Cherokees complained that settlers refused them food and lodging; some whites even stole their horses. Familiarity between Cherokees and their new neighbors led sometimes to violence, as when John Burns mortally wounded a leader of the Cherokee Lower Towns in a drunken brawl, or when Henry Crumy "cruelly whipt" a headman of the steadfastly pro-British town of Hiawassee. The government provided gifts to the headman and arrested Crumy, but sentiments in the backcountry were such that Crumy broke jail and escaped justice.[10]

Backcountry friction was not the only problem. Glen had great difficulty persuading lowcountry legislators to continue his courtship of the Cherokees. In the early fall of 1754, the Carolina backcountry shuddered again as unknown Indians fell upon and killed sixteen settlers who had gathered to celebrate a wedding at Buffalo Creek on the path from the Cherokees to the Catawbas. Ru-

9. S.C. Council, Minutes, July 5, 8, 1753, CO5/469, fols. 142–149, 151–154. Since, later in the year, three of the Shawnees escaped "Through the Negligence of the Centinel" and fled the colony, and since Glen never complained about the escapes, we might credit the Cherokees with convincing Glen to release the Shawnees. See S.C. Council to Dinwiddie, Nov. 12, 1753, DRIA, I, 468.

10. S.C. Council, Minutes, Mar. 24, 1752, CO5/467, fols. 52–55, Sept. 3, 1753, CO5/469, fols. 181–187, Mar. 21, Aug. 12, 1755, CO5/471, fols. 187b2–189, 233–36b; John Chevillette to Glen, Feb. 28, 1756, in SCJHMC, 1754–1756, RSUS, reel 7, 160–161.

mors implicated the Cherokees, and lowcountry legislators let Glen know how gravely they mistrusted Carolina's Indian allies. The Commons House suggested that the Buffalo Creek killings had been "committed by our insidious friends the Cherrockees." In 1755, the Commons House sought to have a scalp bounty placed on all Indians, "of what Nation soever, found in the Province committing any Act of Violence or outrage to the Persons or properties of the Inhabitants." Such an act would have contravened the 1730 treaty of alliance with the Cherokees, which, providing for the legal trial of Cherokee suspects, could not tolerate the extralegal scalping of allies on the mere suspicion of theft. Glen, a trained lawyer, opposed the proposal on the grounds that there was "not the least reason to imagine that [Cherokees] had any hand" in frontier killings. He demanded that the Commons House "communicate to me the Grounds of this suspicion." Although the Commons House promised to send evidence, a full month passed before it sent Glen its weak answer: "If Reports from that very Quarter, where the People in our back settlements were Murdered, are not altogether groundless we are afraid that the Cherrockees are not wholly free from a suspicion of guilt." Such vague allegations nurtured a dangerous sense of ambiguity as Carolinians in the lowcountry plantations and piedmont farmers alike saw latent hostility in the Cherokees.[11]

Even Glen and his Council, foremost advocates of the alliance, sent mixed messages to the Cherokees, and to all Indians. While speaking of mutual love and of common familial subjection to the king, their actions raised Cherokee anxieties about Carolinian intentions. Not only did Glen detain Shawnees— only *potential* enemies in 1753—without evidence of guilt in any crime, he did even worse the next year to three Natchez Indian men who lived in the piedmont under Carolinian protection. One of the three, Sanders (also known as the "Notchee Doctor"), had allegedly killed some Peedees. Admitting that "there was no legal proof against Sanders," the Council nonetheless enslaved him and two alleged accomplices, transporting them all to the West Indies for sale. The record is clear that Sanders had Cherokee acquaintances. While they might have wondered about his forced departure from the colony, other Cherokees still worried in 1754 about Glen's treatment of the six Shawnees. The wisdom of the British alliance became an issue debated within and among Cherokee villages.[12]

11. S.C. Council, Minutes, Oct. 1, 18, 1754, Feb. 7, 14, Mar. 4, 7, 1755, CO5/471, fols. 10b–20, 24–27, 120b–124, 124–130, 135b–146, 146–150.

12. SCJHMC, 1754–1756, *RSUS*, Apr. 3, 22, 23, 28, 1754, reel 7, 181–186, 211, 212–213, 228.

Cherokees held the English responsible for alienating the Shawnees. They insisted that Glen's "imprisoning" of the six Shawnees had caused the rest "to join the French." Shawnees, now hostile to the British, were still welcomed in Cherokee villages, and well into 1755 even Conocorte and Attakullakulla— emerging as the chief advocates of the British alliance—entertained Shawnees and other French-allied diplomats from the pays d'en haut. These two men operated out of the town of Chote, in the Overhills region. Before the end of 1756, other Cherokee factions, particularly out of the Overhills town of Tellico, had sent embassies of their own to speak with the French at Detroit, Fort Toulouse (Alabama), and New Orleans. Though none of these returned satisfied with the poor responses they had received from the ill-supplied French, the missions demonstrate that sentiments among the Cherokees, as among backcountry Carolinians and lowcountry legislators, were divided even as their military alliance took shape and produced results. They also point to Cherokee familiarity with the colonial policies of New France.[13]

Attakullakulla, Chote's speaker or diplomat, understood well the true middle ground, having been held captive for six years in the 1740s by Great Lakes Ottawas allied with France. But as a much younger man, he had also traveled to England and had met George II, with whom the Cherokees concluded the Treaty of 1730. Conocorte, the headman of Chote and the most influential of Cherokees by 1753, became a sometime ally of Attakullakulla, though he retained stronger doubts about the British. In December of that year, an Ottawa delegation entered the southern mountains, seeking to draw the Cherokees into a French alliance. Conocorte and Attakullakulla received the Ottawas hospitably but turned their offers down. "Soon after," a trader informed Glen, "parties of French Indians came to war against the Cherokees." These attacks were especially provocative because among those killed were two women, one of them "a noted War Woman" of the town of Tennessee. Since the "War Woman" bore a title of respect, connoting power over captives, her death called for strong action. By the end of 1754, Cherokees had descended the Tennessee River to hover around the French in the Illinois country, where they killed a French lieutenant and captured at least two prisoners. In 1755, they

13. S.C. Council, Minutes, Oct. 1, 18, 1754, CO5/471, fols. 10b–20, 24–29. On Cherokee factionalism and negotiations with the French see, esp., David H. Corkran, *The Cherokee Frontier: Conflict and Survival, 1740–62* (Norman, Okla., 1962), 85–101; S.C. Council, Minutes, Mar. 21, 1755, CO5/471, fols. 187b–189; SCJHMC, 1754–1756, *RSUS*, July 28, 29, 1756, reel 7, 322–326, 329.

took at least another six French prisoners. Cherokee factions inclined to adhere to the alliance with Britain gained strength.[14]

Carolinians meanwhile reconciled themselves to closer cooperation with their neighbors. British colonists had been promising the Cherokees plentiful supplies "of Powder and Lead" since the eruption of the war in 1754. Northward, General Edward Braddock's defeat in the summer of 1755 forced British officers to recognize that they desperately needed native American auxiliaries to combat the rapidly expanding network of France's Indian allies. Never again should an army march, some warned, without "Indians or other irregulars to give timely Notice of the Enemy's Approach."[15] As Ohioan Indians carried "Desolation and murder" into Virginia, George Washington called for Indian allies, who could "point out the wiles and tracks of the enemy." His own experience gave him a damning respect for the warriors: "Five hundred Indians have it more in their power to annoy the inhabitants, than ten times their number of regulars. For besides the advantageous way they have of fighting in the woods, their cunning and craft are not to be equalled, neither their activity and indefatiguable sufferings." The main concern for the British military was not guerilla combat, as is too often assumed. The concern was intelligence. The insurgence of the Ohioan Delawares and Shawnees had deprived the English of all information regarding the strength and movements of the French and their allies in the Ohio country. Southeastern Indian allies, knowledgeable in the hunting country that separated them from the Ohio, could gather intelligence far more readily than British or Anglo-American troops. When Cherokees and Catawbas supported British arms, as they did in sizable numbers between 1756 and 1758, they lived up to these expectations, plunged deep into enemy country, sneaked about French posts or enemy Indian villages, assessed

14. For the incidents, see Affidavit of Robert Gaudey, June 5, 1751, *DRIA*, I, 71; Cornelius Doharty to Glen, Feb. 23, 1753, SCJHMC, 1752–1754, *RSUS*, reel 6, 314–318; S.C. Council, Minutes, Oct. 19, 22, 1754, Nov. 26, 1755, CO5/471, fols. 27b–29, 30–44, 340–342. On war women, see Hatley, *The Dividing Paths*, 57; Louis De Vorsey, Jr., ed., *De Brahm's Report of the General Survey in the Southern District of North America* (Columbia, S.C., 1971), 109.

15. Dinwiddie to the Sachems and Warriors of the Great Nations of the Cherokees and Catawbas, Nov. 4, 1754, in R. A. Brock, ed., *The Official Records of Robert Dinwiddie, Lieutenant-General of the Colony of Virginia, 1751–1758* (hereafter cited as *Dinwiddie Records*) (Virginian Historical Society, *Collections*, N.S., III [Richmond, Va., 1883]), 391; "Statement of Col. Dunbar and Lieut. Col. Thomas Gage Being Called to Enquire into the Causes . . . of the Bad Behaviour of the King's Troops," Nov. 21, 1755, Loudoun Manuscripts, Henry E. Huntington Library, San Marino, Calif.; Jennings, *Empire of Fortune*, 157–158.

enemy strength, captured an occasional prisoner, struck terror, and returned to British camps with the only information to be had.[16]

Cherokees, too, came to see advantages in the alliance. They might have ignored British inducements and followed the policy of the strongest faction among their Creek neighbors and recent enemies to the south: bargaining for neutrality. But the Seven Years' War brought the Cherokees into serious difficulties. Warriors from the French-allied peoples to the north, determined to strike British Carolina and unconcerned with Cherokee desires, had to be restrained from passing through Cherokee country, else Britain would accuse the Cherokees of complicity in the scorching of the Carolina frontier. Without adequate firepower, Cherokees would be in no position to stop these raids, and, as the northerners swept through Cherokee country, Cherokee neutrality eroded. Already a powerful Cherokee woman had fallen to their attacks. In Chote and other Overhills villages, calls for war, traditionally raised by women, summoned warriors to attack peoples of the Great Lakes. South Carolina, moreover, had always been the main colonial trading partner, and its apparently available arms and supplies promised to provide Cherokees with the wherewithal to defend themselves. The stronger Cherokee faction, with considerable logic, supported the policy of aiding British forces.[17]

Conocorte and Attakullakulla came to promise to aid the British under certain conditions. At Cherokee request, South Carolina had already built Fort Prince George near the Cherokee Lower Town of Keowee. The fort had several purposes: to maintain peace between the Lower Creeks and the Lower Cherokees, to oversee the trade, and to provide a smith for the repair of Cherokee guns. The two Cherokees now demanded that forts be built and garrisoned in the Overhills region of their nation, near the likely entries of Indians allied with France, "for the protection of our wives and Children . . . in the Absence of our Warriors." By 1756, both South Carolina and Virginia agreed to build and gar-

16. Washington to Dinwiddie, Apr. 7, 24, 27, 1755, in John C. Fitzpatrick, ed., *The Writings of George Washington from the Original Manuscript Sources, 1745–1799*, 39 vols. (Washington, D.C., 1931–1944), 300–304, 329–331, 340–344; Governor Horatio Sharpe to Sir Thomas Robinson, Annapolis, Jan. 6, 1756, in William Hand Browne, ed., *Correspondence of Governor Horatio Sharpe*, I, *1753–1757* (Maryland Historical Society, *Archives of Maryland*, VI [Baltimore, 1888]), 337.

17. Michael D. Green, *The Politics of Indian Removal: Creek Government and Society in Crisis* (Lincoln, Nebr., 1982), 21–23; Cherokee Headmen to Glen, Sept. 21, 1754, Ludovic Grant to Glen, Cherokees, Tomatly Town, July 22, 1754, both in *DRIA*, II, 7–8, 15–16.

rison strong houses near Chote. Virginia's fort, as it turned out, was "a mere Bubble, Constructed to Humour the Indians." And, if the Carolinian Fort Loudoun fell short of its promise to provide for the "lodgement, security and protection of the women and Children of the Cherokees," then at least its garrison, an independent company of the king's troops, planted itself as a symbol of a developing union as deep in the Cherokee highlands as it was possible to go. For Glen, who had been arguing for the posts for years, there must have been some satisfaction in seeing his forts straddle the nation over which he hoped to stand as the commander.[18]

Command itself surfaced as the major problem. Since Cherokees would not defer to their allies, command eluded Glen and the British, and issues concerning leadership breached the alliance. Glen had a strong feeling for rank, a feeling he shared with the governing elites of Britain and the British colonies. In 1755, he directly instructed Attakullakulla on British-Carolinian social norms, explaining that, although certain public meetings demanded that a governor consult openly with disreputable deerskin traders, in private settings Glen's elevated "station would have obliged [traders] to stand at a Distance." And he could inadvertently remind Cherokees of South Carolinian ideas about race, promising them equal treatment with settlers even though "they Differed in Colour from the White." These conceptions of status and race would plague Cherokee-British relations as the Seven Years' War became a lesson to Cherokees in the British and colonial elite's brutal certainty of its right

18. On the purposes of forts, see Little Carpenter to Colonel William Byrd and Edmund Randolph, Mar. 14, 1756, Loudoun MSS; Glen to Little Carpenter, Oct. 14, 1755, Feb. 17, 1756, *DRIA*, II, 76, 99; Governor William Henry Lyttelton to Old Hop, June 3, 1756, *DRIA*, II, 115–116. On the agreement between Cherokees and Virginia, see Mar. 17, 1756, Little Carpenter to Byrd and Randolph, Mar. 14, 1756, Loudoun MSS; Grant to Glen, Cherokees, Tomatly Town, Mar. 27, 1755, *DRIA*, II, 40–45. Edmond Atkin, writing in 1755, found it "a great absurdity to imagine, that either the French or ourselves can maintain an Interest and Influence, more especially among the Inland Nations, barely by the Possession of Forts, without being at the same time possess'd of their *Affections*." He recommended that the English follow the French example of giving presents prudently and mending guns freely: "The French in many places have made those two things alone as practices in their Forts . . . almost counterbalance every other disadvantage they labor under." See Jacobs, ed., *The Edmond Atkin Report and Plan of 1755*, 9, 11. On Virginia's fort, see Col. Henry Bouquet to Earl of Loudoun, Charleston, Aug. 25, 1757, CO5/48, fols. 338–340. On Fort Loudoun's shortcomings, see SCJHMC, 1754–1756, *RSUS*, July 29, 1756, reel 7, 322–326. See also Corkran, *Cherokee Frontier*, 82–83, 104.

to mastery over others. Nowhere was hierarchy more important to Europeans, or more cruelly enforced among them, than in the military.[19]

By February 1756, enough Cherokee warriors were willing to commit to Britain to form a significant portion of Virginia's Big Sandy Creek campaign against the Shawnees. The expedition, as Hatley suggests, exhibited difference and tension between the peoples. The Cherokees, who could easily stomach the rough treatment of enemy captives, were nevertheless horrified and bewildered by the colonial force's brutal floggings of its own men, particularly when these authoritarian rituals of punishment took a sadistic turn. In one episode, Cherokees observed one of the leading Virginians, William Preston, supervise the flogging of an undisciplined soldier who had cursed. Cursing, which brought on the flogging, was a crime against God, a direct attack on the source of all authority. If a man could so wantonly mock his Creator, what order could mortal superiors expect? Blasphemy, declared Virginia's lieutenant governor Dinwiddie, was "a Crime which seems to include a Capacity for all others, for what may not be dreaded from the Wretch who reviles infinite Goodness, ridicules consummate Wisdom, and defies unbounded Power[?]"[20]

Preston's own record suggests that, as the mutilation proceeded, he and one of his lieutenants made sport of its victim. The officers' jests "very much Incensed the Indian chiefs then present." This torture and humiliation of a comrade-in-arms violated Cherokee sensibilities. Cherokee war parties were voluntary affairs, led by war captains who made decisions but who lacked the authority to punish. One colonial officer, though overstating the case in 1761, wrote that the Cherokees had "no such thing as coercive power among them." Virginians and British regulars, conversely, expected rank and status to accompany martial endeavors. Virginia permitted its officers to dish out corporal punishment to common soldiers without even the formality of a court martial. The whip, as Lawrence Stone has observed, was a potent symbol of England's social norms. The scene at the whipping was emblematic of the confrontation of two social and ideological orders. The repetition of such demon-

19. S.C. Council, Minutes, Dec. 8, 27, 1755, CO5/471, fols. 367b–372, 383–385b; Douglas Edward Leach, *Roots of Conflict: British Armed Forces and Colonial Americans, 1677–1763* (Chapel Hill, N.C., 1986), 112.

20. Dinwiddie's Fourth Charge to the Grand Jury, Oct. 16, 1753, *Dinwiddie Records,* III, 27; William Preston, Diary of Sandy Creek Expedition, Feb. 9–Mar. 13, 1756, Draper Manuscripts, State Historical Society of Wisconsin, Madison, reel 100, Preston Papers, 1 QQ 96–123 (microfilm at Princeton University, Princeton, N.J.); Hatley, *The Dividing Paths,* 102.

strations of British hierarchy would educate the Cherokees in British ways—and the Indians did not like what they learned.[21]

Cherokees did not enforce status with corporal punishment, nor were they habitually deferential to social superiors. As Cherokees learned that British gentlemen and the aspiring colonial gentry were cocksure of their superiority, as Indians grew to understand the British and provincial officers with whom they increasingly dealt, they objected to fundamental elements of the officers' identity. British officers and colonial elites learned in turn that the Cherokees would not accept the lowly link within the chain of authority that the empire was forging for them. For both parties, the lessons were unhappy. Neither side paid strict attention to them until repeated conflict arose, as it did over the still-understudied issue of gifts among allies. Cherokees and Britons came to blows over the distribution of the spoils of war. The issue had a material dimension, to be sure. But material disputes can be bargained. What made this issue so explosive were its social and cultural dimensions. These included principles so dear to each side that they were beyond negotiation.[22]

21. Preston Papers, 1 QQ 122–123; Colonial officer, quoted in Frederick O. Gearing, *Priests and Warriors: Social Structures for Cherokee Politics in the Eighteenth Century*, American Anthropological Association Memoir no. 93 (Menasha, Wis., 1962), 4. Rennard Strickland, *Fire and the Spirits: Cherokee Law from Clan to Court* (Norman, Okla., 1975), 30, says public punishment was "rare." On Virginia's punishments to soldiers, see George Washington, Orders, May 1, 1756, in Fitzpatrick, ed., *Writings of George Washington*, I, 353. On English norms of punishment, see Lawrence Stone, *The Crisis of the Aristocracy, 1558–1641* (New York, 1966), 29; Roy Porter, *English Society in the Eighteenth Century*, rev. ed. (London, 1990), 86.

22. Wilbur R. Jacobs, *Wilderness Politics and Indian Gifts: The Northern Colonial Frontier, 1748–1763* (Lincoln, Nebr., 1966) (first published as *Diplomacy and Indian Gifts: Anglo-French Rivalry along the Ohio and Northwestern Frontiers, 1748–1763* [Stanford, Calif., 1950]), esp. 11–45; Cornelius Jaenen, "The Role of Presents in French-Amerindian Trade," in Duncan Cameron, ed., *Explorations in Canadian Economic History: Essays in Honour of Irene M. Spry* (Ottawa, 1985), 231–250; White, *Middle Ground*, 180–183. For an episode in the French mismanagement of "spoils," see Ian K. Steele, *Betrayals: Fort William Henry and the "Massacre"* (New York, 1990), 111–116.

There is much room for further investigation of the presents issue. In his seminal study, *Wilderness Politics*, Jacobs concentrates on policy. Although he explores briefly the Indian notion that presents acted as "words" with many symbolic functions in Indian diplomacy, he does not examine what notions the English or French might have brought with them to the giving of presents, beyond an assertion that the gifts were a "type of bribery" (16, 28).

FIGURE 2

*The Three Cherokees Came over from the Head of the River Savanna to London, 1762.*
Osteneco (center) led Cherokees in the Big Sandy expedition but would later lay
siege to Fort Loudoun in the Overhills Cherokee country during the Cherokee War.
After that war, he visited London in the company of two other Cherokees in 1762;
William Shorey (far left), his interpreter, died on the voyage. Osteneco is dressed as
a war leader expected to be outfitted. The source of the engraving is uncertain.
Courtesy, National Anthropological Archives, Smithsonian Institution,
Washington, D.C.

Cherokees had joined Captain Preston of the Virginians in the Big Sandy
Creek expedition (1756) in hopes of both presents from Virginia and plunder
from the Shawnee villages. Plunder failed because the force never made it to
the Shawnee towns. Along the way, Cherokees annoyed Virginians by assuming the right to take food from any pot without first asking permission, and at
half-rations there was not enough food to be had. To this provocation was added
foul weather. Heavy rains and swollen rivers made for extremely difficult travel,
and Virginian canoes carrying the bulk of the ammunition and food capsized.
Cherokees offered to gird their loins and advance on the enemy, but the Virginians faded in small groups into the woods, leaving their commanders with
none to lead. Although Osteneco, the expedition's leading Cherokee, earned

high praise for his men from the Virginians and was personally feted in Williamsburg on April 26, other Cherokees made their way homeward: exhausted, hungry, gainless.[23]

One party, returning through the Virginia backcountry, met stark inhospitality from the settlers, establishing a pattern that would trouble relations until the outbreak of the Cherokee War in 1759. Gifts of food had always been a mark of friendship and hospitality among Cherokees, who provided such gifts to visitors as a matter of obligation and received them as a matter of right, yet many Virginians turned Cherokee supplicants down. It is suggestive of a kind of middle ground that a white woman, an indentured servant who might well have been fleeing her master, joined the party. It is also possible that the party took her by force; the documents tell both stories. Whether by choice or coercion, she helped the warriors find cabins to plunder. Acting out their own moral economy, taking by force what settlers would not give out of friendship, Cherokees left outrage in their wake. In the rumors that followed, the robberies became "horrid Murders," as Virginians blamed Cherokees for outright raids on farmsteads and even for the siege of a fort on the frontier.[24]

Despite the Virginia fiasco of 1756, Osteneco, Attakullakulla, and Conocorte still had reason to believe that a British alliance would provide their people with supplies and gifts. The British certainly continued to promise as much. A Virginian captain who later in the year supplied fine firearms to a band of Cherokees prudently sent a runner "to the [Cherokee] Nation with one of the guns . . . to Aqueant them what is provided." Virginia also offered Cherokees a bounty on enemy scalps in September 1756, and the next January South Caro-

---

23. Corkran, *Cherokee Frontier*, 67.

24. Conocorte put the hospitality ethic this way that very spring, speaking for Overhills people preparing to host the builders of Fort Loudoun: "What little we have we will share it with them and when there is a Want we will all want together." See Connecortee to Glen, Chote, May 20, 1756, in *DRIA*, II, 108. Catawbas later took the woman from the Cherokee party and returned her to the English. Doing so, they asked for lenience toward her, claiming that she had been forced to join the Cherokees. But North Carolina governor Dobbs doubted that, having been informed that Cherokees had acted "at her Instigation." See Dobbs to Board of Trade, June 14, 1756, Newbern, CO5/297, pt. 2, fol. 338; Copy of a Conference Held with the King and Warriors of the Catawbas by Mr. Chief Justice Henley, Salisbury, May 26, 1756, CO5/297, pt. 2, fol. 340. For outrage and rumor, see Dinwiddie to Washington, July 12, 1756, Washington to Dinwiddie, Aug. 4, 1756, and Dinwiddie to Washington, Aug. 19, 1756, in W. W. Abbot et al., eds., *The Papers of George Washington: Colonial Series*, 10 vols. (Charlottesville, Va., 1983–1995), III, 260, 321, 361.

lina's Captain Raymond Demere proclaimed to the Cherokees that colony's bounty on enemy scalps: goods worth thirty doeskins. Although Conocorte complained that the "Reward was too small"—thirty skins would have been a thin season for a Cherokee hunter—impoverished Cherokees took up arms against Great Britain's enemies. The following year, the South Carolina assembly sweetened the deal when it voted to promise to Cherokee warriors "the value of forty weight of Leather which for a Thousand Indians it is estimated will amount to the sum of £30,000 of this money or 4285 . . . 14 . . 3 sterling." South Carolina's new governor, William Henry Lyttelton, authorized the promise.[25]

Against the backdrop of the rising Fort Loudoun, of British promises, and of actual British gifts, the pro-British faction appeared to have triumphed. Attakullakulla must have had high hopes during the spring and summer of 1757 — hopes for the security of his people, hopes for Britain's loyalty to the alliance, and hopes for generous presents that he and Conocorte could redistribute as they consolidated their authority in the divided nation.

In May 1757, with a party of fourteen, Attakullakulla's brother descended the Tennessee River and "discovered" French Fort Massac (Illinois), "on the Ohio." The party returned to Fort Loudoun in July with the scalp of a young French officer. As Demere prepared to give the promised bounty of thirty skins' worth of goods to the warrior who had taken the scalp, Attakullakulla argued that each man in the party should receive some reward. Demere hedged, Attakullakulla prevailed, and the warriors each went home with presents worth about eighteen doeskins. For the Cherokees, it had been a successful expedition, but not excessively so; in fact, when closely examined, the reward reveals clearly the material grounds for Cherokee disillusionment with Britain.[26]

25. For the runner, see Andrew Lewis to George Washington, Augusta, Oct. 28, 1756, Dinwiddie to Washington, Sept. 13, 1756, in Abbot et al., eds., *Papers of George Washington*, III, 445. For Demere and Conocorte, see Raymond Demere to Lyttelton, Fort Loudoun, Jan. 31, 1757, Demere to Old Hop and Upper Cherokee Headmen, Jan. 25, 1757, *DRIA*, II, 325, 332. For the deer harvest, see William Byrd to Loudoun, Apr. 30, 1758, Abercromby Manuscripts, Huntington Library. On South Carolina's promise to the Cherokees, see Lyttelton to Loudoun, Mar. 21, 1758, Abercromby MSS.

26. Bouquet to Loudoun, Charleston, Aug. 25, 1757, CO5/48, fol. 338; Demere to Lyttelton, Fort Loudoun, July 30, 1757, *DRIA*, II, 395. My estimates in this and the following paragraphs are based on a "List of the Prices of Goods for the Cherokee Trade," November 1751, and "Account of Sundries Delivered to the Indians by Sergeant Harrison," August 1756, both in *DRIA*, I, 146–147, II, 172–173. The estimates probably overestimate the value of the gift, since prices for goods had risen in Cherokee country since the 1751 code; see Mankiller to Demere, Jan. 15, 1757, *DRIA*, II, 319.

The reward was uncommonly generous, and valuable from a South Carolinian perspective. Each warrior received about the equivalent of thirteen pounds, ten shillings in South Carolina money. But this, for two months' hazardous service, did little more than provide one set of clothes, a pound of powder, and two pounds of ball or shot for each man on the expedition, plus a gun for the fellow who took the scalp. Although much better than nothing, it left the warriors to face their wives and mothers with nothing for their families. Worse still, most rewards of 1757 failed to live up to even that meager standard. At Fort Cumberland, Maryland, in October, George Washington, meeting Cherokee warriors who had returned with scalps and prisoners from a dangerous mission toward Fort Duquesne, declared his "vast Love and Brotherly Affection" for them but found that he had to explain to them why he had so few presents, hoping they would accept those few "as token of my strong Love." Such explanations increasingly failed to satisfy Cherokee leaders as they looked upon the uniforms, gorgets, and slaves of officers who seemed slow to mount an offensive. Thus it is not surprising that ugly disputes frequently punctuated exchanges between British officers and Cherokee warriors seeking compensation for their raids and reconnaissance.[27]

The British did not confront this very material issue squarely, although they possessed the wherewithal to understand its material dimensions. Few colonial or British officials faced up to the warriors' obligation to clothe their families. When one group of Cherokees requested a full set of clothes for each man, the necessary equipment for the service, "five Stroud Mantles," silver, bead, and cloth ornaments, and goods for their people at home, Colonel Henry Bouquet resorted to hyperbole, calling it "the most extravagant thing that ever was thought of."[28]

In raw economic terms, Bouquet's outrage was unwarranted, a parsimonious response that contributed to Cherokee alienation. One provincial captain with long Indian experience, Thomas Bosomworth, thought the Cherokee

27. George Washington, "Rough Sketch of a Speech Made to the Indians," [October 1757], in Abbot et al., eds., *Papers of George Washington*, V, 27 n. 4; Lachlan Mackintosh to Lyttelton, Nov. 29, 1757, *DRIA*, II, 418–420; William Trent to Bouquet, Virginia, June 5, 1758, in Sylvester K. Stevens and Donald H. Kent, eds., *Wilderness Chronicles of Northwestern Pennsylvania* (Harrisburg, Pa., 1941), 125.

28. Thomas Bosomworth, "Proportion of Presents Agreed to be Given Each Indian . . ." July 23, 1759, British Museum, London, Additional Manuscripts (hereafter BM Add. MSS), 21655, fol. 15, and Bouquet to Washington, Reastown, July 23, 1758, both in S. K. Stevens et al., eds., *The Papers of Henry Bouquet*, II, *The Forbes Expedition* (Harrisburg, Pa., 1951), 260, 263 (hereafter cited as *Forbes Expedition*).

request equaled no "more than the Expense of a Provincial Soldier in the New Levies who have their Arms etc. found them." Bosomworth calculated that its cost, per warrior for the duration of the campaign, would amount to £10 7s immediately plus £8 17s in presents upon the completion of service. On the face of it, that combined £19 4s would have exceeded the pay given to an ordinary Virginia provincial in 1758 by almost £6, much of which would have been made up, as Bosomworth pointed out, by the cost of arming and otherwise providing for the soldier. But several other considerations render the proposal less generous to Cherokees than it at first appears. High-ranking colonial officers received a salary ten times that of the private soldier; figuring all colonial officers into the equation would put the Cherokees at a considerable disadvantage. Cherokee war leaders made effective captains and therefore might rate a higher reward. The exceptional skills of the Cherokees might also be considered. Full-time hunters, with knowledge of stealth and of the ground, Cherokees might have commanded pay commensurate with that of Virginia's mounted troopers. The proposed reward, in any case, never materialized. Few British officials thought Cherokees worthy of equitable recompense. Another set of figures from 1758 underscores the inequity. South Carolina hoped to raise one thousand Cherokees at £4 to £6 sterling each. The province expected its own regiment, by contrast, to cost an average of £30 sterling per soldier, which, after other costs, meant an average annual pay per man of about £10 sterling, roughly twice the proposed Cherokee allocation.[29]

29. Thomas Bosomworth, "Proportion of Presents," July 23, 1759, BM Add. MSS, 21655, fol. 15. A Virginia provincial could expect to receive a £10 bounty (in Virginia's currency) and about £10 5s (currency) in pay for the full seven months of the campaign. Since the currency's exchange rate with sterling gyrated in the neighborhood of 150/100 in 1758 and 1759, the soldier's total draw was about £13 10s. See William Waller Hening, ed., *Statutes at Large, Being a Collection of All the Laws of Virginia*, 18 vols. (Richmond, Va., 1809–1823), VII, 28, 62, 164; and Leslie V. Brock, *The Currency of the American Colonies, 1700–1764: A Study in Colonial Finance and Imperial Relations* (1941; facsimile reprint, New York, 1975), 476–477, fig. XVII. See also James Titus, *The Old Dominion at War: Society, Politics, and Warfare in Late Colonial Virginia* (Columbia, S.C., 1991), 122.

On South Carolinian pay, see Lyttelton to Loudoun, Mar. 21, 1758, CO5/50, fol. 33; Byrd to Loudoun, Mar. 21, 1758, CO5/50, fol. 36; S.C. Council, Minutes, Mar. 17, 1758, CO5/474, fol. 133. For the proposed provincial regiment, see Lyttelton to Pitt, July 12, 1757, CO5/18, fol. 82; Bouquet to Loudoun, Aug. 25, 1757, CO5/48, fol. 338; Lyttelton to Board of Trade, Aug. 7, 1758, CO5/376, fol. 41. By 1759, the colony expected to pay mounted rangers the equivalent of £2 sterling and their officers £5 *per month*. See Message from the Assembly to Lyttelton, July 13, 1759, PRO, War Office Papers, series 34, vol. 35 (hereafter WO34/35), fol. 125.

That a racist logic operated here is suggested by a South Carolinian measure passed in

The Cherokees, it should be remembered, could deliver valuable goods: not only scalps but information about the status of French forces in the Ohio Valley. British officers underscored the point as they worried about losing Cherokee support. Bouquet openly admitted the Cherokees' value. He praised Attakullakulla for the Cherokees' discovery of Fort Massac. He admired the map drawn by a head warrior back from a mission to spy on the targeted Fort Duquesne, a map that "included the smallest details" and revealed the weakness of the French post. He was not alone. In June 1757, Dinwiddie wrote from Williamsburg that 180 Cherokees were "out a Scouting" toward Fort Duquesne and that "a Party of them" had carried to the British "four Scalps and two prisoners" who could be interrogated. When Governor Horatio Sharpe of Maryland reported to William Pitt in May 1758 that French and Indian forces at Fort Duquesne had fallen below five hundred, he credited a Cherokee source. Given the benefits of Cherokee intelligence, the British understanding of Cherokee demands as "extravagant" needs further investigation. We therefore have a problem: Why, when another interpretation was at hand, did the British generally see the Cherokee demands as extravagant?[30]

One historian suggests that the British "failed to recognize that the Cherokees were mercenaries." He blames the word "presents," arguing that the British could not see that presents "constituted an Indian's pay." Though presents were a sore point, this underestimates British perceptiveness and ignores the complexity of gift giving in early modern British culture. Anthropologists have long insisted that gifts carry or fulfill obligations, something Britons, colonists, and Cherokees readily understood. The author of "A Discourse upon the Beginning of Tacitus" (1620), probably Thomas Hobbes, phrased it strongly: "Benefits received are pleasing so long as they are requitable. When once they exceed that, they are an intolerable burden." Among Anglo-Americans in the eighteenth century, this was no less the case than among others. Laurel Thatcher Ulrich has argued that a "present" recorded in the diary of the midwife Martha Ballard was simultaneously "both a gift and a payment, an unsolicited offering and compensation for services performed." In fact, Britons and Anglo-Americans easily mixed up the idea of presents and payments. Vir-

---

1742. Slaves who killed an enemy or took a prisoner (or even the enemy's colors) would gain a fancy livery outfit. Those who performed valorously in other ways would gain an annual holiday! See S.C. Journal of the Upper House of Assembly, July 8, 1742, CO5/443, fols. 35–36.

30. For the map, see Bouquet to Forbes, June 16, 1758, *Forbes Expedition*, 93, 95–96. See also Dinwiddie to William Pitt, June 18, 1757, CO5/18, fol. 78; Bouquet to Loudoun, Aug. 25, 1757, CO5/48, fol. 338; Sharpe to Pitt, May 18, 1758, CO5/18, fol. 446.

ginia's statute books refer to presents to Indians as "rewards for their services." William Lyttelton, who became governor of South Carolina in 1756, wanted all supplies of arms and ammunition given as presents to the Cherokees to be "considered in the light of a Subsidy to a foreign Nation who may be dangerous Enemies or very serviceable allies to us." Washington posed it as a "standing maxim" in 1754 that "all the Indians that come expect presents, . . . for any particular service, they must be bought."[31]

But if the British and colonial officers well understood that presents were payments that carried obligations, by equating Cherokees with paid, "bought" mercenaries they fitted the Indians into an unsuitable category. To the British and British colonists, mercenaries occupied a dangerous social place, low, armed, and potentially disloyal. Britons on both sides of the Atlantic, but perhaps even more so on the American side, despised mercenaries of all nations (except, perhaps, when they found themselves beside such professionals and

---

31. Corkran, *Cherokee Frontier,* 129; Thomas Hobbes, *Three Discourses: A Critical Modern Edition of Newly Identified Work of the Young Hobbes,* ed. Noel B. Reynolds and Arlene W. Saxonhouse (Chicago, 1995), 51; Laurel Thatcher Ulrich, *A Midwife's Tale: The Life of Martha Ballard, Based on Her Diary, 1785–1812* (New York, 1991), 67, 70. Benjamin Franklin considered the importance of obligations when he recalled having offered lodging to evangelist George Whitefield. Whitefield "reply'd, that if I made that kind Offer for Christ's sake, I should not miss of a Reward.—And I return'd, *Don't let me be mistaken; it was not for Christ's sake, but for your sake.*" If Whitefield was attempting to relieve himself of the "Burden of the Obligation . . . and place it in Heaven," said a friend of Franklin's, "I had contriv'd to fix it on Earth." See Benjamin Franklin, *The Autobiography of Benjamin Franklin,* ed. Louis Masur (New York, 1993), 109; Hening, ed., *Statutes at Large,* VII, 165; Lyttelton to Board of Trade, Aug. 7, 1758, CO5/376, fol. 41; Washington to Colonel Joshua Fry, May 23, 1754, in Fitzpatrick, ed., *Writings of George Washington,* I, 52.

The most influential anthropological work on gift giving is Marcel Mauss, *The Gift: The Form and Reason for Exchange in Archaic Societies,* trans. W. D. Halls (London, 1990). Marshall Sahlins's *Stone Age Economics* (Chicago, 1972) contains a discussion of Mauss's *The Gift* that also implies a radical divide, not so much between archaic and civilized societies as between capitalist and "traditional" forms of exchange (181–183). Claude Lévi-Strauss emphasizes the persistence, especially in the United States, of powerful, even elemental ideas surrounding gift giving. See Lévi-Strauss, *The Elementary Structures of Kinship,* rev. ed., trans. J. H. Bell, J. R. Von Sturmer, and Rodney Needham (London, 1970), 56. For a sociology of the gift in the context of capitalism, see David Cheal, *The Gift Economy* (New York, 1988), 3, 11. For our purposes, it is important to remember that "capitalism" was still immature in 1750 and perhaps less powerful ideologically among those who dominated the war effort in the South than among others.

under fire). Their equation of Cherokees with mercenaries, men so desperately poor that they would kill for money, did not do much to raise their estimation of Indians. It hardly inspired much confidence in the alliance; for if the British could buy Cherokees, might not the French? One South Carolinian councillor worried as early as 1745: "There is no Confidence to be put in those Indians, . . . they [are] rather ready to joyn any Enterprize where there is a view of Plunder."[32]

Cherokee men did not suffer the moral slight alone. Colonists regularly referred to Cherokee women as "wenches," a term that suggested both low origins and loose morals. Cherokee men complained, in fact, that Britons saw Cherokee women as sexually available. Mercenaries did for money what better men did for duty and country; wenches might easily do for gain what better women did for duty and family. Though British officers repeatedly attempted to fix Cherokee affections through gifts and professions of love, they were jealous and angry lovers, deeply resenting their need for Cherokee company; they never trusted Cherokees to be constant. Washington, after figuratively and repeatedly embracing Cherokees in the Forbes campaign of 1757–1758, vented his resentment: "The Indians are mercenary; every service of theirs must be purchased; and they are easily offended, beingthoroughly [sic] sensible of their own importance."[33]

British officers might have been professional soldiers, but they were the king's men; they did not identify with mercenaries. For one thing, far from demanding presents from the army, some had themselves paid for their rank. Roy Porter estimates that "in mid-century an ensigncy cost about £400, a lieutenant-colonelcy about £3,500." Others gained rank by virtue of social status and a few by virtue of "a combination of successful violence and political favoritism." Having achieved rank, officers grew "accustomed to deference and

32. "Representation of John Fenwick to Board of Trade, 1745," CO5/371, fol. 61; Porter, *English Society*, 119.

33. Washington to Stanwix, Apr. 10, 1758, in Fitzpatrick, ed., *Writings of Washington*, II, 173. Hatley analyzes the image of Cherokee "wenches" in *The Dividing Paths*, 148, 152 (see also 148). Lt. Richard Coytmore, singled out by Lower Cherokees to be killed by Cherokees in 1760, had been accused by one of their leaders in 1759 of slighting Cherokee manhood while "using" Indian women: "He paints himself and says he is a warrior, but we are not warriors, and has to do with our women at his own pleasure"; see S.C. Council, Minutes, Oct. 19, 1759, CO5/474, fol. 20b; Alexander Miln to Lyttelton, Feb. 24, 1760, *DRIA*, II, 499. Records indicate that Cherokee women held prisoner by British troops during the Cherokee War suffered "daily" sexual abuse; see S.C. Council, Minutes, Jan. 20, 1761, CO5/477, fol. 35.

cherished authority." They offered a low and unsavory place in their social and military hierarchy to the demanding Cherokees. When the Indians refused to show proper subordination, British officers saw only insolence and disloyalty. And, because the British and their colonial counterparts were so confident of their superiority that they thought it must be evident to their allies, they noted, as did Washington, that Cherokees were "easily offended." [34]

Cherokees did not see themselves as mercenaries, certainly not in the sense that word awakened in British minds. The lopsided balance sheet of their service for Britain did not alienate them in material terms alone. There was a critical symbolic component to Cherokee alienation. In addition to firearms, blankets, and other utilitarian items, Cherokees wanted "Silver Plates to go round their arms, and silver Brotches for their Shirt Breasts, and Gorgets for the Breasts of Captains, that they may go to War like White Men." They wanted to reduce the distinction between themselves and British officers, to wear on their bodies the marks of their affinity with men for whom they were risking their lives. The colonial upper echelons seeking a firm Cherokee alliance might have rejoiced; instead, they viewed the Cherokees as disdainfully as they might view prostitutes dressed beyond their status.[35]

It was not, then, a failure to recognize the complexities of gift giving that plagued Cherokee-British relations. Both sides understood that gifts were bonds. Nor were Britons surprised that Cherokees requested gifts. That was something all servants did. It was, rather, the definition of the bond embodied by the gift that differed widely. Ideally, Britons expected gratitude from subordinate beneficiaries, and Cherokees expected generosity from wealthier brothers. As subordination could not be reconciled with brotherhood, these ideals failed: Cherokees became dependent mercenaries in the British view, and the British became poor leaders in the Cherokee view. Each side understood the

34. Washington to Stanwix, Apr. 10, 1758, in Fitzpatrick, ed., *Writings of Washington*, II, 173; Porter, *English Society*, 136; Leach, *Roots of Conflict*, 4, 107.

35. Captain William Thomson to Lieutenant Colonel [John] Armstrong, Fort Loudoun, Apr. 9, 1758, CO5/50, fol. 127; Dening, *Mr Bligh's Bad Language*, interprets the borrowing of Tahitian garb by British sailors. Shannon, "Dressing for Success," *WMQ*, 3d Ser., LIII (1996), 25–26, explains the importance of such articles in the mediations between Mohawks and British colonists. John F. Kasson calls prostitutes "social counterfeits," whose dress portrayed a "deceptive gentility" in the early-nineteenth-century American city, in *Rudeness and Civility: Manners in Nineteenth-Century Urban America* (New York, 1990), 100–103. See also Christine Stansell, *City of Women: Sex and Class in New York, 1789–1860* (New York, 1986), 93–100, 171–192.

other's demands, found them to be unacceptable, and the bonds of alliance grew taut.[36]

The British officers and colonial officials, like the colonists of the Virginia frontier, by holding back the wealth they so manifestly possessed, committed what for Cherokees amounted to a moral and social breach. The British claimed the role of leader but did not act the part. Despite the cultural gulf, many Britons understood this. Edmund Atkin, who became superintendent of the southern Indian department in 1756, knew the uses of the gift in Cherokee diplomacy: "According to their Custom universally an Exchange of Presents is expected and made, at all Meetings or Interviews upon Publick Business, even among themselves. It is that which binds everything that is said on such Occasions. Without it there is no Faith. No Ratification." Glen knew that presents were "given for fixing the affections of Indians." Georgia's governor Henry Ellis went further, speaking to visiting Creeks of the gifts less in contractual terms than in terms of "cementing our Love by new and stronger ties," of "common benefit," of "marks of our unceasing Benevolence."[37]

Understanding that gifts stood as an "expression of love," Glen and Ellis came close to the sociological view that gifts function in modern societies "to construct certain kinds of voluntary social relationships." Britons and Cherokees readily understood broadly that gifts implied obligations and sentiment. But, as they attempted to define those obligations through displays of gift giving and receiving, they came to disagree strongly about the nature of their desperate partnership. For Britons, patronage remained a critical feature of social and political life, and the exchange of material gifts could still mark the elaboration of social and political networks. "Benevolence" did not come freely, as Hobbes understood: "For no man giveth, but with intention of Good to himself; because Gift is Voluntary; and of all Voluntary Acts, the Object is to every man his own Good; of which if men see they shall be frustrated, there will be no beginning benevolence, or trust." Hobbes, speaking from a hierarchical society, recognized that even the most gracious giver demanded "GRATITUDE."[38]

36. Porter, *English Society*, 66, 90. See also entries for July 22, 1709, and Apr. 9, 1711, in Louis B. Wright and Marion Tinling, eds., *The Secret Diary of William Byrd of Westover, 1709–1712* (Richmond, Va., 1941), 62, 327, in which he gives gifts to the servants of others.

37. Edmund Atkin to Board of Trade, June 1756, Colonial Office Papers, series 323, vol. 13, fol. 304; Glen to Board of Trade, December 1751, CO5/373, fol. 175; Georgia Council, Minutes, Nov. 3, 1757, CO5/646, fol. 88.

38. Cheal, *The Gift Economy*, 14, 39; Thomas Hobbes, *Leviathan* (1651), ed. C. B. Macpherson (London, 1968), 209 (quoted also in Sahlins, *Stone Age Economics*, 176).

Religious Britons gave gratitude and praise to God; hierarchically-minded Britons passed such thanks up to their social betters. Lord Chesterfield, the great embodiment of eighteenth-century manners, put careful thought into his thanks to Lord Huntington for the gift to his wife of a flower setting, "which is justly made the capital piece of her dressing room." "It is at once the prettiest and finest thing of the kind that I ever saw in my life." Dinwiddie of Virginia could wax obsequious to his English patron, Horace Walpole: "I shall always think myself in Duty bound to do [your commands], as I shall never forget the Obligat's I am under to Y'r F'dship and Patronage." Further down the chain, George Washington scraped graciously before the lieutenant governor when Dinwiddie seemed "to charge me with ingratitude for your generous, and my undeserved, favours." "Nothing is a greater stranger to my Breast, or a Sin that my Soul more abhors than that black and detestable Ingratitude. I retain a true Sense of your kindnesses, and want nothing but oppertunity to give testimony to my willingness to oblige as far as my life or fortune will extend." Leaders dispensing favors expected obedient returns. The duke of Bedford expected such from South Carolina. The southern secretary of state and "one of the first peers of the Kingdom," Bedford had once supplied South Carolina and Georgia with large quantities of Indian presents and put them under South Carolinian control. Now he asked that the colony appoint the person of his choice as the agent to distribute Georgia's share. Glen persuaded the Council that it had to approve the request, especially given Bedford's past favors and "high station." To oblige "his Grace" could "be no disadvantage." [39]

Extending presents to Indians, royal governors expected to bring Indians into the British interest. Dinwiddie, who knew plenty about slavery, noted that only love or fear would gain Virginia influence over powerful Indians. Of the two, he preferred love, for "fear is a Slavish Passion," more volatile than love, more subject to rebelliousness, whereas "Love and Amity are propagated by Acts of Kindness, the very Exercise of which is Delight." "The Mind is happy under their Influence, and their Influence for that Reason is continually gaining new Strength." The policy he advocated toward Indians was generosity in the Hobbesian sense, which would result in "the advantage of mutual Bounty,

39. Lord Chesterfield to Lord Huntington, London, Nov. 21, 1752, in Philip Dormer Stanhope, *Lord Chesterfield's Letters to His Son and Others,* ed. R. K. Root (London, 1959), 314; Washington to Dinwiddie, May 29, 1754, in Abbot et al., eds., *Papers of George Washington,* I, 107; Dinwiddie to Horace Walpole, Oct. 25, 1754, *Dinwiddie Records,* III, 372; South Carolina Council, Minutes, May 27, June 23, 1749, CO5/459, fol. 33, 76b–79; Franklin, *Autobiography,* ed. Masur, shows a concern for gratitude (50, 109, 145).

Gratitude, and Publick Faith." "Mutual Bounty" did not mean an equal division of the spoils, and, as Cherokees surrendered their autonomy for subordination within a powerful and rich realm, they should have been grateful and performed their services dutifully. Instead, they demanded more gifts.[40]

Gratitude was neither unknown nor unimportant to the Cherokees. Religious Cherokees effusively thanked a variety of sacred beings for having rendered favors, and they thanked Britons for gifts, too. In 1739, after a smallpox epidemic had so raged in the nation that the fields went largely unplanted, General James Oglethorpe sent fifteen hundred bushels of corn to the Cherokees from Augusta. Cherokees had previously let him know that they blamed the epidemic on British traders, but they now told the general that he and "the [Georgia] Trustees treated them as Fathers do their Children." Georgia now "supplied their wants when misfortune came upon them." Although calling themselves "Children," they still lacked deference; they added a hard edge to these thanks. They called Georgia's Trustees "the Preservers of their Nation, as they did the Carolina Traders, the destroyers of it." During the Seven Years' War, Cherokees were not shy about following their thanks with sharp criticism—the ammunition is "but a small quantity"—or with reminders that the English had "promised we never should want goods, notwithstanding that, we have been put to great difficulties." Although Cherokees thanked Britons for good presents, they refused to show a scraping gratitude if they deemed the presents unsuitable compensation for their effective and dangerous services.[41]

Britons could see, because the Cherokees made it plain, that their Indian allies increasingly considered them to be miserly and unloving. The members of one disgruntled Cherokee band dramatized their feelings as they rested in the spring of 1758 at a post on Forbes Road in Pennsylvania. When the commander, whose stocks were low, told them that he could not meet their demands for presents, they threatened to "Rob all the English Houses they met

40. Dinwiddie's Address to the General Assembly [1752], *Dinwiddie Records*, III, 26. David Hackett Fischer notes patterns of gift exchanges in the colonial Chesapeake, and he notes that those who accepted a gentleman's hospitality "tacitly agreed to place themselves under his protection and authority"; see Fischer, *Albion's Seed: Four British Folkways in America* (Oxford, 1989), 279, 393.

41. For a contemporary treatment of Cherokee religious practices, see James Adair, *Adair's History of the American Indians [1775]*, ed. Samuel Cole Williams (New York, 1966), 123–124; Oglethorpe to Harmon Verelst, Savannah, Oct. 19, 1739, CO5/640, fol. 399; Tosate of Tuckasaw and Tosate of Stocke to Glen, Oct. 10, 1754, CO5/471, fols. 44–47; S.C. Council, Minutes, July 5, 1753, CO5/469, fol. 142.

with on their way home" and talked of joining the French. The head warrior
symbolically threatened to break with the British. In the words of the "Indian
scout overseer," William Trent, the Indian "pulled of his shirt and throwed it
to me." "I took it up and jocosely thanked him, and told me I was a poor Man
and wanted a Shirt, he told me he did not give it [to] me, but [to] the Coll.
[Henry Bouquet] and desired me to get it washed. . . . Then a number more
brought their Bundles and throwed them down and told me to keep them and
give them to you [that is, Bouquet] as you loved goods." Bouquet, the warrior
might have added, loved goods more than he loved the Cherokees. To say that,
given Cherokee notions of generosity, was both to insult the British (for no
self-respecting Cherokee leader would hoard goods) and to state a fact. The insult was not wholly lost upon Trent, who recorded it and who was left to persuade the Indians to take back their discarded laundry, a mundane emblem of
the fraying Cherokee-British alliance.[42]

Cherokees interpreted British penury as a clear demonstration of Britain's
disdain for them, which it was. Trent himself "jocosely" jabbed at Cherokee
poverty, ridiculing Cherokees by pointing out that he was above fighting over
a shirt. Britons' ideas of status and their developing conceptions of savagery
and nationality—in short, their certainty of their superiority—permitted, indeed demanded, that officers extend their customary standards of inequality in

42. The post where the dispute took place, Fort Loudoun (also Loudon), should not be
confused with forts of the same name in Virginia and in the Cherokee nation. See Trent to
Bouquet, Fort Loudoun, June 5, 1758, *Forbes Expedition*, 36–38 (quotation). The editors of
the volume believe the reference to the French was a reference to those in the region of Fort
Duquesne; my guess is that the Cherokees, when they spoke of going to the French and the
Creeks, had Fort Toulouse (Alabama) in mind. For Trent, see Paul Woehrmann, "Trent,
William (1715–1787)," in Alan Gallay, ed., *Colonial Wars of North America, 1512–1763: An
Encyclopedia* (New York, 1996), 746–747. For low stocks, see Thomas Bullit to Governor
William Denny, Mar. 31, 1758, in *Pennsylvania Archives*, 1st Ser., III (Philadelphia, 1853), 371.

Harriet Jane Kupferer, "The 'Principal People,' 1960: A Study of Cultural and Social
Groups of the Eastern Cherokee," Smithsonian Institution, *Bureau of American Ethnology
Bulletin*, CXCVI (Washington, D.C., 1966), Anthropological Papers, no. 78, argues that a
strong Cherokee ethic "stipulates giving of oneself and possessions," while at the same time
recognizing the difficulties and disruptive potential of asking and receiving (292). She points
out that Cherokees generally request gifts and thank the giver through a third person. It is
interesting that the Cherokee warrior does not denounce Trent, but a third person, Bouquet.
For a brief, late-nineteenth-century Cherokee woman's views on hospitality, see Jack Frederick Kilpatrick, ed., "The Wahnenauhi Manuscript: Historical Sketches of the Cherokees,
Together with Some of Their Customs, Traditions, and Superstitions," ibid., no. 77, 192.

their dealings with Indians. The reciprocity between the peoples was to reflect the unequal relationship of patron and dependent. Britons, after all, controlled the commodities. As Glen distributed gifts, he attached alienating reminders: "Your dependence for Goods of all kinds has been upon this Province." As Cherokees refused to show the subordinate gratitude Britons expected of loyal servants, the Cherokees themselves became, as they were to Captain Raymond Demere in 1756, a dehumanized "Commodity that are [sic] to be bought and sold." The struggle over gifts drew destabilizing attention to the divergent ideas about command and leadership in the alliance.[43]

Other disputes over generosity shook the alliance in more obvious ways. As in 1756, these confrontations took place in the colonial backcountry. Traveling light from their Smoky Mountain homelands to and from the armies in Virginia, Maryland, and Pennsylvania, Cherokees counted on hospitality from settlers along the way. Too often refused, Cherokees stole what was not offered. Settlers responded with violence. Studies of the origins of the Cherokee War by Hatley, Corkran, and John Phillip Reid point to a series of frontier killings as the critical precipitant of the conflict. Exact numbers are unclear, but between December 1757 and August 1758 settlers killed roughly thirty of their allies. Even Captain William Trent, charged with negotiating with Indians at his post, instead "instigated" the garrison to take up arms against visiting Cherokee parties. In the tidewater, President John Blair of the Council of Virginia called for "War on the Cherokees." Lower Cherokees retaliated for some killings in early 1758, killing two. War did not immediately break out. Cherokees resisted calls for more reprisals, and royal officials attempted to negotiate.[44]

43. S.C. Council, Minutes, Nov. 22, 1754, CO5/471, fols. 61–63; Raymond Demere to Lyttelton, English Camp, Nov. 18, 1756, *DRIA*, II, 249. For an examination of "reciprocal but often unequal" relationships in eighteenth-century Virginia, see Allan Kulikoff, *Tobacco and Slaves: The Development of Southern Cultures in the Chesapeake, 1680–1800* (Chapel Hill, N.C., 1986), 287.

44. Atkin to Loudoun, Mar. 25, 1758, CO5/50, fol. 39; Virginia Council, Minutes, CO5/1429, fol. 173, Oct. 20, 1759, CO5/474, fol. 22. For details on the killings, see Corkran, *Cherokee Frontier*, 142–176; Hatley, *The Dividing Paths*, 100–101; John Phillip Reid, "A Perilous Rule: The Law of International Homicide," in Duane H. King, ed., *The Cherokee Indian Nation: A Troubled History* (Knoxville, Tenn., 1979), 43–44; Reid, *A Law of Blood: The Primitive Law of the Cherokee Nation* (New York, 1970), 66; Depositions and letters in *DRIA*, II, 421, 426–431, 441, 444, 464–470. See also Francis Halkett to Bouquet, Carlisle, Aug. 10, 1758, BM Add. MSS, 21640, fol. 135; John St. Clair to Bouquet, Winchester, May 31, 1758, BM Add. MSS, 21639, fol. 5. The settings of the killings reveal two sources of friction. In the first set-

In September 1758, South Carolina's governor William Henry Lyttelton offered to give presents to the relatives of those Cherokees slain by British subjects. Had his offer been expressed and performed respectfully, even sorrowfully, the act might have done the trick, reconciling Cherokees to the alliance and preventing their attacks on the settlers. In his own culture's terms, he might have condescended to them, but he could only do so to a point. To show too much respect for the Cherokees and to admit British and colonial wrongs would have been to act out a Cherokee point of view with which this British gentleman, accustomed to command, could not abide. Instead, Lyttelton belittled his gift, rendering his sentiments ambiguous: he tied to his offer a threat not well calculated to endow the gift with a promise of love or the expression of grief that might ease tensions. Lyttelton warned that "the Armies of the Great King are strong and mighty." Touching on what was for the numerically decimated and ill-supplied Cherokee warriors a sore point, Lyttelton described the king's troops as "without Number, well armed, well cloathed, well fed and supplied with all the Necessaries of War," and he said that the Cherokees "are few and will soon be in Want of every Thing when once the Trade is withdrawn from you." Take the gift or suffer the consequences of breaking with Britain, that was Lyttelton's way of condoling the families whose relations his people had killed.[45]

Britain's best ally among the Cherokees, Attakullakulla, an influential speaker and warrior, continued to work for an amicable resolution to the crisis and promised Virginia that he would join with the British forces in the fall of 1758. He kept his promise, appearing at the center of activity, Raystown, Pennsylvania. There he again met stiff resistance to his requests for more

---

ting, in late 1757, two Cherokee men and two Cherokee women were killed near the Saluda and Edisto Rivers in South Carolina, an area of recent British settlement. Those killings, not dealt with by the British, provoked a retaliation in March—two South Carolinians were killed and scalped by townspeople of the original Cherokee victims. The location of the killings on land recently taken by South Carolina suggests that the contest for land was not absent as a factor in British-Cherokee friction. The other setting for killings was the path between central Pennsylvania, where British and Cherokee forces were massing for an assault on Fort Duquesne in 1758, and the Cherokee country. In May, Cherokees—disappointed at Britain's lack of generosity and its failure to live up to expectations—plundered the back settlements, drawing Virginian fire. In three engagements, at least nine Cherokees and one Virginian were killed. This setting suggests the importance of the controversy over presents.

45. Lyttelton to the Lower and Middle Cherokee Headmen and Warriors, Sept. 26, 1758, *DRIA,* II, 481. For examples of Southeastern Indian acceptance of such compensation to avoid war, see Reid, *A Law of Blood,* 171–172.

goods. In two letters, British General John Forbes pointedly called him an inferior—"as consummate a Dog," "as great a Rascal to the full as any of his companions"—and he thought his demands for goods "extravagant." He even wondered whether Cherokees were men. Joking with his superiors, he described the woods between his camp and the enemy as "impenetrable almost to anything human, save the Indians, if they be allowed the appellation." However much he might need their skills, he resented them for outperforming British patrols, for rendering ambiguous his claim to superiority.[46]

Three Cherokees, returning from a perilous reconnaissance of Fort Duquesne, also had ambiguities to sort out. They carried both enemy women's scalps and the valuable information that the French post at the Forks of the Ohio was undermanned and practically defenseless. They duly reported all this to George Washington at Fort Cumberland—in spite of being fired on by a party from the garrison. As if to underscore Cherokee abilities, Washington noted that the bumbling soldiers not only had shot at friends, fortunately without result, but had been unable to learn anything of the enemy.[47]

In the fall of 1758, as Forbes's army moved toward Fort Duquesne, a disillusioned Attakullakulla and his warriors decided to return to the nation, abandoning the campaign. Forbes, seeing danger in the party's departure, dispatched expresses to the surrounding British posts to have Attakullakulla and his followers arrested and disarmed. After suffering that indignity, Attakullakulla, on his release, went to Williamsburg to work for peace. Some of his alienated followers, meanwhile, returned to Chote, capital town of the Overhills Cherokees.[48]

Presbyterian missionary William Richardson was there when they arrived. Conocorte, still an ally of Britain, had refused to allow him to preach. Richardson noted in his diary that Forbes's actions against Attakullakulla's party, in addition to the murder of an Overhills Cherokee by an Anglo-American, had

---

46. For Attakullakulla's promise, see Turner to Lyttelton, July 2, 1758, *DRIA*, II, 472. For Forbes's denunciations, see Forbes to General James Abercromby, Raystown, Oct. 16, 1758, Abercromby MSS; Forbes to Peters, Raystown Camp, Oct. 16, 1758, in Alfred Proctor James, *Writings of General John Forbes Relating to His Service in North America* (Menasha, Wis., 1938), 235 (the *Oxford English Dictionary* defines a "rascal" as, among other things, "a man of low birth or station"); Forbes to Pitt, July 10, 1758, CO5/50, fol. 418.

47. Washington to Bouquet, Aug. 19, 1758, BM Add. MSS, 21641, fol. 46.

48. John Richard Alden, *John Stuart and the Southern Colonial Frontier: A Study of Indian Relations, War, Trade, and Land Problems in the Southern Wilderness, 1754–1775* (London, 1944), 79; Corkran, *Cherokee Frontier*, 160–161, 164–165; Jones, *Writings of General Forbes*, 256–257.

fanned a fiery anger in the town. Conocorte "got into a great passion" when he discussed Forbes's disarming of the warriors. The old leader visited conjurers, probably those of the returning war parties, who told him of "very cross Talk in Virginia." The conjurers were preparing "a Physick [which] they say will drive away all their Disorders."[49]

The disorders came fast in the annus mirabilis of the first British empire, 1759. As the British brought Indians to a truce and pushed French troops out of the Upper Ohio, New York, Cape Breton, and much of Quebec, parties of Cherokees began to strike the British colonies. Warriors from the Overhills town of Settico attacked the North Carolina frontier in April, killing at least nineteen people. Warriors from Lower Town Estato killed three Carolinians on the Pacolet River in July. Later that month, the Lower Towns of Toxaway and Conasatchee joined Estato and Settico in sending warriors against the Carolinas, killing more people on the Broad and Pacolet Rivers. In August, Setticoes killed a packhorseman near Overhills Great Tellico and a soldier within a rifle shot of Fort Loudoun. Someone also killed a trader. That month South Carolina embargoed the Cherokee trade and prepared to raise an army.[50]

Although these killings contributed to the outbreak of the Cherokee War, it is important to recognize that they did not make war inevitable. First, the killings were not reflexive: Cherokees had waited half a year before retaliating for their kinsmen's deaths at settlers' hands. Second, even after Cherokee raids South Carolina delayed *its* response, and a tense peace held for several months. It was not a matter of Cherokee leaders' being unable to restrain their warriors from exacting a vengeance mechanistically demanded by customary law. It was rather a matter of each side understanding the other's position, but disputing, challenging, and opposing it. The negotiations over the period—which involved much more than talks—reveal that the search for a just solution involved, for each people, a contest with the other to impose its own version of the structure of their relationship. The Cherokees, understanding (and rejecting) British pretensions to superiority, wanted from the British a flowing of goods in exchange for their warriors' sacrifices. They sought to maintain their political autonomy but within an alliance founded on the rhetoric of brotherly concern. The British, recognizing (and resisting) Cherokee claims to independence, sought to turn Cherokee economic dependence into political dependence. The British colonies, particularly South Carolina, wanted clear authority, even mastery; and they wanted their Cherokee dependents to admit that

49. Samuel C. Williams, "An Account of the Presbyterian Mission to the Cherokee, 1757–1759," *Tennessee Historical Magazine*, 2d Ser., I (1930–1931), 134–135.

50. Corkran, *Cherokee Frontier*, 168, 171, 173–175.

this was for the best—even to be grateful for it. Neither side could accept the other's all-too-clear definition of the partnership. Each called the other "brother," but the word—far from being filled with a variety of interpretations, the kinds of expedient misunderstandings that characterized the pays d'en haut—became instead a thin and hollow reed on which to prop the alliance.[51]

The alliance remained the ideal of important Cherokee headmen. In October, a delegation headed by Oconostota, the Great Warrior of the Overhills town of Chote, arrived in Charleston with gifts to give and with a clear purpose: "I am come hither to strive and do the best I can to make up all matters, I love all the white people and my thoughts are to see goods and things as usual in the nation." And with that, his men placed a pile of deerskins at the governor's feet. Lyttelton, in a knowing violation of etiquette, accepted the gifts while rejecting the commitment they implied: "I do not receive them as a Token of my agreeing to the Peace you propose."[52]

Since presents alone proved incapable of healing the wound, the Cherokee visitors also mooted a daring peace plan based on a reinterpretation of Cherokee traditions. They proposed to extend an internal method of settling homicides to cover this intercultural affair. The internal method Reid has called a "subtle legal doctrine, . . . the rule that a man who went to war should be exonerated for his faults." The headmen proposed that each Indian suspect "should be sent in Quest of a French Scalp or Prisoner for every white Man he had killed; that they looked upon this running the Risque of their Lives as sufficient Retaliation." Normally this form of satisfaction would have operated only within the nation, but the Cherokees were willing to extend their love to the Carolinians if the Carolinians would accept the plan. Lyttelton refused— he could not accept a Cherokee embrace on Cherokee terms, which would have undermined his authority, an authority that required him to protect the king's subjects and to punish those guilty of abusing them. So he took the delegates hostage and marched them under the guard of an army of more than twelve hundred troops to Fort Prince George, on the southeastern flank of the lower Cherokee villages. There Cherokee leaders earnestly attempted to negotiate, but Lyttelton would accept only submission to his demands.[53]

51. Contrast with Reid, "A Perilous Rule," in King, ed., *Cherokee Nation,* 43–44; Reid, *A Law of Blood,* 66.

52. On the desire for peace, see Warriors of Estatoe to Lyttelton, Mar. 20, 1758, and Lachlan Mackintosh to Lyttelton, Fort Prince George, Mar. 21, 1758, *DRIA,* II, 449–450, 451. For Lyttelton's violation, see S.C. Council, Minutes, Oct. 19, 1759, CO5/474, fol. 20b.

53. For the Cherokee proposal, see *South-Carolina Gazette,* supplement, Nov. 17–24, 1759, in Charleston Library Society, *South Carolina Newspapers, 1732–1782* (Charleston, S.C., 1956),

The Cherokees would have to yield up for execution twenty-four "Murderers" of British subjects. In the meantime, the Cherokee delegates would be held in Fort Prince George. Cherokees went so far as to yield up two killers. They managed to persuade Lyttelton to keep only twenty-two others hostage until the Cherokees filled Lyttelton's blood demand. As a strong token of a desire for peace, one Cherokee leader, Round O, voluntarily joined the hostages. Then outbreaks of smallpox and measles alarmed the troops. Before coming to a genuine resolution with the Cherokees, Lyttelton departed with the main body for Charleston, leaving a contingent at the disease-ridden fort to guard the Cherokee prisoners.[54]

It was the end of the misalliance. Ordinary Cherokees rejected their leaders' submission to Britons who clearly despised them. Within two weeks of Lyttelton's departure, open war erupted as Lower Settlement Cherokees killed ten English traders, and Middle Settlement Cherokees pounded the South Carolina borderlands, killing scores of people and sending hundreds fleeing toward the coastline. In February 1760, Attakullakulla stood before Fort Prince George to make a last futile request for the release of those hostages who had not died of smallpox. After the refusal, the garrison learned from a trader that Britain's best allies in the Overhills region would now "join with the Rest having been denied their Hostages." No longer able to find room to adjust to the demands of imperial power, the Cherokees stood united in war against the British.[55]

The issue between the peoples was not one of two alien legal systems unable to understand or adjust to the other. Cherokees, Britons, and colonists had the wherewithal to comprehend one another's demands, even as they viewed one another with caution and a sense of danger. Young Washington had put his finger on the difficulty in July 1758: "The malbehavior," as he saw it, "of our Indians gives me great concern." He wished they were "more hearty in our interest," because he knew that the best of his Virginians were not "equal to them

---

microfilm, reel 4; Corkran, *Cherokee Frontier,* 178–179; Reid, "A Perilous Rule," in King, ed., *Cherokee Nation,* 42–43. For Lyttelton's march, see *South-Carolina Gazette,* Feb. 2–9, 1760, in Charleston Library Society, *South Carolina Newspapers;* Corkran, *Cherokee Frontier,* 181–190.

54. Though Lyttelton used the term "murderers," he had no interest in actually identifying guilty individuals. His number 24 was retributive; it derived from the number of colonial victims of Cherokee violence since the previous year, not from the number of killers. See Lyttelton to Jeffery Amherst, Dec. 27, 1759, WO34/35, fol. 136; Lyttelton to Pitt, Fort Prince George, Dec. 29, 1759, CO5/19, fol. 198; Hatley, *The Dividing Paths,* 124; Corkran, *Cherokee Frontier,* 178–190.

55. Miln to Lyttelton, Feb. 24, 1760, *DRIA,* II, 499.

in the woods." This troubled him because he considered them to be his equal nowhere else, and their skills made them "too sensible of their high importance to us." Exactly how they could have been made to be more "hearty" in the British "interest" he did not say, but in his society, as in England, dependence justly bred subservience and patronage demanded loyalty and gratitude. Illuminating the issues of feeling and rank, Washington's judgment of the difficulty was better than that of Captain Trent or General Forbes, who wished that a clear contract had been made with the Cherokees from the start. For it was not simply the inadequacy of the presents that infuriated the Cherokees; it was the meaning that the British attached to them, a meaning the Cherokees read accurately. The issue between Cherokees and Britons resulted, not from misunderstanding, even over presents, but from tensions that were generated by each party's fairly accurate appraisal of the other's desires. To the British and to the colonial elite, whose concepts of status bore an increasingly racial tinge, Cherokee friendship should have meant a willful, even grateful subordination to British power and wealth: a "hearty" recognition of Cherokee interest in an empire of goods. The British understood Cherokee demands for gifts and claims to respect but took them as both marks of Cherokee dependence and examples of haughty insubordination. The *South-Carolina Gazette* summed up Great Britain's cause against the Cherokees in verse:

> We'll teach the treach'rous Indians how
> With due Humility to bow;
> Their savage Hearts we will subdue
> And make them to our King more true
>
> .    .    .    .    .    .    .    .
>
> Our Fathers often us have told
> How we for Trinkets have been sold.

As long as Cherokee "malbehavior" exhibited a questionable relation to British authority, Cherokee loyalties remained suspect. To the Cherokees, British claims to leadership were convincing only so long as the British behaved as leaders should, with care and generosity. As Cherokees learned what subordination meant to the British, as they came to understand Britain better, they rejected the assigned role, asserted their partnership in an alliance, and demanded that the British admit their worth, their "high importance." [56]

56. *South-Carolina Gazette*, Nov. 1–3, 1759, in Charleston Library Society, *South Carolina Newspapers;* Washington to Bouquet, Fort Cumberland, July 16, 1758, BM Add. MSS, 21641, fol. 13. Trent's idea is reported in Forbes to Bouquet, Philadelphia, June 10, 1758, BM Add. MSS, 21640, fol. 59. The phrase "empire of goods" is T. H. Breen's; see "An Empire of Goods:

Never during the colonial period did British or British-colonial officers establish an alliance in North America closely resembling the French alliance with the Indians of the Great Lakes. The British proved unable to establish close military cooperation with a network of numerous, largely independent peoples, as the French had been able to do with the Ottawas, Ojibwas, Potawatomis, and others. The best British opportunity to do so was in the South, and the linchpin of the alliance they hoped to establish there was the Cherokee nation—as they commonly termed it. Cherokees had had a long history of close relations with South Carolina. In the Seven Years' War, their martial alliance bore promise; at one time in 1758 they fielded some 450–700 warriors for Britain. Not even the Mohawks in friendship with Sir William Johnson could match that record before 1759, when British victory was imminent. Yet the Cherokee relationship with British colonists, officials, and soldiers proved to be a misalliance. Cherokees and Britons had not grown close enough to fabricate institutions and symbols that could command real loyalty. Leaders on both sides not only failed to prevent outbreaks of violence and to mediate successfully the violence when it came; they failed to agree on a relationship that each could wish to protect against internal disorder as well as external threat. In short, they had no shared order to defend.[57]

As Cherokees and Britons came better to understand one another's sense of the relationship, they concluded that they could not work together. They could establish no middle ground, no area in which misunderstandings led to agreement. Claims to obligation, reciprocity, and mutuality failed to take firm root. Wars, writes Claude Lévi-Strauss, "are the result of unsuccessful transactions." In 1759, as the British military tasted victory over France and felt little need for troublesome Cherokee warriors, transactions between Cherokees and Britons had not a prayer of success.[58]

---

The Anglicization of Colonial America, 1690–1776," *Journal of British Studies*, XXV (1986), 467–499.

57. For Cherokee numbers, see Corkran, *Cherokee Frontier*, 148; Jacobs, *Wilderness Politics*, 168. Lyttelton put the numbers even higher: between 660 to 760 warriors going either against the enemy or to join British forces. See Lyttelton to Abercromby, May 16, 1758, Abercromby MSS. Six Nations numbers would not exceed these until 1759; see Jacobs, *Wilderness Politics*, 179. Ian K. Steele, *Warpaths: Invasions of North America* (New York, 1994), puts the number of Six Nations warriors on the British side in the 1755 campaign (the largest number before 1759) at 300 (191). Forbes thought that in May 1758 he had with him some 700 Cherokees, who constituted "the greatest body of Indians that we have ever had join us"; see Forbes to Pitt, May 19, 1758, CO5/50, fol. 412.

58. Lévi-Strauss, *Elementary Structures of Kinship*, 56.

# "Domestick . . . Quiet being broke"

## Gender Conflict among Creek Indians
## in the Eighteenth Century

One day in July 1813, when the Creek Indians of Alabama and western Georgia were in the midst of a violent civil conflict called the Redstick War, a number of warriors fell on Ockfuskee, a Creek town on the Tallapoosa River, some fifty miles above present-day Montgomery, Alabama. There, in addition to killing five chiefs and destroying nearly all of the livestock, they attacked a white resident named Mrs. Grayson, who had been invited by the chiefs to teach the town's women how to spin and weave. The Redsticks, as the dissident Creeks called themselves, slaughtered her cattle and hogs and destroyed her stock of cotton, her loom, and a bolt of cloth. Finally, they turned to Mrs. Grayson herself, stripping her of clothes and leaving the woman with nothing but a shift and petticoat.[1]

Seemingly a conflict between religious nativists and accommodationists, the Redstick War mirrored contemporary native American movements in which Indians tried to purge themselves of European corruptions. In Ockfuskee, the Redsticks thus murdered accommodationist chiefs, slaughtered livestock (which had been introduced by colonists), destroyed looms, and humiliated an American settler. The Redstick War, however, marks the convergence of several different long-running and deep fault lines in Creek society, and the simple division between backward-looking nativists and forward-looking accommodationists obscures as much as it clarifies these fractures. The attack on Mrs. Grayson targeted an agent of what reformers called civilization, but it also undeniably targeted a woman. By stripping Grayson of her clothing and destroying her belongings, Creeks intended to make a statement about how women should behave. In this way, the attack marks a deep fracture in Creek

1. Benjamin Hawkins to John Armstrong, July 28, 1813, in C. L. Grant, ed., *Letters, Journals, and Writings of Benjamin Hawkins*, 2 vols. (Savannah, Ga., 1980), II, 651 (hereafter cited as *LBH*).

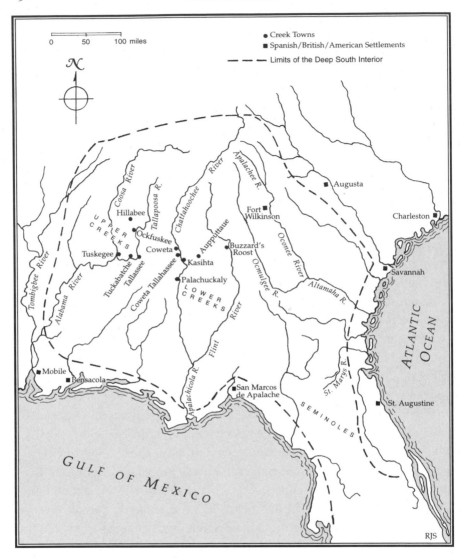

FIGURE 1
The Deep South Interior, circa 1800.
*Drawn by Richard Stinely*

society formed by the stress of redefining gender roles during a century of dramatic change. The formation of this fault line fundamentally shaped Creek history in the second half of the eighteenth century.[2]

2. For a general portrait of the conflict between nativists and accommodationists, see Gregory Evans Dowd, *A Spirited Resistance: The North American Struggle for Unity, 1745–*

Historians have long recognized that colonialism significantly altered relationships between Indian women and men. Generally, the story has been one of decline; capitalism and patriarchy overcame native societies once characterized by gender equality, and, in the end, women became subordinated like their European counterparts. Since the 1990s, however, historians have begun uncovering ways in which women in some native groups actively participated in and took advantage of the economic and social changes wrought by colonization. Eighteenth-century Creek Indians in the Deep South Interior (defined here roughly as the present-day states of Alabama, Georgia, and Florida) are part of this more complex story. Creeks fought each other and white reformers to shape to their satisfaction the rapidly changing gender roles. The story of this struggle is less one of decline than it is a multilayered, shifting narrative of tension and conflict.[3]

The Creek struggle to redefine gender roles opened in the early eighteenth century, when warfare, spurred by the imperial rivalries of France, Spain, and Britain, promoted the power of warriors at the expense of women. By midcentury, the deerskin trade had further aggravated the tensions between women and men. When a particularly abrupt economic shift hit the Creeks after the American Revolution, Creek women used the new market to become once again providers to Creek households. At the same time, as hunting became less tenable and as United States agents circumscribed warfare, Creek men tried to redefine their masculinity in the new economic order. Some joined a new class of wealthy Creek merchants and planters who participated actively in the markets of towns such as Mobile, Pensacola, and Augusta, but many others rejected this pursuit or, just as often, were shut out of it. The mounting stress of these changes ultimately found release in the Redstick War. The warriors who attacked Mrs. Grayson, then, acted not only as nativists but also as men. When they destroyed her loom and livestock and stripped her of clothes, they did so in the context of a century-long struggle to redefine gender roles.

---

*1815* (Baltimore, 1992). Joel W. Martin, *Sacred Revolt: The Muskogees' Struggle for a New World* (Boston, 1991), provides a more detailed look at the religious side of the Redstick War. For a treatment of the Redstick War that breaks down the dichotomy between nativism and accommodationism, see Claudio Saunt, "A New Order of Things: Creeks and Seminoles in the Deep South Interior, 1733–1816" (Ph.D. diss., Duke University, 1996), chap. 11.

3. For an excellent critique of the historiography on native American women, see Nancy Shoemaker, "Kateri Tekakwitha's Tortuous Path to Sainthood," in Shoemaker, ed., *Negotiators of Change: Historical Perspectives on Native American Women* (New York, 1995), 50–52.

## The Opposing Identities of Women and Men

Throughout the eighteenth century, Creek women and men struggled to come to terms with the gendered changes wrought by colonization. In the early and mid-1700s, the imperial struggles between France, Spain, and Britain promoted the power of Creek warriors. Warfare was nearly constant in the Southeast until 1763, when the Peace of Paris finally placed Britain in a dominant position in the eastern half of North America. Before then, Creek warriors had profited immensely, collecting gifts and payments offered by the colonial powers to ensure their allegiance and accumulating war honors in the many battles they fought. The rising fortunes of Creek men encouraged and reinforced the relationship between masculinity and warfare, but such an association, which set the identities of men and women in direct opposition, had long been a central component of Creek culture. A Creek creation story, first recorded in 1735, for example, makes the polarity of men and women a central element of the world.[4]

This polarity led most Southeastern Indians to equate defeat with feminization, thus confirming the expectations and prejudices of European men. Bernard Romans, who worked as an engineer and surveyor for the British in Florida in the late 1760s and early 1770s, noted of the Creeks, "No greater disgrace can be thrown on a man than calling him by the odious epithet of Woman." The neighboring Chickasaws, he wrote, "are horridly given to sodomy, committing that crime on the dead bodies of their enemies, thereby (as they say) degrading them into women." Romans had perhaps mistaken a figurative expression for a literal statement, but his comment about sodomizing the enemy appears to have a metaphorical truth. The Chickasaws and the Creeks both symbolically forced their enemies to become women. In 1773, in a tense meeting with the Cherokees in Augusta, for example, Creek leaders berated their former enemies for ceding Creek land by calling them "old women, and saying they had long ago obliged them to wear the petticoat." The naturalist William Bartram, who observed the proceedings, noted that the insult was a "most humiliating and degrading stroke." Though the Cherokees had long been traditional Creek enemies, and thus regular targets of Creek hostility, Creek warriors might have also been referring to the status of Cherokee women, who wielded a substantial amount of power. In his history of the American Indians, trader James Adair summed up the difference between Cherokee

4. Saunt, "A New Order of Things," chap. 1; Amelia Bell Walker, "The Kasihta Myth," *Anthropology Tomorrow*, XII (1979), 46–63.

and Creek women by contrasting the "petticoat-government" of the Cherokees with the "patriarchal-like" government of the Creeks.[5]

Masculinity was of such importance in times of war that Creek men avoided
touching women, perhaps because they feared compromising their "madness,"
the term Creeks used to describe the asocial yet brave actions of their warriors.
In the Green Corn Ceremony, the annual ritual of renewal, men again refrained
from touching women or even speaking to them for fear of their effect. Similarly, in the period before menstruation and surrounding childbirth, women
withdrew from the rest of the town, but especially from men, who were believed to be particularly susceptible to the effects of menstruating or pregnant
women. This segregation may reflect less men's fear of contamination than
their respect for female power as manifested in menstruation and childbirth.
In fact, in Koasati and Alabama, two Muskogee or Creek languages, the word
for menstruation, "hóllo," was associated with dangerous magic and spiritual
power. Such associations and fears point to the opposing identities of men and
women.[6]

5. Bernard Romans, *A Concise Natural History of East and West Florida . . .* , I (New York,
1775), 41, 70; William Bartram, *Travels of William Bartram* (1791), ed. Mark Van Doren (New
York, 1928), 382; James Adair, *Adair's History of the American Indians* (1775), ed. Samuel Cole
Williams (Johnson, Tenn., 1930), 153. For a direct comparison of the status of women in
Cherokee and Creek societies in the late eighteenth and early nineteenth centuries, see
Richard A. Sattler, "Women's Status among the Muskogee and Cherokee," in Laura F. Klein
and Lillian A. Ackerman, eds., *Women and Power in Native North America* (Norman, Okla.,
1995), 214–229.

6. Adair, *Adair's History,* ed. Williams, 115, 129–130, 171–172; Caleb Swan, "Position and
State of Manners and Arts in the Creek, or Muscogee Nation in 1791," in Henry Rowe
Schoolcraft, ed., *Information respecting the History, Condition, and Prospects of the Indian
Tribes of the United States,* V (1855; reprint, New York, 1969), 272; "A Historical Narration of
the Genealogy, Traditions, and Downfall of the Ispocoga or Creek Tribe of Indians, Written
by One of the Tribe," original in the Draper Manuscripts, State Historical Society of Wis-
consin, microfilm copy (reel 146I), P. K. Yonge Library of Florida History, University of
Florida, Gainesville (hereafter cited as PKY); John R. Swanton, *Social Organization and
Social Usages of the Indians of the Creek Confederacy,* Smithsonian Institution, Bureau of
American Ethnology, Forty-second Annual Report of the U.S. Bureau of American Ethnol-
ogy (Washington, D.C., 1928), 358–361; Amelia Rector Bell, "Separate People: Speaking of
Creek Men and Women," *American Anthropologist,* XCII (1990), 332–346; Martha Harroun
Foster, "Of Baggage and Bondage: Gender and Status among Hidatsa and Crow Women,"
*American Indian Culture and Research Journal,* XVII (1993), 142; Mona Etienne and Eleanor
Leacock, eds., *Women and Colonization: Anthropological Perspectives* (New York, 1980), 4.

Just as Creek men avoided contact with menstruating women, women actively distanced themselves from the violent masculinity of men. Karl Kroeber, a scholar of American Indian literatures, suggests that one Creek tale about greed and violence, traditionally recounted by women, has an element of "feminine ridicule of masculinity." Women perhaps used such ridicule to control warriors, whose rash behavior often endangered entire communities. As the heads of matrilocal households, they had a special interest in protecting their communities, an interest that often clashed with the desires of warriors to prove themselves in battle. In 1757, for instance, South Carolina agent Daniel Pepper refused to relay the assembly's decision to grant rewards for the scalps of Frenchmen or their Indian allies because he had learned from a Creek leader that "such a Thing might breed a good Deal of Disturbance in the Nation, particularly with the Women, who would alledge that I forced them by such Encouragement to a War." The opposition of Creek women to such destructive behavior may explain why they often interposed when Creek men threatened to kill traders or other whites in the Deep South Interior. According to one Creek, in the 1740s when warriors were raiding Spanish and Indian settlements in Florida and returning with scalps "the wise Indians and the women" berated them for killing people "who give us food, clothes, and munitions for free when we go to see them."[7]

The extreme opposition of Creek men and women even manifested itself in the very language they spoke. Creek men accented different syllables and attached distinct endings to verbs. Men, for example, said "okíkas" ("he was"), whereas women expressed the same phrase with the word "okikâ." Boys perhaps picked up this speech difference when they learned the masculine pursuits of hunting and warfare from their uncles, though their mothers might

---

7. Karl Kroeber, "An Introduction to the Art of Traditional American Indian Narration," in Kroeber, ed., *Traditional Literatures of the American Indian: Texts and Interpretations* (Lincoln, Nebr., 1981), 9–13, 23 n. 6; Daniel Pepper to Governor William Henry Lyttelton, Apr. 7, 1757, in William L. McDowell, Jr., ed., *Documents Relating to Indian Affairs,* [I], *May 21, 1750–August 7, 1754* (Columbia, S.C., 1958), [II], *1754–1765* (Columbia, S.C., 1970), Colonial Records of South Carolina (hereafter cited as *DRIA,* I, II), II, 363–365; *A Journal of the Proceedings and Minutes of the Governor and Council of His Majesty's Province of Georgia,* May 26, 1760, in Allen D. Candler et al, eds., *The Colonial Records of the State of Georgia,* 26 vols. (Atlanta, 1904–1916), VIII, 314–317 (hereafter cited as *CRG*); *South-Carolina Gazette* (hereafter cited as *SCG*), May 31, 1760, Mar. 7, 14, 1761; Seymour Feiler, ed. and trans., *Jean-Bernard Bossu's Travels in the Interior of North America, 1751–1762* (Norman, Okla., 1962), 139; Governor of Florida to the King, Feb. 17, 1745, Stetson Collection (hereafter cited as *ST*), bundle 6151, 58-2-13/17, Santo Domingo 862, PKY.

have also participated in its teaching. In the first grammar of the Creek language, published in 1860, the author, Baptist missionary H. F. Buckner, concluded that the "old custom of having one dialect for the men, and another for the women" resulted from "the oppression of the females." Separate gender spheres, according to Buckner, led "to the formation of a dialect peculiar to the women; so that it was regarded indelicate and unwomanly for a female to speak to men in the language of men." Buckner, writing with an obvious Christian bias, failed to consider whether the separate gender spheres were emblematic of women's power rather than weakness, but his observations do suggest that language reflected the opposing identities of women and men.[8]

## The Deerskin Trade and Rising Tensions between Women and Men

In the 1760s, changes in the structure of the deerskin trade further polarized relations between Creek women and men. Before that time, Creeks by necessity had shared the additional labor of the widened deerskin trade. Men had expanded their subsistence hunting to produce excess skins, and women had dressed the skins for export. Beginning in the 1760s, however, the demand for raw deerskins increased significantly in European markets, and young Creek men found that this change, which eliminated the need for women's labor in the preparation of the hides, allowed them to turn the trade into an exclusively masculine pursuit, as separate from women as the distinct dialect they spoke. Free from the direction of women, who had channeled its products into their sphere of the matrilineal and matrilocal household, the deerskin trade rapidly became the province of young and relatively independent men. By the 1780s, the trade was exclusively in raw skins owing to the mutually reinforcing influence of European demand and Creek supply.[9]

On the Creek side of the exchange, men rather than women were the forces of change. Years of warfare, encouraged by European powers, eventually proved debilitating, and young men consequently turned to the deerskin trade to establish and express their masculinity. Because British colonial authorities initially discouraged the purchase of raw skins, this trade originated in the

8. Mary Haas, "Men's and Women's Speech in Koasati," *Language*, XX (1944), 146; Geoffrey Kimball to the Author, Oct. 24, 1996; Henry Frieland Buckner, *A Grammar of the Maskwke, or Creek Language* (Marion, Ala., 1860), 9–10.

9. Kathyrn E. Holland Braund, *Deerskins and Duffels: The Creek Indian Trade with Anglo-America, 1685–1815* (Lincoln, Nebr., 1993), 68–69; Robin F. A. Fabel, *The Economy of British West Florida, 1763–1783* (Tuscaloosa, Ala., 1988), 56; William Panton, June 2, 1787, Papeles Procedentes de Cuba (hereafter cited as PC), legajo 200, 914, reel 277, PKY.

woods between unlicensed traders and hunters who accepted lower prices for their skins in order to purchase rum. These Creeks—young, unmarried men who, as Romans noted, little associated with women—looked to consume the profits of their trade immediately. In 1755, for example, a trader named Williams was accused of illegally trading rum for undressed skins in the woods at a place called Honey Mountain. A year later, Creek leaders asked Governor William Henry Lyttelton of South Carolina to "stop all Out Stores, and lett none of your People at Augusta or any where else trade with our People below for it keeps our young People from coming home and their buying Goods cheaper below makes them often quarrel with the White People in the Nation, besides they often get drunk below which makes them fight and sometimes kill one another." Continued protests by Creek leaders indicate that the problem only worsened. At treaty negotiations in 1763, one Creek chief asked the governors on hand "not to suffer any people to trade in the woods, because the young people there got drunk, and disposed of their skins for that commodity." In spring 1768, Creek warriors, supported by British Indian agent John Stuart, broke up one such site of exchange at Buzzard's Roost on the Flint River, where traders had established stores to intercept young Creek men returning from the hunt. By 1772, despite the efforts of Creek leaders and colonial officials, raw skins were becoming the dominant form of exchange.[10]

The preponderance of rum in the deerskin trade—in the late 1760s, about 80 percent of skins brought into Mobile were traded for sugarcane liquor—reflects the desire of young men to prove themselves. In the eighteenth century, Creeks appear to have associated drunkenness with madness, the quality of bravery and recklessness that warriors sought, and rum was consequently consumed in greater quantities by men than women. A Muskogee-English dic-

10. Saunt, "A New Order of Things," 88–91; Thomas Hatley, "The Three Lives of Keowee: Loss and Recovery in Eighteenth-Century Cherokee Villages," in Peter H. Wood, Gregory A. Waselkov, and M. Thomas Hatley, eds., *Powhatan's Mantle: Indians in the Colonial Southeast* (Lincoln, Nebr., 1989), 235–239; James Beamer to Governor Glen, Feb. 21, 1756, *DRIA*, II, 104–106; *SCG*, Mar. 7, 1761; John Richard Alden, *John Stuart and the Southern Colonial Frontier: A Study of Indian Relations, War, Trade, and Land Problems in the Southern Wilderness, 1754–1775* (London, 1944), 296; Headmen of the Lower Creeks to Lyttelton, Oct. 1756, *DRIA*, II, 212–213; *Journal of the Congress of the Four Southern Governors . . . with the Five Nations of Indians, at Augusta, 1763* (Charlestown, S.C., 1764), 27; Emistesigo to James Wright, Sept. 5, 1768, *CRG*, X, 580–582; John Stuart to Thomas Gage, July 2, 1768, and enclosures, and A Talk from the Lower Creeks to John Stuart, Sept. 19, 1772, enclosed in Stuart to Gage, Nov. 24, 1772, both in Thomas Gage Papers, American Series, reel 140H, PKY; Fabel, *Economy of British West Florida*, 56.

tionary from the late nineteenth century glosses the Creek term "hache" as "drunk, crazy, resolute, daring," a word etymologically related to "hadjo," as in the warrior titles Efau Hadjo, meaning "mad dog" or "drunken dog," and Itcho Hadjo Tassikaya, meaning "mad deer warrior" or, translated another way, "foolish, mad, drunken deer warrior." In 1752, South Carolina agent Thomas Bosomworth heard Old Bracket, a leader of Tuckabatche, tell the young men of that town that "at Best they were all a Parcell of Madman, that when they were drunk they were all Men and Warriors, and thought they shewed their Manhood in insulting, abusing, and threatning to kill the white People, upon the Continuance of whose Friendship the Welfare of them all depended." More than a half-century later, in 1811, one Creek warrior who faced imminent execution would state, "I do not fear death, for I am drunk to numb my feeling if they kill me." The consumption of alcohol not only facilitated the reckless and brave behavior expected of young men, but its acquisition in the deerskin trade also distanced them from the more household-oriented and thus feminine trade in clothing.[11]

The attitude of Creeks toward drunken behavior further suggests that they associated inebriation and madness. Like the mad, asocial behavior of warriors, drunkenness might have been for the Creeks an accepted mood that a warrior ritually entered and exited. In war, Creek men went through a ceremonial transition, donning black and red paint to symbolize their entry into the world of asocial behavior. On their return, they participated in another ceremony to mark their reentry into the social world of the square ground. This transformation allowed Creek men to scalp and mutilate their enemies yet return home as peaceful, social members of their clan and town. Creeks believed alcohol had similar transformative properties. In his report of 1755 on the state of Brit-

11. Alden, *John Stuart*, 315–316; Braund, *Deerskins and Duffels*, 105–106; Peter C. Mancall, "'The Bewitching Tyranny of Custom': The Social Costs of Indian Drinking in Colonial America," *American Indian Culture and Research Journal*, XVII (1993), 28; R. M. Loughridge and David M. Hodge, *English and Muskokee Dictionary: Collected from Various Sources and Revised* (1890; reprint, Okmulgee, Okla., 1964), 140–141; Albert Samuel Gatschet, *A Migration Legend of the Creek Indians, with a Linguistic, Historic, and Ethnographic Introduction*, I (Philadelphia, 1884–1888), Brinton's Library of Aboriginal American Literature, no. 4, 161; Second Journal of Thomas Bosomworth, October–December 1752, *DRIA*, I, 319; Carl Mauelshagen and Gerald H. Davis, eds., *Partners in the Lord's Work: The Diary of Two Moravian Missionaries in the Creek Indian Country, 1807–1813* (Atlanta, 1969), 55. Other native Americans shared similar views with the Creeks about drunkenness. See Peter C. Mancall, *Deadly Medicine: Indians and Alcohol in Early America* (Ithaca, N.Y., 1995), 68–70, 75; Mancall, "'The Bewitching Tyranny of Custom,'" *American Indian Culture and Research Journal*, XVII (1993), 20, 29.

ish relations with Southern Indians, British agent Edmond Atkin wrote: "Their Reason or Will having no share therein, they have no Conception that they are culpable so far as to deserve to suffer for any mischief or outrage committed by them while in that Condition. If complained of, or upbraided for it, they say with great Composure, 'that they are sorry for what hath happened, But that it was not they that did it, 'twas Rum did it.'" By the 1830s, when one longtime Alabama resident noted that both men and women were abusing alcohol, the willingness of Creeks to excuse violent, drunken behavior might have been a result of the earlier association between drunkenness and madness:

> Chiefs common men and women will wallow in filth and mire so long as they can raise the means to purchase spirits to drink during such time of frenzy they will fight each other indiscriminately frequently takeing each others lives, and when such fracus is over they attribute the whole scene to the spirits they have drank, very truly saying it was not them but the liquor what was in them that fought, well knowing and meaning their peaceable disposition toward each other when in their natural state of sobriety.

Like the mad warrior who returned home in peace, a drunk behaved violently, only to return to a "peaceable disposition." [12]

Women voiced their opposition to the consumption of rum both to limit the wanton behavior of warriors and to discourage men from consuming the profits of the deerskin trade. In 1755, Edmond Atkin wrote that as soon as hunting season ends, rum traders "place themselves near the Towns, in the way of the Hunters returning home with their deer Skins." He continued: "The poor Indians in a manner fascinated, are unable to resist the Bait; and when Drunk are easily cheated. After parting with the fruit of three or four Months Toil, they find themselves at home, without the means of buying the necessary Clothing for themselves or their Families. Their Domestick and inward Quiet being broke, Reflection sours them, and disposes them for Mischief." Although Atkin suggested that reflection changed the minds of some warriors, his description of "Domestick" disquiet indicates that women played an im-

12. Benjamin Hawkins, "A Sketch of the Creek Country in the Years 1798 and 1799," *LBH*, I, 324–325; Swanton, *Social Organization*, 436. One trader among the Cherokees reported in the *South-Carolina Gazette* that "it was usual for the Cherokee warriors when they had done michief, to take some kind of drug to ease their minds after it." The use of such drugs by Southeastern Indians further delineated the social from the asocial world. See *SCG*, Feb. 2, 1760; Wilbur R. Jacobs, ed., *The Appalachian Indian Frontier: The Edmond Atkin Report and Plan of 1755* (1954; reprint, Lincoln, Nebr., 1967), 26; "Historical Narration of the Genealogy, Traditions, and Downfall of the Ispocoga," Draper MSS.

portant role in such conversions, especially when the madness of their men came at the expense of clothes and other essential items.[13]

The elimination of women from the deerskin trade made them dependent on men for many necessities. William Bartram noted from his observations in the 1770s that women "still amuse themselves in manufacturing some few things, as belts and coronets for their husbands, *feather cloaks,* moccasons, etc." But the naturalist seems aware that these "few things" manufactured by women, although still significant, were rapidly becoming less crucial to the domestic economy of the Creek Indians as the deerskin trade dramatically altered their way of life. Instead of garments created from deerskins, mulberry tree bark, and tree moss, Creek clothing was increasingly made of strouding, calico, osnaburg, and other European textiles. Men still used moccasins and occasionally leggings fashioned from deerskins, but most of their clothing now consisted of foreign materials. They dressed in breechcloths and leggings made of strouding, and they wore shirts and mantles fashioned from imported calico, decorated, like their breechcloths and leggings, with European gartering, beads, and bells. Women wore petticoats and, at times, calico waistcoats, also richly decorated, and in the winter they donned wool mantles. Duffel, a woolen cloth, replaced deerskins as blankets.[14]

Inventories showing large quantities of thread and needles remained common, reflecting the amount of labor women still invested in sewing clothes. When Charles McLatchy, a trader operating in Apalache, died in 1787, for example, he had on hand twenty-two hundred sewing needles and 291 pounds of thread. In addition, women continued to produce finger-woven garters and belts with elaborate bead decorations. But the labor involved in decorating clothes with beads, gartering, and bells represented less work—and less essential work—for women. Most shirts came ready-made, and breechcloths made of strouding were easier to fashion than those of deerskins, which demanded the laborious preparation of the hide. More important, all of these goods were

---

13. Jacobs, ed., *Appalachian Indian Frontier,* 35. Anthropologist Amelia Rector Bell suggests that today Creek women struggle to control the male anger and violence unleashed by alcohol. She ties the opposition of male anger and female control to deeply rooted cultural beliefs. See Bell, "Creek Ritual: The Path to Peace" (Ph.D. diss., University of Chicago, 1984), 84–85.

14. William Bartram, "Observations on the Creek and Cherokee Indians, 1789, with Prefatory and Supplementary Notes by E. G. Squier," American Ethnological Sociey, *Transactions,* III (New York, 1853), 29; Bartram, *Travels,* ed. Van Doren, 401; Dorothy Downs, "British Influences on Creek and Seminole Men's Clothing, 1733–1858," *Florida Anthropologist,* XXXIII, no. 2 (1980), 48, 51.

purchased by men through the deerskin trade. Women's labor was necessary to finish clothes with beads and gartering, but women themselves had no direct access to the materials. They depended on men.[15]

Women continued to find demand for their cane baskets and mats, but the destruction of canebrakes by growing numbers of hogs and cattle made the collection of this once common grass more difficult. Like their Cherokee counterparts, Creek women might have begun making vine baskets as replacements, though such containers are too fragile to store foods or other goods and can serve only decorative purposes. Creek women also made pots and other earthen and wooden vessels, but these, too, were partially replaced by European goods garnered in the deerskin trade. Though earthen and wooden containers remained in use in towns, Creek men carried the lighter and stronger brass and tin versions when they went hunting or warring. A Creek hunter who was murdered in 1790, for example, had with him forty skins, six new shirts, three calico hunting shirts, two rifles, three saddles and a bridle, five blankets, three kettles, and five pack saddles. Where he once would have depended on women's labor for all of these goods, the kettles, calico shirts, and undressed skins made him less reliant on his wife and female relatives.[16]

15. Luis de Bertucat to Arturo O'Neill, Oct. 14, 1787, PC, legajo 37, bundle 7, doc. 276-272, reel 169, PKY; Downs, "British Influences on Creek and Seminole Men's Clothing," *Florida Anthropologist*, XXXIII, no. 2 (1980), 60–62; Josephine Paterek, *Encyclopedia of American Indian Costume* (Santa Barbara, Calif., 1994), 36–37; Bartram, *Travels*, ed. Van Doren, 393–395; John R. Swanton, *The Indians of the Southeastern United States*, Smithsonian Institution, Bureau of American Ethnology, Bulletin 137 (Washington, D.C., 1946), 456–480.

16. On Cherokee basket making and the replacement of cane baskets by vine baskets, see Sarah H. Hill, "Weaving History: Cherokee Baskets from the Springplace Mission," *William and Mary Quarterly*, 3d Ser., LIII (1996), 129–132. On the influx of European goods, see Vernon J. Knight, Jr., and Marvin T. Smith, "Big Tallassee: A Contribution to Upper Creek Site Archaeology," *Early Georgia*, VIII (1980), 59–74; Knight, *Tukabatchee: Archaeological Investigations at an Historic Creek Town, Elmore County, Alabama, 1984*, Report of Investigations, Office of Archaeological Research, Alabama State Museum of Natural History, University of Alabama (University, Ala., 1985), 121–123, 165–167; L. Ross Morrell, "The Woods Island Site in Southeastern Acculturation, 1625–1800," *Notes in Anthropology*, XI (1965), 66; and Carol I. Mason, "Eighteenth Century Culture Change among the Lower Creeks," *Florida Anthropologist*, XVI, no. 3 (1963), 68–69. On the preference of warriors for brass or tin kettles, see Alexander McGillivray to [?], Feb. 1, 1779, PC, legajo 204, 731, reel 283, PKY; Thomas Perryman to the Governor of Pensacola, Aug. 20, 1812, PC, legajo 2356, 125, reel 172, PKY; and Patricia Dillon Woods, *French-Indian Relations on the Southern Frontier, 1699–1762* (Ann Arbor, Mich., 1980), 151; Louise F. Hays, ed., "A Talk from Six Chiefs of the Lower Towns to the Governor of Georgia, July 17, 1790, Creek Indian Letters, Talks, and Treaties, 1705–1839," typescript, I, 221b–221c, Georgia Department of Archives and History (hereafter cited as CIL).

In contrast to their position in the deerskin trade, women retained their crucial role as farmers, but the emergence of plantations in the Deep South Interior provided unwanted competition. One Creek warrior named Emistesigo explained in 1771: "I am now far advanced in life, and this is the first time I ever saw plantations settled in my nation. The reason of my complaining is this, that formerly our old women and motherless children used by exchanging a little corn for goods to be able to cover their nakedness but they are now deprived of this resource and often obliged on the contrary to purchase corn from the traders." A few months after Emistesigo lodged his complaint, Wolf King also objected to the plantations owned by traders. James Germany, for example, operated a farm on the Tallapoosa River where slaves performed all of the labor. In 1772, Creeks living on the Tallapoosa resolved not to allow traders to establish any more plantations, but such settlements continued to grow. Though Creek women, by raising children, farming, preparing food, ornamenting clothes, and gathering herbs, still played crucial roles in the Creek economy, the deerskin trade, and particularly the change to raw deerskins, took away an important source of their economic power. At the same time, it gave men the means to express a masculinity often hostile to the interests of women.[17]

## The New Economic Order and Women's Search for Autonomy

After the American Revolution, a number of métis Creeks, led by Alexander McGillivray, emerged as important leaders in the Deep South Interior. Familiar with the economic practices of their Anglo fathers, many of them established plantations near Creek towns and developed a lucrative trade between Creek hunters and merchants in Pensacola and Augusta. With the elimination of European rivalries in the Southeast, they soon consolidated their leadership by controlling official communication with American officials. The new economic order that they instituted received further impetus when Benjamin Hawkins, the principal temporary agent for Indian affairs south of the Ohio, assumed office in December 1796. An advocate of what would soon become Jeffersonian Indian policy, Hawkins intended to civilize the Creeks. He explained in 1807: "The plan I persue is to lead the Indian from hunting to the pastoral

17. "At a Congress of the Principal Chiefs and Warriors of the Upper Creek Nation," Oct. 29, 1771, Lockey Collection (hereafter cited as LOC), Public Record Office, Colonial Office 5/589, PKY; David Taitt, "David Taitt's Journal of a Journey through the Creek Country, 1772," in Newton D. Mereness, ed., *Travels in the American Colonies* (New York, 1916), 501, 510, 535, and David Taitt to John Stuart, May 4, 1772, 552–554.

life, to agriculture, household manufactures, a knowledge of weights and measures, money and figures."[18]

Hawkins found allies not only among métis traders and ranchers but also among many Creek women. Like Hawkins himself, these women opposed the dominance of warriors whose fortunes had risen because of the deerskin trade and the near-constant warfare waged by Britain, France, and Spain in the first two-thirds of the eighteenth century. Hawkins observed the effects of this warrior culture in a letter to a woman friend written one year after he had assumed his post: "It is not customary anywhere among the Creeks to associate with the women, and it is a curious fact that there are white men in this land who have been here five years without ever entering an Indian house. I visit them, take them by the hand and talk kindly to them, and I eat with them frequently, and this day I had four Indian women to dine with me with some Chiefs and white men, a thing they tell me unknown before to either of them."[19] Anxious to control the madness of their men, many Creek women at first listened eagerly to Hawkins's talks.

Like men, they tried to parlay their traditional subsistence practices, particularly agriculture, into market-oriented activities. Though Hawkins claimed there was "no market for provisions" before his arrival, he unwittingly revealed otherwise, noting that the "wants of the traders were few and those procured with beads, binding thread or needles." Women used these items to make and decorate clothes, indicating that, even if Hawkins failed to recognize its legitimacy, there existed a significant barter between Creek women and traders. Hawkins further encouraged market production by purchasing agricultural products for his residence and model farm at Coweta Tallahassee, on the Chattahoochee, near present-day Columbus, Georgia. Conceding to the Creek demand for just exchange, he established a list of fixed prices for goods such as pork, bacon, beef, corn, fowl, eggs, butter, cheese, peas, and hickory-nut oil. In 1798, only a year after his arrival, Hawkins observed the effect of his efforts: "The women who are the labourers in this land experience the advantage of having corn for sale, as they have been many of them clothed by it this season." It seemed, then, that women had found a new means to economic independence. The marketplace freed them from their reliance on men and even gave them power over Creek warriors, whose profits in the deerskin trade were beginning to decline.[20]

18. On Alexander McGillivray, see Saunt, "A New Order of Things," chap. 4; Mauelshagen and Davis, eds., *Partners in the Lord's Work*, 7.

19. Hawkins to Elizabeth House Trist, Nov. 25, 1797, *LBH*, I, 164–165.

20. Benjamin Hawkins, "A Sketch of the Creek Country in the Years 1798 and 1799," *LBH*, I, 312–313; Hawkins to Edward Price, Dec. 31, 1798, *LBH*, I, 230.

Hawkins's intention, however, was "to introduce a regular husbandry," meaning plow agriculture practiced by men. The market he created at Coweta Tallahassee was to serve as a "powerful stimulus" to the residents of Coweta, Coweta Tallahassee, and Kasihta who had established farms based on the patriarchal model promoted by the Indian agent. Near Coweta, for example, Hawkins had encouraged trader Thomas Marshall to cultivate cotton, a plan that he and other traders "adopted with spirit." Coweta Tallahassee was the site of Hawkins's model farm, meant to show Creek men how to fence and plow their fields, and Kasihta had several adjacent villages established after European-American patterns. The village of Aupputtaue, for example, was well fenced, and in 1797 Hawkins hired a farmer to tend a corn crop there, inducing the residents to use the plow instead of the hoe. Micco Thlucco's outlying settlement was also well fenced, and in the spring of 1799 Hawkins showed him how to plow, noting that he had already "seen much of the ways of the white people and advantages of the plough over the slow and laborious hoe." The "stimulus" mentioned by Hawkins was thus directed at three towns in which men controlled a significant part of the agricultural production.[21]

Though most Creek women continued to work as farmers through the end of the eighteenth century and beyond, they could compete only in markets such as the one at Coweta Tallahassee, where prices were fixed; ironically, at such markets, Hawkins discouraged them from farming by promoting "regular husbandry," rewarding male farmers with gifts of plows, seed, and livestock. One traveler who visited Hawkins in 1803 wrote, "We have had occular demonstrations of Indians ploughing in their fields." Such promotions had concrete effects on Creek women and men. "I have to regret that our women, with the hoes, are behind us," Creek leader Efau Hadjo told Hawkins in the early nineteenth century, "that they and their children are likely to have poverty and hunger for their lot." In the long run, Creek women would have to find other means to profit in the new economic order.[22]

Cotton perhaps offered the surest way to enter the market; in the emerging new order, the United States encouraged and fostered women spinners and weavers. Many Creek men were in fact wary of giving women the power of eco-

---

21. Hawkins, "Sketch of the Creek Country," *LBH*, I, 308–313.

22. Ibid., I, 291–293; Stephen Folch, "Journal of a Voyage to the Creek Nation from Pensacola in the Year 1803," May 5, 1803, PC, legajo 2372, 1, reel 436, PKY; "Report of Commissioners to the Secretary of War, May and June 1802," in United States Congress, *American State Papers: Documents, Legislative and Executive, of the Congress of the United States . . . ,* 38 vols. (Washington, D.C., 1832–1861), Class II, *Indian Affairs,* 2 vols., ed. Walter Lowrie et al., I, 668–681 (hereafter cited as *American State Papers, Indian Affairs*).

nomic independence. When Hawkins first proposed his civilization program at Kasihta on the Chattahoochee River in 1797, he reported: "They all heard me with attentive silence, untill I mentioned the raising and spinning of cotton." "One of them laughed at the idea, but the Fusatchee Mico assent to all and said it must be done. The objection made to it by the men, is, that if the women can cloathe themselves, they will be proud and not obedient to their husbands." For their part, Hawkins and his assistants used Creek women to spur men to work in the fields, turning the desire of Creek women for economic independence into a tool to subjugate them in the domestic economy of the patriarchal family. Richard Thomas, the agent at the Creek factory, explained: "The females of this nation approve much of Colonel Hawkins's plan of introducing the culture of cotton and the spinning wheel; it may, in the course of a few years, induce the young men to throw away the hungary flute." Thomas believed that when Creek women "are able to cloathe themselves by their own industry, it will render them independent of the hunter, who in turn will be obliged to handle the ax and the plough, and assist the women in the laborious task of the fields, or have no wife."[23]

Despite the long-range plans of Hawkins and his assistants, women initially welcomed the cultivation of cotton. "The women approve much of the plan for introducing the culture of cotton and the spinning wheel," reported Richard Thomas, "and I have had several applications for cotton seed, cards and wheels." He wrote Hawkins in 1798: "Soohahoey brought two gallons [of cotton seed] up, but will not spare to any of her neighbours a single grain; she is determined to plant the whole, and requests me to tell you not to forget the small wheel and cards." In 1799, according to Hawkins, women were spinning in Hillabee, Coweta, Coweta Tallahassee, and Palachuckaly, where two Creek girls had prepared one hundred yards of cotton fit for the loom. "Some of the Indian girls have showed much desire to be instructed and aptness to learn," he wrote. That year, three hundred women and children clothed themselves in homespun, and some women even earned enough money to purchase hogs and cattle. They were, noted Hawkins, "a stimulus to their country women." One machinist and loommaker whom Hawkins had sent into the nation concluded

23. *Journal of Benjamin Hawkins*, Jan. 5, 1797, in *Letters of Benjamin Hawkins, 1796–1806* (Georgia Historical Society, *Collections*, IX [Savannah, Ga., 1916]), 55–56; Richard Thomas to Henry Gaither, Jan. 28, 1798, *Letters of Benjamin Hawkins* (Ga. Hist. Soc., *Colls.*, IX [1916]), 478; Hawkins to Silas Dinsmoor, June 7, 1798, *LBH*, I, 199; Benjamin Hawkins, "Sketch of the Present State of the Objects under the Charge of the Principal Agent for Indian Affairs South of the Ohio," March 1801, *LBH*, I, 354.

that Creek women were "very desirous of being instructed and determined to follow the orders of the agent."[24]

Cotton cultivation and spinning and weaving might have offered Creek women an entrance into the market, but here, too, men began controlling their labor and taking the profits. In his initial tour through the Deep South Interior in December 1796, Hawkins was pleased to note that Robert Grierson, a Scotsman who had settled with his Creek family three miles northwest of Hillabee "had his family around him ginning and picking cotton" on his thirty-acre farm. Grierson reported that he had no problem finding Creek women to pick cotton, paying them half a pint of salt or three strands of mock wampum per bushel, or a half-pint of taffia for two bushels. By the end of the decade, he was employing eleven women, "red, white and black," as Hawkins put it, to spin and weave his product. To pick the cotton, he relied solely on Indian women, most of whom were unskilled at spinning. Hawkins encouraged Grierson to serve as a model to traders and Creek men, and several took up cotton production. Trader Benjamin Steadham's two métis daughters who lived at Palachuckaly were reportedly "good spinners," and Alex Cornels had prepared two acres for cotton in 1801.[25]

Many Creek women, particularly the older generation, who easily perceived that working unremunerated for men was a form of subordination, resisted such work. Lavinia Turner, a weaver whom Hawkins hired to instruct Creek women, reported: "The little Indian girls of Mr. Cornells which you ordered here to be taught to spin, were sent accordingly by their father but I found them very intractable, they had of themselves or from their Grandmothers' advice, conceived that their learning to spin was conferring a singular favour on the agent and as such they must be well paid for it, and they demanded a suit of fine cloths as the price of attempting to spin." Her observation is especially revealing because Cornels had readily adopted the model of the patriarchal,

24. Thomas to Hawkins, Jan. 28, 1798, *Letters of Benjamin Hawkins* [Ga. Hist. Soc., *Colls.,* IX [1916]), 476–477; Hawkins to James Jackson, Feb. 27, 1799, in Louise F. Hays, ed., "Letters of Benjamin Hawkins, 1797–1815," typescript, 41, Georgia Department of Archives and History; Hawkins to William Panton, Feb. 3, 1800, *LBH,* I, 328; Hawkins, "Sketch of the Present State of the Objects under the Charge of the Principal Agent for Indian Affairs," March 1801, *LBH,* I, 353; Hawkins to Panton, Feb. 7, 1801, Cruzat Papers, PKY; Benjamin Hawkins, "Journal of Occurrences in the Creek Agency from January to the Conclusion of the Conference and Treaty at Fort Wilkinson by the Agent for Indian Affairs," *LBH,* II, 407.

25. *Journal of Benjamin Hawkins,* Dec. 9, 10, 1796, Traders in the Upper Creeks, 1797, both in *Letters of Benjamin Hawkins* (Ga. Hist. Soc., *Colls.,* IX [1916]), 29–30, 168–174; Hawkins, "Sketch of the Creek Country," *LBH,* I, 291–293, 301.

nuclear family and had taken agricultural production out of the hands of the women in his family, using slave labor in their place.[26] The métis son of an English trader, he was comfortable with the patriarchy of his father's culture. The women in his wife's lineage, the grandmothers whom Turner mentioned in her report, reacted against Cornels's patriarchy by demanding that their granddaughters receive payment for their work. These young women, by learning domestic chores for which they would not be paid, were in fact doing "a singular favour" for Hawkins and, more directly, Cornels.

Spurred at different times by men and women, cotton production continued to expand, but the market slowly became dominated by male planters. In 1806, for example, the speaker of the Creek nation requested of the Spanish crown that Forbes and Company, the main trading house operating in the Deep South Interior, be allowed to ship cotton free of duty "for the benefit of the Creek nation." Those Creeks involved in shipping cotton to markets on the Gulf Coast were usually men who owned plantations. The market for homespun, in contrast, was only local.[27] As the market expanded, wealthy Creek men increasingly would use the labor of African American slaves and Creek women to export cotton out of the Deep South Interior.

In two areas in the market, women had no real competition from men. The first was the production of nut oil, the only rivals being swine, which ate many of the nuts before they could be gathered. Both Bernard Romans and William Bartram had noted before the Revolution that women made "milk" and "oil" from nuts. In 1797, Edward Price, the storekeeper at the Creek factory at Fort Wilkinson on the Oconee, wrote, "We have been much perplexed with the small trade for groundnuts, chestnuts, and etc., but thought right to accommodate the poor women for their little matters[,] of consequence to them and not of any material amount." The following year, the "material amount" rose to eight gallons and then thirty gallons the year after that. In 1800, when Hawkins raised the price of hickory-nut oil from seventy-five cents per quart to one dollar, women brought in three hundred gallons, ample evidence that they were anxious to enter the market economy and were responding to its incentives. Creek women earned twelve hundred dollars from their trade in hickory-nut oil in 1800, the equivalent value of sixteen hundred deerskins.[28]

26. Hawkins, "Journal of Occurrences in the Creek Agency," *LBH*, II, 411–412; Hawkins, "Sketch of the Creek Country," *LBH*, I, 291–293.

27. Daniel McGillivray to [John Forbes?], Aug. 28, 1806, Forbes-Innerarity Papers, 67/30, reel 147 P, PKY.

28. Bartram, "Observations," Amer. Ethn. Soc., *Trans.*, III (1853), 32; Romans, *Concise Natural History of East and West Florida*, 96; Bartram, *Travels*, ed. Van Doren, 57; Price to

The other area in the market free of competition was the exchange of sexual favors for goods. Romans had observed that Creek women "will never scruple to sell the use of their bodies when they can do it in private; a person who wishes to be accommodated here can generally be supplied for payment, and the savages think a young woman nothing the worse for making use of her body, as they term it." By 1802, after five full years of Hawkins's civilization program, women were clearly using their bodies to enter the male-dominated market economy. Hawkins noted: "The old women who have handsome granddaughters are as adverse to the plan of civilization as the old Chiefs. They think of no support but prostituting their granddaughters or daughters, on this they confidently rely for cloths and food and spoke of it as a cheap and easy way of acquiring both." Two Moravian missionaries who visited the Deep South Interior in 1804 confirmed Hawkins's observations: "A single woman is permitted to reach an agreement with a man, or with several men, if the parties concerned agree. For this she accepts pay. . . . In bargaining with the white men, Creek girls employ interpreters. All matters are discussed frankly and without hesitancy, as though it were the most innocent matter in the world." Prostitution was one of the surest ways women could obtain clothes and food in the market.[29]

Creek men had long tried to control the sexual activities of women. Except "as to the government of the women, there is not law," noted Hawkins, whose sense of the government of women among the Creeks was surely exaggerated by his own blindness toward the oppression of women in European American society. Creek adulteresses did receive a harsher punishment than their male counterparts, but unmarried Creek women had no restrictions on their sexual activities. Nevertheless, Creek men appear to have associated and limited women's sexual and economic independence. The same year in which Hawkins commented on the prevalence of prostitution, Abraham Mordecai, a Jewish man long involved in the deerskin trade, set up a cotton gin just below the

---

Hawkins, Dec. 4, 1797, Records of the Creek Trading House, Letter Book, 1795–1816, reel 94-O, PKY; Florette Henri, *The Southern Indians and Benjamin Hawkins, 1796–1816* (Norman, Okla., 1986), 120.

29. Romans, *Concise Natural History of East and West Florida,* 97; Hawkins, "Journal of Occurrences in the Creek Agency," *LBH,* II, 412; Carl Mauelshagen and Gerald H. Davis, "The Moravians' Plan for a Mission among the Creek Indians, 1803–1804," *Georgia Historical Quarterly,* LI (1967), 363. John Swanton notes that these "temporary marriages" often involved women who had committed adultery and been abandoned by their husbands; see Swanton, *Social Organization,* 384.

confluence of the Coosa and Tallapoosa Rivers. Many of Mordecai's suppliers were Creek women. One visitor to the Upper Creeks reported in 1803 that there were two hundred spinning wheels in the area, and he "saw a list of 100 more bespoken." According to an early historian who interviewed Mordecai, the entrepreneur traded for "pink root, hickory-nut oil and peltries of all kinds." Pink root and hickory-nut oil were the trade goods of women, and it is likely that the lint cotton that Mordecai shipped to New Orleans was made from their crops. Soon after the gin was built, a number of Creek warriors destroyed it in retaliation for Mordecai's relationship with a married Creek woman. They were likely threatened as much by the sexual independence of the adulteress as by her growing economic autonomy. Thirteen years earlier, a visitor to the Deep South Interior had purportedly recorded the words of an old Creek "conjurer," who clearly linked economic and sexual freedom: "Our Women laugh at us and refuse to work: they are Prostitutes and suckle the Children of white Men!"[30]

Though some men, particularly métis, found that cattle, slaves, and specie were ample measures of their masculinity, others felt that the advent of the new order in the postwar years feminized them. Their sense of loss of control over Creek women, their anxiety about their own status in the new order, and their hostility toward the expanding settler population is evident in the way they addressed women. Women "are universally called wenches," one visitor to the Deep South Interior wrote in 1791. Men "who have seldom been abroad, and are not distinguished by war-names, are styled old women, which is the greatest term of reproach that can be used by them." In 1793, Shawnee visitors challenged their Creek hosts to turn out for war by threatening to "twist their ears and noses and take them for old women."[31]

The hostility of such language occasionally manifested itself in rapes and in the symbolic mutilation of white women. In November 1790, for instance, two

30. Hawkins to James McHenry, Jan. 6, 1797, *LBH*, I, 63; Sattler, "Women's Status among the Muskogee and Cherokee," in Klein and Ackerman, eds., *Women and Power in Native North America*, 218–219; Albert James Pickett, *History of Alabama and Incidentally of Georgia and Mississippi, from the Earliest Period* (Sheffield, Ala., 1896), 469–470; Folch, "Journal of a Voyage to the Creek Nation," May 5, 1803, PC, legajo 2372, 1, reel 436, PKY; Dwight M. Wilhelm, *A History of the Cotton Textile Industry of Alabama, 1809–1950* (n.p., n.d.), 25; John Pope, *A Tour through the Southern and Western Territories of the United States of North America; the Spanish Dominions on the River Mississippi, and the Floridas; the Countries of the Creek Nations; and Many Uninhabited Parts* (1792; facsimile reprint, Gainesville, Fla., 1979), 60–62.

31. Swan, "Position and State of Manners," in Schoolcraft, ed., *Information respecting the History, Condition, and Prospects of the Indian Tribes*, 272, 280; Juan Nepomuceno de Quesada to Luis de Las Casas, Apr. 26, 1793, PC, legajo 1436, 5614, reel 158, PKY.

Indians reportedly raped a white woman near the Altamaha River. Two years later, in June 1792, a number of Indians traveling down the Saint Marys River with the Scots Indians George and William Cannard camped near an old house belonging to a settler named George Tillet, who was away from home. According to one Alexander Steele, a guest at Tillet's house, in the evening William Cannard came with a number of other Indians and "desired me to leave the house telling me in English and in the most vulgar language what he intended with Tillet's wife." Steele went for help and when he returned "found they had carried and dragged her a considerable distance into the fields." "We went to rescue her and found her in the possession of about fourteen or fifteen Indians, and with one in such a position and others aholding her that we doubted not but they had ravished her." Another gang rape reportedly nearly occurred on the Saint Marys River in February 1802, when eight Creeks attacked a settler and "made attempts to ravish this man's wife and daughter, pushing him and his son away with their guns, telling them that the land was theirs and that they had no business off the islands." [32]

Symbolic mutilation was never reported as such, of course, but some documents suggest that Creek men responded specifically to the sex of their victims. In 1793, on the disputed fork of the Oconee and Apalachee Rivers in Georgia, for instance, a Mrs. Thrasher was found "alive, scalped, wounded in both her thighs, her right breast, with balls, and stabbed in her left breast with a knife, her left arm cut nearly off, as is supposed with a tomahawk, of which wounds she died in about 24 hours." A year later, in a Creek raid on Colerain on the Saint Marys, a Mrs. Rawlins "received a ball through her body, the Indians then scalped her and cut her in a most barberous manner and left her body on the field." [33] There is no evidence of Creek men treating Creek women with such hostility, but when sexual violence did occur, literate colonists would have rarely, if ever, been witnesses.

## Gender Conflict and the Outbreak of the Redstick War

In May 1811, a Creek woman and man, recently returned from a hunt, met a Moravian missionary named Johann Christian Burckhard, who was exploring

32. Richard Lang to the Governor of St. Augustine, Dec. 8, 1790, East Florida Papers (hereafter cited as EF), bundle 195M15, doc. 1790-25, reel 82, PKY; Alexander Steele, Sept. 12, 1792, EF, bundle 122E10, reel 47, PKY; and Residents of the South Side of Saint Marys River to Juan Nepomuceno de Quesada, Aug. 18, 1792, EF, bundle 122E10, doc. 1792-291, reel 47, PKY.

33. Affidavit of Michael Cupps and Nancy Smith, Apr. 23, 1793, CIL, I, 288; Affidavit of Benjamin Rawlins, Feb. 28, 1794, CIL, II, 359.

the countryside of what would soon become western Georgia and eastern Alabama. Though her male companion offered the missionary some food, the woman remained silent and sullen. Burckhard recorded in his diary: "Neither knew English, but finally she told the reason for her attitude, saying they were unable to get a spinning wheel without having to pay for it. When I told her I wanted nothing without pay, she was satisfied and brought me turkey soup, bread, and salt. She also brought me corn for my horse. Upon receiving payment she vigorously shook my hand."[34] Burckhard questioned the lack of traditional Creek hospitality, but his acquaintance had good reason to be sullen. Unable to purchase a spinning wheel, she could not fully participate in the new economic order that had swept over the region in the previous two generations. The Creek hunter willingly gave Burckhard some food, but this generosity reflected an era bygone, when plentiful game had allowed Creeks to welcome strangers with a share of the hunt. As Burckhard's acquaintance surely knew from experience, deer were scarcer with every new hunting season, and the remaining Creek hunting grounds were rapidly filling with cattle and settlers. Creeks were finding their older gender roles increasingly less tenable and the future of little promise.

Two years later, in 1813, dissident Creek Redsticks murdered and "most cruelly mangled" seven settlers near the mouth of the Ohio River, precipitating the Redstick War. The attack was, in part, a warrior's response to civilization, an assertion of Creek masculinity against the identity imposed by United States Indian agents. At the mouth of the Ohio, for example, Redsticks disemboweled a pregnant woman and impaled her fetus. According to one account, one of the warriors later boasted that "he had killed and eaten white people, and he had killed and cut open the white woman near the mouth of the Ohio." In subsequent battles, Redstick warriors might have displayed extra hostility toward women, though it is difficult to distinguish accurate descriptions of the violence from biased exaggeration. In August 1813, for example, when Redsticks attacked and destroyed a fort on the Alabama River that sheltered métis and white settlers, one witness reported that "he saw 250 dead bodies and the women in a situation shocking to behold or relate."[35] Yet, even if Creeks at-

34. Mauelshagen and Davis, eds., *Partners in the Lord's Work*, 49.

35. Hawkins to Upper Creek Chiefs, Mar. 25, 1813, *LBH*, II, 631; Nimrod Doyell to Hawkins, May 3, 1813, *American State Papers, Indian Affairs*, I, 843–844. As one Creek had stated many years earlier, women give birth and children grow up to become warriors; "consequently, not getting rid of both types, the number of their enemies would grow with time"; see Governor of Florida to Conde de Gálvez, June 12, 1786, EF, bundle 42C4, doc. 6, 39, reel 16, PKY; Hawkins to John B. Floyd, Sept. 26, 1813, *LBH*, II, 667.

tacked and mutilated their male victims with equal force, the violence against women violated white codes of warfare, and Creeks knew it. These were the actions of warriors anxious to reestablish their madness.

Whites interpreted such assertions of Creek masculinity as direct assaults on civilization. In December 1813, in the heat of the war, *Niles' Weekly Register* published a letter from one resident who lived on the Tombigbee River, not far from some of the fiercest fighting in central Alabama:

> Many of [the Creeks] were regular farmers; the men labored in the field, the women plied the wheel and the shuttle at home. Schools, apparently well attended, had been established; one half of the various tribes known by the general name of Creeks, spoke the English language; and very few of them had altogether refused to adopt the habits of civilized man. Much time, labor and money had been spent upon them—their lands and rights had been carefully guarded—they are without excuse, for they had nothing to complain of. They listened to the serpent, and became the murderers of their benefactors—the horrible assassins of women and children.

According to this observer, Redsticks had overturned the proper order—one characterized by male farmers and female weavers—and had committed unnatural acts, such as murdering their benefactors and slaughtering women and children. The serpent mentioned in the letter, although a clear reference to Satan, also brings to mind the sexual discord unleashed by Eve in the Garden of Eden. Andrew Jackson, who led American troops against the Creek dissidents, used similar rhetoric, condemning the leading Redstick prophets as a "matricidical band"; "it is not on defenseless women and children that retaliation will be made," he stated, distinguishing civilized from savage war. Perhaps with the same contrast in mind, United States officers self-consciously reported in published letters that they had spared Creek women and children. After the war, relatives of one half-hearted métis Redstick leader revived his reputation as a respectable planter in part by insisting that he had urged warriors to spare women and children.[36] Though the repeated comments by whites on the savagery of the Creeks betray a one-sided perspective, they also highlight a real

36. Letter to the Editor, *Niles' Weekly Register* (Baltimore), Dec. 18, 1813, J. Coffee to Andrew Jackson, Nov. 4, 1813, Jackson to General Pinckney, Mar. 28, Apr. 23, 1814; Jackson to Mateo González Manrique, Aug. 24, 1814, enclosed in Manrique to Juan Ruiz de Apodaca, Sept. 6, 1814, PC, legajo 1795, 1006, reel 116, PKY; Hawkins to Kendal Lewis, Feb. 16, 1814, in Louise F. Hays, ed., "Unpublished Letters of Timothy Barnard, 1784–1820," typescript, 305c, Georgia Department of Archives and History; J. D. Dreisbach to Lyman Draper, July 1874, Draper MSS, reel 1V62.

part of the conflict: Redsticks refused to abide by European ideals of masculinity and femininity.

Like Redstick warriors, women, too, reasserted their femininity in the war. Some of them became prophets, preaching against the plows and looms that had upset older gender roles. Others reassumed their traditional identity as food makers by gathering berries and nuts to support Redstick adherents. In addition, they repositioned themselves in the heart of the Creek economy by rejecting most European-made goods. They likely also condoned the Redsticks' wholesale slaughter of livestock in the Deep South Interior. Ranching had encouraged the dispersal of towns where women farmed the land, replacing them with outlying ranches owned by Creek men.[37]

The attack on Mrs. Grayson highlights the Redstick animosity toward the gender roles urged on them by white reformers. In Grayson, Creek women faced everything these reformers had told them to become. Similarly, men confronted a proponent of the new economic order that had supplanted the hunting and warring they had long pursued. Creek animosity toward white reformers is only part of the story, however, for the attack on Mrs. Grayson also highlights tensions between Creek women and men. When Creek women watched and perhaps participated in forcefully disrobing Grayson, the recollection of a century of struggle to redefine their identity would have left them troubled. From the war's beginnings, when men disemboweled a pregnant woman and impaled her fetus, they could not have failed to recognize the masculine character of the conflict. Moreover, the women who lived in Ockfuskee shared a great deal with Grayson.[38] Like Grayson, they, too, prepared food and made clothes. In addition, much as Grayson was stripped of her wealth, Creek women themselves had been impoverished in part by men over the course of the preceding five decades. Traditionalist Creeks attacked Mrs. Grayson because she was an agent of assimilation, but, as the multilayered and shifting history of gender conflict makes clear, men also slaughtered her livestock, destroyed her loom, and stripped her of clothes because she was a woman.

37. Alexander Beaufort Meek, *Romantic Passages in Southwestern History; Including Orations, Sketches, and Essays* (New York, 1857), 271; Martin, *Sacred Revolt*, 145; Roy S. Dickens, Jr., *Archaeological Investigations at Horseshoe Bend National Military Park, Alabama,* Special Publications of the Alabama Archaeological Society, no. 3 (University, Ala., 1979); Charles H. Fairbanks, "Excavations at Horseshoe Bend, Alabama," *Florida Anthropologist,* XV (1962), 48; Saunt, "A New Order of Things," 311–318, 501–503.

38. See Tom Hatley, *The Dividing Paths: Cherokees and South Carolinians through the Era of Revolution* (New York, 1993), 89–90, for an insightful description of the bonds between Cherokee women and white women.

# Pigs and Hunters

## "Rights in the Woods" on the Trans-Appalachian Frontier

The history of the trans-Appalachian frontier once unfolded in a linear progression. In the imagined procession from Indian hunter to "American"
farmer, Frederick Jackson Turner sketched the stepped ascent from one mode
of subsistence to the next and from a primitive to a privatized landscape. For
generations of historians inspired by Turner's thesis, this sequential parade
plotted the triumph of civilization over savagery.

Neat successions and triumphalist reckonings have now yielded to a messier
dynamic. Reconstituting the late-eighteenth-century Ohio Valley frontier as a
cultural crossroads, historians have scrambled the worlds of Indians and pioneers. Contrary to Turner and generations of "stage-theorists," scholars have
come to understand that, through the last four decades of the eighteenth century, neither Indian nor European inhabitants of the Ohio Valley depended on
a singular means of subsistence. Instead, numerous woodland Indian groups
and diverse European colonists drew their sustenance from some combination
of hunting, herding, and farming. During these decades of joint occupancy, inhabitants lived in a mixed and mixed-up world where frontier cultures coincided as well as collided.[1]

The crossing of ways emerged most strikingly in hunting. The combination
of European tools and Indian techniques was the most visible evidence of con-
junction, but the merging went beyond means and methods. Borrowing from—
and in fear of—one another, Indian and pioneer hunters devised new rules for

1. For attempts to redefine and resuscitate the frontier as place and process (which in-
form my use of the word), see Howard Lamar and Leonard Thompson, "Comparative
Frontier History," in Lamar and Thompson, eds., *The Frontier in History: North America
and Southern Africa Compared* (New Haven, Conn., 1981), 3–13; William Cronon, George
Miles, and Jay Gitlin, "Becoming West: Toward a New Meaning for Western History," in
Cronon, Miles, and Gitlin, eds., *Under an Open Sky: Rethinking America's Western Past* (New
York, 1992), 3–27; Stephen Aron, "Lessons in Conquest: Towards a Greater Western His-
tory," *Pacific Historical Review*, LXIII (1994), 125–147.

dividing spoils and measuring manhood that suggested the growing congruences between frontier cultures.

These correspondences in hunting ways began to sculpt a common landscape. On the trans-Appalachian frontier in the latter half of the eighteenth century, Indian and pioneer property regimes merged elements of private and collective land tenure. In the *mutual* process of "frontiering," both Indians and pioneers altered existing constructions of property, developing novel arrangements that blended individual and group rights.

The convergence of subsistence systems and property regimes, however, was no basis for peaceful coexistence. What made Indians and pioneers similar did not make them the same. If hunting exemplified the coming together of Indian and backcountry ways, it also exhibited the continuing apartness of the peoples of the Ohio Valley. Those enduring contrasts were apparent in the divergent conceptions of womanhood that prevailed among whites and Indians. On the trans-Appalachian frontier in the last decades of the eighteenth century, constructions of gender not only differentiated men from women but also men from other men.

To gender differences were added the quite opposite attitudes with which white and Indian hunters regarded their prey. These, too, destabilized intercultural relations, especially as the environmental foundations of frontier hunting cultures began to collapse. Hunters from the British American colonies first breached the Appalachians during the 1760s. Within thirty years of the Anglo-American gunfire in Kentucky, the biggest game had disappeared from the country on the south side of the Ohio River, and pioneers had entirely supplanted Indians from their former hunting lands. Accompanying the depletion of game and the displacement of Indians was the replacement of hybrid border customs by more fully privatized and commercialized relations. During the 1790s, wildlife scarcities became increasingly apparent to villagers north of the Ohio as well, and pressure grew on native peoples to extend their commitment to market hunting and private property. But while American settlers in Kentucky adjusted quietly to the privatization of the landscape, Ohio Indians vigorously resisted the further subversion of familiar ways.[2]

2. To call these Kentucky pioneers "Anglo-Americans" suggests an ethnic unity that was not at all the case. In designating ethnically diverse European pioneers as "Anglos," I follow the practice of historians of the American West who collapse a variety of ethnic groups under the "Anglo-American" rubric. Thus, the designation "Anglo-American" includes many pioneers who did not hail from the British Isles. What linked Kentucky's diverse Anglo-American pioneers was not so much a shared English heritage as previous settlement in or passage through the backcountry of the British American colonies. In a similar vein, the

For historians, this contrast between how Indians and pioneers reconciled to a privatized order maps a fault line beneath the common ground that was the eighteenth-century Ohio Valley frontier. Although both Indians and pioneers restrained the practice of private landholding, only Indians denied the principle of it. Therein lay the tragedy of the Ohio Valley commons.

I

Across what Frederick Jackson Turner called the "Greater Pennsylvania" backcountry—the arc of settlement that gradually stretched south and west from Philadelphia to the South Carolina uplands during the half-century before the American Revolution—nearly all white colonists sought private ownership of land. Private ownership, however, did not by customary understanding grant exclusive rights to resident landholders. Although settlers in the interior of Pennsylvania, Virginia, and the Carolinas articulated what Richard Maxwell Brown has called a "homestead ethic," a demand to hold fee-simple title to a "family-sized farm" on the basis of occupancy and improvement, they also insisted that white colonists had a "right in the woods." A reflection of the centrality of open-range herding, especially hog raising, to life in this region, a right in the woods entitled "each person in possession of a plantation . . . to a certain proportion of [the roaming] live stock." Because subsistence rested on a combination of common-ranged stock and privately cultivated produce, the customs of the backcountry balanced rights in the woods and individuated property. Except for enclosing vegetable gardens and cornfields to keep animals out, this was a world in which good fences did not make good neighbors.[3]

---

term "native" is a problematic designation for the Indian peoples of the Ohio Valley, many of whom were relatively recent emigrants to the country.

3. J[ohn] F[erdinand] D[aniel] Smyth, *A Tour in the United States of America*, 2 vols. (London, 1784), I, 144 (quotation). On the "homestead ethic" and its contradictions, see Richard Maxwell Brown, "Back Country Rebellions and the Homestead Ethic in America, 1740–1799," in Brown and Don E. Fehrenbacher, eds., *Tradition, Conflict, and Modernization: Perspectives on the American Revolution* (New York, 1977), 73–99; Stephen Aron, "Pioneers and Profiteers: Land Speculation and the Homestead Ethic in Frontier Kentucky," *Western Historical Quarterly*, XXIII (1992), 179–198. On livestock-herding traditions as an integral component of backcountry subsistence systems, see David Hackett Fischer, *Albion's Seed: Four British Folkways in America* (New York, 1989), 741–743; Terry G. Jordan and Matti Kaups, *The American Backwoods Frontier: An Ethnic and Ecological Interpretation* (Baltimore, 1989), 119–123; Robert D. Mitchell, *Commercialism and Frontier: Perspectives on the Early Shenandoah Valley* (Charlottesville, Va., 1977), 139–149, 183–187. What Frederick Jackson

Although this mixture of herding and cultivation furnished inhabitants with an adequate diet, the explosion of livestock created problems. Cattle, horses, and hogs thrived on the woodland range, but animals often strayed into enclosed fields. These trespasses invited conflict between the owner of the land and the owner of the livestock. Of course, determining the ownership of stock was not always easy. Pigs in particular multiplied rapidly, and unbranded animals proliferated. Settlers also had difficulty keeping their swine domesticated. An occasional handful of salt and regular feedings of corn were the accepted means of maintaining attachments. But on the borders of British American colonization, salt and corn were not always available. In Kentucky in 1779, a pioneer remembered that as pigs were left to forage in the woods they became "so wild that even the wolves dared not attack them."[4]

By the time Anglo-Americans began their colonization of Kentucky in 1775, hunting had joined the ranging of livestock and the raising of crops as a vital contributor to pioneer subsistence. Between the pioneer stations of central Kentucky and the previous borders of British American settlement lay hundreds of miles of what by backcountry parlance was "the wilderness." Isolated from reinforcement and resupply, pioneers had no choice during periods of the 1770s and 1780s but to live "on their guns" and off the land. "Kentucky never could have been settled in the way it was had it not been for the cane and game," affirmed pioneer James Wade.[5]

The cane to which Wade referred was dense clusters of a tall bamboo that were scattered across the central Kentucky landscape. Although pioneers struggled through these "canebrakes," their value as provender for domestic stock and a hideout from Indians made their presence essential. Cane also nourished wild herbivores, especially buffalo, whose abundance saved the first settlers from starvation.[6]

---

Turner described as "Greater Pennsylvania," Jordan and Kaups term "the Midland American backwoods." For further discussion of the geographic expansion and cultural character of this backcountry, see Jordan and Kaups, *The American Backwoods Frontier*, 7–14.

4. William Dodd Brown, ed., "A Visit to Boonesborough in 1779: The Recollections of Pioneer George M. Bedinger," *Register of the Kentucky Historical Society*, LXXXVI (1988), 324.

5. Roseann R. Hogan, ed., "Buffaloes in the Corn: James Wade's Account of Pioneer Kentucky," *Register of the Kentucky Hist. Soc.*, LXXXIX (1991), 30.

6. J. S. McHargue, "Canebrakes in Prehistoric and Pioneer Times in Kentucky," *Annals of Kentucky Natural History*, I (1941), 1–13; Mary E. Wharton and Roger W. Barbour, *Bluegrass Land and Life: Land Character, Plants, and Animals of the Inner Bluegrass Region of Kentucky, Past, Present, and Future* (Lexington, Ky., 1991), 19–32.

Kentucky's huge population of buffalo and other game delighted explorers, traders, soldiers, surveyors, and settlers, but the existence of plentiful wildlife did not in itself ensure success in hunting. Earlier in the eighteenth century, the first generation of settlers in the Greater Pennsylvania backcountry had also come into a game-filled region, yet wild meat constituted an inconsequential portion of their diet. Most emigrants initially lacked the skills to exploit this resource. True, these same Europeans underwent a rapid seasoning process, during which they adapted a host of Old World practices to backcountry conditions. For example, the thick woodlands and thin population of the Pennsylvania, Virginia, and Carolina interiors necessitated that backcountry settlers adjust the traditions of crop raising and stock ranging that had been developed in densely peopled and largely deforested European landscapes. Success in hunting, however, demanded more than a modification of previous routines. Prohibited in the British Isles from engaging in the aristocratic sports of hunting, fishing, and fowling, the majority of emigrants arrived with little if any experience in the techniques of stalking and shooting wildlife.[7]

It took some time for backcountry settlers to master the art of hunting. Scandinavian Pennsylvanians, the descendants of the colonists of New Sweden, had the most experience and provided some guidance in hunting to their backcountry neighbors. For the most part, however, settlers grasped the essentials of woodcraft by watching and listening to Pennsylvania Indians. From neighboring Indians, backcountry men learned how to dress, how to track, how to decoy, and how to live off the land while they chased (or as often awaited) game.[8]

The borrowing of Indian hunting techniques enabled increasing numbers

7. For reports of abundant game in precolonial Kentucky, see J. Stoddard Johnston, ed., *First Explorations of Kentucky: Doctor Thomas Walker's Journal of an Exploration of Kentucky in 1750 . . . also Colonel Christopher Gist's Journal of a Tour through Ohio and Kentucky in 1751 . . .* (Louisville, Ky., 1898), 75; George Butricke to Burnsley, Sept. 25, 1768, in Clarence Walworth Alvord and Clarence Edwin Carter, eds., *Trade and Politics, 1767–1769* (Springfield, Ill., 1921), 409; Elizabeth Thatcher Clough, ed., "Kentucky Ancestors in Pioneer Days: Abraham Thomas—'This Small Legacy of Experience,'" *Kentucky Ancestors,* XXVI (1990), 75; *Felix Walker's Narrative of His Trip with Boone from Long Island to Boonesborough in March, 1775,* in George W. Ranck, *Boonesborough: Its Founding, Pioneer Struggles, Indian Experiences, Transylvania Days, and Revolutionary Annals* (Louisville, Ky., 1901), 163–164.

8. Joseph Doddridge, *Notes on the Settlement and Indian Wars of the Western Parts of Virginia and Pennsylvania from 1763 to 1783* (1824; reprint, Pittsburgh, 1912), 91–93; Smyth, *A Tour in the United States of America,* I, 179–183; Jordan and Kaups, *The American Backwoods Frontier,* 211–232; Harriette S. Arnow, *Seedtime on the Cumberland* (New York, 1960), 76–109; John Mack Faragher, *Daniel Boone: The Life and Legend of an American Pioneer* (New York, 1992), 17–23.

of backcountry folk to add wild meat to their subsistence repertoire. As the borders of British American settlement pushed into the Susquehanna Valley, up the Shenandoah Valley, and across the Carolina upcountry, the capacity of inhabitants to live by hunting expanded. By midcentury, when white colonists pushed into the mountain valleys of southwestern Virginia and northwestern North Carolina, hunting had become a notable component of the backcountry economy. For a small number of men in these parts, the possibilities of even better hunting lured them on lengthier excursions into the mountains—and, beginning in the 1760s, beyond the Appalachians.

The advent of hunting as an element in the backcountry economy distressed colonial officials. Symbolically, the democratization of hunting cost gentry rulers a prominent badge of aristocratic privilege. More troubling, unfettered hunting stirred up trouble with Indians. Especially on their longer hunts across the Appalachians, white hunters poached on Kentucky lands that various Ohio Valley Indian groups claimed. During the 1760s, the meeting of white and Indian hunters in Kentucky and Tennessee resulted in a number of violent encounters, and British American officials feared these might soon escalate into a general border war.

The problem, from the perspective of the colonial gentry, was, not the differences between Indian and backcountry hunters, but their apparent similarities. Drawing on then-current notions of social development, gentlemen concluded that when backcountry whites hunted they reverted to the lowest stage of society. True, gentlemen on both sides of the Atlantic hunted. But, because aristocrats hunted for sport and not subsistence, they escaped being stigmatized as "white Indians." As practiced in Indian country and backcountry, though, hunting produced indigence, indolence, and insolence.[9]

There was "but one remedy" against these evils, avowed J. Hector St. John de Crèvecoeur, and that was to refrain entirely from hunting. "As long as we keep ourselves busy tilling the earth, there is no fear of any of us becoming wild; it is the chase and the food it procures that have this strange effect." Simply banning hunting, however, proved impossible, and efforts to establish lines between Indians and backcountry settlers were widely ignored. Soon after the Proclamation of 1763, which was supposed to keep pioneers from settling or hunting in Indian country across the Appalachian crest, Sir William Johnson,

9. On the eighteenth-century understanding of social progress and decay, see Drew R. McCoy, *The Elusive Republic: Political Economy in Jeffersonian America* (Chapel Hill, N.C., 1980), 13–47. Enlightenment theories of stages of society based on mode of subsistence had remarkable resilience. One need only look at Frederick Jackson Turner's thesis for a late-nineteenth-century updating of eighteenth-century understandings.

the superintendent of Indian affairs, concluded that backcountry people "are not to be confined by any boundaries or limits." [10]

Despite much outcry against troublesome hunters, colonial game laws never duplicated the repressive "bloody code" that intimidated English poachers. Virginia planters aspired to the standing of English lords, but they did so without the latter's crucial monopoly on hunting. Beginning in the seventeenth century, Virginia lawmakers enacted a group of statutes that established deer-hunting seasons in Virginia. But, although English laws made illegal hunting a capital offense, Virginia poachers faced only fines and whippings. And, in spite of the complaints by officials that backcountry hunters disturbed the peace of the realm, the game laws of colonial Virginia always exempted the residents of "frontier" counties from seasonal restrictions on taking venison. [11]

In neighboring North Carolina, lawmakers took a harder line. Anticipating Crèvecoeur's cure for the social ills promoted by hunting, a 1745 statute narrowed the privilege of hunting to residents of the colony who cultivated at least "5,000 hills of corn." To repress vagrant hunters, who were accused of wasting wildlife, murdering livestock, and promoting disorder, the North Carolina Assembly doubled the corn-planting requirement and introduced a one-hundred-acre property qualification in 1766. As in Virginia, however, penalties were too light and enforcement too lax to suppress illegal hunting. [12]

10. J. Hector St. John de Crèvecoeur, *Letters from an American Farmer* (1782), ed. Warren Barton Blake (New York, 1957), 215; Sir William Johnson to Earl of Dartmouth, Sept. 22, 1773, in K. G. Davies, ed., *Documents of the American Revolution, 1770–1783*, 21 vols. (Shannon, Ireland, 1972–1981), VI, 225.

11. William Littell, ed., *The Statute Laws of Kentucky*, 3 vols. (Frankfort, Ky., 1809–1819), II, 548–561, recapitulates the history of hunting laws in Virginia. On the "bloody code" to which eighteenth-century British poachers were subjected, see E. P. Thompson, *Whigs and Hunters: The Origin of the Black Act* (New York, 1975); Douglas Hay, "Poaching and the Game Laws on Cannock Chase," in Douglas Hay et al., *Albion's Fatal Tree: Crime and Society in Eighteenth-Century England* (New York, 1975), 189–253; P. B. Munsche, *Gentlemen and Poachers: The English Game Laws, 1671–1831* (Cambridge, 1981).

12. William L. Saunders, ed., *The Colonial Records of North Carolina*, 25 vols. (Raleigh, N.C., 1886–1905), IV, 745, XXIII, 218–219, 656, 775–776, 801–803, 916, 955–956, XXV, 503–504. On the evolution of colonial game laws and the persecution of hunters, see James A. Tober, *Who Owns the Wildlife? The Political Economy of Conservation in Nineteenth-Century America* (Westport, Conn., 1981), 23–28; Thomas A. Lund, *American Wildlife Law* (Berkeley, Calif., 1980), 19–34; Stuart A. Marks, *Southern Hunting in Black and White: Nature, History, and Ritual in a Carolina Community* (Princeton, N.J., 1991), 28–33; Rachel N. Klein, *Unification of a Slave State: The Rise of the Planter Class in the South Carolina Backcountry, 1760–1808* (Chapel Hill, N.C., 1990), 47–64.

By the 1760s, many inhabitants on the fringes of British American settlement rejected all restrictions on their hunting. Contemptuous of official injunctions and of Indian rights in the woods, parties of backcountry men congregated each autumn at the headwaters of the Holston River in southwestern Virginia to make "long hunts" across the Appalachians. Colonial authorities could do little in the face of such brazen defiance; they had neither the money nor the manpower to police hundreds of miles of frontier.[13]

Many of these long hunters, who often also doubled as land hunters, focused their attentions on the cane-covered, game-filled plain that neighboring Indian peoples called Kentucky. After traversing the Cumberland Gap, most long-hunting bands headed north and west. That course skirted Cherokee homelands and brought long hunters into a region between the Kentucky and Ohio Rivers that was currently devoid of villages. Long hunters encountered Indian hunters there, but they dismissed the claims of seasonal wanderers and discounted any exclusive right to the unimproved flora and fauna. To long hunters, the exuberance of wildlife belonged to all who could live on their guns, and the absence of farmsteads marked the land as available to those who would build a permanent cabin and plant a crop of corn.[14]

Following long hunters into Kentucky, pioneer settlers carried the same expectations about the land and its resources. The idea of "getting land for taking it up," of acquiring fee-simple title to a tract on the basis of occupancy and agricultural improvement, drove the colonization of Kentucky. Still, through

13. John Redd, "Reminiscences of Western Virginia, 1770–1790," *Virginia Magazine of History and Biography*, VI (1899), 338–340; John Haywood, *The Civil and Political History of the State of Tennessee from Its Earliest Settlement Up to the Year 1796* (Nashville, Tenn., 1891), 38–39, 44–49, 88–92; Arnow, *Seedtime on the Cumberland*, 134–171; Ruth Paull Burdette and Nancy Montgomery Berley, *The Long Hunters of Skin House Branch* (Columbia, Ky., 1970).

14. In constructing homestead rights in terms of continuous possession and agricultural improvement, pioneers voided Indian claims, which were based on intermittent occupation of Kentucky. Pioneers also discounted the improvements made by Indian hunters, for it was the torch and not the hoe that Indians used to modify the Kentucky landscape. Throughout the woodlands of North America, Indian peoples periodically burned the forests to clear out underbrush and stimulate the growth of new grasses. This, they hoped, would better nourish large herbivores and make prey less elusive. In what is now southwestern Kentucky, the effects of Indian-set fires were dramatically displayed, as meadows succeeded forests as the landscape's dominant feature. On Indian improvements to woodland hunting grounds, see Samuel N. Dicken, "The Kentucky Barrens," *Bulletin of the Geographical Society of Philadelphia*, XXXIII (1935), 42–51; Wharton and Barbour, *Bluegrass Land and Life*, 33–39; Stephen J. Pyne, *Fire in America: A Cultural History of Wildland and Rural Fire* (Princeton, N.J., 1982), 71–83.

the worst of "Indian times," which coincided in Kentucky with the Revolutionary War, wild meat sustained pioneers.[15]

So long as pioneers were forced to live "on their guns," the importance of hunting inflated the local prestige and authority of the best hunters. During the Revolutionary War years, pioneers turned to hunter-warriors to lead as well as feed them. "To be a brave, skillful warrior and a good hunter was the greatest honor to which any man could attain," recalled one Kentucky frontiersman. When Indians chased pioneers into fortified stations and destroyed their crops and stock, colonists depended on hunters for survival. Under cover of darkness, squads of four or five men slipped out from the stations and rendezvoused in nearby woods. To avoid giving away their positions, these hunters did without fires, exposing themselves to winter cold, summer mosquitoes, and year-round wolves. Without light, they could not engage in fire hunting, the customary means of spotting deer and other game at night; during the day, they also had to restrict their shooting. When Indians were known to be about, hunters dared not shoot at the easiest prey. Keeping the fast became another test of manliness. To a hunting party out of Boonesborough in 1779, "a fine young buffalo" appeared to be a perfect breakfast, until one member "reproached them for their *boyish* conduct" and exhorted his fellows "to exhibit more self denial and fortitude and act like men." Chastened, the rest of the hunters agreed to maintain their silent fast and "see who the *boys* are and who evince[s] the most fortitude."[16]

Demonstrations of manliness won fearless hunters the admiration of neighbors and strangers; so even more did expressions of mutuality. Under normal circumstances, backcountry custom granted an animal to the hunter who drew first blood. But at those times when hunting was the sole source of Kentuckians' subsistence, the spoils were equally divided—and not just among those with a role in the killing. Adept hunters were quick to offer rations to any pioneer in need. The Baptist preacher John Taylor gratefully discovered that after he removed to central Kentucky and found himself ill-equipped to supply his

15. Doddridge, *Notes on the Settlement and Indian Wars,* 85. On "Indian times" as the pioneers' designation of the frontier era, see Elizabeth Perkins, *Border Life: Experience and Perception in the Revolutionary Ohio Valley* (Chapel Hill, N.C., 1998), chap. 5.

16. Levi Purviance, *The Biography of Elder David Purviance, with His Memoirs: Containing His Views on Baptism, the Divinity of Christ, and the Atonement . . .* (Dayton, Ohio, 1848), 204; Brown, ed., "A Visit to Boonesborough in 1779," 321. See also Spencer Records' Narrative, 1842, Draper Manuscripts, 23CC38–39, microfilm, 1980, State Historical Society of Wisconsin, Madison (hereafter cited as DM); Nathaniel Hart, Jr., to M. T. Williams, Dec. 20, 1838, DM, 2CC26.

own meat from the woods. Taylor survived, thanks to the "common generosity of hunters," who "admit[ted] me to share in the profits, so far as meat went." [17]

Taylor was not invited to share in the profits from skins, an omission that underlined the boundaries between mutuality and profit-mindedness. In hunting, one set of rules governed the sale of skins, and another the gifts of meat. As long as these precepts of exchange fell into neat compartments, commercial dealings and good neighborliness coexisted. [18]

So in much the same way did common rights and nominally private property coincide. The indispensability of hunting expanded the scope of rights in the woods. Through the first decade of Anglo-American colonization, an era in which wild meat frequently substituted for other fare, an informal consensus limited private enjoyment of individuated property. As in earlier backcountries, Kentucky pioneers cultivated and enclosed only a small fraction of their fields; the rest, at least temporarily, became like unclaimed woods, a common on which all white inhabitants had certain rights—to cross at will, to range stock, to collect dead timber, and, most important in Revolutionary Kentucky, to hunt game. [19]

With survival at stake, pioneers insisted that collective needs eclipsed exclusive claims. A 1777 petition to the Virginia General Assembly regarding the disposition of Kentucky's salt licks expressed this narrowed conception of private property rights. Signed by Daniel Boone and seventy-five other settlers around Boonesborough, the appeal complained that, although "bountiful Nature hath plentifully furnished this Country with Salt Springs," the inhabitants "have for some time past been almost destitute of the necessary Article Salt." The peti-

17. John Taylor, *A History of Ten Baptist Churches, of Which the Author Has Been Alternately a Member: In Which Will Be Seen Something of a Journal of the Author's Life for More Than Fifty Years* (Bloomfield, Ky., 1827), 44. See also Chester Raymond Young, ed., *Westward into Kentucky: The Narrative of Daniel Trabue* (Lexington, Ky., 1981), 75–77; James Nourse, "Journey to Kentucky in 1775," *Journal of American History,* XIX (1925), 254, 364; John D. Shane interview with Daniel Boone Bryant, 1844, DM, 22C14; John D. Shane interview with Mrs. John Morrison, DM, 11CC152; Spencer Records' Narrative, 1842, DM, 23CC37–38.

18. My argument about compartmental exchange relations in hunting parallels the distinctions between local and long-distance trade drawn by Alan Taylor, *Liberty Men and Great Proprietors: The Revolutionary Settlement on the Maine Frontier, 1760–1820* (Chapel Hill, N.C., 1990), 77–85; and Christopher Clark, *The Roots of Rural Capitalism: Western Massachusetts, 1780–1860* (Ithaca, N.Y., 1990).

19. For a similar argument about the balance between private property and community rights, see Andrew R. L. Cayton, "Marietta and the Ohio Company," in Robert D. Mitchell, ed., *Appalachian Frontiers: Settlement, Society, and Development in the Preindustrial Era* (Lexington, Ky., 1991), 193–195.

tioners then urged the government of Virginia to make prompt improvement as a prerequisite for ownership of essential resources. "If the Claimants do not immediately erect Salt Manufactories at the different Springs claimed by them," the petitioners requested the Virginia assembly declare the springs "publick Property."[20]

The entreaty received a cool response from the Virginia assembly, but pioneers did not wait for legislative blessing. In western Virginia in 1774, Daniel Trabue remembered that, when merchants "hid their salt, . . . People gethered in companys and went and hunted up the salt . . . and Divided it," paying the owners "a reasonble prise." Four years later, Daniel Boone led a party of salt makers to Blue Licks. The Boonesborough settlers had not waited for an answer to their petition. And, because the proprietor had not improved his property, the salt makers planned no compensation.[21]

In the pioneers' attempt to legitimize access to precious resources, their moral economy was at odds with the statutes of Virginia. In the tidewater and piedmont "forecountry," slaveowning planters zealously guarded the sanctity of their property rights. Social order and economic prosperity, they believed, depended on an owner's unrestricted dominion over however much land and slaves he might engross. But this privatized world was hundreds of miles away from the Kentucky frontier; and, where gentry lawmakers were distant, rights in the woods held sway.

II

The usufructuary forest rights fashioned by pioneers brought their conception of land closer to that of neighboring Indians and hinted at the broader convergence of cultures. Indian and pioneer "stages of society," neatly demarcated in Enlightenment theories and Turnerian texts, blurred on the Appalachian frontier. As anxious pioneers learned from Indians how to live on their guns, apprehensive Ohio Indians also borrowed from pioneers. The presence of back-

---

20. James Rood Robertson, ed., *Petitions of the Early Inhabitants of Kentucky to the General Assembly of Virginia, 1769–1792* (Louisville, Ky., 1914), 43–44.

21. Young, ed., *Westward into Kentucky*, 42 (quotation); Nathan Boone Statement, 1851, DM, 6S103; Joseph Jackson Statement, 1844, DM, 11C62; William Waller Hening, ed., *The Statutes at Large; Being a Collection of All the Laws of Virginia, from the First Session of the Legislature, in the Year 1619*, 13 vols. (Richmond, Va., 1809–1823), IX, 122, 310; James R. Bentley, ed., "Letters of Thomas Perkins to Gen. Joseph Palmer, Lincoln County, Kentucky, 1785," *Filson Club History Quarterly*, XLIX (1975), 145–146; Thomas D. Clark, "Salt, a Factor in the Settlement of Kentucky," *ibid.*, XII (1938), 42–52.

country invaders induced Ohio Indians to alter their subsistence system and to experiment with new constructions of rights in the woods *and* the clearings.

Like their backcountry counterparts, the Indians of the Ohio country were a multiethnic agglomeration of refugees. Closest to the pioneer stations in central Kentucky and also recently settled were the Scioto Valley villages of the Shawnee confederacy. Shawnee in name, these villages included an assortment of ethnic groups: Pennsylvania Indians heading west to escape Anglo-American encirclement and Illinois Indians moving east to position themselves between French and British trading orbits. Multilingualism was the rule: in the 1760s at Chillicothe, the principal Shawnee town, residents typically spoke three or more languages.[22]

The 1760s witnessed an influx of Anglo-American traders, captives, and renegades who brought English words and English ways increasingly into the mix. As part of their incorporation into Indian communities, backcountry-born captives learned to live and think as Indians. But adopted captives as well as other "white Indians" also introduced colonial foods, fashions, and furnishings. At the aptly named Newcomer's Town in 1772, missionary David

22. The Shawnees' towns had once been located on the south side of the Ohio River. When French explorers first penetrated the Ohio Valley in the late seventeenth century, they found dozens of hamlets in what is now Kentucky, which was labeled on these maps as Shawnee country. As late as 1736, a French census enumerated 200 Shawnee men at the village of Eskippakithiki on the eastern edge of the central Kentucky plain. The Shawnees, however, were by then a scattered people, living in small contingents and mingling with other Indian groups in Alabama, Georgia, the Carolinas, and Pennsylvania. Eskippakithiki, too, was soon abandoned, probably during the 1750s. But Shawnees, together with other Pennsylvania Indians, had already returned to the Ohio country and established villages on the north side of the Ohio River. See A. Gwynn Henderson, "Dispelling the Myth: Seventeenth- and Eighteenth-Century Indian Life in Kentucky," *Register of the Kentucky Hist. Soc.*, XC (1992), 1–25; Lucien Beckner, "Eskippakithiki: The Last Indian Town in Kentucky," *Filson Club Hist. Qtly.*, VI (1932), 355–382; Michael N. McConnell, "Peoples 'in Between': The Iroquois and the Ohio Indians, 1720–1768," in Daniel K. Richter and James H. Merrell, eds., *Beyond the Covenant Chain: The Iroquois and Their Neighbors in Indian North America, 1600–1800* (Syracuse, N.Y., 1987), 93–112; Charles Callender, "Shawnee," in William C. Sturtevant, gen. ed., *Handbook of North American Indians*, XV, Bruce G. Trigger, ed., *Northeast* (Washington, D.C., 1978), 630–634; Peter H. Wood, "The Changing Population of the Colonial South: An Overview by Race and Region, 1685–1790," in Peter H. Wood, Gregory A. Waselkov, and M. Thomas Hatley, eds., *Powhatan's Mantle: Indians in the Colonial Southeast* (Lincoln, Nebr., 1989), 85–87; Richard White, *The Middle Ground: Indians, Empires, and Republics in the Great Lakes Region, 1650–1815* (New York, 1991), 186–222; Jerry E. Clark, *The Shawnee* (Lexington, Ky., 1977), 5–27.

McClure found traditional bark longhouses adjacent to backcountry-style log cabins. Although the Delaware prophet Neolin envisioned a world cleansed of European things and thinking, his home, with its "stone cellar, stairway, stone chimney and fireplace," reminded McClure "of an English dwelling." [23]

Nowhere were European ways more influential than in the realm of hunting. These ways were inscribed in the discriminations that Ohio Indians began to draw between the rights in the woods of meat hunters and skin hunters. An outsider—a hunter who did not have a right in the woods that surrounded a village's clearings—was generally allowed to take meat. Peltry, on the other hand, which could be turned into things European, belonged exclusively to the families within the claimant town, and outsiders were warned not to take hides. [24]

That distinction held when Ohio Indians ran into long hunters in Kentucky. No towns were then located in eastern and central Kentucky, but villagers to the north and south claimed a right in the woods, and custody of this hunting common was shared—if not always peacefully. Through the middle decades of the eighteenth century, skirmishes among Indian hunters gave the country a reputation as a "Dark and Bloody Ground." Yet, when Indian hunters met backcountry long hunters in the 1760s, they sometimes chose not to exact their own "bloody code." More than once, Indian hunters spared captured poachers. Skins and supplies were confiscated, and long hunters were admonished not to take pelts from Indian country again. The pardoned men then received guns and shot to keep them alive and at least once advice about where to find "plenty [of meat] to kill to go home." In effect, Ohio Indians treated back-

---

23. Franklin B. Dexter, ed., *Diary of David McClure, Doctor of Divinity, 1748–1820* (New York, 1899), 61, 68 (quotations); William Albert Galloway, *Old Chillicothe: Shawnee and Pioneer History; Conflicts and Romances in the Northwest Territory* (Xenia, Ohio, 1934), 44–45; Helen Hornbeck Tanner, "The Glaize in 1792: A Composite Indian Community," *Ethnohistory*, XXV (1978), 15–39; Michael N. McConnell, *A Country Between: The Upper Ohio Valley and Its Peoples, 1724–1774* (Lincoln, Nebr., 1992), 210–220.

24. On distinctions between meat hunting and skin hunting, see White, *The Middle Ground*, 103–104; White, *The Roots of Dependency: Subsistence, Environment, and Social Change among the Choctaws, Pawnees, and Navajos* (Lincoln, Nebr., 1983), 7–13, 69–96. The influence of European ways, it should be emphasized, preceded the physical presence of Europeans in the Ohio Valley. A century before the Anglo-American colonization of Kentucky, before even the French had much knowledge of the Ohio Valley, the consequences of the fur trade reverberated in the country of the Shawnees and their neighbors. Control of peltry inspired the Iroquois invasions of the 1670s and 1680s that desettled Kentucky and destroyed villages across the upper Ohio Valley. On the "beaver wars" that desettled the Shawnees and other Ohio peoples, see Daniel K. Richter, *The Ordeal of the Longhouse: The Peoples of the Iroquois League in the Era of European Colonization* (Chapel Hill, N.C., 1992), 50–74, 144–149.

country hunters much as did the laws of Virginia. Just as Virginia statutes permitted "frontier" hunters to take meat out of season, so Ohio Indians differentiated between hunting for food, which they condoned, and for pelts, which they expropriated.[25]

The intolerance of skin hunters attested to the substantial impact of the fur trade on external relations, but commercial concerns did not as immediately disturb the protocols of intravillage exchange. In the early 1770s, the Reverend David McClure witnessed a ceremony among Delawares in which hunters "present[ed] the skins of the animals and a considerable part of the meat to the widows and the aged." The ritual underscored the preeminence of the common weal within the village. It also suggested the prestige that came with gifts of game. Providing meat for relations roused Ohio Indian men as did no other action, except perhaps skill and stoicism in combat or captivity. In Indian country, as in backcountry, young men took enormous pride in their martial exploits and in the game that they provided for kin, especially for elders who could no longer hunt.[26]

Elaborate ceremonies, allowing hunters to express their respect for fellow villagers, continued to accompany the pursuit, division, and consumption of game. Custom, for example, still dictated that, when two Shawnees hunted together, the first game killed was given to the other man with the remark: "I enliven you as a man." No bargain was struck; the recipient provided nothing in return—though, as in other societies where the rules of the market did not govern, the recipient expected to do the same should the situation ever be reversed.[27]

25. James Knox, "Report on a Hunting Trip," 1769, Photocopy in Special Collections, Margaret I. King Library, University of Kentucky, Lexington. See also John D. Shane interview with Daniel Boone Bryan, 1844, DM, 22C14; Lyman C. Draper interview with Nathan and Olive Boone, 1851, DM, 6S46–52. It was John Filson, *The Discovery, Settlement, and Present State of Kentucke* (1784), ed. William H. Masterson (New York, 1962), 8, who claimed that the Indians knew Kentucky "by the name of the Dark and Bloody Ground, and sometimes the Middle Ground."

26. Dexter, ed., *Diary of David McClure*, 89–90.

27. Thomas Wildcat Alford, *Civilization* (Norman, Okla., 1936), 53 (quotation); Ebenezer Denny, *Military Journal of Major Ebenezer Denny, an Officer in the Revolutionary and Indian Wars* . . . (Philadelphia, 1859), 68; John Heckewelder, *History, Manners, and Customs of the Indian Nations, Who Once Inhabited Pennsylvania and the Neighbouring States,* ed. William C. Reichel (Historical Society of Pennsylvania, *Memoirs,* XII [Philadelphia, 1876]), 100–106, 191–192, 310–311; Henry Harvey, *History of the Shawnee Indians from the Year 1681 to 1854, Inclusive* (Cincinnati, 1855), 151; James H. Howard, *Shawnee! The Ceremonialism of a Native Indian Tribe and Its Cultural Background* (Athens, Ohio, 1981), 43–48, 195–196.

The rule of reciprocity among Shawnee hunters, however, excluded certain prey, an exception that illustrated the intrusion of commercialism into Ohio Indian calculations. If the first animal taken was an otter or a beaver, trappers suspended assumptions about gift giving; the killer retained possession of these pelts, which carried the highest value with European traders.[28]

As European tools and weapons supplanted native technologies and as the demand for liquor grew, the hunting economy of Ohio Indians acquired a dual character that paralleled that of pioneers. By the early 1790s, when adopted captive Jonathan Alder went hunting with his Shawnee kin, he expressed a reduced commitment to redistributive rituals. As in earlier times, Alder provided venison and bear meat to his parents and to fellow villagers. Yet Alder no longer shared his pelts with widows and elders, for "all the profits accruing from the sales of skins and furs" were his alone. Alder's adoption of separate rules to govern the disposition of flesh and hides imitated backcountry conventions, where gifts of meat to neighbors in need coincided with profit-minded marketing of peltry.[29]

It was no accident that Alder, a white Indian, took the boldest plunge into economic individualism. Like many other white captives who chose to remain with their adoptors, Alder lived among Indians, but between worlds. That intermediary position enabled Alder and other white Indians to act as cultural *brokers*. It made them cultural *breakers* too, for they became the witting and unwitting carriers of European practices and values into Ohio Indian country.[30]

Among the transmitted traditions was livestock herding. Well into the eighteenth century, the absence of cattle, sheep, and hogs in Indian country marked a cultural divide across the frontier. Minimizing the distinction, Ohio Indians occasionally likened wildlife to livestock. The analogy served a purpose. By maintaining that "the Elks are our horses, the Buffaloes are our cows, [and] the deer are our sheep," Ohio Indians justified their ownership of game and their right to punish foreign poachers. But the reasoning was flawed, for Shawnees, Delawares, and their Indian neighbors more typically condemned the idea of owning game *and* domesticating stock. Both actions, it was believed, desecrated the spirituality of animals.[31]

28. Alford, *Civilization*, 53.

29. Orley E. Brown, ed., *The Captivity of Jonathan Alder and His Life with the Indians* (Alliance, Ohio, 1965), 62.

30. On white Indians acting as cultural brokers across the trans-Appalachian frontier, see Colin G. Calloway, "Beyond the Vortex of Violence: Indian-White Relations in the Ohio Country, 1783–1815," *Northwest Ohio Quarterly*, LXIV (1992), 16–26.

31. Dexter, ed., *Diary of David McClure*, 85.

These denunciations, however, lost some potency when Ohio Indians began to raise livestock in the second half of the eighteenth century. Already in the 1760s, European visitors to the Ohio country remarked on the Indians' cattle and on their skill in making butter and cheese. After the Revolution, livestock herds increased in size and importance. As overhunting reduced the supply of game and the loss of Kentucky constricted the available hunting territory, Ohio Indians compensated by raising more cattle and hogs. In becoming herders as well as hunters and horticulturists, they embraced the mixed subsistence system of trans-Appalachian pioneers.[32]

To be sure, the introduction of livestock did not undermine traditional beliefs. As with other imports from Europe, Ohio Indians successfully integrated domesticated animals into existing rituals. Thus, ceremonies connected with hunting expanded to pay respect for slaughtered livestock.[33]

Still, the diffusion of livestock heightened the resemblance between Indian villages and pioneer settlements and altered the look of the land. In the backcountry manner, Indians left their stock to graze on the open range, but roving cows, pigs, and horses had to be kept out of cornfields. Advised by officials of the United States government, Christian missionaries, and assorted white intermediaries, Ohio Indians, to varying extents, chopped trees, split rails, and enclosed fields.[34]

32. John W. Jordan, ed., "Journal of James Kenny, 1761–1763," *Pennsylvania Magazine of History and Biography*, XXXVII (1913), 22; Paul A. W. Wallace, ed., *Thirty Thousand Miles with John Heckewelder* (Pittsburgh, 1958), 41, 44; David Jones, *A Journal of Two Visits Made to Some Nations of Indians on the West Side of the River Ohio, in the Years 1772 and 1773* (Burlington, N.J., 1774), 57; Thomas Ridout, "The Narrative of the Captivity among the Shawanese Indians, in 1788, of Thos. Ridout, Afterwards Surveyor-General of Upper Canada," in Matilda Edgar, *Ten Years of Upper Canada in Peace and War, 1805–1815; Being the Ridout Letters* (Toronto, 1890), 361, 366; O. M. Spencer, *The Indian Captivity of O. M. Spencer,* ed. Milo Milton Quaife (Chicago, 1917), 96. For a case study of New England Indians and the introduction of livestock, see Virginia DeJohn Anderson, "King Philip's Herds: Indians, Colonists, and the Problem of Livestock in Early New England," *William and Mary Quarterly,* 3d Ser., LI (1994), 601–624.

33. McConnell, *A Country Between,* 219.

34. Spencer, *The Indian Captivity of O. M. Spencer,* ed. Quaife, 96; Lawrence Henry Gipson, ed., *The Moravian Indian Mission on White River: Diaries and Letters, May 5, 1799, to November 12, 1806,* Indiana Historical Collections, XXIII (Indianapolis, 1938), 297, 338–339; Joseph E. Walker, ed., "Plowshares and Pruning Hooks for the Miami and Potawatomi: The Journal of Gerard T. Hopkins, 1804," *Ohio History,* LXXXVIII (1979), 389–393, 402–403; John Johnston, "Recollections of Sixty Years," in Leonard Uzal Hill, *John Johnston and the Indians in the Land of the Three Miamis* (Piqua, Ohio, 1957), 188–189; R. David Edmunds,

Fence building and other signs of a Europeanized landscape reached their greatest extent in the communities of Christian Indians founded by Moravian missionaries. Having initiated missions among the Delaware in eastern Pennsylvania, Moravian evangelists followed Indian refugees into the Ohio country. There Moravians, like other Christian emissaries, faced opposition from nativist prophets, who saw to it that indifference and hostility greeted proselytizers. Under the zealous stewardship of David Zeisberger, the Moravians persevered where other missionaries failed. At a series of sites, Zeisberger supervised the erection of Christian towns by Indian converts.[35]

For Zeisberger and his brethren, no less than for missionaries of other sects, saving savages required that they be civilized, that their world be remade along European lines. Although Moravians displayed more sensitivity than rival missionaries, they proposed no less thorough a reformation of Ohio Indian life. To facilitate the civilizing process, Moravian missionaries closely regulated the lives of Indian neophytes. Immediately targeted for extinction were beliefs and rituals that competed with Christianity. The banning of dances, sacrifices, and other so-called heathenish festivals manifested this intolerance of syncretism.

Missionaries deemed hunting to be particularly incompatible with a civilized, Christian life, which they predicated on an agriculturally derived subsistence. Ohio Indians, of course, had long cultivated the soil, but farming as well as other aspects of food preparation were controlled by women. This was unacceptable to white reformers, who insisted that men stay out of the woods and work assiduously in the fields. Conversion, then, involved a profound reorientation of the Indians' gendered division of space and labor. To forward this transformation, Moravian missionaries sought to discourage and restrict male hunting. Residents of Moravian towns were prohibited from soliciting supernatural aid in hunting. Men were told not to go on any long hunts without informing the village minister. To give women "more time to attend to their do-

---

"'Unacquainted with the Laws of the Civilized World': American Attitudes toward the Métis Communities in the Old Northwest," in Jacqueline Peterson and Jennifer S. H. Brown, eds., *The New Peoples: Being and Becoming Métis in North America* (Lincoln, Nebr., 1985), 185–193; Joseph A. Parsons, Jr., "Civilizing the Indians of the Old Northwest, 1800–1810," *Indiana Magazine of History*, LVI (1960), 195–216.

35. On Zeisberger's career and the Moravian missions in the Ohio country, see Eugene F. Bliss, ed., *Diary of David Zeisberger: A Moravian Missionary among the Indians of Ohio*, 2 vols. (Cincinnati, 1885); Elma E. Gray, *Wilderness Christians: The Moravian Mission to the Delaware Indians* (Ithaca, N.Y., 1956); Earl P. Olmstead, *Blackcoats among the Delaware: David Zeisberger on the Ohio Frontier* (Kent, Ohio, 1991).

mestic concerns," females were prevented from going at all. By this separation, it was hoped, "the men will be induced to return home sooner." Thus did Moravian missionaries shrink hunting time, while encouraging men to raise more stock and cultivate more crops.[36]

Boasting fine orchards, well-tended gardens, neatly fenced cornfields, and sprawling pastures that supported substantial herds of cattle, horses, and hogs, the landscape surrounding these Moravian Indian villages took on a decidedly European character. Here, by the 1790s, fences not only blocked wandering stock but also demarcated property lines. Although the orchard remained a community concern, adult male converts owned their own homes, raised their own livestock, and fenced and cultivated their own plantations. To missionaries who equated progress with privatization, improvements were apparent.[37]

III

Appearances deceived. Domesticated animals and fenced fields gave the landscape a more European look, and to the Reverend David Zeisberger's delight, Indians from near and far came to inspect the Moravians' improvements. To his dismay, visitors rarely converted, backsliding plagued neophytes, and Indian prophets decried the Moravians' presence. Fulfilling prophecy, nativists expelled Moravians and purged foreign elements from Indian country. Still, the efforts to cleanse their country of European influences accented the difficulties in discriminating between what was native and what was not.

The adaptability of Ohio Indian peoples abetted the comingling of frontier cultures, but it was not a sign of surrender. Into the early nineteenth century, Ohio Indians accepted new beliefs and practices selectively, rejecting those recommendations at odds with their ideas of the good and virtuous life. They refused to give up hunting, disdained instruction in how to labor as white people, and declined to venerate industry. "We do not need anyone to teach us how to work," a Quaker missionary was lectured. "If we want to work, we know how to do it according to our own way and as it pleases us." Most Ohio Indian men scorned appeals to forsake hunting in favor of farming, for the loss of their rights and responsibilities in the woods would have deprived them

36. Gipson, ed., *The Moravian Indian Mission on White River*, 36 (quotation); John Heckewelder, *A Narrative of the Mission of the United Brethren among the Delaware and Mohegan Indians, from Its Commencement, in the Year 1740, to the Close of the Year 1808* (Philadelphia, 1820), 122–124.

37. Wallace, ed., *Thirty Thousand Miles*, 104, 111; Heckewelder, *A Narrative of the Mission*, 103–104, 123, 157; Gipson, ed., *The Moravian Indian Mission on White River*, 226–227.

of the traditional basis for proving manhood. In their view, the conversion demanded by missionaries threatened to change men into women, and few relished this emasculation. Indian men and women also resisted the logic of market relations. After more than a century of trading skins, Ohio Indians remained cold to the untamed pursuit of advantage. "They still think that those who have something are in duty bound to share with them," recorded a frustrated missionary.[38]

Confronted by culture-breaking missionaries, encroaching pioneers, shrinking lands, and disappearing game, Ohio Indians maintained, in historian Gregory Evans Dowd's phrase, "a spirited resistance." In the early years of the nineteenth century, Ohio Indians turned a deaf ear to Christian evangelists. They flocked once more to hear the visions of nativist seers, to hear the dreams of a world restored. If Indians stopped giving "heed to what the white people tell," stopped "imitat[ing] them and keep[ing] horses, cows, [and] hogs," then all could "live again as . . . before the white people came into this land." If Indians dressed in skins, killed their stock, and gave up "everything" they had from the white people, the deer, which were at present a half a tree's length beneath the earth, would return and there would be "wild game enough." In response, men shaved heads, renounced alcohol, and shed European garb. Readying for the return of departed game, they slaughtered cattle and tore down fences.[39]

The crusade, however, stopped short of a completely revitalized landscape. Although the Shawnee prophet Tenskwatawa commanded his followers to kill cattle and hogs, he did not foresee a return to a stockless way of living. When the prophet's followers chased Moravians out of the White River country (what is now northeastern Indiana) in 1806, they were careful not to rid it entirely of European influences. Rather than exterminating the Moravians' stock in a rite of nativist revitalization, crusaders insisted that, since the cattle grazed on Indian land, Indians deserved half of the animals. A similar division governed the disposition of everything made of wood.[40]

In these demands, militants betrayed an attachment to European things and European thinking that made inconceivable a thorough restoration of the

38. Gipson, ed., *The Moravian Indian Mission on White River*, 427, 450.

39. Ibid., 262. The phrase "a spirited resistance" comes from the title of Gregory Evans Dowd's study of the nativist uprising in Ohio Indian country and nicely captures the prophetic sources of pan-Indian militancy. For his interpretation of the nativist movement in the early nineteenth century, see *A Spirited Resistance: The North American Indian Struggle for Unity, 1745–1815* (Baltimore, 1992), 123–147.

40. Gipson, ed., *The Moravian Indian Mission on White River*, 392, 452–453.

landscape. Militant rhetoric played up the differences between Europeans and Indians, but militant behavior displayed a syncretic logic. That had long been true of Ohio Indian nativism. A generation earlier, Neolin preached of the separate origins of Indians and whites—while residing in an English-style house and while propounding a message of cultural reformation that bore the imprint of Christian moralism. Even as Neolin's successors elaborated on the idea of polygenesis and prophesied an Ohio River boundary between Indian country and the United States, their world remained as permeable to Anglo-American influences as ever.

That the worlds of Indians and pioneers could not easily be separated did not mean their ways had become indistinguishable. Consider again hunting, the realm that symbolized the fusing of cultures: in both backcountry and Indian country, hunting contributed to subsistence, established compartmental exchange relations, shaped rights in the woods, offered a venue to demonstrate manhood, and provided an avenue to local authority. But the similarities in how Indian and pioneer men hunted did not erase the differences in how they lived.

The most obvious fork in the ways of hunters was in the sexual composition of parties. In Indian villages and backcountry settlements, the approach of autumn and the completion of the harvest signaled the onset of the hunting season. Once the crops were in and the leaves were down, backcountry farmers "became uneasy at home. Everything about them became disagreeable," remembered a resident of western Virginia, "even the good wife was not thought for the time being a proper companion." Leaving women behind, able-bodied men escaped to the woods for days and, in the case of "long hunters," for months and years at a time. By contrast, the extended fall and winter hunts made by Indians were not single-sex sojourns. Whole families participated, with women responsible for packing necessities and carrying belongings from villages to hunting camps. There they cut wood, hauled water, dressed game, prepared food, and watched over children.[41]

Backcountry parties assigned the hunting-related jobs handled by Indian women to men who were brought along specifically as campkeepers. These were often African American slaves, whose lack of freedom reinforced the perception of Indian women as "squaw drudges." Fixating on "the humiliating condition" of Ohio Indian women, who were treated more "as slaves than as

41. Doddridge, *Notes on the Settlement and Indian Wars,* 98 (quotation); Spencer Records' Narrative, 1842, DM, 23CC5; William Preston (Smithfield) to Arthur Campbell and William Campbell, Dec. 6, 1780, Preston Family Papers, Gray Collection, Filson Club, Louisville, Ky.

companions," Anglo-American commentators insisted that native wives and daughters did the real work during the hunt and during the rest of the annual subsistence cycle. When Indians returned to their villages in early spring, reported one captive, men lounged about, "it being thought disgraceful for an Indian [man] to labor." Meanwhile, Indian women spent their summers toiling in fields and tending to livestock.[42]

More sensitive observers recognized that the Indians' gendered division of labor was not so imbalanced. All things considered, Indian women's work was less onerous than that shouldered by backcountry wives and daughters. On Appalachian frontiers and across the American countryside, pioneer women labored in fields and did what was needed, regardless of the work's gendered designation. In a pinch, some even hunted, and tales abounded of pioneer mothers outshooting pioneer fathers and outfighting Indian marauders. Assumption of male roles and accomplishment in hunting and warring did not, however, elevate these women to positions of local leadership.[43]

Pioneer society had no official equivalent to the female peace and war chiefs of the Shawnees. These posts were customarily, though not always, held by the mother, sister, or another close relative of the corresponding male headmen. The female peace or village chief oversaw the everyday activities of women. She scheduled planting and arranged the feasts that coincided with various seasonal rituals. She was also responsible for conveying the consensus of village women to a male war chief. According to an early-nineteenth-century ethnographer, when the wishes of women opposed those of a male war chief, the female chief "seldom fail[ed] to dissuade him."[44]

42. Mary Kinnan, *A True Narrative of the Sufferings of Mary Kinnan, Who Was Taken Prisoner by the Shawanee Nation of Indians on the Thirteenth Day of May, 1791, and Remained with Them till the Sixteenth of August, 1794* (Elizabethtown, Ky., 1795), 8 (quotation); Spencer, *The Indian Captivity of O. M. Spencer*, ed. Quaife, 75 (quotation); Brown, ed., *The Captivity of Jonathan Alder*, 29–30; Jones, *A Journal of Two Visits*, 55–58; Dexter, ed., *Diary of David McClure*, 68; James Smith, *An Account of the Remarkable Occurrences in the Life and Travels of Col. James Smith, during His Captivity with the Indians, in the Years 1755, '56, '57, '58, and '59*, ed. William Darlington (1799; reprint, Cincinnati, 1870), 44–45; John Brickell, "Narrative of John Brickell's Captivity among the Delawares," *American Pioneer*, I (1842), 47.

43. For an example of white women's taking on the role of hunters and sharpshooters, see Stephen Aron, *How the West Was Lost: The Transformation of Kentucky from Daniel Boone to Henry Clay* (Baltimore, 1996), 34–35.

44. Vernon Kinietz and Erminie W. Voegelin, eds., *Shawnese Traditions: C. C. Trowbridge's Account*, Occasional Contributions of the Museum of Anthropology, University of Michigan, Number 9 (Ann Arbor, Mich., 1939), 12–13.

The authority of Ohio Indian women derived from the access their gender gave them to specific sacred powers. Indian men readily acknowledged that women collectively governed the production of food and the ceremonies associated with subsistence. Pioneer men made no comparable concessions to female power. Although they expected wives and daughters to do their share, all aspects of the backcountry subsistence system remained under patriarchal authority.[45]

Conflicting constructions of womanhood divided Indian and pioneer constructions of manhood, but the distinction between frontier hunting cultures went beyond the relations of men and women. As significant were the relations between people and animals. To be sure, the dissimilarity was not a stark and simple one between Christians and animists. Backcountry and Indian hunters each ascribed magical powers to the nonhuman world. Both wore charms and uttered incantations to ward off evil spirits, reverse bad omens, and cure cursed weapons. But pioneer hunters recognized no kinship with their prey. Whereas Ohio Indians performed elaborate rites to express gratitude and show respect to animal cousins, backcountry men saw the hunt as an act of mastery. In demonstrating their dominion over lesser beasts, pioneer hunters acknowledged no obligation to the game they killed.[46]

That was a recipe for destruction of the hunting commons. Among Ohio Indians, the commodification of skins produced an increase in hunting and a decrease in deer populations. The pressure on game intensified once Indian hunters lost their rights in the Kentucky woods and had to rely on a constricted domain. The declines steepened following American invasions of the Ohio country in the 1780s and 1790s, which left villages and cornfields burned. Facing a subsistence crisis, Ohio Indian hunters covered dietary shortfalls by harvesting more wild meat. Noticeable as the resulting reductions in wildlife were, they were nothing compared to what pioneers accomplished south of the Ohio River. For without an ethic of reciprocity to restrain their exhibitions of mastery, Kentucky's pioneer hunters wasted game "at a mighty rate."[47]

The depletion of Kentucky wildlife inspired a number of proposals to better manage hunting. In the spring of 1775, at the first and only convention of

45. On the gendered character of sacred power, see Dowd, *A Spirited Resistance*, 1–22.

46. Doddridge, *Notes on the Settlement and Indian Wars*, 24; Mann Butler, "Details of Frontier Life," *Register of the Kentucky Hist. Soc.*, LXII (1964), 224; Daniel Linsey Thomas and Lucy Blayney Thomas, *Kentucky Superstitions* (Princeton, N.J., 1920), 241; Fischer, *Albion's Seed*, 708–715.

47. Lucien Beckner, ed., "Reverend John D. Shane's Interview with Pioneer William Clinkenbeard," *Filson Club Hist. Qtly.*, II (1928), 115.

the House of Delegates of the Transylvania Colony, Daniel Boone forwarded a bill for preserving game. Boone's idea was quickly buried, as were other schemes to curb hunters. At Blue Licks in the early 1780s, the increasing scarcity of game prompted an agreement between the settlers to allow only the neighborhood's best hunter to kill buffalo. But this effort was designed more to lessen the stench of rotting buffalo and reduce the magnet for wolves than to save a dwindling resource. About the only ceiling that pioneer hunters observed was that set by the supply of powder and shot.[48]

Neither commercial incentives nor subsistence imperatives fully explain the slaughter of buffalo. Herds of buffalo once roamed east of the Appalachians too. They had been killed, observed Thomas Walker in 1750, not for their hides, but for "diversion." In Kentucky, where herds were even larger and buffalo meat of even greater use value, "some would kill three, four, five, or 1/2 a dozen buffaloes and not take half a horse load from the all." It was, not hunger, but the display of manhood that motivated these sprees. "Many a man killed a buffalo just for the sake of saying so," admitted one pioneer. The squandering persisted until the late 1780s—until there were no more buffalo in the central Kentucky woods for hunters to have a right.[49]

### IV

The destruction of the commons compounded tragedy and irony, for, after stripping Indians of their rights in the Kentucky woods, pioneers let theirs erode as well. "Cane and game," pioneers acknowledged, sustained them, yet

48. *Journal of the Proceedings of the House of Delegates or Representatives of the Colony of Transylvania,* in Ranck, ed., *Boonesborough,* 206; Hogan, ed., "Buffaloes in the Corn," *Register of the Kentucky Hist. Soc.,* LXXXIX (1991), 5; Spencer Records' Narrative, DM, 23CC35; Beckner, ed., "Shane's Interview with Pioneer William Clinkenbeard," *Filson Club Hist. Qtly.,* II (1928), 104; Beckner, ed., "John D. Shane's Interview with Jesse Graddy of Woodford County," ibid., XX (1946), 13.

49. Johnston, ed., *First Explorations of Kentucky,* 37 (quotation); *Judge Richard Henderson's Journal of Trip to "Cantuckey" and of Events at Boonesborough in 1775,* in Ranck, ed., *Boonesborough,* 176 (quotation); John D. Shane interview with Joshua McQueen, DM, 13CC21 (quotation); Otto Rothert, ed., "John D. Shane's Interview with Pioneer John Hedge, Bourbon County," *Filson Club Hist. Qtly.,* XIV (1940), 179; Lucien Beckner, ed., "A Sketch of the Early Adventures of William Sudduth in Kentucky," ibid., II (1928), 47; Clough, ed., "Abraham Thomas," *Kentucky Ancestors,* XXVI (1990), 77; "Some Particulars Relative to the Soil, Situation, Production, etc. of Kentucky: Extracted from the Manuscript Journal of a Gentleman Not Long Since Returned from Those Parts," in Eugene Lincoln Schwaab, ed., *Travels in the Old South, Selected from Periodicals of the Times,* 2 vols. (Lexington, Ky., 1973), I, 60.

settlers maintained neither flora nor fauna. As bluegrass pastures succeeded canebrakes and pedigreed stock supplanted game, the landscape acquired a new face—and new rules came into place that diminished rights in the woods. But, whereas Ohio Indians desperately contested the imposition of foreign ways, pioneers and their offspring staged at best a dispirited resistance against the privatization of property regimes.[50]

The retreat of Indians from the borders of the Bluegrass inflated land values and opened the country to a flood of migrants. Included were numbers of wealthy Virginians intent on establishing their authority and securing their property. Through legislation, litigation, and a bit of extralegal intimidation, they strove to undo frontier arrangements and codify the privatization of natural resources.[51]

During the 1790s, the appearance of "no trespassing notices" in Kentucky's early newspapers broadcast the break with traditions of untrammeled access and the breakdown in the previous consensus. These postings warned readers not to hunt, fish, or fowl on an owner's exclusive domain. Interlopers were also

50. On the destruction of cane and succession of bluegrass *(Poa pratensis)*, see James B. Finley, *Autobiography of Rev. James B. Finley; or, Pioneer Life in the West*, ed. W. P. Strickland (Cincinnati, 1853), 39; Paul Woehrmann, ed., "The Autobiography of Abraham Snethen, Frontier Preacher," *Filson Club Hist. Qtly.*, LI (1977), 316; Lucien Beckner, ed., "Rev. John Dabney Shane's Interview with Mrs. Sarah Graham of Bath County," ibid., IX (1935), 228; Beckner, ed., "Shane's Interview with Pioneer William Clinkenbeard," ibid., II (1928), 115; David Meade (Lexington) to Ann Randolph, Sept. 1, 1796, in Bayrd Still, ed., "The Westward Migration of a Planter Pioneer in 1796," *WMQ*, 2d Ser., XXI (1941), 335; Wharton and Barbour, *Bluegrass Land and Life*, 26–27; Darrell Haug Davis, *The Geography of the Blue Grass Region of Kentucky* (Frankfort, Ky., 1927).

51. The criminalization of custom and the defense of common rights have been the themes of a number of important studies in eighteenth-century British history. See, especially, Hay et al., *Albion's Fatal Tree;* Thompson, *Whigs and Hunters;* and E. P. Thompson, *Customs in Common* (London, 1991), esp. 97–184. On this side of the Atlantic, the conflicts between custom and commercialism are taken up in Gary Kulik, "Dams, Fish, and Farmers: Defense of Public Rights in Eighteenth-Century Rhode Island," in Steven Hahn and Jonathan Prude, eds., *The Countryside in the Age of Capitalist Transformation: Essays in the Social History of Rural America* (Chapel Hill, N.C., 1985), 25–50; Steven Hahn, "Hunting, Fishing, and Foraging: Common Rights and Class Relations in the Postbellum South," *Radical History Review*, no. 26 (October 1982), 37–64; Hahn, *The Roots of Southern Populism: Yeoman Farmers and the Transformation of the Georgia Upcountry, 1850–1890* (New York, 1983), 239–253. For a critique of Hahn's perspective, see Shawn Everett Kantor and J. Morgan Kousser, "Common Sense or Commonwealth? The Fence Law and Institutional Change in the Postbellum South," *Journal of Southern History*, LIX (1993), 201–242.

advised not to let stock roam across privately held lands, nor to remove timber from them, nor even to cross the property without the permission of the owner. One ban ominously promised "to make an example of" any "such strolling transgressors."[52]

Privatizers generally relied on the law to implement and enforce their conceptions. New statutes, particularly a 1798 act "for preventing trespasses," challenged pioneer hunters' constructions of rights in the woods. On its face, this law appeared an innocuous piece of legislation. It did not close the open range. Landowners were still expected to fence in crops, not domesticated animals. The act merely clarified what constituted a "lawful fence" and spelled out a schedule of reparations. But privatizers seized on the letter of the law and lengthened fences. Some owners encircled their entire property with lawful fences, so that unbroken barricades ran for miles through the more densely settled parts of the Bluegrass country.[53]

Lawmakers were not completely blind to the nuisances created by the loss of rights in the woods. To ease the inconveniences caused by extended fences, the Kentucky legislature eventually ratified a law ensuring public passage through private lands. The passway act, approved in December 1820, offered some relief from three decades of privatization. It hardly reversed the trend or restored the pioneers' balance between private property and public necessity. The statute suspended trespassing laws only in places where a jury of "four housekeepers" decreed public crossing "indispensable." The mandated path, measuring no more than fifteen feet wide, was opened to only "those who may be legally and necessarily required to attend courts, elections, etc."[54]

The passway act made no allowance for the rights of hunters. In the manner of English lords, some of the largest landowners had turned a portion of their estates into private hunting parks. Impressed by the neat appearance of

52. See the advertisement signed by "S. Teagarden" in *Kentucky Gazette* (Lexington), Jan. 27, 1817 (quotation); see also ibid., Jan. 5, 1793, July 11, 1799; *Stewart's Kentucky Herald* (Lexington), Nov. 25, 1805; *Reporter* (Lexington), Dec. 12, 1812. On the practice of taking timber from private lands and efforts to combat it, see W. Croghan (near Louisville) to Edmund Rogers, Feb. 7, 1804, Rogers-Underwood Family Papers, Manuscripts Division, Filson Club; Fanney Slaughter (Louisville) to Polly Campbell, May 18, 1809, Slaughter Family Papers, Manuscripts Division, Filson Club; *Benjamin Stansberry v. John Dickerson, James Cochren, and Peter Bonta,* May 1797, Abstract from Bullitt Circuit Court Records, Robert Emmett McDowell Collection, Filson Club.

53. Littell, ed., *The Statute Laws of Kentucky,* II, 27–28.

54. *Acts Passed at the First Session of the Twenty-Eighth General Assembly for the Commonwealth of Kentucky* . . . (Frankfort, Ky., 1820–1821), 114–116.

private forests, a visitor jokingly wondered whether "they sweep the woods here?" Turning custom on its head, the proprietors of these preserves fenced deer *in* and employed hounds to keep hunters *out*. "If any body went in to shoot," recalled one of the excluded, "they would set the dogs on them."[55]

In addition to canine gamekeepers, excluders looked to legislators and jurists for protection of their private woods. When Kentucky became a state, Virginia game laws remained in force. These stipulated fines and whippings for out-of-season hunters, though the statutes had previously exempted meat hunting by residents of frontier counties. As settlement thickened in central Kentucky, privatizers claimed the immunity of meat hunters no longer applied.[56]

Backcountry hunting customs, like open-range herding traditions, persisted in spite of privatizing pressure. Long into the nineteenth century, a rifle hung over the mantle or the door of most Kentucky farmsteads. Indeed, a half-serious European visitor remarked that in choosing a rifle the Kentuckian was "even more particular than in selecting a wife." The placement and choice reflected the abiding contribution that hunting made to the well-being of Kentucky households.[57]

The spot reserved for the rifle was as much symbolic as it was pragmatic. With Indians no longer lurking and livestock and corn satisfying subsistence requirements, rifles did not have to be kept so prominently at hand. For a good part of the year, their use was limited to purging squirrels and other pests from

55. Robert Triplett, *Roland Trevor; or, The Pilot of Human Life; Being an Autobiography of the Author, Showing How to Make and Lose a Fortune, and Then to Make Another* (Philadelphia, 1853), 264 (quotation); John D. Shane interview with Samuel Potts Pointer, DM, 12CC247–248 (quotation); Lewis H. Kilpatrick, "The Journal of William Calk, Kentucky Pioneer," *Mississippi Valley Historical Review*, VII (1921), 375; Richard Laverne Troutman, "Plantation Life in the Antebellum Bluegrass Region of Kentucky" (master's thesis, University of Kentucky, 1955), 20.

56. John Bradford, *The General Instructor; or, The Office, Duty, and Authority of Justices of the Peace, Sheriffs, Coroners, and Constables, in the State of Kentucky* (Lexington, Ky., 1800), 72–74; Littell, ed., *The Statute Laws of Kentucky*, II, 548–549, 554–561, III, 655–661.

57. Christian Schultz, Jr., *Travels in an Inland Voyage through the States of New-York, Pennsylvania, Virginia, Ohio, Kentucky, and Tennessee, and through the Territories of Indiana, Louisiana, Mississippi, and New-Orleans*, 2 vols. (New York, 1810), II, 21 (quotation); David Meriwether, "Memoirs of David Meriwether," 6–7, typescript, Filson Club. The importance of fish and game in the diet of antebellum southerners is explored in Royce Gordon Shingleton, "The Utility of Leisure: Game As a Source of Food in the Old South," *Mississippi Quarterly*, XXV (1972), 429–445; Sam Hilliard, "Hog Meat and Cornpone: Food Habits in the Ante-Bellum South," American Philosophical Society, *Proceedings*, CXIII (Philadelphia, 1969), 2–3, 7–8, 12.

cornfields. In 1795, the Kentucky legislature passed an act requiring every white male more than sixteen to kill a certain number of squirrels and crows annually. To fulfill their obligations, neighbors periodically came together for all-day contests in which rival companies vied to top their opponents' squirrel count. The largest of these competitions netted more than five thousand squirrels in a single day. Afterward the furry prey became the featured course in a festive barbecue and burgoo. On an everyday basis, however, the incessant chore of shooing away pests was left for young boys. That they accomplished with the aid of dogs and shotguns, a weapon conceived "entirely beneath the *dignity* of genuine" Kentucky hunters.[58]

For men confined much of the year to farming and stock raising, shooting matches provided intermittent opportunities to pull down rifles. "Driving nails," "snuffing candles," and "barking squirrels"—that is, shooting just beneath the bushy-tailed rodents so that they were sent flying from their perch— were popular contests in early-nineteenth-century Kentucky. These tournaments, often held with other aggressive and bloody contests on court and militia training days, established pecking orders among neighborhood shooters.[59]

The lingering conflation of marksmanship and manhood heightened the stakes of shooting matches and squirrel hunts. To blast a squirrel anywhere but in the head was "reckoned very unsportsmanlike." Such poor targeting diminished a man's standing among his peers. The best squirrel hunters, though, were the objects of local adulation.[60]

58. *Spirit of the Times and Life in New-York,* Aug. 25, 1832 (quotation); Littell, ed., *The Statute Laws of Kentucky,* I, 336, III, 101–102, IV, 30, 142–143, V, 101–102; *Acts Passed at the First Session of the Third General Assembly for the Commonwealth of Kentucky . . .* (Frankfort, Ky., 1796), 57–58, 64–65; *Acts Passed at the First Session of the Twenty-second General Assembly, for the Commonwealth of Kentucky . . .* (Frankfort, Ky., 1814), 173; John D. Shane interview with Isaac Howard, DM, 11CC253; Charles Anderson, "The Story of Soldier's Retreat: A Memoir," pt. III, 1–3, typescript, Filson Club; Daniel Drake, *Pioneer Life in Kentucky, 1785–1800,* ed. Emmet Field Horine (New York, 1948), 93, 129–131; Charles G. Talbert, ed., "Looking Backward through One Hundred Years: Personal Recollections of James B. Ireland," *Register of the Kentucky Hist. Soc.,* LVII (1959), 109–117.

59. *Western Citizen* (Paris), Dec. 11, 1824; Frances L. S. Dugan and Jacqueline P. Bull, eds., *Bluegrass Craftsman: Being the Reminiscences of Ebenezer Hiram Stedman, Papermaker, 1808–1885* (Lexington, Ky., 1959), 119–120; Talbert, ed., "Looking Backward through One Hundred Years," *Register of the Kentucky Hist. Soc.,* LVII (1959), 108–109; Drake, *Pioneer Life in Kentucky,* 187.

60. [William Newnham Blane], *Travels through the United States and Canada* (London, 1828), 302 (quotation); *Kentucky Gazette,* May 14, 1796, May 18, 1801, Feb. 12, 1816; Drake, *Pioneer Life in Kentucky,* 130.

Momentous as these pastimes were in establishing a man's credentials among his neighbors, the supreme test of male prowess still lay in the pursuit of bigger game. Nails, candles, and squirrels were poor substitutes for multi-pointed bucks or "master" bears. As in the colonial backcountry, the year's biggest, longest, and best hunting awaited the completion of the harvest. These fall and winter excursions often brought together a dozen or more hunters. Packing their horses heavy with guns, tents, blankets, cooking utensils, sugar, coffee, cornmeal, salt, and, of course, bourbon, the hunting party frequently traveled thirty or forty miles to woods where "the country was not fenced up."[61]

A favorite destination for hunters from the Bluegrass country was the mountains of eastern Kentucky. In the Appalachians, deer and bear were plentiful, and the thinly settled country retained the appearance of an open woods. But residents maintained (or tried to maintain) a monopoly on game. As in the early years of colonization, Appalachian hunters still ensured the subsistence of neighbors and shared their homes and their meals with passing strangers. Their generous hospitality, however, did not extend to sharing hunting grounds. Those who came to kill game were made most unwelcome, for rights in the woods, locals insisted, belonged exclusively to residents.[62]

Residential rights in the woods faded more quickly in the Bluegrass. There, on occasion, hogs trespassed into enclosed fields, tenants filched timber without the consent of landlords, and hunters pursued game without regard for man-made boundaries. But these were isolated and individual transgressions that instigated no surge in social crimes and posed no danger to the ascendance of a privatized regime.

By and large, gentry lawmakers masterminded the dismantling of rights in the woods, but the so-called pioneer spirit certainly contributed to the fall of the commons. Even as that temper celebrated the destructive mastery of hunters, it paid ultimate due to the mature manhood, the independence, that came only with the ownership of land. Pressured by Indians, pioneers readily repressed the full expression of exclusive tenure. But these restrictions on pri-

61. Dugan and Bull, eds., *Bluegrass Craftsman*, 185 (quotation) (see also 28–30, 185–194); *Spirit of the Times and Life in New-York,* Aug. 25, 1832; Finley, *Autobiography of Rev. James Finley,* ed. Strickland, 72–73; [Emmanuel Hatfield], *Stories of Hatfield, the Pioneer . . .* (New Albany, Ind., 1889), 115–117, 162; [John Rogers Underwood], "The Life of John Rogers Underwood as Dictated to His Daughter Elizabeth," Underwood Collection, Kentucky Library, Western Kentucky University, Bowling Green.

62. John Palmer, *Journal of Travels in the United States of North America, and in Lower Canada, Performed in the Year 1817* (London, 1818), 114–115; John D. Shane, "The Henderson Company Ledger," *Filson Club Hist. Qtly.,* XXI (1947), 42.

vate rights did not alter the quest for an independence founded on the acquisition of private lands.

To the contrary, the pursuit of land overwhelmed all restraints. At times, some pioneers voiced support for limits on the amount of land an individual might engross. When his family moved with other squatters to the upper Ohio Valley in the 1770s, Joseph Doddridge recalled that locals considered private holdings of more than four hundred acres to be a wrongful expropriation of land. "My father, like many others, believed that having secured his legal allotment, the rest of the country belonged of right to those who chose to settle in it," remembered Doddridge. Presented the opportunity to add two hundred adjoining acres to his farmstead, Doddridge's father secured a patent. "But his conscience would not permit him to retain it in his family; he therefore gave it to an apprentice lad whom he had raised in his house." The self-restraint on land accumulation shown by Doddridge's father, however, was rare in Kentucky. In October 1779, petitioners from Boonesborough complained that the four-hundred-acre settlement right was, in fact, too "small a compensation" for the "loss[,] trouble[,] and risk" of moving to Kentucky. Through much of the 1770s and 1780s, pioneer settlers joined nonresident speculators in the scramble to engross as much land as possible.[63]

"The spirit of speculation was flowing in such a torrent that it would bear down every weak obstacle that stood in its way," wrote the Presbyterian minister David Rice of his first visit to Kentucky in the early 1780s. "I looked forward to fifty or sixty years," he observed, "and saw the inhabitants engaged in very expensive and demoralizing litigations about their landed property." Rice, the father of Kentucky Presbyterianism, displayed remarkable prescience about the consequences of undammed speculation. For more than half a century after the initial American colonization of Kentucky, lawsuits over conflicting land claims clogged the state's courts.[64]

The proliferation of conflicting claims encouraged all landowners to guard their holdings more jealously. Anxious to defend shaky claims, they asserted their exclusive possession and enjoyment more forcefully, even to woodlands

63. Doddridge, *Notes on the Settlement and Indian Wars,* 84; Robertson, ed., *Petitions of the Early Inhabitants of Kentucky to the General Assembly of Virginia,* 47. For an extended discussion of land acquisition and the pursuit of "mature" independence, see Aron, *How the West Was Lost,* 58–81.

64. Robert H. Bishop, ed., *An Outline of the History of the Church in the State of Kentucky, during a Period of Forty Years: Containing the Memoirs of Rev. David Rice, and Sketches of the Origin and Present State of Particular Churches, and of the Lives and Labours of a Number of Men Who Were Eminent and Useful in Their Day* (Lexington, Ky., 1824), 36.

that displayed little if any sign of occupancy and improvement. The result, of course, was the erosion of customary (as well as legal) rights in the woods. In nineteenth-century Kentucky, backcountry traditions of rights in the woods did not vanish, but the worlds of pigs and hunters were not what they once were.

On the trans-Appalachian frontier, Indians and pioneers shaped the construction and destruction of one another's rights in the woods. Like pioneer men, Indian men created a commercial compartment within the hunting economy, and Indian women claimed the right to possess what they cultivated. True, the incursions of pioneers and the depletion of game forced Ohio Indians to reconfigure their subsistence strategies and modify their conceptions of gendered space and labor. But try as missionaries did to remake Indian men into farmers, their message failed to persuade. Indian men and Indian women preferred to preserve their respective rights and responsibilities in the woods and the clearings. And, through all their experimentations with alien creeds, Ohio Indians resisted the idea of an individual's buying, selling, and owning a piece of land.

By contrast, in the absence of Indians, pioneers treated land as a commodity no different than skins. Through all their experimentations with Indian ways, pioneers never lost their devotion to an independent manhood premised on the ownership of land. Indeed, although missionaries preached to Indians that farming was an essential component of civilized manhood, that was really not the case across the frontier. How could it have been when so many independent landowners depended on black slaves or white tenants to clear and cultivate their fields? In Kentucky, in the last decades of the eighteenth century and well into the nineteenth century, the tensions between independent men and their male dependents stirred unrest. So, too, the designs of the most aggressive privatizers did not gain the approval of men who saw their rights in the woods reduced. And yet, because almost all white men shared a belief in private property, the transition to a privatized order never inspired the kind of resistance mounted by Indian men and women.

ELIZABETH A. PERKINS

# Distinctions and Partitions amongst Us
## Identity and Interaction in the Revolutionary Ohio Valley

*You could tell where a man was from, on first seeing him.*
*—John Hedge*

At the beginning of Kentucky's hard winter of 1779–1780, Daniel Trabue and a small party of young men set out to make salt at Bullit's Lick. They carried cast-iron pots and brass kettles to boil the salty spring water, which produced a fine, grayish powder used for food preservation and seasoning. In a little more than two weeks, Trabue's group rendered two bushels of salt per man, enough to preserve a large store of meat for the next spring, when game animals would be thin and tough after surviving on winter forage. As they prepared for their return trip, several men traveling together from the falls of the Ohio asked whether they could join Trabue's party on their way to the upper forts. "As company was good in these times," Trabue observed in his 1827 memoir, they readily agreed.[1]

Their trip began auspiciously. On the first night the men camped, "one of these strangers (his name was Saullivon) . . . killed a cappital Buffelo." With plenty of salt, they "lived well that night for meet." Overnight, however, a deep snow fell, and it turned quite cold; the party was in no hurry to depart the next morning. As they warmed themselves around a good fire, Trabue recalled that "one of these Jentlemen, a stranger, observed, 'This morning is very sutiable to set in a good tavern and have to drink good rum and hot Tea or Coffey for breckfast.'" Sullivan, who had killed the buffalo the night before, ventured that, for his part, "he thought a pan of fryed hommany would suite him best." Trabue recorded a surprising outcome to this seemingly innocuous remark: "It was taken as an insult. Blows insued. They had a very smart scuffle in the snow. We parted them and our Tuckeyho boys laughed hea[r]tyly at it." After separating the disputants, Trabue's party reached home safely with their salt.[2]

1. Chester Raymond Young, ed., *Westward into Kentucky: The Narrative of Daniel Trabue* (Lexington, Ky., 1981), 70–73 (quotation on 73).
2. Ibid., 73.

Quoted raw, in Daniel Trabue's fractured spelling, this passage at first seems baffling. What could possibly prompt two travelers gathered around a campfire on a cold winter's morning to come to blows over an imaginary breakfast? Conventional accounts of backwoods behavior might offer an environmental explanation: far from the restraints of civil society, men became, in the words of French essayist J. Hector St. John de Crèvecoeur, "ferocious, gloomy, and unsociable," ready to challenge any comers on matters of pride or opinion. "By living in or near the woods," he explained, "their actions are regulated by the wildness of the neighbourhood." Such crude explanations of frontier behavior have passed out of fashion; scholars today are more apt to suspect that the social or ethnic origins of these two men had a role to play in their disagreement. And what about the "Tuckeyho boys"? Who were they, and why did they find this exchange so humorous? The answers to these questions lie, not in the proximity of the forest, but in the problem of identity in a fluid social setting.[3]

Eighteenth-century inhabitants of the Ohio Valley lived in a dynamic multicultural environment. Contested by European colonial powers and ultimately seized by Anglo-Americans with force, the region was also the territory of numerous Indian tribes, including the Shawnees, Cherokees, Chickasaws, Miamis, Mingos (Ohio Iroquois), Delawares, and Senecas. A cockpit of competing international interests, the valley also witnessed the convergence of internal migrants from a variety of areas east of the Appalachians. Colonization of the Kentucky country began in the mid-1770s, concurrent with (and fueled by) the Revolutionary contest against the British and their Indian allies. Although many Kentucky settlers made the journey with kin or friends, they also encountered a host of strangers of different races, cultures, and social origins. In a letter home to Massachusetts, one man observed: "We have Inhabitants from almost every part of the world." John Filson explained in *The Discovery, Settlement, and Present State of Kentucke* (1784) that "being collected from different parts of the continent, they have a diversity of manners, customs and religions, which may in time perhaps be modified to one uniform." Filson's guarded prediction of eventual assimilation suggests that, at the time he wrote, cultural diversity was still very much in evidence.[4]

3. J. Hector St. John de Crèvecoeur, *Letters from an American Farmer* (1782; reprint, London, 1971), 51–52. For a reinterpretation of western pugnacity, see Elliott J. Gorn, "'Gouge and Bite, Pull Hair and Scratch': The Social Significance of Fighting in the Southern Backcountry," *American Historical Review*, XC (1985), 18–43.

4. James R. Bentley, ed., "Letters of Thomas Perkins to Gen. Joseph Palmer, Lincoln County, Kentucky, 1785," *Filson Club History Quarterly*, XLIX (1975), 148; John Filson, *The Discovery, Settlement, and Present State of Kentucke . . .* (Wilmington, Del., 1784), 29.

Historians have been relatively slow to explore the dynamics of cultural pluralism in this early western population. Dating from Frederick Jackson Turner's famous dictum that "in the crucible of the frontier the immigrants were Americanized, liberated, and fused into a mixed race," scholars traditionally have viewed western migrants as either a homogeneous population or one divided principally by economic antagonisms between rich and poor.[5] Since the 1980s, scholars have sought to distinguish more precisely the racial, ethnic, and economic characteristics of early Kentuckians. The first federal census in 1790 estimated that 17 percent of Kentuckians, excluding Indians, were nonwhite; almost all of these inhabitants were enslaved African Americans. Historians interested in the European ancestry of white settlers have analyzed surnames on tax rolls to estimate that most migrants to Kentucky were of English or Ulster Scots origin, with smaller numbers coming from families of Irish, Welsh, or German descent (see Table 1). Those interested in the economic rank of white males have calculated land and slaveownership and have found significant evidence of economic inequality (see Table 2). One scholar estimates that in the years after the Revolution the "vast majority, perhaps 75 percent," of the settlers who poured into Kentucky were "poor and without land."[6]

As valuable as this composite profile might be, statistics reveal little about real social and economic relationships. Left unanswered are important questions about how people sorted themselves out, made decisions about each other, and interacted with one another during a period of profound cultural

5. Frederick Jackson Turner, *The Frontier in American History* (1920), foreword by Wilbur R. Jacobs (1947; reprint, Tucson, Ariz., 1986), 23. On cultural pluralism in the early western population, see Gregory H. Nobles, "Breaking into the Backcountry: New Approaches to the Early American Frontier, 1750–1800," *William and Mary Quarterly*, 3d Ser., XLVI (1989), 650–652; Andrew R. L. Cayton, "Land, Power, and Reputation: The Cultural Dimension of Politics in the Ohio Country," *WMQ*, 3d Ser., XLVII (1990), 266–286; Albert H. Tillson, Jr., "The Southern Backcountry: A Survey of Current Research," *Virginia Magazine of History and Biography*, XCVIII (1990), 388–397.

6. United States Bureau of the Census, *A Century of Population from the First Census of the United States to the Twelfth, 1790–1900* (Washington, D.C., 1909), 207; Thomas L. Purvis, "The Ethnic Descent of Kentucky's Early Population: A Statistical Investigation of European and American Sources of Emigration, 1790–1820," *Register of the Kentucky Historical Society*, LXXX (1982), 259; Fredrika Johanna Teute, "Land, Liberty, and Labor in the Post-Revolutionary Era: Kentucky as the Promised Land" (Ph.D. diss., Johns Hopkins University, 1988), 63. On the debate over surname analysis as a guide to ethnicity, see Thomas L. Purvis, "The European Ancestry of the United States Population, 1790," *WMQ*, 3d Ser., XLI (1984), 85–101; Donald H. Akenson, "Why the Accepted Estimates of the Ethnicity of the American People, 1790, Are Unacceptable," *WMQ*, 3d Ser., XLI (1984), 102–119.

TABLE 1
*Racial and Ethnic Origins of Kentucky's Population, 1790*

Race

| | | |
|---|---|---|
| | White | 83.0% |
| | Nonwhite | 17.0% |

Ethnic Origin

| | | |
|---|---|---|
| | English | 42.8% |
| | Scotch-Irish and Scots | 20.6% |
| | African | 17.0% |
| | Irish | 7.5% |
| | Welsh | 5.6% |
| | German | 4.1% |
| | French | 1.3% |
| | Dutch | 1.0% |
| | Swedish | .2% |

*Note:* All percentages are estimates. The 1790 census divided Kentucky's population into white and nonwhite classifications, with Indians excluded from this count. Owing to the imprecision of this language, a few non-Africans may be included in my general classification "African." In the second section of the table, I have recalculated Thomas L. Purvis's statistics on European ethnicity to reflect the geographic origins of the entire population, not just those of European descent. Purvis's estimates are based on surname analysis and must, therefore, be considered highly speculative. It should also be emphasized that the vast majority of Kentucky's early population was native-born. Ethnicity here refers to the ultimate geographic origins of migrant families.

*Sources:* United States Bureau of the Census, *A Century of Population from the First Census of the United States to the Twelfth, 1790–1900* (Washington, D.C., 1909), 207; Thomas L. Purvis, "The Ethnic Descent of Kentucky's Early Population: A Statistical Investigation of European and American Sources of Emigration, 1790–1820," *Register of the Kentucky Historical Society,* LXXX (1982), 259.

TABLE 2

*Wealth of Kentucky Heads of Household, 1792–1800*

| Year | % Landowners | % Slaveowners |
|------|--------------|---------------|
| 1792 | 34.9 | 23.2 |
| 1797 | 40.6 | — |
| 1800 | 43.0–49.2 | 25.2 |
| 1802 | 48.2 | 27.2 |

*Note:* All of the above are estimates based on Kentucky county tax lists, which enumerate all free males more than age 21.

*Sources:* For 1792, 1797, 1802, see Fredrika Johanna Teute, "Land, Liberty, and Labor in the Post-Revolutionary Era: Kentucky as the Promised Land" (Ph.D. diss., Johns Hopkins University, 1988), 263, 275. For 1800, see Lee Soltow, "Kentucky Wealth at the End of the Eighteenth Century," *Journal of Economic History,* XLIII (1983), 620; Joan Wells Coward, *Kentucky in the New Republic: The Process of Constitution Making* (Lexington, Ky., 1979), 55, 63.

flux. Categories of race, ethnicity, and socioeconomic status fit present concerns about the fault lines of American society but did not necessarily possess the same explanatory power for those living two hundred years ago. Attitudes about ethnicity, for example, underwent a profound transformation in the nineteenth century, as theorists of scientific racism speculated about the enduring biological characteristics of the Celtic or Teutonic "species." In the twentieth century, ethnicity became a rallying cry for political assertions of cultural differences between groups who had lived in the same country for generations. Differences in skin color, national origin, and economic standing *were* visible to eighteenth-century inhabitants of the Ohio Valley. Yet, by privileging these social divisions or reducing all such differences to the simple dichotomy of rich and poor, historians overlook more subtle cultural distinctions not easily comprehended within any of these modern categories.[7]

The terms "cohee" and "tuckahoe" encompass one such distinctive structure of social identity. Originally a Powhatan Indian term for a variety of

7. Dale T. Knobel, *Paddy and the Republic: Ethnicity and Nationality in Antebellum America* (Middletown, Conn., 1986), 104–128; Richard Polenberg, *One Nation Divisible: Class, Race, and Ethnicity in the United States since 1938* (New York, 1980), 243–250; Anthony P. Cohen, *The Symbolic Construction of Community* (New York, 1985), 104–107; Werner Sollors, ed., *The Invention of Ethnicity* (New York, 1989), ix–xx.

edible roots, by the late eighteenth century "tuckahoe" became a common name for an inhabitant of the lowlands of Virginia. The tuckahoe's counterpart was the "cohee," a resident living west of the Blue Ridge. Virginians migrating to the Ohio Valley carried this social distinction with them; Daniel Trabue's "Tuckeyho boys" were former residents of the tidewater or piedmont. In 1786, a Kentuckian wrote to the governor of Virginia: "We have two sorts of people in this country, one called tuckyhoes, being Generall. of the Lowland old Virginians. The other class is Called cohees, Generally made up of Backwoods Virginians and Northward men, Scotch, Irish, etc., which seems, In some measure, to make Distinctions and Particions amongst us." A settler similarly explained to western collector John Shane: "Irish mostly from Pa. country, and S. Carolina were called COHEES. Mostly Presbyterians. Virginians were call[ed] Tuckahoes. You could tell where a man was from, on first seeing him." Braiding together a complex skein of social and cultural identities, the distinction between cohee and tuckahoe transcended wealth, ethnicity, or religion alone; depending on the circumstance, the terms implied any, or all, of these meanings.[8]

Historians also need to explore cultural interaction in the Ohio Valley. Within the acknowledged constraints of the border war that convulsed the region from 1774 to 1795, Indians and whites, Germans and Ulster Scots, cohees and tuckahoes encountered one another as individuals, not as abstracted cultures or races. Make no mistake: brutality, rather than mutual comprehension, characterized many of these meetings. Yet, attitudes about others were always contingent, ready to be verified, muted, or altered by actual experience. Encounters with strangers formed a large part of the rich oral lore recorded by John Shane, Lyman Draper, and other nineteenth-century collectors who interviewed surviving settlers of the Ohio Valley in the 1830s and 1840s. Many immigrants retained vivid recollections of their initial contacts with people who looked, spoke, smelled, or acted differently than they did. Along with other personal narratives and contemporary manuscripts, these accounts capture the variety and complexity of human interaction on the borders of early America in a way that statistics alone cannot. Indian reactions to encounters with strangers are more difficult, yet not impossible, to recover in the writings of

8. Robert Johnson to Gov. [Patrick] Henry, Dec. 5, 1786, in William P. Palmer et al., eds., *Calendar of Virginia State Papers and Other Manuscripts* (Richmond, Va., 1875–1893), IV, 191; John D. Shane (hereafter cited as JDS) interview with John Hedge, ca. 1840s, Draper Manuscripts, 11CC19, microfilm, 1980, reel 76, State Historical Society of Wisconsin, Madison (hereafter cited as DM). See also Willard F. Bliss, "The Tuckahoe in New Virginia," *VMHB*, LIX (1951), 387–396.

captives, traders, travelers, and missionaries to the western country. By examining the "Distinctions and Particions" that border inhabitants used to classify themselves and others and then considering how these categories worked in practice, this essay explores the negotiation—and essential ambiguity—of identity in a fluid frontier setting.[9]

## First Impressions

Like many back settlers, Mrs. John Morrison's family enjoyed broad geographic horizons. Her father was born in Cumberland County in the Pennsylvania backcountry; he later moved to southwestern Virginia and then north to Augusta County in the great valley, where he married Morrison's mother, "a Miss Campbell." The couple departed for the settlements on the Holston River (in present-day Tennessee) and eventually traveled to Kentucky in 1779. After staying at Harrodsburg for a few weeks, they moved to the fort in Lexington. Morrison recalled her mother's reaction to the other migrants who soon began arriving: "Told her, when they saw others coming; and asked her if she wasn't glad." Her mother said: "If they were the right kind. Said her heart sunk within her, when the first person she saw, was a rough old dutchwoman. There were others, however, and after awhile some very respectable persons." [10]

Morrison's mother neatly defined the problem of the stranger in a fluid social setting: the need to discover whether she or he is "the right kind." Sociologists describe this process of identification as the "coding" of strangers: using clues of personal appearance, language, and manner to discover other extrinsic and intrinsic characteristics such as rank, nationality, or moral character. The need to evaluate strangers is most commonly seen as an urban dilemma,

9. On the larger context of cultural interaction in early America, see T. H. Breen, "Creative Adaptations: Peoples and Cultures," in Jack P. Greene and J. R. Pole, eds., *Colonial British America: Essays in the New History of the Early Modern Era* (Baltimore, 1984), 195–232. For a useful introduction to the literature of native American testimony, see Colin G. Calloway, ed., *The World Turned Upside Down: Indian Voices from Early America* (Boston, 1994). On the strengths and weaknesses of retrospective settler accounts in reconstructing the mental world of Euramerican settlers, see Elizabeth A. Perkins, *Border Life: Experience and Memory in the Revolutionary Ohio Valley* (Chapel Hill, N.C., 1998), chap. 1.

10. JDS interview with Mrs. John Morrison, ca. 1840s, DM, 11CC150–152. On Pennsylvania's role as a distribution center for migrants to the south and west, see James T. Lemon, *The Best Poor Man's Country: A Geographical Study of Early Southeastern Pennsylvania* (New York, 1972), 71–97.

yet this same decision-making process went on throughout much of early America (with the possible exception of closely knit New England towns) as immigrants from a variety of European countries and African regions came into contact with each other and with native inhabitants of equal, or even greater, ethnic diversity. Making accurate judgments about the character and intentions of strangers was important in small towns and port cities; it could be, literally, a matter of life and death in sparsely settled border regions.[11]

The evaluation of strangers in early America drew upon a rich symbolic code of cultural differentiation. Some distinctions relied on apparent referents such as skin color or language; others, like the food preferences championed by Daniel Trabue's fellow travelers, were normally invisible. All such group boundaries are largely symbolic. Of the hundreds of distinguishing features that human beings can discriminate among, only a few become centrally important in the construction of social identity. Once in place, however, a single distinction like dress or religion can stand for a whole repertoire of other ascribed characteristics. The choice of a cultural marker may be quite arbitrary; what is crucial, writes one anthropologist, is "what the boundary means to people, or, more precisely, . . . the meaning they give to it." Identity, in short, is a cultural construct rather than a biological absolute.[12]

In the border country, culturally relevant attributes took a variety of forms. Personal appearance, especially clothing, played an important role in the rapid appraisal of strangers. As John Hedge informed Shane, "you could tell where a man was from, on first seeing him." The Englishman Nicholas Cresswell discovered the importance of dress when he visited the Ohio Valley in the summer of 1775. After commenting freely on the ragged appearance of his traveling companions, Cresswell, the eldest son of a Derbyshire landowner, found the tables turned when he arrived at Fort Pitt in "very shabby dress" and tried to cash a personal note. Clothing was a sensitive indicator of social position in eighteenth-century Anglo-America; "a periwig and lace-ruffled cuffs," writes one analyst, "proclaimed freedom from manual work in field or workshop."

11. On the "coding" of strangers in antebellum America, see Karen Halttunen, *Confidence Men and Painted Women: A Study of Middle-Class Culture in America, 1830–1870* (New Haven, Conn., 1982), 36. Halttunen drew upon the work of urban sociologist Lyn H. Lofland, *A World of Strangers: Order and Action in Urban Public Space* (New York, 1973), chap. 1. Robert H. Wiebe offers similarly useful insights into the "sifting of newcomers" in antebellum America in *The Segmented Society: An Introduction to the Meaning of America* (New York, 1975), 21–52.

12. Anthony P. Cohen, *The Symbolic Construction of Community* (New York, 1989), 12.

To Nicholas Cresswell's dismay, even backcountry innkeepers judged a man's appearance for indications of his creditworthiness.[13]

Eventually befriended by an Indian trader, Cresswell received a second lesson in the importance of dress when he proposed to accompany the trader across the Ohio River into the Indian country. "Mr. Anderson informs me that the Indians are not well pleased at anyone going into their Country dressed in a Hunting shirt," Cresswell recorded in his journal. The buckskin hunting shirt, widely assumed to be an article of Indian dress, was to Cresswell's Delaware hosts the garb of the backcountry militiaman. As Sarah Graham later explained to John Shane, "The militia in those times had no other shirts than buckskin hunting shirts; and wore moccasins and bear-skin hats." Drawing an important lesson from his first fashion blunder, Cresswell "got a Calico shirt made in the Indian fashion, trimmed up with Silver Brooches and Armplates so that I scarcely know myself." Once properly attired for his trip, Cresswell found a hospitable welcome in the Delaware towns.[14]

As Cresswell's experience suggests, dress served as a potent symbol of identity in an exotic world of strangers. Reading the language of dress became part of the social expertise of every border inhabitant. Native Americans, for example, apparently recognized the status implications of European costume. A former Indian captive related the story of a man who lost his saddlebags on the road between Lexington and Frankfort. "The ind[ian]s found some ruffled shirts in his saddlebags. All the english they co'd say, when they got on the shirts, was, 'Massa,' signifying, I suppose, Gentlemen." Settlers recognized Indians' cultural competence in the symbolism of European attire and attempted to turn it to their own advantage. When an Indian army besieged the fort at Boonesborough in 1778, the badly outnumbered defenders agreed to a parley. Accompanying Daniel Boone outside the stockade was Major William Bailey Smith dressed in British officer's uniform with "a red scarlet coat and maccaroni hat, [with] an ostrich feather in it." Visibly stressing the military credentials of their own side, Boone and Smith reported that there were still more commanders within the fort.[15]

---

13. JDS interview with John Hedge, ca. 1840s, DM, 11CC19; Nicholas Cresswell, *The Journal of Nicholas Cresswell, 1774–1777* (London, 1925), 101; Rhys Isaac, *The Transformation of Virginia, 1740–1790* (Chapel Hill, N.C., 1982), 43.

14. Cresswell, *Journal*, 103; JDS interview with Sarah Graham, ca. 1840s, DM, 12CC45.

15. JDS interview with Alexander Hamilton, ca. 1840s, DM, 11CC295; JDS interview with John Gass, 1843, DM, 11CC12–13.

Euramericans expressed similar interest in, if less comprehension of, Indian costume and ornamentation. James Wade found "a very nice ind[ia]n cap" where a party had camped near Mount Sterling; John Shane included a small sketch with his interview. "The cap was made of cloth; with 2 red tassels hanging down, one on each side of the head, at the corners that stuck up. Coarse, thick, white colored cloth. Two pieces." Another man recalled pursuing an Indian wearing "a coon-skin cap on his head, with a long tail hanging down." Lending scant support to modern stereotypes about frontier dress, this incident was Shane's only record of the now-ubiquitous symbol of the white frontiersman. William Clinkenbeard admired several examples of Indian ornamentation, including "a very nice indn. shot pouch . . . all beaded off" that another man brought in. And, at a prisoner exchange, he encountered the "most splendid looking squaw I ever saw." "I suppose she had [a thousand] ornaments on her. Was all cov[ere]d over w[ith] them." Only a few settlers attempted to interpret the symbolism of Indian bodily decoration, however. In one example, Mrs. Shanklin told of a white prisoner who escaped from his Indian captors and "got into Mann's Lick . . . naked, trimmed, and painted." The Indians had at first painted him black, the captive reported. "But he gave them intimations that he was a gunsmith, and could repair their guns. They then daubed him w[ith] spots of red: an indication of more pleasure." [16]

The passage of apparel across the permeable cultural boundary between native and immigrant complicated visual identification. During a time of relative peace, John Hanks's mother made several "cappo-coats for them to take along and sell among the Indians—made them of blue broadcloth, with a cap or hood to draw over the head: otherwise like a match coat." Hanks added: "I recollect I sowed on them some myself." The "cappo" (capote) was an article of European attire, a long cloak or overcoat with a hood worn by soldiers and travelers. The matchcoat was its native American analogue: a mantle, originally made of furs and skins, later made of imported British broadcloth. In the back settlements, such articles of dress were readily interchangeable among wearers. Benjamin Stites bought a broadcloth "cappo" from the Shawnee war leader Blackfish, which he "had to freeze, to get the lice out." He recalled that "the Indians frequently wore handkerchiefs, cappo, etc." "The one that killed uncle David Jennings had a cappo and cocked hat, he must have gotten at St. Clair's

---

16. JDS interview with James Wade, ca. 1840s, DM, 12CC17; JDS interview with George Fearis, ca. 1840s, DM, 13CC241–242; JDS interview with William Clinkenbeard, ca. 1840s, DM, 11CC60; JDS interview with Mrs. Shanklin, ca. 1840s, DM, 11CC218.

defeat." One suspects that the significance of this officer's cocked hat was not likely lost on its new owner.[17]

Mistakes in reading the language of dress caused endless confusion in border areas. William Clinkenbeard's militia company "killed a white-man dressed fine in ind[ia]n dress." "Cousin to Gen. Clark. Had been wounded, and was making his way in to our camp, and was shot. Had gone to live with the Indians, when, I don't know." Spencer Records's brother once fired at a white captive by mistake: "We supposed that the prisoner was an Indian, on account of his running off from us, and because he wore a calico shirt." Another man shot and killed a white scout in Indian dress who was returning to Cassidy's Station. Children, in particular, seemed to lack sophistication in quickly assessing a stranger's appearance. Indians captured two young boys gathering roasting ears near Short Creek when "one of their moccasins came loose, and he stooped down to tie it." "As he did so, they saw two Indians coming; but they had such clean match coat blankets . . . they thought them whites."[18]

As a symbolic medium, dress also had power to transform identity in the border country. By donning a calico shirt for his visit to the Indian towns, Nicholas Cresswell proclaimed his status as a potential friend, rather than a probable enemy; he became, in the eyes of the Delaware, "the right kind." In a similar fashion, a company of Ottawas helped escaped Shawnee captive Abel Janney to pass unmolested through the Wyandot town of Sandusky by turning him into a "white Indian," a European who had gone over to the Indian side. When their party neared the town, attacked only two months previously by the Pennsylvania militia, Janney recalled that "the Chief of the [Ottawa] company turned about to me, and told me that he must cut my hair in their form, or else those Indians that lived in the town would beat me very much, and perhaps kill me." Having just witnessed the torture and immolation of the militia commander defeated at Sandusky, Janney hastily agreed. "So he took a pair of scissors which they always take with them to war, and began to trim my hair, which they did according to the Indian custom[;] then they painted me

---

17. JDS interview with John Hanks, ca. 1840s, DM, 12CC138; JDS interview with Benjamin Stites, 1842, DM, 13CC60. On the incorporation of selected elements of European dress by Ohio Indians, see Michael N. McConnell, *A Country Between: The Upper Ohio Valley and Its Peoples, 1724–1774* (Lincoln, Nebr., 1992), 211.

18. JDS interview with William Clinkenbeard, ca. 1840s, DM, 11CC66; Donald F. Carmony, ed., "Spencer Records' Memoir of the Ohio Valley Frontier, 1766–1795," *Indiana Magazine of History*, LV (1959), 366; JDS interview with William Clinkenbeard, ca. 1840s, DM, 11CC63; JDS interview with Robert Jones, 1842, DM, 13CC176.

and fixed me as much like themselves as they possibly could, and gave [me] my own gun, and we marched to the town with two scalps on a stick." As a symbolic Indian, Janney passed through the grieving town without incident. Joshua McQueen visited the Spanish river port of Natchez on a trading trip in 1782 and similarly adopted protective coloring. Noting that he was the only American in the boat—"They were all frenchmen but one other man, and he was one of a sort of people that file their teeth [and] live in some hot country way to the west somewhere"—McQueen wore a handkerchief on his head, "the same as a Frenchman."[19]

Native inhabitants seemed particularly sensitive to the transformative capacity of personal apparel. When a party of Shawnees captured Benjamin Allen in 1790, they took him to their camp on the Licking River and told him to pull off his clothes. "They brought two calico hunt[ing] shirts, sort of red with half the arm worn off, and put them on me," Allen recalled. "They then tied on a blanket round me, w[ith] a buffalo tug: and then tied a p[iec]e of blanket round my head. They then patted me on the head, and s[ai]d, ind[ia]n." Native Americans captured prisoners like Allen for a variety of reasons, including torture, exchange, or adoption into the community as replacements for lost family members. By transforming Allen into an "in[di]an," his Shawnee captors signaled that adoption was likely to be his fate.[20]

That this physical transformation had symbolic as well as practical intent is further illustrated by George Yocum's story of a young girl captured by Indians while her party passed through the wilderness. "When they took her, each Indian gave her a broach," Yocum said. One Indian had no silver broach to give, however, "and he took a pewter plate they had dropped in the road, and made her a rude pewter broach and gave [it to] her." While they went off to attack another party along the road, the Indians left the girl behind, and she wandered off; when Yocum's company found her, she was wearing eighteen broaches. "In this way we knew the number of the Indians that attacked the company that McFarlan was with," he noted on her return. Benjamin Allen reported a similar adoption ritual when one of his Shawnee captors asked him if he would go home with him. When Allen agreed, the Indian "put 2 silver rings on my fingers, and a powder horn, w[ith] some yellow lace to it, over my head." "Fr[om] this I supposed he took me to be his." Allen most likely read his cap-

19. Abel Janney, "Narrative of the Capture of Abel Janney by the Indians in 1782," *Ohio Archaeological and Historical Publications,* VIII (Columbus, Ohio, 1900), 470–471; JDS interview with Joshua McQueen, ca. 1840s, DM, 13CC124.

20. JDS interview with Benjamin Allen, ca. 1840s, DM, 11CC71.

tor's actions correctly; in Shawnee cultural practice, such gift exchanges created bonds of mutual obligation and established ties of symbolic kinship.[21]

Europeans held more fixed notions of ethnic identity than did native Americans, yet they also recognized the power of dress to transform or disguise. Settlers, for example, maintained that white captives held for any length of time came to resemble Indians. William Clinkenbeard took part in General George Rogers Clark's campaign against the Shawnee towns on the Miami River in 1782 and recalled: "This white woman that we took h[ad] b[ee]n a long time among the ind[ia]ns. Didn't know her name, or her people's. Looked as much like an ind[ia]n for color and for dress, as an ind[ia]n herself." John Rupard joined a small raiding party across the Ohio River in 1789 and later returned with a much larger force to bury the dead. In addition to the bodies of their own men, Rupard's party found the corpses of two Indians with "chunks thrown over them" and "an ind[ia]n white man" with "a sort of stone wall around him." The latter's identity was not immediately apparent, however, as Rupard made plain: "We examined the place, stripped him, and found him a white man."[22]

In a telling account of the mutability of dress and identity, Daniel Trabue recounted the reunion of several Indian captives with their white families at the Treaty of Greenville in 1795. When introduced to his children after a lapse of fifteen years, one old man "cryed out aloud and fell Down on the floore, Crying and bewailing his condition." "Said he, 'My cheldrin is Indians!'" Upon recovering from his initial shock, the settler gave his sons new clothes and persuaded them to wash off their paint. Significantly, the former captives' reintroduction to European culture began with a change of their clothing; even more significant, within two hours the young men had dressed as Indians again.[23]

In addition to dress, other aspects of appearance aided in the rapid evaluation of strangers. Migrants used a combination of physical referents such as skin color, physique, and demeanor to construct rough categories of racial and ethnic identity. Sarah Graham maintained that skin color and height served as a guide to Indian ethnicity, telling John Shane: "Shawnees were almost-gold-yellow, and small. Choctaws tall and large: 6 feet high and more." Some migrants first encountered individuals of a different skin color upon their arrival in the Ohio Valley; their responses ranged from simple curiosity to expressions

21. JDS interview with George Yocum, ca. 1840s, DM, 12CC150; JDS interview with Benjamin Allen, ca. 1840s, DM, 11CC72.

22. JDS interview with William Clinkenbeard, ca. 1840s, DM, 11CC66; JDS interview with John Rupard, 1843, DM, 11CC99.

23. Young, ed., *Westward into Kentucky*, 140; JDS interview with Asa Farrar, ca. 1840s, DM, 13CC4.

of fear. John Redd met a mulatto man at Martin's Station in Powell's Valley, Virginia, and noted that "notwithstanding his coller he was treated with as much respect as any white man." Tidewater planter David Meade, who journeyed down the Ohio River to Kentucky in 1796, recalled his initial alarm at the sight of "three large keel Boats rowed by naked Copper colored men—of very savage appearance." Meade confided in a letter to his sister in Virginia: "I had little doubt [to] what race of men they belonged and notwithstanding my reason assured me that there was nothing like hostility to be expected from them[,] my fears were all awakened." The planter confessed that he did not feel easy until they were out of sight, "which was in a very short time for they plied their oars with a degree of agility and force unknown on James River." [24]

Skin color, like dress, was not an absolute guide to a stranger's identity, however. Interracial contact and cohabitation were common in the border country, blurring racial and ethnic distinctions. David Meade first thought that "white men" navigated the three Indian keelboats on the Ohio River but later learned that the voyagers were métis—"a mongrel race between French and Indian—they are said to make excellent watermen." Descriptive references to complexion often lacked racial specificity: whites routinely used the general rubric "yellow" to characterize the coloring of Indians, mulattoes, and métis; a fellow European, on the other hand, might be described as "a man of darke skin." Nathaniel Hart attributed the capture of the Boone and Callaway girls to their mistaking Indians for "Simon, a yellow man, who staid at the Fort." Another child described the Indians who waylaid her as "yellow men, with rings and beads." Henry Parvin recalled his own confusion as a child when Indians attacked Constant's Station in 1785. "We saw them, a parcel of swarthy, yellow looking things, with shining pieces of silver on, and we thought they had killed a snake, and thought of going to see what kind of one it was, they were gathered round, taking them to be a parcel of mulattoes." [25]

Racial identities confounded adults as well. Peter Harper, variously described as a "half Indian" or "a sort of yellow man," lived in Strode's Station

24. JDS interview with Mrs. Sarah Graham, ca. 1840s, DM, 12CC49; John Redd, "Reminiscences of Western Virginia, 1770–1790," *VMHB*, VI (1899), 339; Bayrd Still, ed., "The Westward Migration of a Planter Pioneer in 1796," *WMQ*, 2d Ser., XXI (1941), 331.

25. Still, ed., "Westward Migration of a Planter," *WMQ*, 2d Ser., XXI (1941), 331; Redd, "Reminiscences," *VMHB*, VI (1899), 338; JDS interview with Capt. Nathaniel Hart, 1843, DM, 17CC192; JDS interview with Jeptha Kemper, ca. 1840s, DM, 12CC128; JDS interview with Henry Parvin, ca. 1840s, DM, 11CC173. On the frontier as a "marrying ground," see Gary B. Nash, "The Hidden History of Mestizo America," *Journal of American History*, LXXXII (1994–1995), 947.

and served in the settlement's garrison before settling in his own cabin near Mount Sterling, Kentucky. The youngest son of a former Indian captive, Harper "looked as much like an ind[ia]n as could be[—]Black hair and straight walk," according to his neighbor William Clinkenbeard. While hunting one day, "H[arper] got killed, and we never knew how, whether by whites or in[dia]ns"; about the same time, James McMullen reported that he had shot an Indian on Lulbegrud Creek. "Everybody s[ai]d it was H[arper], from [McMullen]'s description: an ind[ia]n on a horse," recalled Clinkenbeard, but McMullen continued to insist that he had shot an Indian. He "never seemed to do well after this," the old settler mused in hindsight. "Everybody believed he thought it was an Indian, but if it was a white man, through mistake, he ought to have told it."[26]

In the midst of a border war that blurred the distinction between military and civilian populations, personal appearance played a crucial role in rapidly distinguishing potential enemies from friends. Border inhabitants—native and immigrant alike—used clues of dress and skin color to make quick judgments about the loyalties and intentions of the strangers they met. Appearance was not always an accurate guide to identity, however. Peter Harper resembled an Indian physically, yet his neighbors considered him a "white man" slain by a careless mistake. That racial identities seemed indeterminate and dress had symbolic power to transform identity hints at the contingency of these social relationships: in the Anglo-Indian borderland, identities of interest were not yet fixed in permanent racial categories but shifted with the free flow of events. Nicholas Cresswell did not become a Delaware with his adoption of Indian clothes, but he did become a friend. Baptist missionary David Jones pushed the logic of this reasoning to a prematurely hopeful conclusion: "It seemed strange to me to see the [white] captives have the exact gestures of Indians. Might we not infer from hence, that if Indians were educated as we are, they would be like us?"[27]

## Words and Customs

Judging a stranger's appearance only began the process of determining whether he or she was "the right kind." Customs, manners, and language also served as relevant attributes in making decisions about others. Western settlers—like many immigrant populations—were culturally conservative, carry-

26. JDS interview with William Clinkenbeard, ca. 1840s, DM, 11CC59.

27. David Jones, *A Journal of Two Visits Made to Some Nations of Indians on the West Side of the River Ohio, in the Years 1772 and 1773* (New York, 1865), 88.

ing to their new homes memories and preconceptions that served as models or templates for conduct in a new geographic setting. Upon their arrival in the Ohio Valley, migrants encountered representatives of other races, cultures, and social groups, all with their own customs and cultural norms. A diversity of behaviors, including habits of speech, social conventions, and preferences in food and drink, served to identify like-minded fellows and distinguish out- siders. If dress or skin color separated strangers into large, crude categories of potential friendship or enmity, customs and manners revealed more subtle cultural distinctions based on perceptions of kinship or otherness.[28]

In the realm of words and customs, intercultural contacts provoked laugh- ter, sometimes disgust, but only rarely real violence. How border inhabitants used language and behavior to define themselves unfolds suggestively in an- other incident from Daniel Trabue's salt-making expedition of 1779. Trabue in- troduced this story by noting: "One of the men we had with us was a young Irishman who was constant contending and Disputeing with the other young men that was from old Virginia about words and customs." One morning on their way to Bullit's Lick, Trabue shot a buffalo bull, a native animal that some of his party had never before encountered. Although he felled the bison with his shot, Trabue soon realized that he "had shot this buffelo too high" and told one of the other men to shoot him again. "This young Irishman said, 'No'; he would kill him and Jumed at him with his tomerhock and strikeing him in the forehead." Trabue warned him that the buffalo's mud-matted wool and thick skull would cushion his blows, but the Irishman "kept up his licks, a nocking

28. In the 1950s, historians searched the colonial era for qualities that unified Americans and distinguished them from their Old World predecessors; today, the recognition of cul- tural conservatism among migrants posits a very different relationship between European cultures and their American offshoots. On transatlantic cultural connections, see, for ex- ample, T. H. Breen, "Persistent Localism: English Social Change and the Shaping of New England Institutions," WMQ, 3d Ser., XXXII (1975), 3–28; David Grayson Allen, In English Ways: The Movement of Societies and the Transferal of English Local Law and Custom to Mas- sachusetts Bay in the Seventeenth Century (Chapel Hill, N.C., 1981); Ned C. Landsman, Scot- land and Its First American Colony, 1683–1765 (Princeton, N.J., 1985); A. G. Roeber, "In Ger- man Ways? Problems and Potentials of Eighteenth-Century German Social and Emigration History," WMQ, 3d Ser., XLIV (1987), 750–774.

David Hackett Fischer made a forceful argument for the primacy of British regional in- fluence in the shaping of American social institutions. His work, however, is flawed by a static concept of cultural diffusion that largely ignores the complex intermingling of cul- tural inheritance and creative adaptation at work in early America. See Fischer, Albion's Seed: Four British Folkways in America (New York, 1989); for a critique, see "Forum: Albion's Seed: Four British Folkways in America—A Symposium," WMQ, 3d Ser., XLVIII (1991), 223–308.

a way." Suddenly, Trabue recalled, "the buffalo Jumped up." "The man run, the buffalo after him. It was opin woods, no bushes, and the way this young Irishman run was rather Desending ground and every Jump he cryed out, 'O lard! O lard! O lard! O lard!'" With the buffalo close on his heels, the Irishman darted behind a beech tree; the animal crashed headlong into its trunk, "the tuckeyho boys laughing, 'Ha! Ha! Ha!'" Later, Trabue wrote, when "these young men would Mimmick him, 'O lard! O l[ard]!' etc. and breack out in big laughter," the "Irishman said he would go no further with such fools as these boys weare," that he could have been killed. After failing to persuade the young man to go on, Trabue and his party finally "bid him a Due [adieu], leaveing him a butchering his buffelo."[29]

As Trabue's account suggests, verbal communication served as an important sorting device in contacts with strangers. Accent or idiom often revealed a newcomer's geographic or ethnic origins; in recalling face-to-face contacts with non-English migrants, memorialists like Trabue frequently attempted to recreate, or at least note, distinctive dialects or usages. Ulster Scots, usually called "Irishmen" in the eighteenth century, evidently spoke with a characteristic brogue or accent, which Trabue's "tuckeyho boys" were quick to mimic. In transcribing the Irishman's speech into his written text, Trabue summarized this linguistic distinction with his phonetic spelling of "O lard!" (as in car) for the exclamation "O lord!" Even more ambitious was Spencer Records's transcription of Highland Scots speech. In recalling the brutal massacre of friendly Moravian Indians at Gnadenhütten in 1782, Records "never heard any person speak of the circumstance, without expressing his abhorrence, excepting one poor old dirty Scotchman, named James Greenlee, who said, 'Owh mon ats a weel cum don thang, fur they suppurted the other Injuns as tha cum and gaad.'"[30]

John Shane's interview notes reflect a similar consciousness of linguistic distinctions. Jacob Stevens narrated the story of Hugh Cunningham and his wife,

29. Young, ed., *Westward into Kentucky*, 72.

30. Carmony, ed., "Spencer Records' Memoir," *Indiana Magazine of History*, LV (1959), 334. In response to nativist hostility toward Irish Catholics, Protestant descendants of Ulster immigrants, formerly known as "Irishmen," began to adopt the name "Scotch-Irish" in the mid-nineteenth century. On the evolution of this term, see Maldwyn A. Jones, "The Scotch-Irish in British America," in Bernard Bailyn and Philip D. Morgan, eds., *Strangers within the Realm: Cultural Margins of the First British Empire* (Chapel Hill, N.C., 1991), 284–285; Kenneth W. Keller, "What Is Distinctive about the Scotch-Irish?" in Robert D. Mitchell, ed., *Appalachian Frontiers: Settlement, Society, and Development in the Preindustrial Era* (Lexington, Ky., 1991), 69–72.

describing them as "both right Irish." After being captured by Indians, Cunningham was absent from the settlement for such a long time that "his wife had made another engagement . . . to a much younger and likelier man." When her husband returned just before her new marriage was to take place, Cunningham's wife could not conceal her disappointment. " 'Well Ugh, are you alive yet?' Hugh, picked [piqued] at this reception, crustily replied, 'Yes you dom fool! Don't you see I am?' " In recounting the capture of the Shawnee leader Blue Jacket, William Clinkenbeard underscored the linguistic distinctiveness of both the Indian and an Irishman who volunteered to kill him. Clinkenbeard's militia company agreed that the famous war leader "sho'd be killed, but no one was will[ing] to do it, but a little Irishman." "Says he, By Jasus, I'll kill him." When the Irishman's "heart failed him to kill a man in cold blood," the militiamen offered their prisoner a drink of whiskey. Blue Jacket replied: "It was 'velly good turn.' " Informants frequently linked Ulster speech patterns with the liberal use of profanity. In a typical example, Josiah Collins characterized Alexander McConnell as "some-sort of irishman" and added that he "swore pretty hard."[31]

Immigrants of German or Dutch descent also spoke with a perceptible accent. Usually lumped together as "Dutchmen" by English settlers, some German- or Dutch-speakers like Michael Stoner (Holsteiner) conversed in what Nathaniel Hart termed "very broken English." Other migrants spoke with only a trace of an accent or a slightly irregular syntax. Challenged for hiding during the siege of Boonesborough, Tice Brock reportedly exclaimed: "Py sure . . . I was not made for a fighter—I was not made for a fighter." Daniel Trabue also hinted at a distinctive German pronunciation in his story of the "poore Dutchman," Jacob Stucker, who wrapped a plundered Indian blanket around himself and declared: "This will keep me worm this winter." Admittedly here, though, Trabue's substitution of the written word "worm" for the spoken word "warm" may also be another example of the memorialist's erratic spelling rather than an intentional linguistic marker.[32]

31. JDS interview with Jacob Stevens, ca. 1840s, DM, 12CC135–136; JDS interview with William Clinkenbeard, ca. 1840s, DM, 11CC64; JDS interview with Josiah Collins, 1841, DM, 12CC70.

32. JDS interview with Capt. Nathaniel Hart, 1843, DM, 17CC191; JDS interview with John Gass, 1843, DM, 11CC13; Young, ed., *Westward into Kentucky*, 137. A. G. Roeber discusses the English use of the name "Dutch" for both German- and Dutch-speakers in " 'The Origin of Whatever Is Not English among Us': The Dutch-speaking and the German-speaking Peoples of Colonial British America," in Bailyn and Morgan, eds., *Strangers within the Realm*, 220 n. 1.

Behavior, like language, helped distinguish familiars from outlandish outsiders. The Irishman's attempt to kill the buffalo with his tomahawk is typical of a whole genre of border stories illustrating the peculiar proclivities of strangers or newcomers. Nathaniel Hart narrated a brief biographical account of Richard Burke, another Ulsterman, who came to Kentucky "as a waiting man to the Shelbys, and obtained a pre-emption" for his own farm. "He commonly went by the name of 'fool Burke,'" Hart recalled, "being very singular in all his ways." Josiah Collins similarly termed German settlers "fools" for working too hard. "These old Dutch fellows were such fools, they couldn't take care of themselves. Thought if they didn't go out and work, they would starve to death, and never thought of danger. Michael Stucker said, d——n the Indians, they had killed his father, and now he should have the corn to work, all by himself." Collins concluded that "most all of the old Dutchmen got killed in those days." Nathaniel Hart concurred: "The dutch were not good soldiers. They understood nothing of Indian warfare."[33]

Unusual customs and awkward words tended to set German and Dutch settlers apart from the Anglo-American majority—even when they lived close by. In an interview conducted in the 1850s, Joseph Ficklin confided to Shane: "We had no irishmen in those days [referring to contemporary nativist stereotypes about Irish Catholics], and it was the amusement of the wits to make fun of the dutch." More cold-blooded was Spencer Records's appraisal of his two German tenants, Abraham Gardner and Rudolph Fuss, who boarded for a time with his family in their log cabin. "They were both Dutchmen, and not used to guns," Records noted in his memoir, "so that I could have no dependence on them, only that they would make a show if Indians came in sight; and if we should be fired on, they might be shot in place of me."[34]

In much the same fashion, humorous stories targeted Irishmen as outsiders. William McClelland, a second-generation Ulster emigrant, related his uncle's account of "Higgany, an irishman," who carried an obsolete blunderbuss on an expedition against the Indian towns above Fort Pitt during the Seven Years' War. Having never fired a gun before, Higgany repeatedly loaded the blunderbuss but hesitated to discharge it. When the captain finally ordered him to fire in an emergency, "the Irishman pulled his trigger, and the fire knocked him full a rod back, and broke his collar bone, and laid him flat on his

33. JDS interview with Capt. Nathaniel Hart, ca. 1843, DM, 17CC193, 17CC208; JDS interview with Josiah Collins, 1841, DM, 12CC102.

34. JDS interview with Joseph Ficklin, ca. 1850s, DM, 16CC267; Carmony, ed., "Spencer Records' Memoir," *Indiana Magazine of History*, LV (1959), 361–362.

back." As Higgany "came to a little, he called to those around him to stand back a little, he had put seven loads in, and but one had come out." McClelland explained that normally "the blunderbuss had to be tied to a log when they went to fire"; the captain had given the heavy gun to the big Irishman to carry because "they did not know what use they might want with it."[35]

Stories illustrating an outsider's lack of experience or sense also invite alternative readings. Considered from another perspective, intercultural contacts with outlandish newcomers often dramatized the efforts of immigrants to replicate familiar cultural forms in a new geographic setting. Actions that seemed inexplicable to migrants of a dissimilar background might well have made perfect sense to members of the same cultural group. Higgany's ignorance of firearms, for example, suggests that he was a recent arrival in America. In eighteenth-century Europe, warfare was the province of trained soldiers rather than the civilian population; most Anglo-American males, on the other hand, participated in some form of militia training. Similarly, in Daniel Trabue's buffalo story, what Trabue interpreted as the Irishman's impetuosity in keeping "up his licks, a nocking a way," was probably from the latter's perspective a logical inference based on his prior agricultural experience. Inexperienced in the handling of North American bison but familiar with a traditional technique for stunning domestic livestock for slaughter, the Irishman struck a rapid blow to the buffalo's forehead just as he might have cudgeled a steer. Unfortunately, the newcomer's cultural inheritance did not serve him well in this instance, much as German American traditions of intensive tillage and peaceful relations with neighboring Indians proved ill-suited to an ongoing border war in a rich hunting territory. By the mid-nineteenth century, the Irishman's impetuosity and the Dutchman's obduracy would become ethnic stereotypes; on the Anglo-Indian border, their actions conformed to more generalized stereotypes about the unpredictability and foolishness of strangers or newcomers.[36]

## Cultures of Rank and Region

Distinctive behavior was by no means limited to the non-English migrant. Class and regional divisions cut across the Anglo-American population, en-

35. JDS interview with William McClelland, ca. 1850s, DM, 11CC182. On the long English tradition of Irish jokes, see Robert Secor, "Ethnic Humor in Early American Jest Books," in Frank Shuffelton, ed., *A Mixed Race: Ethnicity in Early America* (New York, 1993), 177–183.

36. On early American military training, see John E. Ferling, *A Wilderness of Miseries: War and Warriors in Early America* (Westport, Conn., 1980), 78. On "interethnic imagemaking" in the nineteenth century, see Knobel, *Paddy and the Republic,* 21–38.

dowing even the actions of fellow English-speakers with a degree of exoticism. Samuel Potts Pointer, originally from Loudoun County in the Virginia piedmont, helped Eli Cleveland with his harvest for ten days in 1789; fifty years later, Pointer still marveled at Cleveland's manner of living. Cleveland, who owned a mill at the mouth of Boon's Creek, "had hounds to hunt . . . [and] a place posted in to keep in deer." "If any body went in to shoot, they wo'd set the dogs on them. 'Twas s[ai]d the dogs were dangerous, but they never troubled me. C[leveland] was rich! rich! 'Twas s[ai]d he hadn't slept with his wife, for 14 years." From Pointer's remarks, it is difficult to ascertain which caused more comment among Cleveland's neighbors: the mill owner's wealth, his unorthodox marital relations, or his attempt to enforce game laws in what was widely considered a hunting commons. John Wilson encountered another wealthy man living on the banks of Beargrass Creek and was similarly struck by his domestic arrangements. "Captain Prince lived at the old station. A virginian. His wealth consisted mostly in negroes. They had scarcely any furniture. His daughters had servants to wait on them for everything—mean as they lived." [37]

Gentlemen were different, Joseph Ficklin explained to Shane. "There was at that time in Va., a wide distinction between the families of gentlemen, and common people—and the common man when he went to the gentleman's house, didn't pretend to go in, but stood at the door and took off his hat." Taking up residence in the rude settlements of the western country, gentlemen continued to manifest their distinctiveness—what might be termed the "culture of rank"—in a variety of ways: through their more elaborate dress, their ownership of land and slaves, and, frequently, by their relative freedom from manual labor. A female immigrant characterized a member of her river party succinctly: "Runnells was a gentleman. Didn't row any." [38]

Distinctions in housing emerged more slowly. When the tidewater planter David Meade passed through Bourbon County, Kentucky, in 1796, he was surprised to discover that "in these [log] Cabbins many opulent and some Genteel people live . . . even at this time and I am told that they are by the latter made more than barely comfortable." Meade soon founded his own rural

37. JDS interview with Samuel Potts Pointer, ca. 1840s, DM, 12CC247–248; JDS interview with Capt. John Wilson, 1855, DM, 17CC9.

38. JDS interview with Joseph Ficklin, ca. 1850s, DM, 16CC257; JDS interview with [a Cincinnati woman], ca. 1840s, DM, 13CC9. The phrase "culture of rank" comes from Stuart M. Blumin, *The Emergence of the Middle Class: Social Experience in the American City, 1760–1900* (Cambridge, 1989), 30.

seat—which he grandiosely called Chaumière des Prairies—with the construction of a single-story log dwelling divided into four chambers. Largely cut off from the elaborate refinements of tidewater life, Meade nevertheless cultivated a gentleman's reputation for largess. According to a local informant: "Mead[e] spent a great deal in entertaining people. Never would receive pay. Every man was a gentleman, and as such stayed as long as he pleased."[39]

As emigrants from various parts of British America converged on Kentucky, regional differences in cultural norms also became apparent. To a former resident of the Monongahela country, for example, the customs of the tidewater might seem unfamiliar, or even repugnant. How such parochial identities and prejudices influenced social conduct is illustrated by an episode narrated by Mrs. Ephraim January. When Indians captured her twin brothers, January's father decided to return to Pennsylvania. At that time, a company was preparing to go up the river, but its members divided into two different groups, one journeying by water and the other by land. "The co[mpany] my f[ather] and m[other] were in, was a c[ompany] from Va.," January explained. "They had been out, I suppose, looking for land; and were on their way in. Some of them were pretty wild fellows. The land party were [Pennsylvanians], and tho't they wo'dn't stay w[ith] the others." The Pennsylvanians paid dearly for their clannishness, however; Indians attacked their group and killed several of its members. The two parties were not far apart at the time, and one of the Pennsylvanians was able to escape to the riverbank to hail the others for help.[40]

Differences between Virginians and Pennsylvanians formed a meaningful distinction in common culture. At the outbreak of the Revolutionary War, Virginia's Indian commissioners repeatedly insisted to skeptical Shawnee and Delaware diplomats that Virginians were, not "a Distinct People," but "one Flesh and Blood" with Pennsylvanians and the other English colonists. Political and wartime alliances did little to erase such perceptions of cultural difference. When Needham Parry, a Quaker from York County, Pennsylvania, visited a farm near Danville, Kentucky, in 1794, the owner "took a great deal of pains to shew me his improvements, of every sort." Proudly displaying his orchard with fruit-bearing apple trees, the man "said he wished to improve

39. Still, ed., "Westward Migration of a Planter Pioneer," *WMQ*, 2d Ser., XXI (1941), 321, 333; JDS interview with Dr. A. Young, ca. 1850s, DM, 11CC234. For an analysis of the changing taxonomy of the term "gentleman" in colonial and early national society, see Gordon S. Wood, *The Radicalism of the American Revolution* (New York, 1992), 24–42, 194–195.

40. JDS interview with Mrs. Ephraim January, ca. 1840s, DM, 11CC222.

his place like a Pennsylvanian. Although he was a Virginian, from Augusta County." Joseph Ficklin distinguished between the settlement patterns of the two immigrant groups in central Kentucky, claiming: "Lexington was settled principally by [Pennsylvanians]. The south side of the river by the Craigs, [Virginians]." One of the most visible distinctions between Pennsylvanians and Virginians was in the matter of slaveholding. In 1780, the Pennsylvania legislature passed a law providing for the gradual emancipation of the state's slave population; Pennsylvanians moving to Kentucky retained a reputation for holding antislavery sentiments. As an early resident of Fayette County told Shane: "There was a set of [Pennsylvanians] all on one side of me, when I came here. They [Pennsylvanians] were all great abolitionists."[41]

Regional stereotypes were not always benign. Charges of loyalism, for example, dogged the steps of Carolina emigrants. William Clinkenbeard claimed that a "heap of Tories" settled at Strode's Station the first winter he was there. "Everybody coming to Kentucky. Could hardly get along the road for them. And all grand tories, pretty nigh. All from Carolina, tories. Had been treated so bad there, they had to run off or do worse." Numerous reports—both contemporary and retrospective—identified the founders of one of central Kentucky's most prominent stations as loyalists. In a letter written from Boonesborough in 1776, John Floyd noted that "the Bryans and other Tories to the number of 28 men" had sixty-six acres of corn growing on a tract near Elkhorn Creek. Joseph Ficklin, who had lived at Bryan's Station as a boy, confirmed to Shane that "the Bryans rested under the imputation of being tories—and all went back to North Carolina." Although differences between tory and patriot never flamed into the civil war that engulfed other backcountry regions, political sympathies might have led to scattered instances of violence in Kentucky. Recalling yet another mysterious death like that of the métis Peter Harper, Ficklin related that "one Williams, who was in the station, and was regarded as

41. Robert L. Scribner et al., eds., *Revolutionary Virginia: The Road to Independence,* 7 vols. (Charlottesville, Va., 1973–1983), III, 463, IV, 176; Lucien Beckner, ed., "John D. Shane's Copy of Needham Parry's Diary of Trip Westward in 1794," *Filson Club Hist. Qtly.,* XXII (1948), 239; JDS interview with Joseph Ficklin, ca. 1850s, DM, 16CC259; JDS interview with Roger Quarles, ca. 1840s, DM, 11CC148. Pennsylvania's slaveholding population was small in comparison to Virginia's; in 1790, only 2.5% of Pennsylvania families owned slaves, as opposed to 44.9% for Virginia and 17% for Kentucky. See U.S. Bureau of the Census, *A Century of Population Growth,* 135. On the narrow limits of the Pennsylvania emancipation process, see Gary B. Nash and Jean R. Soderlund, *Freedom by Degrees: Emancipation in Pennsylvania and Its Aftermath* (New York, 1991).

a tory . . . went out from the station to hunt . . . and never returned." Hinting obliquely at the possibility of foul play, Ficklin remarked: "It was never known what became of him—whether he went off and joined the Indians, or was killed by them, or killed himself, or how."[42]

Regional distinctions in customs and manners also cut across the political boundaries of states. Informants generally agreed, for example, that migrants from the western districts of the old states were more sophisticated in their dealings with Indians. When John Hedge reached Kentucky in November 1791, he discovered that "Ready Money Jack" kept the only tavern on the road between Mayslick and the Blue Licks; there Hedge's traveling company "got some hot corn cake and milk, which ate admirable." Although other settlers hesitated to settle beyond Mayslick, apparently the innkeeper did not fear for his safety. "Ready Money Jack was from Monongahela country," Hedge explained. "Was less afraid of Indians. The people in that country were more accustomed to them." In nearly identical terms, William Clinkenbeard characterized Major Hood, "a low dutchman" from the Red-Stone country, as "a pretty good hand after ind[ia]ns; expect he had been accustomed to them." Traveling from a greater distance and settling south of the Ohio River in fewer numbers, New England emigrants bore less nuanced identities. One man termed Abijah Brooks "a right Yankee"; a woman described Elias Barbee as simply "a northern man."[43]

## Culinary Geography

In the realm of customary behavior, preferences in food and drink serve as sensitive indicators of social belonging or distance. Immigrants and their descendants routinely seek out the remembered foods of their homelands; con-

---

42. JDS interview with William Clinkenbeard, ca. 1840s, DM, 11CC55; John Floyd to Joseph Martin, in Neal Hammon and James Russell Harris, "'In a Dangerous Situation': Letters of Col. John Floyd, 1774–1783," *Register of the Kentucky Hist. Soc.*, LXXXIII (1985), 213; JDS interview with Joseph Ficklin, ca. 1850s, DM, 16CC259.

43. JDS interview with John Hedge, ca. 1840s, DM, 11CC19–22; JDS interview with William Clinkenbeard, ca. 1840s, DM, 11CC61; JDS interview with Benjamin Allen, ca. 1840s, DM, 11CC76; JDS interview with Mrs. Sarah Graham, ca. 1840s, DM, 12CC47. William Clinkenbeard was one of the few settlers to distinguish between the "High Dutch" (Germans) and the "Low Dutch" (Dutch), explaining to John Shane at one point that a "Good many dutch came abt. Shepherdstown [Va.]; [there is a] diff[erence] between high and low dutch" (DM, 11CC66).

sumers discriminate among a wide array of edible commodities to mark social boundaries, commemorate events, and express personal values.[44] In much the same way, patterns of food and beverage consumption lent cultural meaning to the social universe of Ohio Valley residents. Although Indian corn and wild meat constituted the general provision for all inhabitants during the eighteenth century, subtle culinary distinctions illuminated the complexity of the local cultural geography.

Some backcountry food traditions originated in Europe. Accustomed to plentiful supplies of meat and maize, native-born settlers observed that those of European birth readily ate foods they themselves normally scorned. Angus Ross, from the Highlands of Scotland, ate the marrow from buffalo shank bones and goose eggs with veins that others would not touch. In describing his former poverty, Ross "used to say he hired as a herder one year in the Highlands of Scotland for his board and a pair of shoes." "Never got his shoes, at that. Had never had enough of meat to eat, there." Descendants of Ulster emigrants expressed a fondness for buttermilk, the sour milk left over after churning the butter from whole milk. Here, the invention of tradition transformed the staple of the poor farmer in Europe into a uniquely nourishing American beverage. Josiah Collins overheard John Todd tell his wife not to give their daughter "any sweet milk, but to feed it altogether on Buttermilk, that was the most healthy." Todd's parents were both from Ireland, Collins explained to John Shane.[45]

Tea drinking, the bellwether of an expanding British consumer culture, linked a few immigrant households with the tastes and styles of the metropolis. As in coastal areas, backcountry tea drinking was not the sole prerogative of the genteel, although it did suggest a certain level of social aspiration. Mary Dewees and David Meade both recorded tea parties as part of the polite social round in Pittsburgh and Lexington in the 1780s and 1790s. Mrs. Phillips invoked her polite antecedents for John Shane when she recalled that her mother and Mrs. John Todd took tea together in the fort at Lexington, even though "they had nothing but tea and dried buffaloe meat." Familiarity with the rituals of tea consumption was not yet universal in the back settlements, however. James Stevenson claimed that "the first tea-cups and saucers I ever saw" were

44. On food as a cultural medium, see Mary Douglas and Baron Isherwood, *The World of Goods: Towards an Anthropology of Consumption* (New York, 1979), 66–67.

45. JDS interview with John Hanks, ca. 1840s, DM, 12CC144; JDS interview with Josiah Collins, 1841, DM, 12CC73.

at the home of a transplanted Virginia planter, John Fowler, who moved to Kentucky in 1783. A popular genre of border stories revolved around the blunders of those new to the preparation and service of tea. A Maryland family, for example, drew Daniel Drake's scorn by keeping "a quantity of tea boiling in a large uncovered Dutch oven . . . out of which they were dipping it with a tin cup and drinking it from the breakfast table."[46]

Divergent culinary traditions distinguished cohees from tuckahoes. When Hugh Garret's militia company stopped at a house one day to ask a woman for something to drink, "she sat us out a churn full of cream with cups." "Dupuy said it was mighty rich buttermilk. Craig said he must be a d——d tuckahoe that he didn't know the difference between cream and buttermilk." In a story illustrating the intersection of regional, ethnic, and social distinctions in the realm of food customs—as well as in electoral politics—Joseph Ficklin claimed that Andrew Steel lost a bid to serve in the Virginia legislature because "they ran him off at the election with Cohee." His opponents "Told on him, that his wife came to the door, and said 'Andrew come to your mush. The pegs [pigs] have been in it, and will be in it again.'" Mush, a thick porridge made with cornmeal and water or milk, was a western dish, explained Ficklin. "Knew nothing about mush in eastern Va. Called it hominy in E. Va. It (mush) was a Cohee dish." John Fowler, the candidate with the tea cups and saucers, won the election.[47]

In reflecting upon social divisions in early Kentucky, another of Shane's informants linked habits of food consumption with religious affiliation and social standing. After describing John Fowler's tea equipment and the coach-and-four driven by James Wilkinson, James Stevenson added that the first loaf of bread he had ever seen was at Lewis Craig's Mill. "In those times this was the outside of Presbyterianism," he explained to Shane, "and I looked upon those men as the quality of the land. The Baptists were the great ones." Shane added

46. John L. Blair, ed., "Mrs. Mary Dewees's Journal from Philadelphia to Kentucky," *Register of the Kentucky Hist. Soc.*, LXIII (1965), 206–207; Still, ed., "Westward Migration of a Planter," *WMQ*, 2d Ser., XXI (1941), 335; JDS interview with Mrs. Phillips, 1854, DM, 16CC291; JDS interview with James Stevenson, ca. 1840s, DM, 11CC250; Daniel Drake, *Pioneer Life in Kentucky . . .* (Cincinnati, 1870), 202. On tea drinking and the spread of metropolitan styles to the early western settlements, see Elizabeth A. Perkins, "The Consumer Frontier: Household Consumption in Early Kentucky," *JAH*, LXXVIII (1991–1992), 486–510.

47. JDS interview with Hugh Garret, ca. 1840s, DM, 11CC246; JDS interview with Joseph Ficklin, ca. 1850s, DM, 16CC269–271. After Virginia established Kentucky County in 1776, Kentuckians served in the Virginia legislature until statehood in 1792.

his own observation in an initialed aside: "They came from an older part of the country. [Presbyterianism], therefore, here, was allied with unimposing prospects. Neither great wealth, ostentation, nor influence." In a similar fashion, religious and social tensions might have been at work in the scuffle over breakfast recorded by Daniel Trabue. Breakfast at a tavern with rum toddy, tea, and coffee would likely have been the fare favored by a genteel Anglican; a simple pan of fried hominy was Baptist or Methodist fare.[48]

Anglo-Americans who ventured outside the safety of their settlements discovered the culinary peculiarities of Indians and Frenchmen. The use of salt, like buttermilk, marked a cultural divide in the western country. Soon after a hunting party captured Benjamin Allen and dressed him as an Indian, they came upon a herd of buffalo. Taking this opportunity to kill several animals and pack their meat for transport, the Indians then prepared a portion for cooking. "They gave me a leather purse of salt to salt mine," Allen explained, adding, "[I] never saw any of them use of it." On a militia raid against the Indian towns north of the Ohio River, William Clinkenbeard stopped to sample some boiled dumplings that he found still warm and steaming in a tray. Clinkenbeard recalled thinking that "now I wo'd have my belly full," but he could not eat the Indian food. "They were made of corn and beans with enough of meal in them to make them stick together," he said, but "without any salt."[49]

Disagreements surfaced over preparation techniques and the range of foods considered edible. The culture shock of Euramericans suddenly confronted with Indian foodways was a staple of backcountry captivity narratives. Escaped Shawnee captive Abel Janney had lived on blackberries for four days but still could not eat the meal of roast wolf entrails his Ottawa companions prepared. On a trading voyage to Natchez with a party of Frenchmen, Joshua McQueen similarly traversed alien culinary terrain. For daily fare, "we lived on Bears oil and rice, stewed up," he told Shane. One day, while out hunting for something to add to the pot, McQueen killed a doe, which he cut in half to carry back to the traders' bateaux. As he rounded a bend in the river, he stumbled upon a hunting camp of almost fifty Indians, including women and children. "I dare

48. JDS interview with James Stevenson, ca. 1840s, DM, 11CC250. Presumably, Stevenson means that this is the first loaf of wheat bread that he had seen; cornbread was usually cooked in an iron skillet.

49. JDS interview with Benjamin Allen, ca. 1840s, DM, 11CC72; JDS interview with William Clinkenbeard, ca. 1840s, DM, 11CC66.

not be afraid," McQueen recalled. "They were cooking there, and I just went on and put my half doe across the pole. . . . An Indian took me by the coat into his wigwam, swung his kettle of lie [lye] corn on, and warmed it, and gave me a horn spoon (Buffaloe. Black as [an] ace of spades)." After he had satisfied his immediate appetite, McQueen began to shove aside some of the rich fat that seasoned the porridge. The Indian noticed his gesture "and asked me in French what kind of fat. I answered Mukquaw (bear)." No, it was "sha sha, he said, dog meat. After that I slackened off a good deal," McQueen noted. Later, when the Indians went down to trade with the French boat and to join in a drinking party, the French purchased a "painter" (a colloquial term for a cougar or mountain lion) for their mess. McQueen reported that the painter "ate a good deal like mutton," if you did not see its ribs.[50]

Such cross-cultural contacts could also lead to the appreciation and assimilation of unfamiliar foods. Benjamin Allen termed another dish cooked by his Shawnee captors "elegant," describing it as fat buffalo meat seasoned with dried buffalo meat and thickened with meal. Baptist missionary David Jones enjoyed his first hickory nuts—"much superior to any of that kind in our eastern world"—at the house of a Shawnee headman. Returning the favor to the chief and his friends, Jones served them a breakfast of "fat buffalo, beavers tails and chocolate." The last, a beverage possibly unfamiliar to the Indian guests, was a tropical American food product currently the rage in Europe and Anglo-America.[51]

Food, like clothing, formed a permeable cultural boundary in the border region. Euramericans rapidly adopted maize, local game, and maple sugar as dietary staples; at the same time, native inhabitants learned to appreciate a variety of European dishes. When the trader James Kenny visited the Beaver Creek settlement of Gray Eyes, a Delaware headman, he discovered that he lived in a shingled house and made "Good Butter." Visiting the Moravian mission towns along the Tuscarawas River a little more than a decade later, David Jones similarly found livestock herding and dairying. Shawnee captive Thomas Ridout was astonished to be served tea by Metsigemewa, his captor's wife. In preparing for breakfast, the Shawnee woman "boiled some water in a small copper kettle, with which she made some tea in a tea-pot, using cups and saucers of

50. Janney, "Capture of Abel Janney," *Ohio Archaeological and Hist. Pubs.*, VIII (1900), 471–472; JDS interview with Joshua McQueen, ca. 1840s, DM, 13CC126–127.

51. JDS interview with Benjamin Allen, ca. 1840s, DM, 11CC71; Jones, *A Journal of Two Visits*, 42–54.

yellow-ware. . . . When she had done, she poured some tea in a saucer, which, with some fried meat on a pewter plate, she gave [to] me." The tea proved to be green tea, sweetened with maple sugar. Ridout confessed that "this was a luxury I little expected to meet with," not only because of the distance the tea must have traveled but also because he was a prisoner and "could hardly expect such fare." [52]

That the culinary diplomacy of the western country also had its limits is suggested by the tragic fate of one of the Moravian mission towns, Gnaden-hütten, which was put to the torch by a backcountry militia company in 1782. Falsely accusing the Christian Indians of stealing the European tablewares that they had adopted, the militiamen slaughtered more than ninety of the town's residents, the majority of these women and children. So it was that creative adaptations by Indians and Europeans in matters of dress, housing, and cuisine turned out not to lead very far down the path of cultural syncretism in the Ohio Valley, nor, indeed, in Anglo-America as a whole. In later years, with the crafting of heroic narratives of Indian conquest and American nationhood, even the tentative first steps in this direction would be forgotten but by a few. [53]

In making decisions about strangers, preconceptions about cultural norms helped to group other persons and give them a name. Border residents used clues of appearance, language, and behavior to sort others into simple perceptual categories that emphasized certain differences while underplaying broad similarities in behavior. Local and particular distinctions based on regional or cultural identities continued to have force in the new geographic setting, as did consciousness of ethnic, racial, and class differences. In the minds of old settlers, new local attachments never completely overcame an awareness of living with strangers in one's midst. Joseph Ficklin still recalled making fun of the Dutch, "tuckeyho boys" mimicked the accents of Irishmen, and fellow travelers came to blows over the menu of an imaginary breakfast.

Yet, because migrants sorted themselves out several ways simultaneously— as cohees and tuckahoes, Irishmen and Dutchmen, gentlemen and common

52. John W. Jordan, ed., "Journal of James Kenny, 1761–1763," *Pennsylvania Magazine of History and Biography*, XXXVII (1913), 22; Jones, *A Journal of Two Visits*, 101; Matilda Edgar, ed., *Ten Years of Upper Canada in Peace and War, 1805–1815; Being the Ridout Letters . . .* (Toronto, 1890), 355.

53. Richard White, *The Middle Ground: Indians, Empires, and Republics in the Great Lakes Region, 1650–1815* (New York, 1991), 390.

folk, Presbyterians and Baptists—a collective sense of "us" versus "them" failed to coalesce along socioeconomic, ethnic, regional, or even racial lines. Over time, as frontier outposts evolved into settled agricultural communities, some of these social boundaries hardened; others disappeared. All such "Distinctions and Particions" eventually became subsumed under the largest division, which traced the fault line of border war: encroaching immigrant and dispossessed native. A shared history of border warfare proved a powerful solvent for received cultural categories among migrants, even as it crystallized the perceived racial differences between native and newcomer.

# "Noble Actors" upon "the Theatre of Honour"

## Power and Civility in the Treaty of Greenville

In 1945, the state of Ohio unveiled a large mural in the capitol building in Columbus depicting the 1795 meeting at Fort Greenville between the officers of the Legion of the United States and members of the Miami, Shawnee, Delaware, and other Indian tribes. Like the paintings in the rotunda of the United States Capitol, the mural is an example of what Eric Hobsbawm has called "the invention of tradition." Its purpose is to record a decisive historical moment in a heroic style, overwhelming the viewer with the essential justice of the events it portrays.[1]

The painter was Howard Chandler Christy, a native of Morgan County, Ohio, a frequent illustrator for popular magazines and a former Rough Rider with Theodore Roosevelt during the Spanish and American War. His mural was as grand in size as it was in ambition. Measuring seventeen by twenty-two and three-quarters feet, the painting presented noble men engaged in noble action. At the center, on a small table, is the Treaty of Greenville, the document by which the assembled Indians both renounced their assertion that the Ohio River was the permanent border between them and the United States and ceded much of the land that would become the state of Ohio to the new Republic. Towering above everything is a dark, wild tree pushing into a dramatic sky. On the left, over the Indians, the tree opens to reveal a large American flag standing out in the breeze.[2]

Christy arranged his subjects in a semicircle around two dominant figures, Little Turtle of the Miami on the left and Major General Anthony Wayne on the right. Consciously or not, the artist presented the growth of civilization, as educated eighteenth-century Americans would have understood it, in his place-

---

1. Eric Hobsbawm, "The Invention of Tradition," in Hobsbawm and Terence Ranger, eds., *The Invention of Tradition* (Cambridge, 1983), 1–14.

2. For a brief biography of Christy, see Edna Maria Clark, *Ohio Art and Artists* (Richmond, Va., 1932), 448.

FIGURE 1

*The Treaty of Greenville.* By Howard Chandler Christy. In the foreground are Little Turtle and Anthony Wayne; behind Little Turtle are Blue Jacket and Tarhe. Behind Wayne stand William Clark and William Henry Harrison. Courtesy, Ohio Historical Society, Columbus

ment of people. From half-naked, crouching Indians on the left, we move to a shadowy center occupied by men such as William Wells, who moved back and forth between Indian and European societies. The farther right our eyes travel, the more civilized the men become, from the smartly attired American officers (such as Lieutenant William Henry Harrison) to the seated, literate scribes.

Little Turtle and Wayne stand opposite each other, looking directly into each other's eyes. In their hands, they hold symbols of their respective roles. The almost-naked Miami is offering the American general a calumet (pipe), a token of peace. Wayne, on the other hand, is far from demonstrative; dignified to the point of impassivity, he holds in his right hand a piece of paper, the left grasps his sheathed sword. Both instruments represent the triumph of the United States: the written word has ratified the submission of the Indians coerced by the sword. Although Christy presents the native Americans as complex figures, he emphasizes that Little Turtle is the supplicant and Wayne the man with power.

Whatever the accuracy of Christy's history or the quality of his artistry, he captured the essence of the Greenville meeting. The men who were there saw it above all as a drama, an enactment of cultural roles in what they knew was

FIGURE 2

The Upper Ohio Valley in the Late Eighteenth Century.
*Drawn by Richard Stinely*

one of the most important events in their lives. For them, the negotiation of concrete issues involved a presentation of cultural images. Experiencing considerable social stress, they were profoundly concerned with affirming themselves and their societies.[3]

3. In thinking about the argument of this essay, I have learned much from Jean-Christophe Agnew, *Worlds Apart: The Market and the Theater in Anglo-American Thought, 1550–1750* (Cambridge, 1986); Richard L. Bushman, *The Refinement of America: Persons, Houses, Cities* (New York, 1992); Greg Dening, *Mr Bligh's Bad Language: Passion, Power, and Theatre on the Bounty* (Cambridge, 1992); and Jay Fliegelman, *Declaring Independence: Jef-*

Historians agree that little serious negotiation took place at Greenville. Events in both North America and Europe had conspired to leave the Indians living in what is now Ohio, Indiana, and southern Michigan vulnerable to the encroaching Americans. In the late summer of 1794, General Wayne had led the three-thousand-man Legion of the United States in a campaign of destruction against the Indians of the Maumee Valley, building posts at their villages at the Glaize (Fort Defiance) and Kekionga (Fort Wayne). The Legion's success was made possible in part because Great Britain, which had long encouraged the Indians in their struggles against the Americans, deserted them. Not only did the British refuse to open the gates of Fort Miami to Indians fleeing after the battle of Fallen Timbers on August 18; they agreed to evacuate all of their forts in the Northwest Territory as part of a treaty signed with the American envoy John Jay in November 1794. Although the Indians subsequently accepted supplies from the British, they could not forget that His Majesty's agents were, at best, unreliable allies.

Thus, Little Turtle, the great warrior who had been instrumental in the defeat of American expeditions led by Josiah Harmar in 1790 and Arthur St. Clair in 1791, could protest, but not refuse, Wayne's demands. The general got exactly what he wanted when the treaty was signed on August 3, 1795. He got more than land, however; he also got—or, more important, believed he got—legitimacy. He persuaded himself that he had persuaded the Indians to consent to the establishment of American sovereignty north of the Ohio River.[4]

All of the participants in the Greenville negotiations thought that the events of the summer of 1795 were about much more than establishing boundaries. Both Americans and Indians saw ceremonial occasions as opportunities to

---

*ferson, Natural Language, and the Culture of Performance* (Stanford, Calif., 1993). Gillian Russell, *The Theatres of War: Performance, Politics, and Society, 1793–1815* (Oxford, 1995), esp. 14–25, is particularly good on the importance of drama to late-eighteenth- and early-nineteenth-century British officers.

4. The fullest description of the Greenville negotiations is in Harvey Lewis Carter, *The Life and Times of Little Turtle: First Sagamore of the Wabash* (Urbana, Ill., 1987), 145–153. Other important accounts include Richard White, *The Middle Ground: Indians, Empires, and Republics in the Great Lakes Region, 1650–1815* (Cambridge, 1991), 413–476; Gregory Evans Dowd, *A Spirited Resistance: The North American Indian Struggle for Unity, 1745–1815* (Baltimore, 1992), esp. 111–115; Reginald Horsman, *Matthew Elliott, British Indian Agent* (Detroit, 1964), 92–118; and Dorothy V. Jones, *License for Empire: Colonialism by Treaty in Early America* (Chicago, 1982), 157–186.

mediate conflict and avoid violence. They also likened them to public dramas in which men struggled to define the proper relationship between personal interests and social obligations. Central to the success of their performances was the question of sincerity. They would watch each other (and themselves) like an audience in a theater for evidence of deception, assuming that behind the efforts at decorum lay petty passions and self-interest.[5]

The enormous obstacles to the creation of an atmosphere of mutual respect and friendship, however, only made its realization all the more extraordinary. Civility meant more to the people gathered at Greenville than the disguise of baseness. As many historians have demonstrated, the Miami and other Indians believed that without politeness social relationships were virtually impossible. What the Europeans called refinement was for the Indians the foundation of trustworthiness. The content of public orations was often less important than the emotional impact the speaker had on his audience. His goal was to persuade his listeners of his good faith. Unless he convinced them of his sincerity, nothing else would matter.[6]

The American officers at Greenville were obsessed with what the Indians thought of them. In fact, we miss a critical aspect of Wayne and other officers' understanding of what they were doing as they conquered the Northwest Territory in the 1790s if we see them simply as duplicitous, pausing briefly at Greenville to play at civility while contemplating the removal of defeated Indians. American officials genuinely believed that their triumph was incomplete without the defeated tribes' public acknowledgment of its essential justice. They required the Indians' acceptance of their new republican order as a prerequisite for their right to govern the territory they took from them in the Treaty of Greenville. The acquiescence of peoples excluded from the exercise of power was a critical ratification of their sense of legitimacy as leaders. Only with such consent could they as republicans presume to model the correct behavior of citizens and lead the United States to peace, prosperity, order, and glory. More than a gesture of magnanimity, more than a cloak for subterfuge, civility was as critical to winning a complete victory as any sword, musket, or cannon.

---

5. Fliegelman, *Declaring Independence*, 24; Kenneth Cmiel, *Democratic Eloquence: The Fight over Popular Speech in Nineteenth-Century America* (New York, 1990), 23–54; Bushman, *Refinement of America*, esp. iv–v, 46–58.

6. Daniel K. Richter, *The Ordeal of the Longhouse: The Peoples of the Iroquois League in the Era of European Colonization* (Chapel Hill, N.C., 1992), 41–47; and Colin G. Calloway, ed., *The World Turned Upside Down: Indian Voices from Early America* (Boston, 1994), 11–14.

## A "Great Family" of "Brothers"

The Greenville negotiations took place in a cultural context that centered on developing the symbiotic relationship between civility and power in the United States. If civility was far from uniform in eighteenth-century British America, it was always about manners and appearances; it suggested decorum and restraint in dealing with other peoples. Civility was a decidedly ethnocentric concept, implying that some European Americans were better than everyone else because they were better at attaining standards of conduct they had established as worthwhile. For the most part, as David S. Shields has shown, the "great project of civility" in the eighteenth century was a private affair, enacted in salons, taverns, and meeting rooms, where ambitious people met for education and amusement far from the public world of kings and courtiers. There they discussed and rehearsed new ways of dealing with each other. With the creation of a republican government in the United States, the practice of civility took on a public dimension. The absence of a monarchical court meant that those men and women most interested in demonstrating their good behavior were now in positions of power.[7]

Even as they defined themselves against those they saw as their social inferiors rather than their superiors, the officials of the new Republic craved popular acceptance. Indeed, public affirmations of their legitimacy were the most distinctive feature of republican rule; what made American officials different from British or French ones was that people seemed to accede publicly to their exercise of power. These public affirmations were not limited to ballots. The most mundane official acts became theatrical displays. The 1794 meeting of the General Court of the Northwest Territory was essentially a drama in which the participants played well-defined roles that attempted to order social relationships and political expression on the western edges of the new nation.

On March 21, 1794, John Ludlow, sheriff of Hamilton County, did "proclaim and make known" that, pursuant to a writ from "the honourable George Turner, Esquire, one of the Judges in and over" the Northwest Territory, the court would convene in Cincinnati on the second Tuesday in April. Ludlow, "in obedience" to Turner's order, gave "Notice" to the constables and coroner to appear "then and there in their own proper persons, with their Rolls, Records, Inquisitions, and other remembrances to do those things which to their office in that behalf appertain to be done" as well anyone who wished to "pros-

---

7. The fullest discussion of civility is David S. Shields, *Civil Tongues and Polite Letters in British America* (Chapel Hill, N.C., 1997).

ecute against" the prisoners in the county jail. *"God Save the Territory!"* Ludlow concluded with a flourish.[8]

On the morning of April 8, the appropriate officials duly proceeded from Turner's chambers "to the public ground . . . in the following order, Constables with Battoons, Shiriff and Coroner with white Wonds, Goaler, The Honorable Judge, Clerk with a green bag, Judges of the Common Pleas, Justices of the Peace, Attornies/Messengers etc." This parade of authority made visible the political hierarchy of the territorial government. It was a remarkable display of the importance of status and rank in the new democratic republic. Judge Turner then addressed the assembled jury about the need for justice in an imperfect world and the incompatibility of *"LIBERTY and LICENSCIOUSNESS."*[9]

Regretting that "error is incident to human nature," Turner explained that "misapprehensions and disorders *will* arise under even the *best* systems of government, and in the *best* regulated state of society." Happiness depends on "the possession of liberty," which can only be secured with *"restraining rules."* Thankfully for Americans, they lived in an "enlightened" age when *"Imperial Reason"* held sway. "Far removed" from corrupt Europe, "blessed" with a wonderful soil and climate, they had the power to form a pure government and "transmit" the "blessings" of freedom "to millions yet unborn." The job of jurors was "to try the truth of facts affecting the liberty, the lives, the reputation and the property of their fellow-citizens."[10]

Reason might guide men to the truth, Turner continued, but emotion was as important in helping them to decide how to exercise their power. "Be tender, gentlemen, of the reputation and feelings of your fellow-citizens." They are "part of the same great family with yourselves.—They have feelings, like you;—and, like you, are in the pursuit of human happiness. . . . The object of your meeting is to serve a community which calls you brothers."[11]

With these precepts in mind, the jury considered three indictments. The first two were against African Americans. James Dorsey, "a free negro, convicted of larceny," was sentenced "to be whipped through the principle streets of this city, with one and thirty stripes on the bare back; and during the punishment to wear fastened on his hat a paper with these words in large letters, 'AN INCORRIGIBLE OFFENDER.'" In addition to this public punishment, Dorsey

---

8. "Proclamation," *Centinel of the North-Western Territory* (Cincinnati), Mar. 22, 1794.

9. Ibid., Apr. 12, 1794.

10. "Charge Delivered to the Grand Jury, April 8th. by the Honourable George Turner, One of the Judges in and over This Territory," ibid., Apr. 19, 1794.

11. Ibid.

had to pay court costs and post bond for six months' good behavior. Mingo, allegedly a "run-away negro," was also found guilty of larceny. Apparently, he was not incorrigible, for he only received twenty-nine stripes on his bare back before the jail. Finally, innkeeper Thomas Cochran, convicted of "suffering gaming in his house," had to pay a one-hundred-dollar fine and court costs and lost his license. Satisfied with its work, the court adjourned. A little more than a week later, the high sheriff, the coroner, and the gentlemen of the Bar "gave an elegant entertainment to his Honour, at the house of George Gordon, esq. and to which the Gentlemen who composed the Grand Jury were likewise invited. The day was spent with perfect harmony and decorum." [12]

Like other public ceremonies in the recently created United States, the meeting of the General Court had affirmed its basic social and political structures. In theory, the citizens of the new Republic were a "great family" of "brothers," who defined themselves to a significant extent in the ways in which they dealt with blacks and, by implication, women, Indians, and other inferiors. If their exercise of power was brutal, their public behavior demonstrated that they were reasonable men who could control themselves. Style and content were virtually inseparable; indeed, to a considerable extent, style was content. The court not only punished criminals; it displayed the reasons why the officials of the United States should be "in and over" the other members of their great family, why they should be thought of more as fathers than brothers. As they made public examples of men who were unable to overcome their incorrigibility, they invited their audience to contrast the behavior of those on trial with their own ability to act in ways that promoted "perfect harmony and decorum."

The General Court insisted on such ceremony in part because sovereignty was hotly contested in the Ohio Valley—and the nation in general—in the 1790s. The question of who would direct the future of the region remained in doubt. Territorial officers and military leaders strongly supported the expansion of the power of the national government created by the Constitution of 1787 and the territorial government established by the Northwest Ordinance of 1787. They believed that it was the obligation of educated gentlemen such as themselves to build order and civility into the structures of life in the Northwest Territory.[13]

12. *Centinel of the North-Western Territory,* Apr. 19, 1794.

13. Andrew R. L. Cayton, *The Frontier Republic: Ideology and Politics in the Ohio Country, 1780–1825* (Kent, Ohio, 1986), 12–32; Cayton and Peter S. Onuf, *The Midwest and the Nation: Rethinking the History of an American Region* (Bloomington, Ind., 1990), 1–24.

Indians and American settlers in the Ohio Valley, on the other hand, tended to see national officials as intrusive and arrogant. Indians had every reason to fear the government of the United States. It shamelessly claimed sovereignty over a territory that stretched from the Ohio River to what is now eastern Minnesota, it had established forts northward from the Ohio in the Great Miami and Wabash Valleys, and it had sent military expeditions in 1790 and 1791 to burn cornfields and destroy villages on the Maumee River.

Americans felt just as threatened by the Federalists' insistence on the orderly development of the Northwest Territory. They were particularly upset by land policies that tended to benefit large speculators and by the national government's insistence in the Northwest Ordinance that Americans show "the utmost good faith . . . toward the Indians." Whites defied federal authority by squatting on federal lands. Many ignored or mocked territorial officials, making fun of their pretensions or calling for their removal.[14]

Indeed, Cincinnati, the de facto capital of the United States west of the Appalachian Mountains, was the antithesis of republican visions of "harmony and decorum." Feeding off Fort Washington were dozens of taverns, shops, and brothels. Anthony Wayne refused to station his Legion there in 1793 because of the debauchery. Men attacked Acting Governor Winthrop Sargent in print and refused to obey duly constituted laws. By 1794, some were already denouncing the Northwest Ordinance and calling for an elected state government. Others were simply burning down the Hamilton County jail.[15]

The contradictions between the rhetoric of harmony that characterized the meeting of the General Court and the reality of serious conflict exemplify the general dilemma of American gentlemen in the decades following the American Revolution. They saw themselves as engaged in the construction of a great empire; nothing was more important to its success than the behavior of its citizens. But exactly who was a citizen? And what were his responsibilities? In

14. On the contested nature of authority in the Northwest Territory, see Andrew R. L. Cayton, *Frontier Indiana* (Bloomington, Ind., 1996), 70–165; Cayton, *Frontier Republic,* 33–50; Cayton, "'Separate Interests' and the Nation-State: The Washington Administration and the Origins of Regionalism in the Trans-Appalachian West," *Journal of American History,* LXXIX (June–September 1992), 39–67; and Alan Taylor, "Land and Liberty on the Post-Revolutionary Frontier," in David Thomas Konig, ed., *Devising Liberty: Preserving and Creating Freedom in the New American Republic* (Stanford, Calif., 1995), 81–108. On the Northwest Ordinance, see Peter S. Onuf, *Statehood and Union: A History of the Northwest Ordinance* (Bloomington, Ind., 1987); and Robert M. Taylor, Jr., ed., *The Northwest Ordinance, 1787: A Bicentennial Handbook* (Indianapolis, Ind., 1987).

15. *Centinel of the North-Western Territory,* Feb. 27, 1796.

answering these questions, the members of the General Court and the participants at Greenville helped to elucidate the powerful combination of popular sovereignty and political exclusion that was at the core of American political culture from the Revolution to the second half of the twentieth century.[16]

Their purposes were simultaneously elitist and egalitarian, a contradiction far more glaring to us than to them. Prominent American men, especially veterans of the American War of Independence, saw themselves as sharing an equality based upon fraternity—they were brothers in a new world without kings, priests, or nobles. But their brotherhood rested squarely on the supposedly voluntary subjugation of other human beings. If liberty amounted to autonomy, or personal independence, then it was a privilege enjoyed by only a few. Citizens were fictive brothers because they were also fictive fathers, democratic patriarchs who were equal to each other in large part because they were superior to everyone else.[17]

Gender, race, and class were critical in determining who could enjoy the rights of citizenship. But late-eighteenth-century Anglo-American gentlemen rarely thought of these categories as being as important as we do. Rather, they conceived of the world as divided between civility and savagery, between reasonable and vulgar peoples. The latter category included a multitude of peoples of different genders and races: the white "lawless banditti" who inhabited the frontiers of the Ohio Valley were only marginally more respectable than enslaved African Americans or Miami Indians. To abandon the government of the new nation to any of these peoples was to doom it to chaos and extinction.[18]

As elitist as some American men were, they were also committed to some degree of popular sovereignty. Their democratic patriarchy would be illegitimate and impotent without regular public demonstrations of consent by the

16. For helpful discussions of similar issues in Great Britain, see Linda Colley, *Britons: Forging the Nation, 1707–1837* (New Haven, Conn., 1992), 364–375, esp. 371–372; and Russell, *Theatres of War*, 3–6.

17. Steven C. Bullock, *Revolutionary Brotherhood: Freemasonry and the Transformation of the American Social Order, 1730–1840* (Chapel Hill, N.C., 1996), 120–133; Charles Royster, *A Revolutionary People at War: The Continental Army and American Character, 1775–1783* (Chapel Hill, N.C., 1979), 353–360.

18. Carroll Smith-Rosenberg, "Dis-Covering the Subject of the 'Great Constitutional Discussion,' 1786–1789," *JAH,* LXXIX (June–Sept. 1992), 841–873; Linda K. Kerber, "The Paradox of Women's Citizenship in the Early Republic: The Case of *Martin vs. Massachusetts,* 1805," *American Historical Review,* XCVII (1992), 349–378; Virginia Delegates to Benjamin Harrison, Nov. 1, 1783, in Edmund C. Burnett, ed., *Letters of Members of the Continental Congress,* 8 vols. (Washington, D.C., 1921–1936), VII, 365 (quotation).

vulgar to the rule of the civilized. Ideally, slaves, women, children, uneducated white men, and Indians would all consent to their own degradation on the altar of fraternal citizenship. Men such as Wayne believed that the greatness of the American empire depended on their leadership, that their leadership rested upon their ability to win the approbation of both their peers and their inferiors, and that that approbation had to be granted publicly and without reservation.[19]

Like most of their educated contemporaries in the United States and Europe, the civil and military officers in the Northwest Territory knew that all human beings are imperfect creatures, that they are selfish, ambitious, contentious, and full of passions. The point of civilization, of reason and enlightenment, was not to eliminate nasty behavior, for it could not be done. Rather, they hoped that strong institutions, orderly environments, and, above all, exemplary behavior by natural leaders would encourage people to restrain their brutish natures. The fundamental question was not whether people were inherently good or bad; it was whether people could learn to behave in a civilized fashion, to repress selfish instincts and develop a desire to behave benevolently. The essence of civility was sympathy, the ability to feel as well as reason, to perform in ways that not only met other peoples' expectations but elevated them.[20]

Civility was particularly the responsibility of powerful men. Refinement was not the arrogant foppery of a courtier, the badge of the lazy and effeminate. The ultimate test of a man's worth lay in the ways in which he dealt with his dependents, with slaves, vulgar whites, women, and Indians. And civility was hard work. A man who lost his temper, yelled at his inferiors, or, worse, beat them in a rage was hardly worthy of anyone's respect. To be sure, miscreants had to be punished. But those with power had an obligation to exercise it with a decorum that would earn them respect. Whipping incorrigible blacks in the streets of Cincinnati was acceptable because a duly appointed court had formally reasoned that it was necessary and had ensured that it would be administered in a dignified fashion.

19. Jay Fliegelman, *Prodigals and Pilgrims: The American Revolution against Patriarchal Authority* (Cambridge, 1982), 35–36; Gordon S. Wood, *The Radicalism of the American Revolution* (New York, 1991); and Alan Taylor, *William Cooper's Town: Power and Persuasion on the Frontier of the Early American Republic* (New York, 1995). On Ohio, see Andrew R. L. Cayton, " 'Language Gives Way to Feelings': Rhetoric, Republicanism, and Religion in Jeffersonian Ohio," in Jeffrey P. Brown and Cayton, eds., *The Pursuit of Public Power: Political Culture in Ohio, 1787–1861* (Kent, Ohio, 1994), 31–48.

20. Lawrence E. Klein, *Shaftesbury and the Culture of Politeness: Moral Discourse and Cultural Politics in Early Eighteenth-Century England* (Cambridge, 1994), 1–14, 195–212; Bushman, *Refinement of America*, 46–58.

James Dorsey and Mingo no doubt saw matters differently. It is unlikely that the words "respect" or "dignity" crossed their minds as the lash criss-crossed their backs. But to the gentlemen of Cincinnati, the style of their punishment was as important as the punishment itself. A fine distinction perhaps, but none-theless a critical one to the men who governed the United States in the 1790s. By ostentatiously parading through the city, Judge Turner and his colleagues were demanding that their fellow citizens scrutinize them, confident that their decorum would mark them as civilized men and convey the impartiality of their actions to their republican brothers. No less significant, they were offer-ing the rest of their great family tangible evidence of their superior character and thus the legitimacy of their claim to exercise power over them.

## To "Merit an Eternal Memorial of Applause"

Civility mattered as much to the officers of the Legion of the United States, which was created by Congress in 1792, as it did to the territorial General Court. Americans, after all, despised standing armies as instruments of Euro-pean tyranny. They believed that they promoted immorality and discord and, with their emphasis on rank and obedience, undermined the democratic foun-dations of a republic. The mission of the Legion, therefore, involved more than the defeat of the Indians living in the Maumee Valley, indeed, more than the restoration of American honor after the humiliation of Harmar and St. Clair. Like the members of the court in Cincinnati, the officers of the Legion had to demonstrate that they and the United States were so worthy of their eventual victory that both Indians and whites would voluntarily consent to their sover-eignty and recognize them as the natural leaders of the Northwest Territory.

This was a tough challenge, given that no one in the Legion regularly be-haved like an affectionate brother, let alone a genteel patriarch. Rank-and-file soldiers seemed most interested in contesting any and all authority. The most common transgression, in fact a majority (52 percent, 100 of 190) of the cases brought to a court-martial in 1792 and 1793, was desertion (or intention to desert). Second was the vague charge of "bad conduct" (44, or 26 percent), fol-lowed by drunkenness (25 cases), offenses by sentries (13 percent), and absence without official leave (13, or 17 percent).[21]

Like the gentlemen of the General Court, the officers of the Legion pun-ished incorrigibility with harsh, physical punishment. Although some miscre-

21. Richard C. Knopf, "Crime and Punishment in the American Legion, 1792–1793," Spe-cial Collections, King Library, 2, 3, Miami University, Oxford, Ohio.

ants got away with reductions in rank or losses of pay, the standard penalty was one hundred lashes, often with a "wire-stranned whip." Others suffered brandings or were forced to run a gauntlet. Of the 190 men tried, 19 (10 percent) faced the ultimate penalty, public execution, usually by a firing squad. Fifteen of them were actually killed.[22]

Such brutality had only a limited impact on a Legion whose soldiers were as assertive as any group of American citizens. A few belonged to "the Damnation Club," the members of which took pride in their ability to withstand public whippings. One man claimed to have endured seven hundred lashings. Meanwhile, the Cincinnati newspaper frequently ran advertisements offering rewards for the return of deserters. In the fall of 1793, Captain Edward Butler promised "TWENTY SPANISH MILLED DOLLARS" for each of eight men who had deserted on the march from Fort Washington to Greenville. In April 1795, Captain Zebulon Pike offered fifty dollars for Francis Waldron, a twenty-six-year-old New Jersey–born blacksmith and an apparent master of deception. Waldron "appears to strangers as a man of morality, and not habitual to the vices of hard drinking, swearing etc. he is very industrious and a great imposter. is capable of every immaginable dissimulation." Clearly planning to take full advantage of the social confusion of the early Republic, Waldron had stolen an officer's clothes as well as a rifle.[23]

James Elliot, a prim Vermonter who spent three years as a noncommissioned officer in the Legion, including most of 1795 at Greenville, gave personal testimony to the brutishness of military life. "In an army," Elliot wrote shortly after his service, "every thing invites and leads to dissipation." Had he a son, he would have him serve a "short tour" with an army, for he would learn more about "human nature" there than at a college. It was a risky business, though, because, for every youth who learned a lesson from the experience, nine or ten would be "eternally ruined."[24]

The members of the Legion were at their worst in dealing with the many women who accompanied them on their expedition. Some were wives; some were, in the words of the doctor at Fort Defiance, "Dulcinea[s]," who did much of the work necessary to keep the Legion functioning, ranging from laundry to

22. Ibid., 4.

23. Richard C. Knopf, ed., *A Surgeon's Mate at Fort Defiance: The Journal of Joseph Gardner Andrews for the Year 1795* (Columbus, Ohio, 1957), 16; "One Hundred and Sixty Dollars Reward," *Centinel of the North-Western Territory,* Nov. 30, 1793, "Fifty Dollars Reward," May 24, 1794.

24. James Elliot, "Essay II; On the Moral Consequences of Standing Armies," in Elliot, *The Poetical and Miscellaneous Works of James Elliot . . .* (Greenfield, Mass., 1798), 202.

cooking to what the doctor called "other demands." Although many were paid for their labor, they were often treated badly.[25]

Elliot particularly despised that "the idea of a chaste and permanent connubial connection" was to so many "an object of ridicule." Not only was "adultery . . . always frequent," soldiers took pride in "seducing an innocent virgin, or a simple wife." "Hundreds of once innocent and happy females are to be seen in every army, who have become, from necessity or despair, the most abandoned beings in existence."[26]

Elliot recalled one officer who told "with seeming exultation" a story of his success at sleeping with the wife of his landlord while the landlord was in New York City, escorting some Indian chiefs. "Guilty of treachery in private friendship," this man was nonetheless "as good a character, and . . . apparently as amiable a man, as any officer in the regiment." Elliot could excuse unmarried men their "unlawful pleasures" but not mature officers. It was, he thought, "part of that general system of unjust and contemptuous treatment of women, to which our sex in general are so obstinately attached." More precisely, the men of the Legion were using women both for pleasure and in their competition with each other for status.[27]

Trying to keep human depravity at bay, General Wayne and Secretary of War Henry Knox talked incessantly about the need for discipline in the Legion. Unable to credit the efforts of so-called savages, they attributed the failures of Harmar and St. Clair to the personal defects of officers and men. They had not been righteous enough; they had not paid attention to detail; they had relied on undisciplined Kentucky militia.

It was precisely because the officers expected little from common soldiers that they held themselves and their peers to higher standards. Indeed, they believed that leading exemplary public lives was the key to winning the respect of their men and, with it, their consent to be directed by gentlemen. How could officers expect inferiors to behave well until they had demonstrated that they could restrain their own passions? Like territorial officials, military leaders could not acquire legitimacy through whippings alone. They had to persuade others that they were worthy of leadership. And all of this had to start at the top, with the man most likely to win the coveted title of father.

25. Knopf, ed., *Surgeon's Mate*, 42, 53.

26. Elliot, "On the Moral Consequences of Standing Armies," in Elliot, *Poetical and Miscellaneous Works*, 202.

27. Ibid., 203, 204. See also Russell, *Theatres of War*, 37–41, 161–163; Christine Stansell, *City of Women: Sex and Class in New York, 1789–1860* (New York, 1986), 20–30.

Like many officers who had served during the American War of Independence, Anthony Wayne was a successful man who persisted in perceiving himself as scorned and mistreated. Wayne's military exploits (including leading the American attack at Stony Brook, New York, in 1779) earned him the rank of major general in 1784. But he found life after the war difficult. He was an incompetent rice planter, trapping himself in a web of debt. He was a pompous politician, unable to win key elections or the kind of high appointment he desired. George Washington only reluctantly gave Wayne command of the Legion. The president hoped that the immense responsibility of the task would help the general "correct his foibles," among which were that he was "open to flattery; vain; easily imposed upon; and liable to be drawn into scrapes," and maybe "addicted to the bottle." [28]

As impetuous a human being as he was cautious an officer, Wayne devoted much of his time as commander of the Legion to petty personal squabbles. He was continually feuding with his second-in-command, the estimable James Wilkinson of Kentucky, who made a career out of deception and double-dealing. Wilkinson was always trying to undermine Wayne with both his superiors and his own men. In December 1794, Wilkinson denounced Wayne as "a liar, a drunkard, a Fool, the associate of the lowest order of Society, and the companion of their vices, of desperate Fortune, my rancorous enemy, a coward, a Hypocrite, and the contempt of every man of sense and virtue." [29]

This exorbitant language was typical of the Legion's officers. When General Charles Scott of Kentucky defended Wayne to Washington, Wilkinson called Scott "a fool, a scoundrel and a poltroon." Wayne, for his part, took a long time to catch on to Wilkinson's game, which was to assume command of the Legion. When he did, he could only call his second-in-command "that vile assassin," "that worst of all bad men." And so it went. The correspondence of the officers was a cornucopia of insults and innuendo. Wayne complained bitterly in 1793 that officers were using groundless courts-martial to settle "their private disputes." The courts-martial continued, even during the treaty negotiations. Five days after the signing of the Treaty of Greenville, James Elliot denounced

28. George Washington, "Opinion of the General Officers," Mar. 9, 1792, in John C. Fitzpatrick, ed., *The Writings of George Washington from the Original Manuscript Sources, 1745–1799*, 39 vols. (Washington, D.C., 1931–1944), XXXI, 509–515. For a general discussion of Wayne's character, see Paul David Nelson, *Anthony Wayne: Soldier of the Early Republic* (Bloomington, Ind., 1985), 224–226 (quotation on 225).

29. Quoted in Nelson, *Wayne*, 275.

the "spirit of prejudice and envy, and consequent enmity and discord, [which] appear[ed] to be generally prevalent amongst the officers of the army."[30]

In the summer of 1794, an anonymous writer (probably a former officer in the Legion) sent a long letter to the *Centinel of the North-Western Territory*. Written in the form of a speech that Minerva, goddess of wisdom, had asked Anthony Wayne to deliver to his troops before they embarked on their campaign against the Indians, the letter was a warning to the officers to improve their characters—and quickly, for "the enterprize before you is great, and has already mocked at the toils of two armies." Vice and licentiousness, claimed the author, threatened not only the "character" but the "cause" of the Legion. Wayne's responsibility in this war on immorality was to act "as a father," to "advise and instruct [his men] in duty" and to offer "the law of kindness" to his "children of love." To his speech he must "affix the blood-dipt seal of sincerity." Especially troublesome was the continual quarreling, even dueling, provoked "by vicious resentment" and the surrender of reason "to gratify the humour of a base passion." The writer urged the officers to substitute honor and sympathy for jealousy and ambition. "Patriotism" was the sum of all virtues in a soldier. Those "who do not possess it are like the man who appeared at the feast without the wedding garment." "You have accepted an office which you have not the proper spirit to execute."[31]

The correspondent of the *Centinel* believed that the success of the Legion's mission—to defeat Indians and establish the authority of the United States—depended on its members' ability to act with rectitude. "A martial body," he argued, "should be viewed as a grand pile of finished architecture." "The superior officers should appear like the stately pillars of a royal edifice, wrought with elegant proportions and decorated with the most exact beauties: while all the inferior grades should seem equally essential to the support—symmetry—grandeur and strength of the complete work." In other words, the Legion must be a moral standard-bearer for the nation as well as a military one.

30. Wilkinson, quoted in Nelson, *Wayne*, 256; Wayne to Knox, Jan. 29, 1795, in Richard C. Knopf, ed., *Anthony Wayne, A Name in Arms: Soldier, Diplomat, Defender of Expansion Westward of a Nation, The Wayne-Knox-Pickering-McHenry Correspondence* (Pittsburgh, 1960), 383; Wayne, quoted in Nelson, *Wayne*, 295; Wayne, Sept. 6, 1793, quoted in C. M. Burton, ed., "Wayne's Orderly Book," Michigan Pioneer and Historical Society, *Historical Collections*, XXXIV (Lansing, Mich., 1905), 474; Elliot, "Sketches, Political, Geographical, etc., Extracted from the Journal of James Elliot, during a Period of Three Years Service in the Legion of the United States," in Elliot, *Poetical and Miscellaneous Works*, 144.

31. "For the Centinel. . . . My Dear Officers and Valiant Soldiers," *Centinel of the North-Western Territory*, Sept. 6, 1794.

Like most eighteenth-century gentlemen, the Legion's officers accepted the existence of a disparity between public and private behavior. But the letter writer demanded that they see a connection between the two arenas. He insisted that the antidote to their private foibles was the exercise of sympathy. Let "Friendship," that "stranger indeed in our camps," return. "Let back-biters—scandal-runners—eve-droppers—false-accusers and secret bearers be heard of no more ranging the serpentine round of disappointed envy and the covered-ways of ruthless intrigue. Let your characters be paraded in day-light and examined in scrutiny." In short, "Be therefore noble *actors* upon that field which you may make the theatre of honour."[32]

The reward for transcending in public behavior the dishonor of private life was everlasting fame. In an echo of the speech Shakespeare's Henry V makes to his men before the battle of Agincourt, the author insisted that history would remember what they did only if they were worthy of victory. "Vice" was "a *Hydra* more terrible than the savage foe in front." Its defeat was the prerequisite for victory over the Indians. The Legion must "by one decided and general action convince the world, that [they] were just in the onset" as well as "great in the contest" and therefore "merit[ed] an eternal memorial of applause to [their] magnanimity."[33]

These themes were familiar ones in the eighteenth century. Throughout his career, Wayne frequently reminded his men, especially his officers, of the importance of appearances, that how they carried themselves was as significant as what they did. In October 1793, the general lamented "the Apparent want of Harmony, and Due Subordination" in some of the officers, reminding them that "at this Crisis . . . they ought to Unite as a Band of Brothers." Wayne assumed that gentility in leaders was fundamental to the success of a republican social order. "It is a false Notion," he asserted, "that Subordination and Prompt Obedience to Superiors is any debasement of a Mans Courage or a Reflection upon his Honour, or Understanding."[34]

The Legion of the United States marched to victory in 1794. But its mission was only half-finished. Could it prove in 1795 that it was worthy of its military triumph? Could its officers, especially its putative father, win the respect and acquiescence of the Indians, which, in turn, would help them win the respect and acquiescence of other people in the Ohio Valley?

32. "For the Centinel (cont.)," ibid., Sept. 13, 1794.

33. "For the Centinel (cont.)," ibid., Sept. 20, 1794.

34. Wayne, Oct. 14, 1793, quoted in Burton, ed., "Wayne's Orderly Book," Mich. Pioneer and Hist. Soc., *Hist. Colls.*, XXXIV (1905), 476, 492.

Precisely because he occupied a position of superior power, Anthony Wayne knew that his fame depended on his ability to be the perfect host at Greenville. He was determined to show that he did not deserve his nickname of "mad." He would not deny that he had passions—impulses, often selfish ones—but he could demonstrate that, when it mattered, when his fellow citizens, the Indians, and history were watching most closely, he could control himself and that, by extension, the United States could control itself. Whatever fate that "*Capricious* female" "Fortune" had in store for him, Wayne had assured the widow of Nathanael Greene in 1793, "No conduct of mine, during the Awful and Solemn appeal, will ever require the paliation of a friend, Nor will the sanguine field be disgraced by receiving [me] on its *cold* bosom." To paraphrase the words of the young Nathanael Greene, Wayne claimed to have pursued honor and virtue "in spite of all Opposition," which was "the carrector of a truly great and Noble Soul."[35]

## "In the Most Public Manner"

The Indians living between the Ohio River and the Great Lakes had every reason to exercise anything but self-control in 1795. Worn down by decades of war, famine, and disease, increasingly dependent on the British for food and goods, they were literally witnessing the disintegration of their societies. Alcoholism and depression were eating away at respect for traditional leaders and customs.

After their stunning victories over the Harmar and St. Clair expeditions, some Indians made a great show of unity at the Glaize on the Maumee River in the early fall of 1792. The Glaize was the center of Indian spiritual and political unity, the home to two thousand people. At a council in late September and early October, the Delaware Buckongahelas asserted that all Indians were "animated by one Mind, one Head, one Heart." The council reaffirmed a 1786 contention that "any cession of our lands should be made in the most public manner, and by the united voice of the confederacy." These repeated calls to unity could not disguise, however, that the Indians of the Maumee Valley were increasingly alienated from each other and divided about how to deal with the ever growing numbers of American invaders.[36]

35. Wayne to Catherine Littlefield Greene, Dec. 17, 1793, Greene Papers, William L. Clements Library, Ann Arbor, Mich.; Greene, quoted in Wood, *Radicalism of the American Revolution*, 204.

36. Helen Hornbeck Tanner, "The Glaize in 1792: A Composite Indian Community," *Ethnohistory*, XXV (1978), 16–39; Buckongahelas, "Indian Council at the Glaize, 1792," in E. A. Cruikshank, ed., *The Correspondence of Lieut. Governor John Graves Simcoe . . .* , 5 vols.

Conflict was nothing new to the Indians of the Great Lakes. For more than a century, Europeans and other Indians, most notably the Iroquois, had intruded into the worlds of the Miami, the Potawatomi, and others. With them came trade, technology, diseases, and wars that threatened to destroy the integrity of existing cultures. In response to such crises, Indians had constructed an elaborate system to mediate disagreements and contain tensions. Through adoption, intermarriage, trade, and calumet ceremonies, they had created a diplomatic and commercial world that favored a sense of social obligation, or responsibility, among human beings, even enemies.[37]

Specifically, French and later British intruders had been adopted as fathers in a fictive kinship network that rested on mutual misunderstanding. Before the democratic revolutions of the late eighteenth century, most European males were happy to be called patriarchs; they expected to command their inferiors. But Indians saw a father as an essentially benevolent figure, whose influence flowed from sympathy rather than coercion. He was, according to Richard White, supposed to be "kind, generous, and protecting." "A child owed a father respect, but a father could not compel obedience." In other words, Indians conferred patriarchy only on those men who acted in ways that merited the title of father.[38]

When people dealt with each other in a public forum, they did so in a context suffused with the rhetoric of personal obligation. Ceremonies with both friends and enemies were delicate meetings, fraught with a potential for anger and violence. So Indians tried to construct an atmosphere of what Europeans would call civility, in which angry, frustrated men who had every reason to distrust each other could interact in reasonable ways. Speeches and exchanges might make it possible for people to handle grievances that inspired deep hostility.

The Iroquois, argues Daniel K. Richter, chiefly prized virtues "associated with harmony and consensus: imperturbability, patience, good will, selflessness." In council, speakers emphasized the personal ties among the participants, calling each other "brother" if they were equals or "father" or "son," de-

---

(Toronto, 1923), I, 220; "Speech of the United Indian Nations, . . . 28th November and 18th December, 1786," in United States Congress, *American State Papers: Documents, Legislative and Executive, of the Congress of the United States . . .*, 38 vols. (Washington, D.C., 1832–1861), Class II, *Indian Affairs*, 2 vols., ed. Walter Lowrie et al., I, 8–9 (hereafter cited as *American State Papers, Indian Affairs*).

37. White, *Middle Ground*.

38. Ibid., 84.

pending on the hierarchical character of their relationship. In the quest for harmony, "participants seldom spoke with complete frankness if they disagreed with each other; peace and unity of mind ideally prevailed." Indians especially valued oratory, for, in a system in which coercion rarely worked, persuasion was a man's most powerful skill. Oratory, however, was incomplete without gifts. Writes Richter: "'True' words were always accompanied by presents of symbolically charged or economically valuable items. . . . In a very practical and concrete sense gifts made words true and legitimized the position of the person who conveyed them."[39]

The culture of fictive kinship was strong enough to survive decades of misunderstanding among Indians and Europeans. But it could not withstand the demographic onslaught of tens of thousands of Americans in the 1780s and 1790s. Most American settlers came to the Ohio Valley intending to transform it, although they could not always agree on exactly how. As was evident from their response to the elaborate plans for the development of the Northwest Territory, most were in a hurry to get land. They had no patience for long ceremonies and fictive relationships; they had no interest in the cultural value of creative misunderstanding. The inevitable result was war.

Even by the exceptionally low standards of the North American frontier, the struggle for the Ohio Valley was remarkably nasty. The victory that seems inevitable in retrospect was brutally contested from the 1770s through the 1790s. Notwithstanding the many examples of interaction among whites and Indians, the border war that centered on the Ohio River was horrific, its history replete with tales of uncommon brutality. It was not enough for either side to win; they had to destroy each other's bodies in cathartic rituals of physical violence. When George Rogers Clark captured Vincennes in February 1779, he ordered the murder of a half-dozen wounded Indians. A British officer recorded that "in cold blood [Clark] knocked their brains outs, dipping his hands in their blood, rubbing it several times on his cheeks, yelping as a Savage." In the winter of 1789–1790, the British trader Henry Hay, usually a very merry fellow, watched an Indian, enraged by the murders of some relatives, beat an elderly white captive to death. The next day, Hay saw the man's heart and scalp carried by his killer. At St. Clair's defeat in November 1791, victorious Indians smashed the skull of the American general, Richard Butler. Death alone was not punishment enough for the man who several years earlier had announced to assembled Indians that "this country belongs to the United States." Butler's dried

39. Richter, *Ordeal of the Longhouse*, 41, 47.

skull was sent to the Iroquois, his heart was cut into pieces for every tribe who participated in the battle, and his corpse left for animals to gnaw on.[40]

It was this savage culture of violence that made the gentility of the Greenville meeting so necessary. The Indians and Americans who came to negotiate were more than flawed and divided human beings; they were angry men who had good reason to despise each other. If the officers of the Legion had to struggle to behave well in the role of conquerors, imagine the difficulties facing the Indians. They had every reason to be angry; they were not just performing for history, they were talking about the survival of their way of life. Civility was the means of restoring some sense of order and meaning to a world disintegrating before their eyes.

## Vox Populi? The Performance of Consent

Constructed in November 1793 and named in honor of Wayne's recently deceased friend, Nathanael Greene, Greenville was probably the "most formidable" fort in the Ohio Valley. It sat on the southwestern branch of the Great Miami River on what Wayne described as "a high commanding bold Peninsula, almost surrounded by Beautiful extensive prairies or natural meadows." The fort's perimeters consisted of twelve- to fifteen-feet-high pickets, with a platform behind them at a height of perhaps two feet; at each corner was a blockhouse. Eight or nine temporary structures, or redoubts, stood well beyond the pickets. Inside the walls was a collection of fourteen-feet-square huts located on the west side of the fortification as well as houses for the officers, sutlers, and merchants, a powder magazine, council house, mess hall, and an artillery park. There was also a sizable parade ground in the southeastern corner.[41]

---

40. Bernard W. Sheehan, "'The Famous Hair Buyer General': Henry Hamilton, George Rogers Clark, and the American Indian," *Indiana Magazine of History*, LXXIX (1983), 21; M. M. Quaife, "A Narrative of Life on the Old Frontier: Henry Hay's Journal from Detroit to the Mississippi River," State Historical Society of Wisconsin, *Proceedings*, LXII (Madison, Wis., 1914), 222; Wiley Sword, *President Washington's Indian War: The Struggle for the Old Northwest, 1790–1795* (Norman, Okla., 1985), 187–188. See the discussion of violence in White, *Middle Ground*, 452–453.

41. Frazier Ells Wilson, *James Elliot Explores Primitive Ohio . . .* (Greenville, Ohio, 1992), 6, 7; Wayne to Catherine Littlefield Greene, Dec. 17, 1793, Greene Papers; "Description of the Cantonment of Greenville, in the Western Territory of the United States, in a Letter from the Author to a Friend in Vermont," May 11, 1796, in Elliot, *Poetical and Miscellaneous Works*, 168–173.

Although it was an American fort, Greenville, during the hot summer of 1795, was contested space in which the private and public necessarily mingled. The post and its environs were home to an estimated 1,130 Indians, roughly the same number as the eleven hundred to twelve hundred soldiers on duty in May 1795. These numbers do not include hundreds of women and children. All of these people lived side by side, the Americans in the "Citadel," the Indians outside the walls in and around the temporary redoubts that Wayne had had constructed in 1793. Highly concentrated, the population was also highly uneasy.[42]

Like an anxious host, Wayne remained uncertain that the guests he had invited to meet with him at Greenville would actually come. Although he believed the Indians were serious about peace, he had rejected their offer to hold the negotiations at Kekionga, fearful that their pacific overtures might be "only artifice." What if they should "prove Perfidious" and "artfully procrastinate" until the Americans' supplies ran low? No, better to meet at Greenville, close to other American forts, secure in his supplies and his "Citadel."[43]

As more Indians informed him of their intention to come to Greenville, Wayne began to grow nervous. Did he have enough men? What about "the Nefarious Machinations of those wicked [British] agents" in and around Detroit? Should not the government send troops from the Atlantic Coast to Fort Washington as soon as possible? If he had enough troops, would he have enough "Articles" and "*trinkets*" to impress the chiefs when they arrived? Were the Indians tricking him?[44]

Similar questions preoccupied the Indians who accepted Wayne's invitation. In early 1795, many began visiting the Americans at Fort Wayne and Fort Defiance. On January 29, twenty-six Delawares and Shawnees (including the chief Blue Jacket) brought four prisoners to Fort Defiance. The next day, some of the Indians dined with the officers.[45]

Such a scene became a common occurrence. Occasionally, officers "strolled" over to Indian camps, accepting pancakes and treating the ill. The American

---

42. "A Return of the Numbers of the Different Nations Present at, and Parties to, the Treaty of Greenville, Taken on the 7th August, 1795," *American State Papers, Indian Affairs,* I, 582; Elliot, "Sketches, Political, Geographical," in Elliot, *Poetical and Miscellaneous Works,* 139; *Centinel of the North-Western Territory,* July 25, 1795. On the weather, see Knopf, ed., *Surgeon's Mate,* 45, 51, 58.

43. Wayne to Timothy Pickering, Mar. 8, 1795, Wayne to Knox, Jan. 24, 1795, in Knopf, ed., *Anthony Wayne,* 380, 388.

44. Wayne to Knox, Feb. 12, 1795, Wayne to Pickering, Mar. 8, 1795, in Knopf, ed., *Anthony Wayne,* 385, 387, 388, 389, 390.

45. Knopf, ed., *Surgeon's Mate,* 11.

doctor at Fort Defiance even began to prepare "a Vocabulary of Shawanoese Language." On June 1, Little Turtle arrived at Fort Defiance, for no other purpose, he asserted, than "the gratification of his wish to see his Brothers." The Miami chief lived at the officers' quarters for a few days and impressed them with his intelligence, his "modest and manly" behavior, and his abstention from alcohol.[46]

Little Turtle was not deceiving his hosts. Although many Indians came to the Americans because they were hungry and needed food and shelter, their visits were also social calls. They were attempting to reestablish relationships with the soldiers. The six months between their agreement to meet with the Americans and the actual start of the council in July was an intermediary stage of their relationship, a social frontier. The return of prisoners and professions of friendship and hospitality were designed to persuade the participants of their mutual sincerity. Before they could make peace, they had to make friends.

Obviously, the surface conviviality was something of an illusion. After all, these men had been trying to kill each other just months earlier; some still bore the marks of battle on their maimed bodies. The underlying tension revealed itself in odd moments, as when Little Turtle, enjoying a tour of the Americans' gardens, "soon after assumed a melancholy air and observed that that land was once his own property." Or in a brief tussle over the ownership of a canoe. Or when a drunken Shawnee tried to set fire to Fort Defiance and was almost killed for his "temerity." Or in an attack on cattle drives from Greenville. These incidents were all near misses. Men almost came to blows and then stepped back and stopped themselves, as if they knew that people who had been enemies for so long could not come together in any meaningful way until they first learned to trust each other on some level.[47]

Preceded by flags of peace and accompanied by prisoners and gifts, Indians began arriving at Greenville in late spring. The soldiers of the Legion greeted their guests with cannon fire, which was returned by rifles. Meanwhile, the Americans made preparations for the grand council. On the morning of Monday, June 15, the day on which the meeting was supposed to begin, soldiers fired fifteen cannon and unfurled "a large and beautiful new flag, at the head of an elegant flagstaff lately erected in the citadel." The ceremony enacted the structure of federalism: fifteen cannon for fifteen states, with the flag of the nation as a whole above them.[48]

46. Ibid., 22, 28, 29, 39.

47. Ibid., 28, 35, 39, 41.

48. Elliot, "Sketches, Political, Geographical," in Elliot, *Poetical and Miscellaneous Works,* 140.

Many Indians had not yet arrived. Still, costumed in his full dress uniform, Wayne welcomed those who were there on June 16. The council fire was lit and the calumet of peace smoked. Then the host spoke, using, from the beginning, the language of sympathy. Wayne said he took "all by the hand as brothers" who were committed to "the good work of peace." He remarked on the "clear sky and a refreshing breeze" as auspicious signs and noted that he had had roads cleared in all directions so that "all nations may come in safety and ease." However empty this rhetoric may seem to us, Wayne was trying to demonstrate his good faith by doing things Indians would appreciate. As important as gifts of food were to the Indians in establishing trust, sentimental language mattered to all participants. "Unstained with blood," Greenville was "pure as the heart" of George Washington. Wayne insisted that he wished for "nothing so much as peace and brotherly love." While they awaited the rest of their brothers, they would "rest in peace and love." At the end, Wayne offered "a little drink," with an admonition to be "merry, without . . . passing the bounds of temperance and sobriety."[49]

Privately, Wayne worried that he might not get a treaty signed at all. British goods and blandishments might wean away the Indians at Greenville and prevent others from arriving. He had asked the War Department in December to establish sufficient "trading houses in their Country." Secretary of War Timothy Pickering replied in April that the United States would provide twenty-five thousand dollars' worth of goods (later increased but not by enough, as far as Wayne was concerned) if the treaty were successful, plus ten thousand dollars in annuities. The annuities were something of an innovation, a way for the federal government to secure the permanent dependence of the Indians. "Good policy," according to Pickering, "requires that we endeavour to secure the good will of the Indian Tribes by making it their interest to be our friends, by their dependance on our yearly bounty." The idea was to "create an obligation of which they would feel the force."[50]

The limited number of gifts available to Wayne was only one of the reasons the general had doubts about such a policy. He had to use the 1789 Treaty of Fort Harmar, by which some Wyandots and Delawares had agreed to allow white settlements in what is now southern Ohio, as the basis for any agreement

49. Wayne, June 17, 1795, quoted in "Treaty of Greenville," *American State Papers, Indian Affairs,* 564.

50. Wayne to Knox, Dec. 23, 1794, Pickering to Wayne, Apr. 8, 1795, Pickering to Wayne, May 7, 1795, Wayne to Pickering, May 15, 1795, Pickering to Wayne, June 29, 1795, all in Knopf, ed., *Anthony Wayne,* 371, 394, 414, 418, 433. See also Dowd, *Spirited Resistance,* 114–115.

he might reach. Wayne knew that most Indians refused to recognize the validity of the Fort Harmar treaty. He also knew that, although annuities might buy consent, they could not secure it. As important, purchasing peace was little better than seizing territory. And Wayne wanted much more than land and peace; he wanted genuine consent to the establishment of American sovereignty north of the Ohio River. In this endeavor, words and personal demeanor were critical to his success.

Pickering agreed. He urged Wayne to follow the "One great principle [that] ought to govern all public negociations—*a rigid adherence to truth*—a principle that is essential in negociations with *Indians.*" "Jealousy is strongest in minds uninformed: so that the utmost purity and candor will hardly escape suspicion." In any case, Wayne must never let down his guard, for sympathetic people were often exploited by deceptive enemies. The secretary could not forget the lesson of Pontiac, the Ottawa leader who had led a war of resistance against the British occupation of the Great Lakes region between 1763 and 1765. Pontiac was "a great Chief," who had practiced "treachery" while "Under the guise of friendship." Pickering did not mention that the Americans were past masters at practicing deception through sentimental language.[51]

For their part, Wayne's guests responded to the general's warm welcome with professions of sincerity, the intensity of which only served to underscore their own private fears and divisions. Tetabokshke of the Delaware celebrated "the commencement of our friendship, which," he hoped, "will never end." The Potawatomi New Corn promised that his young men had renounced the British and "henceforth will view the Americans as their only true friends." "We come with a good heart, and hope you will supply us with provision." Less gracious but more honest, the acerbic Asimethe of the Potawatomis pointed out the real reason why he and his colleagues were there. In a word, it was power. "You see us all here," he told Wayne. "You sent for us. The remainder of us are dead, or incapable of coming to see you." He then presented two prisoners, "in compliance with your requisition . . . and as a proof of our sincere wishes for peace."[52]

On June 24, an explosion inside the fort suddenly transformed the Indians' anxiety into fear. A fire in the laboratory that produced ammunition ignited a considerable quantity of powder in cartridges, fireworks, and loaded muskets.

51. Pickering to Wayne, Apr. 8, 1795, Pickering to Wayne, May 7, 1795, in Knopf, ed., *Anthony Wayne*, 400, 413.

52. Tetabokshke, June 16, 1795, New Corn, June 17, 1795, Asimethe, June 21, 1795, all quoted in "Treaty of Greenville," *American State Papers, Indian Affairs*, I, 564.

Although the fire was put out quickly and no one was killed, understandable Indian suspicions of "treachery" provoked Wayne to call his men to arms. He then rode around the citadel, inspecting what one soldier called "the formidable posture of defence." Meanwhile, Indians "left the camp in confusion." "Many of them hid themselves in the woods, and were not easily persuaded to return."[53]

Trying to restore some semblance of trust, Wayne gave the Indians the temporary redoubts he had had built before the fort was finished, thus averting a crisis. Still worried about the number of men and goods at his disposal, he could hardly force the Indians to stay if they chose to leave. Moreover, he did not want to coerce them; he wanted them to acquiesce in American sovereignty voluntarily. Wayne needed his guests to decide to respect him. Promising "large presents" soon, he assured them that they were "as safe here, as if you were in your own villages." As always, Wayne insisted on his sincerity. "I have never yet," Wayne claimed with a significant caveat, "in a public capacity, told a lie." "You will not be deceived, by placing the utmost confidence in what I shall tell you."[54]

Such a statement seems laughable on the face of it. Given the history of the Euramerican conquest of North America, it is tragic. But we fail to understand what was going on at Greenville if we do not accept that Wayne believed what he said. Which is not to say that he was being honest. Giving up the redoubts was part of a contraction of lines designed to improve his position. Worried about the number of soldiers he had available and a dearth of supplies and gifts for the Indians, Wayne was making "a merit of necessity for want of Numbers." As he explained to Pickering, "The Guns of our Bastions . . . look directly into [the redoubts]—so that they will be very *harmless covers*—shou'd the Indians be stimulated to immitate the conduct of the famous *Pontiac* in his attempt upon Detroit."[55]

Here, as elsewhere, the line between deception and sincerity was razor thin. Crucial to understanding Wayne's comment about not lying "in a public capacity" is understanding the immense significance he and others placed on their rhetoric in that particular time and place. Wayne knew that he, like everyone else, was imperfect; he knew that he had lied in the past. His qualification

53. Elliot, "Sketches, Political, Geographical," in Elliot, *Poetical and Miscellaneous Works*, 141.

54. Wayne to Pickering, June 17, 1795, in Knopf, ed., *Anthony Wayne*, 428; Wayne, June 25, 1795, quoted in "Treaty of Greenville," *American State Papers, Indian Affairs*, I, 565.

55. Wayne to Pickering, June 17, 1795, in Knopf, ed., *Anthony Wayne*, 428, 429.

was designed to emphasize how much importance he attached to the public meeting at Greenville, to underline his commitment on such occasions to working to rise above natural human instincts. His reputation, and that of the United States, rested on his sincerity. This meeting, Wayne was saying, is a special event, and he would not behave there as he would under normal, everyday circumstances.

Calming down after their initial panic over the explosion, the Indians demanded concrete evidence of Wayne's good intentions. They asked for larger quantities of food, specifically wine, pork, and mutton. The general complied. He even shared a drink with the Indians, insisting once more that they should think themselves "perfectly at home" and that he wished to see them "happy and contented." [56]

They did not meet again until July 3. Wayne, perhaps fearing a recurrence of the events of June 24, gave a full explanation of the ways in which the Americans would celebrate their national birthday. More than a warning, the speech tried to establish the United States as a bulwark of civility. Wayne took the Indians "by the hand, with that strong hold with which brothers ought to salute each other." "Tomorrow will be the anniversary of the day which gave peace, happiness, and independence, to America; to-morrow, all the people of the Fifteen Fires, with shouts of joy, and peals of artillery, will celebrate the period which gave them freedom." It was the twentieth time Americans would rejoice. Now their friends the Indians could rejoice, too. No one should be frightened by the cannon fire. To the contrary, "our big guns . . . will be the harbingers of peace and gladness, and their roar will ascend into the heavens." "The flag of the United States, and the colors of this legion, shall be given to the wind, to be fanned by its gentlest breeze, in honor of the birth-day of American freedom." Wayne held up his colors. Formerly, "they were displayed as ensigns of war and battle; now, they will be exhibited as emblems of peace and happiness." [57]

Responding politely, the obviously skeptical Indians made it clear that they required more than fancy words if they were going to acquiesce in Wayne's triumph. The Ojibwa Mashipinachiwish announced that he took pleasure in Wayne's words, although he wished the general were more succinct. Was it not

56. Le Gris, New Corn, The Sun, June 30, 1795, Wayne, June 30, 1795, quoted in "Treaty of Greenville," *American State Papers, Indian Affairs,* I, 565.

57. Wayne, July 3, 1795, quoted ibid., I, 565–566. The celebratory events of July 4 are described in Burton, ed., "General Wayne's Orderly Book," Mich. Pioneer and Hist. Soc., *Hist. Colls.,* XXXIV (1905), 625–626 (note the warnings against Indians in the Block Houses, 626, 627–628).

wonderful that Indian and American warriors were "met together in brotherly love?" Wayne could "believe what I say, and what I am going to say." "As we are here on good business, our hearts must dictate what our tongues express. The Great Spirit knows when we speak truth, and punishes falsehood." The Ojibwa was practical as well as eloquent: he wanted two of his young warriors released from what he had heard was a death sentence. Wayne replied with what he claimed was his usual "deliberation," so that they could "depend" on what he said, and granted the request.[58]

Formal negotiations began on July 15. After once again proclaiming his legitimacy as a duly appointed representative of the United States, Wayne proposed that the Treaty of Greenville should be little more than the Treaty of Fort Harmar. Now, after months of watching each other for signs of sincerity, the participants had to deal with concrete issues. Were they going to trust each other or not? Would the Indians consent to Wayne's demands?[59]

No one was ready to provide answers to such questions yet. The Indians were unhappy about the invocation of the Fort Harmar agreement and divided over what to do about it. Whereas a suspicious Little Turtle denounced the previous treaty, Mashipinachiwish and others expressed a tentative faith in Wayne. That evening, Blue Jacket with thirteen Shawnee and Masass with twenty Ojibwas arrived, further complicating matters. The latter acknowledged the Fort Harmar treaty and urged his brothers to "be sincere in their engagements." The more elusive Blue Jacket avoided discussing the treaty directly, content to assure Wayne that "our hearts are open, and void of deceit." Wayne thanked Masass for his "honest, open, and manly heart." "I therefore take you by the hand, with the warmth and friendship of a brother."[60]

On July 20, Wayne gambled that months of gifts and persuasion had had an impact. He decided to press the issue. His trump card was Jay's Treaty, which the United States Senate had ratified on June 24 and Washington would sign on August 14. Wayne had the British agreement to surrender its posts in the Northwest Territory read aloud. The Indians also had to hear the Treaty of Fort Harmar as well as the names of those in attendance during its negotiation. Wayne was certain that they "will have candor sufficient, when they hear their names called over, to acknowledge it as their act and deed, as *Masass* has freely

58. Mashipinachiwish, July 3, 1795, Wayne, July 3, 1795, quoted in "Treaty of Greenville," *American State Papers, Indian Affairs,* I, 566.

59. Wayne, July 15, 1795, quoted ibid., I, 567.

60. Mashipinachiwish, Masass, Blue Jacket, Wayne, July 18, 1795, quoted ibid., I, 568.

and sincerely done, . . . by which he proved himself to be possessed of a manly, undisguised heart." In short, Wayne was calling the bluff of the Indians with regard to sincerity. Were they honest men, worthy of his respect, or were they deceptive liars?[61]

Uncertain of how to respond, many Indians defiantly demanded to know by what authority Wayne claimed land north of the Ohio River. Why should they believe him? In perhaps the tensest moment of the meeting, "mad" Anthony Wayne responded calmly. Taking the anger in stride, he asked for a postponement until the next day when, "after reflecting coolly, and sleeping, the answer may be more dispassionate." In that hope, he was disappointed. The next day, Little Turtle pressed for more details of land cessions. Angry about the Indians' lack of unity and the apparent eagerness of some to placate Wayne, he insisted that the general "pay attention" to his words. The proposed boundary cut off land that his people had "enjoyed . . . [from] time immemorial, without molestation or dispute." "The print of my ancestors' houses are every where to be seen in this portion."[62]

Little Turtle was the only participant to speak so directly. Two hundred years later, his voice sounds the most sincere because he was the most forthright. His colleagues were more circumspect. The Wyandot Tarhe, who had been wounded at Fallen Timbers, was willing to accept the Americans' claims and blame the British for everything. Contending that the United States could be demanding even more land than it was, Tarhe insisted that he spoke from his "heart." He urged everyone to "peruse" his speeches "and see whether or not I have spoken with sincerity," which is precisely what everyone in attendance was doing anyway.[63]

Over the course of the next several days, the Indians debated whether they should accept the Fort Harmar treaty. In public, they talked of unity; in private, they obviously quarreled. Some asked for more gifts, more signs of American good faith. Wayne, in turn, persistently proffered presents and argued that the United States was willing to pay for the land. With the magnanimity that comes more easily to conquerors than the conquered, he urged everyone to forget the past and promised with a "soft, white linen" to wipe "the tears from your

61. Wayne, July 20, 1795, quoted ibid., I, 569.

62. Tarhe, Wayne, Masass, Little Turtle, July 21, 1795, Little Turtle, July 22, 1795, quoted ibid., I, 570, 571.

63. Wayne to Knox, Dec. 23, 1794, in Knopf, ed., *Anthony Wayne*, 370; Tarhe, July 22, 1795, quoted in "Treaty of Greenville," *American State Papers, Indian Affairs*, I, 571.

eyes . . . and the blood from your bodies." On July 24, the general allowed "a double allowance of drink; because we have now buried the hatchet, and performed every necessary ceremony, to render propitious our renovated friendship."[64]

Tensions nonetheless remained high. On July 29, Little Turtle made his case against the treaty. Wayne had said that the president of the United States spoke to them through him and "that, whatever he should say, should be firm and lasting; that it was impossible he should say what was not true." Little Turtle, too, wanted to be as candid as possible. He did "not wish to hide their sentiments. . . . You have told us to speak our minds freely, and we now do it." In his opinion, the proposed treaty line took too much Miami land; he wanted the Americans restricted to a boundary from Fort Recovery to Fort Hamilton.[65]

Tired and ready to go home, many Indians urged their colleagues to take whatever the Americans offered. Asimethe of the Potawatomi lamented: "All our treaties, hitherto, have failed." He could only hope that this one "will be lasting." Yet his acquiescence was more a recognition of reality than consent. Soon more American "forts will be planted thick among us." What choice did they really have?[66]

But Little Turtle would not give in. He produced documents from President Washington assuring him that the Miami could enjoy their hunting grounds, that they could retain their villages, and that "he would place traders among us, who would deal fairly." Wayne could talk all he wanted about "peace and mutual friendship." Little Turtle wanted more than words.[67]

Wayne, however, was unwilling to give much more. Refusing to accept the Miami chief's proposed boundary, he granted him an annuity and some trading concessions. Certain of Little Turtle's growing isolation, he refused to take him very seriously. Since many Indians seemed ready to accept Wayne's terms, Little Turtle was reduced to the role of an obstructionist who refuses to abide by the will of the majority. He had lost, not just to the Americans, but to his fellow Indians. Sensing imminent victory, the ever more confident general began to use the language of paternalism, implicitly warning his guests that fathers were not always kind. Was not "the United States . . . acting the part of a

64. Wayne, July 24, 1795, quoted in "Treaty of Greenville," *American State Papers, Indian Affairs,* I, 573.

65. Little Turtle, July 29, 1795, quoted ibid., I, 576.

66. Asimethe, July 29, 30, 1795, quoted ibid., I, 576.

67. Little Turtle, Wayne, July 30, 1795, quoted ibid., I, 577.

tender father, to them [the Miami] and their children, in thus providing for them, not only at present, but for ever?"[68]

Otherwise ignoring the unmollified Little Turtle, Wayne then had the treaty read and explained its provisions. He declared to his "Brothers" that the "negotiation" was over. Each nation was formally asked if they approved and would sign the treaty. All—Ojibwas, Ottawas, Potawatomis, Wyandots, Delawares, Shawnees, Miamis, Weas, Kickapoos—replied yes, unanimously, except for Little Turtle. Wayne announced that an engrossed treaty would be signed "on parchment" on August 2.[69]

Ninety men affixed their marks on that day. When they were finished, Wayne promised the assembled Indians copies of the treaty and considerable gifts. Four days later, the Americans began to distribute the presents; Wayne also offered private gifts to some of the chiefs "as testimonies of particular regard."[70]

Then Tarhe rose to proclaim the new relationship with the American officers that the Indians believed they had finalized at Greenville. What he said meant different things to the Indians and the Americans. Indeed, the multiple meanings of his words went to the heart of the reason why the negotiations failed to produce a lasting peace in the region. Tarhe formally announced that the Indians "do now, and will henceforth, acknowledge the fifteen United States of America to be our father, and you will all, for the future, look upon them as such: you must call them brothers no more." He took Wayne "by the hand . . . as a pledge of our sincerity, and of our happiness in becoming your children." Tarhe then instructed Wayne on his new role of father:

> Listen to your children, here assembled; be strong, now, and take care of all your little ones. See what a number you have suddenly acquired. Be careful of them, and do not suffer them to be imposed upon. Don't shew favor to one, to the injury of any. An impartial father equally regards all his children, as well those who are ordinary, as those who may be more handsome; therefore, should any of your children come to you crying, and in distress, have pity on them, and relieve their wants.

Meanwhile, all Indians should be "obedient to our father; ever listen to him when he speaks to you, and follow his advice."[71]

68. Wayne, July 30, 1795, quoted ibid., I, 578.
69. Ibid.
70. Wayne, Aug. 3, 7, 1795, quoted ibid., I, 579, 580.
71. Tarhe, August 7, 1795, quoted ibid., I, 580. This is Richard White's interpretation; see *Middle Ground*, 472–473.

In reply, Wayne, not surprisingly, urged everyone to pay attention to Tarhe. "I have hitherto addressed you as brothers. I now adopt you all, in the name of the President and Fifteen great Fires of America, as their children." He gave them medals, which they were to "hand down to your children's children, in commemoration of this day—a day in which the United States of America gives peace to you and all your nations, and receives you and them under the protecting wings of her eagle."[72]

It was not until August 12 that a defiant Little Turtle in a private conference with Wayne offered his qualified approval of the treaty. Bowing to reality, accepting that he had no other viable option, he rhetorically demonstrated his acquiescence by finally calling the general "Father."[73]

Unable to stop the Americans, the Indians were trying to come to terms with their defeat. Some could understand the intruders only in the traditional language of the middle ground; thus the need to turn them into fathers. Most, particularly Little Turtle, recognized the existence of a new reality. The American conquest was more than a seizure of land. Like the French and British and unlike most Americans, federal officials genuinely wanted to reach some kind of accommodation with the inhabitants of the region they already claimed. They wanted the Indians to do more than give up their land; they wanted the conquered to acknowledge the moral superiority of the conquerors, to say, in short, that what had happened—two decades of brutality and death followed by the triumph of the United States—had been for the ultimate good of everyone involved.

From the Indian perspective, Greenville was more than an official recognition of American power. It was also an extended, if fleeting, moment of creative cultural adaptation. It is hardly remarkable that there was tension among the Indians at Greenville. What is remarkable is that, for the most part, they handled themselves with extreme dignity. The way we behave in moments of crisis, even defeat, may be the truest tests of the strengths of our culture and the degree to which we feel integrated into, rather than alienated from, it. The Indian performances at Greenville, in sum, were an effort to mediate the impact of great social upheaval through sentimental language and the creation of traditional fictive relationships.

By bestowing the name of father on Wayne, some of the Indians assumed that the Americans were taking the places of their French and British prede-

72. Wayne, Aug. 7, 1795, quoted in "Treaty of Greenville," *American State Papers, Indian Affairs*, I, 580.
73. Little Turtle, Aug. 12, 1795, quoted ibid., I, 583.

cessors, that they would act with paternal regard for their children, that they were entering into a kind of social obligation with the Americans. In so doing, they revealed that they had fatally misunderstood the meaning of the American Revolution. Little Turtle, on the other hand, knew exactly what had happened, which was why he was so reluctant to consent to the treaty. Giving up on resistance, he spent much of the rest of his life trying to adjust to the new reality.[74]

Meanwhile, Wayne understood his new title of father in the Revolutionary language of popular sovereignty. It was a name he and his fictive military brothers would never win from the mass of Americans, who increasingly insisted that white men were all brothers, or, at best, friends. Wayne failed to understand the invocation of the word father as a sign that he had participated in the mutual creation of the kind of reciprocal social obligations with which the Indians were familiar. The general did not dismiss Tarhe's language as empty rhetoric, however. To the contrary, Wayne took what Tarhe said quite seriously—on his own terms. He was certain that it meant that he had persuaded the Indians that he was as superior morally as he was militarily. When Wayne reported to his superiors, he emphasized their consent as the most important outcome of the negotiations. It was "with infinite pleasure" that he informed Secretary Pickering of the "treaty of peace between the United States of America and all the late hostile tribes of Indians North West of the Ohio, [which] was Unanimously and Voluntarily agreed to, and chearfully signed by all the *Sachams and War Chiefs*." [75]

## Legacy

As the Indians left Greenville, delighted members of the Legion celebrated the signing of the treaty by reenacting on August 20 their "glorious victory . . . over the *late* hostile Indians" at Fallen Timbers. Apparently, they performed "a variety of military evolutions, exhibiting a *miniature* representation of that celebrated action." The diplomatic victory of 1795 sealed the military victory of 1794: the strokes of the pen had finished the work of the sword. Coercion had produced consent.[76]

74. Cayton, *Frontier Indiana*, 196–225; Carter, *Little Turtle*, 156–239.

75. Wayne to Pickering, Aug. 9, 1795, in Knopf, ed., *Anthony Wayne*, 442. See also Wayne, Aug. 7, 1795, quoted in Burton, ed., "Wayne's Orderly Book," Mich. Pioneer Hist. Soc., *Hist. Colls.*, XXXIV (1905), 634–635.

76. Elliot, "Sketches, Political, Geographical," in Elliot, *Poetical and Miscellaneous Works*, 144.

Six months after concluding the treaty, Wayne returned to Philadelphia like a triumphant Roman general. Cavalry escorted him, and fifteen guns saluted his late-afternoon arrival. *Claypoole's American Daily Advertiser* reported that Wayne "was ushered into the city by ringing of bells and other demonstrations of joy, and thousands of citizens crowded to see and welcome the return of their beloved General. . . . In the evening, a display of Fire-Works was exhibited in celebration of the Peace lately concluded with the Western Indians."[77]

Almost two weeks later, the First Troop of Philadelphia gave a gala dinner for Wayne, which was attended by citizens, soldiers, and all of the available officers of the Legion of the United States. The gathering toasted a whole retinue of countries and leaders, including "THE WESTERN ARMY—May they entwine with their Laurels the Blessings of a grateful Country." The very first toast was to the United States of America—"May they continue to exhibit to the World, the solid advantages derived from a free but energetic Government, whose fruits are Peace, Justice, and Universal Benevolence."[78]

Wayne and his comrades believed that they had achieved eternal fame by performing the most basic of American rituals: they had secured popular consent to the exercise of sovereignty. Wayne would always claim that the Indians had freely agreed to the treaty. The Indians did not see their choice as free, and many of them naively hoped that their acquiescence would lead to a revival of the kind of relationships they had had with the French. Wayne did not understand that, of course, and went to his grave fully believing that Greenville had affirmed the injunction in the Northwest Ordinance to observe "the utmost good faith . . . toward the Indians" and never to take "their lands and property . . . without their consent."[79]

Some forty-five years after the signing of the Treaty of Greenville, one of the last surviving participants in the negotiations made a final visit to the place. William Henry Harrison in August 1840 was a candidate for the presidency of the United States. He celebrated the remarkable changes in the Greenville area in the past half-century. Thanks "to the industry and enterprise of Western pioneers," the dark forest had given way to "broad, cultivated fields, flowery gardens, and happy homes." Where once there was a fort, there was now a town. Where once there was contested ground, there was now the state of Ohio. Long

77. "Extracts from the Diary of Jacob Hiltzheimer, of Philadelphia, 1768–1798," *Pennsylvania Magazine of History and Biography*, XVI (1892), 419–420; *Claypoole's American Daily Advertiser* (Philadelphia), Feb. 8, 1796.

78. *Claypoole's American Daily Advertiser*, Feb. 20, 1796.

79. Wayne to Pickering, Sept. 2, 1795, in Knopf, ed., *Anthony Wayne*, 447.

before Wayne enjoyed his Philadelphia triumph, American settlers had begun pushing across the borders the Treaty of Greenville had established. Despite the resistance, both physical and spiritual, of thousands of native Americans in the first decades of the nineteenth century, they were in 1840 no longer a significant presence in the region they had once defended. For them, the Treaty of Greenville was a mark of insincerity, part of an American tradition in which governments promise justice that they rarely deliver.[80]

This was part of the legacy of Greenville, this visible human happiness purchased at the price of invisible human misery. But there was more to its legacy than deception and betrayal. Greenville reminds us of the existence of a spectrum of attitudes among Americans toward Indians in the late eighteenth century. To be sure, virtually all shared a desire to dispossess them and to devalue them as savage others. Still, if American males, in particular, constructed a superior self-image in their dealings with Indians, they did not all do so in the same way. Although brutal Indian-hating machismo predominated, there were also men who affirmed their society and claimed significant places in it by treating Indians in what they considered to be a civilized fashion.

In detailing the myriad ways in which the expansion of the American empire involved the moral failure of innumerable human beings, it is easy to dismiss the periodic attempts of some of its agents as well as those of countless Indians to behave with dignity and grace in moments of crisis. It is true that Wayne and Harrison were at Greenville securing the liberty of republican citizens by securing the acquiescence of Indians in their own subjugation. But it is also true that to justify this action, the American officers had to work hard to subordinate themselves to the highest standards of human conduct that they could imagine possible. Their efforts in that endeavor, however fleeting, keep alive the possibility that powerful human beings can, on occasion, overcome their passions and model a kind of restraint that by doing honor to their opponents does honor to themselves.

80. "Harrison at Fort Greenville," in A. B[anning] Norton, *The Great Revolution of 1840: Reminiscences of the Log Cabin and Hard Cider Campaign* (Mount Vernon, Ohio, 1888), 245, 246.

# To Live among Us
## Accommodation, Gender, and Conflict in the Western Great Lakes Region, 1760–1832

Elizabeth Thérèse Fisher of Mackinac Island received a note from her fiancé one Saturday evening in late March 1824. Henry Baird, the young Irish lawyer, wrote to his fourteen-year-old métis sweetheart to inquire "at what time [she] would be ready to go to the Sugar-Camp tomorrow" and told her, "if you will ride with me and inasmuch as you have said 'If you please' to me I will be happy to have the pleasure of your Company." [1]

In the days and years ahead, Elizabeth and Henry would learn a great deal from each other. In their new home in Green Bay, Wisconsin, the young wife, who spoke French, Ottawa, and Ojibwa but little English, taught her spouse the nuances of the French Creole and native American cultures of the region; the husband helped his wife learn English as she taught herself to read, and he trained her as a legal assistant in his law office, where she served as the interpreter for most of his clients. But first, Henry would experience the joys of maple sugar making. Both the intimacy and the sugar production were typical of the mixed-race Creole communities of the Midwest in the late eighteenth and early nineteenth centuries. [2]

By contrast, in November 1827, just three years later and two hundred miles to the southwest of Green Bay, an Indian woman lay dying. "Her face was much lacerated, and one eye apparently put out," wrote newly appointed Indian agent Joseph Street, who was passing through the lead-mining region known as Fever River when he saw two Indians carrying her away in a blanket.

The author would like to thank Allan Kulikoff, Rebecca Kugel, Neal Salisbury, and Christine Heyrman for their helpful comments on an earlier draft of this essay.

1. Henry S. Baird to Elizabeth T. Fisher, Mar. 20, 1824, Henry Baird Papers, box 1, folder 1, State Historical Society of Wisconsin, Madison. Probably Elizabeth had the note read and translated for her by a family member.

2. Elizabeth T. Baird, "O-De-Jit-Wa-Win-Wing; Comptes du Temps Passe," Henry S. Baird Collection, box 4, folder 9, State Historical Society of Wisconsin.

He was shocked to learn that she "had the evening before been drinking much whiskey, and that a white man knocked her down and stamped on her head with his foot." Although the Menominee woman was "well known at this place, and reputed a good Indian," local officials took no action to investigate the murder. Violence in the lead-mining area had become all too common, and local government agents either could not or would not follow Street's recommendation to keep "a more vigilent eye . . . upon the hetrogenus mass" of white miners.[3] Over the course of a decade, between 1822 and 1832, such men seized the lead region from Indian miners, forcing them out of the area entirely.

Why did some patterns of Indian-white relations lead to peaceful coexistence and integrated communities while others resulted in conflict and Indian removal? This essay examines two communities that existed within the same region during the early nineteenth century: one based on the fur trade and the other on lead mining. There were several similarities between these two. Both were established in the area of southern Wisconsin, northern Illinois, and eastern Iowa among mostly Mesquakie, Sauk, and Winnebago people (although some Menominees, Potawatomis, and other Indians also lived in the region). Both communities were based on exporting partially processed natural resources—animal pelts and pig lead—to be processed further elsewhere. Although the fur-trade towns were founded well before the mining communities, they persisted into the 1820s and existed contemporaneously with the mining camps and towns. Indian miners had aunts and cousins living in the fur-trade towns and often went there to visit or trade.

In one type of community, fur-trade towns, Indians, whites, and métis people coexisted peacefully as neighbors, relatives, employers, and workers; but in another, in the lead-mining region, Indian-white relations degenerated into hopeless conflicts. Examining the dynamics of social and economic interaction in the two communities may help to explain why accommodation succeeded in one place and failed in another. Although the term "accommodation" is sometimes used to suggest that indigenous or minority groups acquiesced in their own exploitation and oppression, I do not mean to use the word in that way here. I do mean "accommodation" as successful integration of Indian people into communities, economies, and societies in which people of European descent also lived and participated.

I will argue that women's actions, gender relations, and the negotiation of gender roles were crucial to the creation of the culturally syncretic fur-trade

---

3. Joseph M. Street to Secretary of War, Nov. 15, 1827, Indian Office Miscellaneous Files, 1826–1827, Pension Building, State Historical Society of Wisconsin.

The Fox-Wisconsin Region, circa 1827. *Adapted from Mrs. John H. [Juliette M.] Kinzie,*
Wau-Bun: The "Early Day" in the North-West *(1856), ed. Louise Phelps Kellogg (Manasha,*
*Wis., 1930), with reference to Helen Hornbeck Tanner, ed.,* Atlas of Great Lakes Indian
History *(Norman, Okla., 1987), 123, 140, 144. Drawn by Terry Sheahan*

communities and that an examination of these same factors can illuminate reasons for Indian removal and the ultimate triumph of monoculturalism in the mining district. Ultimately, the ways that each community expressed domination and mutuality in gender, race, and intracommunity relations determined whether accommodation would be possible.

During the century between the end of the Fox Wars in 1737 and the Black Hawk War of 1832, the land between Lake Michigan and the Mississippi became ethnically diverse, experiencing several waves of immigration. Winnebago, Sauk, Mesquakie, Menominee, and other native peoples living in the region were joined by French Canadian fur traders, who married native women, lived in Indian villages, and then founded Creole fur-trade towns after 1760. Although the region was technically under British control after the Seven Years' War, in reality the residents were practically independent. A few men from England and Scotland moved into the region, but the Creole towns continued to be places where French and native languages prevailed. Finally, Anglophone immigrants from the United States arrived in large numbers after the War of 1812. A particularly intense period of Anglo migration into the lead-mining area took place after 1822, a phenomenon referred to here as the "lead rush."[4]

The fur-trade centers at either end of the Fox-Wisconsin waterway grew after the Seven Years' War and developed a culture that was neither purely European nor native American but had elements of both. This culture will be referred to here as "Creole"—a distinctive regional multiethnic blend having roots in many Indian and European traditions. Virtually all of the husbands were French Canadian, and nearly all of the wives were native American during the 1760s and 1770s, after which grown métis children joined the ranks of householders.[5] These towns were not only multiracial but also multiethnic; a typical

4. I use the term "Creoles" to refer to people who lived in communities such as Prairie du Chien and Green Bay that had a culture neither purely European nor native American but had elements of both. These people included Frenchmen, Indian women, their mixed-race children, and sundry others. "Métis" refers to people of mixed European and native American ancestry. "Anglophones" and "Anglos" refer to English-speakers. In the context of the lead-mining region, it should be understood that these people had immigrated from the United States. I use these labels, with some reservations, in preference to the term "Americans," which can be misleading.

5. Sixty wives and mothers were identified from 1817 Prairie du Chien church records with other sources. Eleven were Dakota, five Mesquakie, two Ojibwa, and one each Pawnee, Sauk, Menominee, and Winnebago. Twenty-two were métis, two were French-African, and one was known to be French. The ethnicity of the other thirteen was not ascertained. See

family might include a French Canadian husband, a wife of mixed Sauk and Mesquakie ancestry, their métis children, and kin, servants, and other employees with Pawnee, Dakota, Menominee, Scottish, or even African ethnic heritages. Their neighbors might represent several different ethnicities. I use the general term "Creoles" to refer to all of the residents who participated in this culture, regardless of race or ethnicity. Although they were participants in a Creole culture, most of them were bicultural, that is, they understood, identified with, and participated in other cultures some of the time. Probably ethnicity and culture were more important concepts than race to Creoles, but outsiders did think in racial terms.

Creole communities were rooted in relationships established when immigrants entered Indians' neighborhoods. Midwestern Indians assimilated newcomers through a process that incorporated individuals into family units, a tradition probably dating from the precontact era. Outsiders became kin through marriage or, less frequently, adoption. Kinship bound strangers to their neighbors through ties of obligation, which regulated conduct. Outsiders who rejected this assimilation could expect no cooperation from Indians, because their rejection would be seen as evidence of bad intentions. Native customs allowed polygyny as well as divorce, making Indian matchmakers suspicious of the European who protested that he was already married or preferred a long courtship to make sure of compatibility. The possibility of divorce might have comforted young women whose marriages were arranged. As a result of the pressure and the opportunities, traders compromised on their own culture's marriage taboos to marry local daughters (sometimes qualifying these unions as "country marriages" in their correspondence with outsiders). As the

---

James L. Hansen, "Prairie du Chien's Earliest Church Records, 1817," *Minnesota Genealogical Journal*, IV (1985), 329–342. Additional information about ethnicity was provided by James H. Lockwood, "Early Times and Events in Wisconsin," State Historical Society of Wisconsin, *Collections*, II (Madison, Wis., 1856), 125–126; and M. M. Hoffmann, *Antique Dubuque, 1673–1833* (Dubuque, Iowa, 1930), 51–59. Nearly all male householders, however, had at least some French ancestry. Only three English names were among twenty-nine householders at Prairie du Chien before 1785. Even among seventy-two adult male residents who lived there about 1820 whose names could be identified, only eleven had English names; all the others, except a Mandan freedman, had French names. See Hansen, "Prairie du Chien's Earliest Church Records," *Minnesota Genealogical Journal*, IV (1985), 329–342; United States Congress, *American State Papers: Documents, Legislative and Executive, of the Congress of the United States . . .* , 38 vols. (Washington, D.C., 1832–1861), Class VIII, *Public Lands*, 8 vols., ed. Walter Lowrie et al., V, 47–98, 270–272, 283–328 (hereafter cited as *American State Papers, Public Lands*).

Indians wished, economic relationships then became personal.[6] Initially, fur traders spent at least some of the year with their Indian kin in the native villages, but after 1760 some of these families established separate towns, maintaining ties with friends and kin in the Indian villages.

Creole culture was created by husbands and wives, parents and children, employers and employees, and neighbors in their everyday lives and personal relationships. They communicated, learned, taught, adapted, and negotiated the details of daily life. Language was the most fundamental skill people needed for accommodation, and many wives were expected to learn, teach, and interpret across cultures, as Elizabeth Baird's experience makes clear.

If outsiders married local Indian and métis women in order to gain entry into the region's economy and to get interpreting assistance, wives had their own set of expectations. They were frequently willing to play the role of "cultural mediator," as Clara Sue Kidwell has explained. This role was a respected one in Indian society; they and their kin expected appropriate treatment. Furthermore, native women were used to a certain amount of autonomy with regard to economic production, and related resources such as sugar groves and cornfields were considered to belong to them. Finally, women in this region were not particularly subordinate to Indian husbands, although younger people were expected to defer to their elders' wishes.[7] We should not be surprised, then, that native-descended women took active roles in shaping the emerging Creole culture and economy, creating accommodation.

The Creole towns were hierarchical systems with a handful of elite fur traders at the top, generally Euramerican and métis men and their métis and Indian

6. Sylvia Van Kirk, *Many Tender Ties: Women in Fur-Trade Society, 1670–1870* (Norman, Okla., 1980); Jennifer S. H. Brown, *Strangers in Blood: Fur Trade Company Families in Indian Country* (Vancouver, 1980); Jacqueline Louise Peterson, "The People in Between: Indian-White Marriage and the Genesis of a Métis Society and Culture in the Great Lakes Region, 1680–1830" (Ph.D. diss., University of Illinois at Chicago Circle, 1981); Tanis Chapman Thorne, "People of the River: Mixed-Blood Families on the Lower Missouri" (Ph.D. diss., University of California, Los Angeles, 1987); Bruce M. White, "Gender and Trade in the Lake Superior Region in the Eighteenth Century," paper presented at the conference "Crucibles of Cultures: North American Frontiers, 1750–1820," sponsored by the Institute of Early American History and Culture, The Historic New Orleans Collection, and the Newberry Library, Nov. 18, 1994, New Orleans; Nancy Oestreich Lurie, ed., *Mountain Wolf Woman, Sister of Crashing Thunder: The Autobiography of a Winnebago Indian* (Ann Arbor, Mich., 1961).

7. Clara Sue Kidwell, "Indian Women as Cultural Mediators," *Ethnohistory*, XXXIX (1992), 97–107; Lucy Eldersveld Murphy, "Autonomy and the Economic Roles of Indian Women of the Fox-Wisconsin River Region, 1763–1832," in Nancy Shoemaker, ed., *Negotiators of Change: Historical Perspectives on Native American Women* (New York, 1995), 72–89.

wives and children. These elites employed "retainers"—contract workers and tenant farm families—and owned a few Indian slaves. In the middle were a few moderately successful traders and small farmers and the occasional artisan or professional. Wives, daughters, sons, and other kin helped with family business activities. Occasionally women traded in their own names if widowed or if their husbands retired, but most frequently men were the official heads of household and business. Similar towns and cultures appeared throughout the Great Lakes and Upper Mississippi Valley at places as far apart as Mackinac and Saint Louis. More than fifty such communities were founded during the late eighteenth century; by the late 1820s, as many as ten to fifteen thousand people called them home, according to Jacqueline Peterson's estimate. The population of Prairie du Chien was probably between six hundred and eight hundred in 1816, and perhaps nine hundred to eleven hundred people lived in Green Bay at that time.[8] Creole towns coexisted with Indian villages nearby.

Accommodation in the Creole communities entailed considerable teaching, learning, adaptation of traditional practices, and negotiation of gender roles. Compromises were made at the personal level. Although the Creoles were, as fur traders, taking part in an international economy, they also created domestic economies, and it is at this level that we can see the dynamics of syncretism.

A look at native and Creole maple sugar production illustrates not only learning and adaptation in domestic production but also women's active roles in the processes. Sugar making had long been part of the seasonal economy of the Great Lakes Indians, whose many homes included the family sugar camps. After the autumn corn harvest, they moved from the summer villages to winter hunting grounds and then, in March, to these sugar camps, situated in a grove of maple trees.[9]

8. For a more thorough discussion of the social order of Creole towns, see Lucy Eldersveld Murphy, "Economy, Race, and Gender along the Fox-Wisconsin and Rock Riverways, 1737–1832" (Ph.D. diss., Northern Illinois University, 1995), chap. 3. Population figures are difficult to estimate because the towns swelled so much during summer months with fur-trade workers, who wintered in Indian hunting regions but summered in town, and hundreds of Indians, who came to town to trade in fall and spring on their journeys from and to their summer villages. However, Jacqueline Peterson estimated the Prairie du Chien population at 370 in 1807 and about 600 in 1816 and the Green Bay population at 533 in 1796 and 900 in 1816. Probably several hundred more could be added during the busy seasons. See Peterson, "People in Between," 133, 136.

9. Donald Jackson, ed., *Black Hawk: An Autobiography* (1955; reprint, Urbana, Ill., 1990), 89–95; H. A. Schuette et al., "Maple Sugar: A Bibliography of Early Records," Wisconsin Academy of Sciences, Arts, and Letters, *Transactions*, XXIX (Madison, Wis., 1935), 209–236; Schuette et al., "Maple Sugar: A Bibliography of Early Records, II," ibid., XXXVIII (1946),

For Indians, the month or so of sugar making was a festive event at which women managed the boiling of maple tree sap, continuing day and night, while children helped or played nearby and men chopped wood for the fires and hunted to provide meat for the whole party. The tree sap was collected in birch-bark buckets. Before metal pots were acquired in trade, women used pottery, wood, or bark vessels and concentrated the sap by dropping hot stones into it, boiling it in birch-bark trays, or freezing it. European-made kettles increased the ease of boiling the sap a great deal, so they were eagerly adopted. The women stored sugar in birch-bark containers of various sizes called mococks, which they sometimes decorated with fancy quillwork and used as special gifts.[10]

Indians had produced commodities for trade to other communities for many centuries before European contact, a practice they continued when the European presence provided additional markets. By the early nineteenth century, Indian women made maple sugar a commodity of major importance. The Indians of northern Illinois and southern Wisconsin sold more than seventy thousand pounds of maple sugar in 1816, for example, not counting what they made for their own consumption. The Indian women around Green Bay alone produced twenty-five thousand pounds of this amount in one season. Fur traders, in their correspondence with one another, speculated on the prospects of a season's sugar, as they did with pelt production. As late as the 1890s, Indians in east-central Wisconsin were still selling maple sugar to their white neighbors.[11]

In the Creole communities of the Great Lakes, families accepted and adapted

---

89–184. For those wishing to study maple sugaring in early America, this extensive bibliography, which quotes relevant sections from primary sources, is a good starting place.

10. Margaret Holman and Kathryn C. Egan, "Maple Sugaring," *Michigan History,* LXXIV (March-April 1990), 30–35; Milo Milton Quaife, ed., *Alexander Henry's Travels and Adventures in the Years 1760–1776* (Chicago, 1921), 69–70, 143–144; Thomas Ridout, "An Account of My Capture by the Shawanese Indians," *Western Pennsylvania Historical Magazine,* XII (1929), 18; Frances Densmore, "Uses of Plants by the Chippewa Indians," *Forty-fourth Annual Report of the Bureau of American Ethnology* (Washington, D.C., 1928), 308–313.

11. Gary A. Wright, "Some Aspects of Early and Mid-Seventeenth Century Exchange Networks in the Western Great Lakes," *Michigan Archaeologist,* XIII (1967), 181–197; Thomas Forsyth Papers, Lyman Draper Manuscripts, microfilm, 3T: 63, State Historical Society of Wisconsin; Mary Maples Dunn to the Author, June 29, 1993. At this time, the native American population of the region was around 12,000. See Helen Hornbeck Tanner, ed., *Atlas of Great Lakes Indian History* (Norman, Okla., 1987), 139–411. For an example of fur traders' correspondence, see John Lawe to [———], Apr. 25, 1824, Green Bay and Prairie du Chien Papers, microfilm, reel 1, 10152, State Historical Society of Wisconsin.

sugar traditions. They continued the spring tradition of moving to sugar camps called *sucreries*. Sugar making was well adapted to a lifestyle of seasonal migration, as practiced not only by native Americans but also by Creoles, many of whom traveled extensively in the fur trade. At Green Bay, the town was deserted during the spring sugar production. An observer, Albert Ellis, commented that Creoles moved "from their home cabins on the River bank, into the deep wood, often many miles distant; taking generally most of their household treasures, even to their chickens." Elizabeth Fisher took Henry Baird to her grandmother's sugar camp, where the family owned more than a thousand trees.[12] Because sugar making was considered women's work, skills—and ownership of sugar bushes—were passed from Indian mothers to métis daughters.

Creole sugar methods were quite similar to Indian techniques and continued to be under women's management. Many of the "better class of the French" preferred to refine their sugar more than did Indians, however, which had the effect of whitening it. They strained the syrup and then added a special clarifying agent, Ellis noted: "Here came in the product of the chickens, to-wit, the eggs, the whites of which were broken in the boiling syrup, when all impurities immediately came to the surface and were removed." Like Indian women, métis women also might sell their excess sugar, the refined sugar being more desirable than the regular. Ellis recorded: "Some of the more enterprising and forehanded, bought syrup and . . . coarse sugar of their Indian retainers, and their less able neighbors, and went into the purifying process on a large scale, and thus largely increased their product for the season. A few families of this class had a preference in the sugar market at the frontier trading posts, their mococks, branded with their names, always being first sought, at advanced prices."[13]

The sugar season neatly coincided with the French Creole Easter celebration, and this festival combined elements from several cultures: day and night sugar boiling and celebrating, feasting on Easter eggs and crêpes with maple syrup, and the ringing of the sugar bush with "the merry violin and the dance."[14]

12. Ebenezer Childs, "Recollections of Wisconsin since 1820," State Hist. Soc. of Wis., *Colls.,* IV (1857–1858), 161; Albert G. Ellis, "Fifty-Four Years' Recollections of Men and Events in Wisconsin," State Hist. Soc. of Wis., *Colls.,* VII (1876), 220; Baird, "O-De-Jit-Wa-Win-Wing," Baird Coll., chap. 5; Schuette et al., "Maple Sugar," Wis. Academy of Sciences, Arts, and Letters, *Trans.,* XXXVIII (1946), 134.

13. Baird, "O-De-Jit-Wa-Win-Wing," Baird Coll., chap. 5; Jacques Porlier to J. Jacques Porlier, Mar. 11, 1815, Green Bay and Prairie du Chien Papers, reel 1; Ellis, "Recollections," State Hist. Soc. of Wis., *Colls.,* VII (1876), 221.

14. Ellis, "Recollections," State Hist. Soc. of Wis., *Colls.,* VII (1876), 221; Baird, "O-De-Jit-Wa-Win-Wing," Baird Coll., chap. 5.

Creoles continued the tradition of special gifts. Métis girls gave their boy-friends maple sugar candy wrapped in a strip of birch bark, which they called a "billet doux" (love letter—literally, a "sweet note"). Mothers such as Marguerite Griesie Porlier, who was part Menominee, expressed their love to distant chil-dren by promising to send a mocock of sugar.[15]

Processes involved in cultural fusion are evident in this description of Cre-ole sugar production. First, teaching took place when Indian women taught their métis daughters and granddaughters the basics of production. Second, the concept of sugar production as an area of women's management was passed from the Indian to the Creole culture. Maple sugar making was not practiced in Europe, so European-descended men had no traditions sex-typing the work differently.[16] That meant men and women did not have to negotiate control over this type of production. Third, even so, European traditions such as Easter celebrations, poultry keeping, and crêpe making could be introduced—pre-sumably by men—to make the endeavor bicultural. Fourth, the Indian and métis women of Creole communities chose to continue producing native com-modities, not only for their own families but sometimes also for market. That is one of the ways that they actively influenced Creole economies. Last, al-though both Creole and Indian communities produced sugar, Creoles also purchased Indian-made sugar either to refine further or to resell. Creoles do not seem to have appropriated native sugar camps, except those that daughters inherited from native foremothers. Thus, there was more cooperation than competition for resources or economic roles.

Other forms of production raised issues that required the negotiation of gender roles. Just as maple sugar production was new to Europeans, dairying and bread making were new to Indians. But although sugar making was passed from Indian women to métis women, transmission of these Euramerican skills in Creole society was more problematic, owing to the gendered nature of work. In all of this region's cultures, some jobs and skills were sex-typed whereas oth-ers were nongendered. For example, interpreting could be done by men or women, whereas hunting was considered by all to be men's work.[17] Creoles en-

15. Ellis, "Recollections," State Hist. Soc. of Wis., *Colls.*, VII (1876), 222; Jacques Porlier to J. Jacques Porlier, Mar. 11, 1815, Green Bay and Prairie du Chien Papers, reel 1; "Life at La Baye" exhibit, Heritage Hill State Park, Green Bay, Wis.

16. The term "sex-typing" is used to refer to gendered concepts of work in Julie A. Matthaei, *An Economic History of Women in America: Women's Work, the Sexual Division of Labor, and the Development of Capitalism* (New York, 1982), 187–197.

17. There was at least one woman hunter in this area, however: an Ojibwa woman named O-cha-own, who lived alone not far from Green Bay during the late eighteenth century. See

countered differences in cultural perceptions about the types of work women ought to do and had to find compromises. Disputes regarding women's production were often solved by hiring others to do certain kinds of work or by purchasing commodities women did not wish to make.

Creoles kept cattle for meat, but other uses for these animals raise interesting issues concerning gender roles in these multicultural, multiracial communities. In European and Euramerican communities, people also used cows for dairying. In Euramerican communities in eastern North America, milking and butter making were usually considered women's work, although men cared for the animals. Native Americans, however, had no such traditions, since they had not kept livestock. In fact, historian Rebecca Kugel has found that, to the northwest, in present-day Minnesota, some Ojibwas were wary of cattle because they believed them to have spiritual power, which could become malevolent.[18]

Some Indian and métis women resisted taking up dairying, as did some white and métis men. The wife of trader Julien Dubuque, appearing only in the written records as "Madame," was said to be Mesquakie. She seems to have avoided learning these skills: when her husband died in 1810, although there were seven cows on their farm, no butter churn or other dairying equipment was listed on his estate inventory.[19]

Several documents demonstrate that some dairying was done during the early nineteenth century in Green Bay and Prairie du Chien. Besides an 1811 letter that mentions a "milkhouse" on land that had belonged to a U.S. agent at Prairie du Chien, legal papers dated 1805 refer to Jacob Franks's "seven milch cows" on his farms at Green Bay.[20] Did Franks's wife, Thérèse LaRose, a métisse, milk these cows? If so, where did she learn how? If not, who did milk them?

Learning sometimes took place outside the region. Some métis daughters of traders went to Mackinac, Montreal, Saint Louis, or other towns to be educated at boarding schools. Elizabeth Baird's mother, Marianne Lasaliere Fisher,

---

Augustin Grignon, "Seventy-Two Years' Recollections of Wisconsin," State Hist. Soc. of Wis., *Colls.*, III (1857), 259.

18. Joan M. Jensen, *Loosening the Bonds: Mid-Atlantic Farm Women, 1750–1850* (New Haven, Conn., 1986), 93; Rebecca Kugel, "Of Missionaries and Their Cattle: Ojibwa Perceptions of a Missionary as Evil Shaman," *Ethnohistory*, XLI (1994), 227–244.

19. Julien Dubuque Estate Inventory, June 11, 1810, Chouteau Maffitt Collection, Missouri Historical Society, Saint Louis.

20. Nicholas Boilvin to William Eustis, Mar. 5, 1811, Prairie du Chien Papers, Nicholas Boilvin Letters, State Historical Society of Wisconsin; Agreement, Jacob Franks and John Lawe, Lawe Collection, item 2151, July 3, 1805, box 1, folder 1, Chicago Historical Society.

ran such a school for teenagers at Mackinac, where "the girls were taught to read, write, and to sew. . . . In addition, they were taught general housekeeping." That could have included some dairying, as there was a "maid who milked" at that home. Some other métis daughters spent time with Euramerican aunts and other family members who lived elsewhere. Girls who brought Euramerican domestic skills into Green Bay or Prairie du Chien were soon wives and mothers, who taught daughters, nieces, and cousins the skills they had learned. Even so, their application of the lessons was bound to be selective: some were ignored, others altered or embellished. For this reason, perhaps, butter continued to be imported into the 1820s.[21]

Elizabeth Baird's memoir reveals some of the difficulties her family encountered as they tried to negotiate dairying. Whether it was because of her Indian ancestry or personal taste, Elizabeth hated dairying. She wrote, "All who know of my great dislike of milk, especially cream, may imagine what I suffered in taking care of milk and making butter." Henry and other family members, however, liked and wanted dairy products, but Elizabeth apparently resisted milking. At first, rather than importing butter and dispensing with milk as other families apparently did, they tried to hire others to do the dairying. She and Henry hired a "man servant" from Montreal, who would chop wood, bring in water, take care of the horse and cow, and milk the cow. "The latter," she recalled, "he considered almost a disgrace."[22] She also remembered: "My husband was an Irishman and of course never milked a cow. His mother in after years used to say 'a gentleman from Dublin never did.'" If the manservant disliked milking because he considered it women's work, Henry resisted because he considered it inappropriate to both his class and gender. When their servants quit several years later, Elizabeth had to milk, which shocked Henry's mother, who apparently thought this inappropriate labor for a "lady." A combination of inherited ideas about the gender- and class-appropriateness of dairying seems to have made everyone in the Baird household try to avoid milking the cows, including Elizabeth, who felt that such work was not rightly part of her wifely duties.[23]

Ultimately, Elizabeth got her wish. A few days after the servants quit and left Elizabeth to milk, she was kicked and injured by an apparently malevolent

21. Baird, "O-De-Jit-Wa-Win-Wing," Baird Coll., chaps. 3, 11; American Fur Company Account Book, 120, 186, 187, 191, Chicago Historical Society.

22. Neither would he do housework "that was considered degrading." See Baird, "O-De-Jit-Wa-Win-Wing," Baird Coll., chap. 13.

23. Ibid., chaps. 11, 26.

cow, so that her husband "declared that I never should milk again, and *I never did.*" Did she consciously or unconsciously provoke the cow? We cannot know. Fortunately, occasional work could sometimes be arranged with Creole women from the local community; one might hire a neighbor to help out for a few days. Thus, the Bairds again turned to hired labor to resolve their gender-role conflicts and engaged a Madame LaRose, who came across the river in her canoe twice a day, her baby strapped in a cradle board, to milk the five cows, until more permanent servants could be found.[24] The negotiations got Henry his dairy products and Elizabeth her freedom from responsibility for them.

The butter at issue in the dairying disputes would be spread on the basic Euramerican staple, bread, which many Indians loved as well. The unique feature of wheat bread was the leavening, usually yeast. Although Indians made a type of unleavened corn bread, wheat bread was introduced into the region by Europeans, for whom bread baking was often housewives' work. But if husbands wanted wheat bread, that could be a problem for native and métis wives, whose mothers generally had not passed along these skills. At Prairie du Chien, the problem of bread baking was effectively solved when Michel Brisbois, a prominent trader and farmer, set up a bakery. He traded bread tickets worth fifty loaves of bread for each one hundred pounds of flour, and the tickets became a kind of circulating medium "to buy trifles of the Indians with."[25] Again, gender-role conflicts were solved by buying the product rather than expecting women to produce it.

At Green Bay, there were fewer ways to negotiate, and, somehow, people learned to bake bread. Residents ground locally grown wheat with two-person hand mills to make flour until the first horse mills were set up in 1809. An Ojibwa wife of an interpreter made bread in a bake kettle at a fireplace.[26] Eliza-

24. Ibid., chaps. 25, 26. (Madame LaRose might have been the estranged wife of Jacob Franks, owner of the "milch cows.")

25. One Yankee woman who moved into the area in 1830 claimed that a common greeting of Indians to whites at that time was "I have no bread." See [Juliette M. Kinzie], *Wau-Bun: The "Early Day" in the North-West* (1856), ed. Nina Baym (Urbana, Ill., 1992), 92; Lockwood, "Early Times," State Hist. Soc. of Wis., *Colls.*, II (1856), 125.

26. Augustin Grignon, "Seventy-Two Years' Recollections," State Hist. Soc. of Wis., *Colls.*, III (1857), 254; William Arundell, "Indian History," *Miners' Journal* (Galena), Oct. 30, 1830, typescript, Archives, file 1809, State Historical Society of Wisconsin; Lockwood, "Early Times," State Hist. Soc. of Wis., *Colls.*, II (1856), 120; John Shaw, "Personal Narrative of Col. John Shaw, of Marquette County, Wisconsin," State Hist. Soc. of Wis., *Colls.*, II (1855), 229–230; Thomas Anderson, "Personal Narrative of Capt. Thomas G. Anderson, 1800–28," State Hist. Soc. of Wis., *Colls.*, IX (1892), 149.

beth Baird's experiences as a fourteen-year-old bride learning to make bread—a food she liked much more than milk or butter—suggest one way the skill was transmitted.

As a third-generation métisse, Elizabeth had eaten plenty of bread in her short life growing up in Mackinac, but she had never learned how to make it. There, as at Prairie du Chien, people bought bread from bakeries, so she had never seen it made. Her first biscuits were "heavy," and her crumpets—"laid in a dry pan and baked by an open fire"—were "a little more palatable." Fortunately, "we were young and healthy, nothing hurt us, and we did not become the victims of dyspepsia, as one might imagine." At last, a neighbor befriended her: "Good old Mrs. Irwin . . . gave me my first instruction in bread-making, telling me the secret of light bread and giving me a cup of yeast to experiment with." Elizabeth was not completely satisfied with the results, but she kept trying and one day invited Mrs. Irwin's husband for dinner. She recalled: "I cannot now tell what we had for dinner, but I do know we had *bread,* which lies heavy upon me yet in memory. However, our new friend assured me that he liked just such bread, an assertion which put an end to my apologies, that were made in such broken English, that they were not soon forgotten, being a great source of amusement in after years." [27]

Although there were virtually no white women in these Creole communities before the War of 1812, Creole men wanted Euramerican women's products. Some native and métis women learned to milk cows, make butter, and bake bread, whereas others resisted. Compromises between European-descended men and native-descended women sometimes included either buying bread and butter rather than producing them at home or hiring others to produce them. The scattered resistance suggests that it was more difficult to negotiate domestic production across culture and gender lines than it was to adapt native women's production, such as sugar making, to Creole society.

Farming also required compromise, and in this case the solutions that Creoles worked out were influenced by gender, race, and class. Negotiation across cultures was difficult enough when one taught skills to—or organized an activity with—people for whom the type of production was new. But Creoles also confronted conflicting gender roles in their fields and gardens, and their actions were complicated by the ambivalence that many of them seem to have felt toward farming.

Indigenous people of the Midwest considered farming to be women's work, and the Winnebago, Sauk, and Mesquakie women were apparently quite suc-

27. Baird, "O-De-Jit-Wa-Win-Wing," Baird Coll., chap. 12.

cessful at it. For example, during the 1760s, Jonathan Carver recorded, the women at Lake Winnebago raised "a great quantity of Indian corn, beans, pumpkins, squash, and water melons." They planted beans among the corn, letting the cornstalks support the winding vines, and, because they used no tools more complicated than a hoe, they had no need for draft animals. The Sauk women's production was substantial enough to make the "Great Town of the Saukies" famous as "the best market for traders to furnish themselves with provisions of any within eight hundred miles of it." From 1805 into the 1820s, Sauk and Mesquakie women at the Turkey River and around Rock Island raised thousands of bushels of corn annually, cultivated more than three hundred acres, and raised "sufficient corn to supply all the permanent and transient inhabitants of the Prairie des Chiens," according to another observer.[28]

With this degree of agricultural success, it is little wonder, then, that Sauk and Mesquakie men were not the least bit interested in learning what U.S. government agents termed "the advantages of employing the plough, harrow, etc." In fact, Indian men showed their contempt for the efforts of agricultural agent William Ewing in 1806 by shooting his draft animals full of arrows.[29] They rejected not just the adoption of new tools but a complete change of gender roles that would have meant adopting Euramerican systems of property relations and concentration of wealth while completely reorienting a worldview that linked women, land, and reproduction.

In spite of European and Euramerican traditions in which farm wives kept a "kitchen garden," missionaries and government policy makers could not imagine Indian agriculture as successful so long as women and not men were in charge of it. They clung to their own gendered ideas about farming even when these ideas were not particularly effective.

28. Norman Gelb, ed., *Jonathan Carver's Travels through America, 1766–1768* (New York, 1993), 71–72. Both Carver and Peter Pond commented on the "great quantities" and "Grate Crops" raised by the Sauk women during the 1760s and 1770s. See Charles M. Gates, ed., *Five Fur Traders of the Northwest* (Saint Paul, Minn., 1965), 41; P[ierre] de Charlevoix, *Journal of a Voyage to North-America*, 2 vols. (London, 1761), II, 121; Gelb, *Carver's Travels*, 74 (quotation); Elliott Coues, ed., *The Expeditions of Zebulon Montgomery Pike*, 3 vols. (New York, 1895), I, 294; Major Morrell Marston to Rev. Jedidiah Morse, November 1820, in Emma Helen Blair, ed., *The Indian Tribes of the Upper Mississippi Valley and Region of the Great Lakes*, II (Cleveland, Ohio, 1912), 151; James H. Lockwood, "Early Times," State Hist. Soc. of Wis., *Colls.*, II (1856), 112.

29. Marston to Morse, in Blair, ed., *Indian Tribes of the Upper Mississippi Valley*, II, 179–180; Donald Jackson, "William Ewing, Agricultural Agent to the Indians," *Agricultural History*, XXXI (April 1957), 4–7.

With the exception of Indian women, most Creoles seem to have had mixed feelings about the actual farming work. Indian women living in the Creole towns did farm there, and, as mentioned earlier, Indian women from neighboring villages provided produce to Creoles wishing to buy it. Métis women were often wives in middling or elite families who hired help whenever possible and, like other Creoles, bought food from Indians living nearby. Métis men had as uncles and grandfathers Indian men who scorned the idea of men's farming, and they had as fathers white and métis traders who had selected their occupations based on personal preference.

For example, John W. Johnson, who ran a U.S. government trading post at Bellevue on the Mississippi River, wrote to his superior in 1809 that, although he wanted "to improve the mind of the Indians particular in so valueable a point as agriculture" and had apparently been asked to take charge of a demonstration farm at the garrison, he felt that the twelfth of April was too late in the season "to Commence for the present year," since he had neither "hands" nor a "team." If Tapassia, Johnson's Sauk and Mesquakie wife, read the letter, she must have laughed.[30] While her kinswomen were preparing their fields nearby, Euramerican men's reliance on the supposedly superior white agricultural methods meant that grain could not be grown without draft animals or hired men.

Did Tapassia teach John native agricultural methods or, perhaps, did she set up her own garden? Did he eventually teach her to use a plow? What were the work arrangements in bicultural, multiracial marriages in which traditional gender roles denominated each partner the proper farmer?

Unfortunately, the evidence for this couple and for others like them is scanty. John doubtless knew of Ewing's humiliation three years earlier and preferred simply to trade peacefully at Bellevue without enduring the additional hard work of farming and possible ridicule of his Indian customers and in-laws. But after moving to Prairie du Chien seven years later, John apparently did have some input with regard to planting, since he wrote to a friend in 1816 asking for some garden seed and commented, "I have an ellegant situation for a garden."[31]

30. John W. Johnson to William Clark, Apr. 12, 1809, Clark Papers, Missouri Historical Society. The land had previously been tilled. If Tapassia was like most other full-blood Indians of this time, of course, she would have been illiterate. See Thomas Forsyth Papers, Draper MSS, 2T:22a. It is unclear when they married, but they had the first of three children in 1811.

31. Johnson to Theodore Hunt, July 6, 1816, Lucas Collection, Missouri Historical Society. John wrote that he had inherited a garden when he moved, leading us to assume that he could have saved seed for the following year, but perhaps he wanted a greater variety. One wonders if Tapassia asked her friends and relatives for seed too.

Most farming was for home consumption before 1816. By one account, Green Bay families of that era had on average only two or three acres under cultivation. Before the War of 1812, most husbands were, at best, part-time farmers; some might have agreed with Missouri métis men, who, Tanis Thorne argues, "firmly held the idea that agriculture was the work of slaves and women."[32] How did they organize the farm work?

The elite families owned a number of farms, which were farmed by tenant families, the men of which worked for the elites as voyageurs and laborers. Since these men were often called away in their capacities as boatmen or other fur-trade workers during the growing season, their wives did a substantial amount of the farm work. Morgan L. Martin, who moved to Green Bay in 1827, wrote, "All these enclosures of men more or less employed as laborers by the traders, were cultivated by their women, whom they called *wives,* but really Indian women with whom they lived after the Indian custom."[33]

A few records of mixed couples in which the wives were métis do exist. Like middling and elite couples elsewhere, these couples hired others to do the farm work whenever possible, but sometimes family members had to work together. Henry and Elizabeth Baird hired men to do their farm work; when all the hired help quit, owing to the meddling of Henry's parents, Elizabeth and her father-in-law had to take care of the vegetable gardening (Henry was too busy with his law practice). But Elizabeth's mother-in-law, a city woman, "could not see how a lady could put her hands into the dirty ground." In addition, Elizabeth wrote: "My husband always planned a flower garden which I was expected to attend. I tried to do so but my cares were too great." She resisted enough to get some help, she remembered: "Yet we did have a flower garden for I planted the seeds and father Baird would help me in weeding."[34]

Another couple, the Gagniers, lived near Prairie du Chien in 1827 and had a slightly different approach. The wife, Teresa, was French and Sioux, and the husband, Regis, was French and African. They had as a boarder an elderly "discharged American soldier by the name of Solomon Lipcap," according to an early resident who knew them. Apparently their white Anglo boarder helped

32. Ellis, "Recollections," State Hist. Soc. of Wis., *Colls.,* VII (1876), 218; Grignon, "Seventy-two Years," State Hist. Soc. of Wis., *Colls.,* III (1857), 254; Thorne, "People of the River," 199.

33. *American State Papers, Public Lands,* V, 47–98, 270–272, 283–328; "Lawe and Grignon Papers, 1794–1821," State Hist. Soc. of Wis., *Colls.,* X (1888), 139–140.

34. Other such couples include the Rolettes and the Lawes. See Elizabeth Baird, "O-De-Jit-Wa-Win-Wing," Baird Coll., chaps. 14, 18, 26; Jeanne Kay, "John Lawe, Green Bay Trader," *Wisconsin Magazine of History,* LXIV (1980), 2–27.

with the cultivating, as he was reportedly "at work hoeing in the garden near the house" when they were all attacked by Indians during the Winnebago Revolt of 1827.[35]

Creoles created accommodation within families, neighborhoods, and towns. They adapted native assimilation customs by intermarrying but forming their own communities. Native-descended women mediated between Euramerican immigrants and indigenous people, as eventually did their husbands and children. By teaching, learning, and adapting languages and lifeways, they created syncretism on a personal level. Gender relations were clearly at the center of this process.

Gender roles were an area of potential conflict for Creoles, who responded in a variety of ways. Some Indian wives took charge of the farming; some couples in mixed marriages counted on tenant families, boarders, or hired workers to cultivate their land or milk their cows. Some, like the Dubuques, dispensed with dairying altogether. Some bought bread and butter with furs and other products—even maple sugar. The spirit of creative accommodation took a variety of forms. If Indian wives' farm work differed from métis women, the native women were probably less interested in dairying or raising poultry, and their husbands were probably less active cultivators. Conversely, métis wives seemingly incorporated more Euramerican domestic activities into their routines, such as laundry and butter and bread making, which gave them less time to cultivate their land.

Native-descended women shaped these towns in economic as well as social ways. The economies of Creole communities did not exactly mirror Euramerican patterns, and fur-trade families did not confine their activities solely to securing pelts in exchange for dry goods. Women as well as men determined what would be produced, and how.

Long-term accommodation like that in the Creole towns could have prevailed at the lead mines but did not. After the 1820s—a decade of Indian-Anglo coexistence at the mines during which conflict became endemic—the Indians were forced out. A number of factors contributed to this outcome, but unsuccessful gender relations were central to the discord.

Clear similarities existed between the fur-trade economy and lead production. As in the fur trade, mining meant extracting the region's natural resources for export. At first, also like the fur trade, indigenous workers gathered the product to be exported by white traders. Lead mining was a part of the Indi-

---

35. Lockwood, "Early Times," State Hist. Soc. of Wis., *Colls.,* II (1856), 161.

ans' seasonal economy in this region, as was hunting for fur-bearing animals. The sex ratio among immigrants who participated in the mining economy was imbalanced, only slightly less so than among fur-trade immigrants. And yet, in spite of these similarities and in spite of a few exceptional instances of intermarriage, cooperation, and integration, Indians and Euramericans could not find common ground in the mining district.

Native Americans had dug lead (also known as "galena") in the Upper Mississippi Valley for at least four thousand years and traded it as far away as the present states of Ohio, Mississippi, Georgia, and the province of Ontario and used it to make ornaments and sparkling paint. Generally this was a midsummer activity that took place while young men were away on the summer hunt. During the seventeenth century, the French learned about the Upper Mississippi Valley lead mines and apparently taught Indians to smelt ore and to make molds for crafting objects out of melted lead.[36]

The French colonial presence increased both native and French demand for lead in several ways. First, to the south in the Illinois country, French traders accepted lead along with furs in exchange for trade goods beginning in the seventeenth century. Second, one of the most important items traded to the Indians was the gun, valued because the technology both enhanced men's ability to hunt and increased their military prowess. Although Indians depended on Europeans for gunpowder, they could make their own musket balls with lead, so native demand for galena increased with Indian men's participation in the fur trade during the eighteenth century. Furthermore, both international wars and

36. Ronald M. Farquhar and Ian R. Fletcher, "The Provenience of Galena from Archaic/Woodland Sites in Northeastern North America: Lead Isotope Evidence," *American Antiquity*, XLIX (1984), 774–785; John A. Walthall et al., "Galena Analysis and Poverty Point Trade," *Midcontinental Journal of Archaeology*, VII (1982), 133–148; John A. Walthall, Stephen H. Stow, and Marvin J. Karson, "Ohio Hopewell Trade: Galena Procurement and Exchange," in David S. Brose and N'omi Greber, eds., *Hopewell Archaeology: The Chillicothe Conference* (Kent, Ohio, 1979), 247–250; John A. Walthall, *Galena and Aboriginal Trade in Eastern North America* (Springfield, Ill., 1981), 20. Other useful sources on native mining include Janet Doris Spector, "Winnebago Indians, 1634–1829: An Archeological and Ethnohistorical Investigation" (Ph.D. diss., University of Wisconsin, Madison, 1974); Karl J. Reinhard and A. Mohamad Ghazi, "Evaluation of Lead Concentrations in Eighteenth-Century Omaha Indian Skeletons Using ICP-Ms," *American Journal of Physical Anthropology*, LXXXIX (1992), 183–195; Reuben Gold Thwaites, "Narrative of Spoon Decorah," State Hist. Soc. of Wis., *Colls.*, XIII (1895), 458–459; Kristin Hedman, "Skeletal Remains from a Historic Sauk Village (11RI81), Rock Island County, Illinois," in Thomas E. Emerson, Andrew C. Fortier, and Dale L. McElrath, *Highways to the Past: Essays on Illinois Archaeology in Honor of Charles J. Bareis, Illinois Archaeology*, V, (1993), 537–548.

local intertribal conflicts stepped up demand. Sauks, Mesquakies, and Winnebagos traded the lead within their own communities, to members of other tribes, and to Euramerican traders.[37]

During the late eighteenth century, Indians increased their lead mining, thereby diversifying their economies and reducing their dependence on furs as commodities to be sold for trade goods. Anticipating the interest of the U.S. government and individual Anglophone miners, they tried to forestall Euramerican encroachment on the mining lands by keeping all whites out of the mining area except a few traders who became kin through marriage to Indian women. These men also traded for furs, and their wives were traditional mediators.[38]

One such wife was the Sauk-Mesquakie woman Mawwaiquoi, who married Samuel C. Muir, a Scottish lead trader and physician. After their marriage, Muir resigned his position as a surgeon with the U.S. army. By 1820, they had a post on an island opposite the Mesquakie village at present-day Dubuque, Iowa, where Indian women could sell the lead they dug. Later, Muir and Mawwaiquoi moved to Puck-e-she-tuk at present-day Keokuk, Iowa, and then to the mining center at Galena. They had five children. Galena's early history records that Muir treated Mawwaiquoi "with marked respect." "She always presided at his table, and was respected by all who knew her, but never abandoned her native dress."[39]

From 1788 to 1832, a few wives like Mawwaiquoi and husbands like Samuel Muir linked the Sauk, Mesquakie, and Winnebago lead miners to markets in

37. Phillip Millhouse, "A Chronological History of Indian Lead Mining in the Upper Mississippi Valley from 1643 to 1840," 1–5, Collections of the Galena Public Library, Galena, Ill.; Jeanne Kay, "The Land of La Baye: The Ecological Impact of the Green Bay Fur Trade, 1634–1836" (Ph.D. diss., University of Wisconsin, Madison, 1977), 175–176; Thwaites, "Narrative of Spoon Decorah," State Hist. Soc. of Wis., *Colls.*, XIII (1895), 458; Jackson, ed., *Black Hawk*, 92.

38. Murphy, "Economy, Race, and Gender," chap. 4; Thomas Auge, "The Life and Times of Julien Dubuque," *Palimpsest*, LVII (1976), 2–13; William E. Wilkie, *Dubuque on the Mississippi, 1788–1988* (Dubuque, Iowa, 1987).

39. Thomas Forsyth, "A List of the Names of the Half-Breeds, Belonging to the Sauk and Fox Indians, Who Claim Land according to the Treaty Made at Washington City, on the 4th August 1824 . . . ," Forsyth Papers, Draper MSS, 2T: 23; Isaac R. Campbell, "Recollections of the Early Settlement of Lee County," *Annals of Iowa*, 1st Ser., V (1867), 889–890; Henry Rowe Schoolcraft, *Travels through the Northwestern Regions of the United States* (1821; reprint, Ann Arbor, Mich., 1966), 344–345; Sac-Fox Halfbreeds, Thomas Forsyth, 1830, vol. 32, *Records of the Superintendent of Indian Affairs, St. Louis*, 11, 15, Kansas State Historical Society, Topeka; *History of Jo Daviess County, Illinois* (Chicago, 1878), 234–235.

Saint Louis, Prairie du Chien, and elsewhere. As long as Euramerican men like Muir were more interested in trading than mining lead, the Indians continued to specialize as producers, maintaining an active role and the ability to control the region and its trade. Indian women were central to mining and consequently to the diversity of production it represented.

Early-nineteenth-century observers uniformly described the principal Indian lead miners as female, although children or elderly men might help out. For example, in 1818 a traveler passed by the Mesquakie lead mines near the Mississippi River and remarked, "The women dig the ore, carry it to the river where they have furnaces, and smelt it." The strongly sex-typed nature of this work is clear from another traveler's observation that "the warriors and young men, hold themselves above it." A white miner recalled: "When the Indians mined, . . . there were often fifty or a hundred boys and squaws at work, on one vein. They would dig down a square hole, covering the entire width of the mine leaving one side not perpendicular, but at an angle of about forty-five degrees, then with deer skin sacks attached to a bark rope, they would haul out along the inclining side of the shaft, the rock and ore."[40] The Indians' tools also included pickaxes, hoes, shovels, crowbars (some of them made out of old gun barrels), and baskets. Eventually they also bought tin pails to replace the homemade containers. They broke up mineral deposits by heating the rocks with fire and then dashing cold water on them.[41]

In 1822, the U.S. government sent troops to force the Indians to allow Anglophone miners to dig there. The first group included James Johnson and eight of his male workers, four black and four white. At least some of these blacks were probably slaves. About four dozen other Anglos came in that year.[42]

From 1822 through the Black Hawk War of 1832, the mineral region east of the Mississippi experienced a full-fledged lead rush. About four thou-

40. Edward Tanner, "Wisconsin in 1818," State Hist. Soc. of Wis., *Colls.*, VIII (1879), 288; Schoolcraft, *Travels*, 344–345; Lucius H. Langworthy, "Dubuque: Its History, Mines, Indian Legends, Etc.," *Iowa Journal of History and Politics*, VIII (1910), 376.

41. Schoolcraft, *Travels*, 343–344; Moses Meeker, "Early History of the Lead Region of Wisconsin," State Hist. Soc. of Wis., *Colls.*, VI (1872), 281; Reminiscences of Esau Johnson, Group C, 1–3, Esau Johnson Papers, State Historical Society of Wisconsin, Branch, Wisconsin Room, Karrmann Library, University of Wisconsin, Platteville.

42. Joseph Schafer, *The Wisconsin Lead Region* (Madison, Wis., 1932), chaps. 3, 4; Reuben Gold Thwaites, "Notes on Early Lead Mining," State Hist. Soc. of Wis., *Colls.*, XIII (1895), 271–292; Meeker, "Early History of the Lead Region," ibid., VI (1872), 271–296; *History of Jo Daviess County*, 226–257.

sand whites and one hundred blacks arrived in the region seeking wealth and adventure, founding towns such as Galena, Mineral Point, Hardscrabble, and New Diggings and spreading out in twos and threes across the rolling countryside.[43]

For a few years, the Indians, blacks, and whites lived and mined as neighbors, but by 1827 accommodation began to fall apart. The U.S. federal government supported and protected the Anglophone miners in exchange for 10 percent of the lead they produced, but it implemented policies that tolerated and encouraged lawlessness and trespass on Indians' rights and resources. During the course of this decade, the self-styled Americans seized the lead mines and the exploitation process from the Sauk, Mesquakie, and Winnebago people. The Winnebago Revolt of 1827 and the Black Hawk War were, in part, protests against this seizure.

But at the beginning of Euramerican involvement in the mining district, conflict was not foreordained. For a few years in the early 1820s, Indians, blacks, and whites lived and worked in the area of Fever River (later called Galena River) in relative peace. In August 1823, between five hundred and two thousand Indians tolerated their neighbors, seventy-four whites and blacks. Anglo mining techniques differed from Indian: the men sank shafts, placed windlasses across the openings to control buckets for the lead and workers, and used explosives to break up large concentrations of the mineral. One observer found the contrast entertaining: "The Indian women proved themselves to be the best as well as the shrewdest miners. While Col. Johnson's men were sinking their holes or shafts, in some instances the squaws would drift under them and take out all the mineral or ore they could find. When the men got down into the drift made by the women, the latter would have a hearty laugh at the white men's expense."[44] Some of these early miners described the community for a writer in the 1870s, a half-century later. They remembered that about 1823 there were perhaps eight log cabins in the immediate vicinity of "the Point"—later called the town of Galena—"but the river bottoms, ravines and

---

43. United States, Census Office, *Fifth Census; or, Enumeration of the Inhabitants of the United States, 1830* ... (Washington, D.C., 1832), Michigan Territory, Iowa County and State of Illinois, Jo Daviess County; Consolidated Returns of Mineral and Lead Manufactured, 1827–1829, Historical Collections of the Galena Public Library.

44. *History of Jo Daviess County*, 243; Meeker, "Early History of the Lead Region," State Hist. Soc. of Wis., *Colls.*, VI (1872), 280–281, 282; Thwaites, "Notes on Early Lead Mining," ibid., XIII (1895), 271–292; Henry R[owe] Schoolcraft, *A View of the Lead Mines of Missouri* ... (New York, 1819), 90–106.

hillsides were thickly dotted with the wigwams of the Sacs and Foxes, who . . . were engaged in hunting and fishing, and supplied the whites with a large portion of their meats, consisting of venison, game, fish, etc. The squaws and old men, too old to hunt, raised the most of the mineral which supplied the furnaces." Indian and white boys fished and prospected together.[45] Native economic practices continued apace, while the newcomers proved to be customers for Indian hunters. For a few years, Indians and whites were able to mine side-by-side, yielding accommodation. The small number of Anglos during this early period probably contributed to tolerance on both sides.

A settlement at Gratiot's Grove seemed to promise that accommodation was possible at the mines. The small Creole community, founded by the Gratiot brothers and their families, was central to the rapid acceleration of the lead rush in 1826. The impetus for this sudden expansion of mining began when Winnebago miners discovered a particularly rich prospect about fifteen miles northeast of Galena in 1825 or 1826. At the same time, Henry and John Gratiot of Saint Louis decided to seek opportunities in a free state because they opposed slavery; they arrived in the mining region in 1825 and were joined by their families in 1826.

The Gratiots were in some ways typically Creole. The brothers were American-born men of French ancestry, and they spoke French in addition to English. Women in the Gratiot family connected them to established midwestern Creole communities: their mother was a member of the powerful Chouteau fur-trade family of Saint Louis, a connection the Indians acknowledged when they respectfully dubbed Henry "Chouteau"; Henry's wife, Susan Hempstead Gratiot, had kin at Prairie du Chien. No doubt through the Chouteau fur-trade empire they had many other connections there. Clearly, they knew well the French Creole culture with which the region's Indians had become familiar.[46]

Another woman, an interpreter named Catherine Myott, brought the Gratiots and the Winnebagos together. Myott was a Winnebago métisse and an important woman in several communities. Her father, Nicholas Boilvin, was the U.S. Indian agent at Prairie du Chien until his death in 1827. She was between thirty and forty years old, according to the 1830 census, with a daughter between five and ten years old. A skilled linguist, she spoke Winnebago and

45. *History of Jo Daviess County*, 243.

46. [Marie G. Dieter], *The Story of Mineral Point, 1827–1941* (1941; reprint, Mineral Point, Wis., 1979), 17–18; Elihu B. Washburne, "Col. Henry Gratiot—A Pioneer of Wisconsin," State Hist. Soc. of Wis., *Colls.*, X (1888), 244–245; George Davenport to O. N. Bostwick, Jan. 29, 1826, Chouteau-Papin Collection, Missouri Historical Society.

French and possibly English as well; Winnebago leaders had great respect for her.[47]

Interpreters who could speak Winnebago and English were rare in the region, which created problems for Anglophone immigrants. Winnebago, a Siouan language, is unrelated to Algonquian languages of the region such as Sauk, Mesquakie, Ojibwa, and Ottawa, so it was difficult for people who spoke Algonquian tongues to pick up. Boilvin's successor as agent at Prairie du Chien, Joseph Street, who spoke only English, was extremely frustrated by this problem.[48]

With the help of Catherine Myott, the Gratiots negotiated for rights to mine and live in the region, paying three hundred dollars in trade goods and provisions. No one recorded what promises the Gratiot brothers made to the Winnebagos, but the agreement probably stated that the Gratiots would accept Winnebago lead, furs, and other products in trade for the high-quality merchandise Indians knew their Chouteau family connections commanded. In addition, the Winnebagos likely realized that, with Anglo miners flocking to the area throughout the summer of 1826, it would be impossible to keep whites completely out and so decided to accept the elite French Creole Gratiots in the hope that the Gratiots would be able to maintain peaceful relations there. Susan Hempstead Gratiot's kin ties at Prairie du Chien, where Catherine Myott also had relatives, were probably an important consideration from the Winnebago point of view, since Prairie du Chien residents had proven themselves to be tolerable neighbors. In 1831, Henry Gratiot's appointment as U.S. Indian subagent to the Winnebagos formalized existing relations between them and the Creoles.[49]

47. Washburne, "Col. Henry Gratiot," State Hist. Soc. of Wis., *Colls.*, X (1888), 235–245; Hansen, "Prairie du Chien's Earliest Church Records," *Minnesota Genealogical Journal*, IV (1985), 330; Elizabeth Taft Harlan, Minnie Dubbs Millbrook, and Elizabeth Case Erwin, eds., *1830 Federal Census: Territory of Michigan* (Detroit, Mich., 1961), 244; Henry Dearborn to Nicolas Boilvin, Apr. 10, 1806, State Hist. Soc. of Wis., *Colls.*, XIX (1910), 314–315; Ellen M. Whitney, ed., *The Black Hawk War, 1831–1832*, 2 vols. (Springfield, Ill., 1973), II, 324 n. 5, White Crow speeches, Apr. 28, June 3 1832, II, 321, 507, 509. However, she didn't speak Sauk (II, 319 n. 1); Adèle Gratiot, "Mrs. Adèle P. Gratiot's Narrative," State Hist. Soc. of Wis., *Colls.*, X (1888), 267.

48. Joseph Street to James Barbour, Jan. 8, 1828, Joseph Street, "An Estimate of Expenses," Sept. 1, 1828, Letters Received by the Office of Indian Affairs, microcopy 234, reel 696, National Archives, Washington, D.C.

49. Thomas Forsyth to William Clark, Aug. 15, 1826, Draper MSS, 4T:259; Gratiot, "Gratiot's Narrative," State Hist. Soc. of Wis., *Colls.*, X (1888), 267; Washburne, "Col. Henry Gratiot," ibid., X (1888), 253; Whitney, ed., *Black Hawk War*, II, 36 n. 4, 77 n. 1.

After 1826, a multilingual community grew up around Gratiot's Grove, including perhaps twenty Francophone families (both Creole and Swiss) and Anglos such as Esau and Sally Johnson. (The Swiss were refugees from the Selkirk colony of Canada's Red River.) Residents included a few sons of Prairie du Chien families, including the Heberts, who had Mesquakie kin, the Gagniers, who had Dakota kin, and the St. Cyrs, who had Winnebago relatives and were stepcousins of Catherine Myott.[50] Gratiot's Grove was not ethnically typical—in terms of the demographics of the whole lead-mining region, Francophones and foreign-born immigrants represented only a very small minority of lead rushers—but the settlement gave whites a foothold in the Winnebago mineral area.

News of the wealth of the lead deposits around Gratiot's Grove did stimulate migration markedly by 1827. According to one estimate, the mining region's white and black population increased from two hundred in 1825, to one thousand in 1826, to four thousand by 1827. No more than 3 percent of these were African American. Some blacks in the region were slaves, although the legality of slavery was repeatedly challenged in the new courts, and Indian slavery was being phased out gradually.[51]

In what was a typical prologue to native assimilation, many Indians made special efforts to observe and befriend blacks and whites, monitoring their activities as they established relationships. For example, James Beckwourth, one of the African American men working for James Johnson as a hunter and miner, later recalled being befriended by the Indians, who showed him "their choicest hunting-grounds" and often accompanied him. Beckwourth remarked that this increased his "knowledge of the Indian character," and, no doubt, the relationships were equally educational for his native companions.[52]

Another relationship arose when Old Buck—a Mesquakie leader whose

50. Caleb Atwater, *Remarks Made on a Tour to Prairie du Chien; Thence to Washington City in 1829* (Columbus, Ohio, 1831), 190; Alvin M. Josephy, *The Artist Was a Young Man: The Life Story of Peter Rindisbacher* (Fort Worth, Tex., 1970), 47–55; Harlan, Millbrook, and Erwin, eds., *1830 Federal Census: Territory of Michigan,* 109; Hansen, "Prairie du Chien's Earliest Church Records," *Minnesota Genealogical Journal,* IV (1985), 330.

51. [Dieter], *The Story of Mineral Point,* 17–18; R. W. Chandler, "Map of the Lead Mines on the Upper Mississippi River," 1829, copy in author's possession; *Fifth Census . . . 1830,* Jo Daviess County, Illinois, and Iowa County, Michigan Territory; Murphy, "Economy, Race and Gender," chap. 5; Russell M. Magnaghi, "Red Slavery in the Great Lakes Country during the French and British Regimes," *Old Northwest,* XII (1986), 201–217.

52. James P. Beckwourth, *The Life and Adventures of James P. Beckwourth as Told to Thomas D. Bonner* (1852; reprint, Lincoln, Nebr., 1972), 22.

band had for years worked the famous mines called the "Buck Lead"—made friends with a Yankee smelter named Horatio Newhall, who wrote to his brother in 1828 that the Mesquakie leader had camped the previous winter near his Sinsinawa River furnace. "Himself and sons often visit me in town. . . . I have been at his lodge twice." Old Buck took the next logical step by trying to arrange a marriage between his daughter and Newhall, but Newhall refused.[53]

Such associations helped the Indians to understand the immigrants and to observe and police men like Newhall and Beckwourth. By the late 1820s, native American men spent more and more of their time and energy policing the region, trying to control the lead rushers.[54]

In spite of intruding Anglophone miners, Indians continued to mine for lead through the 1820s. Mesquakies mined at and around the old Mines of Spain west of the Mississippi (from which whites were excluded until 1832) and around the Fever River until the mid-1820s. Winnebagos, and to a lesser extent the Sauks, mined between the Rock and Wisconsin Rivers, east of the Mississippi. They sold lead to merchants and smelters like Muir, Newhall, and the Gratiots and also to other Indians.[55]

Women continued through this period to be the principal Indian miners. Young and middle-aged Indian men might prospect, smelt, and guard the mines, but exposure to Anglophone views that digging ore was men's work did not alter Indian men's convictions that mining was for women and their assistants, the elderly and children. Native mining techniques continued to differ from whites', indicating that Indians and Anglos did not mine together. Sometimes Indians prospected for whites, but beyond that Indians and whites did not cooperate in mining. Indian men, for their part, showed little interest in playing more than auxiliary roles even in native mining.[56]

That Indian and white miners did not incorporate each other's mining techniques underscores the extent to which each worked independently from people of the other race. Not only did Indians and Anglos fail to cooperate in lead mining, after 1826 they also failed to achieve peaceful relations, integration, or toleration.

53. Horatio Newhall to Isaac Newhall, Mar. 1, 1828, 4, Horatio Newhall Papers, microfilm, Illinois State Historical Library, Springfield.

54. On native American police work, see Murphy, "Economy, Race, and Gender," chap. 5.

55. George Davenport to O. N. Bostwick, Jan. 29, 1826, Chouteau-Papin Collection; Nicholas Boilvin to William Eustis, Feb. 11, 1811, typescript, State Historical Society of Wisconsin, Branch, Wisconsin Room, Karrmann Library; Thwaites, ed., "Narrative of Spoon Decorah," State Hist. Soc. of Wis., *Colls.*, XIII (1895), 458.

56. Reminiscences of Esau Johnson, C-2, Esau Johnson Papers.

Instead, relations between Indians and Anglos became increasingly hostile. Anglo miners invaded even areas the U.S. government acknowledged belonged to the Indians, destroyed their cornfields, and killed and scared away the game. Blood was spilled during the Winnebago Revolt of 1827 and the Black Hawk War of 1832. Both of these conflicts expressed Indian resistance to Anglo immigration and incursions on Indian land, and both resulted in more Indian land cessions.[57]

This outcome was not, however, inevitable. Even once the U.S. government had made clear that it would back whites' mining efforts in the region, accommodation was possible. Gratiot's Grove serves as an example of what might have been much more pervasive. There mining operations resembled Creole sugar production: both Indians and whites dug lead, just as Indians and Creoles both made maple sugar. Whites bought minerals from Indians and whites, just as Creole traders bought sugar from both. Indians kept some of both their sugar and their lead for their own use and to trade with other Indians. In both Gratiot's Grove and the fur-trade towns, kinship linked residents to the local Indians and their friends; communication was possible by way of bilingual residents. Although there is no evidence the Gratiots married native women, they employed Catherine Myott to mediate with their Winnebago neighbors and took pains to be on friendly terms with them. Other métis people also were residents. Not surprisingly, relations at Gratiot's Grove were apparently much more peaceful than elsewhere at the mines.

By contrast, Anglos at the mines did not make the connections that could have permitted negotiation leading to peaceful coexistence or even cultural syncretism. When Indians tried to assimilate them, they resisted. Their economic organization, abusive behavior, and traditional gender relations isolated them.

One reason that Anglos and Indians were more often in conflict than accord at the mines after the mid-1820s was that they generally had no relationships other than those of neighbor. If they had been coworkers, they might have developed lasting patterns of cooperation, but they did not work together. Indian

57. Gov. Lewis Cass to the Secretary of War, July 10, 1827, in Clarence Edwin Carter, ed., *The Territorial Papers of the United States*, XI, *The Territory of Michigan* (Washington, D.C., 1943), 1101–1103. General works on the Black Hawk War include Cecil Eby, *"That Disgraceful Affair": The Black Hawk War* (New York, 1973); Anthony F. C. Wallace, *Prelude to Disaster*, ed. Ellen M. Whitney (Springfield, Ill., 1970); Roger L. Nichols, *Black Hawk and the Warrior's Path* (Arlington Heights, Ill., 1992); and Black Hawk's autobiography, Jackson, ed., *Black Hawk*.

women were not among the wage workers or slaves mining for white bosses such as James Johnson—owing, no doubt, to disinterest on the women's part and to sex-typed notions of mining on the part of the small number of mining entrepreneurs—so they were not coworkers. Indian men clearly had no interest in digging for ore under any circumstances, because they considered it women's work.

In addition, most Anglo miners were self-employed and in no position to recruit employees. U.S. government policy makers aimed for a system of exploiting the mines that would be egalitarian—that is, open to men of all social ranks. In fact, Lieutenant Martin Thomas, superintendent of the U.S. lead mines, with his resident agents and the approval of the secretary of war, constructed a system that they hoped would discourage speculators and favor individual miners. Rather than selling the mineral lands outright, the government established the leasing system, so that men with little or no capital could profit alongside the elites.[58] The leasing system made land titles unavailable, discouraging the permanent settlement that might have encouraged marriage.

Although Creoles negotiated gender roles, Anglo and Indian lead miners did not. One might suppose a husband-wife mining team composed of an Indian wife and a white or black husband could have been extremely productive, but if this ever occurred there is no record of it. For that matter, white and black women apparently never mined. Sally Johnson, Esau's wife, for example, provided domestic support but did not dig. Anglophone men did not think that wives should dig lead. Gender roles with regard to mining were at least as rigid for whites as for Indians.

In addition to the fact that Anglo lead rushers and Indians were not coworkers, accommodation was hampered by their having no language in common. The Indians spoke their own languages, of course: Winnebago (a Siouan language) or Sauk/Mesquakie (Algonquian dialects). Some of them also spoke

58. James E. Wright, *The Galena Lead District: Federal Policy and Practice, 1824–1847* (Madison, Wis., 1966), 19–20. "The working men are those that suit us best and not the speculators," one of Thomas's agents wrote, a sentiment all policy makers seem to have shared (19). Although Indians continued to mine in the region up to the Black Hawk War of 1832, they did not figure in this system. (Apparently, Indians did not have to pay the 10 percent of their lead that whites and blacks did.) Unfortunately, egalitarian ideals in the mining region brought chaos in social relations, and the government failed to put in place any controls. No fort was built in the region; the court system was remote and weak. The system turned several thousand white men loose in Indian country, and the system's agent consciously encouraged conflict and violence.

French and Ojibwa, the latter being the lingua franca of the region up to this point. But most of the immigrants who came to dig lead spoke little besides English.

One exception was Horatio Newhall, the Yankee smelter and physician who was befriended by his neighbor Old Buck. In 1827, Newhall wrote to his brother: "I have made me a Dictionary of the most common words in their language so that by the help of this I can understand them tolerably well."[59] Old Buck recognized the potential for mediation, but when Newhall declined to marry Old Buck's daughter, he missed an opportunity to form a lasting alliance. Yet Newhall was only adhering to his culture's marriage customs of monogamy, endogamy, and strong distaste for divorce.

For others, marriage could have bridged the language barrier, as Elizabeth and Henry Baird learned. Mawwaiquoi and Samuel Muir were among only a handful of biracial couples at the mines; it seems that only the earliest Anglo men in the lead region married native women, and they were traders rather than miners. Like Newhall, few lead rushers planned to stay in the region for very long; most expected to make some money and return home in a season or a few years. In addition, many of them harbored prejudices against the "Heathen" and "savage" indigenous people.[60] Both of these factors—impermanence and intolerance—tended to deter marriages with local women, who preferred to stay and no doubt resented the racism.

Native women in the lead-mining region did not leave records of their impressions of the Anglo men. Initially, they might have viewed men who mined lead as effeminate and therefore not likely husbands. Records left by others, however, indicate that male miners' relations with Indian women during the 1820s were increasingly exploitative and violent, treatment that Indian men protested vehemently.

The immigrants used and abused Indian women sexually. For example, about 1823 mining boss Moses Meeker recalled, "Indians . . . offer[ed] lewd women to the whites for whisky, which too many of the young men accepted to their sorrow." A few years later, Winnebago leaders complained to their Indian agent that "some of the white people are insulting to the Indians and take liberties with their women." In 1827, after a drinking party Anglo boatmen had sponsored, several Winnebago women were abducted and taken aboard a boat

59. Horatio Newhall to Isaac Newhall, Mar. 1, 1828, Horatio Newhall Papers.

60. For example, ibid.; Edward Langworthy, "Autobiographical Sketch of Edward Langworthy," *Iowa Journal of History and Politics,* VIII (1910), 346.

ascending the Mississippi to supply Fort Snelling, provoking an attack by Winnebago men on the boat as it descended the river.[61]

Many Anglo miners also exhibited patterns of misogynistic violence. It was also in 1827 that a white miner in Galena knocked down the Menominee woman and stamped on her head, killing her. White and black men in the mining area also abducted, enslaved, and beat black women and girls on occasion, and a few white wives found themselves abused and abandoned by husbands who became alcoholics and gambling addicts.[62] It is little wonder, then, that many Indian women avoided contact with the Anglophone miners.

Who were these immigrants, and why did they think and act in these ways? Of the adult lead rushers, 97 percent were white and 77 percent male in 1830 (although they perceived 95 percent of their population to be male). They were generally restless young people of all social ranks participating in a cultural rite, the customary wandering that young Anglo men performed during their late teens and twenties before settling down and forming families. Some of them sought wealth, some were just adventurous, others were seeking both excitement and fortune. Going to the lead mines was only one of several journeys many of the young men had undertaken; others included visiting friends and relatives on different parts of the frontiers, working as a farm hand, seeing the sights of such cities as Cincinnati or Saint Louis, riding a flatboat to New Orleans, serving in the army, even engaging as a clerk to a Missouri River fur trader. The women were generally adventurous sisters and wives, and a few were servants.[63]

61. Meeker, "Early History of the Lead Region," State Hist. Soc. of Wis., *Colls.*, VI (1872), 290; Forsyth to Clark, June 10, 1828, Draper MSS, 6T:84; Reminiscences of Esau Johnson, B-43, Esau Johnson Papers; Whitney, ed., *Black Hawk War*, II, 793 n. 3; [Dieter], *The Story of Mineral Point*, 18.

62. *Miners' Journal*, Sept. 13, 1828; *Louisa I. Holmes v. Roland R. Holmes*, April term, 1832, *Sally George v. Alexander George*, April term, 1832, *Dunkey v. William Morrison, Leonard Bryant and Mary Bryant v. Alexander Neavill and Elias Griggs*, all in Jo Daviess County Court Records, Galena Public Library, on loan to the Karrmann Library.

63. *Fifth Census . . . 1830*, Michigan Territory, Iowa County and State of Illinois, Jo Daviess County; Chandler, "Map of the United States Lead Mines on the Upper Mississippi River"; Edward Langworthy, "Autobiographical Sketch," *Iowa Journal of History and Politics*, VIII (1910), 347. Some sources on the lead-mining region are Schafer, *The Wisconsin Lead Region;* Wright, *Galena Lead District;* Gratiot, "Gratiot's Narrative," State Hist. Soc. of Wis., *Colls.*, X (1888), 261–275; Reminiscences by the Langworthy brothers in the *Iowa Journal of History and Politics*, VIII (1910); Meeker, "Early History of the Lead Region," State Hist. Soc. of Wis., *Colls.*, VI (1872), 281; Horatio Newhall Papers and early Galena newspapers, Illinois

For many of these young men, going to Fever River, as the lead district was generally called, also meant escaping from parental and social control and from the conventions and comforts of life with women. Slightly more than half of the households in the lead-mining region in 1830 consisted of young men only. They called this way of living "keeping Bachelor's Hall," and it meant a man could leave his dirty clothes wherever he wanted, drink and gamble to his heart's content, and do whatever he wanted on the Sabbath. When they wearied of keeping Bachelor's Hall, these men waxed sentimental about womanhood.[64] But in the meantime, they sometimes beat, raped, killed, kidnapped, and abandoned the women in the region. They also fought and killed each other. Although they might sometimes have fantasies about beautiful young Indian women, keeping Bachelor's Hall by definition excluded females. That may explain why they perceived the region's sex ratio to be even more skewed than the census takers reported. Under other circumstances and later in life, many if not most of these men would be restrained, law-abiding citizens, but during the 1820s too many of them were rude, brash, violent, and racist, as they sought to dominate others. Their experience at the mines was strongly gendered.

For every Horatio Newhall or Henry and Susan Gratiot who made friends with an Indian or métis neighbor and tried to find links of communication and negotiation, dozens of other lead rushers made no connections. Part of their difficulty was the incompatibility of their gender role expectations with native patterns. Their vision of the possible did not include women—particularly women of color—in roles of mediation, certain commodity production, teaching across cultures, or interpreting; neither did they consider intermarriage an option. Their patterns of dominating and exploiting women were too strong to be replaced by the mutuality of negotiation and compromise.

In both the Creole towns and the mining district, social relations were characterized by domination and subordination on the one hand and mutuality on

State Historical Society, Springfield; Friedrick G. Hollman, *Auto-Biography of Friedrick G. Hollman* (Platteville, Wis., [1870?]); Reminiscences of Esau Johnson, Esau Johnson Papers; Jo Daviess County Court Records, Galena Public Library; Letters in various collections of the Missouri Historical Society.

64. For example, Langworthy, "Dubuque," *Iowa Journal of History and Politics*, VIII (1910), 383; Reminiscences of Esau Johnson, B-28, Esau Johnson Papers. See, for examples of sentimentality, Coelebs, "Home," *Advertiser* (Galena), Aug. 16, 1829, Coelebs, "Marriage," "Sonnet to Miss M**** C*****," Aug. 30, 1828, W., "The Indian Girl," July 25, 1828.

the other. The patterns of these relations differed markedly, however. Creole communities were socially, politically, and economically stratified societies in which a few elite families exercised considerable control over the middling and poorer sort and the small number of slaves. Paradoxically, gender, intercultural, and race relations were characterized by negotiation and compromise indicative of mutuality if not equality.

By contrast, during the lead rush of the 1820s, Anglo men too often tended to dominate and exploit women rather than seek compromise. In addition, they resisted mutuality in race relations, ultimately seeking to conquer and displace the indigenous people. However, egalitarian ideals for intragroup relations created a society that had a few weak elites, a few slaves, and a mass of uncontrolled equals seeking to assert themselves over others, especially women and Indian men. Of course, Indians and non-native women often objected, resisted, and withdrew from negotiation. Ironically, those who tended toward mediation rather than confrontation, such as Horatio Newhall and the Gratiots, were the lead rush district's weak elites.

Accommodation required personal relationships: communication, teaching, learning, cultural understanding, compromise, and commitment. Creole communities could incorporate Indians, whites, and métis people and could coexist peacefully with nearby Indians not only because they depended on one another economically but also because the former included kin and friends of the latter. In centers where cultures combined, people worked out compromises in negotiations that were frequently gendered. Usually, women were central to accommodation, and when it broke down both gender roles and gender relations explain important elements of its failure.

The Creole mining community at Gratiot's Grove demonstrates that accommodation might have succeeded at the mines. There sincere effort, kin ties, and mediation brought people together. Catherine Myott linked the Gratiots and their local lead rushers to the Winnebago residents, as her mother had linked the Indians to her father, Indian agent Nicolas Boilvin, in a country marriage. Characteristic of Anglo unwillingness to recognize native-descended women's powerful roles as mediators, Boilvin's successor Joseph Street blasted the custom of country marriages between agents or traders and local women. The monolingual Street, who apparently did not try to enlist Catherine Myott's aid, was unable to find an English-Winnebago interpreter. He declared that it was "almost impossible to hold a council with the" Winnebagos and had to try communicating by speaking English to his interpreter, who rendered the speech into Mesquakie or Ojibwa. These words were then translated into Winnebago by a bilingual Winnebago. "Much, tho, is entirely lost on both sides," he found. Street never saw the connection between his rejection of women as mediators and his frustration with trying to understand the Indians. Not surprisingly, the Winnebagos seemed to prefer Henry Gratiot, to Street's chagrin.[65]

The Anglo miners were forerunners and representatives of the expanding United States. They were also people who failed to reach accommodation with Indians; a look at native and Anglo mining demonstrates how gendered the experience of their failure was. They could neither specialize nor cooperate to reach accommodation with the indigenous people, for reasons that had a good deal to do with Indian women's experiences, with gender relations between groups, and with conflicting gender roles. Gender certainly cannot explain all aspects of human relations on this frontier, but it can illuminate a great deal.

Mawwaiquoi and Samuel Muir and their children moved back to Puck-e-she-tuk from Galena around the time of the Black Hawk War. We may wonder whether their move was motivated by growing racism at the mines. According to an early history of the region, Muir died in the cholera epidemic of 1832 soon after the family moved, leaving "his property in such condition that it was wasted in vexatious litigation." Mawwaiquoi was "left penniless and friendless, became discouraged, and, with her children . . . returned to her people on the Upper Missouri." [66] Clearly the region had become inhospitable to some women and children of color.

Although the Anglos of the lead-mining region failed to develop a society in which Indians had a role, the multicultural Creole communities persisted. Although Anglos, to a greater extent in Green Bay and a lesser extent in Prairie du Chien, swelled the population, came to dominate in business and politics, and imposed the use of English as the court language, the Creole people and culture continued to play an important, if poorly recognized, role in Wisconsin. Elizabeth Baird, like thousands of other holdovers from the Creole frontier, lived out her life in the American Republic that had taken over her homeland.

Some Indians found ways to triumph over the government policies of removal. Officially relocated after 1827 to a series of reservations in Iowa, Min-

65. Street to Barbour, Secretary of War, Jan. 8, 1828, Sept. 1, 1828 (quotations), Letters Received by the Office of Indian Affairs, Prairie du Chien, microfilm, Newberry Library, Chicago; Street to Cass, Aug. 26, 1831, in Whitney, ed., *Black Hawk War*, II, 147–154.

66. Campbell, "Recollections of the Early Settlement of Lee County," *Annals of Iowa*, 1st Ser., V (1867), 890; Sac-Fox Halfbreeds, Thomas Forsyth, 1830, vol. 32, 11, 15; *History of Jo Daviess County*, 235 (quotation).

nesota, North Dakota, and Nebraska, hundreds of Winnebagos quietly resisted and returned to Wisconsin. Following the Black Hawk War, the Sauk and Mesquakie people were forced west of the Mississippi, confined to Iowa, and later moved to Kansas. During the early 1850s, however, a group of about one hundred Mesquakies, fed up with Kansas, returned to Iowa, bought land, and established a community at Tama, which is still in existence. By 1869, another two hundred had joined them.[67] In a sense, a degree of accommodation was restored with the return of these Indians.

After Henry and Susan Gratiot died, their daughter kept in touch with many Winnebagos, according to her husband. "For many years after [her] marriage . . . and up to 1860, many of the surviving members of the tribe would come almost annually to visit her at her home in Galena. . . . Bringing their blankets with them, they would sometimes remain for several days, sleeping on the floor of her parlors."[68] Even in the midst of the mining district, where accommodation lost out during the 1820s, remnants of the personal relationships that persisted in nearby Creole communities could occasionally, briefly, be found.

67. Nancy Oestreich Lurie, *Wisconsin Indians* (Madison, Wis., 1987), 10, 18–20; Lurie, "Winnebago," in William C. Sturtevant, gen. ed., *Handbook of North American Indians*, XV, *Northeast*, ed. Bruce G. Trigger (Washington, D.C., 1978), 700; Kay, "The Land of La Baye," 416–418; William T. Hagan, *The Sac and Fox Indians* (Norman, Okla., 1958), 205–232, 261.

68. Washburne, "Col. Henry Gratiot," State Hist. Soc. of Wis., *Colls.*, X (1888), 258.

JOHN MACK FARAGHER

# "More Motley than Mackinaw"

## From Ethnic Mixing to Ethnic Cleansing on the
## Frontier of the Lower Missouri, 1783–1833

"Our Father: We, a deputation of about 400 of your children of the Shawnee nation, would respectfully lay our situation before you." So began the 1831 memorial of the chiefs of the Black Bob Band of Shawnees to President Andrew Jackson. "For the last forty years we have resided in Upper Louisiana," they wrote (using the old territorial designation for the region that had since become the state of Missouri), "peaceably following our usual occupations for the support of our families." These Shawnees had been among the first of their tribe to leave the Ohio Valley and cross the Mississippi, seeking refuge from the violent conflict between Indians and Americans that wracked the trans-Appalachian West in the last quarter of the eighteenth century. During the ensuing decades, these absentee Shawnees had been reliable and loyal residents of Missouri, but now state and federal authorities were pressing them to exchange their homes and farms for a reservation established for all the Shawnee people on the western plains of Kansas. That place, they wrote, was a "climate colder than we have been accustomed to, or wish to live in," and they would be "surrounded by people strangers to us." No longer did they feel strong connections with their Shawnee brethren from Ohio: "So long a period has elapsed since we separated from them, that there is now but little of a common feeling of blood and friendship existing between us and them." William Clark, superintendent of Indian affairs in Saint Louis, had heard their appeal, they wrote, "but he says that he has not the power to grant our request, and he tells us to apply to you as the only person able to assist us. Our Father: Have pity on us; take our situation into consideration, and send us a favorable answer."[1]

I want to thank Elizabeth Perkins, Jean O'Brien, Peter Wood, Andrew Cayton, Fredrika Teute, Rob Forbes, Stephen A. Aron, and my colleagues in the Yale American Studies Faculty Seminar for their helpful comments on earlier drafts of this essay.

1. Shawnee Chiefs to President Andrew Jackson, Nov. 20, 1831, in U.S. Senate, *Correspondence on Removal of Indians West of Mississippi River, 1831–1833, and Accounts of Dispersing*

The plight of the Black Bob Band was but one of dozens of wrenching cases of dispossession and dislocation that mark the history of Indian removal during the second quarter of the nineteenth century, and it would seem to confirm an important difference in the comparative history of North American frontiers. Colonial societies on the fringe of the French and Spanish North American empires frequently assumed a form that the historical geographer Marvin W. Mikesell calls *"frontiers of inclusion,"* in which strong affiliations developed between native and colonist communities, including a good deal of cultural and social mixing, even intermarriage. The British and subsequently the American empires, however, established *frontiers of exclusion,* confining indigenous peoples to separate and distinct territories and eventually requiring them to remove further west. "All European peoples were selfishly pursuing their own ends in North America," writes Carl J. Ekberg in his history of successive colonial regimes in the community of Sainte Genevieve, Missouri; but "the Anglo-Americans found it expedient to try to eliminate the red man, whereas Frenchmen and Spaniards found it more profitable to tolerate him." [2]

Yet, what is most striking about the bitter removal of the Black Bob Band—as well as the other Indian communities banished during the era of ethnic cleansing that American historians have antiseptically labeled the "Removal Period"—is that it came at the end of a long history of generally good relations in eastern Missouri between American settlers, French-speaking residents known as Creoles, and emigrant Indians. For a generation following the American acquisition of Upper Louisiana, the local commentary on ethnic relations tended to emphasize the benefits of diversity and the positive character of intercommunal connections. It was not until the movement for Indian removal got under way, in the years surrounding Missouri statehood, that this colloquy of inclusion gave way to one of exclusion.

Shawnees, Delawares, and other Algonquian-speaking peoples of the southern Great Lakes region first emigrated to the lower Missouri River country during the 1780s. Anticipating that they would "soon be hemmed in on all Side[s] by the White people, and then be at their mercy," delegations of Ohio Valley

---

*Agents in Five Counties,* 2 vols., 23d Cong., 1st sess., [1835], S. Doc. 512, II, 706. For the political and social context of this letter, see Grant Foreman, *The Last Trek of the Indians* (Chicago, 1946), 54.

2. Marvin W. Mikesell, "Comparative Studies in Frontier History," *Annals of the Association of American Geographers,* L (1960), 62–74; Carl J. Ekberg, *Colonial Ste. Genevieve: An Adventure on the Mississippi Frontier* (Gerald, Mo., 1985), 124.

chiefs came to Saint Louis in 1780 and 1782, the Spanish governor Francisco Cruzat reported, "to beg the protection of our Catholic sovereign, with the intention, as they assured me, of establishing a firm and sincere peace with the Spaniards." The chiefs declared: "The Americans, a great deal more ambitious and numerous than the English, put us out of our lands, forming therein great settlements, extending themselves like a plague of locusts in the territories of the Ohio River. They treat us as their cruelest enemies are treated, so that to-day hunger and the impetuous torrent of war . . . have brought our villages to a struggle with death." Believing it impossible to reach an accommodation with American expansionism, these Indian peoples crossed the Mississippi, in the words of one Shawnee descendant, "because they were weary of warfare with the Americans and wished to settle in a region in which they could live at peace."[3]

Spanish authorities were interested in using emigrant Indian warriors as an armed force for the protection of Upper Louisiana. Still fresh was the memory of the British-led assault of northern Indian warriors on Saint Louis in 1780, during the American Revolution, and the Spanish hoped to shore up the security of their colony by organizing an effective local militia among the Shawnee and Delaware communities. By 1787, some eighteen hundred emigrant Indians, mostly Shawnees and Delawares, had settled in towns along the Mississippi, south of the village of Sainte Genevieve. With them was the Canadian Louis Lorimier, a trader long associated with the Shawnees, who emigrated to Missouri with his métis wife and family after being burned out of his Ohio trading post by the Americans. In 1793, the Spanish granted Lorimier a trading monopoly among the emigrant Indians in exchange for his "bringing as many as possible over to this side, by posting them as conveniently as may be to our settlements, . . . with a view to their rendering us aid in case of war with the whites as well as with the Osages." From his post on the Mississippi—which later grew into the town of Cape Girardeau—Lorimier was able to call into the

3. Richard White, *The Middle Ground: Indians, Empires, and Republics in the Great Lakes Region, 1650–1815* (New York, 1991), 356; Francisco Cruzat to Estevan Miro, Mar. 19, 1782, in Louis Houck, ed., *The Spanish Regime in Missouri: A Collection of Papers and Documents Relating to Upper Louisiana . . .* , 2 vols. (Chicago, 1909), I, 209; Cruzat to Miro, Aug. 23, 1784, quoted in Ekberg, *Colonial Ste. Genevieve,* 93; Lyman Draper interview with Charles Tucker, Shawnee, June 26–27, 1868, in Draper Manuscripts, 23S172–177, microfilm, 1980, State Historical Society of Wisconsin, Madison (hereafter cited as DM). See also Daniel H. Usner, Jr., "An American Indian Gateway: Some Thoughts on the Migration and Settlement of Eastern Indians around Early St. Louis," *Gateway Heritage,* XI (Winter 1990–1991), 47.

field in service for Upper Louisiana at least two hundred armed men from these Indian communities.[4]

The use of emigrant Indians as a colonial militia was a principal feature of Spanish frontier Missouri. It was a pattern that continued well into the American territorial period, with Lorimier continuing to act, until his death in 1812, as intermediary between the territorial government and communities of emigrant Indians. In 1805, on the recommendation of Louisiana's territorial governor James Wilkinson, Lorimier became Indian agent for the Shawnees and Delawares. "This Man is from long habit a savage," Wilkinson condescended, yet "has, I believe, always discharged the trust reposed in Him with Zeal and Integrity." More to the point, Lorimier could "muster 600 men, . . . over whom he holds absolute controul." According to Amos Stoddard, who preceded Wilkinson as chief American officer in Louisiana, the Shawnees and Delawares, counting several hundred warriors among them, were "considered as a safe-guard to the whites." Because "the country about them is too much settled to afford plenty of game," he wrote, "they mostly hunt on the waters of the St. Francis and White river; and sometimes they penetrate into the territories of the Osages, between whom a predatory war has been maintained for many years." Stoddard praised the Shawnees and Delawares whom, he said, had "generally conducted themselves to the satisfaction of the whites." William Clark—in charge of Indian affairs from 1807 and territorial governor of Missouri from 1813 until statehood in 1821—believed these emigrant Indian warriors performed a "great service to our frontier settlements in that quarter, in preventing roberies of the Osage and in bringing in horses which had either Strayed or had been Stolen from the frontiers." Historian Lynn Morrow argues that the Shawnee and Delaware struggle with the Osages "helped make the Missouri Ozarks region a safe place for new settlements."[5]

During the War of 1812, emigrant Indians fought alongside Americans

4. Zenon Trudeau to Louis Lorimier, May 1, 1793, in Houck, ed., *Spanish Regime in Missouri*, II, 50.

5. Governor James Wilkinson to Secretary of War Henry Dearborn, Aug. 10, 1805, Governor William Clark to President James Monroe, in Clarence Edwin Carter and John Porter Bloom, eds., *The Territorial Papers of the United States*, 28 vols. (Washington, D.C., 1934–1975), XIII, 183, XIV, 445–446; Amos Stoddard, *Sketches, Historical and Descriptive, of Louisiana* (Philadelphia, 1812), 215; Lynn Morrow, "Trader William Gilliss and Delaware Migration in Southern Missouri," *Missouri Historical Review*, LXXV (1981), 150. On Lorimier's tenure as Indian agent, see James F. Keefe and Lynn Morrow, eds., *The White River Chronicles of S. C. Turnbo: Man and Wildlife on the Ozarks Frontier* (Fayetteville, Ark., 1994), 265.

against tribes allied with the British. When the Boone's Lick country of central Missouri was under siege by Osages in 1814, Governor Clark "sent out the Showoness and Delaways" to protect the frontiers. The Indians formed a critical component of a three-hundred-man expeditionary force from the eastern Missouri settlements under the command of Henry Dodge, sheriff of the Sainte Genevieve district. Many of these Indians were veterans of bitter battles fought against Americans during the Revolution, but they put those old hatreds aside. As the expedition traveled up the Missouri River, passing the community where the American frontiersman Daniel Boone had retired with his large, extended family, an ancient Shawnee warrior named Pappiqua recounted to Dodge how thirty-five years before "he had aided in capturing Col. Daniel Boone." It was a credible claim. Louis Lorimier himself had accompanied the Shawnee war party that had taken Boone hostage in 1778.[6]

Boone's son Nathan, in charge of the American defense of the lower Missouri country during the war, counted these Shawnee veterans, including those who had participated in the capture of his father, among his most trusted scouts. In the late 1820s, when the army was making plans to organize the first American cavalry company for western duty, Indian agent Benjamin O'Fallon, nephew of William Clark, suggested recruiting emigrant Indians. "When Indians Are equally mixed with White Troops," he advised, the result is "the finest light troops in the world." Cautioning that regular army officers were "too bigoted in their own opinions to learn enough of the Indian character," O'Fallon insisted that such a company needed the leadership of an officer with experience among Indian people. When the army finally created a company of American dragoons to patrol the plains a few years later, Nathan Boone was placed in command. Boone recruited "Shawnee friends," as he called them, to be his scouts and aides.[7]

The acculturation of emigrant Indians to colonial ways seldom failed to impress visitors. The Shawnees of Missouri, wrote Nicolas de Finiels of France

6. Clark to Monroe, Aug. 25, 1814, in Carter and Bloom, eds., *Territorial Papers*, XIV, 786; Draper interview with Henry Dodge, June 29, 1855, DM, 11C81, 15C99[1]; John Mason Peck, *Forty Years of Pioneer Life: Memoir of John Mason Peck D.D.*, ed. Rufus Babcock (Philadelphia, 1864), 138; M. M. Quaife, "Louis Lorimier," *Missouri Historical Review*, XXI (1926–1927), 616–618. For background on Boone and his family, see John Mack Faragher, *Daniel Boone: The Life and Legend of an American Pioneer* (New York, 1992).

7. Benjamin O'Fallon to Willis M. Green, Dec. 8, 1829, in Benjamin O'Fallon Letterbook (transcript copy), 2 vols., Beinecke Library, Yale University, II, 228–229; Nathan Boone's report, 1843, in Louis Pelzer, *Marches of the Dragoons in the Mississippi Valley* (Iowa City, 1917), 230.

during a tour of Upper Louisiana in 1797, are "capable of more civilization than has generally been thought possible for Indians." He found their villages "more systematically and solidly constructed than the usual Indian villages," with fields fenced "in the American style in order to protect their harvests from animals." Five years later, François Perrin Du Lac noted that the residents of the Indian communities near Cape Girardeau were "active, industrious, and good hunters" and that "they breed cows and pigs, and cultivate maize, pumpkins, melons, potatoes, and corn sufficient for their support the whole year." Likewise, American commandant Amos Stoddard approvingly observed: "The houses of all the [Indian] villages are built of logs, some of them squared, and well interlocked at the ends, and covered with shingles. Many of them are two stories high; and attached to them are small houses for the preservation of corn, and barns for the shelter of cattle and horses, with which they are well supplied. Their houses are well furnished with decent and useful furniture."[8]

Not that these Indian people had abandoned their own culture. Finiels shrewdly called attention to what he termed the "mingling" of customs among them, the way, for example, in which the Shawnees would appear "sometimes in European garb and sometimes in the dress of these children of nature," depending on the occasion. Indeed, cultural mingling was a two-way street, with settlers taking up Indian ways as well. "The proximity of the Indians," wrote Finiels, "had no small influence on the character of the colonists." "Breechclout took the place of culottes; leggings replaced stockings; doeskin moccasins succeeded European shoes; a loosefitting tunic covered the rest of the body; a blue kerchief wrapped about the head completed the costume." Recalling a childhood spent in Sainte Genevieve during the 1790s, Henry Brackenridge described how Indian "boys often intermingled with those of the white village, and practiced shooting with the bow and arrow; an accomplishment which I acquired with the rest, together with a little smattering of the Indian language."[9]

This intermingling continued unabated during the first generation of American settlement. The emigrant Indian community known as Rogerstown—first sited west of Saint Louis on the south side of the Missouri River at a place now

8. Nicolas de Finiels, *An Account of Upper Louisiana,* ed. Carl J. Ekberg and William E. Foley (Columbia, Mo., 1989), 34, 35; François Marie Perrin Du Lac, *Travels through the Two Louisianas and among the Savage Nations of the Missouri . . .* (London, 1807), 45; Stoddard, *Sketches,* 215.

9. Finiels, *Account of Upper Louisiana,* 35, 112; H[enry] M. Brackenridge, *Recollections of Persons and Places in the West* (Philadelphia, 1834), 26.

known as Bridgeton, then relocated up the Meramack River valley near the present city of Union—included a few Americans, some Delawares and Miamis, and many Shawnees, a number of whom had known Daniel Boone during the Ohio and Kentucky days. Boone's home was several dozen miles north, across the Missouri River, and family members later remembered the visits of Shawnees to Boone's cabin as well as the old man's trips to Rogerstown to go hunting with Indian friends.[10]

The leader of this community of some forty families was a man named Jimmy Rogers, an American who had been captured as a child and reared, in the words of one settler, to be "a perfect Indian." It was said that, during the long period of warfare with the Americans, Rogers had commanded a marauding party that plundered Ohio River flatboats and murdered their owners. After the Treaty of Greenville in 1795, however, he led his group out of the United States and across the Mississippi to Upper Louisiana. Baptist preacher John Mason Peck, who was a regular visitor at Rogerstown during his missionary travels, testified that Rogers had become a Christian and transformed himself into "a man of strong sense, industrious, generous, and a firm friend to his white neighbors." Several of those neighbors later remembered the people of Rogerstown fondly. James Long described the Indians as "strong and straight, and fine specimens of manhood." "The women were beautiful, and swift on foot." According to Elizabeth Musick, daughter of an American pioneer family who farmed land nearby: "The squaws made baskets and moccasins and sold them to the whites. The Indians were kind." The people of Rogerstown raised subsistence crops and grazed substantial herds of livestock. They were "thrifty farmers," wrote Peck, "and brought the best cattle to the St. Louis market the butchers had received." In 1811, the residents of Rogerstown discovered near their town a lead mine "in sufficient quantity to induce them to work it," and they requested Governor Clark to grant them "a license of Three Miles Square including the Town, with promission to raise and Sell the Lead Ore imediately in and about the Town." Receiving approval from the War Department, the Indians added mining to their list of successful enterprises. Rogerstown grew prosperous, even wealthy, by contemporary pioneer standards.[11]

These emigrant Indians shared subsistence strategies with their American

10. Faragher, *Daniel Boone*, 313–314.

11. Draper interviews with James Long and Elizabeth Musick, May 1868, DM, 24S164–165, 22S168–170; John R. Musick, *Stories of Missouri* (New York, 1897), 31; Peck, *Forty Years*, ed. Babcock, 112; Clark to Monroe, Apr. 10, 1811, Secretary of War William Eustis to Clark, May 31, 1811, in Carter and Bloom, eds., *Territorial Papers*, XIV, 445–446, 452.

neighbors. Each spring, the people of Rogerstown burned the open range, a practice condemned by the investors of the nearby Maramec ironworks, who feared the destruction of their facilities in the annual conflagrations. This was not an exclusively Indian practice, however, for American pioneers in the area also carried out spring burnings in the belief that it improved grazing conditions and held down the populations of snakes, ticks, and chiggers. Henry Brackenridge provided a description of the American homesteads along the Missouri that sounds much like descriptions of Indian farms: "These usually consist of a few acres cleared on the borders of the river, with a small log hut or cabin, and stables for horses, etc. They raise a little Indian corn, pumpions, potatoes, and a few vegetables. But they have abundance of hogs and horned cattle." By outward appearance, there was little to distinguish Daniel Boone's settlement of Femme Osage on the north side of the Missouri from the village of Rogerstown on the south. Both were settled by farming and stock-raising people who loved horses and hunting.[12]

To be sure, not all the inclusive commentary was positive. Although Amos Stoddard praised the military prowess of emigrant Shawnees and Delawares, measured against his ideal of the noble savage he found them "wonderfully degenerated" and particularly prone to problem drinking. "They have gradually imbibed all the vices of the whites," he believed, "and forgotten their own virtues." The historical evidence suggests that alcoholism was indeed a considerable problem for these emigrant Indian communities. The wife of Chief Rogers of Rogerstown told a missionary that "her husband, when sober, was an amiable and good husband, but that when drunk he was terrible, and not at all to be trusted," and Elizabeth Musick recalled that sometimes the communal dances of the Rogerstown folk would degenerate into a "drunken spree," and "a death would occasionally occur." But the evidence documents at least as much alcohol abuse among Americans as among Indians. John Mason Peck complained bitterly of "scenes of drunkenness and profane revelry" among settlers. "One-half, at least, of the Anglo-American population," he believed, "were infidels of a low and indecent grade, and utterly worthless for any useful purposes of society."[13]

---

12. Keefe and Morrow, eds., *White River Chronicles,* 298; H[enry] M. Brackenridge, *Journal of a Voyage up the River Missouri; Performed in Eighteen Hundred and Eleven* (Baltimore, 1816), 17.

13. Stoddard, *Sketches,* 445; Timothy Flint, *Recollections of the Last Ten Years in the Valley of the Mississippi,* ed. George R. Brooks (1826; reprint, Carbondale, Ill., 1968), 108–109; Draper interview with Elizabeth Musick, May 1868, DM, 22S168–170; Peck, *Forty Years,* ed. Babcock, 87.

Indeed, accounts of native vice are matched by others in which Americans suffered in the contrast with emigrant Indians. Traveling through the Missouri country before the War of 1812, Henry Brackenridge was appalled at the indolence of backcountry settlers. At an isolated shack in a cane break, an American "gave us some hogmeat and coarse hominy for supper [and] threw a bearskin on the ground for us," then shocked his guests by admitting that he did not know the name of the president of the United States, and, moreover, didn't give a damn about finding out. Resuming their travels, and coming to a nearby Shawnee town, Brackenridge and his companions put up at the well-built and comfortable house of an emigrant Indian, who offered them fine hominy and venison steak. "He not only knew the name of the president," Brackenridge noted with approval, "but even made particular inquiries respecting our affairs with England and France, and the prospect of peace or war with either!" [14]

Although, for the most part, emigrant Indians and American settlers maintained separate communities, a good deal of intermingling went on between them. With the assistance of missionaries, Chief Rogers organized a community school at Rogerstown, and, because it offered the best educational opportunity in the area, a number of American settlers sent their own children. "The white and Indian boys were at their books in the school house," John Mason Peck wrote, and, echoing Henry Brackenridge's memory of late-eighteenth-century Sainte Genevieve, he recalled how the students of this "half-Indian seminary" would play "bow and arrow and other Indian pasttimes during intermission." Chief Rogers's oldest boy, Lewis, took very well to schooling and so impressed his teachers with his progress that they arranged for his transfer to an academy in Kentucky. Chief Rogers's other son, however, showed no interest in school. "Lewis would speak to the paper," Rogers declared, but "God damn, I think Indian make it Jim, [he] won't go to school." There were also Americans at the school who "made it Indian." Lewis Williams, later a prominent Baptist minister, so mastered the recess lessons of his Indian friends "in hunting and their own dangerous games" that he became a locally renowned rifleman and woodsman. During the War of 1812, when young Williams was serving as a marksman with one of the militia companies, a Shawnee compatriot challenged him to a contest of skill. Williams won the shooting match, to the Shawnee's chagrin. "Pale face, silver hair," he complained, "but Indian inside." [15]

14. Brackenridge, *Recollections*, 236–239.

15. Peck, *Forty Years*, ed. Babcock, 113; Draper interview with James Long, c. 1868, Draper interview with Uel Musick, c. 1868, DM, 24S164–165, 24S190–191; Robert E. Parkin, *Overland Trails and Trials and Your Community Today* (Overland, Mo., [1956]), 6.

Interviewing old settlers in the mid-nineteenth century, the antiquarian collector Lyman Draper accumulated local lore concerning relations between American settlers and the Indian residents of Rogerstown. According to Elizabeth Musick, Chief Rogers promised half a bushel of silver to any white man who would marry his daughter. One settler was said to have taken up the offer, but he soon died, and his place was taken by another. "But neither," Musick said, "got the promised dowry, old Rogers saying he would wait and see if they proved worthy husbands, for it might be that they would desert her if they should get the money." Musick also told a tale of the attempt of the chief's son Lewis Rogers to find himself a white wife. He courted a local girl, but things didn't work out. "Ah," Musick quoted Lewis, the woman "was mighty nice." "She wanted to know when I come again—I tell her, but didn't go then. Me thought me go when she not expecting me. Did so and found her dirty, everything all scattered around, ashes on hearth. Then think it best I'll not marry her, and did not go anymore." Although these tales reveal, perhaps, a strain of resentment about having rich Indians for neighbors, they suggest the intimate connections between the two communities of Indian and American emigrants.[16]

Although most Missouri communities maintained their character as principally American, French, or Indian, there were also multiethnic villages. Charette, a settlement on the north side of the Missouri River about fifty miles from Saint Louis, was founded by French Creoles in the late 1790s, but over the next few years quite a few Americans, including a number of Boone kin, established farms on the river bottom and in the nearby fertile valleys. Gradually the community came to include Indian men and women as well. By the time the United States acquired Louisiana, Charette had become a thoroughly mixed village of backcountry Americans, French-speaking Creoles, emigrant and native Indians, free and enslaved African Americans, and the growing progeny of their various combinations. Boone kinsman Elijah Bryan called Charette "a French and Indian village," but among the early residents he remembered families with Anglo surnames. "I know the names of other Charette village men," Bryan replied to queries from Lyman Draper. "John Manley—had an Indian woman for a wife . . . [and] John Manial was one I could not think of [before]. Had an Osage woman for a wife with four or five children." Charette, where Daniel Boone's daughter Jemima lived with her husband and chil-

16. Draper interview with Elizabeth Musick, May 1868, DM, 22S168–170; Musick, *Stories of Missouri*, 31. For similar stories detailing the continuing positive interactions between Shawnees and American settlers in the Ozarks, see Keefe and Morrow, eds., *White River Chronicles*, 7, 265.

dren, and where old Boone himself was buried, was the site of a great deal of intermingling.[17]

This "syncretic society," as historian William Unrau labels it, characterized the frontier of the lower Missouri Valley during the first two decades of American rule. The inhabitants of the territory, wrote Henry Brackenridge in 1817, "are composed of whites, Indians, metiffs, a few civilized Indians, and negro slaves." It was a population, declared Washington Irving after touring the region in the early 1830s, that was "more motley than Mackinaw," the old Great Lakes trading post. Looking back on the relations between emigrant Indians and settlers many years later, John Musick wrote that "justice was practiced by both races, and the colonists long lived by the side of the Indians in peace." Musick's view might have been softened by the nostalgia he felt for his youth, but he was more right than wrong.[18]

These relatively good interethnic relations were attributable in part to the modest numbers of Americans who moved across the Mississippi during the first decade of the territorial period. The tangle of unresolved French and Spanish land grants in Missouri kept the legal title of private lands in limbo for more than a decade. The federal land commission appointed to settle these claims did not finish its work until 1813, and the War of 1812 further delayed the surveying that federal law required before officials could open Missouri's public domain to legitimate settlement. Indeed, President Thomas Jefferson had initially proposed keeping settlers out altogether, arguing that Missouri could be used exclusively as a reserve for emigrant Indians from the east. Privately he suggested to his aides that all the non-Indians on the west side of the Mississippi be relocated to the Illinois country. This radical notion horrified the president's advisers, and they quickly persuaded him to drop it, but the protection of emigrant Indian communities from the encroachments of squatters remained a priority of the territorial administration. "Exert your utmost vigi-

17. Elijah Bryan to Lyman Draper, Oct. 23, 1884, DM, 4C34. Farther west, in the Ozarks region, this mingling included the use of common cemeteries, and it is likely that this pattern also characterized multiethnic communities such as Charette; see Keefe and Morrow, eds., *White River Chronicles*, 1.

18. William E. Unrau, *Mixed-Bloods and Tribal Dissolution: Charles Curtis and the Quest for Indian Identity* (Lawrence, Ky., 1989), 14; H[enry] M. Brackenridge, *Views of Louisiana; Containing Geographical, Statistical, and Historical Notices of That Vast and Important Portion of America* (Baltimore, 1817), 208; Washington Irving, *Astoria; or, Anecdotes of an Enteprise beyond the Rocky Mountains*, 2 vols. (1836; reprint, Philadelphia, 1961), I, 107–108; Musick, *Stories of Missouri*, 31.

lance in detecting unauthorised settlements the moment they are made or discovered," Jefferson instructed Secretary of War Henry Dearborn in November 1804, and Dearborn passed the president's orders down the chain of command to territorial officers. A year later, Governor Wilkinson wrote Jefferson of his continuing efforts to eliminate the scattered squatter settlements encroaching on Shawnee and Delaware lands between Sainte Genevieve and Cape Girardeau, and, anticipating the removal of even more eastern native peoples to Missouri in conformance with Jefferson's plan, he argued that the "depopulation [of Americans] must precede the transfer of the Indians." Wilkinson argued for harsh measures against the squatters; "it is not by preparing Beds of down, that we are to get rid of unwelcome Guests," he wrote the president.[19]

Unwelcome guests continued to be a problem. John Musick labeled these squatters "branch-water men," the kind who would take their water from a "branch" or creek "in preference to digging a well, because to dig a well would cost him some exertion, and he is an enemy to anything like labor." This "shiftless sort," wrote Musick, invaded the lands of emigrant Indians, established preemption claims, and sold their improvements to ignorant newcomers, who then had to contend with angry Indian neighbors. In 1807, Indian agent Louis Lorimier asked acting governor Joseph Browne to forward to the president a petition signed by leaders of the Shawnee and Delaware communities complaining that "incroachments on their Boundaries remain unchecked." Fearing that "those intrusions, if too long unnoticed, might become actual claims injurious to them, and their silence or inaction should be construed as consent," the chiefs urged Jefferson to "put an end to their state of suspence and uneasiness." Without waiting for presidential instructions, Browne "directed Prosecutions to be immediately commenced against Intruders on the Land claimed by those Indians," and Sheriff Henry Dodge was ordered to remove the squatters, along with their "companions, Followers, Dependents, Servants, or Slaves." It is important to recall here that Sheriff Dodge frequently called upon the Shawnees and Delawares themselves to act as his deputies.[20]

19. D[onald] W. Meinig, *The Shaping of America: A Geographical Perspective on 500 Years of History*, II, *Continental America, 1800–1867* (New Haven, Conn., 1993), 79; President Thomas Jefferson to Dearborn, Nov. 1, 1804, Wilkinson to Jefferson, Nov. 6, 1805, in Carter and Bloom, eds., *Territorial Papers*, XIII, 54, 266.

20. Jefferson to Dearborn, Nov. 1, 1804, Wilkinson to Jefferson, Nov. 6, 1805, in Carter and Bloom, eds., *Territorial Papers*, XIII, 55, 266; Musick, *Stories of Missouri*, 178–180; Lorimier to Acting Governor Joseph Browne, Feb. 19, 1807, Browne to Dearborn, Mar. 23, 1807, Secretary of Louisiana Territory Frederick Bates to Sheriff Henry Dodge, Nov. 5, 1807, in Carter and Bloom, eds., *Territorial Papers*, XIV, 111, 112, 175.

Such federal actions against squatters aroused considerable fear and loath-
ing among newcomer Americans in Missouri. "White people are at liberty to
settle where they please," one newly arrived group angrily insisted to Indian
agent James McFarlane when he attempted to warn them off Indian lands in
1808. Displaying their firearms, they dared him to "let them see who would prevent it." The territorial administration stood up to the challenge. Jefferson instructed Governor Meriwether Lewis to act against squatters, to "prohibit them
rigorously." In 1809, noting "that certain intruders are settling and making improvements at and near Rogers' town," Lewis issued an antisquatter proclamation and ordered it printed in the *Missouri Gazette,* the territory's principal
newspaper. He would not allow "the peace and tranquillity so happily subsist-
ing between the United States and those tribes [to] be thus wantonly interrupted," and he directed "the said intruders on the public lands of the United
States, at towns and places aforesaid, or within five miles or either of the same,
to depart therefrom, at their peril." "And I do also require the sheriffs of the respective districts aforesaid, in the event of this requisition not being punctually
complied with, to return to me the names of said intruders, in order that they
may be proceeded against according to law." Thus, although there were persistent problems of encroachments on the lands of emigrant Indians, they were
countered by vigorous actions by territorial officials to warn squatters off.[21]

The problem of illegal squatting became much harder to handle following
the War of 1812. In the aftermath of the fighting, Americans "came like an avalanche," in the words of missionary John Mason Peck. "It seemed," he wrote,
"as though Kentucky and Tennessee were breaking up and moving to the 'Far
West.'" Population statistics are telling. In 1804, when the United States acquired Louisiana, the Creole, African American, and American population of
the Missouri district totaled about ten thousand and the emigrant Indians
about two thousand more. Population grew slowly over the next decade, reaching a total of just twenty-five thousand by 1814. But over the next six years,
more than forty thousand settlers crossed the Mississippi and took up lands in
the territory. By 1824, the respective settler and emigrant Indian populations
stood at ninety-seven thousand and eight thousand. This process—in which
incoming settlers overwhelm previously established communities—historical
geographer Donald W. Meinig calls the creation of a "minorated society."[22]

21. James McFarlane to Governor Meriwether Lewis, Dec. 11, 1808, Proclamation by Governor Lewis, Apr. 6, 1809, in *Territorial Papers,* XIV, 261, 267–268.
22. Peck, *Forty Years,* ed. Babcock, 146; Hattie M. Anderson, "Missouri, 1804–1828: Peopling a Frontier State," *Missouri Historical Review,* XXXI (1937), 150–180; Meinig, *Continental America,* 172–175.

Only a few months after the war, Shawnees and Delawares complained to Governor Clark that hordes of strangers were taking their lands and appropriating their improvements. Clark laid the problem to the newly arriving Americans who "encroach upon the Indians nearest them" and acknowledged Indian claims for damages "against the citizens of the United States, to a large amount, for spoliations of various kinds, but which they have not been able to support by the testimony of white men." Several contingents of Cape Girardeau Delawares decided to relocate westward, some to the headwaters of the White River in the Ozarks, where Clark set aside a large tract for them, others to the Arkansas Valley, where they joined Cherokee migrants who had founded communities there some years earlier. Most residents of the Indian communities of eastern Missouri, however, refused to give up their lands, continuing to tough it out. French Creole communities fell victim to American squatters as well. Residents of the village of Cardondelet petitioned Congress, complaining that Americans were "intruding daily . . . , destroying the timber which is scarce in most places here, and which once destroyed leaves the land of no value."[23]

In December of 1815, Clark responded to squatter encroachments with a proclamation. "Our government, founded in justice, will effectually extend its protection to the Native inhabitants within its limits," the governor bravely asserted. "I do hereby require that all white persons who have intruded and are settled upon the Lands of the Indians within this territory depart therefrom without delay—Should they neglect this last and peaceful warning the military power will be called upon to compel their removal." Clark's proclamation echoed the one issued six years before by his late comrade Meriwether Lewis.[24]

But political conditions in Missouri had changed fundamentally during the war. An elected House of Representatives, created in 1812 when Congress advanced Missouri to territorial status of the "second grade," was dominated by

23. Foreman, *Last Trek of the Indians,* 34–35, 54; C. A. Weslager, *The Delaware Indians: A History* (New Brunswick, N.J., 1972), 353, 371–372, 410; Clark to John C. Calhoun, Sept. 5, 1823, quoted in Foreman, *Last Trek of the Indians,* 48–49; William Clark, "Treaty with the Shawnees," Nov. 7, 1825, in United States Congress, *American State Papers: Documents, Legislative and Executive, of the Congress of the United States . . . ,* 38 vols. (Washington, D.C., 1832–1861), Class II, *Indian Affairs,* 2 vols., ed. Walter Lowrie et al., II, 591 (hereafter cited as *American State Papers, Indian Affairs*); Petition of the Inhabitants of Cardondelet, Oct. 30, 1818, in Carter and Bloom, eds., *Territorial Papers,* XV, 451.

24. Proclamation of Governor William Clark, Dec. 4, 1815, in Carter and Bloom, eds., *Territorial Papers,* XV, 191–192.

newcomer delegates, and they balked at Clark's invocation of traditional policy. In January 1816, the legislators protested that the "Tract Claimed by those Indians includes a Considerable portion of the richest and most fertile part" of Missouri and that the Indian communities were "entirely Surrounded with flourishing Settlements of White people." Explicitly rejecting Clark's proclamation, the assembly passed a resolution urging Congress to resolve the problem "by giving those Indians lands some where Else in the unsettled parts of the Territory." Indian removal, they argued, "would much contribute to the population of that part of the Country and secure tranquillity to the neighboring Inhabitants."[25]

In the face of this challenge to federal territorial policy, officials in Washington remained adamant. "The President expects the most prompt and perfect execution of the proclamation," Secretary of War William H. Crawford instructed Governor Clark. "Orders have been issued to the military commanders to furnish the necessary aid, where it shall be required." It was one thing, however, to order the eviction of squatters, quite another to succeed in having the orders carried out. Lacking federal marshals or troops, Clark had to rely on the state militia, whose ranks were filled with newly arrived American emigrants. "It is my opinion, justified by the statements of many," wrote Alexander McNair, registrar of the federal Land Office in Saint Louis, "that five Militiamen of this Territory would not march against the intruders on public lands." Although there is no discussion of the composition of the Missouri militia in the years after the War of 1812, it seems clear that with the arrival of hundreds of new American settlers authorities had discontinued calling upon emigrant Shawnees and Delawares for service. Meanwhile, the territorial assembly renewed their demand for the removal of Indians to "some more remote part of the Territory which is better adapted to Indian persuits." In 1818, after two years of this stalemate, and with squatters continuing to invade Indian lands, Secretary of War John C. Calhoun finally instructed Clark to open negotiations with the Shawnees and Delawares on the possibility of removal.[26]

By 1820, Clark had reached an agreement with a substantial number of emigrant Indians, who took this opportunity to exchange their Mississippi River lands for tracts on the Arkansas River. "The Land proposed to be received in exchange is not of an equal quality by a great difference," Missouri's territorial

25. Resolution of the Missouri Territorial Assembly, Jan. 1, 1816, ibid., XV, 105–107.

26. Secretary of War William H. Crawford to Clark, Feb. 5, 1816, Registrar Alexander McNair to Commissioner Josiah Meigs, Jan. 27, 1816, Memorial of the Territorial Assembly of Missouri, Jan. 24, 1817, Calhoun to Clark, May 8, 1818, all ibid., XV, 111–112, 113, 234–235, 390.

delegate to Congress, John Scott, wrote candidly to Secretary Calhoun. "The Land which those Indians now inhabit is Very Valuable—The Soil is excellent —it is in the middle of the Settlements and fronting on the Mississippi—Those Indians have their Houses, Towns, and farms thereon—Their Animals are domesticated to the place—and all their property there." In conclusion, Scott wrote, "I really think the Bargain to U States a good one."[27]

The controversy over Missouri's admission to the Union as a slave state had important implications for emigrant Indians. In 1818, the territorial legislature adopted a memorial praying for Missouri statehood, but, when the enabling legislation came to the floor of Congress early in 1819, it was defeated by antislavery members of the House of Representatives, setting off two years of debate over the western extension of slavery that seemed to threaten the foundations of the Union. Finally, in 1821, Congress agreed to the famous Missouri Compromise, pairing the admission of slave Missouri with free Maine and agreeing thereafter to the prohibition of slavery in all territory of the Louisiana Purchase north of parallel 36°30′. The ideological and practical issues at stake for Missourians in this struggle worked against the interests of emigrant Indians.

The principal spokesman for the proslavery party in Missouri, Thomas Hart Benton, editor of the Saint Louis *Enquirer,* framed the conflict as a struggle over sovereignty. Missourians, he declared in 1819, were "the first to whose lot it had fallen to make a fair and regular stand against the encroachment of Congress upon the Sovereignty of the States." Benton even took the radical stand that, had the territory's petition for statehood been denied a second time, its residents would have been justified in forming a republic of their own. Such a zealous defense of sovereignty continued after the achievement of statehood, for, although the conflict might have been resolved in Congress through compromise, there was no hint of compromise in the attitude of the state's leaders, who saw threats to their prerogatives at every turn. Quickly the new state government embarked on a concerted campaign to eliminate any trace of competing sovereignty that inhered in the emigrant Indian communities, which technically remained part of "Indian Country"—territory overseen by federal officials of the Indian Office and outside the state's jurisdiction. "I would beg leave to draw your attention to the views of the State of Missouri," Indian agent Richard Graham wrote to Secretary Calhoun in late 1821. "She will evidently urge the extinguishing of the Indian title as far as the western boundary line."

27. John Scott to Calhoun, Sept. 21, 1820, ibid., XV, 646.

Graham predicted trouble, for "those Indians who are some little advanced in civilization, may have farms that they would be unwilling to relinquish."[28]

Benton, who had been elected one of Missouri's first two senators, understood full well the practical dimensions of this land grab. "Extending the area of slavery," he wrote in his memoirs, required "converting Indian soil into slave soil." In Missouri, as in all the western states, the principal way to wealth was through speculation in land. Settlement created a demand for land and thus increased its value, and in Missouri that process was being driven by emigrants from the slave states, many thousands of them accompanied by slaves of their own. As Floyd Calvin Shoemaker, historian of the Missouri statehood struggle, has argued, "the business man, the surveyor, the politician, believed that his business was bound up with more southern settlers and more slaves." Benton put it starkly: "To remove the Indians would make room for the spread of slaves."[29]

As Jefferson's earlier ideas about Indian removal suggest, there had long been sympathy in Washington for Indian removal. But now the territory that Jefferson had proposed as a refuge for emigrant Indians was itself to be cleansed of them. In 1817 and 1820, prompted by pleas from the state of Georgia as well as the territory of Missouri, President James Monroe recommended plans for voluntary Indian removal, but these proposals failed to muster sufficient support in Congress. Prodded by Senator Benton, Monroe reintroduced the plan in 1824. It would promote "the security and happiness of the tribes within our limits," he argued in an official message to Congress. "Surrounded as they are, and pressed as they will be on every side by the white population, it will be difficult if not impossible for them, with their kind of government, to sustain order among them[selves]." Monroe also made it clear, however, that Indians could not be forcibly removed from their lands, a founding principle of Indian affairs enunciated first in the promise of the Northwest Ordinance of 1787 (Indian "land and property shall never be taken from them without their consent") and reiterated by every president since Washington. "It is the duty of the United States," Monroe concluded, not "to

28. Floyd Calvin Shoemaker, *Missouri's Struggle for Statehood, 1804–1821* (Jefferson City, Mo., 1916), 84–86; Richard Graham to Calhoun, Nov. 11, 1821, Richard Graham Papers, Missouri Historical Society, Saint Louis. The Indian Office (later called the Bureau of Indian Affairs) was part of the Department of War until 1849, when it was transferred to the newly created Department of the Interior.

29. Thomas Hart Benton, *Thirty Years' View; or, A History of the Working of the American Government for Thirty Years, from 1820 to 1850*, 2 vols. (New York, 1854), I, 28, 626; Shoemaker, *Missouri's Struggle for Statehood*, 134.

commit any breach of right or of humanity, in regard to the Indians, repugnant to the judgment and revolting to the feelings of the whole American people." [30]

The lofty rhetoric, however, only served to underline the contradiction embedded in Monroe's text, the kind of self-serving conundrum that consistently tore at the seams of American Indian policy. The American people, he offered, would revolt at the thought of forced Indian removal; yet, he also admitted, they would continue to surround and press against the lands and resources of Indian communities. At precisely the point where his analysis called for genuine moral leadership, the president fell silent. Of course Monroe was not alone in seeking to avoid a confrontation with this American Janus. The contradiction was left for Indians to resolve by deciding themselves upon voluntary removal for their own "security and happiness." It was clear from what Monroe *didn't say* that the federal government had resolved to turn a blind eye to the efforts of states like Missouri to use squatters as a club to beat emigrant Indians into submission.

This was not a policy enunciated by a vote of the Missouri legislature or a decree of its governor. It is observable only in the breach. With impunity the state allowed squatters to steal Indian farms and appropriate their improvements. The contrast with the actions of the territorial administration under the leadership of governors Lewis and Clark is palpable. An incident at Rogerstown, preserved in the papers of Indian agent Richard Graham, offers such evidence. A Shawnee farmer named Petatwa, known to Americans as Shotpouch, complained to subagent Pierre Menard that a squatter by the name of William Fulbright had stolen his farm. "He has been four years in possession of a plantation on Courtois fork on the Maramek about twenty five miles from Rogerstown," Menard recorded in Petatwa's deposition. "He was ordered off by Fulbright, aleging that he had not [the] wright to Staic. . . . This Fulbright ordered him off from his place and took possession of it, on wich was a good Cabin and fifteen hundred rails," which Petatwa had just finished splitting, making ready to fence his fields. As the Shawnee owner retreated from his property, the squatter Fulbright shouted that he owed him nothing for these improvements, that the farm "was on government land," by which he meant it was free for the taking from the public domain. Some time later, Petatwa told Menard, he returned to his farm but was severely beaten by another squatter, one John Scaggs, who "maltreated him by violently knocking him over the

---

30. James Monroe, "Extinguishment of Indian Title to Lands in Georgia," Apr. 2, 1824, in *American State Papers, Indian Affairs*, II, 460 (punctuation edited slightly for clarity).

head with a rifle and otherwise beating him." "Scaggs broke his ribs and cut him across the head twice with a Tomahawk after which he tied him by both arms."[31]

Menard attempted to use state offices to redress this clear injustice. That would be difficult to accomplish, for by state law Indians could not testify in court. "If you take this man's property," he wrote to Fulbright, "I will be forced to prosecute you according to law." "If you want his field, buy it of him, and pay him the worth of it. You would not like to pay your Self for a House Stolen by another white man from the Indians." Menard's colleague, Indian agent Richard Graham, wrote to state prosecutors that a number of American witnesses had come forward and were willing to testify against Fulbright. Indeed, it was a neighboring American farmer who had rescued Petatwa from his imprisonment at the hands of Scaggs. Meanwhile, Petatwa's brother, a man known as Little Captain, had also been assaulted. Justice of the Peace Lovel Thompson wrote Graham that "one white man by the [name] of John Martin have taken A gun of Little Captain by force with the pretence that he owed him." The American abused Little Captain's wife and squatted on his farm. "I will att[est] all I can for the Ind[ian]," Thompson promised.[32]

Thus, a number of American neighbors supported the Rogerstown Indians in their attempt to preserve their lands. Yet, despite the letters written on Petatwa's behalf by Menard, Thompson, and Graham, the state obstructed the prosecution with technicalities and delayed initiating proceedings until the statute of limitations had run out. The people of Rogerstown, and indeed all the emigrant Indians of eastern Missouri, were left legally defenseless. The fundamental problem was not simply the illegal action of squatters against Indians but the action—or rather the *inaction*—of the state itself. Petatwa's testimony shrewdly suggested this. Asked by Menard to provide the date of Scaggs's attack, the Shawnee farmer remembered that it had taken place on "the day on which the first election for Governor of the State of Missouri was held." The state, he seemed to be saying, was responsible.[33]

There were Americans in Missouri who considered removal unfair and un-

31. Deposition of Petatwa or Shotpouch, c. 1821, Pierre Menard to Paul Bright, Aug. 7, 1822, Deposition of Petatwa, c. 1826, Graham Papers.

32. Menard to William Fulbright, Sept. 10, 1821, Lovel Thompson to Graham, Dec. 19, 1823, Deposition of Petatwa or Shotpouch, c. 1826, ibid. Menard became the subagent for the Shawnees, Delawares, and Cherokees west of the Mississippi in 1813, after the death of Louis Lorimier; see Keefe and Morrow, eds., *White River Chronicles*, 265.

33. Graham to Col. Rufus Easton, Sept. 18, 1823, Easton to Graham, Sept. 30, 1823, Deposition of Petatwa or Shotpouch, c. 1826, Graham Papers.

wise. "How mistaken (it seems to me) is the policy of our Government in proposing to remove any more Indians to this already impoverished country," Benjamin O'Fallon wrote from Council Bluffs. "Its present inhabitants can scarcely keep soul and body together. Their Tomehawks and sculping knives are already quarreling for something to eat." To Missouri officials, however, the issue at stake was sovereignty. "To the State," declared the Missouri assembly in a memorial to the federal government in 1824, "the existence of separate communities within its bosom, and independent of its laws, is a palpable evil, an anomaly in government, and direct inconsistency with the policy and jurisdiction of a sovereign State." This document concluded with an ominous threat that suggests the forces at work in Indian removal. The emigrant Indians "are fully sensible of the disadvantages of their present position," read the memorial.

> They have suffered too much from the contact and pressure of a white population not to know its effect. They are too few in number to oppose any resistance to the moral and physical causes which must operate to their degradation, and to the further diminution of their numbers. They must know that their present position is temporary; that an effort to remove them is incessantly made; that *the power of the State is against them;* and that, sooner or later, they must go.

The refusal of the state of Missouri to protect Indians in the face of squatter violence was the brutal stick of American policy.[34]

It remained for the federal government to offer the carrot. Secretary of War Calhoun directed Clark—now serving as superintendent of Indian affairs of the Western District—to expedite removal with liberal applications of annuities and rations. In 1825, the whipsaw of squatter violence and federal inducement finally persuaded delegations of emigrant Indians to sign treaties ceding their lands in Missouri in exchange for tracts on the Kansas River. The exodus of Shawnee and Delaware families that took place the next year was the first of hundreds of deportations during the era of Indian removal. "The treaties of 1825 were the beginning of the system of total removal," Benton proudly wrote. "It was a beginning which assured the success of the whole plan, and was followed up . . . until the entire system was accomplished." Indian removal in Missouri, in other words, was the necessary prelude to the violent removals of

34. O'Fallon to Clark, May 9, 1825, O'Fallon Letterbook; General Assembly of the State of Missouri, "Proposition to Extinguish Indian Title to Lands in Missouri," May 14, 1824, in *American State Papers, Indian Affairs,* II, 512 (emphasis added).

the Creeks, the Cherokees, the Seminoles, and dozens of other Indian peoples over subsequent decades.[35]

Yet, even in the face of violence, many Indians remained in eastern Missouri, refusing to give up the struggle to maintain their communities. In 1829, another round of treaties paved the way for the removal of several more communities, but it was not until 1833, when President Jackson denied the petition of the Black Bob Band, that the last remnant of the emigrant Indians left the eastern part of the state, heading either for isolated valleys in the Ozarks or the reservations in Kansas.

Among the casualties of Indian removal in Missouri was the inclusive colloquy that had characterized most of the commentary on interethnic relations during the territorial period. In its memorial of 1824, the Missouri legislators offered an exclusionist reading of the state's history:

> The experience of centuries has shown that Indian tribes, placed in small masses, in the midst of a white population, are constantly exposed to the influence of causes which operate to the degradation of their character, and to the diminution of their numbers. The contact of two races of people, differing in language and character, and each retaining a recollection of former wars and massacres, gives rise to collisions, both of persons and property, in which the weaker party are most usually the sufferers, both in the first wrong, and in the final punishment.

There was in this memorial no acknowledgment of the contribution of Indian warriors to the military history of territorial Missouri, no recognition of the participation of Indian cattlemen and farmers in the early markets of Saint Louis, nothing of the years of good relations between different ethnic communities, not even a hint that for forty years Indians and Americans had been intermingling and mixing in Missouri. As emigrant Indians moved west, leaving their lands to new settlers ignorant of Missouri's history, an exclusionist reading of the past took hold.[36]

No one did more to disseminate this interpretation than Timothy Flint, whose memoir of the decade he spent as a missionary in Missouri from 1815 to 1825, *Recollections of the Last Ten Years*, was one of the most influential books

35. Foreman, *Last Trek of the Indians*, 34–35, 51–52, 54; Weslager, *Delaware Indians*, 430–433; Benton, *Thirty Years' View*, 29.

36. "Proposition to Extinguish Indian Title," in *American State Papers, Indian Affairs*, II, 512.

on the West in antebellum America. One of the persistent themes of Flint's narrative was his denunciation of "amalgamation." Describing a visit to the cabin of a Creole and his Indian wife, for example, Flint warned his readers that "no words can reach the description of the filthiness and apparent misery of this wretched place." "For supper the husband had a terrapin, the squaw an opossum, and we had biscuit and uncooked mackerel, which we carried with us." Despite Flint's disgust with this domestic scene, "the man persisted in declaring himself happy in his condition and in his wife," which the missionary took to be a confirmation of his savagery. In the métis children of these intermarriages, Flint wrote, "the lank hair, the Indian countenance and manners predominate." Like the authors of the Missouri memorial, Flint took a racial rather than a cultural view of intermingling. "It is a singular fact that the Indian feature descends much farther in these intermixtures, and is much slower to be amalgamated with that of the whites than that of the negro." Between the French Creoles and the Indians, he wrote, there seemed to be a "natural affinity," but American settlers would have nothing to do with mingling and mixing. "The antipathy between the two races seems fixed and unalterable. Peace there often is between them when they are cast in the same vicinity, but any affectionate intercourse, never." Flint had to admit that "monstrous exceptions sometimes occur" to this rule of antipathy, but "even the French themselves regard it as a matter of astonishment." Indeed, from his perspective the whole interethnic history of territorial Missouri must have seemed a "monstrous exception." Flint went on to become, in the scholarly assessment of James K. Folsom, "one of the most influential western men of letters of the first half of the nineteenth century." In his many popular works on western topics, Flint read his racial exclusionism back onto the American frontier experience.[37]

This exclusionist reading of the frontier past had become commonplace by the time Francis Parkman published the first volume of his epic "history of the American forest," *The Conspiracy of Pontiac,* in 1851. "The French showed a tendency to amalgamate with the forest tribes," he wrote; but "the borders of the English colonies displayed no such phenomena of mingling races. . . . Scorn on the one side and hatred on the other still marked the intercourse of the hostile races." For Parkman, there were not even any monstrous exceptions to this rule. "With the settlers of the frontier it was much the same. Rude, fierce and contemptuous, they daily encroached upon the hunting-ground of

37. Flint, *Recollections of the Last Ten Years,* 96–97, 119–120; Howard R. Lamar, ed., *The Reader's Encyclopedia of the American West* (New York, 1977), 380.

the Indians, and then paid them for the injury with curses and threats. Thus the native population shrank back from before the English, as from an advancing pestilence." The rhetoric of exclusion had reached high tide, and no margin remained for a history of mingling in places like territorial Missouri. By the 1850s, memories of ethnic cooperation in early Missouri were all but forgotten. Taking their place was a cant of exclusion that suppressed the history of peaceful and stable relations between communities that is such an important part of our usable past.[38]

38. Francis Parkman, *The Conspiracy of Pontiac and the Indian War after the Conquest of Canada*, 2 vols. (1851; reprint, Boston, 1888), I, 77–80.

# Remembering American Frontiers
## King Philip's War and the American Imagination

South of the Kickamuit River, on the shore of Mount Hope Bay in Bristol, Rhode Island, a large, graywacke rock sits at the tide line. Its surface is low and flat and worn and scarred and, much of the time, underwater. But when the tide is low and the sun is high, the rock's surface reveals the shallow, faded marks of an inscrutable inscription: vague outlines of a boat above a row of mysterious, narrowly carved characters. In 1845, a Bristol historian proposed that the inscription had been made by Norsemen in the eleventh century, and, even though he recanted his attribution in decades to come, when the American infatuation with Viking visitors began to wane, the rock soon became widely known as "Northmen's Rock." In 1919, the Rhode Island Historical Society even held a ceremony to christen it with corn, wine, and oil, taking the occasion to rename it "Lief's Rock," an act that so galled Brown University psychology professor and inscribed-rock enthusiast Edmund Delabarre that he set about to disprove the theory of the inscription's Norse origins.[1]

Delabarre began by pointing out that the inscription had not been observed or described before about 1835 and, as he claimed, there is no reason to believe it was made much before then; the ancient appearance of its characters was due to their shallowness when first carved rather than to centuries of erosion. The theory of the inscription's Norse origins, Delabarre concluded, was an elaborate myth, built upon the equally mythical, unsound, and improbable assertion that Vikings visited southern New England in 1007. In place of the Norse myth, Delabarre offered a new theory, one that, on the surface of things, seems even more improbable and wildly fanciful than its predecessor. Delabarre proposed the inscription's characters belonged, not to the ancient runic alphabet, but to the Cherokee syllabary. Not only that, but the inscription could be read. According to Delabarre's reconstruction, when the row of char-

1. Edmund B. Delabarre, "The Inscribed Rocks of Narragansett Bay," Rhode Island Historical Society, *Collections*, XIII (Providence, R.I., 1920), 1–28.

FIGURE 1

The Mount Hope Rock, Bristol, R.I. *Photograph by Jill Lepore*

acters is correlated with Cherokee syllabic symbols it produces a combination of sounds that is pure nonsense. But if it is taken to be a Cherokee transcription of spoken Algonquian in the Wampanoag dialect and then translated into English, it reads: "Metacomet, Great Sachem." And Metacom is the Wampanoag name for King Philip, who, in 1675 and 1676, led a loose confederation of southern New England Algonquians in an effort to oust the English settlers, a conflict that later became known as "King Philip's War" or, more recently, "Metacom's Rebellion."[2]

The inscription, then, had to have been made after 1821, when the Cherokee syllabary was invented, but before 1835, when the curious rock was first no-

2. Ibid., 9–21. On King Philip's War, see Douglas Edward Leach, *Flintlock and Tomahawk: New England in King Philip's War* (New York, 1958). What to call the war, and what to call Philip, has been the subject of considerable controversy. For a full discussion of this controversy, and of my reasons to stick with "Philip" and "King Philip's War," see Jill Lepore, *The Name of War: King Philip's War and the Origins of American Identity* (New York, 1998), xv–xxi.

FIGURE 2

Inscription on Mount Hope Rock, Bristol, Rhode Island. *Photograph by John R. Hess,*
*1919. Courtesy, Harvard College Library, Cambridge, Mass.*

ticed. Among his conjectural explanations, Delabarre suggested that the inscription might have been carved in 1833, when a group of Penobscot Indians
from Maine visited southern New England. Many Wampanoags had joined
the Penobscots and other neighboring tribes at the end of King Philip's War,
and, as they would do in later years, they might well have made a pilgrimage to
Mount Hope, Philip's former home, in 1833. There, Delabarre proposed, one
of them made the inscription on the rock, memorializing Philip as "Metacomet, Great Sachem." How they knew the syllabary and why they carved in
Cherokee are questions Delabarre left unanswered.[3]

3. Delabarre, "Inscribed Rocks," Rhode Island Hist. Soc., *Colls.,* XIII (1920), 22–24. On
the Cherokee syllabary, see Willard Walker and James Sarbaugh, "The Early History of the
Cherokee Syllabary," *Ethnohistory,* XL (1993), 70–94. I have attempted to corroborate Delabarre's theory with anthropologists and linguists but can offer no conclusion. Since characters carved in rock are necessarily crude and often distorted (and those on this rock are
vastly eroded), it is unlikely that anyone will ever be able to actually *disprove* Delabarre's at-

|  | 1 | 2,3 | 4 | 5 | 6 | 7 | 8 | 9 |  |
|---|---|---|---|---|---|---|---|---|---|
| 1. Miller | | | | | | | | | |
| 2. Munro | | | | | | | | | |
| 3. Bacon | | | | | | | | | |
| 4. Chapin | | | | | | | | | |
| 5. Delabarre | | | | | | | | | |
| 6. Cherokee | | | | | | | | | |
| 7. Photograph | | | | | | | | | |
| 8. Warren | | | | | | | | | |
| 9. New Jersey | | | | | | | | | |
| 10. Tennessee | | | | | | | | | |

FIGURE 3

Chart of Recordings of the Inscription on Mount Hope Rock, Bristol, Rhode Island. *Lines 1–4 are the transcriptions of observers before Edmund Delabarre; line 7 is from John R. Hess's 1919 photograph. Courtesy, Harvard College Library, Cambridge, Mass.*

Whether Edmund Delabarre's theory about the inscription on Mount Hope Rock is poppycock or genius, it nevertheless introduces a pivotal pair of themes in early American history—the significance of the frontier and of its myths. In 1893, Frederick Jackson Turner famously argued that "one frontier served as a guide for the next," and, in 1973, Richard Slotkin claimed that stories about the frontier are "the foundation stones of the mythology that informs our history."[4] In other words, new frontiers are always understood in relation to old frontiers. This essay will argue that, in the early nineteenth century (at the very time when the inscription on Mount Hope Rock was made), no frontier experience was more mythologized than what happened in

---

tribution, which remains plausible even though some of his analysis of Cherokee syllabic forms seems somewhat dubious (Willard Walker, personal communication, Dec. 4, 1994). It is also possible that the inscription on the rock was actually "some sort of nineteenth-century antiquarian joke or hoax" (Ann McMullen, personal communication, July 22, 1992).

4. Frederick Jackson Turner, *The Frontier in American History* (New York, 1920), 9; Richard Slotkin, *Regeneration through Violence: The Mythology of the American Frontier, 1600–1860* (Middletown, Conn., 1973), 4.

New England in 1675 and 1676. Even as America's borders swelled toward the Mississippi and beyond, many Americans' ideas about the frontier lagged far behind, dwelling, most of all, on romantic retellings of the story of a man named Philip and of the war that bears his name.

Myths have consequences, and, in the 1820s and 1830s, myths about King Philip's War helped shape Americans' ideas about the dominant Indian policy of their day: Indian removal. The plan, endorsed by Andrew Jackson in 1829, proposed to relocate large numbers of Southeastern Indians—Cherokees, Choctaws, Chickasaws, Creeks, and Seminoles—to lands west of the Mississippi, by force if necessary. Such a move would at once clear eastern tribal lands for white settlers and rid southern states—Georgia, Alabama, Louisiana, Mississippi, Florida, and Jackson's home state, Tennessee—of their pernicious "Indian problems," illicit trading, violent skirmishes, and fraudulent land sales. In the 1830s, Jackson's Indian removal policy would divide the nation, its Congress, and its highest court. It would also bring untold misery to thousands of native peoples. Most infamously, the Trail of Tears would claim the lives of one of four Cherokees marching from Georgia to Oklahoma in 1838. Disease, malnutrition, and exposure would cut the population of other tribes in half.[5]

Yet, at the very same time white Americans began supporting the removal of Indians to a more western frontier, they came to define themselves in relation to an imagined Indian past in a now-vanished (and vanquished) eastern frontier. The imagined past made the present-day policy possible: as the historian Brian W. Dippie has astutely argued, "the belief in the Vanishing Indian was the ultimate cause of the Indian's vanishing."[6] Few historians, however, have investigated how not only whites but Indians understood new frontiers in relation to old ones; they, too, made policy from myth. In New England, Penobscots and Wampanoags turned mythical tales of King Philip's War to their own

5. Notable works on Indian removal include Ronald N. Satz, *American Indian Policy in the Jacksonian Era* (Lincoln, Nebr., 1975); William G. McLoughlin, *Cherokee Renascence in the New Republic* (Princeton, N.J., 1986); Michael Paul Rogin, *Fathers and Children: Andrew Jackson and the Subjugation of the American Indian* (New York, 1975); Francis Paul Prucha, *American Indian Policy in the Formative Years* (Cambridge, Mass., 1962); and Reginald Horsman, *The Origins of Indian Removal: 1815–1824* (East Lansing, Mich., 1970).

6. Brian W. Dippie, *The Vanishing American: White Attitudes and U.S. Indian Policy* (Middletown, Conn., 1982), 71. Or, as Robert F. Berkhofer, Jr., has argued, "No matter how inapplicable in this case, traditional Indian imagery rationalized the needs of the United States in the continued push of Native Americans from lands desired by Whites" (Berkhofer, *The White Man's Indian: Images of the American Indian from Columbus to the Present* [New York, 1978], 160).

advantage, negotiating the tangled logic of the noble savage and adapting the rhetoric of Indian removal to hold on to their own tribal lands. What makes the connection between King Philip's War and Indian removal so startling is that it was made by whites and Indians alike: both linked myths and memories of a seventeenth-century Indian war to the brutalities of a nineteenth-century Indian policy. And, intriguingly, the connection itself may contain the answer to an otherwise bewildering mystery: an inscrutable inscription on a large, graywacke rock on the sandy shores of Mount Hope Bay.

What Edmund Delabarre did not know when he devised his Cherokee theory about Mount Hope Rock is that the Penobscots and former Wampanoags who visited southern New England in 1833 had other memorial activities on their itinerary. On November 6, they spent the evening at the Tremont Street Theater in Boston, attending a performance of *Metamora; or, The Last of the Wampanoags,* a wildly popular play that told the story of King Philip's War with Philip (here known as "Metamora") at center stage. The Penobscots, who had been invited to attend, arrived noticeably late. The *Boston Morning Post* reported, "It was thought that when their box remained so long empty they did not intend coming: and the motives attributed to their absence was that their presence might have some bias on the present difficulties between Alabama and the Government!"[7] That a group of Penobscots attending a play about King Philip's War in Boston could be expected to affect Alabama's negotiations with the federal government regarding Indian removal suggests just how profound a connection existed between the play and the policy—a connection that had been there from the beginning. *Metamora* had debuted in New York on December 15, 1829, just a week after the newly elected president Andrew Jackson delivered his first annual address, announcing his intention to vigorously pursue Indian removal. Admittedly, presidents before Jackson had advocated Indian removal, just as plays about Indians had been performed before *Metamora*. But *Metamora*'s debut and Jackson's address, separated by seven short days in December 1829, intensified and accelerated two developments: the popularity of plays about past frontiers and the removal of Indians from pres-

7. John Augustus Stone, *Metamora; or, The Last of the Wampanoags: An Indian Tragedy in Five Acts as Played by Edwin Forrest,* in Eugene R. Page, ed., *Metamora and Other Plays* (Princeton, N.J., 1941), 40; *Boston Morning Post,* Nov. 8, 1833. This account is briefly discussed in Rosemarie K. Bank, "Staging the 'Native': Making History in American Theatre Culture, 1828–1838," *Theatre Journal,* XLV (1993), 481.

ent ones.[8] If there is more to the matter than mere coincidence, it can best be discovered by investigating the history of both.

*Metamora* was most famously performed by Edwin Forrest, far and away the most celebrated American actor of the nineteenth-century stage. Forrest had himself commissioned the play, and the title role had been designed to exploit his unique acting talents. In 1828, in the spirit of cultivating native American literature dealing with distinctly American themes, Edwin Forrest offered five hundred dollars for "the best tragedy, in five acts, of which the hero, or principal character, shall be an aboriginal of this country." The Committee of Award, headed by William Cullen Bryant, selected a script written by John Augustus Stone, a playwright and actor originally from Concord, Massachusetts. At the close of the debut performance in New York, a poetic epilogue lauded Stone, this "native bard," who, along with Forrest, "a native actor too, / Have drawn a native picture to your view."[9]

8. Andrew Jackson to the Speaker of the House, Dec. 15, 1829, in James D. Richardson, ed., *A Compilation of the Messages and Papers of the Presidents*, III (New York, 1897), 1026. Indian plays had been written and performed in America since the late seventeenth century but only became widely popular in the 1830s and 1840s. *Metamora* is often considered the catalyst for this development, since it led to copycat plays "from which," as Laurence Hutton put it, "theatergoers throughout the country suffered between the years 1830 and 1840" (Hutton, *Curiosities of the American Stage* [New York, 1891], 13). On Indian drama, see Bank, "Staging the 'Native,'" *Theatre Journal*, XLV (1993), 461–486; Marilyn J. Anderson, "The Image of the Indian in American Drama during the Jacksonian Era, 1829–1845," *Journal of American Culture*, I (1978), 800–810; Don B. Wilmeth, "Noble or Ruthless Savage? The American Indian on Stage and in the Drama," *Journal of American Drama and Theater*, I (1989), 39–78; Richard E. Amacher, "Behind the Curtain with the Noble Savage: Stage Management of Indian Plays, 1825–1860," *Theatre Survey*, VII (1966), 101–114; Richard Moody, *America Takes the Stage: Romanticism in American Drama and Theatre, 1750–1900* (Bloomington, Ind., 1955), 78–109; Eugene H. Jones, *Native Americans as Shown on the Stage, 1753–1916* (Metuchen, N.J., 1988). On *Metamora* and Indian removal, see B. Donald Grose, "Edwin Forrest, *Metamora*, and the Indian Removal Act of 1830," *Theatre Journal*, XXXVII (1985), 181–191; and Jeffrey D. Mason, "The Politics of *Metamora*," in Sue-Ellen Case and Janelle Reinelt, eds., *The Performance of Power: Theatrical Discourse and Politics* (Iowa City, 1991), 92–110.

9. The prize was advertised in the *Critic: A Weekly Review of Literature, Fine Arts, and the Drama*, Nov. 28, 1828. On the search for a national drama, see David Grimsted, *Melodrama Unveiled: American Theater and Culture, 1800–1850* (Chicago, 1968), chap. 7. Edwin Forrest's prize might have been in part inspired by George Custis's 1827 *Indian Prophecy* (see George Washington Parke Custis, *The Indian Prophecy, a National Drama in Two Acts, Founded upon a Most Interesting and Romantic Occurrence in the Life of General Washington* [George

FIGURE 4
Poster for *Metamora. Courtesy, Crawford Theatre Collection, Yale University, New Haven, Conn.*

Although seventeenth-century chroniclers of King Philip's War—most notably the Puritan ministers Increase Mather and William Hubbard—had demonized Philip as a monstrous, barbarous, blasphemous villain, *Metamora* popularized the image of Philip as a distinctly American hero. This new image, ushered in by *Metamora,* was well expressed in 1831 by a writer for the prominent *North American Review,* who praised Philip as a leader who "did and endured enough to immortalize him as a warrior, a statesman, and we may add, as a high-minded and noble patriot." That same year, members of the Worces-

___

town, D.C., 1828]). See Murray H. Nelligan, "American Nationalism on the Stage: The Plays of George Washington Parke Custis (1781–1857)," *Virginia Magazine of History and Biography,* LVIII (1950), 299–324. The text of the epilogue is reprinted in *New-York Mirror, and Ladies' Literary Gazette,* Dec. 29, 1829.

ter Historical Society baldly acknowledged their break with the past when they offered a two-part toast to *"Philip of Pokanoket—*Had we lived in the days of our forefathers, as an enemy we would have slain him.*"* Yet, *"*the *present* generation may safely express their respect for his sagacity and patriotism.*"* In *Metamora,* Philip was even made to echo Patrick Henry: *"*Our lands! Our nation's freedom! Or the grave!*"* [10]

In soliciting and performing *Metamora,* Edwin Forrest saw himself at the vanguard of American literary independence. *"*Our literature should be independent,*"* he declared in 1834, boasting of his own efforts *"*to give to my country, by fostering the exertions of our literary friends, something like what might be called an American national drama.*"* Happily for Forrest, *Metamora,* his greatest contribution to this *"*American national drama,*"* was also his most successful money-maker. When Forrest had a lengthy engagement in Mobile, Alabama, in 1844, for instance, his theater receipts for *Metamora* were far greater than for any other performance, twice the receipts for *Macbeth* and *King Lear* in an age when Shakespeare typically thrilled the theatergoing public. In twenty-five years, Philadelphia had only two seasons without *Metamora.* Its success inspired dozens of imitators in the same role and a spate of Indian plays on similar themes, leading one observer to complain in 1846 that Indian dramas *"*had become a perfect nuisance.*"* [11]

10. Increase Mather, *A Brief History of the War with the Indians in New-England . . .* (Boston, 1676); William Hubbard, *A Narrative of the Troubles with the Indians in New-England . . .* (Boston, 1677); *"*Indian Biography,*"* review of *The Fall of the Indian, with Other Poems,* by Isaac McLellan, Jr., *North American Review,* XXXIII (1831), 407–449; *Massachusetts Spy* (Worcester), Oct. 12, 1831 (my thanks to Kenneth Moynihan for pointing me to this event); Stone, *Metamora,* in Page, ed., *Metamora and Other Plays,* 36.

11. Forrest, quoted in Mason, *"*The Politics of *Metamora,"* in Case and Reinelt, eds., *Theatrical Discourse,* 99; Richard Moody, *Edwin Forrest: First Star of the American Stage* (New York, 1960), 99. A 12-day schedule in Saint Louis, for example, brought a record profit of $2,157. Receipts for Forrest's opening night in Mobile performing *Othello* were $528.50. Subsequent performances were: *Macbeth,* $330.50, *King Lear,* $324.50, *Metamora,* $656, *Damon,* $319.75, and *Richard III,* $448. See N[oah] M[iller] Ludlow, *Dramatic Life as I Found It: A Record of Personal Experience and Company* (St. Louis, 1880), 559. On the popularity of Shakespeare in America, see Lawrence Levine, *Highbrow/Lowbrow: The Emergence of Cultural Hierarchy in America* (Cambridge, Mass., 1988), 11–82. Also, some scholars have argued that Forrest's success in Shakespearean roles was largely because they were *"*extensions of his stage Indian, Metamora transplanted to another time and place, but still the proud, doomed individual*"* (Grose, *"*Edwin Forrest,*"* *Theatre Journal,* XXXVII [1985], 185). See also Page, ed., *Metamora and Other Plays,* 4; James Rees, quoted in Hutton, *Curiosities of the American Stage,* 18.

FIGURE 5

*Metamora*-inspired Dime Novel. *Courtesy,*
*John Hay Library, Brown University,*
*Providence, R.I.*

At its peak, in the 1830s and 1840s, *Metamora* held unprecedented popular appeal. Lines from the play became household words, "as familiar upon the public's tongue as the name of Washington." In the frontier states of Indiana, Ohio, Illinois, and Michigan, towns (and probably children too) were named after the play's Indian hero. In Pennsylvania, chapters of the Improved Order of Red Men organized themselves into "Metamora Tribes." King Philip fever ran high. Antiquarians collected and displayed newly discovered relics from the war—King Philip's bowl, King Philip's war club, King Philip's pipe and belt—and a *Metamora*-inspired Philip became the subject of everything from dime novels to nursery rhymes. Such excesses prompted the complaint made in 1838 that the "bloody Indian" was now "glorified in Congress; canonized by philanthropists; autobiographed, and lithographed, and biographed, by authors, artists, and periodicals." [12]

12. Gabriel Harrison, *Edwin Forrest: The Actor and the Man* (Brooklyn, N.Y., 1889), 39; Dennis P. Walsh, "Many Metamoras: An Indian Drama in the Old Northwest," *Old Northwest*, XII (1986), 459. See Frank R. Abate, ed., *Omni Gazetteer of the United States of America*, 11 vols. (Detroit, 1991); Constitution and Bylaws of Metamora Tribe, No. 2, of the City of Lancaster (Lancaster, Pa., 1848), Beineke Library, Yale University, New Haven, Conn. Bowls allegedly owned by Philip were owned by the Massachusetts Historical Society and "King

King Philip was a warrior bold,
Whose deeds are writ in records old;
He through New England's woods did
roam,
And sorrow brought to many a home.

FIGURE 6

King Philip Nursery Rhyme. *Courtesy, American Antiquarian Society,*
*Worcester, Mass.*

Although Edwin Forrest prepared for the role of Metamora well before the proliferation of Philip paraphernalia, he was not wholly without source material. The most promising clues about what those sources might have been come from an inventory of Forrest's library taken in 1863 (the year he had many of his books and personal effects cataloged and sold, including his Metamora wardrobe). Forrest owned more than a few books about King Philip's

---

Philip's War Club" at the Connecticut Historical Society. My thanks to Joanne Chaison of the American Antiquarian Society for pointing me to the King Philip nursery rhyme, which is quoted in Sherry Sullivan, "Indians in American Fiction, 1820–1850: An Ethnohistorical Perspective," *Clio,* XV (1986), 244–245.

War. The bulk of these were published before 1829, and it seems likely that Forrest purchased them while studying for *Metamora*. Among these works, for instance, was James Fenimore Cooper's 1827 novel about King Philip's War, *The Wept of Wish-ton-Wish* (which failed as a novel but became a successful play and even a ballet). More significant, Forrest owned an essay by Washington Irving called "Philip of Pokanoket," first published in 1814 and widely reprinted in Irving's popular *Sketch Book* collection (1819–1820). Irving's portrait of Philip would come to be closely associated with *Metamora*—some newspapers went so far as to reprint Irving's "Philip of Pokanoket" alongside reviews of the play, and the Princess Theatre included a lengthy excerpt from the essay on its advertising poster for *Metamora*.[13]

Washington Irving had himself decided to write about Philip after consulting several early histories of King Philip's War and finding himself disgusted with the colonists' original accounts, especially Boston minister Increase Mather's history of the war. Irving claimed that Mather "dwells with horror and indignation on every hostile act of the Indians, however justifiable, whilst he mentions with applause the most sanguinary atrocities of the whites." "Philip is reviled as a murderer and a traitor without considering that he was a true born prince, gallantly fighting at the head of his subjects to avenge the wrongs of his family; to retrieve the tottering power of his line; and to deliver his native land from the oppression of usurping strangers." Offering a corrective to Mather's history, Irving urged his readers to see beyond the prejudices of the early historians of the war to better appreciate Philip's virtue and mourn that he had died "like a lonely bark foundering amid darkness and tem-

---

13. Joseph Sabin, comp., *Catalogue of the Library of Edwin Forrest* (Philadelphia, 1863), 52; James Fenimore Cooper, *The Wept of Wish-ton-Wish* . . . (Philadelphia, 1829). As Cooper wrote in a letter to Rufus Wilmot Griswold in 1844, "Wish-ton-Wish appeared in 1829. It did not succeed" (James Franklin Beard, ed., *The Letters and Journals of James Fenimore Cooper*, IV [Cambridge, Mass., 1964], 461). Nonetheless, the dramatic version of the novel, which bears little relation to it (see *The Wept of the Wish-ton-Wish, a Drama in Two Acts, from J. Fennimore Cooper's Celebrated Novel of the Same Name, as Performed at All the Principal Theatres in the United States* [New York, n.d.]), was widely performed (for example, see playbills in the Crawford Theatre Collection, box 12, folder 70, box 27, folder 206, Yale University). See also Constance Rourke, *American Humor: A Study of the National Character* (New York, 1931), 114. Forrest owned Irving's essay in a multivolume edition of his *Sketch Book* (Sabin, comp., *Catalogue*, 54). See also Metamora Clippings File, Harvard Theatre Collection, The Houghton Library, Harvard University, Cambridge, Mass.; Edwin Forrest Poster Box, Harvard Theatre Collection, Harvard University.

pest—without a pitying eye to weep his fall, or a friendly hand to record his struggle."[14]

In addition to Irving's *Sketch Book,* Edwin Forrest's library also included copies of two epic poems about King Philip's War: Robert Southey's unfinished *Oliver Newman, a New England Tale* (begun in 1815) and James Eastburn and Robert Charles Sands's *Yamoyden, a Tale of the Wars of King Philip* (published in 1820). Although Irving's essay partly inspired these endeavors, the original seventeenth-century chronicles remained their chief source of information. Recalling how he and Eastburn came to write *Yamoyden,* Sands explained, "We had then read nothing of the subject; and our plot was formed from a hasty glance into a few pages of [Puritan minister William] Hubbard's Narrative." Finally, Forrest owned a copy of colonial army officer Benjamin Church's original history of the war (first printed in 1716) in an 1827 reprint edition. How this book's text might have influenced Forrest is unclear, but its chief illustration, a copy of Paul Revere's 1772 engraving of Philip, seems to have caught Forrest's eye.[15] That Revere's engraving influenced Forrest's costuming is

14. Washington Irving, "Philip of Pokanoket," in *The Works of Washington Irving,* II, *The Sketch Book* (New York, 1851), 364, 372. Irving's Philip was "a patriot attached to his native soil—a prince true to his subjects, and indignant of their wrongs—a soldier, daring in battle, firm in adversity, patient of fatigue, of hunger, of every variety of bodily suffering, and ready to perish in the cause he had espoused" (382–383).

15. Sabin, comp., *Catalogue,* 42, 48. See the unfinished poem, *Oliver Newman, a New-England Tale,* in Robert Southey, *The Poetical Works of Robert Southey, with a Memoir,* V (Boston, 1880), 263–358. See also Albert Keiser, *The Indian in American Literature* (New York, 1933), 38–44. It is possible that Southey never finished his King Philip's War poem because of the bad advance reaction in the United States. When rumors spread that Robert Southey, the British poet laureate, was planning to write an epic poem about Philip, at least one American was outraged at the prospect of an Englishman's writing on this very American subject. "It would be strange, indeed," an irate reader wrote to the *New-York Literary Magazine,* "when the people of Great Britain, even those who are the best informed on other important subjects, are so extremely ignorant of this country, of its character, manners, and government, and in many instances even of its geographical divisions, if they should understand the Indian character. We know of no subject that could occupy the attention and talents of a literary stranger, in which he would be less likely to succeed, than that which Mr. Southey is said to have chosen" (Robert Jarvis, "Southey's New Poem," *New-York Literary Magazine,* III [May 15, 1820], 54 [see also 55–56]). See also James Wallis Eastburn [and Robert Charles Sands], *Yamoyden, a Tale of the Wars of King Philip: In Six Cantos . . .* (New York, 1820), 1; Sabin, comp., *Catalogue,* 80. Forrest later obtained an 1855 edition of Cotton Mather's *Magnalia Christi Americana . . .* (London, 1702); see ibid., 87.

PHILIP. *KING* of Mount Hope.

*P Revere sc*

FIGURE 7

Paul Revere's King Philip, 1770. *Courtesy, American Antiquarian Society,*
*Worcester, Mass.*

Edwin Forrest as Metamora. *Courtesy, Harvard Theatre Collection, The Houghton Library, Harvard University, Cambridge, Mass.*

powerfully suggested by comparing it to Matthew Brady's photograph of Forrest as Metamora. Forrest's "Last of the Wampanoags"—his belt, moccasins, headband, and even posture—seems to echo Revere's "King of Mount Hope."

To portray Philip, then, Edwin Forrest borrowed from Washington Irving (who borrowed—if begrudgingly—from Increase Mather), from Eastburn and Sands (who borrowed from William Hubbard), and from Paul Revere (who had himself copied his Philip from John Simon's 1710 engraving of Mohawk chief Joseph Brant).[16] Metamora was a strange hybrid indeed. Clearly, although Forrest's Metamora flowered in the nineteenth century, he was nonetheless rooted in the rich soil of myth, memory, and history.

Armed with an abundance of sources, and with his own theatrical talents, Forrest was ideally suited to inaugurate an "American national drama" and, ultimately, to found a new kind of American identity derived from the representation of the American Indian. In the early decades of the newly minted nation, an age obsessed with a search for American identity, Forrest's theatrical performances were, in a sense, at the forefront of establishing what it was to be American. His expansive acting style was itself based on an explicit contrast with the more reserved style of English actors. To American eyes, Forrest was forceful and passionate; to English eyes, he was vulgar and bombastic. A critic for *Albion* wrote of Forrest in 1848: "He has created a school in his art, strictly American, and he stands forth as the very embodiment, as it were, of *the masses of American character*." Ironically, Forrest was never more "strictly American" than when he played an Indian. Only by appropriating Indianness did Forrest most effectively distinguish himself from all that was English. Without its aboriginal heritage, America was only a more vulgar England, but with it America was its own nation, with a unique culture and its own ancestral past.[17] Only by anchoring the nation to a romantic (Indian) past could Americans like Forrest steer clear of the rocky shoals of civilization and all its corruptions. Meanwhile, of course, real Indians were thrown overboard and, sooner or later, the anchor was bound to break.

Critics called Edwin Forrest the "very embodiment . . . of the masses of American character," even as they called him, as Metamora, "the complete embodiment of our idea of King Phillip." Forrest was at once "strictly Ameri-

---

16. Branford F. Swan, *An Indian's an Indian; or, The Several Sources of Paul Revere's Engraved Portrait of King Philip* (Providence, R.I., 1959).

17. *Albion, or, British, Colonial, and Foreign Weekly Gazette* (New York), Sept. 2, 1848. As Brian Dippie has remarked, "The Indian, as the First American, was necessary to any such attempt at self-definition. He *was* the American past" (Dippie, *The Vanishing American*, 16).

can" and "wholly Indian." "For the portraying of such personages, we say again Mr. F is peculiarly suited," a critic for the New York *Morning Herald* stated in 1837. "His hoarse voice, uncontrolled by art—his sullen features, his dogged walk, his athletic frame, and his admirable personations of the transitions of the mind from calmness to passion, are lofty and enviable qualifications for the attainment of excellence in this range of the drama." William Alger, Forrest's friend as well as his earliest biographer, claimed that Forrest as an Indian "ap peared the human lord of the dark wood and the rocky shore, and the natural ruler of their untutored tenants; the soul of the eloquent recital, the noble appeal, and the fiery harangue; the embodiment of a rude magnanimity, a deep domestic love, an unquivering courage and fortitude, an instinctive patriotism and sense of justice, and a relentless revenge." [18]

A distinctive feature of Forrest's Indian American was the strength and passion of his oratory. English actor George Vandenhoff saw Forrest perform the role of Metamora in 1842 and wrote: "His voice surged and roared like the angry sea, lashed into fury by a storm; till, as it reached its boiling, seething climax, . . . it was like the falls of Niagara." But if Forrest was widely known for his trademark bellowing, he was almost as often criticized for it (one parody of *Metamora* went by the name *Metaroarer*). In part, criticism of Forrest's loudness served as a racial slur aimed at the savagery of the Indian character he represented. A particularly vituperative attack claimed:

> The *Metamora* of Mr. Forrest is as much like a gorilla as an Indian, and in fact more like a dignified monkey than a man. . . . We are told by that celebrated traveller that upon the approach of an enemy this ferocious baboon, standing upright on his hind legs, his eyes dilated, his teeth gritting and grinding, gives vent to divers snorts and grunts, and then, beating his breast fiercely with his hands till it sounds like a muffled drum, utters a loud roar. What a singular coincidence. The similarity needs scarcely be pointed out. Substitute the words 'great tragedian' for 'ferocious baboon,' omit the word 'hind,' and you have as accurate a description of Mr. Forrest in *Metamora* as any reasonable man can wish. [19]

Seeing Forrest's Indian primitiveness as vulgar and animalistic was a view most often held by European critics, or by Americans who preferred the more

---

18. *Albion*, Sept. 2, 1848; *New-York Mirror*, Dec. 14, 1833; *Morning Herald* (New York), Dec. 28, 1837; William Rounseville Alger, *Life of Edwin Forrest, the American Tragedian* (1877; reprint, New York, 1972), 238–240.

19. Barnard Hewitt, *Theatre U.S.A., 1668 to 1957* (New York, 1959), 107–108; Rourke, *American Humor*, 123; Alger, *Life of Edwin Forrest*, 476–477.

reserved acting style of the English. In England, Forrest was often poorly received (especially in the role of Metamora), and his English counterpart, Charles Macready, did not always fare well in the United States. The cultural and class allegiances that lay behind the endorsement of these two opposing acting styles led, in 1849, to the infamous Astor Place Riot, in which supporters of Forrest protested outside the Astor Place Opera House, where Macready was performing. By the time the riot had ended, at least 22 people were killed and 150 wounded. Clearly, the Astor Place Riot was a product of class antagonisms engendered in the two personalities of Forrest and Macready, one representing the hardy, common man and the other the delicate aristocrat. But within these class antagonisms was a broader concern with national identity; to his supporters, Forrest's style embodied all that was good about America, Macready's all that was bad about England. As one of the protesters later explained, "I was not hostile to Mr. Macready because he was an Englishman, but because he was full of his country's prejudices from the top of his head to his feet." [20]

If Macready's body, from the top of his head to the bottom of his feet, was filled with Englishness, then Forrest's was filled with Americanness. National identity, like gender identity, is itself partly performative; that is, one's political allegiances and cultural inheritances are expressed, in part, in a person's way of moving, talking, walking, and eating. In an age obsessed with a search for American identity, Forrest's theatrical performances were, in a sense, at the forefront of establishing what it was to be American. And for Forrest, being American meant taking on the attributes of Indianness. In playing Metamora, Forrest underwent a profound transformation. "Never did an actor more thoroughly identify and merge himself with his part than Forrest did in Metamora. . . . The carriage of his body, the inflections of his voice, his facial expressions, the very pose of his head and neck and shoulders, were new." He took on not only the costuming but the bearing and accents of an Indian (or his idea of an Indian). "So accurate had been his observations that he caught the very manner of their breathing. . . . Everything that could be absorbed by one nature from another was absorbed and embodied and represented." [21]

Forrest himself often attributed his success in the role of Metamora to time

20. Grimsted, *Melodrama Unveiled*, 68–75; Richard Moody, *The Astor Place Riot* (Bloomington, Ind., 1958); Levine, *Highbrow/Lowbrow*, 63–68 (quotation on 66).

21. Alger, *Life of Edwin Forrest*, 238–240; Harrison, *Edwin Forrest*, 37. (Forrest took on the role in more ways than one; in a letter he referred to a woman he was having an affair with only as "Nahmeokee" [Moody, *Edwin Forrest*, 342]).

spent with a close friend, a Choctaw Indian named Push-ma-ta-ha. As Alger wrote, "A genuine friendship grew up between this chief and Forrest, not without some touch of simple romance." Forrest's love for Push-ma-ta-ha was based on admiration (Push-ma-ta-ha was "a natural orator of a high order") and on physical attraction. During the 1820s, when Forrest briefly lived with Push-ma-ta-ha, the two men are said to have been lying around a campfire, far from the Choctaw village, when "Forrest asked [Push-ma-ta-ha] to strip himself and walk to and fro before him between the moonlight and the firelight, that he might feast his eyes and his soul on so complete a physical type of what man should be. The young chief, without a word, cast aside his Choctaw garb and stepped forth with a dainty tread, a living statue of Apollo in glowing bronze." (Alger claims Forrest later commonly recalled, "My God, what a contrast he was to some fashionable men I have since seen, half made up of false teeth, false hair, padding, gloves, and spectacles!") [22]

A trifle uncomfortable with Forrest's longing for Push-ma-ta-ha's body, Alger felt compelled to explain, "Like an artist, or like an antique Greek, Forrest had a keen delight in the naked form of man, feeling that the best image of God we have is nude humanity in its perfection, which our fashionable dresses so travesty and degrade." But the "simple romance" between Forrest and Push-ma-ta-ha is far more complicated; in essence, it speaks to the broader attraction the idealized manly Indian held for Americans in the first half of the nineteenth century. (Indeed, Forrest—or Alger—might have invented the story of Push-ma-ta-ha to further promote the actor's Indian authenticity.) Forrest admired Push-ma-ta-ha for his primitiveness but also for his unfettered masculinity. In the spirit of the writings of James Fenimore Cooper, Forrest saw Push-ma-ta-ha as man uncompromised by the feminizing forces in American life—the constraints of living in a city, the dictates of (mostly European) fashion, the etiquette of civilized society. In contemplating Philip's life, Washington Irving had himself reflected on the opposition between the artifices of civilized man and the naturalness of the Indian, "free from the restraints and refinements of polished life." Now, in the fine form of Push-ma-ta-ha's body (imagined or otherwise), Forrest and others like him saw a new way for Americans to define themselves, to forge a national—and decidedly masculine— identity by taking on the unique Americanness of America's indigenous inhabitants. In performing Indianness, Forrest, in a sense, imagined himself into a new national identity; he performed Americanness. Forrest became Metamora in the same way he wished for Americans to become Indian, to take on

22. Alger, *Life of Edwin Forrest*, 126–127, 137–139.

their unique American inheritance, thereby distinguishing themselves from Europeans and European culture, and especially from its feminizing forces.[23]

In taking on the attributes of Indianness by playing a seventeenth-century Wampanoag leader, Forrest's Metamora, and the literary portraits it borrowed from, rested on the assumption that there were no more Indians in New England, an assumption that had become a commonplace by the second decade of the nineteenth century. (Forrest, after all, based his portrayal of Philip, not on a New England Wampanoag, but on a Louisiana Choctaw.) In a letter to Thomas Jefferson in 1812, John Adams wrote from Massachusetts: "We scarcely see an Indian in a year. I remember the Time when Indian Murders, Scalpings, Depredations and conflagrations were as frequent on the Eastern and Northern Frontier of Massachusetts as they are now in Indiana, and spread as much terror." In 1828, Supreme Court justice Joseph Story, speaking in Salem, Massachusetts, mourned the loss of New England's Indians: "We hear the rustling of their footsteps, like that of the withered leaves of autumn, and they are gone forever." Although lamenting the fate of Northeastern Indians had become a cliché by the 1820s, Story applied his remarks not just to New England's Indians but to Indians all along the eastern seaboard. "Two centuries ago," he declared, "the smoke of their wigwams and the fires of their councils rose in every valley, from Hudson's Bay to the farthest Florida," whereas today "the winds of the Atlantic fan not a single region, which they may now call their own." "Already the last feeble remnants of the race are preparing for their journey beyond the Mississippi."[24] By the 1820s, the once terrifying warriors who had threatened John Adams's childhood had become, for Story, "feeble." And, as eastern Indians disappeared or became feeble and defeated (and feminized), white Americans assumed their mantle of rough, natural masculinity.

After delivering his Salem address, Justice Story sent a copy of it to John Marshall, the Supreme Court's chief justice, and Marshall made the same connection Story had, between the vanished Indians of New England and the vanishing Indians of the Southeast: "The conduct of our forefathers in expelling

23. Ibid.; Irving, "Philip of Pokanoket," in *Works of Irving*, II, 363–364. David Grimsted points out that early-nineteenth-century critics looking for a distinctive American literature argued that in drama the "first essential" was "nationality," because it was "addressed to the people immediately" (Grimsted, *Melodrama Unveiled*, 138).

24. Lester J. Cappon, ed., *The Adams-Jefferson Letters: The Complete Correspondence between Thomas Jefferson and Abigail and John Adams*, 2 vols. (Chapel Hill, N.C., 1959), II, 310–311; Joseph Story, *The Miscellaneous Writings, Literary, Critical, Juridical, and Political, of Joseph Story* (Boston, 1835), 78–79.

the original occupants of the soil grew out of so many mixed motives that any censure which philanthropy may bestow upon it ought to be qualified," Marshall remarked. And yet, he continued, "I often think with indignation on our disreputable conduct . . . in the affair of the Cherokees in Georgia." Marshall's distinction—exonerating the conduct of seventeenth-century New England Puritans while criticizing contemporary Indian policy—was not uncommon in the debate about Indian removal. Opponents of Indian removal characterized it as a radical break with history. "Nothing of this kind has ever yet been done," Jeremiah Evarts wrote in 1829. "To us, as a nation, it will be a new thing under the sun." Meanwhile, advocates of Indian removal claimed it was entirely consistent with the past. "The present policy of the Government," Andrew Jackson wrote, "is but a continuation of the same change by a milder process."[25]

In constructing their arguments, however, both advocates and opponents of Indian removal collapsed all Indian tribes, past and present, into one. Since "nearly the same principles are involved in the claims of all the Indian nations," Jeremiah Evarts argued, "let the case of a single tribe or nation be considered." That tribe, taken to stand for all others, was the Cherokee nation, whose resistance to removal was elaborated in the tribe's newspaper, the *Cherokee Phoenix,* printed in both English and the Cherokee syllabary. In his decision in *Cherokee Nation v. Georgia* in 1831, Chief Justice Marshall would declare, "If courts were permitted to indulge their sympathies, a case better calculated to excite them can scarcely be imagined." Yet, as suggested in his correspondence with Story, Marshall, like many Americans, understood the Cherokee case largely in relation to earlier Indian-white conflicts, especially the events of seventeenth-century New England, which dominated the popular historical imagination in late-eighteenth- and early-nineteenth-century America. (Marshall was also a bit of a historian; he had written a history of the colonies and had studied King Philip's War.) In 1829, when Andrew Jackson first articulated his Indian removal policy, he himself compared the contemporary Indians of the Southeast with the historical Indians of New England. "Surrounded by the whites with their arts of civilization, which by destroying

25. John Marshall to Joseph Story, Oct. 29, 1828, cited in G. Edward White, *History of the Supreme Court of the United States,* III–IV, *The Marshall Court and Cultural Change, 1815–35* (New York, 1988), 713–714; [Jeremiah Evarts], *Essays on the Present Crisis in the Condition of the American Indians* (Boston, 1829), 101; Andrew Jackson, Second Annual Message, Dec. 6, 1830, in Richardson, ed., *Papers of the Presidents,* III, 1084.

the resources of the savage doom him to weakness and decay, the fate of the Mohegan, the Narragansett, and the Delaware is fast overtaking the Choctaw, the Cherokee, and the Creek."[26] For Jackson, this same fate awaited white Americans, too, unless they themselves expanded to spread out across the continent—and across Indian lands.

One week after Jackson made this speech, when *Metamora* debuted, Edwin Forrest underwent a profound transformation, one that he would undergo night after night for decades to come. As Alger would write, "When [Forrest] came to impersonate Metamora, it was the genuine Indian who was brought upon the stage, merely idealized a little in some of his moral features." But Edwin Forrest was not, after all, an Indian. As one critic explained, Forrest was only "the impersonation of the Indian of romance." "The Indian in his *true* character never *can* find a representative among the whites. Disgust, rather than admiration, would ensue." At times, disgust was indeed forthcoming. Writing in 1830, one critic proposed that perhaps Forrest's stature gave the role of Metamora the legitimacy it did not otherwise deserve:

> Mr. Forrest, by virtue of some considerable reputation as an actor, carried this heavy play on his shoulders, from one end of the Union to the other; and its performance is nightly witnessed by crowded theaters, applauding with strange enthusiasm the reckless cruelties of a bloody barbarian, who stabs his subjects like pigs, and delights the white men of the present day, by burning the villages of their forefathers. . . . Let us hope, for the honour of humanity, that this applause is bestowed on Mr. Forrest, rather than the ferocious savage whom he impersonates.[27]

Indeed, when Forrest's portrayal seemed, to some white audiences, too true, too authentic, disgust was indeed forthcoming. In Augusta, Georgia, in 1831, a

26. [Evarts], *Essays*, 6; *Cherokee Nation v. Georgia*, 30 U.S. 1, 1831. For review and analysis of this case, see White, *The Marshall Court*, 703–740; and Priscilla Wald, "Terms of Assimilation: Legislating Subjectivity in the Emerging Nation," in Amy Kaplan and Donald E. Pease, eds., *Cultures of United States Imperialism* (Durham, N.C., 1993), 59–84. See also, John Marshall, *A History of the Colonies Planted by the English on the Continent of North America* (Philadelphia, 1824), 166–167; Andrew Jackson, quoted in Satz, *American Indian Policy*, 19.

27. Alger, *Life of Edwin Forrest*, 240; *Morning Herald* (New York), Dec. 28, 1837; "Dramatic Literature," *American Quarterly Review*, VIII (September 1830), 145. Though Forrest was, according to Moody, "the only actor who ever gained much distinction from acting the noble red man" (Moody, *America Takes the Stage*, 96).

full house turned tempestuous during the "council-scene" of Act 2, when Metamora delivers perhaps the most dramatic speech of the play:

> White man, beware! The mighty spirits of the Wampanoag race are hovering o'er your heads; they stretch out their shadowy arms to me and ask for vengeance; they shall have it. . . . From the east to the west, in the north and in the south shall cry of vengeance burst, till the lands you have stolen groan under your feet no more![28]

The crowd was not pleased. As one member of the audience recalled, "Evident dissatisfaction had begun to find expression long before the climax was reached, and as the chief rushed from the stage he was followed by loud yells and a perfect storm of hisses from the excited audience, who seemed in their fury to tear everything to pieces." The following day, a local judge declared: "Any actor who could utter such scathing language, and with such vehemence, must have the whole matter at heart. Why, his eyes shot fire and his breath was hot with the hissing of his ferocious declamation. I insist upon it, Forrest believed in that d——d Indian speech, and it is an insult to the whole community." No one showed up for the next night's performance, and the play's run in Augusta was eventually canceled.[29]

Most likely, the people of Augusta had taken Forrest's "d——d Indian speech" as a direct indictment of their own Indian policy of forcing the Cherokees out of the state. In 1831, when *Metamora* was performed in Georgia, the Cherokee nation was appealing its case to the Supreme Court (headed by Marshall), and, as the *Cherokee Phoenix* had declared on New Year's Day of that year: "No one can now remain neutral. Each individual in America must be either for the Indians or against them." And, indeed, the nation was divided, with southerners generally supporting removal and northerners opposed. In the vote on Jackson's Indian removal bill in 1830, New England senators had voted eleven to one against the bill, whereas southerners voted eighteen to zero in favor; in the House, New Englanders voted twenty-eight to nine against, southerners sixty to fifteen in favor. And, although Marshall ruled in *Cherokee Nation v. Georgia* that "the laws of Georgia can have no force" over the Cherokee nation, Jackson simply ignored the ruling, since it did not prevent the fed-

---

28. Stone, *Metamora*, in Page, ed., *Metamora and Other Plays*, 23.

29. James E. Murdock, *The Stage; or, Recollections of Actors and Acting from an Experience of Fifty Years* (Philadelphia, 1880), 298–300; Montrose J. Moses, *The Fabulous Forrest: The Record of an American Actor* (New York, 1929), 332–333.

eral government from acting on Georgia's behalf. The president was even ru-
mored to have remarked, "John Marshall has made his decision: now let him
enforce it." [30]

Whatever the politics of his audience, Forrest himself was an ardent sup-
porter of Jackson, who no doubt saw *Metamora* as an endorsement of Indian
removal, illustrating the wisdom of protecting Indians from the incursions of
white culture. What *Metamora* celebrated, after all, was Philip's death. A tragic
death, yes, but a necessary one. *Metamora* mourned the passing of Philip and
the disappearance of New England's Indians, but it mourned these losses as inevitable, and right. In this, *Metamora* had much in common with the fiction,
verse, and painting of its day, including, most famously, Cooper's *Last of the
Mohicans*. *Yamoyden*, for example, mourned "a departed race,— / Long vanished hence," and in John Greenleaf Whittier's 1830 poem, "Metacom," the dying chief moans about his tribe's decay:

> The scorched earth—the blackened log—
> The naked bones of warriors slain,
> Be the sole relics which remain
> Of the once mighty Wampanoag.

Philip's death is also the most commonly depicted scene of the war, and most
illustrations, like G. I. Brown's painting, *The Last of the Wampanoags*, show
him falling or fallen, alone in the wilderness. In Brown's painting and in Whittier's poem, as in the final scene of *Metamora* ("Rocks, bridge and waterfall"),
Philip is closely associated with the wilderness and with a rocky landscape.
Most critics supposed that "Metamora" was simply a poetic rendering of
"Metacom"; in fact, it is bad Greek for "big rock." [31] And by the end of the play,
Metamora *is* a rock, a speechless, motionless, memorial. In paintings, plays,
poems, and prose, Philip is similarly petrified—dead but symbolically transformed into a mute rock, a stage prop. (A popular engraving of Forrest in the
role of Metamora pictured him leaning on a massive boulder.) When the cur-

30. *Cherokee Phoenix, and Indians' Advocate* (New Echota, Ga.), Jan. 1, 1831; McLoughlin, *Cherokee Renascence*, 436–437.

31. Grose, "Edwin Forrest," *Theatre Journal*, XXXVII (1985), 183–185. And, as Werner
Sollors has argued, Metamora's curse was also, implicitly, a blessing; instead of condemning Americans for their harsh treatment of Indians, cursing stage Indians, like parents im-
parting a dying wish to their children, actually gave Americans permission to enter a new
national era. See Sollors, *Beyond Ethnicity: Consent and Descent in American Culture* (New
York, 1986), 115–125, 126. See also Berkhofer, *White Man's Indian*, 88; Eastburn [and Sands],
*Yamoyden*, 4; John Greenleaf Whittier, "Metacom," *Ladies Magazine*, III (1830), 58.

tain fell, Metamora was dead, and Forrest was only a stage Indian who did not, in the end, believe in "that d——d Indian speech," and, outside of the people of Augusta, Georgia, neither did most of his audience. But only most.

Forrest's promoters were fond of claiming that his portrayal of Metamora was so authentic "it might have deceived nature herself"—in other words, bona fide, real-live Indians might be deceived by Forrest's performance and, naively misapprehending the line between representation and reality, might believe that an actual war was being waged before their own eyes. Just as amusing and entertaining as their supposed credulity, Forrest's promoters implied, was the Indians' presence itself, not uncommon at performances of *Metamora*. "Many a time delegations of Indian tribes who chanced to be visiting the cities where [Forrest] acted this character—Boston, New York, Washington, Baltimore, Cincinnati, New Orleans—attended the performance, adding a most picturesque feature by their presence, and their pleasure and approval were unqualified." [32]

The Penobscots who attended *Metamora* at the Tremont Street Theater in Boston in November 1833 arrived late, but they stayed until the end of the performance, when Forrest, as Metamora, delivered his impassioned dying speech to the audience:

> My curses on you, white men! May the Great Spirit curse you when he speaks in his war voice from the clouds! Murderers! The last of the Wampanoags' curse be on you! May your graves and the graves of your children be in the path the red man shall trace! And may the wolf and panther howl o'er your fleshless bones, fit banquet for the destroyers! Spirits of the grave, I come! But the curse of Metamora stays with the white man!

White audiences were typically reported to break out in wild and "rapturous" applause at the end of this speech, and William Alger claimed that in Boston in 1833 the Penobscots were "so excited by the performance that in the closing scene they rose and chanted a dirge in honor of the death of the great chief." More believable is the contemporary report in the *Boston Morning Post* that the Penobscots "doubtless do not wish to peril their popularity and consequently

---

32. Alger, *Life of Edwin Forrest*, 240. Indian attendance was an enhancement of the performance; in a sense, they were part of it and could be a tremendous draw, helping fill the house with curious onlookers. In 1834, the Sauk chief Black Hawk attended a one-night-only performance of *Black Hawk* at the Bowery Theater in New York. But, just two years after his capture by Jackson's forces, *Black Hawk,* the play, was not the performance; Black Hawk, the man, was (Jones, *Native Americans as Shown on the Stage,* 86).

made no speeches." The popularity of "vanished" Indians depended on their silence. As Justice Joseph Story had declared in 1829, New England's Indians "shed no tears; they utter no cries; they heave no groans. There is something in their hearts, which passes speech." (And, of course, as the *Post* claimed, many suspected the Penobscots might be not only silent but, by simply failing to appear, invisible because they feared "their presence might have some bias on the present difficulties between Alabama and the Government!") [33]

Whether they "chanted a dirge" or "made no speeches" at the Tremont Street Theater, the Penobscots were not silent at the Massachusetts State House, just on the other side of Boston Common. In 1829, in a (failed) effort to garner the support of northern congressmen for Indian removal, Andrew Jackson had posed what he believed to be an absurd question: "Would the people of Maine permit the Penobscot tribe to erect an independent government within their State?" Yet Jackson's rhetorical question was not nearly as absurd as he imagined: the Penobscots who traveled to Boston in 1833 petitioned to do just that, to regain territory and political autonomy that had eroded in the first third of the century. (Maine had been part of Massachusetts until 1820, and many of the Penobscots' treaties fell under Massachusetts jurisdiction.) The Penobscots' claims were largely ignored (and the delegation was instead hustled to the theater). But that same year, the Mashpee Wampanoags of Cape Cod had a bit more success when they, too, filed claims against the Massachusetts government. [34]

In May 1833, William Apess, a Pequot minister, traveled to Mashpee and found there a community of Indians dispossessed of their own meetinghouse. (The Mashpee Wampanoag community had absorbed many Algonquians in the immediate aftermath of King Philip's War and constituted, in 1833, the largest single group of Indians living in Massachusetts.) A minister paid by Harvard to convert the Mashpees to Christianity preached to a congregation almost entirely made up of white parishioners while neighboring whites made

33. Stone, *Metamora,* in Page, ed., *Metamora and Other Plays,* 40; *Morning Courier and New-York Enquirer,* Dec. 16, 1829; Alger, *Life of Edwin Forrest,* 240; *Boston Morning Post,* Nov. 8, 1833; Story, *Miscellaneous Writings,* 79.

34. Richardson, ed., *Papers of the Presidents,* III, 1020. On the Penobscot claims and controversies of 1833, see Paul Brodeur, *Restitution: The Land Claims of the Mashpee, Passamaquoddy, and Penobscot Indians of New England* (Boston, 1985), 78 (on the Mashpee, see 16–19); Donald M. Nielsen, "The Mashpee Indian Revolt of 1833," *New England Quarterly,* LVIII (1985), 400–420; Francis G. Hutchins, *Mashpee: The Story of Cape Cod's Indian Town* (West Franklin, N.H., 1979), 95–112; Jack Campisi, *The Mashpee Indians: Tribe on Trial* (Syracuse, N.Y., 1991), 101–106.

liberal use of Mashpee land. Appalled at this state of affairs, Apess, after being formally adopted into the tribe, led the Mashpees in sending a petition to the governor and Council of Massachusetts, demanding that the tribe be allowed to rule itself and to protect its property. The Mashpee declared: "That we as a tribe will rule ourselves and have the rights so to do for all men are born free. . . . That we will not permit any white man to come upon our Plantation to cut . . . wood . . . hay or any other article. . . . That we will have our own Meeting House, and place in the pulpit whom we please." In July, Apess and several Mashpees prevented a white man from taking wood from Mashpee land and were later arrested for inciting riot when they protested. Their trial brought the Mashpee case into the spotlight, and, in the weeks and months to follow, the "Mashpee Revolt" generated a host of petitions, newspaper editorials, and court pronouncements, many of which countered anti-Mashpee sentiment by invoking the specter of Georgia's treatment of the Cherokees and pointing out the hypocrisy of Massachusetts in much the same way as Jackson had attempted to do five years earlier. When Apess was sentenced to thirty days in prison, Benjamin Franklin Hallett, editor of the *Boston Daily Advocate* asked, "Where are all our Cherokee philanthropists, at this time?" Playing on New Englanders' knowledge that the Mashpees, like the Penobscots, had fought alongside the colonists against the British in the American Revolution, Hallett also resurrected the Irvingesque image of Philip's descendants as Revolutionary patriots: "The persons concerned in the riot, as it was called, and imprisoned for it, I think were as justifiable in what they did, as our fathers were, who threw the tea overboard." Much of Hallett's rhetoric seems to have been inspired by *Metamora* itself. In February 1834, during or soon after the run of *Metamora* at Boston's Tremont Street Theater, Hallett editorialized on behalf of the Mashpees in phrases that echo Metamora's dying curse: "Give us a chance for our lives in acting for ourselves. O white man! white man! the blood of our fathers, spilt in the Revolutionary War, cries from the ground of our native soil to break the chains of oppression and let our children go free." [35]

35. Massachusetts Senate, Document 1833, Doc. 14, 5; *Boston Daily Advocate*, Sept. 11, 1833, quoted in William Apess, *On Our Own Ground: The Complete Writings of William Apess, A Pequot*, ed. Barry O'Connell (Amherst, Mass., 1992), 202. Hallett employed this rhetorical device on several other occasions as well: "While our mouths are yet full of bitterness against Georgian violence, upon the Indians, we shall not imitate their example" (July 12, 1833, quoted ibid., 192); "We have had an overflow of sensibility in this quarter toward the Cherokees, and there is now an opportunity of showing to the world whether the people of Massachusetts can exercise more justice and less cupidity toward their own Indians than the Georgians have toward the Cherokees" (Aug. 5, 1833, 196; see also 167); Brodeur, *Restitution*, 18.

FIGURE 9
William Apess. *Courtesy, Harvard College Library, Cambridge, Mass.*

   Regional differences—between the industrialized North and the expansionist South—had played themselves out in congressional voting on the Indian removal bill, but the Mashpee revolt would reveal that, for all their support of
Cherokee resistance and their nostalgia for a heroic King Philip, northerners
were just as reluctant as their southern neighbors to recognize native sovereignty. Nonetheless, the Mashpees themselves wisely and quickly employed the
rhetoric of anti-Indian removal sentiment in advancing their cause. In a petition to Harvard complaining about their minister's negligence, for instance,
the tribe's representatives wrote: "Perhaps you have heard of the oppression of
the Cherokees and lamented over them much, and thought the Georgians
were hard and cruel creatures; but did you ever hear of the poor, oppressed and
degraded Marshpee Indians in Massachusetts, and lament over them?" Simi-

larly, on December 19, well after Apess had been released and just a few weeks after the Penobscots sat through a performance of *Metamora,* the Mashpees presented an "Appeal to the White Men of Massachusetts":

> As our brethren, the white men of Massachusetts, have recently manifested much sympathy for the red men of the Cherokee nation, who have suffered much from their white brethren; as it is contended in this State, that our red brethren, the Cherokees, should be an independent people, having the privileges of the white men; we, the red men of the Marshpee tribe, consider it a favorable time to speak. We are not free. We wish to be so, as much as the red men of Georgia. How will the white man of Massachusetts ask favor for the red men of the South, while the poor Marshpee red men, his near neighbors, sigh in bondage? Will not your white brothers of Georgia tell you to look at home, and clear your own borders of oppression, before you trouble them? Will you think of this? What would be benevolence in Georgia, the red man thinks would be so in Massachusetts. You plead for the Cherokees, will you not raise your voice for the red man of Marshpee?[36]

No doubt largely owing to the poignancy of such rhetoric, the Mashpees eventually achieved an agreement by which they might govern themselves: their land was redefined as an independent district. Their cause's indebtedness to a *Metamora*-inspired resurrection of King Philip, however, was not forgotten. Two years later, William Apess reappeared in Boston to deliver a popular lecture titled *Eulogy on King Philip* at the Odeon, just a few blocks away from the Tremont Street Theater. Like Forrest, Apess borrowed from the conventions established in the writings of men like Irving and Cooper. He declared King Philip's War "as glorious as the *American* Revolution," compared Philip to George Washington, and pronounced him "the greatest man that was ever in America."[37]

More than any other early-nineteenth-century American writing about Philip, Apess collapsed the century-and-a-half divide between King Philip's War and the Indian removal act. By his mere existence, Apess falsified *Metamora*'s title. Standing in front of the Odeon before, we must assume, a largely white audience, Apess (like the Penobscots watching *Metamora*) was himself evidence that New England's Indians did not die out with Philip in August 1676. Unlike Forrest, Apess was an authentic Indian, as he made clear in

36. Apess, *On Our Own Ground,* ed. O'Connell, 177, 205.

37. Nielsen, "The Mashpee Indian Revolt," *NEQ,* 416; William Apess, *Eulogy on King Philip, as Pronounced at the Odeon in Federal Street, Boston* (Boston, 1836), 6, 47.

his address, again and again, referring to Indians as "we." And unlike Forrest, Apess addressed contemporary Indian rights issues directly. After citing the prejudice he had faced in his own life and the unjust legislation Indians were subject to, Apess offered an ultimatum. At the peak of the Second Seminole War, Apess advised, "Give the Indian his rights, and you may be assured war will cease." Moreover, Apess proposed a radical legacy for King Philip's War. Quoting "Dr. Mather," who had called Philip a man "of cursed memory," Apess addressed the possibility that, in vindicating Philip's memory, his Indian descendants might seek vengeance through attacks on Mather's descendants. "Now we wonder if the sons of the pilgrims would have us, poor Indians, come out and curse the doctor, and all their sons, as we have been, by many of them. And suppose that, in some future day, our children should repay all these wrongs, would it not be doing as we, poor Indians, have been done to?" (After making this threat, however, Apess retracted it: "We sincerely hope there is more humanity in us, than that.")[38]

Yet, for all his revolutionary ferment, Apess nonetheless participated in the romanticization of the vanishing Indian, as had Irving, Cooper, and Forrest before him. Almost all early-nineteenth-century Americans who wrote about King Philip's War included in their productions a rousing speech made by Philip (in 'Metamora, his counselors even urge him, "Speak, Metamora, speak!").[39] And Apess, too, could not resist this convention: "BROTHERS,—You see this vast country before us, which the great spirit gave to our fathers and us; you see the buffalo and deer that now are our support." Buffalo in New England? Clearly, Apess borrowed extensively from the writings and conventions of Indian fiction and of the reported laments of real Indians. Like every other authentic speech by Philip, Apess's is a fiction.

Perhaps uncomfortable with his fictitious Philip speech, however, Apess decided to provide something even more authentic. At the end of his lecture, Apess offered "a specimen of Philip's language," reciting the Lord's Prayer in an Algonquian dialect, perhaps as a means of distinguishing himself from stage Indians like Edwin Forrest. (Tellingly, this was the one feature of Apess's "performance" that was mentioned in a newspaper advertisement for the event: "At the close he will give a specimen of Philip's language.")[40] By speaking in Philip's language, Apess attempted to mediate between authentic Indian and stage Indian. Forrest's rendering of Indian speech was translation and inven-

38. Apess, *Eulogy*, 14.
39. Stone, *Metamora*, in Page, ed., *Metamora and Other Plays*, 25.
40. *Daily Evening Transcript* (Boston), Jan. 6, 1836.

tion, and so was much of Apess's, but in speaking in the nearly extinct Massachuset language Apess attempted to establish his own Indian authenticity.

William Apess used the fascination with Indian speech to find a broader audience for his unapologetically political addresses, whereas the Mashpees learned the lesson of *Metamora* and effectively targeted New Englanders' consciences in comparing their plight to that of the Cherokees. While the romantic Indian remained popular, men like William Apess and groups like the Mashpees used that image to their advantage. If whites were willing to say Indians fighting for their land were patriotic heroes, the Mashpees were willing to take them at their word and press their own claims. (The heroic Philip might have even inspired a Seminole resistance leader in Florida to take the name "King Philip.")[41] In these Indians' protests, they took Indianness back from performers like Forrest and laid the foundation for new generations of Indian activists in New England. Just when the noble savage was falling out of favor and Philip was becoming less useful as an American hero, Indians in New England, especially Wampanoags and Narragansetts, began embarking on a road toward cultural renewal and revival, a road that would lead them, eventually, to their own public and private commemorations of the events of King Philip's War.

If a Penobscot Indian really did carve an inscription on the Mount Hope Rock in 1833, it might well have been in response to the passionate performance of *Metamora,* which the delegation had just attended in Boston. Perhaps whoever wrote the inscription acted from the same impulse as William Apess, choosing to write in the Cherokee syllabary rather than in English as a means of establishing the inscription's Indian authenticity and participating in a kind of Indian nationalism to counter Forrest's American nationalism. Sitting in the audience at the Tremont Street Theater, someone among the Penobscot delegation might have contemplated the links between Cherokee removal and King Philip's War and found a way to spell it out. (The gesture, in fact, prefigures twentieth-century Pan-Indianism.) There are other possibilities, too. Thomas Mitchell, a full-blooded Cherokee, was also living near Boston at the time with his Wampanoag wife, Zerviah Gould, a direct descendant of Massasoit, Philip's father, and either of them might have been responsible for the inscription on Mount Hope Rock. Meanwhile, the Cherokee press was itself constructed in

41. For accounts of the capture of the "distinguished brave of the Seminole tribe," who was called "King Philip" during the Seminole wars, see *Niles' National Register* (Washington City), Aug. 4, 1838; and *Army and Navy Chronicle* (Washington, D.C.), July 6, 1837.

Boston in the 1820s, and someone associated with that endeavor might also have marked the rock. (Elias Boudinot, soon to become the editor of the *Cherokee Phoenix,* was living in Connecticut.)[42] Or, Edmund Delabarre's theory about the Cherokee attribution of the inscription may be poppycock, in which case we are left with yet another myth about the frontier.

To get to the rocky beach where the Mount Hope Rock sits, Edmund Delabarre had to travel down Metacom Avenue in Bristol, Rhode Island. Taking the same road today, we would pass by the King Philip Inn, at 400 Metacom Avenue. "King Philip" is a popular theme in Bristol, the name of streets, schools, and automotive repair shops. But Delabarre's theory about the rock's inscription has gone unnoticed; people in town call it "Viking's Rock," and, though everyone has heard of it, no one seems to remember exactly where it is. And almost no one, of course, remembers Edmund Delabarre, a young psychology professor who arrived at Brown University in 1892, just a year before Frederick Jackson Turner delivered his address on "The Significance of the Frontier in American History." Delabarre had trained at Harvard with William James, and, though his interests shifted from rapid movement (the subject of his dissertation) to inscribed rocks (his newfound New England hobby), he remained true to his Jamesian education. That is, he prided himself on his rigor in debunking romantic Victorian myths; he considered his investigation of inscribed rocks "an exceedingly valuable discipline in scientific method and an enlightening commentary on the psychology of . . . the differing ways in which the same object may be seen by different observers."[43]

The current controversy about the American frontier would have fascinated Edmund Delabarre. The frontier—a place, an idea, a moment—is one of the most contested elements of the American imagination. Frederick Jackson Turner suggested its significance, Richard Slotkin described its mythology, and both have been heavily and widely debated. What I have tried to do here is to understand the *significance of its mythology,* to explore, in a small and particular instance, the role of myths of earlier American frontiers in constructing responses to later ones. *Metamora,* the play, is a tragedy. Metamora, the Indian

42. Delabarre also considers the Mitchell possibility ("Inscribed Rocks," Rhode Island Hist. Soc., *Colls.,* XIII [1920], 21–22). On Zerviah Gould Mitchell, see Ebenezer W. Pierce, *Indian History, Biography, and Genealogy: Pertaining to the Good Sachem Massasoit of the Wampanoag Tribe, and His Descendants* (North Abington, Mass., 1878).

43. Delabarre, "Inscribed Rocks," Rhode Island Hist. Soc., *Colls.,* XIII (1920), 2.

FIGURE 10

King Philip Inn, Bristol, Rhode Island. *Photograph by Jill Lepore*

removal–era phenomenon, is a many-layered mystery. Old cruelties, new cruelties. Peel back all the layers—the play's origins, its actors, its audiences, its
critics—and what remains is a struggle for America's frontiers, both real and
mythical. With Edwin Forrest in its title role, *Metamora* was one of the most
important vehicles by which Indian removal was made palatable to the Ameri-

can public. Its themes and the responses to its production tell the story, not of King Philip's War, but of Cherokee and American nationalism.[44] And William Apess and the Mount Hope Rock, with its inscrutable inscription, suggest both the importance and the challenge of understanding how Indians, too, made use of frontier myths. Perhaps those Indians don't bellow at us across the centuries as loudly as Edwin Forrest does, but they are never, ever as silent as a rock.

44. See McLoughlin, who argues persuasively that Cherokee and American nationalism developed in tandem (*Cherokee Renascence,* xv–xvi).

# SELECTED BIBLIOGRAPHY

The following list of printed primary and secondary sources includes mainly works that relate to the historical period and regions covered by the essays in this volume. Although not inclusive, the bibliography provides a guide for further study of North American frontiers east of the Mississippi from about 1750 to 1830.

## PRIMARY SOURCES

Abbott, W. W., et al., eds. *The Papers of George Washington: Colonial Series.* 10 vols. Charlottesville, Va., 1983–1995.

"Account of the Famine among the Indians of the North and West Branch of the Susquehanna, in the Summer of 1748, An." *Pennsylvania Magazine of History and Biography,* XVI (1892), 430–432.

Adair, James. *Adair's History of the American Indians* (1775). Edited by Samuel Cole Williams. New York, 1966.

Albion, Robert Greenhalgh, and Leonidas Dodson, eds. *Philip Vickers Fithian: Journal, 1775–1776; Written on the Virginia-Pennsylvania Frontier and in the Army around New York.* Princeton, N.J., 1934.

Apess, William. *Eulogy on King Philip, as Pronounced at the Odeon in Federal Street, Boston.* Boston, 1836.

———. *On Our Own Ground: The Complete Writings of William Apess, a Pequot.* Edited by Barry O'Connell. Amherst, Mass., 1992.

Atwater, Caleb. *Remarks Made on a Tour to Prairie du Chien; Thence to Washington City in 1829.* Columbus, Ohio, 1831.

Babcock, Rufus, ed. *Forty Years of Pioneer Life: Memoir of John Mason Peck, D.D.* Philadelphia, 1864.

Bailey, Kenneth P., ed. *Journal of Joseph Marin: French Colonial Explorer and Military Commander in the Wisconsin Country, August 7, 1753–June 20, 1754.* N.p., 1975.

Bartram, John. *Observations on the Inhabitants, Climate, Soil, Rivers, Productions, Animals, and Other Matters Worthy of Notice; Made by John Bartram, in His Travels from Pensilvania to Onondago, Oswego, and the Lake Ontario, in Canada.* . . . London, 1751.

Bartram, William. "Observations on the Creek and Cherokee Indians, 1789, with Prefatory and Supplementary Notes by E. G. Squier." American Ethnological Society, *Transactions,* III (New York, 1953), 1–81.

———. *Travels of William Bartram* (1791). Edited by Mark Van Doren. New York, 1928.

Beauchamp, William M., ed. *Moravian Journals Relating to Central New York, 1745–1766.* Syracuse, N.Y., 1916.

Beckwourth, James P. *The Life and Adventures of James P. Beckwourth as Told to Thomas D. Bonner.* 1856; reprint, Lincoln, Nebr., 1972.

Bibb, Henry. "Narrative of the Life and Adventure of Henry Bibb, an American Slave Written by Himself." In Gilbert Osofsky, ed., *Puttin' on Ole Massa: The Slave Narratives of Henry Bibb, William Wells Brown, and Solomon Northrup*, 51–171. New York, 1969.

Blair, John L., ed. "Mrs. Mary Dewees's Journal from Philadelphia to Kentucky." *Register of the Kentucky Historical Society*, LXIII (1965), 195–217.

[Blane, William Newnham]. *Travels through the United States and Canada*. London, 1828.

Bliss, Eugene F., ed. *Diary of David Zeisberger: A Moravian Missionary among the Indians of Ohio*. 2 vols. Cincinnati, 1885.

Boyd, Julian P., ed. *The Susquehannah Company Papers*. Vols. I–IV. Wilkes-Barre, Pa., 1930–1933.

Brackenridge, H. M. *Journal of a Voyage up the River Missouri; Performed in Eighteen Hundred and Eleven*. Baltimore, 1816.

———. *Recollections of Persons and Places in the West*. Philadelphia, 1834.

———. *Views of Louisiana; Containing Geographical, Statistical, and Historical Notices of that Vast and Important Portion of America*. Baltimore, 1817.

Brown, Orley E., ed. *The Captivity of Jonathan Alder and His Life with the Indians*. Alliance, Ohio, 1965.

Buckner, Henry Frieland. *A Grammar of the Maskwke, or Creek Language*. Marion, Ala., 1860.

Calloway, Colin G. *The World Turned Upside Down: Indian Voices from Early America*. Boston, 1994.

Carmony, Donald F., ed. "Spencer Records' Memoir of the Ohio Valley Frontier, 1766–1795." *Indiana Magazine of History*, LV (1959), 323–377.

Charlevoix, P[ierre] de. *Journal of a Voyage to North-America*. 2 vols. London, 1761.

Cooper, James Fenimore. *The Wept of Wish-ton Wish*. Philadelphia, 1829.

———. *The Wept of Wish-ton Wish; a Drama in Two Acts, from J. Fennimore Cooper's Celebrated Novel of the Same Name, as Performed at All the Principal Theatres in the United States*. [New York, n.d.].

Coues, Elliott, ed. *The Expeditions of Zebulon Montgomery Pike*. 3 vols. New York, 1895.

Cresswell, Nicholas. *The Journal of Nicholas Cresswell, 1774–1777*. London, 1925.

Croghan, George. "Croghan's Journal, 1754." In Reuben Gold Thwaites, ed., *Early Western Travels, 1748–1846 . . .* , I, 72–81. Cleveland, Ohio, 1904–1907.

Cruikshank, Ernest Alexander, ed. *The Correspondence of Lieut. Governor John Graves Simcoe. . . .* 5 vols. Toronto, 1923–1926.

Denny, Ebenezer. *Military Journal of Major Ebenezer Denny, an Officer in the Revolutionary and Indian Wars. . . .* Philadelphia, 1859.

De Vorsey, Louis, Jr., ed. *De Brahm's Report of the General Survey in the Southern District of North America*. Columbia, S.C., 1971.

Dexter, Franklin B., ed. *Diary of David McClure, Doctor of Divinity, 1748–1820*. New York, 1899.

Doddridge, Joseph. *Notes on the Settlement and Indian Wars of the Western Parts of Virginia and Pennsylvania from 1763 to 1783*. 1824; reprint, Pittsburgh, 1912.

Drake, Daniel. *Pioneer Life in Kentucky, 1785–1800*. Edited by Emmet Field Horine. New York, 1948.

Dugan, Frances L. S., and Jacqueline P. Bull, eds. *Bluegrass Craftsman: Being the Reminiscences of Ebenezer Hiram Stedman, Papermaker, 1808–1885.* Lexington, Ky., 1959.

Eastburn, James Wallis [and Robert Charles Sands]. *Yamoyden, a Tale of the Wars of King Philip: In Six Cantos. . . .* New York, 1820.

Edgar, Matilda, ed. *Ten Years of Upper Canada in Peace and War, 1805–1815; Being the Ridout Letters. . . .* Toronto, 1890.

Elliot, James. "Essay II; On the Moral Consequences of Standing Armies." In Elliot, *The Poetical and Miscellaneous Works of James Elliot.* Greenfield, Mass., 1798.

[Evarts, Jeremiah]. *Essays on the Present Crisis in the Condition of the American Indians.* Boston, 1829.

Feiler, Seymour, ed. and trans. *Jean-Bernard Bossu's Travels in the Interior of North America, 1751–1762.* Norman, Okla., 1962.

Filson, John. *The Discovery, Settlement, and Present State of Kentucke* (1784). Edited by William H. Masterson. New York, 1962.

Finiels, Nicolas de. *An Account of Upper Louisiana.* Edited by Carl J. Ekberg and William E. Foley. Columbia, Mo., 1989.

Finley, James B. *Autobiography of Rev. James B. Finley; or, Pioneer Life in the West.* Edited by W. P. Strickland. Cincinnati, 1853.

Fitzpatrick, John C., ed. *The Diaries of George Washington, 1748–1799.* 4 vols. New York, 1925.

——, ed. *The Writings of George Washington from the Original Manuscript Sources, 1745–1799.* 39 vols. Washington, D.C., 1931–1944.

Flint, Timothy. *Recollections of the Last Ten Years in the Valley of the Mississippi.* Edited by George R. Brooks. 1826; reprint, Carbondale, Ill., 1968.

Gates, Charles M., ed. *Five Fur Traders of the Northwest.* Saint Paul, Minn., 1965.

Gelb, Norman, ed. *Jonathan Carver's Travels through America, 1766–1768.* New York, 1993.

Gipson, Lawrence Henry, ed. *The Moravian Indian Mission on White River: Diaries and Letters, May 5, 1799, to November 12, 1806.* Indiana Historical Collections, XXIII. Indianapolis, 1938.

Grant, Anne. *Memoirs of an American Lady: With Sketches of Manners and Scenery in America, as They Existed Previous to the Revolution.* 2 vols. 1808; reprint, New York, 1970.

Grant, C. L., ed. *Letters, Journals, and Writings of Benjamin Hawkins.* 2 vols. Savannah, Ga., 1980.

Gratiot, Adèle. "Mrs. Adèle P. Gratiot's Narrative." State Historical Society of Wisconsin, *Collections,* X (Madison, Wis., 1888), 261–275.

Grignon, Augustin. "Seventy-Two Years' Recollections of Wisconsin." State Historical Society of Wisconsin, *Collections,* III (Madison, Wis., 1857), 197–295.

Hammon, Neal, and James Russell Harris, eds. " 'In a Dangerous Situation': Letters of Col. John Floyd, 1774–1783." *Register of the Kentucky Historical Society,* LXXXIII (1985), 202–236.

Heckewelder, John. *History, Manners, and Customs of the Indian Nations, Who Once Inhabited Pennsylvania and the Neighbouring States.* Rev. ed. Edited by William C. Reichel. 1876; facsimile reprint, Bowie, Md., 1990.

————. *A Narrative of the Mission of the United Brethren among the Delaware and Mohegan Indians, from Its Commencement, in the Year 1740, to the Close of the Year 1808.* Philadelphia, 1820.

Hodges, Graham Russell, and Alan Edward Brown, eds. *"Pretends to Be Free": Runaway Slave Advertisements from Colonial and Revolutionary New York and New Jersey.* New York, 1994.

Hogan, Roseann R., ed. "Buffaloes in the Corn: James Wade's Account of Pioneer Kentucky." *Register of the Kentucky Historical Society,* LXXXIX (1991), 1–31.

Hubbard, William. *A Narrative of the Troubles with the Indians in New-England.* . . . Boston, 1677.

Irving, Washington. *Astoria; or, Anecdotes of an Enterprise beyond the Rocky Mountains.* 2 vols. 1836; reprint, Philadelphia, 1961.

————. "Philip of Pokanet." In *The Works of Washington Irving.* Vol. II. *The Sketch Book.* New York, 1851.

Jackson, Donald, ed. *Black Hawk, an Autobiography.* Urbana, Ill., 1955.

Jacobs, Wilbur R., ed. *The Appalachian Indian Frontier: The Edmond Atkin Report and Plan of 1755.* 1954; reprint, Lincoln, Nebr., 1967.

Janney, Abel. "Narrative of the Capture of Abel Janney by the Indians in 1782." Ohio Archaeological and Historical Society, *Publications,* VIII (Columbus, Ohio, 1900), 465–473.

Johnston, J. Stoddard, ed. *First Explorations of Kentucky: Journals of Dr. Thomas Walker, 1750, and Christopher Gist, 1751.* Louisville, Ky., 1898.

Jones, Alfred Porter. *The Writings of General Forbes Relating to His Service in America.* Menasha, Wis., 1938.

Jones, David. *A Journal of Two Visits Made to Some Nations of Indians on the West Side of the River Ohio, in the Years 1772 and 1773.* 1774; reprint, New York, 1865.

Jordan, John W. "Rev. John Martin Mack's Narrative of a Visit to Onondaga in 1752." *Pennsylvania Magazine of History and Biography,* XXIX (1905), 343–358.

————, ed. "Bishop J.C.F. Cammerhoff's Narrative of a Journey to Shamokin, Penna., in the Winter of 1748." *Pennsylvania Magazine of History and Biography,* XXIX (1905), 160–179.

————, ed. "Journal of James Kenny, 1761–1763." *Pennsylvania Magazine of History and Biography,* XXXVII (1913), 1–47, 152–201.

————, ed. "Spangenberg's Notes of Travel to Onondaga in 1745." *Pennsylvania Magazine of History and Biography,* II (1878), 424–432, III (1879), 56–64.

Keefe, James F., and Lynn Morrow, eds. *The White River Chronicles of S. C. Turnbo: Man and Wildlife on the Ozarks Frontier.* Fayetteville, Ark., 1994.

Kilpatrick, Jack Frederick, ed. "The Wahnenauhi Manuscript: Historical Sketches of the Cherokees, Together with Some of Their Customs, Traditions, and Superstitions." Smithsonian Institution, *Bureau of American Ethnology Bulletin,* CXCVI (Washington, D.C., 1966), Anthropological Papers, no. 77.

Kilpatrick, Lewis H., ed. "The Journal of William Calk, Kentucky Pioneer." *Mississippi Valley Historical Review,* VII (1921), 363–377.

King, Duane, H., ed. *The Cherokee Indian Nation: A Troubled History.* Knoxville, Tenn., 1979.

Kinietz, Vernon, and Erminie W. Voegelin, eds. *Shawnese Traditions: C. C. Trowbridge's Account.* Occasional Contributions of the Museum of Anthropology, University of Michigan, Number 9. Ann Arbor, Mich., 1939.

Kinnan, Mary. *A True Narrative of the Sufferings of Mary Kinnan, Who Was Taken Prisoner by the Shawanee Nation of Indians on the Thirteenth Day of May, 1791, and Remained with Them till the Sixteenth of August, 1794.* Elizabethtown, Ky., 1795.

[Kinzie, Juliette M.]. *Wau-Bun: The "Early Day" in the North-West* (1856). Edited by Nina Baym. Urbana, Ill., 1992.

Knopf, Richard C. *Anthony Wayne, a Name in Arms: Soldier, Diplomat, Defender of Expansion Westward of a Nation; The Wayne-Knox-Pickering-McHenry Correspondence.* Pittsburgh, 1960.

———. *A Surgeon's Mate at Fort Defiance: The Journal of Joseph Gardner Andrews for the Year 1795.* Columbus, Ohio, 1957.

*Letters of Benjamin Hawkins, 1796–1806.* Georgia Historical Society, *Collections,* IX (Savannah, Ga., 1916).

Loudon, Archibald. *A Selection of Some of the Most Interesting Narratives, of Outrages, Committed by the Indians, in Their Wars, with the White People. . . .* 2 vols. Carlisle, Pa., 1808–1811.

Loughridge, R. M., and David M. Hodge. *English and Muskokee Dictionary: Collected from Various Sources and Revised.* 1890; reprint, Okmulgee, Okla., 1964.

Lowry, Jean. *A Journal of Captivity of Jean Lowry and Her Children. . . .* Philadelphia, 1760.

Mather, Increase. *A Brief History of the Warr with the Indians in New-England. . . .* Boston, 1676.

Mauelshagen, Carl, and Carl H. Davis, ed. *Partners in the Lord's Work: The Diary of Two Moravian Missionaries in the Creek Indian Country, 1807–1813.* Atlanta, Ga., 1969.

"Military Letters of Captain Joseph Shippen of the Provincial Service, 1756–1758." *Pennsylvania Magazine of History and Biography,* XXXVI (1912), 367–378, 385–463.

Palmer, John. *Journal of Travels in the United States of North America, and in Lower Canada, Performed in the Year 1817.* London, 1818.

Perrin du Lac, François Marie. *Travels through the Two Louisianas and among the Savage Nations of the Missouri. . . .* London, 1807.

Pope, John. *A Tour through the Southern and Western Territories of the United States of North America; the Spanish Dominions on the River Mississippi, and the Floridas; the Countries of the Creek Nations; and Many Uninhabited Parts.* 1792; facsimile reprint, Gainesville, Fla., 1979.

Pownall, T[homas]. *A Topographical Description of the Dominions of the United States of America.* Edited by Lois Mulkearn. Pittsburgh, 1949.

Purviance, Levi. *The Biography of Elder David Purviance, with His Memoirs: Containing His Views on Baptism, the Divinity of Christ, and the Atonement. . . .* Dayton, Ohio, 1848.

Quaife, Milo Milton. "Henry Hay's Journal from Detroit to the Mississippi River." State Historical Society of Wisconsin, *Proceedings,* LXII (Madison, Wis., 1914), 208–261.

———, ed. *Alexander Henry's Travels and Adventures in the Years 1760–1776.* Chicago, 1921.

"Ranger's Report of Travels with General Ogelthorpe, 1739–1742, A." In Newton D. Mereness, ed., *Travels in the American Colonies,* 215–236. New York, 1916.

*Record of the Court at Upland, in Pennsylvania, 1676 to 1681, and a Military Journal Kept by Major E. Denny, 1781–1795, The.* Philadelphia, 1860.

Redd, John. "Reminiscences of Western Virginia, 1770–1790." *Virginia Magazine of History and Biography,* VI (1899), 337–346.

Ridout, Thomas. "An Account of My Capture by the Shawanese Indians." *Western Pennsylvania Historical Magazine,* XII (1929), 3–31.

Romans, Bernard. *A Concise Natural History of East and West Florida. . . .* New York, 1775.

Schoolcraft, Henry Rowe. *Travels through the Northwestern Regions of the United States.* 1821; reprint, Ann Arbor, Mich., 1966.

Schultz, Christian, Jr. *Travels in an Inland Voyage through the States of New-York, Pennsylvania, Virginia, Ohio, Kentucky, and Tennessee, and through the Territories of Indiana, Louisiana, Mississippi, and New-Orleans.* 2 vols. New York, 1810.

Schwaab, Eugene Lincoln, ed. *Travels in the Old South, Selected from Periodicals of the Times.* 2 vols. Lexington, Ky., 1973.

Seaver, James E., comp. *A Narrative of the Life of Mrs. Mary Jemison. . . .* 1824; reprint, Syracuse, N.Y., 1990.

Smith, James. *An Account of the Remarkable Occurrences in the Life and Travels of Col. James Smith, during His Captivity with the Indians, in the Years 1755, '56, '57, '58, and '59.* Edited by William Darlington. 1799; reprint, Cincinnati, 1870.

Smyth, J[ohn] F[erdinand] D[aniel]. *A Tour in the United States of America.* 2 vols. London, 1784.

Southey, Robert. "Oliver Newman, A New-England Tale." In Southey, *The Poetical Works of Robert Southey,* V, 263–358. Boston, 1880.

Spencer, O. M. *The Indian Captivity of O. M. Spencer.* Edited by Milo Milton Quaife. Chicago, 1917.

Stevens, S. K., et al., eds. *The Papers of Henry Bouquet.* Harrisburg, Pa., 1951–.

Stevens, Sylvester K., and Donald H. Kent, eds. *Wilderness Chronicles of Northwestern Pennsylvania.* Harrisburg, Pa., 1941.

Still, Bayard, ed. "The Westward Migration of a Planter Pioneer in 1796." *William and Mary Quarterly,* 2d Ser., XXI (1941), 318–343.

Stoddard, Amos. *Sketches, Historical and Descriptive, of Louisiana.* Philadelphia, 1812.

Stone, John Augustus. *Metamora; or, The Last of the Wampanoags: An Indian Tragedy in Five Acts as Played by Edwin Forrest.* In Eugene R. Page, ed., *Metamora and Other Plays.* Princeton, N.J., 1941.

Sullivan, James, et al., eds. *The Papers of Sir William Johnson.* 14 vols. Albany, N.Y., 1921–1965.

Swan, Caleb. "Position and State of Manners and Arts in the Creek, or Muscogee Nation in 1791." In Henry Rowe Schoolcraft, ed., *Information respecting the History, Condition, and Prospects of the Indian Tribes of the United States . . . ,* V, 251–283. 1855; reprint, New York, 1969.

Taitt, David. "David Taitt's Journal of a Journey through the Creek Country, 1772." In Newton D. Mereness, ed., *Travels in the American Colonies,* 493–565. New York, 1916.

Talbert, Charles G., ed. "Looking Backward through One Hundred Years: Personal Recollections of James B. Ireland." *Register of the Kentucky Historical Society,* LVII (1959), 109–117.

Taylor, John. *A History of Ten Baptist Churches, of Which the Author Has Been Alternately a Member: In Which Will Be Seen Something of a Journal of the Author's Life for More Than Fifty Years.* Bloomfield, Ky., 1827.

[Thomson, Charles]. *An Enquiry into the Causes of Alienation of the Delaware and Shawanese Indians from the British Interest.* 1759; reprint, Philadelphia, 1867.

Thwaites, Reuben Gold, ed. *Early Western Travels, 1748–1846.* . . . 32 vols. Cleveland, Ohio, 1904–1907.

Triplett, Robert. *Roland Trevor: or, The Pilot of Human Life; Being an Autobiography of the Author, Showing How to Make and Lose a Fortune, and Then to Make Another.* Philadelphia, 1853.

Van Horne, John C., ed. *Religious Philanthropy and Colonial Slavery: The Correspondence of the Associates of Dr. Bray, 1717–1777.* Urbana, Ill., 1985.

Walker, Joseph E., ed. "Plowshares and Pruning Hooks for the Miami and Potawatomi: The Journal of Gerard T. Hopkins, 1804." *Ohio History,* LXXXVIII (1979), 361–407.

Wallace, Paul A. W., ed. *Thirty Thousand Miles with John Heckewelder.* Pittsburgh, 1958.

Whitelaw, James. "Journal of General James Whitelaw, Surveyor-General of Vermont." Vermont Historical Society, *Proceedings* (St. Albans, 1905–1906), 119–157.

Williams, Samuel C., ed. "An Account of the Presbyterian Mission to the Cherokee, 1757–1759." *Tennessee Historical Magazine,* 2d Ser., I (1930–1931), 134–135.

Wright, Louis B., and Marion Tinling, eds. *The Secret Diary of William Byrd of Westover, 1709–1712.* Richmond, Va., 1941.

Young, Chester Raymond, ed. *Westward into Kentucky: The Narrative of Daniel Trabue.* Lexington, Ky., 1981.

SECONDARY SOURCES

Abernethy, Thomas Perkins. *Three Virginia Frontiers.* Baton Rouge, La., 1940.

Alden, John Richard. *John Stuart and the Southern Colonial Frontier: A Study of Indian Relations, War, Trade, and Land Problems in the Southern Wilderness, 1754–1775.* London, 1944.

Amacher, Richard E. "Behind the Curtain with the Noble Savage: Stage Management of Indian Plays, 1825–1860." *Theatre Survey,* VII (1966), 101–114.

Ambrose, Stephen E. *Undaunted Courage: Meriwether Lewis, Thomas Jefferson, and the Opening of the American West.* New York, 1996.

Anderson, Hattie M. "Missouri, 1804–1828: Peopling a Frontier State." *Missouri Historical Review,* XXXI (1927), 150–180.

Anderson, Karen. *Chain Her by One Foot: The Subjugation of Native Women in Seventeenth-Century New France.* London, 1991.

Anderson, Marilyn J. "The Image of the Indian in American Drama during the Jacksonian Era, 1829–1845." *Journal of American Culture,* I (1978), 800–810.

Anderson, Virginia DeJohn. "King Philip's Herds: Indians, Colonists, and the Problem of Livestock in Early New England." *William and Mary Quarterly,* 3d Ser., LI (1994), 601–624.

Anson, Bert. *The Miami Indians.* Norman, Okla., 1970.

Aquila, Richard. *The Iroquois Restoration: Iroquois Diplomacy on the Colonial Frontier, 1701–1754.* Detroit, 1983.

Arnow, Harriette S. *Seedtime on the Cumberland.* New York, 1960.

Aron, Stephen. *How the West Was Lost: The Transformation of Kentucky from Daniel Boone to Henry Clay.* Baltimore, 1996.

———. "Lessons in Conquest: Towards a Greater Western History." *Pacific Historical Review,* LXIII (1994), 125–147.

Axtell, James. *The European and the Indian: Essays in the Ethnohistory of Colonial North America.* New York, 1981.

———. *The Invasion Within: The Contest of Cultures in Colonial North America.* New York, 1985.

———. "The Scholastic Philosophy of the Wilderness." *William and Mary Quarterly,* 3d Ser., XXIX (1972), 335–366.

Bailyn, Bernard, and Philip D. Morgan, eds. *Strangers within the Realm: Cultural Margins of the First British Empire.* Chapel Hill, N.C., 1991.

Bank, Rosemarie K. "Staging the 'Native': Making History in American Theatre Culture, 1828–1838." *Theatre Journal,* XLV (1993), 461–486.

Barnhart, John D. *Valley of Democracy: The Frontier versus the Plantation in the Ohio Valley, 1775–1818.* Bloomington, Ind., 1953.

Beckner, Lucien. "Eskippakithiki: The Last Indian Town in Kentucky." *Filson Club History Quarterly,* VI (1932), 355–382.

Beeman, Richard R. *The Evolution of the Southern Backcountry: A Case Study of Lunenburg County, Virginia, 1746–1832.* Philadelphia, 1984.

Bell, Amelia Rector. "Separate People: Speaking of Creek Men and Women." *American Anthropologist,* XCII (1990), 332–346.

Bellesiles, Michael A. *Revolutionary Outlaws: Ethan Allen and the Struggle for Independence on the Early American Frontier.* Charlottesville, Va., 1993.

Berkhofer, Robert F., Jr. "Space, Time, Culture, and the New Frontier." *Agricultural History,* XXXVIII (1964), 21–30.

———. *The White Man's Indian: Images of the American Indian from Columbus to the Present.* New York, 1978.

Billington, Ray Allen. *The American Frontier Thesis: Attack and Defense.* Washington, D.C., 1971.

Bliss, Willard F. "The Tuckahoe in New Virginia." *Virginia Magazine of History and Biography,* LIX (1951), 387–396.

Boyd, Steven R., ed. *The Whiskey Rebellion: Past and Present Perspectives.* Westport, Conn., 1985.

Braund, Kathryn E. Holland. *Deerskins and Duffels: The Creek Indian Trade with Anglo-America, 1685–1815.* Lincoln, Nebr., 1993.

Brooks, Charles E. *Frontier Settlement and Market Revolution: The Holland Land Purchase.* Ithaca, N.Y., 1996.

Brown, Jeffrey P., and Andrew R. L. Cayton, eds. *The Pursuit of Public Power: Political Culture in Ohio, 1787–1861.* Kent, Ohio, 1994.

Brown, Jennifer S. H. *Strangers in Blood: Fur Trade Company Families in Indian Country.* Vancouver, 1980.

Brown, Richard Maxwell. "Back Country Rebellions and the Homestead Ethic in America, 1740–1799." In Brown and Don E. Fehrenbacher, eds., *Tradition, Conflict, and Modernization: Perspectives on the American Revolution,* 73–99. New York, 1977.

Burdette, Ruth Paull, and Nancy Montgomery Berley. *The Long Hunters of Skin House Branch.* Columbia, Ky., 1970.

Calloway, Colin G. *The American Revolution in Indian Country: Crisis and Diversity in Native American Communities.* Cambridge, 1995.

———. "Beyond the Vortex of Violence: Indian-White Relations in the Ohio Country, 1783–1815." *Northwest Ohio Quarterly,* LXIV (1992), 16–26.

———. *Crown and Calumet: British-Indian Relations, 1783–1815.* Norman, Okla., 1987.

———. *The Western Abenakis of Vermont, 1600–1800: War, Migration, and the Survival of an Indian People.* Norman, Okla., 1990.

Carter, Harvey Lewis. *The Life and Times of Little Turtle: First Sagamore of the Wabash.* Urbana, Ill., 1987.

Cashin, Joan E. *A Family Venture: Men and Women on the Southern Frontier.* New York, 1991.

Cayton, Andrew R. L. *Frontier Indiana.* Bloomington, Ind., 1996.

———. *The Frontier Republic: Ideology and Politics in the Ohio Country, 1780–1825.* Kent, Ohio, 1986.

———. "Land, Power, and Reputation: The Cultural Dimension of Politics in the Ohio Country." *William and Mary Quarterly,* 3d Ser., XLVII (1990), 266–286.

———. "'Separate Interests' and the Nation-State: The Washington Administration and the Origins of Regionalism in the Trans-Appalachian West." *Journal of American History,* LXXIX (June–September 1992), 39–67.

———, et al. *Pathways to the Old Northwest: An Observance of the Bicentennial of the Northwest Ordinance.* Indianapolis, 1988.

"Centennial Symposium on the Significance of Frederick Jackson Turner, A." *Journal of the Early Republic,* XIII (1993), 133–249.

Cheal, David. *The Gift Economy.* New York, 1988.

Cheyfitz, Eric. *The Poetics of Imperialism: Translation and Colonization from* The Tempest *to* Tarzan. New York, 1991.

Clark, Christopher. *The Roots of Rural Capitalism: Western Massachusetts, 1780–1860.* Ithaca, N.Y., 1990.

Clark, Jerry E. *The Shawnee.* Lexington, Ky., 1977.

Clark, Thomas D., and John D. W. Guice. *Frontiers in Conflict: The Old Southwest, 1795–1830.* Albuquerque, N.M., 1989.

Clifton, James, ed. *Being and Becoming Indian: Biographical Studies of North American Frontiers.* Chicago, 1989.

Cohen, Anthony P. *The Symbolic Construction of Community.* New York, 1985.

Comaroff, John, and Jean Comaroff. *Ethnography and the Historical Imagination.* Boulder, Colo., 1992.

Corkran, David H. *The Cherokee Frontier: Conflict and Survival, 1740–62.* Norman, Okla., 1962.

Countryman, Edward. *Americans: A Collision of Histories.* New York, 1996.

———. "Indians, the Colonial Order, and the Social Significance of the American Revolution." *William and Mary Quarterly,* 3d Ser., LIII (1996), 342–362.

Coward, Joan Wells. *Kentucky in the New Republic: The Process of Constitution Making.* Lexington, Ky., 1979.

Cronon, William. *Changes in the Land: Indians, Colonists, and the Ecology of New England.* New York, 1983.

Cronon, William, George Miles, and Jay Gitlin, eds. *Under an Open Sky: Rethinking America's Western Past.* New York, 1992.

Davis, Natalie Zemon. "Iroquois Women, European Women." In Margo Hendricks and Patricia Parker, eds., *Women, "Race," and Writing in the Early Modern Period,* 243–258. London, 1994.

Demos, John. *The Unredeemed Captive: A Family Story from Early America.* New York, 1994.

Dening, Greg. *Mr Bligh's Bad Language: Passion, Power, and Theatre on the Bounty.* New York, 1992.

Dennis, Matthew. *Cultivating a Landscape of Peace: Iroquois-European Encounters in Seventeenth-Century America.* Berkeley, Calif., 1992.

Dippie, Brian W. *The Vanishing American: White Attitudes and U.S. Indian Policy.* Middletown, Conn., 1982.

Douglas, Mary, and Baron Isherwood. *The World of Goods: Towards an Anthropology of Consumption.* New York, 1979.

Dowd, Gregory Evans. "The Panic of 1751: The Significance of Rumors on the South Carolina-Cherokee Frontier." *William and Mary Quarterly,* 3d Ser., LIII (1996), 527–560.

———. *A Spirited Resistance: The North American Indian Struggle for Unity, 1745–1815.* Baltimore, 1992.

Downes, Randolph Chandler. *Council Fires on the Upper Ohio: A Narrative of Indian Affairs in the Upper Ohio Valley until 1795.* Pittsburgh, 1940.

———. *Frontier Ohio, 1788–1803.* Ohio State Archaeological and Historical Society, *Collections,* XIV (Columbus, Ohio, 1935).

Downs, Dorothy. "British Influences on Creek and Seminole Men's Clothing, 1733–1858." *Florida Anthropologist,* XXXIII, no. 2 (1980), 46–65.

Drake, St. Clair. *Black Folk Here and There: An Essay in History and Anthropology.* 2 vols. Los Angeles, Calif., 1987.

Earle, Carville, and Changyong Cao. "Frontier Closure and the Evolution of American Society, 1840–1890." *Journal of the Early Republic,* XIII (1993), 163–179.

Eby, Cecil. *"That Disgraceful Affair," the Black Hawk War.* New York, 1973.

Eccles, W. J. *The Canadian Frontier, 1534–1760.* Rev. ed. Albuquerque, N.M., 1983.

Edmunds, R. David. *The Potawatomis: Keepers of the Fire.* Norman, Okla., 1978.

———. *The Shawnee Prophet.* Lincoln, Nebr., 1983.

———. *Tecumseh and the Quest for Indian Leadership.* Boston, 1984.

Edmunds, R. David, and Joseph L. Peyser. *The Fox Wars: The Mesquakie Challenge to New France.* Norman, Okla., 1993.

Egnal, Marc. *A Mighty Empire: The Origins of the American Revolution.* Ithaca, N.Y., 1988.

Ekberg, Carl J. *Colonial Ste. Genevieve: An Adventure on the Mississippi Frontier.* Gerald, Mo., 1985.

Ekirch, A. Roger. *"Poor Carolina": Politics and Society in Colonial North Carolina, 1729–1776.* Chapel Hill, N.C., 1981.

Elkins, Stanley, and Eric McKitrick. "A Meaning for Turner's Frontier: Part I, Democracy in the Old Northwest." *Political Science Quarterly,* LXIX (1954), 321–353.

———. "A Meaning for Turner's Frontier: Part II, The Southwest Frontier and New England." *Political Science Quarterly,* LXIX (1954), 565–602.

Etienne, Mona, and Eleanor Leacock, eds. *Women and Colonization: Anthropological Perspectives.* New York, 1980.

Fabel, Robin F. A. *The Economy of British West Florida, 1763–1783.* Tuscaloosa, Ala., 1988.

Faragher, John Mack. *Daniel Boone: The Life and Legend of an American Pioneer.* New York, 1992.

———. *Sugar Creek: Life on the Illinois Prairie.* New Haven, Conn., 1986.

———, ed. *Rereading Frederick Jackson Turner: "The Significance of the Frontier in American History," and Other Essays.* New York, 1994.

Finger, John R. *The Eastern Band of Cherokees, 1819–1900.* Knoxville, Tenn., 1984.

Finkelman, Paul. "Evading the Ordinance: The Persistence of Bondage in Indiana and Illinois." *Journal of the Early Republic,* IX (1989), 21–51.

———. "Slavery and the Northwest Ordinance: A Study in Ambiguity." *Journal of the Early Republic,* VI (1986), 343–370.

Fischer, David Hackett. *Albion's Seed: Four British Folkways in America.* New York, 1989.

Forbes, Jack D. *Africans and Native Americans: The Language of Race and the Evolution of Red-Black Peoples.* Chicago, 1993.

———. "Frontiers in American History and the Role of the Frontier Historian." *Ethnohistory,* XV (1968), 203–235.

Foreman, Grant. *The Last Trek of the Indians.* Chicago, 1946.

Foster, Martha Harroun. "Of Baggage and Bondage: Gender and Status among Hidatsa and Crow Women." *American Indian Culture and Research Journal,* XVII (1993), 121–152.

Foster, Michael K., Jack Campisi, and Marianne Mithun, eds. *Extending the Rafter: Interdisciplinary Approaches to Iroquoian Studies.* Albany, N.Y., 1984.

Gallay, Alan. *The Formation of a Planter Elite: Jonathan Bryan and the Southern Colonial Frontier.* Athens, Ga., 1989.

Galloway, Patricia. *Choctaw Genesis, 1500–1700.* Lincoln, Nebr., 1995.

Galloway, William Albert. *Old Chillicothe: Shawnee and Pioneer History; Conflicts and Romances in the Northwest Territory.* Xenia, Ohio, 1934.

Gearing, Fred O. *Priests and Warriors: Social Structures for Cherokee Politics in the Eighteenth Century.* American Anthropological Association Memoir no. 93. Menasha, Wis., 1962.

Gilbert, Bil. *God Gave Us This Country: Tekamthi and the First American Civil War.* New York, 1989.

Goodstein, Anita Shafer. *Nashville, 1780–1860: From Frontier to City.* Gainesville, Fla., 1989.

Gorn, Elliott J. " 'Gouge and Bite, Pull Hair and Scratch': The Social Significance of Fighting in the Southern Backcountry." *American Historical Review,* XC (1985), 18–43.

Gray, Elma E. *Wilderness Christians: The Moravian Mission to the Delaware Indians.* Ithaca, N.Y., 1956.

Gray, Susan E. *The Yankee West: Community Life on the Michigan Frontier.* Chapel Hill, N.C., 1996.

Graymont, Barbara. *The Iroquois in the American Revolution.* Syracuse, N.Y., 1972.

Green, Michael D. *The Politics of Indian Removal: Creek Government and Society in Crisis.* Lincoln, Nebr., 1982.

Griffis, William Eliot. *Sir William Johnson and the Six Nations.* New York, 1891.

Guice, John D. W. "Cattle Raisers of the Old Southwest: A Reinterpretation." *Western Historical Quarterly,* VIII (1977), 167–187.

Gutiérrez, Ramón A. *When Jesus Came, the Corn Mothers Went Away: Marriage, Sexuality, and Power in New Mexico, 1500–1846.* Stanford, Calif., 1991.

Hagan, William T. *The Sac and Fox Indians.* Norman, Okla., 1958.

Hagedorn, Nancy L. " 'A Friend to Go between Them': The Interpreter as Cultural Broker during Anglo-Iroquois Councils, 1740–70." *Ethnohistory,* XXXV (1988), 60–80.

Hahn, Steven, and Jonathan Prude, eds. *The Countryside in the Age of Capitalist Transformation: Essays in the Social History of Rural America.* Chapel Hill, N.C., 1985.

Hamell, George R. "Mythical Realities and European Contact in the Northeast during the Sixteenth and Seventeenth Centuries." *Man in the Northeast,* no. 33 (Spring 1987), 63–87.

Hanna, Charles A. *The Wilderness Trail; or, The Ventures and Adventures of the Pennsylvania Traders on the Allegheny Path.* . . . 2 vols. New York, 1911.

Harvey, Henry. *History of the Shawnee Indians: From the Year 1681 to 1854, Inclusive.* Cincinnati, 1855.

Hatley, Thomas. *The Dividing Paths: Cherokees and South Carolinians through the Era of Revolution.* New York, 1993.

Haywood, John. *The Civil and Political History of the State of Tennessee from Its Earliest Settlement Up to the Year 1796.* Nashville, Tenn., 1891.

Henderson, A. Gwynn. "Dispelling the Myth: Seventeenth- and Eighteenth-Century Indian Life in Kentucky." *Register of the Kentucky Historical Society,* XC (1992), 1–25.

Henri, Florette. *The Southern Indians and Benjamin Hawkins, 1796–1816.* Norman, Okla., 1986.

Hill, Sarah H. "Weaving History: Cherokee Baskets from the Springplace Mission." *William and Mary Quarterly,* 3d Ser., LIII (1996), 115–136.

Hinderaker, Eric. *Elusive Empires: Constructing Colonialism in the Ohio Valley, 1673–1800.* Cambridge, 1997.

———. "The 'Four Indian Kings' and the Imaginative Construction of the First British Empire." *William and Mary Quarterly,* 3d Ser., LIII (1996), 487–526.

Hoffman, Ronald, and Peter J. Albert, eds. *Launching the "Extended Republic": The Federalist Era.* Charlottesville, Va., 1996.

Hoffman, Ronald, Thad W. Tate, and Peter J. Albert, eds. *An Uncivil War: The Southern Backcountry during the American Revolution.* Charlottesville, Va., 1985.

Horsman, Reginald. *Expansion and American Indian Policy, 1783–1812.* East Lansing, Mich., 1967.

———. *The Frontier in the Formative Years, 1783–1815.* New York, 1970.

———. *Matthew Elliott, British Indian Agent.* Detroit, 1964.

———. *The Origins of Indian Removal: 1815–1824.* East Lansing, Mich., 1970.

———. *Race and Manifest Destiny: The Origins of American Racial Anglo-Saxonism.* Cambridge, Mass., 1981.

Howard, James H. *Shawnee! The Ceremonialism of a Native Indian Tribe and Its Cultural Background.* Athens, Ohio, 1981.

Hoxie, Frederick E. *Parading through History: The Making of the Crow Nation in America, 1805–1935.* New York, 1995.

Hurt, R. Douglas. *The Ohio Frontier: Crucible of the Old Northwest, 1720–1830.* Bloomington, Ind., 1996.

Hutton, Paul A. "William Wells: Frontier Scout and Indian Agent." *Indiana Magazine of History,* LXXIV (1978), 183–222.

Isaac, Rhys. *The Transformation of Virginia, 1740–1790.* Chapel Hill, N.C., 1982.

Jacobs, Wilbur R. *On Turner's Trail: One Hundred Years of Writing Western History.* Lawrence, Kans., 1994.

———. *Wilderness Politics and Indian Gifts: The Northern Colonial Frontier, 1748–1763.* Lincoln, Nebr., 1966.

Jaenen, Cornelius. "The Role of Presents in French-Amerindian Trade." In Duncan Cameron, ed., *Explorations in Canadian Economic History: Essays in Honour of Irene M. Spry,* 231–250. Ottawa, 1985.

Jennings, Francis. *The Ambiguous Iroquois Empire: The Covenant Chain Confederation of Indian Tribes with English Colonies from Its Beginnings to the Lancaster Treaty of 1744.* New York, 1984.

———. *Empire of Fortune: Crowns, Colonies, and Tribes in the Seven Years War in America.* New York, 1988.

———. "The Indians' Revolution." In Alfred F. Young, ed., *The American Revolution: Explorations in the History of American Radicalism,* 319–348. De Kalb, Ill., 1976.

———. *The Invasion of America: Indians, Colonialism, and the Cant of Conquest.* Chapel Hill, N.C., 1975.

———, et al., eds. *History and Culture of Iroquois Diplomacy.* Syracuse, N.Y., 1985.

Johnston, James Hugo. "Documentary Evidence of the Relations of Negroes and Indians." *Journal of Negro History,* XIV (1929), 21–43.

Jones, Dorothy V. *License for Empire: Colonialism by Treaty in Early America.* Chicago, 1982.

Jones, Eugene H. *Native Americans as Shown on the Stage, 1753–1916.* Metuchen, N.J., 1988.

Jordan, Terry G., and Matti Kaups. *The American Backwoods Frontier: An Ethnic and Ecological Interpretation.* Baltimore, 1989.

Katz, William Loren. *Black Indians: A Hidden Heritage.* New York, 1986.

Kay, Marvin L. Michael. "The North Carolina Regulation, 1766–1776: A Class Conflict." In Alfred F. Young, ed., *The American Revolution: Explorations in the History of American Radicalism,* 71–123. De Kalb, Ill., 1976.

Kelsay, Isobel Thompson. *Joseph Brant, 1743–1807: Man of Two Worlds.* Syracuse, N.Y., 1984.

Kent, Barry C. *Susquehanna's Indians.* Harrisburg, Pa., 1989.

Kidwell, Clara Sue. "Indian Women as Cultural Mediators." *Ethnohistory,* XXXIX (1992), 97–107.

Klein, Rachel N. *Unification of a Slave State: The Rise of the Planter Class in the South Carolina Backcountry, 1760–1808.* Chpael Hill, N.C., 1990.

Knight, Vernon J., Jr. *Tukabatchee: Archaeological Investigations at an Historic Creek Town, Elmore County, Alabama, 1984.* Report of Investigations, Office of Archaeological Research, Alabama State Museum of Natural History, University of Alabama. University, Ala., 1985.

Kolodny, Annette. *The Land Before Her: Fantasy and Experience of the American Frontiers, 1630–1860.* Chapel Hill, N.C., 1984.

Kroeber, Karl. "An Introduction to the Art of Traditional American Indian Narration." In Kroeber, ed., *Traditional Literatures of the American Indian: Texts and Interpretations,* 1–24. Lincoln, Nebr., 1981.

Kugel, Rebecca. "Of Missionaries and Their Cattle: Ojibwa Perceptions of a Missionary as Evil Shaman." *Ethnohistory,* XLI (1994), 227–244.

Kulikoff, Allan. *The Agrarian Origins of American Capitalism.* Charlottesville, Va., 1992.

———. *Tobacco and Slaves: The Development of Southern Cultures in the Chesapeake, 1680–1800.* Chapel Hill, N.C., 1986.

Kunitz, Stephen J. "Benjamin Rush on Savagism and Progress." *Ethnohistory,* XVII (1970), 31–42.

Kuppermann, Karen Ordahl. "Presentment of Civility: English Reading of American Self-Presentation in the Early Years of Colonization." *William and Mary Quarterly,* 3d Ser., LIV (1997), 193–228.

———. *Settling with the Indians: The Meeting of English and Indian Cultures in America, 1580–1640.* Totowa, N.J., 1980.

Lamar, Howard, and Leonard Thompson, eds. *The Frontier in History: North America and Southern Africa Compared.* New Haven, Conn., 1981.

Landsman, Ned C. *Scotland and Its First American Colony, 1683–1765.* Princeton, N.J., 1985.

Larson, John Lauritz, and David G. Vanderstel. "Agent of Empire: William Conner on the Indiana Frontier, 1800–1855." *Indiana Magazine of History,* LXXX (1984), 310–328.

Leach, Douglas Edward. *Roots of Conflict: British Armed Forces and Colonial Americans, 1677–1763.* Chapel Hill, N.C., 1986.

Lepore, Jill. *The Name of War: King Philip's War and the Origins of American Identity.* New York, 1998.

Limerick, Patricia Nelson. *The Legacy of Conquest: The Unbroken Past of the American West.* New York, 1987.

Littlefield, Daniel F., Jr. *Africans and Seminoles: From Removal to Emancipation.* Westport, Conn., 1977.

Lund, Thomas A. *American Wildlife Law.* Berkeley, Calif., 1980.

Lurie, Nancy Oestreich. *Wisconsin Indians.* Madison, Wis., 1987.

McConnell, Michael N. *A Country Between: The Upper Ohio Valley and Its Peoples, 1724–1774.* Lincoln, Nebr., 1992.

McCoy, Drew R. *The Elusive Republic: Political Economy in Jeffersonian America.* Chapel Hill, N.C., 1980.

McLoughlin, William G. *Cherokee Renascence in the New Republic.* Princeton, N.J., 1986.

Magnaghi, Russell M. "Red Slavery in the Great Lakes Country during the French and British Regimes." *Old Northwest,* XII (1986), 201–217.

Mancall, Peter C. *Deadly Medicine: Indians and Alcohol in Early America.* Ithaca, N.Y., 1995.

———. *Valley of Opportunity: Economic Culture along the Upper Susquehanna, 1700–1800.* Ithaca, N.Y., 1991.

Mandell, Daniel R. *Behind the Frontier: Indians in Eighteenth-Century Eastern Massachusetts.* Lincoln, Nebr., 1996.

Marks, Stuart A. *Southern Hunting in Black and White: Nature, History, and Ritual in a Carolina Community.* Princeton, N.J., 1991.

Martin, Joel W. "Indians, Contact, and Colonialism in the Deep South: Themes for a Postcolonial History of American Religion." In Thomas W. Tweed, ed., *Retelling U.S. Religious History,* 149–180. Berkeley, Calif., 1997.

———. *Sacred Revolt: The Muskogees' Struggle for a New World.* Boston, 1991.

Mason, Carol I. "Eighteenth-Century Culture Change among the Lower Creeks." *Florida Anthropologist,* XVI (1963), 65–80.

Mauelshagen, Carl, and Gerald H. Davis. "The Moravians' Plan for a Mission among the Creek Indians, 1803–1804." *Georgia Historical Quarterly,* LI (1967), 358–363.

Mauss, Marcel. *The Gift: The Form and Reason for Exchange in Archaic Societies.* Translated by W. D. Halls. London, 1990.

Meinig, D. W. *The Shaping of America: A Geographical Perspective on Five Hundred Years of History,* I, *Atlantic America, 1492–1800.* New Haven, Conn., 1986.

———. *The Shaping of America: A Geographical Perspective on Five Hundred Years of History,* II, *Continental America, 1800–1867.* New Haven, Conn., 1993.

Merchant, Carolyn. *Ecological Revolutions: Nature, Gender, and Science in New England.* Chapel Hill, N.C., 1989.

Merrell, James H. "'The Cast of His Countenance': Reading Andrew Montour." In Ronald Hoffman, Mechal Sobel, and Fredrika J. Teute, eds., *Through a Glass Darkly: Reflections on Personal Identity in Early America,* 13–39. Chapel Hill, N.C., 1997.

———. *The Indians' New World: Catawbas and Their Neighbors from European Contact through the Era of Removal.* Chapel Hill, N.C., 1989.

Mikesell, Marvin W. "Comparative Studies in Frontier History." *Annals of the Association of American Geographers,* L (1960), 64–74.

Miller, Jay. "The Delaware as Women: A Symbolic Solution." *American Ethnologist,* I (1974), 507–514.

Mitchell, Robert D. *Commercialism and Frontier: Perspectives on the Early Shenandoah Valley.* Charlottesville, Va., 1977.

―――, ed. *Appalachian Frontiers: Settlement, Society, and Development in the Preindustrial Era*. Lexington, Ky., 1991.

Moody, Richard. *America Takes the Stage: Romanticism in American Drama and Theatre, 1750–1900*. Bloomington, Ind., 1955.

Mooney, James. *Historical Sketch of the Cherokee*. Chicago, 1975.

Morgan, Edmund S. *American Slavery, American Freedom: The Ordeal of Colonial Virginia*. New York, 1975.

Morgan, Lewis Henry. *League of the Ho-de-no-sau-nee, or Iroquois*. 1851; reprint, New Haven, Conn., 1954.

Mulroy, Kevin. *Freedom on the Border: The Seminole Maroons in Florida, the Indian Territory, Coahuila, and Texas*. Lubbock, Tex., 1993.

Murray, David. *Forked Tongues: Speech, Writing, and Representation in North American Indian Texts*. Bloomington, Ind., 1991.

Nash, Gary B. "The Hidden History of Mestizo America." *Journal of American History*, LXXXII (1994–1995), 941–962.

―――. *Red, Black, and White: The Peoples of Early America*. Englewood Cliffs, N.J., 1974.

Nelson, Paul David. *Anthony Wayne: Soldier of the Early Republic*. Bloomington, Ind., 1985.

Nichols, Roger L. *Black Hawk and the Warrior's Path*. Arlington Heights, Ill., 1992.

Nielsen, Donald M. "The Mashpee Indian Revolt of 1833." *New England Quarterly*, LVIII (1985), 400–420.

Nobles, Gregory. *American Frontiers: Cultural Encounters and Continental Conquest*. New York, 1996.

―――. "Breaking into the Backcountry: New Approaches to the Early American Frontier, 1750–1800." *William and Mary Quarterly*, 3d Ser., XLVI (1989), 641–670.

―――. "Straight Lines and Stability: Mapping the Political Order of the Anglo-American Frontier." *Journal of American History*, LXXX (June–September 1993), 9–35.

O'Brien, Jean M. *Dispossession by Degrees: Indian Land and Identity in Natick, Massachusetts, 1650–1790*. Cambridge, 1997.

Olmstead, Earl P. *Blackcoats among the Delaware: David Zeisberger on the Ohio Frontier*. Kent, Ohio, 1991.

Onuf, Peter S. *Statehood and Union: A History of the Northwest Ordinance*. Bloomington, Ind., 1987.

Parkman, Francis. *France and England in North America*. 2 vols. 1851; reprint, New York, 1983.

Perdue, Theda. "Cherokee Women and the Trail of Tears." *Journal of Women's History*, I (1989–1990), 14–30.

―――. *Slavery and the Evolution of Cherokee Society, 1540–1866*. Knoxville, Tenn., 1979.

Perkins, Elizabeth. *Border Life: Experience and Memory in the Revolutionary Ohio Valley*. Chapel Hill, N.C., 1998.

―――. "The Consumer Frontier: Household Consumption in Early Kentucky." *Journal of American History*, LXXVIII (1991–1992), 486–510.

Peterson, Jacqueline, and Jennifer S. H. Brown, eds. *The New Peoples: Being and Becoming Métis in North America*. Lincoln, Nebr., 1985.

Porter, Kenneth W. "Relations between Negroes and Indians within the Present Limits of the United States." *Journal of Negro History,* XVII (1932), 287–367.

Prucha, Francis Paul. *American Indian Policy in the Formative Years.* Cambridge, Mass., 1970.

———. *The Great Father: The United States Government and the American Indians.* 2 vols. Lincoln, Nebr., 1984.

———. *The Sword of the Republic: The United States Army on the Frontier, 1783–1846.* Bloomington, Ind., 1969.

Puglisi, Michael J., ed. *Diversity and Accommodation: Essays on the Cultural Composition of the Virginia Frontier.* Knoxville, Tenn., 1997.

Purvis, Thomas L. "The Ethnic Descent of Kentucky's Early Population: A Statistical Investigation of European and American Sources of Emigration, 1790–1820." *Register of the Kentucky Historical Society,* LXXX (1982), 253–266.

Pyne, Steven J. *Fire in America: A Cultural History of Wildland and Rural Fire.* Princeton, N.J., 1982.

Reid, John Philip. *A Law of Blood: The Primitive Law of the Cherokee Nation.* New York, 1970.

Richter, Daniel K. *The Ordeal of the Longhouse: The Peoples of the Iroquois League in the Era of European Colonization.* Chapel Hill, N.C., 1992.

———. " 'Some of Them . . . Would Always Have a Minister with Them': Mohawk Protestantism, 1683–1719." *American Indian Quarterly,* XVI (1992), 471–484.

Richter, Daniel K., and James H. Merrell, eds. *Beyond the Covenant Chain: The Iroquois and Their Neighbors in Indian North America.* Syracuse, N.Y., 1987.

Ricoeur, Paul. *The Rule of Metaphor: Multi-disciplinary Studies of the Creation of Meaning in Language.* Translated by Robert Czerny, with Kathleen McLaughlin and John Costello. Toronto, 1977.

Roeber, A. G. "In German Ways? Problems and Potentials of Eighteenth-Century German Social and Emigration History." *William and Mary Quarterly,* 3d Ser., XLIV (1987), 750–774.

Rogin, Michael Paul. *Fathers and Children: Andrew Jackson and the Subjugation of the American Indian.* New York, 1975.

Rohrbough, Malcolm J. *The Land Office Business: The Settlement and Administration of American Public Lands, 1789–1837.* New York, 1968.

———. *The Trans-Appalachian Frontier: People, Societies, and Institutions, 1775–1850.* New York, 1978.

Ronda, James P. *Lewis and Clark among the Indians.* Lincoln, Nebr., 1984.

Roth, Randolph A. *The Democratic Dilemma: Religion, Reform, and the Social Order in the Connecticut River Valley of Vermont, 1791–1850.* Cambridge, 1987.

Royce, Anya Peterson. *Ethnic Identity: Strategies of Diversity.* Bloomington, Ind., 1982.

Sahlins, Marshall. *Stone Age Economics.* Chicago, 1972.

Salisbury, Neal. "The Indians' Old World: Native Americans and the Coming of Europeans." *William and Mary Quarterly,* 3d Ser., LIII (1996), 435–458.

Sattler, Richard A. "Women's Status among the Muskogee and Cherokee." In Laura F.

Klein and Lillian A. Ackerman, eds., *Women and Power in Native North America,* 214–229. Norman, Okla., 1995.

Satz, Ronald N. *American Indian Policy in the Jacksonian Era.* Lincoln, Nebr., 1975.

Schuette, H. A., et al. "Maple Sugar: A Bibliography of Early Records." Wisconsin Academy of Sciences, Arts, and Letters, *Transactions,* XXIX (Madison, Wis., 1935), 209–236.

———, et al. "Maple Sugar: A Bibliography of Early Records, II." Wisconsin Academy of Sciences, Arts, and Letters, *Transactions,* XXXVIII (Madison, Wis., 1947), 89–184.

Shannon, Timothy J. "Dressing for Success on the Mohawk Frontier: Hendrick, William Johnson, and the Indian Fashion." *William and Mary Quarterly,* 3d Ser., LIII (1996), 13–42.

Sheehan, Bernard W. " 'The Famous Hair Buyer General': Henry Hamilton, George Rogers Clark, and the American Indian." *Indiana Magazine of History,* LXXIX (1983), 1–28.

———. *Seeds of Extinction: Jeffersonian Philanthropy and the American Indian.* Chapel Hill, N.C., 1973.

Shoemaker, Nancy. "How Indians Got to Be Red." *American Historical Review,* CII (1997), 625–644.

———, ed. *Negotiators of Change: Historical Perspectives on Native American Women.* New York, 1995.

Shuffleton, Frank, ed. *A Mixed Race: Ethnicity in Early America.* New York, 1993.

Sider, Gerald M. *Lumbee Indian Histories: Race, Ethnicity, and Indian Identity in the Southern United States.* Cambridge, 1990.

Silver, Timothy. *A New Face on the Countryside: Indians, Colonists, and Slaves in South Atlantic Forests, 1500–1800.* Cambridge, 1990.

Slaughter, Thomas P. *The Whiskey Rebellion: Frontier Epilogue to the American Revolution.* New York, 1986.

Slotkin, Richard. *Regeneration through Violence: The Mythology of the American Frontier, 1600–1860.* Middletown, Conn., 1973.

Snapp, J. Russell. *John Stuart and the Struggle for Empire on the Southern Frontier.* Baton Rouge, La., 1996.

Sollors, Werner. *Beyond Ethnicity: Consent and Descent in American Culture.* New York, 1986.

———, ed. *The Invention of Ethnicity.* New York, 1989.

Sosin, Jack M. *The Revolutionary Frontier, 1763–1783.* New York, 1967.

———. *Whitehall and the Wilderness: The Middle West in British Colonial Policy, 1760–1775.* Lincoln, Nebr., 1961.

Steele, Ian K. *Betrayals: Fort William Henry and the "Massacre."* New York, 1990.

———. *Warpaths: Invasions of North America.* New York, 1994.

Strickland, Rennard. *Fire and the Spirits: Cherokee Law from Clan to Court.* Norman, Okla., 1975.

Sturtevant, William C., gen. ed. *Handbook of North American Indians.* 17 vols. to date. Washington, D.C., 1978–.

Sullivan, Sherry. "Indians in American Fiction, 1820–1850: An Ethnohistorical Perspective." *Clio,* XV (1986), 239–257.

Sword, Wiley. *President Washington's Indian War: The Struggle for the Old Northwest, 1790–1795.* Norman, Okla., 1985.

Tachau, Mary K. Bonsteel. *Federal Courts in the Early Republic: Kentucky, 1789–1816.* Princeton, N.J., 1978.

——. "The Whiskey Rebellion in Kentucky: A Forgotten Episode of Civil Disobedience." *Journal of the Early Republic,* II (1982), 239–259.

Tanner, Helen Hornbeck. "The Glaize in 1792: A Composite Indian Community." *Ethnohistory,* XXV (1978), 15–39.

——, ed. *Atlas of Great Lakes Indian History.* Norman, Okla., 1987.

Taylor, Alan. "Land and Liberty on the Post-Revolutionary Frontier." In David Thomas Konig, ed., *Devising Liberty: Preserving and Creating Freedom in the New American Republic,* 81–108. Stanford, Calif., 1995.

——. *Liberty Men and Great Proprietors: The Revolutionary Settlement on the Maine Frontier, 1760–1820.* Chapel Hill, N.C., 1990.

——. " 'To Man Their Rights': The Frontier Revolution." In Ronald Hoffman and Peter J. Albert, eds., *The Transforming Hand of Revolution: Reconsidering the American Revolution as a Social Movement,* 231–257. Charlottesville, Va., 1995.

——. *William Cooper's Town: Power and Persuasion on the Frontier of the Early American Republic.* New York, 1995.

Taylor, George Rogers, ed. *The Turner Thesis concerning the Role of the Frontier in American History.* Rev. ed. Boston, 1956.

Taylor, Robert M., Jr., ed. *The Northwest Ordinance, 1787: A Bicentennial Handbook.* Indianapolis, 1987.

Thompson, E. P. *Customs in Common.* London, 1991.

——. *Whigs and Hunters: The Origin of the Black Act.* New York, 1975.

Tillson, Albert H., Jr. *Gentry and Common Folk: Political Culture on a Virginia Frontier, 1740–1789.* Lexington, Ky., 1991.

——. "The Southern Backcountry: A Survey of Current Research." *Virginia Magazine of History and Biography,* XCVIII (1990), 387–422.

Turner, Frederick Jackson. *The Frontier in American History* (1920). Foreword by Wilbur R. Jacobs. 1947; reprint, Tucson, Ariz., 1986.

Ulrich, Laurel Thatcher. *A Midwife's Tale: The Life of Martha Ballard, Based on Her Diary, 1785–1812.* New York, 1991.

Unrah, William E. *Mixed-Bloods and Tribal Dissolution: Charles Curtis and the Quest for Indian Identity.* Lawrence, Kans., 1989.

Usner, Daniel H., Jr. *Indians, Settlers, and Slaves in a Frontier Exchange Economy: The Lower Mississippi Valley before 1783.* Chapel Hill, N.C., 1992.

Van Kirk, Sylvia. *Many Tender Ties: Women in Fur-Trade Society, 1670–1870.* Norman, Okla., 1980.

Wald, Priscilla. "Terms of Assimilation: Legislating Subjectivity in the Emerging Nation." In Amy Kaplan and Donald E. Pease, eds., *Cultures of United States Imperialism,* 59–84. Durham, N.C., 1993.

Walker, Juliet E. K. *Free Frank: A Black Pioneer on the Antebellum Frontier.* Lexington, Ky., 1983.

Walker, Willard, and James Sarbaugh. "The Early History of the Cherokee Syllabary."
  *Ethnohistory*, XL (1993), 70–94.

Wallace, Anthony F. C. *The Death and Rebirth of the Seneca*. New York, 1972.

———. *The Long, Bitter Trail: Andrew Jackson and the Indians*. New York, 1993.

———. *Prelude to Disaster*. Edited by Ellen M. Whitney. Springfield, Ill., 1970.

Wallace, Paul A. W. *Indians in Pennsylvania*. 2d ed. Revised by William A. Hunter.
  Harrisburg, Pa., 1986.

Walsh, Dennis P. "Many Metamoras: An Indian Drama in the Old Northwest." *Old
  Northwest*, XII (1986), 457–468.

Walsh, Margaret. *The American Frontier Revisited*. Atlantic Highlands, N.J., 1981.

Walthall, John A. *Galena and Aboriginal Trade in Eastern North America*. Springfield, Ill.,
  1981.

Watlington, Patricia. *The Partisan Spirit: Kentucky Politics, 1779–1792*. New York, 1972.

Weber, David J. *The Spanish Frontier in North America*. New Haven, Conn., 1992.

Weiss, Timothy F. *On the Margins: The Art of Exile in V. S. Naipaul*. Amherst, Mass., 1992.

Weslager, C. A. *The Delaware Indians: A History*. New Brunswick, N.J., 1972.

White, Richard. *The Middle Ground: Indians, Empires, and Republics in the Great Lakes
  Region, 1650–1815*. New York, 1991.

———. *The Roots of Dependency: Subsistence, Environment, and Social Change among the
  Choctaws, Pawnees, and Navajos*. Lincoln, Nebr., 1983.

Whittenberg, James P. "Planters, Merchants, and Lawyers: Social Change and the Origins
  of the North Carolina Regulation." *William and Mary Quarterly*, 3d Ser., XXXIV
  (1977), 215–238.

Wilmeth, Don B. "Noble or Ruthless Savage? The American Indian on Stage and in the
  Drama." *Journal of American Drama and Theater*, I (1989), 39–78.

Windley, Lathan Algerna. *A Profile of Runaway Slaves in Virginia and South Carolina from
  1730 to 1787*. New York, 1995.

Wood, Peter H., Gregory A. Waselkov, and M. Thomas Hatley, eds. *Powhatan's Mantle:
  Indians in the Colonial Southeast*. Lincoln, Nebr., 1989.

Woods, Patricia Dillon. *French-Indian Relations on the Southern Frontier, 1699–1762*. Ann
  Arbor, Mich., 1980.

Woodward, Grace Steele. *The Cherokees*. Norman, Okla., 1969.

Wright, Gary A. "Some Aspects of Early and Mid-Seventeenth Century Exchange
  Networks in the Western Great Lakes." *Michigan Archaeologist*, XIII (1967), 181–197.

Wright, J. Leitch, Jr. *Creeks and Seminoles: The Destruction and Regeneration of the
  Muscogulge People*. Lincoln, Nebr., 1986.

———. *The Only Land They Knew: The Tragic Story of the American Indians in the Old
  South*. New York, 1981.

Wright, James E. *The Galena Lead District: Federal Policy and Practice, 1824–1847*.
  Madison, Wis., 1966.

Wyckoff, William. *The Developer's Frontier: The Making of the Western New York
  Landscape*. New Haven, Conn., 1988.

Young, Mary. "The Cherokee Nation: Mirror of the Republic." *American Quarterly*,
  XXXIII (1981), 502–524.

# CONFERENCE PROGRAM

*Crucibles of Cultures: North American Frontiers, 1750–1820, November 18 and 19, 1994, Sponsored by the Institute of Early American History and Culture, The Historic New Orleans Collection, and the Newberry Library*

SESSION 1. *Crossing Cultural Terrains.* Chair: Charles T. Cullen, Newberry Library. William B. Hart, Middlebury College, "Black 'Go Betweens' and the Mutability of 'Race,' Status, and Identity on New York's Frontier, 1750–1775." Elizabeth A. Perkins, Centre College, "'To Make Distinctions and Particions Amongst Us': Identity and Interaction in the Revolutionary Ohio Valley." John Mack Faragher, Yale University, "'Even More Motley than Mackinaw': Pioneer Communities of the Lower Missouri." R. David Edmunds, Indiana University, "Native American Entrepreneurs: Potowatomi Métis in the Old Northwest and Kansas." Commentators: Jean M. O'Brien, University of Minnesota, and Peter H. Wood, Duke University.

SESSION 2. *Gendering Order.* Chair: Ronald Hoffman, Institute of Early American History and Culture. Sara G. Parker, University of California, Santa Cruz, "Breaching the Gap: Henderson's Purchase and the Transformation of the Cherokee Cultural Matrix." Bruce M. White, University of Minnesota, "Gender and Trade in the Lake Superior Region in the Eighteenth Century." Lucy E. Murphy, Northern Illinois University, "Frontier Production, Cross-Cultural Skill Exchange, and Gender Relations in the Western Great Lakes, 1740–1832." Commentators: Christine Leigh Heyrman, University of Delaware, and Neal Salisbury, Smith College.

SESSION 3. *Placing the Land.* Chair: Alan Taylor, University of California, Davis. James H. Merrell, Vassar College, "'Shamokin, the very seat of the Prince of Darkness.'" Charles E. Brooks, Texas A & M University, "From Old Growth Forests to Cultivated Wood Lots: Land Use and Ecology on the Western New York Frontier." Stephen A. Aron, Princeton University, "Rights in the Woods: The Privatization of Land on the Trans-Appalachian Frontier." Commentators: William Cronon, University of Wisconsin, and Carville Earle, Louisiana State University.

SESSION 4. *Empowering Domains.* Chair: Fredrika J. Teute, Institute of Early American History and Culture. Jane T. Merritt, University of Washington, "The Power of Language: Cultural Meanings and the Colonial Encounter on the Pennsylvania Frontier." Andrew R. L. Cayton, Miami University, "Contextualizing Power: The Rituals of Public Ceremony in Trans-Appalachia, 1787–1815." Steven W. Hackel, Institute of Early American History and

Culture, "Politics in the Mission: Indian Authority in Spanish California, 1779–1830." Jill Lepore, Yale University, "Remembering American Frontiers: King Philip's War and the American Imagination." Commentators: Duane Champagne, University of California, Los Angeles, and Karen Ordahl Kupperman, University of Connecticut.

SESSION 5. *Final Commentary.* Chair: Frederick E. Hoxie, Newberry Library. Richard White, University of Washington, "Crucibles of Cultures: North American Frontiers, 1750–1820."

# INDEX

Abiel, John, 102
Adams, John, 346
Addongat, 89–90, 103
African Americans, 40, 194, 207–208; free, 88–113; corporal punishment of, 241–242, 245; and mining, 294
Agriculture, 191–192, 283–286, 321–322; cotton cultivating, 165–168; maple sugar making, 270, 276–279; dairying, 279–282
Alabama, 142n, 153, 172–173, 331
Alder, Jonathan, 189
Alger, William, 343, 345, 351
Algonquian Indians, 8; and language, 69, 293, 297, 328
Allan, Ebenezer, 113
Allen, Benjamin, 216, 231–232
Antislavery, 227, 319
Apess, William, 352–357
Architecture: fort, 31, 52, 255; and frontier housing, 47, 186–187, 225–226, 309
Armstrong, John, 43
Asimethe (Potawatomi Indian), 259, 264
Atkin, Edmond, 139, 159–160
Attakullakulla, 124, 126–127, 131–132, 135, 144–146, 148

Backcountry, 1, 10
Baird, Elizabeth Fisher, 270, 278, 281–283, 286
Baird, Henry, 278, 281–282, 286
Bard, Peter, 35
Bartram, John, 25
Bartram, William, 154, 161, 168
Beatty, Charles, 33
Beckwourth, James, 294–295
Benton, Thomas Hart, 319–320, 323
Bethlehem, Pa., 18, 44–46, 60–61, 64, 66
Bibb, Henry, 96
Black Bob Band (Shawnee), 304–305, 324
Black Hawk War, 273, 290–291, 296
Blair, John, 143
Blue Jacket, 222, 262
Boilvin, Nicholas, 292, 301

Boone, Daniel, 184, 197, 213, 308, 310, 311
Boone, Nathan, 308
Bosomworth, Thomas, 133–134, 159
British: and slaveownership, 97; and military authority, 127–129, 137–138; and colonial game laws, 180–182
Browne, Joseph, 315
Bryan, Elijah, 313
Bryant, William Cullen, 333
Buffalo, 197, 220, 232
Burckhard, Johann Christian, 171–172
Burd, James, 21, 35, 55
Burke, Richard, 223
Butler, Edward, 247
Butler, Richard, 254–255

Calhoun, John C., 318–319, 323
Cammerhoff, John Christopher Frederick, 65
Campbell, John, 110
Canassatego (Iroquois chief), 78–79
Cape Girardeau, 306, 315, 317
Carver, Jonathan, 284
Catawba Indians, 78, 121, 125
Cayuga Indians, 22
Ceremony: condolence, 75–76; Green Corn, 155; and civility, 239–240, 245, 253, 257–269
Cherokee Indians, 88–89; and Seven Years' War, 114–150; and women, 137, 154–155; removal of, 317, 324, 331, 347–349, 353–357; syllabary of, 327–328
*Cherokee Nation v. Georgia*, 347, 349–350
Chickasaw Indians, 154, 206, 331
Choctaw Indians, 331, 345
Christianity, 65–66; conversion to, 44–45, 95, 352–353. *See also* Moravians
Christy, Howard Chandler, 235–236
Church, Benjamin, 339
Civility: and rank, 224–226, 241; and tea drinking, 229–230, 232; and ceremony, 239–240, 245, 253, 257–269
Clapham, William, 29, 33, 51

# NOTES ON THE CONTRIBUTORS

Stephen Aron is Associate Professor of History at the University of California, Los Angeles. He is the author of *How the West was Lost: The Transformation of Kentucky from Daniel Boone to Henry Clay*.

Andrew R. L. Cayton is Professor of History at Miami University, Oxford, Ohio. He is the author of *Frontier Indiana*, *The Midwest and the Nation: Rethinking the History of an American Region* (with Peter S. Onuf), and *The Frontier Republic: Ideology and Politics in the Ohio Country, 1780–1825*.

Gregory Evans Dowd is Associate Professor of History at the University of Notre Dame. He is the author of *A Spirited Resistance: The North American Indian Struggle for Unity, 1745–1815*.

John Mack Faragher is Arthur Unobskey Professor of American History at Yale University. He is the author of *Daniel Boone: The Life and Legend of an American Pioneer*, *Sugar Creek: Life on the Illinois Prairie*, and *Women and Men on the Overland Trail*.

William B. Hart is Assistant Professor of History at Middlebury College. He is the author of *The United States and World Trade*.

Jill Lepore is Assistant Professor of History at Boston University. She is the author of *The Name of War: King Philip's War and the Origins of American Identity*.

James H. Merrell is Lucy Maynard Salmon Professor of History at Vassar College. He is the author of *The Indians' New World: Catawbas and Their Neighbors from European Contact through the Era of Removal* and editor (with Daniel K. Richter) of *Beyond the Covenant Chain: The Iroquois and Their Neighbors in Indian North America, 1600–1800*.

Jane T. Merritt is Assistant Professor of History at Old Dominion University. She is the author of "Dreaming of the Savior's Blood: Moravians and the Indian Great Awakening in Pennsylvania," *William and Mary Quarterly*, 3d Ser., LIV (1997), 723–746.

Lucy Eldersveld Murphy is Assistant Professor of History at DePaul University. She is the editor of *Midwestern Women: Work, Community, and Leadership at the Crossroads* (with Wendy Hamand Venet).

Elizabeth A. Perkins is Assistant Professor of History at Centre College. She is the author of *Border Life: Experience and Memory in the Revolutionary Ohio Valley*.

Claudio Saunt is a Mellon Fellow at the Society of Fellows in the Humanities, Columbia University.

Fredrika J. Teute is Editor of Publications at the Omohundro Institute of Early American History and Culture. She has been an editor of *The Papers of John Marshall* and *The Papers of James Madison*.